PROPERTY

EIGHTH EDITION

STEVEN L. EMANUEL

Founder & Editor-in-Chief, *Emanuel Law Outlines* and
Emanuel Bar Review
Harvard Law School, J.D. 1976
Member, NY, CT, MD and VA bars

The *Emanuel® Law Outlines* Series

Published by Wolters Kluwer Law & Business in New York.

Wolters Kluwer Law & Business serves customers worldwide with CCH, Aspen Publishers, and Kluwer Law International products. (www.wolterskluwerlb.com)

To contact Customer Service, e-mail customer.service@wolterskluwer.com, call 1-800-234-1660, fax 1-800-901-9075, or mail correspondence to:

> Wolters Kluwer Law & Business
> Attn: Order Department
> PO Box 990
> Frederick, MD 21705

Printed in the United States of America.

1 2 3 4 5 6 7 8 9 0

ISBN 978-1-4548-0915-9

Library of Congress Cataloging-in-Publication Data

Emanuel, Steven.
   Property / Steven L. Emanuel. -- 8th ed.
      p. cm. -- (Emanuel law outlines series)
   ISBN 978-1-4548-0915-9
   1. Property--United States--Outlines, syllabi, etc. 2. Real
property--United States--Outlines, syllabi, etc. I. Title.
   KF561.E47 2012
   346.7304--dc23

                                    2012017024

About Wolters Kluwer Law & Business

Wolters Kluwer Law & Business is a leading global provider of intelligent information and digital solutions for legal and business professionals in key specialty areas, and respected educational resources for professors and law students. Wolters Kluwer Law & Business connects legal and business professionals as well as those in the education market with timely, specialized authoritative content and information-enabled solutions to support success through productivity, accuracy and mobility.

Serving customers worldwide, Wolters Kluwer Law & Business products include those under the Aspen Publishers, CCH, Kluwer Law International, Loislaw, Best Case, ftwilliam.com and Medi-Regs family of products.

CCH products have been a trusted resource since 1913, and are highly regarded resources for legal, securities, antitrust and trade regulation, government contracting, banking, pension, payroll, employment and labor, and healthcare reimbursement and compliance professionals.

Aspen Publishers products provide essential information to attorneys, business professionals and law students. Written by preeminent authorities, the product line offers analytical and practical information in a range of specialty practice areas from securities law and intellectual property to mergers and acquisitions and pension/benefits. Aspen's trusted legal education resources provide professors and students with high-quality, up-to-date and effective resources for successful instruction and study in all areas of the law.

Kluwer Law International products provide the global business community with reliable international legal information in English. Legal practitioners, corporate counsel and business executives around the world rely on Kluwer Law journals, looseleafs, books, and electronic products for comprehensive information in many areas of international legal practice.

Loislaw is a comprehensive online legal research product providing legal content to law firm practitioners of various specializations. Loislaw provides attorneys with the ability to quickly and efficiently find the necessary legal information they need, when and where they need it, by facilitating access to primary law as well as state-specific law, records, forms and treatises.

Best Case Solutions is the leading bankruptcy software product to the bankruptcy industry. It provides software and workflow tools to flawlessly streamline petition preparation and the electronic filing process, while timely incorporating ever-changing court requirements.

ftwilliam.com offers employee benefits professionals the highest quality plan documents (retirement, welfare and non-qualified) and government forms (5500/PBGC, 1099 and IRS) software at highly competitive prices.

MediRegs products provide integrated health care compliance content and software solutions for professionals in healthcare, higher education and life sciences, including professionals in accounting, law and consulting.

Wolters Kluwer Law & Business, a division of Wolters Kluwer, is headquartered in New York. Wolters Kluwer is a market-leading global information services company focused on professionals.

For my mother
Judith Emanuel

Abbreviations Used in Text

CASEBOOKS

B,C&S — Browder, Cunningham, et. al., *Basic Property Law* (5th Ed. 1989)

C&J — Cribbet, Johnson, et. al., *Cases and Materials on Property* (6th Ed. 1990)

C&L — Casner and Leach, *Cases and Text on Property* (3d Ed. 1984, with 1989 Supplement)

D&K — Dukeminier and Krier, *Property* (3d Ed. 1993)

DKA&S — Dukeminier, Krier, Alexander & Schill, *Property* (7th Ed. 2010)

RKK&A — Rabin, Kwall, Kwall and Arnold, *Fundamentals of Modern Real Property Law* (6th Ed. 2011)

Singer — Joseph W. Singer, *Property Law: Rules, Policies and Practices* (5th Ed. 2010).

HORNBOOKS AND TREATISES

A.L.P. — A.J. Casner, Ed., *American Law of Property* (1952, with 1976 Supplement)

Brown — Ray Brown, *The Law of Personal Property* (3d Ed. 1975)

Burby — William Burby, *Handbook of the Law of Real Property* (3d Ed. 1965)

Cribbet — John Cribbet, *Principles of the Law of Property* (3d Ed. 1989)

C,S&W — Cunningham, Stoebuck & Whitman, *The Law of Property* (2nd Ed. 1993)

Land Use Nutshell — Wright and Webber, *Land Use in a Nutshell* (2d Ed. 1985)

Moynihan — Cornelius Moynihan, *Introduction to the Law of Real Property* (1962)

Nutshell — Roger Bernhardt, *Real Property in a Nutshell* (2d Ed. 1981)

Powell — Powell and Rohan, *Powell on Real Property* (Abridged Ed., 1968)

S&W — Stoebuck & Whitman, *The Law of Property* (3d Ed. 2000)

Williams — Norman Williams, *Amer. Planning Law: Land Use and the Police Power* (1974)

RESTATEMENTS

Rest. — *Restatement of the Law of Property* (1936)

Rest.2d — *Restatement of the Law Second, Property (Landlord & Tenant; Donative Transfers)* (1977-79; 1983, 1986)

Rest.3d (Mortgages) — *Restatement of the Law Third, Property (Mortgages)* (1997)

Rest.3d (Servitudes) — *Restatement of the Law Third, Property (Servitudes)* (2000)

SUMMARY OF CONTENTS

TABLE OF CONTENTS

Chapter 1

INTRODUCTION

Chapter 2

TWO TYPES OF NON-REAL PROPERTY: PERSONAL PROPERTY AND INTELLECTUAL PROPERTY

Chapter 3

ADVERSE POSSESSION

Chapter 4

FREEHOLD ESTATES

Chapter 5

FUTURE INTERESTS

Chapter 6

MARITAL ESTATES

Chapter 7

CONCURRENT OWNERSHIP

Chapter 8

LANDLORD AND TENANT

Chapter 9

EASEMENTS AND PROMISES CONCERNING LAND

Chapter 10

ZONING AND OTHER
PUBLIC LAND-USE CONTROLS

Chapter 11

LAND SALE CONTRACTS, MORTGAGES AND DEEDS

Chapter 12

THE RECORDING SYSTEM AND TITLE ASSURANCE

Chapter 13

RIGHTS INCIDENT TO LAND

TABLE OF FLOW CHARTS
AND CHECKLISTS

Preface

Thanks for buying this book. I've worked hard on this new edition, to make it more tightly focussed on just those topics that are important in today's Property courses and to incorporate new Flow Charts and Tables.

Here are some of this book's special features:

- **"Casebook Correlation Chart"** — This chart, located just after this Preface, correlates each section of the Outline with the pages covering the same topic in the four leading Property casebooks.

- **"Capsule Summary"** — This is an 86-page summary of the key concepts of the law of Property, specially designed for use in the last week or so before your final exam.

- **"QuizYourself"** — At the end of nearly every chapter I give you short-answer questions so that you can exercise your analytical muscles. There are over 100 of these questions, each written by me. I also provide detailed answers.

- **"Exam Tips"** — These alert you to the issues that repeatedly pop up on real-life Property exams, and the factual patterns commonly used to test those issues. I created these Tips by looking at literally hundreds of multiple-choice and essay questions asked by law professors and bar examiners. You'd be surprised at how predictable the issues and fact-patterns chosen by professors really are!

- *Flow Charts and Tables* — I've distilled many of the legal principles in this book into special visual aids that help you see how the pieces fit together. These include Flow Charts and Tables. You'll find them at various places in most chapters, usually after the full treatment of the material in question. The list of Flow Charts and Checklist Tables on p. xxxv will help you quickly locate these new features when you're studying for your exam.

I intend for you to use this book both throughout the semester and for exam preparation. Here are some suggestions about how to use it:[1]

1. During the semester, use the book in preparing each night for the next day's class. To do this, first read your casebook. Then, use the *Casebook Correlation Chart* to get an idea of what part of the outline to read. Reading the outline will give you a sense of how the particular cases you've just read in your casebook fit into the overall structure of the subject. You may want to use a yellow highlighter to mark key portions of the *Emanuel*.

2. If you make your own outline for the course, use the *Emanuel* to give you a structure, and to supply black letter principles. You may want to rely especially on the *Capsule Summary* for this purpose. You are hereby authorized to copy small portions of the *Emanuel* into your own outline, provided that your outline will be used only by you or your study group, and provided that you are

---

1. The suggestions below relate only to this book. I don't talk about taking or reviewing class notes, using hornbooks or other study aids, joining a study group, or anything else. This doesn't mean I don't think these other steps are important — it's just that in this Preface I've chosen to focus on how I think you can use this outline.

the owner of the *Emanuel*.

3. When you first start studying for exams, read the *Capsule Summary* to get an overview. Also, review the *Flow Charts* and *Tables*. These two tasks will probably take you all or part of two days.

4. Either during exam study or earlier in the semester, do some or all of the *Quiz Yourself* short-answer questions. You can find these quickly by looking for *Quiz Yourself* entries in the Table of Contents. When you do these questions: (1) record your short "answer" on the small blank line provided after the question, but also: (2) try to compose a "mini essay." Remember that the only way to get good at writing essays is to write essays.

5. Three or four days before the exam, review the *Exam Tips* that appear at the end of each chapter. You may want to combine this step with step **4**, so that you use the Tips to help you spot the issues in the short-answer questions. You'll also probably want to follow up from many of the Tips to the main outline's discussion of the topic.

6. The night before the exam: (1) do some *Quiz Yourself* questions, just to get your thinking and writing juices flowing; and (2) re-scan the *Exam Tips* (spending about 2-3 hours).

Good luck in your Property course. If you'd like any other publication of Wolters Kluwer Law & Business, you can find it at your bookstore or at **www.wolterskluwerlb.com.**

Steve Emanuel
Larchmont, NY
April 2012

CASEBOOK CORRELATION CHART

(**Note:** general sections of the outline are omitted from this chart. **NC** = not directly covered by this casebook.)

Emanuel's Property Outline *(by chapter and section heading)*	Dukeminier, Krier, Alexander & Schill **Property** (7th Ed. 2010) (Wolters Kluwer)	Cribbet, Findley, Smith & Dzienkowski **Cases and Materials on Property** (9th Ed. 2008) (Foundation)	Rabin, Kwall, Kwall & Arnold **Fundamentals of Modern Property Law** (6th Ed. 2011) (Foundation)	Singer **Property Law: Rules, Policies and Practices** (5th Ed. 2010) (Wolters Kluwer)
CHAPTER 2 **TWO TYPES OF NON-REAL PROPERTY: PERSONAL PROPERTY AND INTELLECTUAL PROPERTY**				
I. Rights of Possessors	18-55, 70-88, 97-116	103-153	860	152-59, 168-77, 231-39
II. Accession	15	193-202	NC	319-28
III. *Bona Fide* Purchasers	162-63	203-212	NC	885
IV. Bailments	99	153-158	860	NC
V. Gifts	164-81	213-235	NC	151-52
VI. Intellectual Property	56-70	NC	1259-1355	131-46, 187-254
CHAPTER 3 **ADVERSE POSSESSION**	116-64	153-191	859-903	281-311
CHAPTER 4 **FREEHOLD ESTATES**				
I. Introduction	183-91	251-254	179-82	NC
II. Fee Simple	191-98, 222-51 206-23	254-267, 281-300	182-07	607-10, 616-25
III. Fee Tail	198-201	300-305	NC	614-15
IV. Life Estates	202-22, 249-50	267-281	187-88	610-11
CHAPTER 5 **FUTURE INTERESTS**				
II. Possibility of Reverter and Right of Entry	256-57	308-309	185-86	605, 608-09
III. Reversions	255-56	309-311	188	610, 754-55
IV. Remainders	259-63, 280-83	312-323	188-92	611-13
V. Rule in Shelley's Case	283-84	323-328	NC	614
VI. Doctrine of Worthier Title	284	328-334	NC	613-14
VII. Statute of Uses and Executory Interests	264-80	334-355	192-93	605, 610, 615
VIII. Waste	217-21, 505-56	276-281	239-56	650-54
IX. Rule Against Perpetuities	285-317	355-370	201-38	628-50
X. Restraints Upon Alienation	208-09, 249-50	NC	257-76	551-71, 658-62

CASEBOOK CORRELATION CHART (Continued)

Emanuel's Property Outline (*by chapter and section heading*)	Dukeminier, Krier, Alexander & Schill **Property** (7th Ed. 2010) (Wolters Kluwer)	Cribbet, Findley, Smith & Dzienkowski **Cases and Materials on Property** (9th Ed. 2008) (Foundation)	Rabin, Kwall, Kwall & Arnold **Fundamentals of Modern Property Law** (6th Ed. 2011) (Foundation)	Singer **Property Law: Rules, Policies and Practices** (5th Ed. 2010) (Wolters Kluwer)
CHAPTER 6				
MARITAL ESTATES				
I. **Rights During Marriage**	359-69	383-385	321-22, 323-24	688-90
II. **Effect of Divorce**	369-84	NC	324-38, 341-43	691, 694-707
III. **Death of a Spouse**	384-87	379-380	324	691
IV. **Community Property**	387-95	381-383	322-23, 338-340	691-92
V. **Domestic Partnerships, Same-Sex Marriages and Other Variations on Traditional Marriage**	395-418	383-385	342-43	707-22
CHAPTER 7				
CONCURRENT OWNERSHIP				
I. **Joint Tenancy**	320, 322-37	372-376, 385-420	277, 280-94, 309-19	665-66
II. **Tenancy in Common**	319-20	372	277	664-65
III. **Tenancy by the Entirety**	321	376-378, 402-405	277-78	670-71, 682-88
IV. **Relations between Co-tenants**	337-58	420-432	279-80, 295-307	667-70, 671-82
CHAPTER 8				
LANDLORD AND TENANT				
II. **Various Tenancies and Their Creation**				
Estate for Term of Years	421	475	81	734
Periodic Tenancies	421-22	475-476	82	734
Tenancy at Will	422-26	474-475	82	734-35
Tenancy at Sufferance	427	476-480	83	735
III. **Tenant's Right of Possession and Enjoyment**	438-42	468-474	48-56	747-48, 782-91
IV. **Condition of the Premises**	482-503	449-458, 488-501	57-81	791-829
V. **Tort Liability of Landlord and Tenant**	504-05	517-525	85-107	830-33
VI. **Tenant's Duties**	505-08	507-517	NC	749-54
VII. **Landlord's Remedies**	459-81	525-546	159-78	768-82
VIII. **Transfer and Sale by Lessor; Assignment and Subletting by Lessee**	442-59	546-558	135-58	754-68
IX. **Fair Housing / Rent Control Laws**	431-38, 508-15	458-468, 501-507	109-33	782, 925-1026

CASEBOOK CORRELATION CHART (Continued)

Emanuel's Property Outline *(by chapter and section heading)*	Dukeminier, Krier, Alexander & Schill **Property** (7th Ed. 2010) (Wolters Kluwer)	Cribbet, Findley, Smith & Dzienkowski **Cases and Materials on Property** (9th Ed. 2008) (Foundation)	Rabin, Kwall, Kwall & Arnold **Fundamentals of Modern Property Law** (6th Ed. 2011) (Foundation)	Singer **Property Law: Rules, Policies and Practices** (5th Ed. 2010) (Wolters Kluwer)
CHAPTER 9 **EASEMENTS AND PROMISES CONCERNING LAND**				
I. Easements Generally	765-68, 842-47	559-560	347-51	456-61, 463-71
II. Creation of Easements	768-73, 774-812	561-603	351-69, 441-60	56-66, 311-19, 426-63
III. Scope of Easements	820-30	603-612	371-91	463-75
IV. Repair and Maintenance of Easements	NC	NC	376	NC
V. Transfer and Subdivision of Easements	812-20	606-607	393-411	461-62, 472-73
VI. Termination of Easements	831-42	612-617	413-39	475
VII. Licenses	773-74	560-561, 575-576	39-47	425-26, 743-44
VIII. Covenants Running with the Land	847-53, 859-88	618-634	461-526	475-501, 573-91
IX. Equitable Servitudes	853-59, 888-924	634-672	345-46, 462-85, 545-62	423-25, 501-18, 532-51
X Modifications and Termination of Covenants and Servitudes	882-896	667-672	527-44	519-32
CHAPTER 10 **ZONING AND OTHER PUBLIC LAND-USE CONTROLS**				
I. Taking Clause	1081-1195	791, 807-879	645-713	1097-1205
II. Zoning Generally	925-40	753-762	619-21	1027-28
III. Legal Limits of Zoning	968-1010, 1019-36	763-767	625-30, 719-32, 738-41	1055-62
IV. Zoning Administration	941-68	772-790	621-44	1028-55
V. Exclusionary Zoning	1037-60	883-914	715-747	1014-26
VI. Regulation of Subdivision	NC	767-772	NC	NC
VII. Historical and Environmental Preservation	1010-18, 1113-31	820-855	825-58, 1237-57	1062-68
VIII. Eminent Domain	1061-80	791-807	591-615	1074-96

CASEBOOK CORRELATION CHART (Continued)

Emanuel's Property Outline *(by chapter and section heading)*	Dukeminier, Krier, Alexander & Schill **Property** (7th Ed. 2010) (Wolters Kluwer)	Cribbet, Findley, Smith & Dzienkowski **Cases and Materials on Property** (9th Ed. 2008) (Foundation)	Rabin, Kwall, Kwall & Arnold **Fundamentals of Modern Property Law** (6th Ed. 2011) (Foundation)	Singer **Property Law: Rules, Policies and Practices** (5th Ed. 2010) (Wolters Kluwer)
CHAPTER 11 **LAND SALE CONTRACTS, MORTGAGES, AND DEEDS**				
I. Land Sale Contracts	519-85	917-997, 1002-1067	1187-1207	837-72
II. Mortgages and Installment Contracts	616-44	974-1002	915-33, 973-1046	84-95, 893-923
III. Deeds	585-615	432-448, 1069-1127, 1190-1246	1047-79	872-76
IV. Conveyancing by Will: Ademption, Exoneration and Lapse	NC	NC	905-15, 935-72, 1081-1101, 1209-35	151
CHAPTER 12 **RECORDING SYSTEM AND TITLE ASSURANCE**				
I. Recording Statutes	645-704	1129-1188	1103-41	876-92
II. Title Registration (Torrens System)	709-13	1246-1254	1116-17	892-93
III. Methods of Title Assurance	551-52, 704-09, 714-27	1254-1299	1143-72	892
CHAPTER 13 **RIGHTS INCIDENT TO LAND**				
I. Nuisance	731-61	673-691	563-90	368-421
II. Lateral and Subjacent Support	738-39	691-698	NC	348-67
III. Water Rights	37-38	698-724	773-824	164-67, 337-48
IV. Air Rights	NC	730-750	NC	384-411

CAPSULE SUMMARY

This Capsule Summary is intended for review at the end of the semester. Reading it is not a substitute for mastering the material in the main outline. Numbers in brackets refer to the pages in the main outline where the topic is discussed. The order of topics is occasionally somewhat different from that in the main outline.

CHAPTER 2

TWO TYPES OF NON-REAL PROPERTY:
PERSONAL PROPERTY AND INTELLECTUAL PROPERTY

I. RIGHTS OF POSSESSORS

A. Wild animals: Once a person has gained possession of a *wild animal*, he has rights in that animal superior to those of the rest of the world.

B. Finders of lost articles: The finder of *lost property* holds it *in trust for the benefit of the true owner,* as a bailee. But the finder has rights *superior* to those of everyone except the true owner. [4-7]

> **Example:** P finds logs floating in a bay. He takes them and moors them with rope. The logs break loose, and are found by D, who takes them and refuses to return them to P. P may recover the value of the logs from D. P's possession is the equivalent of ownership as against anyone but the true owner.

1. Statutes of limitations: Although the possessor of goods holds them in trust for the true owner, all states have *statutes of limitations*, at the end of which the true owner can no longer recover the good from the possessor. Usually, the statute of limitations does not start to run until the true owner knows or with reasonable diligence should know the possessor's identity. [7-8]

II. *BONA FIDE* PURCHASERS

A. *Bona fide purchasers:* The problem of the *"bona fide purchaser"* arises when one who is in *wrongful possession of goods* (e.g., a thief, defrauder, finder, etc.) sells them to one who *buys for value* and *without knowledge* that the seller has no title. (This buyer is the "bona fide purchaser" or *b.f.p.*)

1. General rule: The general rule is that *a seller cannot convey better title than that which he holds* (but subject to exceptions summarized below).

a. Stolen goods: This general rule is always applied when the seller (or his predecessor in title) has *stolen* the property. [9]

> **Example:** X steals a car from P and sells it to Y, who ultimately sells it for fair value to D, who does not know it is stolen. P may recover the car from D, because a possessor of stolen goods can never convey good title, even to a b.f.p.

2. Exceptions: But where the goods are acquired from the original owner not by outright theft, but by less blatant forms of dishonesty and/or crime, the b.f.p. may be protected. [9]

a. "Voidable" title: First, a b.f.p. who takes from one who has a *"voidable"* title (as opposed to the "void" title that a thief has) will be protected. Thus if B obtains goods from A by *fraud* (e.g., B pays with counterfeit money or a bad check), B gets a voidable title, and if he immediately re-sells the goods to C, a b.f.p., A cannot get them back from C.

b. Estoppel: Also, the owner may lose to the b.f.p. by the principle of *estoppel*. If A expressly or impliedly represents that B is the owner of goods or has the authority to sell them, A cannot recover if C buys the goods in good faith from B. Today, one who entrusts goods to a *merchant* who deals in goods of that type gives the merchant power to transfer full ownership rights to a b.f.p. See UCC §2-402(2).

Example: Consumer leaves his watch with Jeweler for repairs. Jeweler is in the business of selling used watches as well as repairing them. Jeweler sells the watch to Purchaser, who pays fair market value and does not suspect that Jeweler does not own the watch. Consumer may not recover from Purchaser.

III. BAILMENTS

A. Bailments: A *bailment* is the *rightful possession* of goods by one who is *not their owner*. [11]

B. Duty during custody: During the time that the bailee (the person holding the goods) has the object in his possession, he is *not an insurer* of it. He is liable only for *lack of care*, but the precise standard depends on who is benefitted:

1. Mutual benefit: If the bailment is beneficial to *both parties*, the bailee must use *ordinary diligence* to protect the bailed object from damage or loss. [12]

Example: A hotel which takes guests' possessions and keeps them in its safe is liable for lack of ordinary care, such as where it fails to use reasonable anti-theft measures.

2. Sole benefit of bailor: If the benefit is solely for the bailor's benefit, the bailee is liable only for *gross negligence*. [12]

3. Sole benefit of bailee: If the bailment is solely for the benefit of the *bailee* (i.e., the bailor lends the object to the bailee for the latter's use), the bailee is required to use *extraordinary care* in protecting the goods from loss or damage (but he is still not an insurer, and is liable only if some degree of fault is shown). [12]

4. Contractual limitation: The modern trend is that the parties may change these rules by *contractual* provisions. But even by contract, the bailee generally may not relieve himself from liability for *gross* negligence. [12]

a. Acceptance: Also, for such a provision to be binding, the bailor must know of it and *"accept"* it. [13]

Example: P puts his car into a commercial garage run by D. The claim check asserts that D has no liability for negligence. The provision will be binding only if D can prove that P knew of and accepted this provision — D probably cannot make this showing, since P can argue that he regarded the claim check as merely a receipt.

IV. GIFTS

A. Definition: A gift is a *present transfer* of property by one person to another *without any consideration* or compensation. [13]

B. Not revocable: A gift is generally ***not revocable*** once made; that is, the donor cannot "take back" the gift. (But gifts "*causa mortis*," i.e., made in contemplation of death, are revocable if the donor escapes from the peril of death which prompted the gift.)

C. Three requirements: There are three requirements for the making of a valid gift: (1) there must be a ***delivery*** from the donor to the donee; (2) the donor must possess an ***intent*** to make a present gift; and (3) the donee must ***accept*** the gift.

    1. Delivery: For the ***delivery*** requirement to be met, ***control*** of the subject matter of the gift must pass from donor to donee. Thus a mere oral statement that a gift is being made will not suffice. [14]

       Example: O says orally to P, "I'm hereby giving you ownership of my valuable painting," but O does not give P the painting or any written instrument referring to the painting. There is no gift, and O still owns the painting.

       a. Symbolic and constructive delivery: *"Symbolic"* or *"constructive"* delivery will suffice in the case of property which cannot be physically delivered (e.g., ***intangibles***, such as the right to collect a debt from another person), or which would be very inconvenient to deliver (e.g., heavy furniture). That is, delivery of something ***representing*** the gift, or of something that gives the donee a ***means of obtaining*** the gift, will suffice. [14-15]

       Example: O is bedridden and cannot get to his locked bank safe-deposit box in another city. O gives P the key to the box, and tells P that the contents of the box now belong to P. Probably the transfer of the key will meet the delivery requirement as a "constructive delivery" of the box. [14]

       b. Written instrument: Most courts today hold that a ***written instrument*** (even if it is not under seal) is a valid substitute for physical delivery of the subject matter of the gift. [15]

       Example: O writes a letter to P saying, "I am hereby giving you my 500 shares of ABC stock as a present." Most courts today will hold that this letter is a written instrument the delivery of which to P meets the delivery requirement, so that physical transfer of the shares themselves is not necessary to make a gift of the shares. But a minority of courts would disagree.

       c. Gifts *causa mortis*: Courts are generally hostile to gifts *causa mortis* (in contemplation of death). Therefore, they frequently impose ***stricter requirements*** for delivery in such cases than where the gift is made *inter vivos* with no expectation of death. For instance, courts are less likely to accept symbolic and constructive delivery in lieu of actual physical transfer of the subject matter of the gift.

         i. Revocation: Also, gifts *causa mortis* may be ***revoked*** if the donor does not die of the contemplated peril (and most courts hold that revocation is ***automatic*** if the donor recovers). [16-17]

    2. Intent: In addition to delivery, there must be an ***intent*** on the part of the donor to make a gift. The intent must be to make a ***present*** transfer, not a transfer to take effect in the future. (A promise to make a ***future*** gift is not enforceable because of lack of consideration.) [17]

       a. Present gift of future enjoyment: However, a gift will be enforced if the court finds that it is a present gift of the ***right*** to the subject matter, even though the ***enjoyment*** of the subject matter is postponed to a later date. [17]

       Example: O writes to P, "I am now giving you title to my valuable painting, but I want to keep possession for the rest of my life." Most courts would hold that the gift is enforceable, because it was a present gift of ownership, even though enjoyment was postponed to the future. [17]

3. **Acceptance:** The requirement that the gift be *accepted* by the donee has little practical importance. Even if the donee does not know of the gift (because delivery is made to a third person to hold for the benefit of the donee), the acceptance requirement is usually found to be met. However, if the donee *repudiates* the gift, then there is no gift. [18]

V. INTELLECTUAL AND OTHER INTANGIBLE PROPERTY

A. Property in ideas and expressions: So-called *"intellectual property law"* — the regulation of products of intellectual work — forms a major and growing area of law. [21]

1. **Three core types of IP:** There are three core types of intellectual property ("IP"): *copyrights, patents* and *trademarks*. Copyrights and patents are almost exclusively the product of federal statutory law. Trademarks are a mixture of federal and state law. After our treatment of these three core types of IP, we briefly consider "publicity rights," which are almost solely a creature of state law.

B. Copyrights: *Copyright* law is regulated by a federal statute, the Copyright Act, that essentially preempts state law. The Act, 17 U.S.C. § 101 et seq, protects the *expression of ideas*, whether embodied in books, articles, musical forms, works of painting and sculpture, motion pictures, or the like. [21]

1. **Rights given to copyright holder:** The Copyright Act gives certain rights to owners of *"original works of authorship"* that are *"fixed in any tangible medium of expression."* A partial list of the copyright owner's exclusive rights includes:

   [1] the right to *reproduce* the copyrighted work (e.g., to print books or make sound recordings).

   [2] the right to prepare *"derivative works"* based on the copyrighted work (i.e., to create works that start from the original work and vary it; thus the owner of the copyright to *Gone With the Wind* has the right to create a sequel using the same characters).

   [3] the right to *sell, rent or lease copies* of the copyrighted work to the public.

   [4] the right to *perform* the copyrighted work publicly (in the case of literary, musical, dramatic, motion-picture, and other types of work that are capable of performance).

   [5] the right to *display* the copyrighted work publicly (e.g., the right to display a painting or sculpture, or a motion picture).

2. **Material must be "original" but not necessarily "novel":** To be protected by copyright, the material must be *"original"* in the sense that it was created by the author rather than copied from someone else. But the material does not have to be *"novel,"* in the sense that it never existed before. (That makes copyright law quite different from patent law, where only novel inventions may be patented.) [22]

   Example: Assume that two poets, each ignorant of the other, compose identical poems. Neither work is novel, yet both are original and, hence, copyrightable.

3. **Ideas and facts not copyrightable:** *Ideas* and *facts* narrated by an author are *not* protected by copyright — only original *"expressions"* of ideas or facts can be protected. [22]

   a. **Compilations:** On the other hand, *compilations* of facts are protected, but only if the compilation represents some *"minimal degree of creativity."* [*Feist Publications*] Typically, for a compilation of uncopyrightable facts to possess the minimum required creative element, the author must *select, coordinate or arrange the facts* in a somewhat *original* way.

   Example: A compilation of the names and addresses of telephone-company subscribers, listed alphabetically by last name, does not involve sufficient selection or arrangement to meet the "creativity" requirement. Therefore, such a compilation may not be copyrighted. [*Feist Publications*] [22]

4. **When copyright protection begins:** Copyright protection in a work begins as *soon as the work is created* in a tangible medium (e.g., writing on a page). That's true *whether or not there is a copyright notice* on the work. [22]

5. **Duration of protection:** The *duration* of copyright protection depends on what type of person owns the copyright. [23]

   a. **Owned by author:** Normally, the human *"author"* of the work owns the copyright. In that case, the copyright lasts for the *life of the author plus 70 years*, after which the work enters the public domain and may be used by anyone.

   b. **Works for hire:** But the Copyright Act recognizes the special category of a *"work for hire."* A work is a "work for hire" if either: (1) the work was prepared by an *employee* within the scope of his or her employment; or (2) in certain circumstances (e.g., collective works and movies), the work was specially ordered or commissioned.

      i. **Different duration:** If the work is a work for hire, the copyright lasts for *95 years from the year of its first publication*, or *120 years from the year of its creation*, whichever comes *first*. So normally, the work for hire will enter the public domain 95 years after its first publication.

6. **Fair use:** Even if the defendant's work is shown to have been copied from, and is substantially similar to, the plaintiff's copyrighted work, the defendant has an important affirmative defense: *fair use*. The Copyright Act says that "the fair use of a copyrighted work ... for purposes such as *criticism, comment, news reporting, teaching ... scholarship* or *research*, is *not an infringement of copyright*." 17 U.S.C. § 107. [23]

   a. **Multi-factor test:** The Copyright Act lists *four factors* that the court is to consider in determining whether the use qualifies for the fair use exemption:

      "(1) the *purpose and character* of the use, including whether such use is of a *commercial nature* or is for nonprofit *educational* purposes;

      (2) the *nature* of the copyrighted work;

      (3) the *amount and substantiality of the portion used* in relation to the copyrighted work as a whole; and

      (4) the effect of the use upon the *potential market for or value of* the copyrighted work."

   b. **Use as parody:** One type of use that is often found to constitute fair use is *parody*. In parody cases, the fact that the parody usually does not materially *decrease the market for or value of* the original copyrighted work (factor (4) above) weighs heavily towards a finding that the use is fair. [24]

7. **Contributory infringement:** The Copyright Act itself does not expressly provide for liability for *"contributory infringement."* But under general common-law principles, one who *intentionally induces or encourages another to infringe* a copyright can be civilly liable for contributory infringement. [*Metro-Goldwyn-Mayer Studios Inc. v. Grokster, Ltd.*] [24]

   Example: The Ds are two software companies that make and distribute free software that allows users to share files over peer-to-peer networks. The vast majority of filesharing acts by users are acts of infringement. Furthermore, each of the defendants actively encourages infringement (e.g., they each advertise themselves as the "best alternative to Napster," a prior clearly-infringing application). *Held*, the Ds are liable for contributory infringement, even though some of the uses to which the customers put the software were non-infringing. [*Metro-Goldwyn-Mayer Studios Inc. v. Grokster, Ltd.*]

C. Patents: The U.S. *patent* system is so complex and specialized that we cannot really even summarize it here. Here are a few of the most superficial points about patent law:

   1. Inventions: Patent law protects, in essence, *inventions and discoveries*. [25]

   2. Novel, useful and nonobvious: To be patentable, an invention must be: (1) *novel*; (2) *nonobvious*; and (3) *useful*. [25]

      a. Novelty: The requirement of *novelty* means, in essence, that the invention must be *"new,"* i.e., *not previously invented or discovered* anywhere. Only the first to file a patent application for the invention or discovery can receive a patent.

      b. Nonobviousness: The requirement of *nonobviousness* means that the invention is not patentable if the improvement it represents over prior art *"would have been obvious* at the time the invention was made to a *person having ordinary skill in the art"* in question.

      c. Usefulness: The requirement of *usefulness* means that an invention that could never "work" (e.g., a perpetual-motion machine) would not be patentable.

   3. Application process: The inventor applies to the U.S. Patent and Trademark Office for a patent. The application must follow a prescribed format, including a written description of the invention and a set of *"claims."* [26]

      a. Search of prior art: A Patent Examiner conducts a search of prior art to determine whether the requirements of novety, nonobviousness, etc. are satisfied. Often, the Examiner requires that the claims be narrowed, or their number reduced, to account for prior art.

   4. Duration: Once the patent is granted, the patent term is *20 years* from the earliest *filing date* of the patent application. 35 U.S.C. § 154. [26]

D. Trademarks: A *trademark* is a name, symbol, type of packaging or other means of *identifying the producer of a good or service.* Trademarks are protected under both federal and state law. The federal statute protecting trademarks is called the *Lanham Act*, 15 U.S.C. §§ 1051-1127. [26]

   1. Definition of "trademark": Under the Lanham Act, a "trademark" applies only to goods (not services). A trademark can consist of "any *word, name* [or] *symbol*," when used to *"identify and distinguish"* a person's goods from those produced by others, and to "indicate the *source*" of the goods. [26]

      a. "Service mark": A *"service mark,"* under the Lanham Act, is the same as a trademark, except that it is used to identify a service rather than a good.

   2. Function: Trademark law gives the owner of a "mark" the *exclusive* right to *use that mark* in connection with the sale of a particular good or service in a particular *geographic area.* The main purpose of trademark law is to protect *consumers* from being *confused* by the fact that two companies are using the same or similar names for their products. [26]

   3. Federal and state law: It is very common for plaintiffs (owners of marks) to join a federal Lanham Act infringement claim together with a claim for violation of *state* trademark laws. A suit for federal Lanham Act violations may be brought in *either* state or federal court. [27]

   4. Trademark Register: Federal law gives the owner of a trademark a way to *"register"* it, so that the *the world is put on notice* that of who owns the mark for a particular geographic area and type of use. The U.S. Patent and Trademark Office (PTO) maintains a "Principal Register" of trademarks. A mark that appears on the Principal Register is known as a *"registered trademark"* (indicated by the ® symbol). Having a registered trademark not only allows the owner to put the world on constructive notice of the mark, but entitles her to get an *injunction* against anyone else who adopts the same or a confusingly-similar mark. [27]

    a. Procedure for registration: The trademark applicant must say, in her application, *either:*

      [1] that she is *already using* the mark in interstate commerce, or

      [2] that she has a bona fide *intent to use the mark* in commerce in the future.

      i. Already in use: If the mark is *already* in use (an *"actual use"* application), the PTO issues a *certificate of registration*, and registers the mark on the Principal Register. The owner is then immediately entitled to use the ® symbol in connection with the mark, and to enjoin others from using the mark.

      ii. Intent to use: But if the applicant merely *intends* to use the mark in the future (an *"intent to use"* application), the PTO issues a "Notice of Allowance." Then, the applicant must begin to use the mark in interstate commerce, and must, within 36 months of the Notice, file a verified statement that such use has occurred.

5. "Distinctive" vs. "generic" marks: A mark must be *"distinctive"* in order to be registrable. That is, the mark must tend to *identify the precise source* of the goods or services. Therefore, designations that are merely *"generic"* — i.e., that are common names for the products or services in question — may not be registered. [28]

    Example: A maker of candies would not be permitted to register "Candy" as a trademark for the candies — the term "candy" is a generic term used to describe the whole category, so it must be kept available for other manufacturers to refer to their products without infringement.

    a. Descriptive terms: Similarly, terms that are *"descriptive"* of the type of goods or services in question generally may not be trademarked. For instance, *geographical* words or phrases that merely indicate the place of origin of the product or service generally cannot be trademarked.

    b. Secondary meaning: Even if a market is not *inherently* distinctive, it may *become distinctive* through the way it is *used in the marketplace*. In that event, the mark is said to have developed *"secondary meaning."* To say a mark has developed secondary meaning is to say that in the mind of the consuming public, the primary significance of the mark is now to indicate the precise source of the product, rather than to describe the product. [28]

    Example: The mark "Kool," used on cigarettes, is no longer mostly descriptive; it has developed a secondary meaning (as identifying a particular brand of cigarette), and has become registrable. After registration, the owner of the brand can now prevent anyone else from selling cigarettes under the "Kool" mark.

6. Anti-cybersquatting statute: The federal *Anticybersquatting Consumer Protection Act (ACPA)* prohibits anyone from registering or using an Internet domain name that is identical to or confusingly similar to a trademark, if the person "has a *bad faith intent to profit from that mark."* [29]

    a. Function: The ACPA tries to suppress a practice in which a person uses another's trademark as part of a website's name, and then in effect holds the domain registration for that name *hostage* so that it can be sold at a profit to the trademark owner. If the Act is violated, the court can impose civil liability, and can also order the domain name to be *transferred* to the owner of the mark. [29]

E. The right of "publicity": Most states today recognize, either by common law or statute, a *"right of publicity."* As a practical matter, the right is only of economic value to *celebrities*. [29]

1. **Right to exclusive use of name and likeness:**   The right of publicity is usually defined as a person's right to the *exclusive use of her name and likeness.* In its most basic form, the right entitles a celebrity to prevent others from using the celebrity's name or photograph for *commercial purposes*, including the advertising of products.

2. **Right during lifetime:** Where the right is recognized, it always extends throughout the *lifetime* of the celebrity.

3. **Right after death:**   In most states that recognize the right of publicity, the right *persists after the celebrity's death*, generally for a period *between 20 and 100 years*. The right is usually held to *descend by will or by intestacy.* [30]

CHAPTER 3
ADVERSE POSSESSION

I.   ADVERSE POSSESSION GENERALLY

A. Function: All states have *statutes of limitation* that eventually bar the owner of property from suing to *recover possession* from one who has wrongfully entered the property. (Suits to recover property are called *"ejectment"* suits.) Once the limitations period has passed, the wrongful possessor effectively gets *title* to the land. This title is said to have been gained by *"adverse possession"* (or *"AP"*). [31]

1. **Clears title:**   The doctrine of adverse possession also furnishes the additional benefit of *clearing titles to land*.

   Example: A state has a 20-year statute of limitations on ejectment actions. X claims that he holds title to Blackacre, and wants to sell it to Y. Y will only have to check the land records going back 20 years — plus perhaps some additional period to cover the possibility that the running of the statute of limitations might have been "tolled" for some reason — in order to check X's claim of ownership. The fact that, say, 100 years ago X's alleged "predecessor in title" took the property by wrongfully entering on it, is irrelevant, since the right of the rightful possessor to regain possession has long since been barred by the statute of limitations.

B. Components of adverse possession: To obtain title by adverse possession, the possessor must satisfy *five main requirements*:

   [1]   the possession must be *"open, notorious and visible"*;

   [2]   the possession must be *"actual"*;

   [3]   the possession must be *"hostile,"* i.e., without the owner's consent;

   [4]   the possession must be *continuous*; and

   [5]   the possession must be for at least the *length of the statutory period* (perhaps longer if the owner was under a disability).

   [31]

II.   "OPEN, NOTORIOUS AND VISIBLE" POSSESSION

A. "Open, notorious and visible" requirement: The adverse possessor's use of the land must be *"open, notorious and visible."* Usually, this means that the possessor's use of the property must be similar to that which a typical owner of *similar property* would make. [32]

Example: Blackacre is undeveloped wild land suitable only for hunting and fishing. If D builds a small hunting cabin on the land, and enters several times per year to hunt and fish, this will meet the "open, notorious and visible" requirement if a typical owner of similar property would make such limited use. But it would not qualify if a typical owner would use the property more extensively, build a much bigger dwelling, etc.

III. "ACTUAL" POSSESSION

A. Actual possession: Courts often say that the possession must be *"actual."* But this requirement overlaps largely with the requirement that possession be "open, notorious and visible." [33]

    1. Occupation by tenant of adverse possessor: The adverse possessor does not necessarily have to be in possession of the property *personally*. For instance, if he leases his possessory interest to a *tenant*, the tenant's possession may suffice for meeting the "actual possession" requirement. [33]

        Example: O owns Blackacre. A physically occupies the property for a short while. A then purports to lease the property to T. A collects rents from T for the statutory period, and does not remit any of this rent to O or otherwise acknowledge that O is the record owner. T's possession will be imputed to A, and A will therefore become the owner by AP at the end of the statutory period. That's because although T's possession was not hostile (see below for the meaning of "hostile") as to A, A's constructive possession (via T) was hostile as to O.

IV. "HOSTILE" POSSESSION

A. "Hostile" possession: The adverse possession must be *"hostile."* This merely means that possession must be *without the owner's consent*. [33]

    Example: T occupies Blackacre under a lease from O, the record owner. T's possession of the premises is not "hostile" since it is with O's consent, so even if T resides for more than the statutory period, he does not become the owner by adverse possession.

    1. Starts as permissive and then becomes hostile: A possession that *starts as a non-hostile* one can *become hostile*. When this happens, the period of possession starts running as of the moment the possession turns hostile. [34]

        a. Life estate *per autre vie* or fee simple determinable: For instance, the possessor might be someone who holds a *life estate per autre vie*, or a *fee simple determinable* — if the holder continues in possession after the end of the life estate or fee simple determinable, this period of additional possession will typically count for adverse-possession purposes. [35]

B. Bad faith possessor: A *minority* of courts impose the additional requirement that the possessor must have a *bona fide belief* that he has *title* to the property. Thus in these minority states, a mere *"squatter"* never gets title. [34]

C. Boundary disputes: Adverse possession is most frequently used to resolve mistakes about the location of *boundary lines*. Most courts hold that one who possesses an adjoining landowner's land, under the mistaken belief that he has only possessed up to the boundary of his own land, meets the requirement of "hostile" possession and can become an owner by adverse possession. [35]

    Example: O is the true owner of Blackacre, and A is the true owner of the adjoining parcel, Whiteacre. When A moves onto Whiteacre, he mistakenly believes that his land goes all the way up to a creek, but the creek is in fact 15 yards into Blackacre. Accordingly, A builds a fence up to the creek, and uses the enclosed portion of Blackacre for farming. At the end of the statutory period, most courts would hold that A becomes the owner of the 15-yard portion by adverse possession.

V.   CONTINUITY OF POSSESSION

A. Continuity of possession: The adverse possession must be *"continuous"* throughout the statutory period, as a general rule. [36]

    1. Interruption by owner: Thus if the owner *re-enters the property* in order to regain possession, this will be an interruption of the adverse possession. When this happens, the adverse possessor must start his occupancy *from scratch*. [37-37]

B. Seasonal possession: *Seasonal use* may qualify, if that's the only kind of use *most owners of similar property would make*. If so, the entire twelve months of the year will be counted towards the statute of limitations. [37]

> **Example:** Blackacre consists solely of forest. An adverse possessor, *X*, comes onto the land each year and cuts the timber during the standard timber-cutting season for that region. *X* will probably meet the continuity-of-possession requirement — he has behaved as an average owner of such forested land would behave. Therefore, the entire 12 months of the year will count towards *X*'s adverse possession.

    1. Intermittent activities like hunting: But *intermittent activities* that are *not the sort of activities done only by true owners* — like occasional *hunting* on the property — are generally *not* enough to constitute continuous possession.

C. Tacking: Possession by two adverse possessors, one after the other, may be *"tacked"* if the two are in *"privity"* with each other. That is, their periods of ownership can be *added together* for purposes of meeting the statutory period. [37]

> **Example:** *A*, who owns Whiteacre, adversely possesses a small strip of the adjacent Blackacre, due to confusion about boundaries. *A* adversely possesses that piece of Blackacre for 15 years; he then sells Whiteacre to *P*, who holds for another seven years (and who adversely possesses the same strip). *A*'s 15 years of possession can be "tacked" to *P*'s seven years, so that *P* meets a 20-year limitations period. (In most courts, this is true whether *A*'s deed to *P* recited the false boundary lines that *A* and *B* believe to be correct, or recited the true boundary lines that do not include part of Blackacre.) [37]

    1. No privity: But if the two successive adverse possessors are not in *"privity,"* i.e., do not have some continuity of interest, then *tacking will not be allowed*. [37]

> **Example:** *A* adversely possesses Blackacre for 15 years. He then abandons the property. *B* then enters for another seven years. *B* cannot "tack" his holding period to *A*'s holding period, since they had no continuity of interest. But if *A* had purported to give *B* his interest by oral gift, deed, bequest or inheritance, then *B* could tack.

VI.   MISCELLANEOUS

A. Length of time: The length of the holding period for adverse possession varies from state to state. It is usually 15 years or longer.

    1. Disabilities: If the true owner of property is under a *disability*, in nearly all states he is given *extra time* within which to bring an ejectment action. [38]

> **Example:** Statutes often hold that the running of the limitations period is suspended until the true owner becomes 21. Usually, the person is given an additional time, say 10 years, to sue after he reaches 21.

    2. Tacking on owner's side: There is effectively "tacking" on the *owner's* as well as the possessor's side. [38]

Example: *O* is the owner of Blackacre in 1980, when *A* enters and begins to adversely possess. In 2000, *O* conveys to *X*. Under a 21-year statute, *A* will gain adverse possession in 2001, even though he has not by then held for 21 years against either *O* or *X* separately.

B. Rights of adverse possessor: Once the statutory period expires, the adverse possessor effectively gets *title*. However, the possessor usually cannot *record* title (since he has no deed). But he can apply for a judicial determination of adverse possession, and if he gets it, that determination can be recorded as if it were a deed. [39]

    1. Need to inspect: Since a title gained by adverse possession usually cannot be recorded, a buyer of property cannot be sure that the record owner still owns it (and that the record owner can therefore convey a good deed) unless the buyer *physically inspects* the property. [39]

    2. Scope of property obtained: Normally, the possessor acquires title only to the portion of the property *"actually"* occupied. [40]

        a. Constructive adverse possession: But there is one important exception: by the doctrine of *"constructive"* adverse possession, one who enters property under *"color of title"* (i.e., a written instrument that is defective for some reason) will gain title to the *entire area described in the instrument*, even if he "actually" possesses only a portion. [40]

C. Conflicts: If there is a conflict between two person's whose interests are solely possessory, the general rule is that the *first possessor has priority over the subsequent one*. [41]

Chapter 4

FREEHOLD ESTATES

I. INTRODUCTION

A. Estates generally: One does not really "own" Blackacre. Instead, one owns an "estate in Blackacre." Traditionally, there are two types of estates: *freehold* and *non-freehold*.

    1. Freehold estates: The three freehold estates are:

        [1] the *fee simple* (which may be either absolute or defeasible);

        [2] the *fee tail*; and

        [3] the *life estate*. [49]

    2. Non-freehold: The non-freehold estates are:

        [1] the estate for *years*;

        [2] the *periodic estate*; and

        [3] the *estate at will*. [49]

II. THE FEE SIMPLE

A. Fee simple absolute: The *fee simple absolute* is the most unrestricted and longest estate. [50]

    1. Inheritable: The fee simple absolute is *inheritable* under intestacy statutes. Thus if the owner of a fee simple absolute dies, the property passes to the people deemed to be his "heirs" under the intestacy statute of the state where the land is located.

2. **Words to create:** Generally, a fee simple absolute is created by using the words *"and his heirs."* Thus at common law, the only way for O to convey a fee simple absolute to A is for O to convey "to A and his heirs." [50]

   a. **Abolished:** But most states have *abolished* the requirement that the phrase "and his heirs" be used. Thus in most states, if O conveys *"to A,"* this will give A a fee simple absolute. [51]

B. **Fee simple defeasible:** The holder of a fee simple *defeasible* may hold or convey the property, but he and those who take from him must use the property *subject to a restriction.* [51-55]

   1. **Three types:** There are three types of fee simple defeasible:

      [1] the fee simple *determinable*;

      [2] the fee simple *subject to a condition subsequent*; and

      [3] the fee simple *subject to an executory limitation*.

      We'll look at each one separately.

   2. **Determinable:** A fee simple *determinable* is a fee simple which *automatically* comes to an end when a stated event occurs (or, perhaps, fails to occur). [51-53]

      a. **Restriction on uses:** Most often, the fee simple determinable is used to *prevent the property from being put to a certain use* which the grantor opposes. The limitation controls even after the property changes hands numerous times.

         Example: *O* owns Blackacre in fee simple. He sells the property "to *A* and his heirs so long as the premises are not used for the sale of alcoholic beverages." *A* then purports to convey a fee simple absolute to *B*, who builds a bar. When the first alcoholic beverage is sold, *B*'s interest *automatically* ends, and the property reverts to *O* (or his heirs).

      b. **Words needed for creating:** Words with a *"durational aspect"* typically signal a fee simple determinable. That is, the words used to create it generally make it clear the estate is to have a particular duration, and is then to end *automatically* upon the occurrence of the stated event. [51]

         i. **"So long as":** Most commonly, the fee simple determine is created by use of the phrase *"so long as"* (or "as long as"), as in the above Example where *A* takes "so long as the premises are not used for the sale of alcoholic beverage."

         ii. **"Until or "during":** Other common formulations are *"until* [Event X happens]," *"during* [the time when Event X has *not* yet happened]," or "*while* [Event X has not yet happened]."

         iii. **Statement of motive or purpose not enough:** On the other hand, a mere statement of the transferor's *motive or purpose* in making the transfer is *not* usually enough to create a fee simple determinable — typically, a fee simple absolute results from such a statement. [52]

            Example: *O* conveys "To City for the purpose of operating a public library." *O*'s statement of purpose isn't enough to make City's interest a fee simple determinable — City gets a fee simple absolute. [52]

      c. **Possibility of reverter:** The creator of a fee simple determinable is always left with a *"possibility of reverter,"* i.e., the possibility that title will revert to him if the stated event occurs.

         Example: In the example in 2(a) above, *O*, following the conveyance, is left with a possibility of reverter if alcohol is sold.

   d. **Rule Against Perpetuities not applicable:** The Rule Against Perpetuities (RAP) is usually held ***not to apply to a possibility of reverter following a fee simple determinable.*** (For more about the RAP, see C-22.) [53]

      Example: *O* owns Blackacre in fee simple. He sells the property "to *A* and his heirs so long as the premises are not used for the sale of alcoholic beverages." *A* has a fee simple determinable, and *O* has a possibility of reverter. Since the RAP doesn't apply to the possibility of reverter, *O*'s distant heirs can get the property back automatically 200 years from now if *A*'s heirs sell alcoholic beverages on the site. (This result assumes that there's no statute of limitations on possibilities of reverter, as discussed immediately below.)

      i. **Statute of limitations:** For this reason, some states have enacted ***statutes of limitation*** that bar a possibility of reverter after a certain period after the fee simple determinable is created. (But other states' statutes don't start to run until the stated event occurs, which won't avoid the 200-year problem in the above example.)

3. **Fee simple subject to condition subsequent:** The fee simple ***subject to a condition subsequent*** is also geared to the happening of a particular event, but unlike the fee simple determinable, the fee simple subject to a condition subsequent ***does not automatically end*** when the event occurs. Instead, the grantor has a ***right of entry,*** i.e., a right to ***take back*** the property — but nothing happens until he ***affirmatively exercises that right.*** [53]

   a. **Words creating:** The words that create a fee simple subject to condition subsequent usually have a "conditional" flavor, such as ***"upon express condition that …,"*** or ***"provided that …"*** Also, most courts require that there also be a statement that the grantor may ***enter the property*** to terminate the estate if the stated event occurs.

      Example: *O* conveys Blackacre to *A* and his heirs "but upon condition that no alcohol is ever served; if alcohol is served, Grantor or his heirs may re-enter the property and terminate the estate." *A* has a fee simple subject to condition subsequent.

   b. **Distinguishing from fee simple determinable:** A key difference between the fee simple subject to condition subsequent and the fee simple determinable relates to the ***statute of limitations.*** When an f.s. determinable is involved, the holders of the possibility of reverter often have a long or unlimited time to sue (see above). But in the case of an f.s. subject to condition subsequent, the statute of limitations usually starts to run upon the occurrence of the stated event, and usually is for a very ***short*** period — so if the holder of the right of entry does not promptly re-enter or sue, he will lose the right. [54]

   c. **Rule Against Perpetuities not applicable:** The Rule Against Perpetuities (RAP) doesn't ***apply to a right of entry*** following a fee simple subject to condition subsequent. (For more about the RAP, see C-22.) [54]

4. **Fee simple subject to executory limitation:** A fee simple ***subject to an executory limitation*** provides for the estate to pass to a ***third person*** (one other than the grantor) upon the happening of the stated event. [55-56]

      Example: *O* conveys "to *A* and his heirs, but if *A* dies without children surviving him, then to *B* and his heirs." *A* has a fee simple subject to an executory limitation.

   a. **Perpetuities:** The ***Rule Against Perpetuities (RAP) applies*** to executory interests following a fee simple subject to executory limitation. (For more about the RAP, see p. C-22.) If the RAP makes the executory interest void, the preceding fee simple may become absolute. [54]

      Example: *O* conveys a building "to City, but if City ceases to use the building as a public school, to *A* and his heirs." City has a fee simple subject to executory limitation, and *A* has an executory interest. Because executory interests are subject to the Rule Against Perpetuities, *A*'s interest is subject to the Rule. Since *A*'s (purported) executory interest might not vest until after all lives in being at the time *O* conveyed plus 21 years, the executory interest is void as a violation of the RAP. Consequently, City has a fee simple absolute.

III. THE FEE TAIL

A. Fee tail generally: The *fee tail* allows the owner of land to ensure that the property **remains within his family** indefinitely. If *O* conveys a fee tail to his son, *A*, and the fee tail is enforced, then upon *A*'s death the property will go to *A*'s heir, then to that heir's heir, etc. — *A* and his decedents can never convey the property outside the family line. (If they try to do so, then the property reverts to *O*'s heirs.) [56]

   1. Words to create: The most common way of creating a fee tail is by a grant "to A and the **heirs of his body.**" [57]

B. Modern treatment: Today, in most states a grant or bequest that would be a fee tail at common law is simply **converted** by statute to a **fee simple absolute.** (But a minority of states follow various approaches, including life estate to the grantee, with a remainder in fee simple to his issue.) No states today fully enforce the fee tail as a method of ensuring that property will descend along bloodlines and will not be conveyed outside the family tree. [57]

IV. THE LIFE ESTATE

A. Life estate generally: A *life estate* is an interest which lasts for the lifetime of a person. Ordinarily, the lifetime by which the life estate is "measured" is that of the holder of the life estate. [57]

   Example: *O* conveys "to *A* for his lifetime, then to *B* in fee simple."

   1. Phrase creating: A life estate is usually created by the words "to A during his life" or "to A for life."

   2. Defeasible: A life estate may be **defeasible**, just as a fee simple may be. [58]

   Example: *O* conveys "to *A*, for so long as she shall remain my widow, then to my son *B*." *A* has a life estate determinable.

   3. Life estate *per autre vie*: There can be a life estate that is measured by the life of someone other than the grantee. This is called a life estate *"per autre vie"* ("by another life"). [59]

   Example: *O* conveys "to *A* for the life of *B*, then to *C* and his heirs." *A* has a life estate per autre vie.

   a. Grantee dies before end of measuring life: Today, if the grantee of a life estate per autre vie dies before the end of the measuring life, the balance of the estate is treated as personal property, which passes by will or by intestacy. Thus in the above example, if *A* died before *B*, *A*'s interest would pass as provided in *A*'s will or under the intestacy statute.

B. Duties and powers of life tenant: Here's a summary of the **powers and duties** of the life tenant.

   1. Powers of life tenant The life tenant's powers to deal with the property are more **restricted** than for the holder of a fee simple, because the life tenant cannot act in a way that would damage the remainder or other future interest.

   a. Right to keep income: The life tenant has the exclusive right to **lease out** the premises (but not beyond the term of the life tenant's own life), and the exclusive right to **keep all rents.** [59]

    i. **Must pay expenses:** But the life tenant's right to keep all rents is subject to her obligation, discussed below, to pay all current expenses.

  b. **Conveyance of interest:** The life tenant may **convey** any interest in the property, up to and including the entirety of his own interest. [61]

    Example: If *A* holds a life estate, he may convey to *B* either for the life of *A* (in which case *B* has an life estate *per autre vie; see supra*, p. C-14), or for a term of years.

    i. **No greater:** But the life tenant **cannot** convey a **fee simple**, or any other estate **greater than the life estate he holds.** If he does purport to convey a greater interest (e.g., a fee simple), the conveyance will be effective, but only to convey the **entirety of the grantor's life estate.**

      Example: *O* conveys a life estate to *A*. *A* purports to convey "to *B* and her heirs." *A*'s conveyance will be interpreted to pass *A*'s life estate to *B* (so that *B* has an estate for the life of *A*).

    ii. **Lease by life tenant for term of years:** This principle means that if a life tenant makes a **lease for a term of years**, that lease will **immediately be cut short** if the life tenant **dies**. And that's true even if the holder of the reversion acquiesced to the lease.

      Example: *O* conveys Blackacre "to my son Sam for life." Sam then makes a 15-year lease of the property to Tenant. *O* is aware that the lease is being made, and tacitly approves. Two years later, Sam suddenly dies. Tenant's lease is immediately over, and *O* can have him ejected from the premises.

2. **Duties of life tenant:** The life tenant has a number of **duties** vis-à-vis the future interest. These include the following:

  a. **No waste:** The life tenant may not commit **waste**, i.e., an **unreasonable impairment of the value** which the property will have when the holder of the future interest takes possession. [62]

    Example: If the property includes a *structure* that has significant value, the life tenant may ordinarily *not demolish* it.

    i. **Demolition and rebuilding:** But most courts in America now allow at least some **"ameliorative waste."** [62] That is, the life tenant may demolish an existing structure and build a new one provided that:

      [1] the **value** of the **reversion** is **not decreased** (i.e., the waste really *is* "ameliorative"); and

      [2] because of **changes to the neighborhood**, or for other reasons, it is very **unlikely that a rational person** in the position of the future-interest-holder would, if she owned the property outright today, want to **continue the prior use.**

  b. **Current operating expenses:** The life tenant must **pay all current operating expenses** of the property.

    i. **Repairs:** Thus the life tenant must **make (and pay for) reasonable "maintenance-style" repairs** (though probably not major structural repairs like a new roof).

    ii. **Taxes:** The life tenant must **pay all property taxes**.

    iii. **Limited to rental or occupancy value:** In the case of a dispute between the life tenant and the holder of the future interest, the life tenant's responsibility for current operating expenses like repairs and taxes applies **only** to the extent the life tenant **received rents** from the property, or the extent of the property's **fair rental value** if the life tenant herself occupies it. That is, the life tenant has **no personal liability** for current operating expenses beyond the **net financial benefits** she has received. [63]

c. **Payment of mortgage:** When a **mortgage** is put on the property before the life tenancy is created, most courts **allocate** the duty to pay mortgage interest and principal **between the life estate and the future interest.** Usually the allocation of both interest and principal is done more or less **in ratio to the present value** of the life estate versus the present value of the future interests. [63]

   i. **No personal obligation:** But as with repairs or taxes, neither the holder of the life estate nor the holder of the future interest is **personally liable** for his or her allocated share of the mortgage, except to the extent that the share is more than covered by the net operating income of the property. Therefore, if the property doesn't earn enough in any given year to cover the life tenant's fairly-allocated share of mortgage interest and principal, the remainderman is **not entitled to an order compelling the life tenant to make up the shortfall;** instead, the remainderman's sole remedy is to lay out the money and then get it back "off the top" if the property is sold while the life estate is still in force. [64]

CHAPTER 5

FUTURE INTERESTS

I. FUTURE INTERESTS GENERALLY

A. **Five future interests:** There are five future estates:

   [1] the *possibility of reverter*;

   [2] the *right of entry*;

   [3] the *reversion*;

   [4] the *remainder*; and

   [5] the *executory interest.*

II. POSSIBILITY OF REVERTER; RIGHT OF ENTRY

A. **Possibility of reverter and right of entry:** The *possibility of reverter* and the *right of entry* follow the fee simple determinable and the fee simple subject to a condition subsequent, respectively. [69-71]

   1. **Possibility of reverter:** When the owner of a fee simple absolute transfers a fee simple **determinable**, the grantor automatically retains a **possibility of reverter**. All states allow this possibility of reverter to be **inherited**, or to be devised by will; most but not all states also allow it to be conveyed *inter vivos*. [69-71]

   2. **Right of entry:** If the holder of an interest in land (e.g., a fee simple absolute) conveys his interest but attaches a **condition subsequent**, the transferor has a **"right of entry"** (sometimes called, more elaborately, a **"right of entry for condition broken"**) Most commonly, one who holds a fee simple absolute and who then conveys a fee simple subject to condition subsequent has a right of entry. [70]

      Example: *O* owns Blackacre in fee simple absolute. He conveys "to *A* and his heirs, on condition that liquor never be sold on the premises; if liquor is sold thereon, *O* or his heirs may re-enter the premises." The conveyance to *A* is a fee simple subject to condition subsequent, and *O* therefore reserves a right of entry.

(Capsule Summary — C A P S U L E S U M M A R Y, printed vertically in left margin)

   a. **Incident to reversion:** Often, a transferor who holds a right of entry also holds a *reversion*. Thus the typical lease contains various right of entry clauses (e.g., the right to re-enter if the tenant does not pay rent), as well as a reversion at the end of the lease term. [70]

   b. **Alienability:** If the right of entry is incident to a reversion (as in the prior paragraph), it *passes with the reversion*. (Thus if a landlord sells his property, he will be deemed to have also sold his right of entry to the buyer.) If the right of entry is *not* incident to a reversion, in most states the right of entry may be left by will and passes under the intestacy statute, but may not be conveyed *inter vivos*. (But some states allow even the *inter vivos* conveyance). [70]

III. REVERSIONS

A. Reversions generally: A *reversion* is created when the holder of a vested estate transfers to another a *smaller estate*; the reversion is the interest which *remains in the grantor*. [71]

> **Example:** *A* holds a fee simple absolute in Blackacre. *A* conveys "to *B* for life." *A* is deemed to have retained a "reversion," which will become possessory in *A* (or his heirs) upon *B*'s death.

   1. **Distinguishing from possibility of reverter:** Distinguish between a reversion and a possibility of reverter. If the grantor has given away a fee simple determinable, he retains only a possibility of reverter. If he has given away something *less* than a fee simple, he retains a reversion. [72]

   2. **Alienability:** Reversions are completely alienable: they may pass by will, by intestacy or by *inter vivos* conveyance. [72]

IV. REMAINDERS

A. Remainders generally: A *remainder* is a future interest in someone other than the grantor or the grantee of a possessory interest, if the future interest can become possessory only upon the *expiration* of the *prior possessory interest*, created by the *same instrument*. [72]

   1. **Requirements:** There are three requirements for a future interest to be a remainder:

     [1] the grantor must convey a *present possessory* estate to one transferee;

     [2] the grantor must create a *non-possessory* estate in *another* transferee by the *same instrument*; and

     [3] the second, non-possessory, estate (the remainder) must be capable of becoming possessory only on the *"natural"* expiration (as opposed to the cutting short) of the prior estate. [72]

> **Example:** *O* conveys "to *A* for life, then to *B* and his heirs." *B* has a remainder because: (1) a present interest was created in *A*; (2) a future interest was created in someone other than *A*, by the same instrument; and (3) the second interest (the remainder) will become possessory only after the natural expiration of the first one (i.e., after *A*'s death).

   2. **Following a term of years:** Today, we refer to an estate *following a term of years* as a remainder. [72]

> **Example:** *O* conveys "to *A* for 10 years, then to *B* and his heirs." Today, *B* is said to have a remainder, even though this would not have been called a remainder at common law.

   3. **Distinguished from reversion:** Distinguish between the remainder and the reversion. Most importantly, the remainder is created in someone *other than the transferor*, whereas the reversion is an interest left in the transferor after he has conveyed an interest to someone else. [73-73]

C
A
P
S
U
L
E

S
U
M
M
A
R
Y

4. No remainder after fee simple determinable: There cannot be a remainder after any kind of fee simple, including after a *fee simple determinable*. If an interest is created in a third person to follow a fee simple determinable, that interest is called an "executory interest," not a remainder. [73]

B. Vested vs. contingent remainders: Remainders are either *"vested"* or *"contingent."* Here's a brief summary of the distinction (with more detail to come below):

❑ **Vested:** A *vested remainder* is one that is **certain to become possessory** whenever and however the prior estate terminates, and we can say at the moment of creation who will take possession whereas ...

❑ **Contingent:** A *contingent remainder* is one that is **not certain** to become possessory. The uncertainty can be caused either (a) by the fact that the remainder's ever becoming possessory is subject to the *occurrence of a condition precedent* that might not occur by the time the prior estate terminates or (b) by the fact that the remainder has been created in favor of a person who is at the time of creation either *unborn or unascertained*. [73]

C. Vested remainders: A remainder is *"vested"* (as opposed to "contingent") if: (1) no *condition precedent* is attached to it; and (2) the person holding it has already been *born*, and his identity is *ascertained*. [74]

> **Example:** *O* conveys Blackacre "to *A* for life, remainder to *B* and his heirs." *B* has a vested remainder, since his identity is ascertained, and there is no condition precedent which must be satisfied in order for his interest to become possessory.

1. Meaning of "condition precedent": No condition precedent is deemed to exist so long as the remainder will become possessory *"whenever and however the prior estate terminates."* Thus in the above example, no matter how and when *A*'s life estate ends, *B*'s estate will immediately become possessory; therefore, *B*'s remainder is vested. [76]

D. Contingent remainders: All remainders that are not vested are contingent. [76] The remainder will be contingent rather than vested if *either* of two things is true:

[1] the remainder is subject to a *condition precedent*; or

[2] the remainder is created in favor of a person who at the time of creation is either *unborn* or *unascertained*.

1. Condition precedent: The "condition precedent" branch of "contingent" means that if some condition must be met before the remainder could *possibly become possessory*, the remainder is contingent. [76-78]

> **Example:** *O* conveys "to *A* for life, then, if *B* is living at *A*'s death, to *B* in fee simple." *B* must meet the condition precedent of surviving *A*, before his remainder can possibly become possessory. Therefore, *B*'s remainder is contingent.

a. Distinguish from condition subsequent: Distinguish between condition precedent (making the remainder contingent) and condition subsequent (making the remainder vested). If the condition is incorporated into the clause which gives the gift to the remainderman, then the remainder is contingent. But if one clause creates the remainder and a separate *subsequent* clause takes the remainder away, the remainder is vested (subject to divestment by the condition subsequent). [76]

> **Example:** *O* conveys "to *A* for life, remainder to *B* and his heirs, but if *B* dies before *A*, to *C* and his heirs." *B*'s remainder is vested, not contingent, because the condition is not part of the clause giving *B* his interest, but is instead part of a second added clause. But if the conveyance was "to *A* for life, then if *B* survives *A*, to *B* and his heirs; otherwise to *C* and his heirs" *B*'s

remainder would be contingent because the condition is incorporated into the very gift to *B*, making it a condition precedent.

Note: The key phrase *"but if"* indicates a condition subsequent rather than a condition precedent, so it's a clue to a vested rather than a contingent remainder.

2. **Unborn or unascertained:** A remainder is also contingent rather than vested if it is held by a person who, at the time the remainder is created, is either (1) *unborn* or (2) *not yet ascertained*. [78]

    Example of unborn: *O* conveys "to *A* for life, then to the children of *B*." At the time of the conveyance, *B* has no children. Therefore, the remainder in the unborn children is contingent. (But a remainder in favor of unborn children, like any other contingent remainder, may *become vested* due to later events. Thus if prior to *A*'s death, *B* has a child, *X*, *X* will now have a vested remainder "subject to open" (in favor of any other children of *B* born before *A*'s death).)

    Example of unascertained: *O* conveys "to *A* for life, then to *A*'s heirs." Assuming that the Rule in Shelley's Case (discussed below) is not in force, the heirs have a remainder, and it is contingent. That's because until *A* dies, it is impossible to say who his heirs are. (At *A*'s death, the remainder will both vest and become possessory.)

3. **Destructibility of contingent remainders:** At common law, a contingent remainder is deemed *"destroyed"* unless it *vests at or before the termination of the preceding freehold estates*. This is the doctrine of *"destructibility of contingent remainders."* [79-81]

    Example: *O* conveys "to *A* for life, remainder to the first son of *A* who reaches 21." At *A*'s death, he has one son, *B*, age 16. Since *B* did not meet the contingency (becoming 21) by the time the prior estate (*A*'s life estate) expired, *B*'s contingent remainder is destroyed. Therefore, *O*'s reversion becomes possessory.

    a. **Normal expiration:** One way the contingent remainder can be destroyed is if the preceding freehold estates *naturally terminate* before the condition precedent is satisfied. This is the case in the above example. [79]

    b. **Destruction by merger:** A contingent remainder can also be destroyed because the estate preceding it (usually a life estate) is *merged into* another, larger, estate. The doctrine of merger says that whenever *successive vested estates* are owned by the *same person*, the smaller of the two estates is *absorbed* by the larger. [80]

        Example: *O* conveys "to *A* for life, remainder to *A*'s first son for life if he reaches 21, remainder to *B* and his heirs." When *A* has a 19-year-old son, *A* conveys his life estate to *B*. Since *B* now has two successive vested estates (the life estate and *B*'s own vested remainder in fee simple), the smaller estate — the life estate — is merged into the fee simple and disappears. Since the son's remainder has not yet vested when *A*'s life estate disappears, the son's contingent remainder is destroyed. [80]

    c. **Destructibility rule today:** About half the states have passed statutes *abolishing the destructibility of contingent remainders*. Some additional states reach this result by case law. [80]

E. **Why it makes a difference:** Here are the main consequences of the vested/contingent distinction:

    1. **Rule Against Perpetuities:** The consequence that most significantly lives on today relates to the *Rule Against Perpetuities*. Contingent remainders are subject to the Rule Against Perpetuities, but vested remainders are not.

2. **Transferability:**   At common law, the two types of remainders differed sharply with respect to *transferability*. Vested remainders have always been transferable *inter vivos*. Contingent remainders, on the other hand, were basically not transferable *inter vivos*. But today, in most states, contingent remainders, too, are transferable *inter vivos*.

3. **Destruction:**   At common law a contingent remainder was *destroyed* if it did not vest upon termination of the proceeding life estate (the doctrine of "destruction of contingent remainders" discussed above). There was no comparable doctrine destroying vested remainders. But this distinction is not as significant today, because as noted above most states have abolished the doctrine of destruction of contingent remainders.

V.   THE RULE IN SHELLEY'S CASE

A. **Rule generally:**   The *Rule in Shelley's Case* provides: *if a will or conveyance creates a life estate in A, and purports to create a remainder in A's heirs* (or in the heirs of A's body), and the estates are *both legal or both equitable, the remainder becomes a remainder in A*. Usually, the result is that A ends up getting a fee simple. [81]

> **Example:** *O* conveys "to *A* for life, remainder to *A*'s heirs." If there were no Rule in Shelley's Case, the state of the title would be: life estate in *A*, contingent remainder in *A*'s heirs, reversion in *O*. But by operation of the Rule in Shelley's Case, the state of the title becomes: life estate in *A*, remainder in *A* (not *A*'s heirs). Then, by the doctrine of merger, *A*'s life estate will merge into his remainder in fee simple, and *A* simply holds a present fee simple.

B. **Step-by-step approach:**   Here's a *step-by-step approach* to deciding whether the Rule in Shelley's Case applies, and for carrying it out if it does apply [82]:

[1] Is there a *single instrument* that creates: (a) a *life estate* in land in *A* (with *A* being the "ancestor"); and (b) a *remainder* in persons described in the instrument as "*A's heirs*" (or a remainder in "the heirs of *A*'s body")? (If the answer is "no," the Rule in Shelley's Case can't apply, so no need to go further.)

[2] If the answer to [1] is yes, are the life estate in *A* and the remainder in *A*'s heirs (or in the heirs of *A*'s body) either *both legal*, or *both equitable*?

[3] If the answer to [2] is yes, the Rule in Shelley's case *applies*, to make the remainder in "*A*'s heirs" a remainder in fee simple in *A*. (Or, if the instrument gave a remainder in "the heirs of *A*'s body," the Rule makes the remainder into a remainder in fee tail in *A*.)

[4] If the Rule applies, then the doctrine of *merger* (see *supra*, p. C-19) will usually apply — but that's a separate operation, not part of the Rule. Thus in the above example, all the Rule does is to make the title be a life estate in *A*, with remainder in *A* (rather than in *A*'s heirs). Now, by separate operation of the merger doctrine, *A*'s life estate merges into his remainder in fee simple, leaving *A* with a present fee simple.

C. **Modern treatment:**   The Rule has been *abolished in the overwhelming majority of American states*. [82]

VI.   DOCTRINE OF WORTHIER TITLE

A. **Doctrine generally:**   The Doctrine of Worthier Title provides that *one cannot, either by conveyance or will, give a remainder to one's own heirs*. [82] (We are interested only in the "conveyance," or "*inter vivos*," aspect of the Doctrine, since that is the only aspect that remains important today.)

1. **Consequence:**   The consequence of the Doctrine of Worthier Title is that if the owner of a fee simple attempts to create a life estate or fee tail estate, with a remainder to his own heirs, the

remainder is *void*. Thus the grantor *keeps a reversion*. (This is why the Doctrine is sometimes called the *"rule forbidding remainders to grantors' heirs."*) [83]

> **Example:** *O* conveys "to *A* for life, remainder to *O*'s heirs." The Doctrine of Worthier Title makes the remainder void. Consequently, *O* is left with a reversion. He is thus free to convey the reversion to a third party; if he does so, his heirs will get nothing when he dies, even if he dies intestate.

B. Rule of construction: In most states, the Doctrine has been transformed into a *rule of construction*. That is, the Doctrine only applies where the grantor's language, and the surrounding circumstances, indicate that he *intended to keep a reversion*. So in most states, the Doctrine today just establishes a presumption that a reversion rather than a remainder in the grantor's heirs is really intended. [83]

VII. THE STATUTE OF USES AND EXECUTORY INTERESTS

A. Statute of Uses: The Statute of Uses provides that any *equitable estate* is *converted into the corresponding legal estate*. [88]

1. Equitable estates: An equitable estate is similar to a trust: if O conveys "to T and his heirs, to the use of A and his heirs," then T's estate is "legal" and A's estate is "equitable." (So look for the phrase *"to the use of,"* which means that the person named following the phrase gets an equitable interest.)

2. Operation of Statute: The Statute of Uses converts any equitable estate into the corresponding legal estate.

> **Example:** *O* conveys Blackacre "to *T* and his heirs, to the use of *A* and his heirs." The Statute of Uses transforms *A*'s equitable fee simple into a legal fee simple. *T*'s legal estate is nullified. So the state of title is simply: legal fee simple in *A*.

a. Bargain and sale deed Sometimes creation of a use is done by using a *"bargain and sale"* deed. So if a fact pattern says that *O* "bargains and sells" Blackacre to *A*, you know that *A* received an equitable title (which would then be converted to a legal title in *A* by the Statute of Uses).

B. Modern executory interests: The Statute of Uses makes possible modern "shifting" *executory interests*. [89-90]

1. Shifting executory interests: A "*shifting* executory interest" is a legal estate in someone other than the grantor, that *cuts short* a prior legal interest. [89]

> **Example:** *O*, who owns Blackacre, "bargains and sells" it — i.e., he creates an equitable estate in it — "to *A* and his heirs, but if the premises are ever used for other than residential purposes, then to *B* and his heirs." The bargain and sale raises a use in *A* in fee simple subject to condition subsequent, and a use in *B*. The Statute of Uses executes both of these uses, so title becomes: fee simple in *A* subject to an executory limitation, and a shifting executory interest in fee simple in *B*. If *A* or his heirs fail to use the property for residential purposes, the gift over to *B* will take effect.

2. Distinguish equitable interest from remainder: Distinguish between an equitable interest and a remainder. The difference is that a remainder *never cuts off* a prior interest, but merely awaits the prior interest's *natural termination*. An executory interest, by contrast, *divests* or *cuts off* a prior interest before the latter's natural termination. [90]

> Example 1: *O* bargains and sells "to *A* for life, then to *B* and his heirs if *B* survives *A*, otherwise to *C* and his heirs." *B* and *C* each have contingent remainders.

Example 2: *O* bargains and sells "to *A* for life, then to *B* and his heirs, but if *B* should die before *A*, to *C* and his heirs." Here *B*'s interest is vested subject to divestment because the "but if..." divesting language comes in a separate clause, and *C*'s interest is therefore an executory interest.

3. **Statute of Uses today:** The Statute of Uses is still in force. Thus a "bargain and sale" deed will generally create a legal estate. Even where the Statute is not in force, the modern deed can be used to produce the same result (e.g., shifting executory interests, which will cut off prior interests). [91]

VIII. THE RULE AGAINST PERPETUITIES

A. Rule Against Perpetuities generally:

1. **Statement of Rule:** The Rule Against Perpetuities can be summarized as follows: *"No interest is good unless it must vest, if at all, not later than 21 years after some life in being at the creation of the interest."* Try to memorize this phrase. [96]

2. **Paraphrase:** Paraphrasing, an interest is invalid unless it can be said, with absolute certainty, that it will either *vest or fail to vest*, before the end of a period equal to: (1) a life in existence (and specified in the document creating the interest) at the time the interest is created plus (2) an additional 21 years.

> **Example:** *O* conveys Blackacre "to *A* for life, remainder to the first son of *A* whenever born who becomes a clergyman." At the date of the conveyance, *A* has no son who is presently a clergyman. Viewing the matter from the date of the conveyance, it is possible to imagine a situation in which the remainder to the son could vest later than lives in being plus 21 years. Thus *A*'s son could be born to *A* after the date of the conveyance, and this son could become a clergyman more than 21 years after the death of *A*, and more than 21 years after the death of all of *A*'s sons living at the time of the conveyance. (*A* and *A*'s sons living at the time of the conveyance are the "measuring lives," since they're living people specifically mentioned in the conveyance.)
>
> Since this remote vesting is possible — even though unlikely — the contingent remainder is *invalid*. This is so even though it *actually turns out* that *A* has a son alive before the date of the conveyance who ultimately becomes a clergyman.

3. **"Rule of logical proof":** The *burden* is on the person seeking to uphold the validity of the interest to *prove that it could not possibly vest remotely.* The Rule is a *rule of logical proof.* The interest holder must prove that a contingent interest is certain to *vest or terminate* no later than 21 years after the death of some person alive at the creation of the interest. If the holder cannot prove that, the contingent interest is void from the outset. [97]

   a. **Judged in advance:** This means that the validity of the interest be judged *at the time it is created*, not at the time the interest actually vests. So if it is *theoretically possible* (even though very unlikely) that the interest will vest later than 21 years after the expiration of lives in being, the interest is invalid. This is true even if it actually turns out that the interest vests before the end of lives in being plus 21 years. (But see the discussion of "wait and see" statutes below.) [97]

4. **Effect of Rule when it applies:** When an interest violates the Rule, the interest is *struck out* and the *remaining valid interests stand.* [97]

   a. **Effect on prior interest:** If the interest that is invalidated by the rule is the last interest in the sequence, the effect of the Rule's application will often be to *"upgrade"* the immediately-prior interest to a *fee simple absolute.*

Example: *O* conveys Blackacre "to *A* and his heirs, but if *A* or his heirs shall ever use the premises for a non-residential purpose, then to *B* and his heirs." As written, *A* has a fee simple subject to an executory interest, and *B* has a (purported) executory interest. But *B*'s interest might vest later than lives in being plus 21 years. (*A*'s great-great-great-grandchild might make a non-residential use 200 years from now, after any life in being at the time *O* conveyed to *A* had ended, and the executory interest in *B*'s distant descendants would become possessory.) Therefore, *B*'s executory interest is invalid. The court will re-write the document so as to strike the language "then to *B* and his heirs." The effect will be to leave *A* with a fee simple absolute.

B. Applicability of Rule to various estates:

1. **Contingent remainders:** The Rule applies to ***contingent remainders***. [97]

    Example: *O* conveys "to *A* for life, remainder to the first son of *A* to reach the age of 25 and his heirs." At the time of the conveyance, *A* does not have a son who has reached the age of 25. The remainder in the unborn son is contingent, rather than vested, since it is not yet known which son if any will reach the age of 25. Since there is a possibility of remote vesting, the gift to the oldest son violates the Rule and is invalid.

2. **Vested remainder:** A *vested* remainder, by contrast, can *never* violate the Rule, because a vested remainder ***vests at the moment it is created***. [98]

    Example: *O* conveys "to *A* for life, remainder to *A*'s children for life, remainder to *B* and his heirs." The gift to *B* and his heirs does not violate the Rule, because that gift is a vested remainder, which vested in interest (though not in possession) on the date of the conveyance. Therefore, even though the remainder to *B* and his heirs might not become possessory until later than lives in being plus 21 years (as where *A*'s last surviving child is one who was not born on the date of conveyance, and who dies after age 21), the gift to *B* is valid. [98]

3. **Reversion:** The Rule does *not* apply to ***reversionary interests*** (reversions, possibilities of reverter, and rights of entry). These are deemed to vest as soon as they are created. [98]

4. **Executory interests:** The Rule applies to ***executory interests***, because such interests are ***not vested*** at their creation. [98]

    Example: *O* conveys "to the City of Klamath Falls, so long as the city maintains a library on the property, then to *A* and his heirs." The executory interest in *A* violates the Rule, because it might vest beyond lives in being plus 21 years — the city might maintain a library on the property longer than any life in being at the time of the gift plus 21 years. Therefore, instead of the executory interest in *A* being valid, *O* and his heirs have a possibility of reverter which will become possessory if the city ever stops using the library.

5. **Options to purchase land:** An ***option*** to ***purchase land*** will often be subject to the Rule. [99-100]

    a. **Option as part of lease:** If an option to purchase property is part of a ***lease*** of that property and is exercisable only during the lease term, then the option is ***not*** subject to the Rule.

    b. **Option "in gross":** But if the option is ***not*** part of a lease or other property interest, the common-law approach (and that of most states) is that the Rule *does* apply. Such an unattached option is called an option ***"in gross."*** [*Symphony Space v. Pergola Prop.*] [99]

    Example: *O* sells Blackacre to *A*, with the condition that if at any time the property is used for the sale of alcohol, *O* or his heirs may repurchase the property for the amount originally paid by *A*. Since there is no time limit to this option, and since the option is not attached to any lease or continuing interest by *O*, the option is void as a violation of the Rule.

6. Right of first refusal (the RAP may apply): Courts are *split* about whether a *right of first refusal* to purchase or re-purchase the property is subject to the Rule. [100]

> **Example:** *A* conveys Blackacre to *B*. The deed says that if *B* or his heirs or assigns at any time desires to sell the property on particular terms and conditions, the property must first be offered to *A* or his heirs and assigns on those same terms and conditions.
>
> Of those jurisdictions applying the RAP, some, but not all, will apply the Rule to *A*'s right of first refusal here. If the jurisdiction applies the RAP to *A*'s right of first refusal, the right will be invalid. That's because the right could be exercised later than all measuring lives (here, *A*'s and *B*'s) plus 21 years. For instance, *B*'s heirs might own the property for 200 years, then try to sell it (triggering the purported right of first refusal in *A*'s heirs), at which point all lives in being at the time of the *A*-to-*B* conveyance have long ended.

7. Land-use restrictions (the RAP doesn't apply): *Land-use restrictions,* such as *equitable servitudes* (p. C-54 *infra*), are *not covered* by the RAP.

> **Example:** *O* owns both Whiteacre and Blackacre, two adjacent parcels. *O* sells Whiteacre to "*A* and his heirs." In the deed, *O* and *A* agree that neither will ever use their property for anything other than single-family residential use, and that this "equitable servitude" will apply to *O*'s and *A*'s successors in interest. The deed to *A* is properly recorded.
>
> These restrictions are not only enforceable against *A* and his assigns (see *infra*, p. 239), they are also not subject to the RAP. Therefore, if *A*'s descendants or assigns use the property for non-residential uses 200 years from now, the court will grant *O*'s successors an injunction against the use.

C. Table: The table below summarizes when the RAP does and doesn't apply.

RECAP: Interests to Which the Rule Against Perpetuities Does or Doesn't Apply

Future Interest	Does the RAP Apply?	Example of Gift that Violates or Doesn't Violate the RAP
Contingent Remainder	Yes	*O* "to *A* for life, remainder to his first son to turn 30," made when no son of *A* has turned 30. Remainder violates the RAP even if son turns 30 one year later.
Vested Remainder	No (vests at creation)	*O* "to *A* for life, then to *A*'s last surviving child for life, then to *C* and his heirs." Remainder in *C* is vested (since subject to no contingency), and thus doesn't violate the RAP, even though it may not become possessory for 100 years in hands of *C*'s successors.
Reversion	No (vests at creation)	*O* "to *A* for life." *O*'s reversion doesn't violate the RAP.
Possibility of Reverter	No (vests at creation)	*O* "to *A* and his heirs so long as property is used as a church." *O* has a possibility of reverter that cannot violate the RAP even though it might become possessory in 200 years.

RECAP: Interests to Which the Rule Against Perpetuities Does or Doesn't Apply

Future Interest	Does the RAP Apply?	Example of Gift that Violates or Doesn't Violate the RAP
Right of Re-Entry	**No** (vests at creation)	*O* "to *A* and his heirs, but if property ceases to be used as church, grantor and his heirs may re-enter." *O* has a right of re-entry that cannot violate the RAP even though it might become exercisable in 200 years
Executory Interest	**Yes**	*O* "to *A* and his heirs so long as property is used for a church, then to *B* and his heirs." Executory interest in *B* violates the RAP, even if *A* stops using as a church one year later.
Option to purchase, in lease	**No**	*O* rents to Corp, Corp gets right to purchase during lease-term. Corp's right can't violate the RAP even if lease lasts 99 years.
Option to purchase, in gross (i.e., not in lease)	**Yes**, in some but not all courts	*O* sells *A* "right to purchase property for $100,000 at any time." Some courts say this violates the RAP even if *A* tries to exercise one year later.
Right of First Refusal	**Yes**, in some but not all courts	*O* gives *A* right to match any offer at any time. Some courts say this violates the RAP even if *A* asserts it means it's only exercisable by him during his lifetime (not by his successors).
Land-Use Restriction (e.g., Equitable Servitude)	**No**	*O* conveys Lot 1 to *A* while keeping Lot 2; *O* and *A* agree that each lot will have a single-family-use restriction, binding on their "assigns." Neither restriction will ever violate the RAP, so each can bind for 200 years.

C
A
P
S
U
L
E

S
U
M
M
A
R
Y

D. Meaning of "lives in being" ("measuring lives"): Since the RAP requires that the interest vest within "lives in being" plus 21 years, you need to know what lives count as "lives in being" (or, *"measuring lives"* or *"validating lives,"* as they're often called).

1. Persons causally connected: A measuring life is any life that is found among people whose lives are *somehow causally connected with the vesting or termination* of the interest.

Examples: Measuring lives can include the preceding *life tenant*, a taker of a *contingent interest*, anyone who can *affect the identity of the takers* (e.g., *B* in a gift to "*B*'s grandchildren"), and anyone else who can *affect events relevant to a condition precedent to the vesting of the interest in question*. [102]

a. Person named in document: Normally, the measuring life will be a person *named or directly referred to* in the document that creates the interest.

Example: *O* conveys "to my daughter Dot for life, then to her first child to reach the age of 21." Dot is childless at the date of the conveyance. Dot is the "life in being" or "measuring life." The contingent remainder to Dot's oldest child is valid, because we know that any child Dot may eventually have will reach 21 within 21 years after Dot's death.

   i. **Person not named:** But there is *no logical requirement* that to be a measuring life, the person be mentioned in the document: sometimes the measuring life will be a person (or a group) that the document *doesn't mention,* but whose life is nonetheless *causally related* to vesting or termination of the interest. For instance, if a person's *grandchild* is referred to, this will likely mean that the parent of that grandchild (even if not mentioned) can be a measuring life.

   Example: *O* devises "to the first of my grandchildren to reach the age of 21." *O* is survived by two sons and one daughter (none of whom is mentioned in the will), as well as by four grandchildren.

   The measuring life is the survivor of *O*'s three children. That is, we know that any grandchild will have to turn 21 no more than 21 years after the last of *O*'s three children dies. Consequently, even though we don't know precisely *which* child of *O* will serve as the measuring life, and even though none of *O*'s children is mentioned in the will, we know that the gift to the "first grandchild to reach 21" will inevitably vest or fail within *some* life-in-being-plus-21-years (i.e., within the life of *O*'s last surviving child plus 21 years). Therefore, the gift to the first grandchild to turn 21 is valid. [103]

E. Special situations: At common law, there are some remote possibilities that nonetheless count for the purposes of the Rule:

   1. **Fertile octogenarian:** There is a conclusive presumption that any person, regardless of age or physical condition, is capable of *having children*. This is the *"fertile octogenarian"* rule, which will sometimes make a reasonable gift invalid. [103]

   Example: *T* conveys "to *A* for life, then to *A*'s surviving children for life, then to the surviving children of *B*." At the time of *T*'s death, *B* has three children, and *B* herself is 80 years old. But it is conceivable that *B* could now have another child, and that that child would take after lives in being plus 21 years — for instance, all of *A*'s children might be born after *T*'s death, and might die more than 21 years after *T*'s death. Therefore, *B*'s three now-living children will not take anything since their interest violates the Rule. It doesn't matter that *B* could not possibly have any further children as a medical matter.

   2. **Unborn widow:** Similarly, if an interest is created which will flow through the *"widow"* of X (by naming and relying on her in determining when the interest will vest), the common-law view is that the interest *must fail*. This is the *"unborn widow"* rule. [103]

   Example: In 2005, *T* bequeaths Blackacre "to *A* for life, then to *A*'s widow, then to the issue of *A* and *A*'s widow who survive them." At *T*'s death, *A* is married to *B*. It is possible that *B* will either predecease or divorce *A*, and *A* will then marry someone born after 2005 (we'll call her *C*.) *C* would be not be a life-in-being in 2005, the time of the bequest. Since the contingent remainder to the issue can't vest without referring to the life of *C*, it is not certain to vest within 21 years of the relevant lives that were in being *at the time the remainder was created* (*C* might live longer than 21 years after the death of *A*). Therefore, the contingent remainder to the issue of *A* and "*A*'s widow" must fail.) (But a modern court might accept evidence that *T* intended "*A*'s widow" to refer to *B* in particular, in which case the gift will be valid.)

   3. **Class gifts:** If a gift is made to all members of a *class*, the entire gift fails unless it can be said that *each member of the class* must have his interest vest or fail within lives in being plus 21 years. This rule will be triggered if the class could *obtain new members* following a testator's death. [104]

> **Example:** *T* bequeaths property "to *A*, then to *A*'s surviving children who attain the age of 25." At the time of the bequest, *A* has two children, *B* and *C*. It is possible that another child (called hypothetically "*D*"), will be born after *T*'s death. Since *A*, *B* and *C* might all die prior to *D*'s fourth birthday, *D*'s interest would then vest too remotely (more than 21 years after the deaths of *A*, *B* and *C*, the measuring lives). Therefore, not only is the gift invalid as to children born after *T*'s death, but it is also invalid as to *B* and *C*, according to the strict common-law approach.

F. **"Wait and see" statutes:** Many states reject the common-law principle that if a scenario could be imagined whereby the interest might vest too remotely, it is invalid regardless of how things actually turn out. These states have adopted *"wait and see"* statutes, by which if the interest *actually vests* within lives in being at the time of creation plus 21 years, the interest is valid — the fact that things might have worked out differently is irrelevant. [105]

> **Example:** *O* conveys Blackacre "to *A* and his heirs, but if *A* or his heirs ever uses Blackacre for other than residential purposes, to *B* and his heirs." At common law, the executory interest in *B* is void, since the premises might stop being used for residential purposes more than lives in being plus 21 years. But under the wait-and-see test, if the property ceases to be used for residential purposes within 21 years after the death of the survivor of *O*, *A* and *B*, the gift over to *B* and his heirs is valid.

     1. **Effect on fertile octogenarian and unborn widow cases:** The wait-and-see approach virtually knocks out the fertile octogenarian and unborn widow cases. So long as the octogenarian does not in fact have a child, or the widow referred to in the instrument in fact turns out to be someone born prior to the instrument, the Rule Against Perpetuities is not violated.

IX. RESTRAINTS ON ALIENATION

A. **Restraints generally void:** A *restraint on the alienation* of a *fee simple* is generally *void*. [106]

> **Example:** *O* conveys Blackacre "to *A* and his heirs, but no conveyance by *A* to any third party shall be valid." Since this restricts the alienation of a fee simple, the restriction will be void, and *A* may convey to whomever he wishes.

     1. **Life estates:** But a *life estate may* be subjected to restraints on alienation. [106]

> **Example:** *O* conveys "to *A* for life, but *A* shall have no right to convey his interest; then to *B* and his heirs." The restraint upon *A*'s life estate will generally be upheld.

     2. **Use restrictions:** *Use restrictions* will generally be *upheld*.

> **Example:** *O* conveys "to *A* and his heirs, provided that the property not be used for non-residential purposes." This use restriction will be upheld, and will not be struck down as a restraint upon alienation.

     3. **Defeasible estates:** The defeasible estates (e.g., fee simple determinable) are also enforced, even though they are in a sense restraints on alienation. [106]

> **Example:** *O* conveys "to *A* and his heirs, but if the property is ever used for the purposes of sale of alcohol, Grantor or his heirs may re-enter." This will be enforced even though it to some extent restrains alienability.

CHAPTER 6
MARITAL ESTATES

I.   THE COMMON-LAW SYSTEM — RIGHTS DURING MARRIAGE

A. The common-law system generally: All but eight states govern marital property in a way that is derived from traditional common-law principles. [119]

B. The feudal system: The feudal system gave the husband extreme dominion over his wife's property, by means of the doctrines of coverture and *jure uxoris*. [119]

    1. Personal property (coverture): Under the doctrine of *"coverture"*, all personal property owned by the wife at the time of the marriage became the property of the husband.

    2. Real property (*jure uxoris*): Under the doctrine of *"jure uxoris"*, the husband had the right to *possess* all his wife's lands during the marriage, and to spend the rents and profits of the land as he wished.

C. Married Women's Property Acts: All states have enacted Married Women's Property Acts, which undo couverture and *jure uxoris*, give the woman equality, and protect her assets from her husband's creditors. [120]

II.   THE COMMON-LAW SYSTEM — EFFECT OF DIVORCE

A. Traditional "title" view: Under traditional common-law principles, if the parties were *divorced*, the division of their property depended heavily on who held formal legal *"title"* to the property. [120]

    1. Title in husband's name: Most significantly, if the legal title to property was held by one spouse alone, that spouse *retained title upon divorce*. This was usually to the husband's advantage.

B. Modern "equitable distribution": Today, every common-law property state has *abolished* the "title" approach to property division at divorce. Instead, all have substituted by statute a doctrine called *"equitable distribution,"* by which property is divided by the court according to the demands of fairness, not based on who has title. [121]

    1. What property is covered: Most states allow the court to divide only *"marital property"* under equitable distribution principles. Usually, marital property is defined to include only property *acquired during the marriage from the earnings of the parties.* (So property acquired *before marriage*, or acquired by one spouse through a *gift or bequest* to that spouse, is not included in the assets to be distributed.) [121-122]

III.   THE COMMON-LAW SYSTEM — DEATH OF A SPOUSE

A. Dower and curtesy: At common law, the surviving spouse was provided for by the doctrines of "dower" and "curtesy".

    1. Dower: A widow (W) received *"dower."* This was defined as a *life estate* in *one-third* of the *lands* of which H was seised at any time during the marriage, provided that H's interest was *inheritable by the issue* of the marriage (if any). So any land owned in *fee simple* by H alone, or by H and a third person as tenants in common, qualified for dower. (But there was no dower in a life estate held by H, even a life estate per autre vie.) [123]

        a. Dower inchoate: While H was alive, W got a right of *dower inchoate* as soon as H became seized. This meant that any *conveyance* of the freehold by H to a third party did not affect the right of dower inchoate, so after H died W could still demand her dower rights from the person who bought from H. [123]

2. **Curtesy:** A widower (H) was entitled to *"curtesy."* This was a life estate in *each piece* of real estate in which W held a freehold interest during their marriage, provided the freehold was inheritable by issue born alive of the marriage. (So if H and W were childless, and W predeceased H, H had no right of curtesy). [123]

3. **Abolished in most jurisdictions:** In all but six American jurisdictions, dower and curtesy have been *abolished*. [124]

4. **Practical importance:** Where dower and curtesy still exist, the main consequence is that *both husband and wife* must *sign any deed* if the recipient is to take free and clear of the right, even if only one spouse holds title. [124]

   a. **Elective share available:** In the six remaining dower and/or curtesy states, the survivor may take an "elective share" (see below) instead, which is almost always more generous.

B. **Modern "elective share" statutes:** The modern substitute for dower and curtesy is the *"elective share."* The surviving spouse has the right to *renounce the will*, and instead receive a designated portion of the estate. [124]

   1. **Effect:** The effect of an elective share statute (which all common-law property states but Georgia have) is that *one spouse cannot "disinherit" the other.*

   2. **Size of share:** Most commonly, the elective share is *one-half* or *one-third*. Both personal and real property are covered.

   3. **Length of marriage irrelevant:** Most elective share statutes treat the *length of marriage* as *irrelevant* — a woman widowed after one day of marriage gets the same share of her husband's estate as one married for 50 years.

IV. COMMUNITY PROPERTY

A. **Community property generally:** In nine states, the rights of husband and wife in property is governed by the *civil-law* concept of *"community property."* These states are Arizona, California, Idaho, Louisiana, New Mexico, Nevada, Texas, Washington and Wisconsin. (In Alaska, couples may elect to hold their property as community property.) [125]

   1. **General approach:** The key tenet of community property is that property acquired during the marriage (with exceptions) belongs *jointly* to husband and wife from the moment it is acquired. Thus upon *divorce* or *death*, the property is treated as belonging *half to each spouse*.

B. **What is "community property":** All property acquired during the marriage is *presumed* to be community property (though this presumption may be rebutted by showing it falls within one of the classes of "separate property" described below). [126-126]

   1. **Before marriage:** Property acquired by either spouse *before marriage* is separate, not community, property.

   2. **Gift or inheritance:** Property acquired by *gift, inheritance or bequest*, even *after marriage*, is separate property.

   3. **Earnings:** Income produced by either spouse's *labor* is community property.

      Example: H is an employee. His salary is community property. Also, if he gets stock in his employer, pension rights, or insurance as part of his job, these probably also are fruits of his labor and therefore community property.

C. Divorce: Generally, if *divorce* occurs, the community property is *evenly divided*. [128]

D. Death: Upon the *death* of one of the parties, the community property is treated as having belonged half to the deceased spouse and half to the surviving spouse. A deceased spouse's half is thus subject to his right to devise it by will to whomever he wishes. [128]

> **Example:** H and W hold Blackacre as community property. H dies, and his will gives whatever interest he has to S, his son by a prior marriage. S and W will hold the property as tenants in common, each with an undivided one-half interest.

V.   VARIATIONS ON TRADITIONAL MARRIAGE

A. Common-law marriage: There are 11 states that still recognize *"common-law"* marriage (Alabama, Colorado, Idaho, Iowa, Kansas, Montana, Oklahoma, Pennsylvania, Rhode Island, South Carolina and Texas, plus the District of Columbia). [129]

1. Definition: The concept of common-law marriage is that if two people *cohabit*, and *hold themselves out to the public as being husband and wife*, they will be *treated as married*.

2. Consequence: In states still recognizing common-law marriage, a couple that is deemed to be common-law married is *treated exactly the same as a couple married pursuant to a marriage license.* For example, if one member of the couple dies without a will, the other will take by intestate succession.

B. State law on same-sex partnerships: Here is a brief summary, as of early 2012, of state law on the right of *same-sex couples* to marry or otherwise receive marriage-like treatment. [129-133]

1. Right to marry: *Six states* currently allow same-sex couples to marry: *Connecticut, Iowa, Massachusetts, New Hampshire, New York and Vermont, plus Washington D.C.* Two additional states, Washington and Maryland, have passed laws to begin granting marriage licenses in 2012.

a. Decisions based on state constitutions: Three of the above states that allow same-sex marriage — Connecticut, Massachusetts and Iowa — have reached that result directly or indirectly as a result of *judicial decisions* finding that the state's prior ban on same-sex marriages *violated the state constitution.* [*Varnum v. Brien*] [130]

b. Statutes: Other states (e.g., Vermont) have legalized same-sex marriage by purely *legislative* means.

2. Civil unions and domestic partnerships: A number of states have passed statutes giving gay couples the right to elect to enter into a *"civil union"* or a *"domestic partnership,"* by which electing couples get some or all of the same state-law rights and responsibilities that they would have if they were married. Civil unions and domestic partnerships vary widely from state to state in their effects. [131]

a. Near-equivalent to marriage: Some civil unions and domestic partnerships (e.g., in California and New Jersey) have state-law effects that are *virtually identical to marriage*.

3. Bans on same-sex marriage: On the other hand, more than 40 states have either statutes or constitutional provisions explicitly *restricting marriage to two persons of opposite sex.* This roster includes some states that allow civil unions or domestic partnerships that confer some or most of the rights and responsibilities of marriage.

a. State constitutional-law rulings: A number of state supreme courts have *upheld these bans* against state-constitutional attack. [132]

i. California: In California, a complicated scenario is still unfolding: (1) the state supreme court found in 2008 that the state constitution gives same-sex couples the right to marry;

(2) voters responded by passing, that same year, "Proposition 8," which amended the state constitution to *take away* that same-sex marriage right; and (3) the federal Ninth Circuit held in early 2012 that Proposition 8 was an intentional discrimination against same-sex couples that was invalid under the U.S. Constitution's Fourteenth Amendment Equal Protection clause, because the legislation was not passed for the purpose of pursuing a "legitimate" state objective. [*Perry v. San Francisco*] [132]

VI. HOMESTEAD EXEMPTION

A. Homestead exemptions: Most states have enacted *"homestead exemptions."* Exempted property may not be seized and sold by *creditors*. Usually, the family's *residence* is exempt from seizure, but only up to a certain dollar limit. Also, homestead exemptions do not bar a *mortgagee* from foreclosing — the exemption only protects against seizure by "general" or "unsecured" creditors. [133]

CHAPTER 7
CONCURRENT OWNERSHIP

I. CONCURRENT OWNERSHIP GENERALLY

A. Three types: There are three ways in which two or more people may own present possessory interests in the same property: (1) joint tenancy (which includes the right of survivorship); (2) tenancy in common (which does not have the right of survivorship); and (3) tenancy by the entirety (which exists only between husband and wife, and which includes not only survivorship but "indestructibility.") [137]

II. JOINT TENANCY

A. Joint tenancy generally: In a *joint tenancy*, two or more people own a *single, unified* interest in real or personal property. [137]

   1. General attributes: Here are the most important attributes of a joint tenancy:

   a. Survivorship: Each joint tenant has a *right of survivorship*. That is, if there are two joint tenants, and one dies, the other becomes *sole owner* of the interest that the two of them had previously held jointly.

   b. Possession: Each joint tenant is entitled to *occupy* the *entire* premises, subject only to the same right of occupancy by the other tenant(s).

   c. Equal shares: Since the joint tenants have identical interests, they must have "equal shares." Thus one joint tenant cannot have a one-fourth interest, say, with the other having a three-fourths interest.

B. Creation: A joint tenancy must be created by a *single instrument* (deed or will), and must be created in both or all joint tenants at the *same time*. [138]

   1. Language used: Usually, a joint tenancy is created by specific language: "To A and B as joint tenants with right of survivorship."

   2. Conveyance by A to A and B: At common law, A (owner of a fee simple) *cannot* create a joint tenancy between himself and another by conveying "to A and B as joint tenants." But many states, by statute or case law, now permit this result. [138]

C. Right of survivorship: Here are some consequences of the *"right of survivorship"* that is the distinguishing feature of a joint tenancy:

1. Heirs and devisees take nothing: When a joint tenant dies, her *heirs* (if she dies intestate) or her *devisees* (if she leaves a will that purports to leave her joint tenancy interest) *take nothing* — the interest is *extinguished* at the moment of the decedent / joint tenant's death, so there is nothing to pass by will or intestacy. [139]

2. Creditors: An unsecured or judgment-lien *creditor* of *one* joint tenant *does not have rights* against the interest of the *other joint tenant.* Therefore, if the debtor joint tenant dies first, the surviving joint tenant usually takes the property *free and clear* of the deceased tenant's creditor — the decedent's interest (and thus the creditor's "interest in that interest") simply *ceases to exist* at the moment of the debtor/joint-tenant's death. [140]

> **Example:** *A* and *B* own Blackacre as joint tenants. Finance Co., which has lent money to *A* unsecured, gets a judgment against *A*, which under local law becomes a lien against all of *A*'s real property. *A* dies. In most states, Finance Co. has no rights against Blackacre — at *A*'s death, his joint tenancy interest is simply extinguished, resulting in an unencumbered fee simple in *B*.

> **a. Statutes:** However, some states have statutes preserving an attachment, mortgage, or other lien on a joint tenant's interest after that tenant's death.

D. Severance: There are a number of ways in which a joint tenancy may be *severed*, i.e., *destroyed*. Severance normally results in the creation of a *tenancy in common*. [140]

1. Conveyance by one joint tenant: A joint tenant may *convey* his interest to a *third party*. Such a conveyance has the effect of destroying the joint tenancy. [140]

> **Example:** A and B hold Blackacre as joint tenants. A conveys his interest to C. This conveyance destroys the joint tenancy, so that B and C now become tenants in common, not joint tenants.

> **a. Motive irrelevant:** This principle applies even where a joint tenant is acting for the *sole purpose* of severing the tenancy, and even where the recipient of the conveyance *immediately reconveys back* to the severing joint tenant — the *motive* of the conveying joint tenant is irrelevant. [140]

> **b. Three or more joint tenants:** If there are *three* or more original joint tenants, a conveyance by one of them to a stranger will produce a tenancy in common as between the stranger and the remaining original joint tenants, but the joint tenancy will continue as between the original members.

> **Example:** A, B and C hold Blackacre as joint tenants. A conveys his interest to X. Now, X will hold an undivided one-third interest in the property as a tenant in common with B and C. B and C hold a two-thirds interest, but they hold this interest as joint tenants with each other, not as tenants in common. Thus if X dies, his interest goes to his heirs or devisees. But if B dies, his interest goes to C.

2. Granting of mortgage: Courts are *split* as to whether the *granting of a mortgage* by one joint tenant severs the joint tenancy.

> **a. "Title theory" states:** In so-called *"title theory"* states, the mortgage is treated as a conveyance, and thus *severs* the joint tenancy (so that the mortgagee can foreclose on the undivided one-half interest of the mortgagor, but the interest of the other party is not affected).

  b. **"Lien theory" states:** In *"lien theory"* states (which represent a majority of states), the mortgage does *not* sever the joint tenancy. In some but not all lien theory states, if the mortgagor *dies first*, the other joint tenant takes the whole property free and clear of the mortgage. [142]

3. **Lease:** Most courts seem to hold that a *lease* issued by one joint tenant does not act as a severance. [142-143]

III. TENANCY IN COMMON

A. **Tenancy in common:** Whereas in a joint tenancy each party has an equal interest in the whole, in a "tenancy in common" each tenant has a *separate "undivided"* interest. [143]

1. **No right of survivorship:** The most important difference between the tenancy in common and the joint tenancy is that there is *no right of survivorship* between tenants in common. Thus each tenant in common can make a *testamentary transfer* of his interest; if he dies intestate, his interest will pass under the statute of descent. [144]

   Example: A and B take title to Blackacre as tenants in common. They have equal shares. A dies, without a will, leaving only one relative, a son, S. Title to Blackacre is now: a one-half undivided interest in S, and a one-half undivided interest in B.

2. **Unequal shares:** Tenants in common may have *unequal shares* (unlike joint tenants). [143]

   Example: A and B may hold as tenants in common, with A holding an "undivided one-quarter interest" and B an "undivided three-quarters interest."

   a. **Rebuttable presumption of equality:** If the conveyance does not specify the size of the interests, there is a *rebuttable presumption* that *equal* shares were intended.

3. **Presumption favoring:** Most states have a *presumption* in *favor* of tenancies in common, rather than joint tenancies, so long as the co-tenants are not husband and wife. But this can be rebutted by clear evidence showing that the parties intended to create a joint tenancy. [144]

4. **Heirs:** Apart from a conveyance directly creating a tenancy in common, a tenancy in common can result from operation of law, including the *intestacy* statute: if the intestacy statute specifies that two persons are to take an equal interest as co-heirs, they take as tenants in common. [144]

   Example: A, fee simple owner of Blackacre, dies without a will. His sole surviving relatives are a son, S, and a daughter, D. The intestacy statute says that heirs who are children take "equally." S and D will take title to Blackacre as tenants in common, each holding an undivided one-half interest.

B. **Conveyance by one co-tenant:** One tenant in common may *convey* his interest to a third person *without the consent* of the other tenant in common. After the conveyance, the grantee simply *steps into the conveying co-tenant's shoes*, and holds as tenant in common with the non-conveying co-tenant. [144]

   Example: *A* and *B* hold Blackacre as tenants in common with equal shares. *A* conveys his interest to *C*. *C* and *B* are now tenants in common with equal shares.

1. **Can't bind absent co-tenant:** But a tenant in common may *not* make a conveyance that in any way *binds another tenant in common* who does not participate in that conveyance. [144]

   Example: *A* and *B* hold Blackacre as tenants in common with equal shares. *A* purports to convey the entire fee simple to Blackacre to *C*. This conveyance has no effect on *B*'s tenancy in common. And that's true even if *B* knew of the conveyance and did not object. Therefore, the conveyance is effective to pass *A*'s interest to *C*, but not to pass *B*'s interest to *C*. Consequently, *B* and *C* now hold as tenants in common.

2. **Grant of mortgage or judgment lien:** Similarly, if one tenant in common purports to grant a *mortgage* on the property, or allows a *judgment* to be entered against him that is a lien on his property, the mortgage or lien will be *effective only against that tenant's own undivided interest*, not the interests of the other co-tenant. Then, if the property is eventually sold or partitioned, the mortgage or lien will be effective only against the first co-tenant's proceeds. [144]

    > **Example:** *A* and *B* own Blackacre, a house and lot, as tenants in common. *A* grants to Bank a mortgage on "Blackacre." Since *B* has not joined in granting the mortgage, Bank's mortgage is good only against *A*'s undivided one-half interest in Blackacre. Therefore, if Blackacre is sold, Bank's mortgage entitles it to be satisfied only out of *A*'s one-half interest in the proceeds. The same is true if Blackacre is sold in a partition action.

3. **Creation of easement or settlement of boundary dispute:** Similarly, if one tenant in common attempts to grant an *easement*, *settle a boundary dispute* with a neighbor, or do anything else that would affect title, the action does not affect the legal rights of any other tenant(s) in common who does not sign the grant or agreement. [145]

    a. **Sole occupancy doesn't matter:** This is true even where one tenant in common has *sole occupancy* of the premises, and the attempt to change title by grant of an easement, settlement of a boundary dispute, etc., is done by that occupying tenant in common.

IV.   TENANCY BY THE ENTIRETY

A. Tenancy by the entirety generally: At common law, any conveyance to two persons who were *husband and wife* resulted automatically in a *"tenancy by the entirety."* [145]

1. **Usually abolished:** Only 22 states retain the tenancy by the entirety. Even in these states, it is no longer the case (as it was at common law) that a conveyance to husband and wife necessarily creates a tenancy by the entirety — instead, there is usually just a rebuttable *presumption* that a conveyance to a husband and wife is intended to create a tenancy by the entirety. [145]

2. **No severance:** The key feature of the tenancy by the entirety is that it is *not subject to severance*. So long as both parties are alive, and remain husband and wife, neither one can break the tenancy. Most significantly, each spouse knows that if he or she survives the other, he/she will get a *complete interest*. [146]

    > **Example:** H and W hold Blackacre as tenants by the entirety. H conveys his interest to X. In all states, if W survives H, W will get the property outright and X will get nothing. (But in some states, the conveyance will be effective to the limited extent that if H survives W, X, not H, will get the property.)

3. **Divorce:** If the parties are *divorced*, the tenancy by the entirety *ends*. The parties are then treated as owning equal shares (usually as tenants in common). [146]

V.   RELATIONS BETWEEN CO-TENANTS

A. Possession: Regardless of the form of co-tenancy, each co-tenant has the *right to occupy the entire premises*, subject only to a similar right in the other co-tenants. (But the parties may make an *agreement* to the contrary.) [147]

1. **No duty to account:** If the property is solely occupied by one of the co-tenants, he normally has *no duty to account* for the value of his exclusive possession (e.g., he has no duty to pay the non-occupying co-tenant one-half of what a normal rent would be). But there are two main exceptions: [147]

    a. Ouster: If the occupying tenant *refuses to permit* the other tenant equal occupancy, then he is said to have *"ousted"* the other tenant, and must *account* to the ousted co-tenant for the latter's share of the *fair rental value* of the premises. [147]

    b. Depletion: Also, the occupying tenant will have a duty to account if he *depletes the land*. [148]

        Example: A and B are co-tenants of Blackacre; A mines coal from the property. A must split the profits with B.

B. Payments made by one tenant: If one tenant makes *payments* on behalf of the property (e.g., property tax, mortgage payments, repairs, etc.), that tenant does *not* have an automatic right to *collect* the share from the other tenants. However, the tenant making the payment may *deduct* the payment from rents he collects from third parties; also, he will be reimbursed for these payments "off the top" before any proceeds from a *sale* are distributed. [148-149]

C. Acquisition of outstanding interest: Co-tenants are required to act towards each other in *good faith*. If they receive their interests at the same time (e.g., from the same will or by the same conveyance), they will usually be held to be in a *fiduciary relationship*. One important consequence is that if one of them *buys an outstanding interest*, he at least temporarily *holds that interest on behalf of all of them*. [149]

    a. Buying at foreclosure or tax sale: This principle applies to a co-tenant who buys the property at a *foreclosure sale* or *tax sale*. The foreclosure or tax title is not automatically held for the benefit of the other tenants, but they have a *right to elect to contribute* within a reasonable time after the sale; if they do so, they maintain their ownership interest. [149]

D. Partition: Any tenant in common or joint tenant (but not a tenant by the entirety) may bring an equitable action for *partition*. By this means, the court will either *divide* the property, or order it *sold* and the proceeds distributed. [150-151]

    1. Preference for partition in kind: Most courts state a preference for partitioning the property *in kind* rather than by sale, and say that they will approve a partition by sale only if the *physical characteristics* of the property prevent division of the property in kind, or if division in kind would be *extremely unfair* to one party. [150]

        Example: The property is in a residential zone that requires 100 feet of street frontage for any house. The property is vacant and has 150 feet of frontage. *A* owns two-thirds and *B* one-third, as tenants in common. *A* proposes to divide the property so that he gets two-thirds of the square footage, and so that he gets 100 feet of frontage. The court probably won't order partition in kind because this would leave *B* with 50 feet of frontage, too little to build a house on. Therefore, the court will probably order the land sold. [150]

    a. Where opponent of partition lives or works on the property: Where the party who is opposing partition by sale *lives on the property* or *uses it for a business*, courts are especially *reluctant* to in effect evict that party by requiring that the entire parcel be sold.

CHAPTER 8
LANDLORD AND TENANT

I. INTRODUCTION

A. Various types: There are four estates that involve a landlord-tenant relationship: (1) the tenancy for *years*; (2) the *periodic* tenancy; (3) the tenancy *at will*; and (4) the tenancy at *sufference*. [157]

B. **Statute of Frauds:** Under the original English Statute of Frauds, any lease for ***more than three years*** must be ***in writing***. (Otherwise, it merely creates an "estate at will.") In the U.S., most statutes now require a writing for all leases for ***more than one year***. [158]

   1. **Option to renew:** In calculating whether a lease is for more than one year (so that it probably has to be in writing), most courts add together the fixed term and any period for which the tenant has the ***option*** to ***renew***. [158]

C. **The estate for years:** Most leases are ***estates for years***. An estate for years is any estate which is for a ***fixed period of time***. (So even a six-month lease is an "estate for years.") [159]

   1. **Certain term:** For a lease to be an estate for years, the beginning date and end date must be ***fixed***.

   2. **Automatic termination:** Because an estate for years contains its own termination date, ***no additional notice of termination*** need be given by either party — on the last day, the tenancy simply ends, and the tenant must leave the premises.

D. **Periodic tenancy:** The ***periodic tenancy*** is one which ***continues*** from one period to the next ***automatically***, unless either party terminates it at the end of a period by notice. Thus a year-to-year tenancy, or a month-to-month one, would be periodic. [159-161]

   1. **Creation by implication:** Normally a periodic tenancy is created by ***implication***. Thus a lease with no stated duration (e.g., T agrees to pay L "$200 per month," but with no end period) creates a periodic tenancy. Also, if a tenant ***holds over***, and the landlord accepts rent, probably a periodic tenancy is created. [160]

   2. **Termination:** A periodic tenancy will automatically be ***renewed*** for a further period unless one party gives a valid ***notice of termination***. [160]

      a. **Common law:** At common law, six months' notice was needed to terminate a year-to-year tenancy, and a full period's notice was necessary when the period was less than a year (e.g., 30 days notice for a month-to-month tenancy). Also, at common law, the notice had to set the ***end of a period*** as the termination date.

      b. **Modern:** Most states today require only 30 days notice for any tenancy, even year-to-year. Notice today must still generally be effective as of the end of a period, but if the notice is not sufficiently in advance of one period, it is automatically applicable to the following period.

         Example: L and T have a month-to-tenancy; if one gives the other notice of termination on January 4, this will be effective as of February 28.

E. **At-will tenancy:** A ***tenancy at will*** is a tenancy which has ***no stated duration*** and which may be ***terminated at any time*** by either party. [160-161]

   1. **Implication:** Usually a tenancy at will, like a periodic tenancy, is created by ***implication***. For instance, if T takes possession with L's permission, with no term stated and no period for paying rent defined (so that the lease is not even a periodic one), it will probably be at will. Also, a few courts hold that if one party has the option to terminate at will, the other party has a similar option so that the tenancy is at will.

F. **Tenancy at sufferance:** There is only one situation in which the "tenancy at sufferance" exists: where a tenant ***holds over*** at the end of a valid lease. Here, the landlord has a ***right of election***, between: (1) ***evicting*** the tenant; and (2) holding him to ***another term*** as tenant. (If L elects to hold T to another term, most courts hold that a periodic tenancy is then created, and the length of the period is determined by the way rent was computed under the lease which terminated.) [161-162]

II. TENANT'S RIGHT OF POSSESSION AND ENJOYMENT

A. Tenant's right of possession: Courts are split about whether L impliedly warrants to T that he will deliver *actual possession* at the start of the lease term. The question usually arises when a prior tenant *holds over*.

  1. "American" view: The so-called *"American"* view is that the landlord has a duty to deliver *only* legal possession, *not actual possession*. Despite the name, at most a slight majority of American courts follow this rule. [163]

  2. "English" rule: Other courts follow the so-called *"English"* rule, by which L *does* have a duty to deliver actual possession. In courts following this rule, T has the right to *terminate the lease* and recover damages for the breach if the prior tenant holds over and L does not oust him. Alternatively, T may continue the lease and get damages for the period until the prior tenant is removed. [163]

B. Quiet enjoyment: T has the right of *"quiet enjoyment"* of the leased premises. This right can be violated in two main ways: (1) by claims of *"paramount title"*; and (2) by acts of L, or persons claiming under him, which interfere with T's *possession or use* of the premises. [163]

  1. Claims of paramount title: L, by making the lease, impliedly warrants that he has *legal power* to give possession to T for the term of the lease. If someone else successfully asserts a claim to the property which is superior to T's claim under the lease (a claim of *"paramount title"*), L has breached this warranty. Thus suppose that X shows that L does not have title to the premises at all (because X has title), or that X shows that L has previously leased the premises to X, or that X shows that X holds a mortgage on the premises, and is entitled to foreclose because L has not made mortgage payments — in all of these instances, X's claim of paramount title constitutes a breach by L of his implied warranty. [163]

  a. Can't terminate without eviction: Assuming T has taken possession, he may *not* terminate the lease (or refuse to pay rent) merely on the grounds that a third person *holds* a paramount title. (It is sometimes said that T is *"estopped to deny L's title"* to the leased property.) On the other hand, if the third person then *asserts* his paramount title in such a way that T is *evicted*, T may terminate the lease and recover damages.

  2. Interference by landlord or third person: If L himself, or someone claiming under L, *interferes* with T's *use* of the premises, this will be a breach of the covenant of quiet enjoyment. [164]

  a. Conduct by other tenants: If the conduct of *other tenants* makes the premises uninhabitable for T, the traditional view is that L is *not* responsible (unless the other tenants use their portion for immoral or lewd purposes, or conduct their acts in the *common areas*). But the *modern trend* is to impute the acts of other tenants to L where these acts are *in violation of the other leases*, and L could have prevented the conduct by eviction or otherwise.

  Example: Suppose that other tenants make a great deal of noise in violation of their leases, so that L could evict them, but does not. The modern trend, but not the traditional rule, is that T may terminate the lease.

  b. Constructive eviction: If T's claim is merely that his *use* or *enjoyment* of the property has been substantially impaired (e.g., excessive noise, terrible odors) the eviction is *"constructive"*. When T is constructively evicted, even if this is L's fault, T is generally not entitled to terminate or stop paying rent unless he *abandons the premises*. [166]

  Example: Other tenants make so much noise that T's use is severely impaired. If T remains in the premises, most courts say that T may not reduce the rent payments to L; he must leave and terminate the lease, or else pay the full lease amount.

C. Condemnation: If the government uses its right of eminent domain to *condemn* all or part of the leased premises, T may have a remedy. [166]

    1. Total taking: If the *entire* premises are taken, the *lease terminates*, and T does not have to pay the rent.

    2. Partial: But if only a *portion* of the premises is taken (even a major part), at common law the lease is *not terminated*. Also, T must *continue paying the full rent* (though he gets an appropriate portion of any condemnation award which L collects from the government). However, the modern trend is to let T terminate if the condemnation *"significantly interferes"* with his use, and to give him a reduction in rent even for a small interference.

D. Illegality: If T intends to use the property for *illegal purposes*, and L knows this fact, the court will probably treat the lease as *unenforceable*, especially if the illegality would be a serious one (e.g., crack distribution). [167-168]

    1. Variance or permit: If the use intended by T requires a *variance* or *permit*, and T is unable to get the variance or permit after the lease is signed, most courts hold that the lease *remains valid*.

III. CONDITION OF THE PREMISES

A. Common-law view: At common law, T takes the premises *as is*. L is *not* deemed to have made any implied warranty that the premises are *fit* or *habitable*. Nor does L have any *duty to repair* defects arising during the course of the lease (unless the parties explicitly provide that he does). [168]

    1. Independence of covenants: Also, the common law applies the doctrine of *"independence of covenants"* in leases. Thus even if L does expressly promise to repair (or warrants that the premises are habitable), if he breaches this promise T must still pay rent. T may sue for damages, but he is stuck in the uninhabitable living conditions. [169]

    2. Constructive eviction: However, even at common law, T can raise the defense of *"constructive eviction"* — he can terminate the lease if he can show that the premises are virtually uninhabitable. But he can only assert constructive eviction if he first *leaves the premises*, something which a poor tenant in uninhabitable residential space can rarely afford to do. [169]

B. Modern implied warranty of habitability: But today, the vast majority of states (either by statute or case law) impose some kind of *implied warranty of habitability*. That is, if L leases residential premises to T, he impliedly warrants that the premises are in at least *good enough condition to be lived in*. If L breaches this warranty, T may (among other remedies) withhold rent, and use the withheld rent to make the repairs himself. [169]

    1. Waiver of known pre-existing defects: Some (but by no means all) courts hold that if T *knows* of the defect *before he moves in*, he will be held to have *waived* the defect, so that the implied warranty of habitability does not apply to that defect. (If the defect is one which T neither discovered nor reasonably could have discovered before moving in, then all courts agree that an otherwise-applicable implied warranty of habitability protects T against the defect.) [169]

    2. Standards for determining "habitability": All courts agree that the existence of a *building code violation* is at least *evidence* of uninhabitability. However, most courts require that to prove uninhabitability, T must show that the conditions not only violate the building code, but are also a *substantial threat to T's health or safety*. (Conversely, most courts hold that if conditions *are* a substantial threat to T's health or safety, the warranty is breached even if there is no building code violation.) [170]

        a. Relevance of nature of building: Some (but not all) courts hold that the *age of the building* and the *amount of rent charged* may be considered in determining whether there has been a breach. Thus a given condition might be a breach of the warranty as to a new luxury high rise, but not as to an old low-rent structure.

3. **Kinds of leases:**

   a. **Residential:** Most *statutes* imposing an implied warranty of habitability apply to *all residential* leases (though some apply merely to units in multiple dwellings, so that a single-family house would not be covered). [170]

   b. **Commercial leases:** Most statutes and cases do *not* impose an implied warranty of habitability as to *commercial* leases. [170]

4. **Waiver in lease:** Generally, a clause in the lease expressly stating that there is no implied warranty is usually *not effective*. (But some statutes, such as the URLTA, will enforce a deal in which T promises, in a *separate writing*, and for adequate consideration such as a lower rent, to *make repairs himself*.) [171]

5. **Remedies:** If T shows a breach of the implied warranty of habitability, he may have a number of *remedies*:

   a. **Terminate lease:** T may usually *vacate the premises* and *terminate* the lease (after he puts L on notice and L still refuses to make the repairs). [171]

   b. **Withhold rent:** T may also *withhold rent* until the defects have been cured. (But most statutes, and some cases, require T to *deposit* the rent in some sort of escrow account.) [171]

   c. **Use rent for repairs:** Many cases and statutes allow T to *make the repairs* and then to *deduct the reasonable costs* of those repairs from the rent. T must usually give L advance notice of his intent to make the repairs and to deduct (so that L can make the repairs himself to avoid the loss of rent). [172]

6. **Retaliatory eviction barred:** By the doctrine of *"retaliatory eviction,"* L usually may not terminate a periodic lease, or deny T's request for a new lease at the conclusion of a tenancy for years, on account of T's assertion of the right to habitable premises. The doctrine is most likely to be applied where L tries to terminate the tenancy in retaliation for T's complaints made to a housing authority about *code violations*. Also, some courts apply the doctrine where the non-renewal or termination is in retaliation for T's withholding of rent or his joining in a tenants' organization. [172]

C. **Destruction of premises:** If the premises are suddenly *destroyed* or *damaged* (by fire, flood, lightning or other natural elements), at common law T must *keep paying rent*, and may not terminate the lease. [172]

   1. **Modern view:** But most states have now passed *statutes* changing this common-law rule — if the premises are destroyed or damaged so that they are no longer habitable, T may now usually *terminate the lease* and stop paying rent. Also, some courts have reached this result by case law. (But T usually cannot recover damages, so termination of the lease is his only remedy.)

IV. TORT LIABILITY OF LANDLORD AND TENANT

A. **Tenant's tort liability:** T, during the time he is in possession of the premises, is treated *like an owner*, for purposes of his *tort liability* to others who come onto the property. [173]

> **Example:** Since L would have a duty to warn a social guest, or licensee, of known dangers, T has a similar duty to warn of dangers that he is aware of.

B. **Landlord's liability:**

C
A
P
S
U
L
E

S
U
M
M
A
R
Y

1. **Common law:** At common law, L is generally ***not liable*** for physical injury to T, or to persons who are on the leased property with T's consent. That is, L has no general duty to use reasonable care to make or keep the premises safe. [174] However, there are a number of ***exceptions*** (including some developed by courts recently), including the following:

    a. **Concealment:** L is liable if he ***conceals***, or ***fails to disclose***, a dangerous defect existing at the start of the lease of which he is ***aware***. [174]

        i. **L should know but does not:** Most courts also hold that if L does not have actual knowledge but ***should know*** about the danger, based on facts that he does know, he will be liable for failing to warn.

        ii. **No duty of inspection:** But L has ***no duty of inspection***, i.e., no obligation to inspect the property to find out whether there are hidden defects.

    b. **Liability to persons other than T:** Nearly all courts hold that if L would be liable to T, he is also liable to ***persons on the premises with T's consent***. (But if L has told T about the defect, L will not be liable to T's guests even if T did not pass on the warning.) [174]

    c. **Areas under L's control:** L has a duty to use ***reasonable care*** to keep the ***common areas*** safe (e.g., lobbies, elevator, corridor, etc.). [174]

        i. **Security against criminals:** Most courts now require L to use reasonable care to prevent ***unauthorized access*** to the building.

            Example: L, the owner of an apartment building, fails to repair the building's outer lock after being told that it is broken. X enters, and mugs T. Most courts would hold L liable for not using reasonable care to secure the building.

    d. **Repairs negligently performed:** If L ***attempts*** to make a repair, he will be liable if the repair is done negligently, and L has made the condition more dangerous or lulled T into a false feeling of security. (But if L's negligent repair does not make the condition worse or lull T, the courts are split as to whether L is liable if T is injured.) [175]

    e. **L contracts to repair:** If a ***clause in the lease*** requires L to make ***repairs*** or otherwise keep the premises safe, L will be liable in tort if he fails to use reasonable care and T is injured. Also, L is probably liable to ***third persons*** on the premises with T's consent in this situation. [175]

    f. **L's legal duties:** If ***building codes*** or other laws impose a duty on L to keep the premises safe, L will generally be liable in tort if he fails in this duty. Probably L will also be liable if he breaches an implied warranty of habitability, and the uninhabitable condition causes injury to T or T's guest. [175-176]

    g. **Admission of public:** If L has reason to believe that T will ***hold the premises open to the public***, and L has reason to know that a dangerous condition exists, L will be liable for resulting physical harm to the public. (L usually has an affirmative ***duty to inspect*** in this situation.) [176]

2. **General "reasonable care" theory:** Some recent cases have simply ***rejected*** the common-law view that L has no general duty to use reasonable care. Under these cases, P does not have to fit within one of the above exceptions, and merely has to show that: (1) L failed to use reasonable care and (2) the lack of reasonable care proximately caused P's injury. [176]

3. **Exculpatory clauses:** At least in the case of a ***residential*** lease, most courts today ***refuse*** to enforce an ***"exculpatory clause"*** in a lease, that is, a clause purporting to relieve L of tort liability for his negligence. About half the states accomplish this by statute, and some others by case law. [176]

V. TENANT'S DUTIES

A. Duty to pay rent: T of course has a duty to **pay rent**.

    1. Breach of L's duties: Most courts today hold that if L **materially breaches** his implied or express obligations (e.g., the implied warranty of habitability), T is temporarily **relieved** from continuing to pay rent. [177-178]

B. Duty to repair: At common law, T had an implied duty to make **minor repairs**. [177]

    1. Modern rule: However, most courts today do not impose this duty on T (and indeed, most impose it on L under the doctrine of implied warranty of habitability, at least for residential leases).

C. Fixtures: A **fixture** is an item of personal property that is **attached** to the land (e.g., lighting, built-in bookcases, etc.). [178]

    1. Right to affix: T is usually allowed to **attach** fixtures if this would not unfairly damage the value of L's reversion.

    2. Right to remove: If T has attached an item to L's property so **tightly** that it's fair to regard it as **part of the real estate** (i.e., it's properly called a "fixture)," as a general rule T **may not remove it** at the end of the lease term. [178]

        Examples: Common examples of chattels that are likely to be found to be fixtures (and thus not removable by T) are *construction materials* incorporated into the structure (e.g., bricks, nails, or lumber used in repairs), *electrical wiring and plumbing*, and *built-in bookcases and cabinets* specially designed to fit only the particular space they occupy.

        Conversely, items like **carpeting** and **kitchen appliances** are likely *not* to be deemed fixtures. [178]

        a. Factors: The following factors, if present, argue in favor of a finding that the item is a fixture (and thus **not removable** at lease-end by the tenant) [178]

            ❏ the item is **firmly imbedded** in the real estate;

            ❏ the item is **peculiarly adapted or fitted** to the real estate; or

            ❏ the item's removal would **destroy** the chattel, or significantly damage the real estate.

            i. Contrary lease provision: But L and T are always free to specify, in the lease, a different treatment on this issue of removeability, and if they do so, **the lease treatment will control.**

        b. "Trade fixtures": Where the item is a so-called **"trade fixture"** — an item attached to the real estate by a **commercial tenant** for use in the tenant's **business** — there is a very strong **presumption** that the trade fixture is **removable** as long as T restores the premises to their original condition. In other words, the **"firmly imbedded"** and **"peculiarly adapted or fitted"** factors described above **do not count for much** in the case of trade fixtures. [179]

            Example: T rents a building from L in which T plans to run a restaurant. T installs a custom refrigeration system that is attached to the building's ductwork. The lease is silent on whether T may remove the system at the end of the lease.

            As long as T has restored the premises to their original condition (e.g., by repairing the ceilings, walls and floors to remove any holes where the items were attached), T may remove the refrigeration system. All of the items were "trade fixtures," i.e., items specially adapted for use in the tenant's trade or business, and there is a strong presumption that trade fixtures are removable as long as the premises are restored to their pre-lease condition. [179]

D. Duty to behave reasonably: T has the implied duty to *behave reasonably* in his use of the premises. (*Examples*: T must not unreasonably disturb other tenants, and must obey reasonable regulations posted by the landlord.) [180]

VI.   LANDLORD'S REMEDIES

A. Security deposits:

1. **Interest:** In many states, L is required by statute to pay *interest* on the security deposit. [180]

2. **Right to keep:** Once the lease terminates, L must *return* the deposit to T, after subtracting any damages. If T abandons the lease before the end of the lease term and L re-lets, L must *immediately* return the deposit (after subtracting damages).

3. **Commingle:** L may normally *commingle* the security deposit with his own funds.

B. Acceleration clause: Most leases contain an *acceleration of rent* clause, by which if T fails to pay rent promptly or otherwise breaches the lease, L may require that all of the rent for the rest of the lease term is payable at once. [181]

1. **Generally valid:** Most courts *enforce* such acceleration clauses. (But if L decides to sue for enforcement of the acceleration clause, he may not also demand possession of the premises.)

C. Eviction:

1. **Express forfeiture clause:** Most leases explicitly give L the right to *terminate the lease* if T fails to pay rent or violates any other lease provision. Such clauses will be enforced, but only if T's breach is *material*. [181]

   Example: If T is merely a couple days late with the rent on one or two occasions, the court will probably not allow L to terminate the lease.

2. **Summary proceedings:** In most states, if L is entitled to terminate the lease and regain possession (or if T holds over at the end of the lease term and L wants to get him out), L may do so by *"summary proceedings,"* which provide for a *speedy trial* of L's right to immediate possession. Summary proceedings usually work by *limiting the defenses* which T may assert. [181-182]

   Example: Some summary proceeding statutes prevent T from asserting the breach of the implied warranty of habitability as a defense in L's action to regain possession for non-payment of rent.

D. Damages for holdover: If T *holds over* after the lease terminates, L is entitled to *damages* as well as eviction. [182]

E. Abandonment: If T *abandons* the premises (and defaults on the rent) before the scheduled end of the lease term, L has three basic choices: (1) to *accept a surrender* of the premises, thus terminating the lease; (2) to *re-let* on T's behalf; and (3) to leave the premises *vacant* and sue for rent as it comes due. [182-183]

1. **Accept surrender:** L may treat T's abandonment as a *surrender*, and accept it. This has the effect of *terminating* the lease, so that *no further rent becomes due from T*. (If T takes possession and/or leases to someone else, and does not notify T that he is acting on T's behalf, then this will probably be held to be an acceptance of surrender, causing T's rent obligation to end.) [182]

2. **Re-letting on T's account:** L may *re-let on T's behalf*, if he notifies T that he is doing so. This has two advantages to L: (1) T remains liable for all rents coming due, if no new tenant is found; and (2) if a new tenant is found who pays a lesser rent, T is still liable for the difference between this and the original rent due under the L-T lease. [182]

   3. **Leave vacant:** Courts are split on whether L has the right to *leave the premises vacant*, and hold L to the lease. Usually, the question is phrased, "Does L have the duty to mitigate?"

      a. **Traditional view:** The traditional view is that L has *no duty to mitigate*, i.e., no duty to try to find a new tenant. [183]

      b. **Duty to mitigate:** But an increasing minority of courts now hold that L *does have a duty to mitigate*, by attempting to find a suitable replacement tenant. In these courts, if L does not make such an effort, T is off the hook. [183]

VII. TRANSFER AND SALE BY LESSOR; ASSIGNMENT AND SUBLETTING BY LESSEE

A. Generally allowed: Unless the parties to a lease agree otherwise, either may *transfer* his interest. Thus L may sell his reversion in the property, and T may either *assign* or *sublease* his right to occupy. [183]

   1. **Distinguish assignment from sublease:** Be sure to distinguish *sublease* from *assignment*. An assignment is the transfer by T of his *entire interest* in the leased premises. Thus he must transfer the *entire remaining length* of the term of his lease. A *sublease* is the transfer by T of *less* than his entire interest. [184]

      Example: T's lease has one year to go. T transfers the first 11.5 months of this interest to T1. In most states, this is a sublease, not an assignment.

      a. **Significance:** The main significance of this distinction is that if T assigns to T1, T1 is *personally liable* to *pay rent* to L, even if he makes no express promise to L or T that he will do so. If T merely subleases to T1, T1 is not personally liable to L for the rent (absent an explicit promise). [185]

B. Running of benefit and burden: Determine whether a particular promise *runs with the land*, either as to benefit or burden. If the *benefit runs*, then an assignee of the promisee can sue to enforce; if the *burden runs*, an assignee of the promisor will be liable. If neither the burden nor benefit runs, then the promisor's assignee is not liable, and promisee's assignee cannot sue. [185]

      Example 1 (benefit runs): In the L-T lease, T promises to make repairs. This promise "touches and concerns the land" both as to benefit and burden, so benefit and burden run. Thus if T assigns to T1, T1 is personally liable for making the repairs. Conversely, if L assigns to L1, L1 can sue T (and T1 if T has assigned to T1) to enforce this promise.

      Example 2 (burdens runs, but benefit does not): In the L-T lease, T promises not to compete with L's use of certain other property. If T assigns to T1, T1 is liable not to compete. But if L assigns to L1, in most states L1 cannot enforce the promise against either T or T1.

   1. **"Touch and concern" test:** The burden runs if the promise *"touches and concerns"* the promisor's assignee's interest in the land. Similarly, the benefit runs if the promise "touches and concerns" the promisee's assignee's interest in the property. [185]

   2. **Normally both or neither:** Normally, either the benefit and burden will both run, or neither will run. (The non-competition situation described in Example 2 above is one of the few examples where this is not true.) [185-186]

C. Rights after T assigns: Here are the rights of the parties after T assigns to T1 his rights under the L-T lease:

   1. **T's liability to L:** After the assignment, T *remains liable* to L (whether T's promise to L does or does not "touch and concern" the land). [187]

Example: T remains liable for the rent after assignment to T1. This is true even if L consents to the assignment, and even if L accepts some rent payments from T1.

2. T's rights against T1: After the assignment, T1 becomes ***primarily liable***, and T is only secondarily liable. Therefore, if L sues T when T1 does not make the rent payments, T can then sue T1 for the amount that T has had to pay (even if T1 never expressly assumed the lease duties at the time of the assignment). [187]

3. L's rights against T1: Assuming that T1 does not make any specific promises of performance when he takes the assignment, T1 is liable only for those promises made by T whose burden ***runs with the land***. [187]

> **Example 1:** T1 is liable to L for *rent*, since the burden of T's original rent promise ran with the land. Thus T1 must make the rent payments even if he did not expressly promise either T or L that he would make these payments.

> **Example 2:** In the original L-T lease, T promises to keep the premises insured. Assume that the burden of this promise does not run with the land (the majority rule). If T assigns to T1 and T1 does not make any promise of insurance, T1 is not liable for failing to insure the property (though L can terminate the lease for breach if T1 does not do so).

a. Assignment by assignee: But T1 remains liable (even on promises whose burdens run with the land) only for the period when he is in ***actual possession***. If he ***re-assigns***, he is ***not liable*** for breaches by the subsequent assignee. [188]

> **Example:** T assigns to T1. T1 remains in possession for six months, then assigns to T2. T1 is liable for the rent that accrued during the six months he was in possession, but not for any rents accruing after he left possession and T2 took possession.

b. Assumption: However, if T1 ***assumes*** the lease (i.e., expressly promises T that T1 will obey all terms of the L-T lease), then T1 is liable both to T and L for all T's obligations, including those accruing after T1 re-assigns to T2. [188]

D. Assignment by L: Now, assume that L assigns his rights to L1. Here, the same rule applies: L1 has the burden of covenants whose burden runs with the land, and has the benefit of covenants whose benefit runs with the land. [189]

1. Repair obligation: Thus if L promised T that he would keep the premises in repair, L1 is liable for making the repairs after the sale. (Also, the implied warranty of habitability, if it applies at all, probably binds L1 just as it bound L.)

E. Agreement by the parties about transfer: All of the above assumes that the lease itself contains no provisions restricting transfer. Most leases, however, contain a promise by T that he will ***not assign or sublease his interest without L's consent***. [189-191]

1. Generally enforced: Most states ***enforce*** such a clause, even if L is completely ***unreasonable*** in refusing to consent to the transfer.

a. Strict construction and waiver: However, courts construe such anti-transfer clauses strictly, and are quick to hold that L ***waived*** the benefit of the clause.

> **Example:** If L knowingly accepts rents from T1 he will probably be held to have waived his right to refuse to consent to the transfer.

b. Consent to second transfer: Also, if L consents (or waives his objection to) a particular transfer, he is usually held to have also waived his right to a ***subsequent*** transfer, under the rule of *Dumpor's Case*. [189]

Example: L consents to T's assignment to T1. In most states, L is also held to consent to T1's further assignment to T2.

2.   **Modern trend:** An increasing minority of states hold (often by statute) that even if the lease says that L has an *unconditional* right to refuse to consent to a transfer by T, the *consent may not be unreasonably withheld*. (In such a state, L should get a lease provision giving him the right to *make his own deal* directly with T1 — this way, if T1 is willing to pay more than the original lease amount, L, not T, gets the benefit.) [190]

CHAPTER 9

EASEMENTS AND PROMISES CONCERNING LAND

I.   EASEMENTS GENERALLY

A.   Definition: An *easement* is a privilege to *use the land of another*. [203]

1.   **Affirmative easement:**   An *affirmative* easement is one entitling its holder to *do a physical act* on another's land.

   Example: *A*, who owns Blackacre, gives *B* a *right of way* over Blackacre, so that *B* can pass from his own property to a street which adjoins Blackacre. *B* holds an affirmative easement.

2.   **Negative easement:**   A *negative* easement is one which enables its holder to *prevent* the owner of land from making certain uses of that land. These are rare.

   Example: *A* owns Whiteacre, which is next to the ocean; *B* owns Blackacre, which is separated from the ocean by Whiteacre. *A* gives *B* an easement of "light and air," which assures *B* that *A* will not build anything on Whiteacre which would block *B*'s view of the ocean. *B* holds a negative easement.

B.   Appurtenant vs. in gross: Distinguish between easements that are *appurtenant* to a particular piece of land, and those that are *"in gross."* [203]

1.   **Appurtenant:**   An easement *appurtenant* is one which benefits its holder in the use of a *certain piece of land*. The land for whose benefit the appurtenant easement is created is called the *"dominant tenement."* The land that is burdened or used is called the *"servient tenement."*

   Example: Blackacre, owned by *S*, stands between Whiteacre, owned by *D*, and the public road. *S* gives *D* the right to pass over a defined part of Blackacre to get from Whiteacre to the road. This right of way is an easement that is appurtenant to Whiteacre — Blackacre is the servient tenement, and Whiteacre is the dominant tenement.

   a.   **Test for:**   For an easement to be appurtenant, its benefit must be intimately *tied to a particular piece of land* (the dominant tenement). Usually, for the easement to be appurtenant, the dominant tenement and the servient tenement will need to be *adjacent* to each other.

2.   **Easement in gross:**   An easement *in gross* is one whose benefit is *not tied* to any particular parcel. [204]

   Example: *O*, who owns Blackacre, gives *E*, who lives across town, the right to come onto Blackacre anytime he wants, and use *O*'s swimming pool. Since the grant is not given because of *E*'s ownership of nearby land, the easement is in gross.

3.   **Profit:**   Related to easements is something called the *"profit a prendre."* A profit is the right to go onto the land of another and *remove the soil or a product of it*. Thus the right to mine *minerals*,

drill *oil*, or capture wild game or fish, are all profits. (In the U.S., profits are functionally identical to easements.)

II.   CREATION OF EASEMENTS

A. Four ways to create: There are five ways in which an easement may be created [205]:

[1] by an *express* grant (which generally must be in writing);

[2] by *implication*, as part of a land transfer;

[3] by strict *necessity*, to prevent a parcel from being landlocked;

[4] by *prescription*, similar to the obtaining of a possessory estate by adverse possession; and

[5] by *estoppel*.

B. Express creation: If a easement is created by a *deed* or a *will*, it is *"express."* [205]

1. Statute of Frauds: An express easement *must be in writing*. This is required by the Statute of Frauds.

2. Reservation in grantor: Often, an express easement is created when the owner of land conveys the land to someone else, and *reserves for himself* an easement in it. This is called an "easement by reservation." [205-206]

Example: *A* deeds Blackacre to *B*, with a statement in the deed that "*A* hereby retains a right of way over the eastern eight feet of the property."

3. Creation in stranger to deed: At common law, it was *not* possible for an owner to convey land to one person, and to establish by the same deed an easement in a *third person*. (Thus an easement could not be created in a *"stranger to the deed."*)

a. Modern courts abandon rule: But most modern courts have *abandoned* this "no easement for stranger to the deed" rule. The Third Restatement agrees with the modern approach. [206]

Example: *O* owns two parcels, 1 and 2. *O* sells parcel 1 to *P*, without recording any easement over parcel 2 in favor of parcel 1. *O* then deeds parcel 2 to *D*, with a statement in the deed, "Easement reserved in favor of *P* or his successors to parcel 1." Today, in most courts (and under the Third Restatement) this easement will be enforced even though *P* was not a party to the *O-D* deed.) [206]

C. Creation by implication: An easement by *implication* may sometimes be created. If so, it does *not have to satisfy the statute of frauds*. [206-207]

1. Summary of requirements: For an easement by implication to exist, these three requirements must all be met [206]:

[1] Land is being *"severed"* from its common owner. That is, it's being *divided up* so that the owner of a parcel is either selling part and retaining part, or is subdividing the property and selling pieces to different grantees.

[2] The use for which the implied easement is claimed *existed prior to the severance* referred to in [1], and was apparent and continuous prior to that severance.

[3] The easement is at least *reasonably necessary* to the enjoyment of what is claimed to be the dominant tenement.

Example: *O* owns two vacant side-by-side lots, Blackacre and Whiteacre. Blackacre (but not Whiteacre) adjoins a public street that contains a public sewer main. *O* constructs a house on Whiteacre, and runs a sewer line from that house underneath Blackacre to the public main. *O* then sells Whiteacre to *A*, without mentioning the existence of the sewer line either orally or in the deed. Later, *A* sells Whiteacre to *B* and *O* sells Blackacre to *C*. *C* blocks the sewer line from Whiteacre as it enters Blackacre. *B* sues to have the blockage removed.

B will win, because *O* created an easement by implication, since (1) *O* owned both parcels simultaneously; (2) the use existed (i.e., the sewer line passed under Blackacre) while *O* still owned both; and (3) the easement remains reasonably necessary to the owner of Whiteacre. [207]

2. **Severance from common owner:** An easement will only be implied where the owner of a parcel *sells part and retains part*, or *sells pieces simultaneously* to more than one grantee. This is the requirement of *"severance."* [207]

> **Example:** *A* and *B* are neighboring landowners. A new street is built adjoining *B*'s property, and *A* can only get to this street by crossing *B*'s property. *A* crosses *B*'s property at a particular spot for several years, then sells to *C*. *C* has no easement by implication across *B*'s property, because there was never any conveyance between *A* and *B* ("severance"), required for the creation of an easement by implication.

3. **Prior use:** The use for which the easement is claimed must have existed *prior* to the severance of ownership. [208]

> **Example:** In the next-to-previous example, involving the underground sewer line, the fact that the sewer line existed while *O* owned both Blackacre and Whiteacre means that this "prior use" requirement is satisfied.

4. **Necessity:** According to most courts, the easement must be *reasonably necessary* to the enjoyment of what is claimed to be the dominant tenement.

> a. **Easement by grant vs. by reservation:** Courts require a *lesser showing* of necessity where the easement is created by *grant* (i.e., in favor of the grantee), than where the easement is *reserved* (i.e., in favor of the grantor). [209]
>
> > **Example:** *A* owns both Blackacre and, adjacent and to the east of Blackacre, Whiteacre. A driveway runs from the east side of Blackacre east across Whiteacre, and then to a well-traveled public road. *A* customarily uses this driveway to leave Blackacre. There is a separate much longer driveway running from the south side of Blackacre through a neighbor's land (covered by an express easement) to a much less-well-traveled and less-well-paved public road. *A* conveys Blackacre to *B*. The deed says nothing about any easement across Whiteacre.
> >
> > A court would likely hold that *B* has an implied easement over Whiteacre to get to the more-travelled road. That is, the court would likely require that *B* show merely a "reasonable necessity" for the easement, and hold that this showing is met here — the fact that a much less convenient easement exists from the south to a different road probably won't prevent *B*'s necessity from being deemed sufficiently great.
>
> > i. **Easement reserved:** But where the easement is *reserved* (i.e., created in favor of the *grantor* rather than the grantee), most courts require that it be *"strictly"* or *"absolutely"* necessary.
> >
> > > **Example:** On the facts of the above example, suppose *A* sells Whiteacre (while keeping Blackacre) and then claims that Whiteacre is now subject to an implied easement in favor of Blackacre. *A* will probably lose — the easement he's claiming is one that would have been created by reservation, and since the easement here is not strictly necessary (the owner of Blackacre can use the less-convenient south alternative), a court will likely conclude that the easement by implication does not exist.

5. **Easement of light and air:** An easement of *"light and air"* (the right to have one's view remain unobstructed) *cannot* be created by implication, in most states. [210]

D. Easement by necessity: The courts will sometimes find an "easement by *necessity*" if two parcels are so situated that an easement over one is *"strictly necessary"* to the enjoyment of the other. [210]

1. **Requirements:** Unlike the easement by implication, the easement by necessity does *not require that there have been an actual prior use* before severance. But three requirements must be met [210]:

    [1] The necessity must be *"strict"* rather than "reasonable" (the usual standard for implied easements);

    [2] the parcels must have been under *common ownership* just before a conveyance; and

    [3] the necessity must *come into existence at the time of,* and be *caused by*, the *conveyance* that breaks up the common ownership.

2. **Landlocked parcels:** The most common example of an easement by necessity is where a parcel is *"landlocked,"* and access to a public road can only be gained via a right of way over adjoining property.

3. **"Strict" necessity:** While courts say that the necessity must be *"strict,"* they don't mean that the property must have absolutely no use without the access. Instead, they mean that it must be the case that without the easement, the property must not be able to be *"effectively"* used *without disproportionate effort or expense.* But this is a tougher-to-meet standard than the "reasonably necessary" standard for easements by implication created by a grant. [210]

4. **Pre-conveyance actual use not required:** As long as the need for the easement was created by the severance from common ownership, it does not matter that *no actual use* of the claimed right of way occurred before the conveyance.

5. **Need must be caused by conveyance:** For the easement by necessity to exist, the *necessity* must *come into existence exist at the moment of the conveyance*, and be *caused by* that conveyance — a necessity that comes into existence *post-conveyance* will *not* suffice. [211]

    a. **Alternative exists, then disappears:** So if the would-be dominant parcel has some *alternative means of access* at the time of the conveyance, and that alternative means *disappears at some later date*, the dominant holder does not get an easement by necessity. [211]

        Example: *O* owns Blackacre and Whiteacre. The eastern border of Blackacre adjoins the western border of Whiteacre. *O* conveys Whiteacre to *A*, with the deed silent as to any right of *A* or his successors to cross Blackacre. At the moment of the conveyance, there are two public roads that serve the parcels: Main Street runs along the western border of Blackacre, and Broadway runs east-west along the northern border of both Whiteacre and Blackacre. (Therefore, prior to the conveyance nobody on Whiteacre ever needed to cross Blackacre to get to Main Street — they left the parcel by using Broadway instead.) Two years later, the city unexpectedly closes Broadway completely. *A* now sues *O* for a declaration that *A* has an easement by necessity to cross Blackacre to get to Main Street.

        A will lose. An easement by necessity will only be found to exist when the necessity (1) exists at the *moment of conveyance* by the joint owner of the two properties, and (2) is *caused* by that conveyance. Here, because the necessity did not exist at the moment of the conveyance (due to the availability of access via Broadway), *A* is out of luck. [211]

E. Easement by prescription: An easement by *"prescription"* is one that is gained under principles of *adverse possession*. If a person uses another's land for more than the statute of limitations period governing ejectment actions, he gains an easement by prescription. [211]

Example: In state X, the statute of limitations on actions to recover possession of real estate (ejectment actions) is 21 years. *A*, the owner of lot 1, uses a path over lot 2, owned by *B*, for 21 years. Assuming that the use meets the requirements discussed below (e.g., use must be "adverse," not "permissive"), after the 21 years *A* gains an easement by prescription, and may use the path as a right of way forever afterwards.

1. **When statute starts to run:** The statutory period does not begin to run until the owner of the servient tenement *gains a cause of action* against the owner of the dominant tenement. Therefore, an easement of *"light and air"* cannot be acquired by prescription (since the owner of the servient tenement never can sue the owner of the dominant tenement, because the latter merely looks out over the former's property, rather than trespassing upon it). [210]

2. **Adverse use:** The use must be *adverse* to the rights of the holder of the servient tenement, and without the latter's *permission*. [212-213]

    Example: *P* and *D* are next-door neighbors. Solely out of friendship, *D* agrees that *P* may use *D*'s driveway to get to *P*'s garage. *P* thanks *D* for this, and does not say that he is asserting an actual legal right to use the driveway. *P*'s use is therefore not adverse, so even if the usage continues longer than the statute of limitations, no easement by prescription will be gained. Instead, the use is merely a *license*, which is revocable at will by *D*.

3. **Continuous and uninterrupted:** The use must be *continuous and uninterrupted* throughout the statutory period. Thus if the use is so *infrequent* that a reasonable landowner would not be likely to protest, the continuity requirement is not satisfied. [213]

4. **Tacking:** There can be *tacking* on the dominant side of the prescriptive easement. [214]

    Example: In a state with a 21-year statute of limitations on ejectment actions, *A*, the owner of Blackacre, uses a path across Whiteacre for 12 years. He then sells Blackacre to *B*, who uses the same path for an additional 9 years. At the end of this 9 years, *B* will have an easement by prescription, because he is in privity of estate with *A* and therefore can tack his use onto *A*'s use.

F. **Easement by estoppel:** One last way an easement may be created is by *"estoppel."* An easement by estoppel is created where *A* allows *B* to use *A*'s land under circumstances where *A* should reasonably foresee that *B* will *substantially change position* believing that this permission will not be revoked, and *B* in fact changes position. An easement can come into existence by this method even though the parties never mention the word "easement," or mention the possibility of revocation. [215]

    Example: *A* and *B* have adjacent vacant lots, with only *A*'s lot having access to the public road. *A*, knowing that *B* wants to build a house, tells *B* orally that if *B* builds the house, *B* can use a path along *A*'s parcel to get from the house to the road. *B* builds the house. *A* will be deemed to have given *B* a permanent easement by estoppel, since *B* has reasonably and foreseeably relied on *A*'s promise of continuing access.

    1. **Can be oral:** An easement by estoppel may occur *even where there is no writing.* In other words, the usual Statute of Frauds for easements does not apply to easements by estoppel. That's what happens in the above example, in which an easement by estoppel occurs based on *O*'s oral grant to *A* of permission to use the road across Blackacre. [215]

G. **Tidelands and the "public trust" doctrine:** The *public as a whole* has something like an easement on the *navigable waterways* and on *seashores*. Under the *"public trust"* doctrine, in force in most states, the state holds title to navigable waterways and *tidelands* in trust for the public, and must safeguard the public's interest in these lands. [215]

    1. **Access to seashore:** The most important aspect of the public trust doctrine is that, in states that apply it, the doctrine guarantees to members of the public the right to *use* the *"tidelands"* portion

of the **ocean shore** for **swimming**, **bathing**, and other **recreational purposes**. Tidelands are the shore lands covered by the tides, i.e., the land between the mean high-tide mark and the mean low-tide mark of the ocean.

    a. Right of access through private lands: Most courts applying the public trust doctrine have not just given the public the right to swim in the tidelands, but have held that for this right to be meaningful, the public must have an easement-like **right of access**, **through private dry-sand property,** to **get to** the tidelands. Some have even given the public the right to use (not just cross) the entire dry-sand portion of privately-owned beaches. [*Raleigh Avenue Beach Ass'n. v. Atlantis Beach Club*] [219-219]

III. SCOPE OF EASEMENTS

A. Prescriptive easement: If the easement is created by **prescription**, the **scope** of the allowable use is determined by looking at the use that took place during the statutory period. Therefore, a use that is substantially **broader** (or more burdensome to the servient tenement) than existed during the time when the statute of limitations was running, will **not** be allowed. [220]

B. Development of dominant estate: Regardless of how the easement was created (e.g., whether by implication, prescription, etc.), the court will allow a use that increases dues to the **normal, foreseeable development** of the dominant estate. [220]

    Example: A right-of-way easement is created by prescription in favor of the sole house then located on a dominant tenement. After the easement is created, two more houses are built on the dominant property. The residents of all three houses may use the right of way, since the basic use — as a pedestrian right of way — remains unchanged, the increased use is a function of normal development, and the increase in the burden is slight.

    1. Excessive use: On the other hand, an increased use that **unreasonably interferes with the use of the servient estate,** viewed in light of the parties' original understanding about how the easement would be used, will **not** be allowed. [221]

        Example: Steve owns Whiteacre, and Don owns the adjacent Blackacre. Each has a single-family house located on a 1/4 acre parcel. Both parcels are zoned single family. Steve gives Don a 10-foot wide easement to drive to the public way abutting Whiteacre. Years later, Don's property is re-zoned to allow a 40-story apartment building. Don erects a 39-story building with 300 apartments. Tenants use the easement to cross Steve's property an average of 400 times per day, including late at night. A court would probably hold that the expanded use is so beyond that contemplated by the parties, and so unreasonably interferes with Steve's use of the servient tenement, that it is beyond the scope of the easement. [221]

C. Use for benefit of additional property: The holder of the dominant estate is normally **not** allowed to **extend his use** of the easement so that **additional property** owned by him (or by others) is benefit-ted. [221]

    Example: *W*, the owner of Whiteacre, gives *B*, the owner of Blackacre, an express easement by which *B* may cross *W*'s property to get from the road to a house on Blackacre. *B* then buys an adjoining parcel, Greenacre, tears down the house on Whiteacre, builds a new house on Greenacre, and extends the path represented by the easement through Blackacre (which he still owns) to get to the new house on Greenacre. *W* will be able to enjoin this extended use, since the easement is now being used to benefit additional property beyond Blackacre, the origi-nally-contemplated dominant estate.

D. Servient owner's right to relocate easement: Courts are in dispute about whether the servient owner may **relocate** the path of the easement to a **different part of the servient owner's property**. [222]

1. **Common-law approach:** At common law, the rule has been that the path of the easement is *fixed*, and the servient owner *may not relocate* the easement to a different portion of the servient owner's property, even if this doesn't cause an extra burden to the dominant owner. [222]

2. **Modern approach:** But the modern approach (and that of the Third Restatement) is that the servient owner *may relocate* the easement, if this doesn't materially inconvenience the dominant owner. [222]

   Example: *A* gives *B* a recorded easement over *A*'s property to get to the public road; the conveyance says that the easement is over a particular 10-foot-wide strip on the east side of *A*'s property. Later, *A* wants to build a house on the east side, and wants to shift the easement to a 10-foot-strip on the west side of *A*'s property. At common law, *B* would be able to block this change, even if using the west-side path wouldn't harm him. But under the modern approach, if using the west-side strip wouldn't be materially harder for *B*, *A* may make the change, even if *B* objects.

IV. REPAIR AND MAINTENANCE OF EASEMENTS

A. **Servient owner not obligated to maintain:** The owner of the *servient estate* is *not required to repair or maintain* the property used in the easement (e.g., a road or driveway), unless the parties expressly provide otherwise. [222]

   Example: *A*, the owner of Blackacre, grants an easement to *B*, the owner of the adjacent Whiteacre, whereby *B* may use a 10-foot strip of Blackacre to drive his car from Whiteacre to the public road. At the time the easement is granted, there is a bridge that the strip crosses. The easement document is silent about repairs. After the grant of the easement, the bridge washes out. *A* has no obligation to restore the bridge, even if the lack of maintenance means that *B* cannot use the easement as the parties intended. [222]

B. **Dominant owner has right to maintain:** Conversely, the *holder of the easement* has an implied *right* to maintain the property used in the easement, if that maintenance is compatible with the intended use of the easement and does not unreasonably interfere with the servient owner's use of the servient estate. [223]

   Example: Same facts as in the above example. *B*, the holder of easement, has a right to rebuild the bridge at his own expense.

   1. **Limited right to contribution:** If the holder of the easement *does* exercise his right to spend money to repair the easement property, normally that holder has the right to *contribution* from the holder of the servient estate, but only in an amount that is proportional to the servient holder's *share of the overall usage benefit* from the repairs. Thus if all the benefits from using the easement are enjoyed by easement holder, the dominant holder will have no reimbursement obligation. [223]

V. TRANSFER AND SUBDIVISION OF EASEMENTS

A. **Transfer of burden:** When the title to the *servient estate* is *transferred*, the burden of the easement *remains* with the property. [223]

   Example: *O*, the owner of Blackacre, gives *A*, a neighboring landowner, an express right of way over Blackacre. *O* then sells Blackacre to *B*. After the sale, *A*'s easement remains valid against Blackacre.

B. Transfer of benefit: Whether the *benefit* of an easement "runs with the land" (i.e., is *enforceable by an assignee*) depends on whether the easement is appurtenant or in gross.

    1. Transfer of easements appurtenant: An easement *appurtenant* (one where the benefit applies to particular land only) normally *passes with the transfer of the dominant estate*. (Thus in the above example, if *A* sells his land to *X*, *X* may enforce the easement against either *O* or one who bought from *O*.) [223]

        a. Where deed is silent: This rule — that the easement appurtenant passes with the transfer of the dominant estate — applies even if the deed of transfer *does not mention the easement*. [224]

        b. Subdivision: If the dominant estate is *sub-divided* into smaller lots sold to different people, and the geography is such that each of the smaller lots can benefit from the easement, then each will generally be permitted to do so. (But this will not happen if this would result in an extreme *increase* in the burden to the servient estate.)

    2. Easements in gross: But easements *in gross* are different. [224]

        a. Common law: At common law, easements in gross are *not transferable*. [224]

        Example: *O* owns Blackacre, which adjoins a public beach. *O* sells *A*, who lives in a different city, the permanent right to park in *O*'s driveway and walk across *A*'s land to the beach. Since this easement is "in gross" — it is not intimately tied to particular land held by *A* — at common law it is not transferable by *A* to anyone else.

        b. Modern view: Today, courts make it easier to transfer easements in gross.

            i. Commercial easements: Nearly all modern courts allow assignment of *"commercial"* easements in gross, i.e., easements that are intended to be used for economic purposes.

            Example: *O* gives the telephone company the right to string wires over his land. Today, because of the commercial nature of this easement in gross, nearly all courts would hold that the phone company can assign this right to some other outfit that takes over the phone operations.

            ii. Non-commercial easement: Some but not all modern courts allow assignment of some *non-commercial easements in gross*. But even these courts won't allow assignment where the *close relationship* of the parties, or the lack of compensation for the easement, suggests that the parties didn't intend to allow assignment. [224]

            Example: *A* owns property abutting a lake, with a path running from the public road to the lake. *A* gives to his close friend *B*, who lives 10 miles away, a free easement to go from the road to the lake so that *B* can swim and boat. Even in courts following the more liberal modern rule — under which easements in gross are generally assignable whether of a commercial nature or not — the close personal relationship between *A* and *B*, and the lack of consideration, would lead to the conclusion that *B* cannot assign his easement to *C*, since *A* and *B* probably intended that the easement would remain personal to *B*. [225]

VI. TERMINATION OF EASEMENTS

A. Natural expiration: If the term of the easement is not specified, the easement will be for an *unlimited duration* (subject to certain exceptions, such as abandonment). [226]

B. Abandonment: Unlike estates in land, an easement may be *terminated* by *abandonment* in some circumstances. [227]

1. **Words alone insufficient:** The easement holder's *words alone* will *never* be sufficient to constitute an abandonment. [227]

2. **Intent plus conduct:** But if the easement holder *intends* to abandon an easement, and takes *actions* manifesting that intent, he will be held to have abandoned the easement, and it will be extinguished. [227]

   a. **Mere non-use not enough:** Mere *non-use* of the easement, even for a long period, is typically *not enough* to show the requisite intent to abandon. However, *affirmative conduct* by the easement holder, *coupled with non-use*, *can* be enough. [230]

   Example: *A* conveys to *B* the right to use a strip on *A*'s land as a driveway to get to the public road that abuts *A*'s property. Several years later, a different public road is built adjacent to *B*'s property. *B* stops using the driveway for a period of three years, during which *B* uses only the new public road.

   This cessation of use would probably *not* be enough to constitute abandonment, because it does not constitute unequivocal evidence that *B* intended to relinquish the benefits of the servitude. If, however, *B* also built a masonry wall between his property and *A*'s, blocking *B*'s access to the driveway over *A*'s property, this act would be unequivocal enough to constitute abandonment, and the easement would be extinguished. [230]

VII. LICENSES

A. **Definition:** A *license* is a right to use the licensor's land that is *revocable* at the will of the licensor. This revocability is the main thing that distinguishes licenses from easements. (But there are a couple of exceptions to the revocability of licenses, described below.) [230-232]

   1. **No Statute of Frauds:** A license is *not* required to satisfy the *Statute of Frauds*, so it may be created *orally*.

   2. **Illustrations:** Some licenses are much like easements, except for revocability (e.g., *O* orally gives *A* the right to use *O*'s driveway to get from *A*'s land to the public highway; this would be an easement if it were in writing, but is a license because it is oral). Other licenses are much more transitory. For instance, a *ticket* to a sports event or concert is a license; similarly, the right to use a *parking lot* is generally only a license.

B. **Exceptions to revocability:** There are a couple of exceptions to the general rule that licenses are revocable at the grantor's will.

   1. **Oral license acted upon:** Most important, a license is *irrevocable* if its use would have been an easement except for failure to meet the Statute of Frauds, and the licensee makes *substantial expenditures* on the land in *reliance* on the licensor's promise that the license will be permanent or of long duration. [232]

      Example: *P* orally gives *D* permission to build a roadway across *P*'s land so that *D* can get from his land to the public highway. *D* expends substantial money digging and paving the road. *P* attempts to revoke, and sues *D* for trespass. A court would probably hold that the license, though oral, was irrevocable because of *D*'s substantial reliance expenditures.

VIII. COVENANTS RUNNING WITH THE LAND

A. **Definition:** Like easements, *"covenants"* may under some circumstances run with the land. A covenant running with the land is simply a contract between two parties which, because it meets certain technical requirements, has the additional quality that it is *binding against one who later buys the promisor's land*, and/or *enforceable by one who later buys the promisee's land*. [232]

1. **Legal relief:** When we use the term "covenant," we are talking about a promise that is subject to *legal* rather than equitable relief. That is, when a covenant is breached the relief granted is *money damages*, not an injunction or decree of specific performance. (An injunction or specific performance may be granted for breach of what is called an "equitable servitude," discussed below.)

B. **Statute of Frauds:** For a covenant to run with the land, it must be *in writing*.

C. **Assume that it runs with the land:** You don't have to worry too much about the special rules for these "covenants at law." [233-237] In most instances, you can safely assume that the rules governing covenants (promises the breach of which is compensated by money damages) in modern courts are mostly the same as the rules governing servitudes (promises the breach of which is redressed by injunction or decree of specific performance), discussed below.

IX. EQUITABLE SERVITUDES / RESTRICTIVE COVENANTS

A. **Generally:** *"Equitable servitudes,"* also referred to as *"restrictive covenants"* are a special type of *restriction on how the land will be used* (e.g., "residential only" or "no use that competes with the filling station on Blackacre"). [237]

1. **Enforced at equity:** Restrictive covenants are enforced *at equity*, by the award of an *injunction* (ordering the defendant not to do something) or a decree of *specific performance* (ordering the defendant to do something). When a court not only gives equitable relief, but applies it against an *assignee* of the original promisor, the promise is referred to as an *"equitable servitude"* against the burdened land. We will use the general term "servitude" here to cover the whole category of equitable servitudes and restrictive covenants. [238]

2. **Enforced:** Equitable servitudes generally *run as to both burden and benefit.* That is, they can generally be enforced *by* whoever the *current owner* is of any parcel that was intended to be *benefitted*, and *against* whoever the current owner is of the parcel that was intended to be burdened. However, on the "running of burden side," servitudes are subject to one important special rule: the current owner will be bound only if he had *some form of notice* of the restriction at the time he took ownership — see p. C-54 *infra*.

3. **Affirmative vs. negative:** Most agreements for which equitable enforcement is sought are *negative* in nature — they are usually agreements not to violate certain *building restrictions*. But occasionally, an equitable servitude may involve an *affirmative* promise (e.g., the promise to pay dues to a homeowners' association, or the promise to make certain repairs).

B. **Privity not required:** The requirements of *privity* are virtually *non-existent* in connection with equitable servitudes. For instance, two *neighboring landowners* that never had any land-transfer relationship between them can, by agreement, impose land-use restrictions that will be binding on assignees. [239]

> **Example:** *A* and *B*, who own adjacent parcels, agree that neither will tear down his house without the other's consent. *A* and *B* sell their properties to *X* and *Y*, respectively. Assuming requirements of notice are met, *X* can get an injunction against *Y* to stop a threatened demolition in violation of the restriction, even though *Y* may not have expressly agreed to honor the restrictions.

C. **Running of benefit and burden:** A servitude normally *runs with the land* on *both the benefitted and the burdened sides.* That is, unless there is evidence that the original parties intended otherwise, the *burden will be binding* upon any successor to the original owner of the burdened parcel, and the *benefit will be enforceable* by any successor owner of the benefitted parcel. [238-238]

1. **Requirement of notice:** But the single most important thing to remember about equitable servitudes is that equity will not enforce an agreement *against a subsequent purchaser* of the burdened

C
A
P
S
U
L
E

S
U
M
M
A
R
Y

parcel unless he had **notice** of the restriction. Notice may be either **"actual"** or **"constructive."** [241]

> **Example:** Devel, a developer, owns a 40-lot subdivision. He intends to file a plat showing that all lots are limited to single-family use, but never gets around to doing so. He sells Lot 1 to *A* with a single-family restriction contained in the deed (and with a reciprocal promise that he, Devel, will also restrict his other 39 lots). He then sells Lot 2 to *B* without any restriction in the deed (and without *B*'s having an actual knowledge that any lot is burdened or promised to be burdened). Even though Devel has created a single-family restriction on Lot 2 (and all other lots) by his arrangement with *A*, *B* will not be bound by that restriction, because he took without "actual" or "constructive" notice (both terms are discussed below) of the restriction on Lot 2.

a. **Actual notice:** The concept of **"actual"** notice means that if the subsequent purchaser of the burdened land happens to know about the restriction, it is irrelevant that the restriction is not recorded anywhere.

> **Example:** *A* and *B* each agree in writing not to use their properties for anything but residential premises. Neither records this promise in the land records. *B* assigns to *X*, and orally tells *X*, "You should know that I have promised *A* that I'll never use the property for non-residential purposes." *A* will be able to enjoin *X* from making non-residential use of the property, because *X* was on actual notice of the restriction at the time he bought.

b. **Constructive:** Also, the subsequent purchaser will be deemed to be on notice if he has **"constructive"** knowledge of the restriction. Most importantly, if the restriction is properly **recorded** in the land records that fall within the purchaser's chain of title (see *infra*, C-81, for more about chain of title), the purchaser is bound even if he does not in fact discover the restriction by the time he buys. ("Inquiry" notice, discussed *infra*, C-82, is another form of constructive notice.)

   i. **Lack of notice:** Conversely, if the restriction is **not recorded** (or is recorded but is not part of the subsequent purchaser's chain of title), then the subsequent purchaser will **not** be bound unless he happens to have actual notice, or some non-record form of constructive notice, of the restriction. The example involving Devel in C(1) above is an illustration of how the subsequent purchaser (*B* in that example) won't be bound because the restriction on his lot wasn't in his chain of title and he didn't have actual notice of it when he took.

c. **Check for notice:** So whenever you have a restrictive covenant that is sought to be enforced against a subsequent party who was not party to the conveyance that originally created the restriction, the most important thing for you to do is to **make sure that the subsequent party had either actual notice, record notice**, or some form of non-record **constructive notice**, of the restriction: if she didn't, then **she can't be bound by the restriction no matter what else happened.**

D. **Developer's building plan:** A general **building plan** formulated by a developer will often bind all parcels in the development. The developer records the plan in the form of a subdivision **"plat"** or map, and includes a use or building restriction in the filed subdivision plan. [242]

1. **Significance of plat:** The significance of the plat is this: if the plat was filed before third person *X* bought a parcel, and the plat disclosed the restriction, then *X* is **bound by the restriction** even if it's not reflected in his own deed.

> **Example:** In 2001, Dev, a developer, files a plat for Black Acres, a 40-lot subdivision, reciting that all 40 lots must be used for single-family purposes. Dev sells Lot 1 to *A*, and Lot 2 to *B*. The deed to *A* contains the restriction, but the deed to *B* omits it on account of clerical error (and *B* does not have actual knowledge of the restriction at the moment he buys). *B* now tries

to build an apartment building on his lot, and *A* sues for an injunction. The court will likely conclude that: (1) the filed plat gave *B* "record notice" of the restriction; (2) the restriction is therefore binding on *B*; and (3) *A*, as the holder of a parcel intended to be benefitted by the restriction, is entitled to an injunction against the non-single-family use.

   a. **Plan filed without restriction:** But if the building plan filed before the conveyance of a lot to third person *X* did ***not*** contain the building restriction (and the conveyance to *X* did not contain the restriction) *X* would ***not*** be bound. That would be true even if the building plan was ***later amended*** to include the restriction, and/or all post-*X* transfers were made subject to the restriction. In other words, once a lot is transferred free and clear of a restriction, ***it will remain free and clear forever*** no matter what restrictions are later put on all other lots in the subdivision, unless some owner of the parcel in question voluntarily and in writing agrees to be bound by the plan-wide restriction.

   Example: In the Example involving Devel on p. C-55, once *B* took Lot 2 free and clear, any purchaser from *B* would take free and clear as well, even if Devel got around to filing a subdivision plat before *B* re-sold.

2. **"Implied reciprocal servitudes":** Courts often employ the doctrine of ***"implied reciprocal servitude"*** — if Purchaser 1 acquires his land in expectation that he will get the benefit of subsequently-created servitudes by Developer, there is immediately created in him the benefit of an implied reciprocal servitude against Developer's remaining land (even if Developer then does ***not*** put the restriction in later deeds). [243]

   Example: Devel, a developer, owns a 40-lot subdivision. He intends to file a plat showing that all lots are limited to single-family (SF) use, but never does. He sells Lot 1 to *A* with an SF restriction contained in the deed (and with a reciprocal written promise that he, Devel, will also restrict his other 39 lots). Devel then sells Lot 2 to *B* without any restriction in the deed. However, at the moment *B* takes, *B* is aware that Lot 1 was bound by the SF restriction in the deed from Devel to *A*.

   A court would likely hold that: (1) when Devel sold Lot 1 to *A* with the SF restriction, an implied reciprocal servitude arose in favor of *A* and against Devel's remaining 39 lots; (2) *B*, since he has actual knowledge of the Lot 1 restriction, also has actual notice of the reciprocal restriction on Lot 2; (3) *B* is therefore bound; and (4) *A* has the benefit of the Lot 2 restriction, so that *A* can sue *B* for an injunction if *B* tries to use Lot 2 for non-SF purposes.

   a. **Reciprocal servitude must be in later buyer's chain of title:** But keep in mind that even if the developer burdens Lot 1 when it's sold to Purchaser 1, and reciprocally burdens his retained lot (call it Lot 2), the later buyer of Lot 2 won't be bound by this reciprocal servitude unless the developer-to-Purchaser-1 restriction is found to be ***in Lot 2's chain of title***, or the buyer of Lot 2 has ***actual notice*** of the reciprocal restriction on Lot 2. In other words, no matter how definitively the developer burdens his own land (Lot 2) with a reciprocal servitude, a later ***"innocent" buyer*** of that burdened lot (one who neither knows nor has reason to know of the reciprocal servitude) ***cannot be held to that servitude.***

   Example: In the above example, if *B* didn't check the records for Lot 1, and didn't have actual knowledge of the fact that Devel had imposed the SF restriction when he sold Lot 1 (or of the fact that Devel made the reciprocal promise as to the other 39 lots), *B* would not be bound by the restriction on Lot 2, even though the lot was burdened by an implied reciprocal servitude when Devel consummated the sale-with-restriction of Lot 1.

E. **Selection of neighbors:** Equitable restrictions (as well as covenants at law) may be used to facilitate the ***selection of neighbors***. Such agreements will generally be enforced as long as they are ***reasonable*** in scope (so that they do not constitute an unreasonable "restraint on alienation") and are not in violation of any anti-discrimination law. [244]

> **Example:** Each deed executed by a developer provides that the purchaser must become a member of the homeowners' association, and that the purchaser may not sell his land to anyone who is not a member of the association. It also provides that the association has the right of first refusal to buy any property offered by a member. Such a restriction will generally be enforced, and will give the association's other members (providing that the association has enough money) the practical ability to keep property out of the hands of anyone deemed undesirable. Such a provision is often used by *condominiums* and *co-ops*.

X. MODIFICATION AND TERMINATION OF COVENANTS AND SERVITUDES

A. Modification and termination generally: Covenants and servitudes can be modified or terminated under a number of circumstances. (For simplicity, we'll refer to modification or termination of a "servitude," but we mean "covenant or servitude.") [247]

1. Agreement by all parties: The servitude can be *modified* or *terminated* if all parties to it so *agree*. But they must do so in a document that satisfies the *required formalities for creation* of the servitude in the first place (e.g., it must be in writing, and in most states must be notarized). [247]

  a. Oral agreement: So an *oral agreement*, even by all affected parties, to terminate or modify a servitude will *not* suffice, because the statute of frauds requires that the modification or termination be in writing, just as the original servitude had to be in writing.

2. Abandonment: The servitude can be extinguished by *abandonment* by the benefitted party. But abandonment is hard to establish, and requires unequivocal evidence of an intent to abandon. Mere *cessation of use* is typically *not* enough. [247]

3. Changed conditions: The servitude may be modified or terminated by court order when *conditions have so changed* that it is *impossible to accomplish the purposes* for which the servitude was created. [247]

> **Example:** Developer owns 10 adjacent parcels, which he sells to 10 separate buyers. In each deed, he inserts a restriction that the property be used only for single-family purposes. Lots 1-8 are condemned for use as a public multilane highway. The resulting noise and traffic make Lots 9 and 10 no longer suitable for residential use. The owner of Lot 9 wants to transform his house into a retail store. The owner of Lot 10 wants both lots to remain residential.
>
> A court would be justified in terminating the servitude, because the purposes for which it was created (maintenance of a viable residential neighborhood) can no longer be accomplished.

4. No expiration from passage of time: But the *mere passage of time*, without more, will *not* cause a covenant or servitude to be extinguished. [247]

CHAPTER 10

ZONING AND OTHER PUBLIC LAND-USE CONTROLS

I. THE "TAKING" CLAUSE, AND LAND-USE CONTROLS AS IMPLICIT TAKINGS

A. The "Taking" Clause generally: State and federal governments may take private property for public use — this is the power of "eminent domain." However, the Fifth Amendment to the U.S. Constitution provides that "private property [shall not] be taken for public use, without just compensation." This is the so-called "Taking" Clause, made binding on the states by means of the Fourteenth Amendment. [261]

    1. Land-use control as taking: Normally, land-use controls will *not* constitute a taking for which the government must pay compensation. But very occasionally, a regulation may so drastically interfere with the private owner's use of his property, or with the value of that property, that the court will conclude that there has been an *implicit* "taking."

    2. Damages vs. injunction: If the court does find an implicit "taking," it will award one or both of the following remedies: (1) it will strike down the regulation, i.e., *enjoin* the government from enforcing it any more; or (2) it will award *damages* to the owner for his lost use or value.

B. Taking/regulation distinction: If the state merely *regulates* property use in a manner consistent with the state's *"police power,"* then no compensation needs to be paid, even though the owner's use of his property or even its value has been substantially diminished. Thus zoning regulations, environmental protection rules, landmark preservation schemes, etc., will usually not constitute a compensable "taking." But if the regulation goes too far, it will become a "taking" even though the state calls it a regulation. Here are some of the principles the courts look to when deciding whether a regulation has become a compensable "taking": [261]

    1. Substantial advancement of legitimate state interests: The land regulation will be a taking unless it *"substantially advances legitimate state interests."*

        a. Broad range of legitimate interests: A *broad range* of governmental purposes constitute "legitimate state interests." These include maintaining residential uses (often done by zoning), preserving landmarks, protecting the environment, etc.

        b. Tight means-end fit: In order for the regulation to substantially advance legitimate state interests, there must be a fairly *tight fit* between the state interest being promoted and the regulation chosen (more than a mere "rational relation" between means and end).

        Example: The Ps, owners of beach front property, want to replace their bungalow with a larger home. D, a government body that regulates beach front construction, prevents the Ps from doing the rebuilding unless the Ps first give the public an easement across the property along the ocean, which would permit people to walk along the beach from the north of the Ps' property to the south and vice versa. D claims that the easement is needed to prevent public views of the beach from being worsened.

        Held, for the Ps. The government may have had an interest in encouraging public views of the beaches, but the easement requirement was not substantially related to achievement of that objective, because the easement would only help those already on the beach (who already had good views). [*Nollan v. California Coastal Comm.*] [267]

        c. "Rough proportionality" for give-backs: When a city conditions the owner's right to develop his property on some *"give-back"* by the owner, there must be a *"rough proportion-*

ality" between the burdens on the public that the development would bring about, and the benefits to the public from the give-back.

> **Example:** Owner wants to expand her store. City says, "You may do that, but only if you deed to the public a 15-foot strip of land to be used as a bike pathway." *Held*, this trade-off was an unconstitutional taking of Owner's property, because City didn't show that the public burdens from the extra traffic to Owner's bigger store were "roughly proportional" to the public benefits from the bike path. [*Dolan v. City of Tigard*] [267]

2. **Deprivation of all economically viable use:** If a regulation is found to deny the landowner of *all economically viable use* of his land, this will make the regulation a "taking." [263]

> **Example:** Regulations prevent a particular owner of vacant land from building any structure on the property. This will probably deprive him of all economically viable use, and will thus be a compensable taking unless necessary to serve some overriding governmental interest, such as prevention of flooding or erosion.

3. **Physical occupation:** If the government makes or authorizes a permanent *physical occupation* of the property, this will automatically be found to constitute a taking. [262]

> **Example:** The state orders O to give the public a permanent *easement* across his property so that the public can get to a beach — this would be a permanent physical occupation, automatically amounting to a compensable taking.

4. **Diminution in value:** The more drastic the *reduction in value* of the owner's property, the more likely a taking is to be found.

> **Example:** Particular land is valuable mostly for the coal to be found under it. The state bars the owner of the mineral rights from doing any coal mining under the land. *Held*, the value of the mining rights was so completely impaired as to amount to a taking.

5. **Prevention of harm:** A taking will probably *not* be found where the property use being prevented is one that is *harmful* or *"noxious"* to others.

> **Example:** A zoning ordinance may properly prevent the operation of a steel mill in the middle of a residential neighborhood.

C. **Damages for temporary taking:** If a land-use regulation is so broad that it constitutes a taking, the owner may be able to bring an *"inverse condemnation"* suit. Under such a suit, he may receive *damages* for the *temporary* taking (temporary because the regulation is eventually struck down by the court). See *First English Evangelical Lutheran Church v. L.A. County.* [268-269]

1. **Use in moratoriums:** This principle means that local governments do *not* have the unlimited right to put *temporary moratoriums* on development — an owner who, because of the moratorium, can't make any economically viable use of his property for some period of time may well be able to recover damages on the theory that his property has been "taken," even though the taking was not permanent. [264]

> **Example:** City puts a five-year moratorium on the building of any structure in the City. An owner of vacant land in City, who can't derive any revenue from the property, would likely be able to recover damages for this temporary "taking" of all economically viable use of his property.

a. **Significance:** But there is no *automatic* right to compensation for a temporary ban on all economically-viable use of one's property — instead, the *surrounding circumstances* must be considered when the court decides whether the interference with use was so severe that it amounts to a temporary taking for which compensation must be paid. [*Tahoe-Sierra Preservation Council v. Tahoe Regional Planning Agency*] [264]

> **Example:** Suppose *O*'s vacant property actually increased substantially in value during a several-year moratorium on all development. A court, in considering the "surrounding circumstances," would likely decide that the injury to *O* has not been severe enough to require that this be treated as a compensable "taking" under *Tahoe-Sierra, supra.* [265]

D. Subsequent owner who takes with notice of restriction: Suppose the case is one of those relatively uncommon ones in which the land-use restriction is so great that a taking will be deemed to have occurred. Even if the person who owns the property at the time the regulation is put into effect does not sue, a *subsequent buyer* — who buys the property *with knowledge* of the restriction — *may proceed* with the suit just as the original owner could have. [*Palazzolo v. Rhode Island*] [269]

II. ZONING

A. Generally: The main type of public land-use regulation is *zoning*. Zoning is generally done on the local, municipal, level. The municipality's power to zone comes from the state "police power," or power to act for the general welfare, which is delegated by state statute to the municipality.

1. **Use zoning:** Most zoning is *"use zoning,"* by which the municipality is divided into districts, in each of which only certain uses of land are permitted (e.g., a residential-only district, a commercial district, etc.) [269]

2. **Density controls:** Other zoning laws govern the *density* of population or construction. Thus a town might establish a *minimum lot size* for single-family homes, minimum *set-back* requirements (requiring a certain amount of unbuilt land on some or all sides of the structure), *minimum square footage* for residences, and *height* limits. [270]

B. Legal limits on zoning:

1. **Constitutional limits:** Several different federal constitutional provisions may limit a city's ability to zone in a particular manner:

   a. **Taking Clause:** First, the Fifth Amendment's "Taking" Clause means that if a zoning regulation is so overreaching that it deprives the owner of all economically viable use of his land, or is not substantially related to some legitimate public purpose, the zoning will be treated as a taking for which compensation must be paid. (See the discussion of the Taking Clause above.)

   b. **Procedural due process:** The Fourteenth Amendment's Due Process Clause imposes certain *procedural requirements* on the zoning process. For a zoning action that is *administrative* rather than legislative (e.g., the granting of a variance or special-use permit for a particular property), an owner is entitled to a *hearing*, an impartial tribunal, and an explanation of the government's decision. [271]

   c. **Substantive due process:** If the zoning law fails to bear a *rational relation* to a *permissible state objective*, it may violate the *substantive* aspect of the Due Process Clause. [272-273]

   > **Example:** A zoning law that limits a district to single-family occupancy, and defines "family" so as to exclude most extended families, violates substantive due process. See *Moore v. City of East Cleveland.* [272]

   d. **Equal protection:** A zoning law that is adopted for the purpose of excluding racial minorities will trigger strict judicial scrutiny, and will probably be found to be a violation of the *Equal Protection* Clause of the Fourteenth Amendment. [273]

2. Aesthetic zoning: Most courts hold today that *aesthetic* considerations may constitute *one factor* in a municipality's zoning decision. But aesthetics may not be the *sole* factor. [275-275]

> **Example:** A city provides that only Georgian Colonial-style houses may be built, because these structures are the most beautiful. A court would probably strike down this regulation on the grounds that although aesthetics may be one factor, they may not be the sole factor.

C. Administration of zoning:

1. Bodies involved in: Several governmental bodies generally get involved in zoning: [276]

    a. Town council: The *zoning code* is enacted by the *municipal legislature*. Usually this is the *town council*.

    b. Board of zoning appeals: A "board of adjustment" or "board of zoning appeals" usually exists to award or deny *variances*, and to hear appeals from the building department's enforcement of the zoning laws.

    c. Planning or zoning commission: The town council generally appoints a *planning commission* or zoning commission. The commission generally *advises* the town council on (but does not independently determine) the contents of the zoning code.

2. Variances: Virtually all zoning ordinances have a provision for the granting of *variances*, i.e., relief in a particular case from the enforcement of an ordinance. [278-279]

    a. Requirements for: Most states impose these requirements for a variance: (1) denial would result in *"unnecessary hardship"* to the owner; (2) the need for the variance is caused by a problem *unique to the owner's lot* (not one shared by many lots in the area); and (3) the variance would not be *inconsistent* with the overall purpose of the ordinance, or inconsistent with the general welfare of the area.

3. Special uses: Zoning ordinances also usually provide for *"special use"* permits. Typically, a special use permit must be obtained for such things as private schools, hospitals and churches. Generally, an applicant is not entitled to a special use permit "as of right," but only in the discretion of the zoning board; however, usually no showing of "special hardship" has to be made (as is the case for a variance). [280]

4. Conditional zoning: Many ordinances provide for *"conditional" zoning*. Under this device, the rezoning of a particular parcel is made subject to the developer's promise to comply with certain conditions, which will protect neighbors. [282]

> **Example:** O owns a parcel in an area zoned residential-only. If the ordinance allows for conditional zoning, the town might rezone O's parcel for light industry, but only if O agrees to large set-backs, a low floor-space-to-land-area ratio, or other condition.

5. Non-conforming uses: When a zoning ordinance is enacted or made more stringent, the pre-existing uses that are now banned by the ordinance are called *"non-conforming uses."* Virtually all ordinances either: (1) grant a non-conforming user a *substantial period* within which he may continue his use; or (2) let him continue that use *indefinitely*. [282]

    a. Constitutional issue: Probably it would be a violation of an owner's due process or other constitutional rights for him not to be given at least a substantial period within which to phase out the non-conforming use.

    b. Amortization: If the ordinance does give an owner a substantial period to phase out his use (called an *"amortization"* provision), most courts hold that no violation of the owner's constitutional rights results from the fact that he must eventually cease the non-conforming use.

CAPSULE SUMMARY

D. Exclusionary zoning: *"Exclusionary* zoning" is the use of zoning laws to exclude certain types of persons and uses, particularly *racial and ethnic minorities* and *low-income* persons. [284]

1. **Examples of exclusion:** A town might exclude certain types of people by putting tight restrictions on the kinds of allowable *residential uses*. Thus a high minimum-acreage requirement, a ban on multiple dwellings, a ban on mobile homes, or a ban on publicly-subsidized housing are all ways a town could try to keep out poor people (and, to the extent that blacks, say, are on average poorer than whites, a way to keep out black people).

2. **Equal Protection law:** Exclusionary zoning may be attacked as a violation of the *Equal Protection* Clause of the U.S. Constitution. An equal protection argument has the best chance of success when it argues that a town is discriminating on the basis *race* or *national origin*, since these are "suspect classes"; an attack based on the claim that the town is discriminating against the *poor* will probably not succeed (because poverty is not a suspect class).

   a. **Effect vs. purpose:** Also, the plaintiff in an equal protection case will probably only win if the court applies *"strict scrutiny"* to the ordinance. This, in turn, will happen only if the court believes that the town acted with the *purpose* of discriminating on racial or ethnic grounds, not if the ordinance merely has the *effect* of making it harder for minorities to live there. [286]

3. **Federal statutory suits:** Zoning may also be attacked in federal court suits based on federal statutory law, especially the Fair Housing Act. Zoning enacted for the purpose of limiting access by racial or ethnic minorities violates the Act. [286]

   a. **Effect vs. purpose:** In a Fair Housing Act suit, P does not have to show a discriminatory purpose behind the zoning enactment. Instead, he merely has to show a discriminatory *effect*; then, the burden shifts to the defendant town to show that its enactment serves legitimate governmental interests rather than discriminatory ones.

4. **State case law:** A number of *states*, by case law, have held that zoning may not be used to *exclude the poor*.

   a. *Mt. Laurel* **cases:** The most important such cases are the two *Mt. Laurel* cases, in which the New Jersey Supreme Court held that a town must allow its *"fair share"* of the region's demand for low and middle-income housing. According to the *Mt. Laurel* principle, not only may zoning not be used to keep out the poor, but affirmative measures must be taken by a town to cause such housing to be built (e.g., density bonuses given to developers who build some low income housing; cooperation with developers seeking federally-subsidized housing; allowing of mobile homes, etc.) Also, builders must be allowed to seek *site-specific relief* (in which the court orders the builder's parcel to be rezoned to allow the particular project, if the court finds for the developer). [288-290]

E. Statutory protection against religious discrimination — RLUIPA: To protect religious institutions against burdensome or discriminatory land-use regulation, Congress enacted the *Religious Land Use and Institutionalized Persons Act ("RLUIPA")*. [291]

1. **What the statute says:** RLUIPA prohibits federal, state and local governments from applying a land-use regulation in a way that *"imposes a substantial burden* on the *religious exercise* of a person" (including a religious institution or group) unless the government carries the burden of proving that the imposition of this burden:

   [1] "is in furtherance of a *compelling governmental interest*"; and

   [2] "is the *least restrictive means of furthering* that compelling governmental interest."

   a. **Individualized assessments:** RLUIPA applies mostly to *"individualized assessments"* of proposed uses for property. Typically, the statute applies where a religious group applies for a *special-use permit* to build a place of worship, and the local authorities deny the permit application, often in response to community opposition. If the group asserting the RLUIPA claim can show that its religious rights have been substantially burdened by the permit denial, the court must **apply strict scrutiny**, and will almost invariably **invalidate** the regulation as applied to the group. That's true even if government does not discriminate against the religious user (i.e., puts non-religious users through the same difficult permit process). [293]

III. REGULATION OF THE SUBDIVISION PROCESS

A. Subdivision regulation: Towns often extensively regulate the process of **subdivision**. This is the process of dividing a parcel into two or more smaller ones, for resale to different purchasers. [293]

    1. Sewers and water mains: For instance, towns usually have detailed requirements that the developer put in water mains, sewers, gutters, and other drainage facilities.

    2. Street design: Similarly, towns regulate **street design**, and require the developer not only to furnish the land for streets, but to build the streets himself.

IV. HISTORICAL AND ENVIRONMENTAL PRESERVATION

A. Historical preservation: Municipalities often try to protect buildings or districts of great **historical** or **architectural** interest. [294]

    1. Districts and landmarks: Sometimes, an entire **historical district** is protected. Alternatively, sometimes a particular **structure** will be protected because of its historical or architectural significance. In either event, historical preservation schemes generally prohibit the owner from **altering** or **demolishing** the building without a special **permit**.

    2. Generally upheld: A historic preservation ordinance will generally be **upheld** so long as: (1) it gives reasonably precise **standards** to the board charged with enforcement, so that the board does not behave in an **arbitrary** or **discriminatory** manner; and (2) it does not constitute a "taking" without compensation, in violation of the Fifth Amendment. [294]

        a. Taking: The owner's best chance of attacking a scheme is by arguing that it deprives him of all economically viable use of his land, without compensation, in violation of the Fifth Amendment's Taking Clause. But even such arguments are hard to win. For instance, in the **Penn Central** case, the Supreme Court held that a New York City ordinance preventing major changes to Grand Central Terminal, but allowing the owners to continue their present use of the property (as a terminal with office space above it) did not amount to a taking. (But a prohibition on *all* development of a building beyond the current use might be found to deny the owner all economically viable use of the property, in which case the preservation scheme would be a taking for which compensation must be paid.) [295-296]

        b. Transferable Development Rights (TDRs): Some ordinances avoid "taking" problems by giving the owner "Transferable Development Rights" or "TDRs," by which he may transfer his development rights from the preserved building to other nearby parcels. If in the particular real estate market the TDRs have substantial economic value, this may turn what would otherwise be a "taking" (because the owner is deprived of all economically viable use of his land) into a non-taking. [296]

B. Environmental preservation: Towns and regions also frequently attempt to protect the **environment**. Of special interest are regulations that attempt to maintain **open areas** by limiting or prohibiting certain kinds of development. [296]

    1. Urban park land: Occasionally, a city may prohibit the development of privately-owned urban **park land**. But prohibiting all development of otherwise-valuable vacant land in the middle of a downtown area is likely to constitute a compensable "taking," because the owner is being deprived of all economically viable use of his land. (But the problems might be eased by allowing TDRs, as discussed above.)

2. **Wetlands and coastlands:** More frequently, towns and regions try to limit or prohibit development on *wetlands* and *coastland*. By and large, such preservation schemes have been *upheld*, on the grounds that preservation of these areas is a goal of great social importance, outweighing the landowner's interest in land development. (But a permanent ban on development might be a compensable "taking," unless the government shows that construction would be dangerous, as in the case of a coastal area subject to heavy flooding and erosion.)

C. **CERCLA and hazardous waste sites:** One federal environmental statute of special interest to landowners (and their lawyers) is *CERCLA*, the Comprehensive Environmental Response, Compensation and Liability Act. CERCLA, also known as the *"Superfund"* law, lets the federal Environmental Protection Agency (EPA) *clean up abandoned hazardous waste sites.* [296-297]

1. **Who can be liable:** Once the EPA identifies a hazardous waste site and classifies it as a Superfund site, the Agency may hold various private parties *liable for cleanup costs.* People who can be held liable include:

   [1] the *current owner or operator* of the site; and

   [2] the person who owned or operated the site *at the time any disposal of hazardous waste onto the site occurred*.

   a. **Successor liability:** Category [1] above means that if a person *buys a site* that turns out (even *unbeknownst* to her) to contain hazardous waste due to the actions of *prior owners, the buyer can be liable for possibly-massive cleanup costs even though she had nothing to do with the original contamination!* [297]

      i. **"Bona fide prospective purchaser" defense:** However, CERCLA gives buyers of already-contaminated property a *"bona fide prospective purchaser" (BFPP)* defense. To be a BFPP, the buyer must, before buying, make *"appropriate inquiries* into the *previous ownership and uses* of the facility," usually by commissioning an expert environmental study of the site. The buyer must also, after closing, make reasonable efforts not to worsen the environmental problems. [297]

V. EMINENT DOMAIN

A. **Generally:** State and federal governments have the power of *eminent domain*, i.e., the power to take private property for public use. Usually this is done through *condemnation proceedings*, in which the government brings a judicial proceeding to obtain title to land that it needs for some public use. Alternatively, the government occasionally simply makes *use* of a landowner's property without bringing formal condemnation proceedings; here, the landowner may bring an *"inverse condemnation"* action, in which he seeks a court declaration that his property has been taken by the government and must be paid for. The two requirements for the government to use its eminent domain power are: (1) the property must be put to a *"public use"*; and (2) *"just compensation"* must be paid. [298]

B. **"Public use":** The requirement of *"public use"* (imposed by the Taking Clause of the Fifth Amendment) is very *loosely* interpreted. Here are the main rules:

   ❏ So long as the state's use of its eminent domain power is *"rationally related* to a *conceivable public purpose,"* the public use requirement is satisfied. [*Hawaii Housing Authority v. Midkiff*]

   ❏ The property *need not be open to the general public after the taking.* As the first rule above suggests, all that "public use" means is that the property be used for a *"public purpose."* [*Kelo v. New London,* discussed immediately *infra.*] Therefore, the fact that the property is **turned over to some private user** does not prevent the use from being a public one as long as the public can be expected to derive some benefit (e.g., economic development) from the use. [298]

Example: D (the city of New London, Connecticut) wants to redevelop an area by assembling land and building a research facility for a big pharmaceutical company. To get the land, it condemns 15 properties that are owner-occupied and in good condition. The Ps claim that the condemnation violates the requirement that any taking under eminent domain laws be for "public use."

Held, for D. To be a constitutional use of eminent domain, all that's required is that there be a *"public purpose"* behind the taking. Furthermore, the concept of "public purpose" is to be broadly defined, and the Court will generally defer to the legislature's judgment about whether the taking will aid the public good. Where, as here, the government rationally believes that its plan will create new jobs and increase tax revenue, that's sufficient. [*Kelo v. New London*] [299]

C. **"Just compensation":** In general, the requirement of *"just compensation"* means that the government must pay the *fair market value* of the property at the time of the taking. [300]

    1. **Highest and best use:** This fair market value is usually based on the *"highest and best use"* that may be made of the property (at least under current zoning regulations). Thus if a vacant parcel is zoned for subdivision, the value that must be paid is the value the land would have to a subdivider, not the value based on the current rental value of vacant land.

CHAPTER 11

LAND SALE CONTRACTS, MORTGAGES AND DEEDS

I. LAND SALE CONTRACTS

A. **Statute of Frauds:** The *Statute of Frauds* is applicable in all states to any contract for the sale of land, or for the sale of any interest in land. Therefore, either the contract itself, or a memorandum of it, must be *in writing*. [305]

    1. **Memorandum satisfying:** A *memorandum* of the parties' agreement, summarizing some terms but not the entire oral agreement, will satisfy the Statute if it specifies the following: (1) the *names* of the parties; (2) the *land* to be conveyed; (3) normally, the *purchase price*; and (4) the *signature* of the party to be charged (i.e., the party against whom enforcement is sought). [305-306]

        Example: Seller writes a letter to Buyer, confirming the provisions of their oral contract for the sale of Blackacre. This letter will constitute a sufficient memorandum if Buyer seeks to enforce the contract against Seller, but not if Seller seeks to enforce it against Buyer.

    2. **Part performance exception:** There is one major exception to the Statute of Frauds for land sale contracts: under the doctrine of *part performance*, a party (either buyer or seller) who has taken action in *reliance* on the contract may be able to gain at least limited enforcement of it. [306-308]

        a. **Acts by vendor:** If the vendor *makes a conveyance* under the contract, he will then be able to sue for the agreed-upon price, even if the agreement to pay that price was only oral.

        b. **Acts by purchaser:** Courts are split as to what acts by the *purchaser* constitute part performance entitling him to specific performance.

i. **Possession plus payment:** Many states hold that if the buyer takes *possession*, and also *makes payments*, this will be sufficient part performance that the seller will be required to convey the property.

ii. **Improvements:** Also, in many states, a buyer who takes possession and then either makes permanent *improvements*, or changes his position in *reliance*, can require the seller to convey.

iii. **"Unequivocally referable" requirement:** Most courts say that the buyer's part performance must be *"unequivocally referable"* to the alleged contract. Thus the buyer must show that the part performance was clearly *in response* to the oral contract, and not explainable by some other aspect of the parties' relationship.

Example: D orally promises to convey Blackacre to P if P will move in with D and care for D in his old age. P does so. P is distantly related to D. D dies without ever having made the conveyance. If P sues D's estate to enforce the alleged oral agreement, P will probably lose because P's part performance (moving in and caring for P) is not "unequivocally referable" to the oral contract, since P may have been doing it out of affection for a relative.

B. Time for performance: In a suit for damages, the *time* stated in the contract will be deemed to be *of the essence*, unless the parties are shown to have intended otherwise. [308-309]

Example: Seller refuses to close on the date specified in the contract. Buyer may bring a suit for damages for the delay, even if it is only a few days.

1. **Equity:** But in a suit in *equity* (i.e., a suit for *specific performance*), the general rule is that time is *not* of the essence. Therefore, even if the contract specifies a particular closing date, either party may obtain specific performance though he is unable to close on the appointed day (so long as he is ready to perform within a reasonable time after the scheduled day).

Example: The sale contract specifies a November 1 closing date. Buyer has trouble lining up his financing, so he can't close on November 1. The contract is silent about whether time is of the essence. By November 15, Buyer has his financing lined up, and asks Seller to close. Seller now refuses. In the absence of strong evidence that the parties intended time to be of the essence, Buyer will probably get a court to order Seller to convey even though Buyer missed the November 1 closing date.

C. Marketable title: Nearly all land sale contracts require the vendor to convey a *marketable* title. (Even if the contract is silent on this issue, an obligation to convey a marketable title will be *implied* by the court.) [310]

1. **Definition of "marketable title":** A marketable title is one that is *free from reasonable doubt* about whether the seller can convey the rights he purports to convey. Thus it is *not* sufficient that a court would probably hold the title good in a *litigation*. Instead, the title must be *free from reasonable doubt* so that the buyer will be able to resell in the future. The purchaser is not required to *"buy a lawsuit"*. [310]

2. **Defects making title unmarketable:** Here are some of the defects that might make title unmarketable: [311]

a. **Record chain:** First, anything in the prior chain of title indicating that the vendor does not have the *full interest* which he purports to convey, may be a defect. (*Examples:* A substantial variation between the *name* of the grantee of record in one link and the name of the grantor in the following link is a defect. Similarly, a substantial variation in the *description of the land* between one deed and the next may be a defect.)

CAPSULE SUMMARY

    b. Encumbrances: Second, even if the vendor has valid title to the property, an *encumbrance* on the property will normally constitute a defect. [312-313]

       i. Mortgage or lien: Thus an outstanding *mortgage* would be an encumbrance making the title unmarketable. (However, the vendor has the right to *pay off the mortgage at the closing*, out of the sale proceeds.) Similarly, *liens* (e.g., a lien for unpaid taxes, or a lien gotten by a judgment creditor) are defects.

       ii. Easement: An *easement* will be a defect if it reduces the *"full enjoyment"* of the premises.

       iii. Use restrictions: Similarly, privately-negotiated *use* restrictions (e.g., a covenant whose burden runs with the land, to the effect that only residential structures will be built) can be a defect.

       iv. Land-use and zoning violations: Most courts hold that violations of *building codes* are *not* encumbrances on title. But a violation of a *zoning ordinance* usually *is* treated as an encumbrance.

3. Agreement: But the parties may *agree* that certain kinds of defects will *not* constitute unmarketable title. This agreement will normally take place in the contract of sale.

    Example: Buyer and Seller agree that a particular easement held by X across the property will not render title unmarketable. The court will enforce this agreement.

    a. Buyer on notice of defect: Also, the buyer may be held to be on *notice* of certain defects, and therefore held to have implicitly agreed to take subject to them (e.g., where a right of way across the property is very visible to anyone who looks even casually at the property).

4. Time for measuring marketability: Unless the contract specifies otherwise, the vendor's title is not required to be marketable *until the date set for the closing*. Thus the vendor may sign a contract to sell property he does not yet own (or on which there are several defects in title), and the purchaser cannot cancel the contract prior to the closing date because of this fact. [313]

    a. Installment contracts: Even if the contract is an *installment agreement*, by which the vendor is required to convey title only after all installments of the purchase price have been paid, the buyer can't cancel merely because she finds out there's an outstanding mortgage that the seller proposes to keep outstanding during the installment period. Unless the buyer can carry the burden of showing *reasonable and serious doubt* about whether the seller will be *able and willing to make the mortgage payments while the contract is in force*, the fact that there is an outstanding mortgage won't render title unmarketable. [313]

    Example: Suppose the outstanding mortgage principal is considerably less than the present value of the property, and the seller has never missed mortgage payments in the past. On these facts, the buyer probably won't persuade the court that the seller's title is not marketable, so the buyer will have to keep on paying the installments.

D. Tender: In the usual transaction, the seller's duty to deliver the deed and the buyer's duty to pay the money are *concurrent*. Therefore, if one party is expected to default, the other party must be sure to *tender his own performance*, in order to be able to hold the other party in default, and sue for damages and/or specific performance. The party who tenders must also make a formal *demand* that the other party *perform*. If the non-defaulting party *doesn't* tender performance, she is likely to be found to have waived her right to claim damages for the default (and may lose her right to reclaim any deposit). [313]

    Example: Seller and Buyer contract for the sale of Blackacre, closing to occur April 1, for $300,000. The contract requires Seller to deliver marketable title, and time is of the essence. On March 15, Buyer learns of an easement that would render title unmarketable, but does not say anything about this to Seller. By April 1, Seller hasn't made arrangements to remove the easement, of which he was aware (and which could have been removed by a small payment to the easement-holder). On April 1, Buyer does not offer to pay, or show any ability to pay, $300,000. Because Buyer did not "tender" his own performance on the closing date, Buyer may well be found to have waived his right to damages for Seller's failure to deliver marketable title.

1. **Effect of other party's repudiation:** But a tender is necessary only where there is some chance that it would be effective. Thus if the other party has *repudiated*, or if the other party's inability to perform is *incurable*, no tender and demand for performance is necessary.

E. **Remedies for failure to perform:** Where one party fails to perform a land sale contract, the other party may have two remedies: (1) a suit for *damages*; and (2) a suit for *specific performance*. [314-317]

1. **Damages:** If one party breaches a land sale contract, the other may almost always sue for *money damages*. Generally, P recovers the *difference between the market price and the contract price* (the "benefit of the bargain" rule).

2. **Specific performance:** Usually, an action for *specific performance* may be brought against the defaulting party, whether the defaulter is buyer or seller. Most commonly, the seller changes his mind, and buyer is able to get a decree of specific performance ordering seller to convey the property. (Each parcel of land is deemed unique, so the court presumes that money damages would not be adequate to compensate the buyer.)

3. **Deposit:** If buyer is unable to close on the appointed date, most courts do *not* allow him to recover his *full deposit.* [315]

    a. **Contract contains liquidated damages clause:** In the vast majority of sale contracts today, the contract typically says that in the event of a breach by the buyer, the seller can *keep the deposit.* So the deposit is in effect a *prepaid liquidated damages clause.* In such a case:

        i. **Reasonable estimate:** If the deposit is a *reasonable estimate* (viewed *either* as of the time the contract was made or at the time of suit) of the damages that the seller would likely incur if the buyer breached, most courts will hold that it is not a penalty, and will allow the seller to *keep* the full amount. The typical "*10%* of the purchase price" deposit, when accompanied by a clause saying that if buyer breaches, seller can keep the deposit, will generally by *valid* under this approach. [316]

        ii. **Unreasonable estimate:** But if the deposit is so *large* that it is *neither* a reasonable estimate of seller's actual damages viewed as of the moment of the contract signing nor a reasonable estimate of his actual damages viewed as of the time of the suit, nearly all courts will *refuse to enforce it*, on the grounds that it is a *penalty.* [316]

F. **Equitable conversion:** For many purposes, the courts treat the *signing of the contract* as vesting in the purchaser *equitable ownership* of the land. (Conversely, the vendor is treated as becoming the equitable owner of the purchase price.) [316]

1. **Risk of loss:** Most courts hold that since the vendee acquires equitable ownership of the land as soon as the contract is signed, the *risk of loss* immediately *shifts to him*. This is true even if the vendee never takes *possession* prior to the casualty. [317-318]

    Example: S contracts to sell land to B. Prior to the closing, while S is still in possession, a hurricane destroys the house located on the land. Most courts hold that the loss falls upon B — B must still pay the agreed-upon purchase price, and does not receive any abatement of price, nor does he get his deposit back.

a. **Exceptions:** But courts following this majority rule have a couple of key *exceptions* to it: (1) the vendor bears any loss resulting from his own *negligence*; and (2) the vendor bears the loss if at the time it occurred, he could not have conveyed title (e.g., because his title was *unmarketable*).

b. **Insurance:** But very importantly, courts who place the risk of loss on the purchaser give him the *benefit of the vendor's insurance*. [318]

G. **Real estate broker's role:** Most sales of real estate involve a real estate broker.

1. **"Ready, willing and able":** Most states hold that the broker is entitled to his commission merely by finding a buyer who is *"ready, willing and able"* to consummate the transaction — in other words, the broker who finds such a buyer can collect his commission *even if the transaction never goes through*, at least where the reason it doesn't is that the seller changes his mind. [319]

2. **Fiduciary duty:** The broker will typically have a *fiduciary duty* to the seller.

   a. **Duty of listing broker:** First, consider the listing broker, i.e., the broker who *contracts directly with the seller* to list the property. It's easy to see that the listing broker's *sole fiduciary duty is to the seller*. [320]

      Example: The listing broker must try to get the seller the best price, must disclose all material facts to the seller about the various bids, and can't favor a lower-paying buyer over a qualified higher-paying one.

   b. **Duties of selling broker:** Now, consider the *selling* broker (the broker who meets with a potential buyer, shows her various potential properties, and in the event that she buys is compensated by receiving a portion of the listing broker's commission). Perhaps surprisingly, the selling broker, like the listing broker, *owes a fiduciary duty solely to the seller*. That's because the selling broker is, technically speaking, a *"subagent"* of the listing broker, and thus inherits the listing broker's duty to the seller. [320]

II. MORTGAGES AND INSTALLMENT CONTRACTS

A. **Nature of mortgage:** A *mortgage* is a financing arrangement, in which the person buying property (or one who already owns property) receives a loan, and the property is pledged as security to guarantee repayment of the loan. [321]

1. **Two documents:** There are two documents associated with every mortgage: (1) the *"note"* (or "bond"); and (2) the *mortgage* itself.

   a. **The note:** The *note* is the buyer's personal *promise to make the repayments*. If there is a foreclosure against the property and the foreclosure sale does not yield enough to cover the outstanding mortgage debt, the note serves as the basis for a *deficiency judgment* against the borrower for the balance still due.

   b. **Mortgage:** The *mortgage itself* is a document which gives the lender the right to *have the property sold* to repay the loan if the borrower defaults. Since the mortgage in effect gives the mortgagee an interest in the land, the mortgage is *recorded*.

2. **Sale of mortgaged property:** Usually, when mortgaged property is sold the mortgage is paid off at the closing. But property can be sold without paying off the mortgage, either by: (1) having the purchaser take "subject to" the mortgage; or (2) having the purchaser "assume" the mortgage. [321]

   a. **Sale "subject to" mortgage:** If the purchaser merely takes *"subject to"* the mortgage, he is *not personally liable* for payment of the mortgage debt. True, the mortgagee can foreclose if the buyer does not make the payments. But the mortgagee may not sue the buyer for any balance still remaining on the loan after foreclosure; that is, the mortgagee may not get a deficiency judgment against the purchaser. (But the mortgagee may in this instance sue the original mortgagor for this balance.)

   b.   Assumption: If the new buyer *assumes* payment of the mortgage, he is liable, both to the original mortgagor and to the mortgagee, for re-payment of the mortgage loan. Thus the mortgagee can get a deficiency judgment against the assuming purchaser.

3.   Foreclosure: *Foreclosure* is the process by which the mortgagee may reach the land to satisfy the mortgage debt, if the mortgagor defaults. [325]

   a.   Judicial foreclosure: Usually, foreclosure is *judicially supervised* — the foreclosing mortgagee must institute a lawsuit, and the actual foreclosure sale takes place under supervision of a government official (usually a sheriff).

   b.   Private foreclosure sale: Some states allow the mortgage lender to use a document called a *"deed of trust"* rather than a "mortgage." The deed of trust allows the lender (or a third person) to hold the property as *"trustee,"* and to sell it in a *private sale* if the borrower defaults.

      i.   Commercially reasonable manner required: However, the private sale must be held in a *commercially reasonable manner* so as to bring the highest price possible — if the lender does not do this, he will owe damages to the borrower in the amount that the borrower might have gotten back (representing the borrower's equity above the mortgage amount) had the sale been a commercially reasonable one. [325]

   c.   Not binding on senior mortgagee: *No foreclosure is ever binding on a mortgagee whose interest is senior to the foreclosing creditor's interest.* In other words, if a *junior creditor* forecloses, that foreclosure proceeding can only wipe out the equity and any interest(s) *junior* to that of the foreclosing creditor. [326]

      Example: On April 1, Bank lends *O* $100,000, secured by a promptly-recorded mortgage on Blackacre. On May 1, Finance Co. lends *O* $200,000 secured by a promptly-recorded mortgage on the same property. On June 1, Cred lends *O* $50,000, also secured by a promptly-recorded mortgage. In November, *O* falls behind on the payments to Finance Co. but not the payments to Bank or Cred. Finance Co. starts a foreclosure proceeding, and purports to join Bank and Cred in that foreclosure.

      Bank will be entitled to have the action dismissed as to it. Therefore, what will be foreclosed is merely *O*'s equity, plus any interest junior to Finance Co.'s, including Cred's interest. Thus if *X* purchases at a foreclosure sale, *X* will own the property, but subject to Bank's mortgage. And, still assuming that Bank elects not to join the foreclosure proceeding, any amounts paid by *X* will go first to pay off Finance Co., then Cred, then *O*. [326]

   d.   Equitable subrogation: Under the doctrine of *equitable subrogation*, a person other than the mortgagor who pays off a mortgage can *step into the shoes* of the now-paid-off mortgagee, and maintain that mortgage in place for the payor's benefit, as if it hadn't been paid off. This lets the payor keep the priority level of the paid-off mortgage. [328]

      i.   Where relevant: The most common scenario for subrogation is where there are *three creditors* (let's identify them from most senior as #1 down to most junior as #3). #3 pays off the debt held by #1, and the question then becomes who has priority, #3 or #2? By use of the doctrine of equitable subordination, #3 "inherits" the priority of #1 as if the #1 mortgage had never been dissolved; this lets #3 take ahead of #2. So you should only need to worry about equitable subordination when there are at some point *three claimants in the picture*. [328]

4. **Absolute deed as substitute for mortgage:** Sometimes an arrangement that is really in economic function a loan is cast in the documents as a *sale by the borrower to the lender,* together with some sort of *repurchase right* by the borrower. Where this happens, courts will treat the arrangement as *being a mortgage*, and the lender will *have to use foreclosure procedures.* [323]

> **Example:** Investor pays Owner $200,000, and Owner simultaneously conveys Blackacre to Investor. The parties intend this as a financing device. They do this by orally agreeing, at the same time as the conveyance, that if before the first anniversary of the conveyance Owner pays Investor $200,000 plus a 10% profit, Investor will re-convey Blackacre to Owner.
>
> If Owner doesn't make the payment on time, the court will treat this as a mortgage. The consequence is that Investor won't be able to just sit on the deed — instead, Investor will have to start state-law foreclosure proceedings, and Owner will have until the end of those proceedings to pay Investor the $100,000 + 10% and get the property back.

5. **Mortgagee in possession:** There are a few situations in which the mortgagee will be entitled to *take possession of the property* until the mortgage is paid off or the property foreclosed upon. If the mortgagee does so, it is referred to as a *"mortgagee in possession."* [324]

   a. **Abandonment:** The most important scenario in which the mortgagee will have the right to take possession prior to a complete foreclosure proceeding is the *"abandonment"* scenario. That is, if the mortgagor stops paying and *abandons the premises*, the mortgagee is entitled to take possession and administer the property to maintain the value of his security interest.

   b. **Missing payments not enough:** But the mere fact that the mortgagor has *stopped making payments,* standing alone, does *not* entitle the mortgagee to take possession.

   c. **Duties of mortgagee in possession:** Once the mortgagee takes possession, he has *duties* that are roughly parallel to those of the actual owner. For instance, he must *maintain the property in reasonable condition*, and must credit any rents (less reasonable expenses of managing and repairing the property) against the mortgage debt. [325]

B. **Installment contracts:** Land can be bought under an *installment contract*. The buyer makes a down payment, and pays the rest of the purchase price in installments (usually monthly). Here, the buyer does *not receive his deed* until after he has paid all (or, sometimes, a substantial portion) of the purchase price. [330-331]

1. **Forfeiture:** If the installment buyer defaults, the seller does not need to go through complex foreclosure proceedings — he can just exercise his contractual right to declare the contract *forfeited* (in which case the seller theoretically gets to keep whatever has been paid on account). But modern courts often hold that if the buyer has paid a *substantial portion* of the purchase price, and the seller would be unjustly enriched by a complete forfeiture, ordinary *foreclosure proceedings* (applicable to mortgages) must be used.

III. DEEDS

A. **Nature of deed:** The *deed* is the document which acts to *pass title* from the grantor to the grantee. [331]

1. **Merger:** Under the doctrine of *merger*, most obligations imposed by the contract of sale are *discharged* unless they are repeated in the deed. [331]

> **Example:** The contract calls for merchantable title, in the form of a warranty deed. Buyer carelessly accepts a "quitclaim" deed which makes no warranties. Buyer will not be able to sue Seller on the contractual provision if the title turns out to be defective — the contractual provi-

sions are extinguished and replaced by whatever provisions are contained in the deed, under the merger doctrine.

2. **Two main types of deeds:** There are two basic types of deeds: (1) the *quitclaim* deed, in which the grantor makes no covenant that his title is good (he merely passes on to the grantee whatever title he in fact has); and (2) the *warranty deed*, in which the grantor makes one or more promises about the state of the title.

B. Description of the property:

1. **Types of description:** There are different ways of *describing* land in a deed. [332-332] Here are two common ones:

   a. **Metes and bounds:** A *"metes and bounds"* description begins by establishing a starting point (usually based on a visible landmark or "monument"). Then a series of "calls and distances" is given, each of which represents a line going in a certain direction for a certain distance. [332]

      Example: "From the southwest corner of East and Main Street, then running north 50 degrees 26 minutes for 273 feet, then west 59 degrees 8 minutes for 100 feet," etc.

   b. **Plat:** The *"plat"* method relies on the recording of a map or "plat" of property by a developer, in which the plat shows the location of individual lots. [332]

      Example: "Lot 2 in Block 5 in Highwood, a subdivision platted on a map filed in the Register's Office of the County of Westchester on June 13, 1910." [332]

2. **Inadequate description:** If the description is *not sufficiently specific or accurate* to let a court determine what property is meant, the *entire deed* will be found to be *invalid*. [332]

   Example: *O* owns a 100-acre farm. He hands a deed covering "the 15 acres along the creek" to his son. There are 25 acres each of which could be said to be "along the creek." A court is likely to hold that the description is so imprecise (exactly which acres are covered?) that the deed is invalid. [332]

   a. **Subsequent actions of parties:** But the court will try to resolve ambiguities, so that it can uphold the deed. [332]

   b. **Construction in grantee's favor:** Courts tend to interpret the deed in a way which is *most favorable to the grantee* (i.e., the document is construed against the grantor, since the grantor usually drafts the deed). [333]

C. Formalities: Deeds must meet certain *formalities*, which vary from state to state. [333]

1. **Identification of parties:** The deed must correctly *identify the parties* (the grantor and the grantee). [333]

   a. **Void if not satisfied:** A deed that does not correctly identify the parties is *void*, i.e., of no effect at all. Similarly, if the identification is so *imprecise* that the court can't tell who is being referred to, the deed will be treated as void. [333]

      i. **Imprecise identification:** This is most likely to be an issue on the *grantee* side, since circumstantial evidence will usually help identify the grantor.

   b. **Deceased grantee:** If the grantee listed on the deed is *dead* at the time the deed is "delivered" (see *infra*, p. C-73, for a discussion of delivery), the deed is deemed not to identify the parties correctly, and therefore to be *void*.

c. **Non-existent entity:** Similarly, if the grantee is a *corporation* or other entity that *does not exist* at the time the deed is delivered, and never comes into existence, the court will likely hold that the deed is void. [333]

2. **Signature:** The grantor must place her *signature* on the deed. The signature of the *grantee* is generally *not* necessary.

3. **Attestation or acknowledgment:** In most states, statutes require the deed either to be *"attested"* to (i.e., *witnessed* by one or more persons not parties to the transaction) or to be *notarized*.

D. **Delivery of deed:** For a deed to be valid, it must not only be executed, but also *"delivered."* But this "delivery" requirement does not refer solely to physical delivery. The concept of "delivery" includes two sub-requirements: [334-334]

[1] that there be a *physical transfer* of the deed by the grantor to someone else (even if only to an agent of the grantee rather than to the grantee herself); and

[2] that the grantor use *words or conduct* evidencing his *intention* to make the deed *presently operative* to vest title in the grantee.

1. **Presumption of delivery from physical transfer:** *Physical transfer* of the deed by the grantor *to the grantee* will create a *strong presumption* that the "intent to make presently operative" requirement (requirement [2] above) has been satisfied.

a. **Must take effect immediately:** But remember that the requirement that the deed be "delivered" is just an *abbreviated* way of expressing the idea that the conveyance does not occur unless the grantor intends that it *take effect immediately.*

2. **Presumption from fact of recording:** The fact that the deed has been *recorded* raises a strong *presumption* that the grantor *intended delivery to occur* prior to the moment of recording. (But this presumption can be *rebutted* by clear evidence of a contrary intent by the grantor.) [334]

a. **Request not to record:** The *converse is not true* — as long as the grantor intends that the conveyance be effective immediately (i.e., intends for delivery to occur now), the fact that the grantor asks the grantee *not to record* the deed until some later date *doesn't prevent immediate delivery* from occurring. Again, remember that delivery is always a question of the *grantor's intent,* and the mere fact that the grantor requests the grantee to wait until recording typically will not mean that the grantor intends for there to be a postponement of delivery. [334]

Example: *O* hands his son Sam a deed, saying, "I want you to have Blackacre. You can move in tomorrow. But don't record the deed until I've had a chance to tell your sister that I gave the property to you instead of her." Delivery will be found to have occurred immediately (especially given the strong presumption of present delivery that applies whenever there is a physical transfer of the deed directly to the grantee).

3. **Delivery to a third party (escrows):** Physical transfer of the deed might be made by the grantor not to the grantee himself, but to a *third party,* to be re-transferred to the grantee if certain conditions are met. Assuming that the third party is not an agent of either the grantor or grantee, the transaction is referred to as an *escrow.* [335]

a. **When title passes:** The deposit of the deed with the escrow agent usually *does not act to transfer legal title.* Thus legal title remains in the grantor until the performance of the stated *conditions* or the happening of the stated *event.* Once the event or condition occurs, title *automatically vests in the grantee*; re-delivery of the deed by the escrow agent to the grantee is not necessary.

        i. Unauthorized delivery: Thus if the escrow agent delivers the deed to the grantee before the condition or event has occurred, this delivery is ***ineffective to pass title***. [336]

    4. Not revocable: If the delivery occurs, title passes immediately to the ***grantee***. Thereafter, return of the deed to the grantor has ***no effect*** either to ***cancel*** the prior delivery or to reconvey the title to him. The only way the title can get back to the grantor is if a new, formally satisfactory, conveyance takes place.

E. Covenants for title in warranty deed: If the deed is a *"warranty"* deed (as opposed to a "quitclaim" deed, which merely conveys whatever interest the grantor has without making any promises), the grantor is held to be making various promises about the state of his ownership. These promises are called *"covenants for title."* [336]

    1. The covenants: The covenants fall into three basic groups: [336-337]

        a. Seisin and conveyance: The covenants of *"seisin"* and of *"right to convey"* mean that the grantor is warranting that he holds the ***type of estate*** which he purports to convey.

        Example: These covenants might be breached if the grantor purported to convey a fee simple absolute, but actually only owned and conveyed a fee simple subject to condition subsequent or a fee simple subject to an executory limitation.

        b. Against encumbrances: The covenant *"against encumbrances"* is a promise that there are no encumbrances against the property, that is, no impediments to title which do not affect the fee simple but which diminish the value of the land.

        Examples: *Mortgages*, *liens*, *easements* and *use restrictions* are all encumbrances, so if the grantor gives a deed containing a covenant against encumbrances, the existence of any of these will constitute a breach of that covenant.

        c. Quiet enjoyment and warranty: The covenants of *"quiet enjoyment"* and *"warranty"* represent a ***continuing contract*** by the grantor that the grantee will be entitled to ***continued possession*** of the land in the future.

        Example: These covenants would be breached if a third person not only asserted that he had paramount title, but commenced proceedings to *eject* the grantee.

    2. Present vs. future covenants: Be sure to distinguish between: (1) ***present*** covenants; and (2) ***future*** covenants. [337]

        a. Present covenants: The covenants of *seisin*, *right to convey*, and *against encumbrances* are ***present covenants***. They are breached, if at all, at the ***moment the conveyance is made***. Thus a breach can occur ***even though there is no eviction*** — all the grantee needs to do to recover on the claim is to show that title was in fact defective on the date of the conveyance.

        b. Future covenants: By contrast, the covenants of ***quiet enjoyment*** and ***warranty*** are ***future covenants***. They are breached ***only when an eviction occurs***.

        Example: Grantor conveys Blackacre to Grantee under a warranty deed. Ten years later, Grantee discovers that X has always had a better title than Grantor had. This is a breach of the present covenants (seisin, right to convey and against encumbrances), even though there is no eviction. But it is not a breach of the future covenants (quiet enjoyment and warranty), because X has not tried to evict Grantee.

    3. No protection against having to defend invalid claim: None of the six covenants is deemed breached merely because someone ***files a claim*** against the grantee asserting facts that, if proved, would demonstrate that the grantee has been given imperfect title. In other words, no covenant of title gives any protection at all against the grantee's *costs, such as legal fees, in having to defend an invalid claim* by a third party. [338]

4. **Statute of limitations:** The main reason for distinguishing between present and future covenants involves the *statute of limitations*. [338]

   a. **When it starts to run:** The statute starts to run on a *present* covenant *at the time the conveyance is made*. But it starts to run on a *future* covenant only *when an eviction occurs.*

   b. **Consequence:** Therefore, if many years pass from the time of the conveyance, and the grantee discovers that someone has paramount title, the grantee is likely to be out of luck: the time for suing on the *present* covenants is likely to have *passed* (since that clock started running at the time of the conveyance), yet there will be no breach of the future covenants if the holder of the paramount title has not attempted to eject the grantee.

      Example: On the facts of the above example involving paramount title held by X, Grantee is likely to be out of luck, with his present covenants time-barred and his future covenants not yet breached due to the absence of any ejectment action by X. [338]

5. **Enforcement by future grantee (running of covenants):** A second reason for distinguishing between the present and future covenants concerns whether the covenant *runs with the land*, i.e., whether it is *enforceable by subsequent grantees*. [339]

   a. **Present covenants:** The present covenants usually *do not run with the land*.

   b. **Future covenants:** But the future covenants *do run with the land*.

      Example: O conveys to G1 under a warranty deed. G1 conveys to G2. G2 discovers that X has always held a paramount title superior to O's. G2 cannot sue O on the present covenants (seisin, right to convey and against encumbrances), because these do not run with the land. But he may sue O for breach of the future covenants (warranty and quiet enjoyment). (But remember that these future covenants will not be breached unless X actually sues to eject G2.)

6. **Measure of damages:** If the grantor breaches any of these warranties, the grantee's recovery is generally limited to the *purchase price paid* — the grantee may *not* recover for any *appreciation* in the value of the land since the conveyance. [339]

F. **Warranty of habitability:** Most courts today recognize an *implied warranty of habitability* on behalf of the purchaser of a *new residence* against a *professional builder* who built the house. [339]

   Example: Developer, who is in the business of building homes, sells a home to P. Shortly after P moves in, he discovers that the foundation is cracked and the roof is structurally unsound. In most states, P may sue Developer for breach of the implied warranty of habitability.

1. **Used homes:** The buyer of a *used home cannot* sue the prior "amateur" owner. But the second buyer may, in most states, sue the *original builder* for breach of the implied warranty of habitability, provided that: (1) the defect was *not obvious* at the time of the second purchase, and (2) the defect occurred within a *reasonable time* after construction of the house. [340]

   Example: On the facts of the above example, if P sold the house to P1, P1 could sue Developer if the foundation and roof problems were not obvious at the time of the P-P1 sale, and occurred within a reasonable time after Developer built the house.

G. **Co-ops and condos:**

1. **Co-ops:** The term *"co-operative"* or *"co-op"* usually refers to a means of owning an apartment house. The building is owned by a co-operative *corporation*. What the lay-person thinks of as an "owner" of an individual apartment unit is really a *shareholder* in the corporation. Each shareholder is entitled to enter into a *"proprietary lease,"* in which the corporation is lessor and the

shareholder is lessee. The lessee is generally required to pay his portion of the building's **mortgage** interest and principal, and various **"carrying charges"** used to defray the maintenance and operating costs of the building. [342]

2. **Condominium:** The **condominium** or **"condo"** is a form of ownership in which each individual resident holds a **fee simple** in a certain physical space or parcel, but all the residents collectively own certain **"common areas."** In the typical "horizontal" condo structure (e.g., two-story townhouses spread over a large parcel), each individual resident might own the soil upon which his townhouse stands, but he would not own the surrounding lawns, swimming pool, etc. — these would be held by the condominium association. [342]

IV. CONVEYANCING BY WILL: ADEMPTION, EXONERATION AND LAPSE

A. **Conveyancing by will generally:** There are three common-law doctrines that are specific to conveyances of property by **will**:

❑ **ademption**;

❑ **exoneration**; and

❑ **lapse**

B. **Ademption:** The common-law doctrine of **"ademption"** deals with those cases in which a testator makes a devise of specified property — personal property or realty — and the specified property is **no longer part of the testator's estate** at the time of death. The ademption doctrine says that the bequest **completely fails** in this situation, and the legatee **gets nothing.** The specific gift is said to have "adeemed," i.e., failed. [343]

> **Example:** At the time Test writes her will, she owns Blackacre. The will recites that Test "hereby bequeaths Blackacre to my daughter Dee." The will gives all other real and personal property to Test's son Sam. One year later, Test sells Blackacre for $400,000, and does not modify the will. Test then dies. At common law, Dee will get nothing, because the gift of Blackacre is adeemed. The $400,000 in proceeds will go to Sam as the residuary legatee.

1. **Statutes:** Most states have statutes that at least cut back on the doctrine of ademption.

2. **Equitable conversion:** If the specifically-devised property is, at the moment of the testator's death, under a **contract to be sold,** and you are not told of the existence of any relevant statute, you should assume that by the doctrine of equitable conversion (*supra*, p. C-68) the purchase price will be personal property, not real estate, and will go to the person identified as the recipient of personal property under the will.

> **Example:** In the above example, if Blackacre is under contract to be sold at the time Test dies, the $400,000 proceeds will go to Sam as legatee of the personal property, not to Dee as recipient of the specific bequest of Blackacre.

C. **Exoneration:** Under the common-law doctrine of **"exoneration,"** a person who receives a bequest of property that is **subject to a lien or mortgage** is entitled to receive the property **"free and clear,"** if there is no evidence that the testator intended a contrary result. When exoneration applies, the estate's personal property — i.e., its cash — is used to pay off the lien or mortgage. [343]

> **Example:** Test's will bequeaths Blackacre to her son *S*, and all of her other property, real and personal (including $500,000 in cash), to her daughter *D*. At the time of Test's death, Blackacre is subject to a $100,000 mortgage. Assume that all relevant common-law doctrines apply,

and that there is no evidence of Test's desires regarding the handling of the mortgage at her death. When *S* takes Blackacre, who is responsible for the mortgage?

S takes free-and-clear of the mortgage, under the common-law doctrine of exoneration. By that doctrine, if the testator does not indicate a contrary intent, any specific devise of real or personal property is to made free and clear of any mortgage or lien. So here, the mortgage on Blackacre will be paid off with some of the cash that would otherwise have gone to *D* as residuary legatee.

1. **Statutes:** Most states have *statutes* altering the common-law exoneration doctrine.

D. Lapse: Under the common-law doctrine of *"lapse,"* if a beneficiary named in a will *pre-deceases the testator,* the *bequest fails*, rather than go to that beneficiary's next-of-kin. Instead, the bequeathed property becomes part of the testator's residuary estate. [344]

1. **Statutes:** Most states have enacted *"antilapse"* statutes. These generally have the effect of abolishing the lapse doctrine — and allowing the dead beneficiary's heirs to take — in certain situations, typically those in which the pre-deceased beneficiary is a *relative* of the testator. [344]

> **Example:** Test writes a will leaving Blackacre to "my good friend Fred," who is not a relative of Test. The will leaves all the rest of Test's estate to a daughter Dee. Fred dies intestate after Test's will is executed; Fred is survived by a single heir at law, a son Sam. One year later, Test dies. Assume that the state has a statute providing that in the case of a bequest to a person who is a lineal descendant of the testator's grandparent, if the beneficiary has pre-deceased the testator then the heirs at law of the beneficiary shall take so long as there is no indication that the testator intended a contrary result. In all other respects, the common law applies. Who takes Blackacre, Sam or Dee?
>
> Dee takes Blackacre. Since Fred is not a lineal descendent of Test's grandparent (the facts say that Fred and Test are not relatives), the antilapse statute does not apply. Consequently, the common-law lapse rule applies, so as to cause the bequest to Fred to fail because Fred pre-deceased Test. Therefore, Blackacre becomes part of Test's residuary estate, which goes to Dee.

CHAPTER 12

THE RECORDING SYSTEM AND TITLE ASSURANCE

I. COMMON-LAW PRIORITIES

A. Conflicts in real estate: Most of the time when there are two or more conflicting claims to a particular piece of real estate, the conflict is resolved by use of recording acts, discussed below. However, occasionally the recording act will not govern a particular situation, and it becomes important to understand the *common-law* system of priorities. [357]

1. **First in time, first in right:** The basic common-law rule of priorities is *"first in time, first in right."* In other words, in a contest between successive grantees, the one who received her interest first *has priority over any later taker.* This rule applies not only to conflicts between two grantees of estates in land, but also to a conflict between a grantee of an estate and the beneficiary of an *encumbrance* like a mortgage or an easement. [357]

> **Example:** *O* borrows $100,000 from Bank, and gives Bank a mortgage on Blackacre, which *O* owns in fee simple. *O* then sells Blackacre to *B* for the fair market value it would have if unencumbered. At the time *B* buys, he has no idea that a mortgage is outstanding. At common law,

Bank's mortgage, since it's earlier in time, has priority over *B*'s interest. Therefore, under the common-law approach, if *B* doesn't pay the mortgage, Bank can foreclose.

II.   RECORDING STATUTES

A. General function of: The main function of ***recording acts***, which are in force in every jurisdiction, is to give a purchaser of land a way to check whether there has been an ***earlier transaction*** in the property inconsistent with his own. Even if there has been an earlier transaction, if it is not recorded the later purchaser will generally gain priority — thus the recording acts give a buyer a way to be sure that he is getting good title. [357]

> **Example:** Consider the facts of the above Example. Under virtually any modern recording act, if Bank did not record, *B* would, as one who took without actual notice of Bank's mortgage and paid valuable consideration, not be subject to Bank's mortgage, assuming *B* recorded promptly after buying. [358]

1. Bona fide purchasers (BFPs): Modern recording acts generally protect only ***"bona fide purchasers"*** (***"BFPs"***). In brief, a person is a BFP, and is thus eligible for protection against an unrecorded prior interest, only if the person took ***"for value"*** and ***"without notice"*** of the prior interest. We examine the "for value" requirement *infra*, p. C-80, and the "without notice" requirement *infra*, p. C-81. For now, just remember that only BFPs are protected. [358]

2. Relations between original parties: Recording acts only govern the relationship between a grantee and a subsequent purchaser of the same property. They do ***not*** govern the relation between the ***grantor and the grantee under a particular conveyance***.

> **Example:** D conveys Blackacre to P. D then conveys it again to X, who doesn't know about the D-P conveyance. X records his deed before P can record his. Because of the recording act, X's deed takes priority over P's. P sues D for his double-dealing. P will be able to recover against D, because the recording act has no effect upon the relations between both parties to a particular deed (i.e., P and D), only the relationship between two grantees under different deeds (i.e., P and X).

B. Different types of acts: There are three basic types of recording acts: (1) ***"pure race"*** statutes; (2) ***"pure notice"*** statutes; and (3) ***"race-notice"*** statutes. [358]

1. Pure race statutes: A ***race*** statute places a premium on the ***race to the recorder's office***. The subsequent purchaser must ***record before the earlier purchaser***, but he is protected ***regardless of whether he has notice*** of the earlier conveyance. Very few pure race statutes remain on the books.

2. Pure notice statute: A pure ***notice*** statute provides that an unrecorded instrument is invalid against ***any*** subsequent purchaser without notice, ***regardless of whether the subsequent purchaser records prior to the first purchaser***.

3. Race-notice statute: A ***race-notice*** statute protects the subsequent purchaser only if he meets ***two*** requirements: (1) he ***records before*** the earlier purchaser records; and (2) he takes ***without notice*** of the earlier conveyance.

Illustration: Here's an illustration of how each of the three types of statute would operate: [359]

Assume that in 2005, *O* conveys Blackacre to *A*. In 2006, *O* conveys to *B*. In 2007, *B* records. In 2008, *A* records. Here is how the rights of *A* and *B* to Blackacre would be resolved under the three statute types:

> *Race:* Under a pure race statute, *B* wins automatically, without regard to whether he had actual notice of the earlier conveyance to *A* — *B* recorded his deed before *A* did, so that is the end of the

matter. (Had *A* recorded in 2007 and *B* in 2008, *A* would have won, even though at the time *B* took, he had no way to find out about the earlier conveyance to *A*.)

Notice: Under a pure notice statute, *B* wins. In fact, *B* would have won even if he never recorded at all, or recorded after *A* — the mere fact that *B* took after *A*, and without notice of *A*'s interest, would be enough to give him the victory.

Race-notice: Under a race-notice statute, *B* will win only if he took without actual notice of *A*'s interest. Furthermore, if *B* had recorded after *A* (instead of before *A*, as really happened), *B* would have lost due to his late recording even if he took without actual notice of *A*'s interest. So under the race-notice statute (probably the most common kind of statute), the subsequent purchaser (here, *B*) has two obstacles to overcome: (1) he must record first; and (2) he must take without actual notice of the earlier interest.

C. **Mechanics:** Here is a summary of the mechanics of recording: [359]

   1. **Deposit:** The grantee (or the grantee's title insurance company) brings the deed to the recording office (usually located in the county where the land lies). The recorder stamps the date and time of deposit, and then places a photocopy of the deed in a chronological book containing all recorded deeds.

   2. **Indexing:** Then, the deeds are **indexed**. Usually there is both a **grantor** index (enabling a searcher to find all conveyances made by a particular grantor) and a **grantee** index (permitting the searcher to find all conveyances made *to* a particular grantee).

D. **What instruments must be recorded:** Recording acts generally allow (and in effect require) the recording of *every instrument by which an interest in land*, whether legal or equitable, is *created* or *modified*. Thus not only fee simple conveyances, but also *life estates*, *mortgages*, *restrictive covenants*, and *tax liens*, are all required to be recorded. [360-360]

   1. **Not recordable:** Some types of interests are usually *not recordable:*

      a. **Adverse possession:** Thus titles based upon *adverse possession* are usually not recordable (since there is no instrument to record).

      b. **Some easements:** Similarly, an *easement* by *implication or necessity* usually does not have to be recorded (since it does not give rise to a recordable document). (But in some instances, a conveyance of the property to a bona fide purchaser who takes without notice of the easement may cut the easement off.) On the other hand, an *express* easement is recordable.

      c. **Short leases:** In many states, a *short term lease* (e.g., less than three years) may not be recorded. If so, that lease will be valid against a subsequent bona fide purchaser.

      d. **Contracts:** Similarly, some states do not allow executory *contracts of sale* to be recorded. (But the vendee's rights will be subordinate to that of a subsequent claimant who actually buys the property.)

         i. **Contract of sale:** On the other hand, most states *allow* a contract of sale to be recorded (assuming that the contract otherwise meets the jurisdiction's requirements for a recordable interest in land, such as being signed, witnessed and/or notarized) even though they don't *require* recordation. In such a state, if the contract is recorded the rights of the contract vendee to close under the contract will be *superior* to the rights of any subsequent grantee, mortgagee, judgment creditor, etc., of the vendor. [360]

E. **Parties protected:** The subsequent grantee, to get the protection of the recording act against a prior grantee, must either be: (1) a *"purchaser for value"* or (2) a *creditor* meeting certain standards. [361-363]

1. **Purchaser for value:** In most states, a grantee gets the benefit of the recording act (i.e., he takes priority over an earlier unrecorded conveyance) only if he *gives value* for his interest. [361]

   a. **Donee:** Thus a *donee* is usually *not protected* by the recording act.

   Example: O conveys to A. O then purports to give the property, for no consideration, to B. B records, A never does. Under most statutes, B still loses to A, because B — although he is a subsequent grantee who recorded first — did not give valuable consideration.

   b. **Less than market value:** Although consideration is required, it does *not* have to be an amount *equal to the market value of the property* (but it must be more than *nominal* consideration).

   Example: On the facts of the above example, if B had paid half the market value of the property, he would probably have prevailed against A; but if he only paid $1, he would not.

   c. **Purchase from or through grantee:** One who purchases for valuable consideration from the record owner is of course protected. But also, one who buys from the *heirs or devisees* of the record owner will also be protected.

   Example: O conveys to A. O then conveys to B for value. B records, A does not. B then bequeaths the property to C. C conveys to D. D will prevail against A — even though B in one sense took "nothing," his right to prevail under the recording act against a prior unrecorded deed is itself devisable.

2. **Creditors:** A landowner's *creditors* may also receive the protection of the recording act. [362]

   a. **Mortgage:** If a creditor receives a *mortgage* from the landowner, he is treated as a "purchaser," but he must still meet the "for value" requirement.

      i. **New value given:** This means that if the creditor is giving something of *new value* (e.g., cancelling part of the debt in return for the mortgage, or extending the owner's time to pay), he will probably be deemed to have taken for value, and will thus be protected against a prior unrecorded conveyance.

      ii. **No new value given** But if the creditor merely retains the same rights he always had (to be paid the full amount of his debt, at the time promised), then he is not giving new value, and his mortgage will not be protected against a prior unrecorded conveyance.

   b. **Unsecured creditors:** An *unsecured*, general, creditor gains *no protection at all* from the recording acts. [362]

   Example: *O*, in return for receiving a loan from Bank, simultaneously gives Bank a mortgage on *O*'s house. Bank does not promptly record. Finance Co. then makes an unsecured loan to *O*, not knowing of Bank's mortgage. Now, Bank finally records. The state has a pure notice statute.

   Even though Bank had not recorded prior to Finance Co's extending unsecured credit to *O*, Finance Co. doesn't get the benefit of the recording act, because Finance Co's unsecured loan is not an interest in *O*'s real property. Therefore, Bank's interest has priority under the common-law "first in time" principle (*supra*, p. C-77). [362]

   c. **Judgment and execution creditors:** A previously-unsecured creditor who obtains a *judgment*, or who is allowed to *attach* his debtor's property at the beginning of the lawsuit, gets a *lien* against the debtor's property. This lien may or may not be protected under the recording act against a prior unrecorded purchase, depending on how the statute is drafted. (If the statute only protects "purchasers," the lien creditor probably does not get protection against the prior unrecorded deed.)

3. **Eligible to be recorded:** The subsequent purchaser who wants the protection of the recording act must record his own deed, and that deed must be one which is in fact *eligible to be recorded*. If it is not, the purchaser will not be protected even if the recording clerk makes a mistake and accepts the document. [364]

   a. **Must record whole chain:** Also, the subsequent grantee must see to it that his *entire chain of title* is recorded. (Thus if one of the subsequent grantee's predecessors in interest submitted, say, an improperly-notarized document that was therefore not eligible for recording, the subsequent grantee would lose.)

4. **Forged deeds:** Recording acts do not protect purchasers (even BFPs) who receive *forged deeds*. [364]

   Example: In 2005, *O* is the record owner of Blackacre. In 2006, *A* forges a deed reading "from *O* to *A*," and records it. In 2007, *A* purports to sell Blackacre to *B* (and receives from *B* the full market value of the property), via a deed reading "*A* to *B* in fee simple." *B* records. In an action between *O* and *B*, *B* loses, even though *B* is a BFP and has perfect record title. [364]

   a. **Satisfaction of mortgage:** The same principle operates in connection with a forgery of a *release or satisfaction of a mortgage.* In other words, if the owner of mortgage property forges a satisfaction-of-mortgage document from the lender and records it, any purchaser of the property from that owner *takes subject to the mortgage.* [365]

F. **Notice to subsequent claimants:** In virtually all jurisdictions (that is, jurisdictions having notice or race-notice statutes, but not those very few having pure race statutes) the subsequent purchaser will lose if he was on *notice* of the earlier deed. A purchaser can be on notice in three ways: (1) *actual notice*; (2) *record notice*; and (3) *"inquiry"* notice. [365]

   1. **Actual notice:** If the subsequent purchaser is shown to have had *actual* notice of the existence of the prior unrecorded interest, he will not gain the protection of the recording act in a notice or notice-race jurisdiction.

   2. **Record notice:** The subsequent grantee is deemed to have *"record"* notice if the prior interest is *adequately recorded.* However, the mere fact that a deed is recorded somewhere in the public records does not mean that the recording is "adequate" — the document must be recorded in a way that a reasonable searcher would *find* it. [365-369]

      a. **Defective document:** A document which is *not entitled to be recorded* will not give record notice, even if it is mistakenly accepted for recording.

         Example: If the jurisdiction requires the deed to be *notarized*, and it is not, it will not give record notice. However, states often treat certain formal defects in deeds as being "cured" after the passage of a certain amount of time.

      b. **Imputed knowledge:** If proper recording of the earlier document took place, subsequent purchasers are on "record notice" even if they *never actually see* the document that has been filed. That is, the court *imputes* to the subsequent purchaser the knowledge which he *would have obtained* had he conducted a diligent title search.

      c. **"Chain of title":** Therefore, the recording of an instrument gives record notice to a subsequent searcher only if that searcher *would have found the document* using generally-accepted searching principles (use of the grantor and grantee indexes). A recorded instrument which would not be found by these principles is said to be outside the searcher's "chain of title," and prevents the giving of record notice. [367-369]

         Example: O conveys to A; A never records. A then conveys to B; B records. O conveys the same property to C; C records. Assume that C has no knowledge of the O-to-A or A-to-B conveyances. C will have priority over B, even though B's interest is recorded. This is because C, when searching title, has no way to know of the A-to-B deed — C would never find the original O-to-A conveyance, and thus cannot know to look under A's name in the grantor index to discover whether he ever conveyed to anyone else. (Nor would C have any way to know to look for B's name in the grantee index.) The A-to-B deed is said to be "outside C's chain of title"; C is therefore not on record notice of the A-to-B deed, and will take priority over B.

i. **Estoppel by deed:** Chain-of-title issues arise when the doctrine of *"estoppel by deed,"* applies. That doctrine holds that where a person (call him O) makes a conveyance of property to another (call him A) before O has ever obtained title, and then subsequently O does obtain title, this title *passes immediately* to the grantee (A). If the estoppel by deed doctrine is applied, and the estoppel is held to be binding upon a subsequent *bona fide* purchaser, then that purchaser's failure to check the records for conveyances by a record owner *prior to the date that owner obtained record title* will be ruinous. Therefore, most courts hold that even though the estoppel by deed doctrine may apply as between the original grantor and grantee, the doctrine is *not binding against a subsequent good-faith purchaser.* [368-369]

Example: O is the son of X, the record owner of Blackacre, who has promised to leave the property to O in X's will. In 2004, while X is still alive, O purports to convey the property to A; A believes O is already the owner, and gives valuable consideration. A properly records the deed. In 2005, X dies and, as promised, leaves the property to O. In 2006, O conveys to B, who is a purchaser for value and is without notice of the prior O-to-A transfer. Right before taking, B checks the grantor index to make sure that O didn't convey the property at any time after he took in 2005 (but B feels no need to check the index for conveyances by O prior to the date in 2005 when O became the record owner). The jurisdiction applies the estoppel-by-deed doctrine, at least as between the grantor and the grantee.

The estoppel-by-deed doctrine means that as soon as O takes in 2005, title is deemed immediately vested in A. Yet B, even though he has checked the grantor index for all times when O was the record owner, never had reason to discover the O-to-A deed. If the O-to-A deed is deemed to be within O's chain of title, then B would lose (since recording acts protect only against conveyances that have not been properly recorded within the grantor's chain of title), even though B "did everything right" when he checked the records.

Therefore, most courts would refuse to apply the estoppel-by-deed doctrine against B. So under the majority approach B would win — the O-to-A deed would be deemed not within B's chain of title, and B would consequently get the protection of the recording act as against A. [369]

3. **Inquiry notice:** Even if a purchaser has neither record notice nor actual notice of a prior unrecorded conveyance, he may be found to have been on *"inquiry" notice* of it. Inquiry notice exists where a purchaser is in *possession of facts that would lead a reasonable person in his position* to make an *investigation*, which would in turn advise him of the existence of the prior unrecorded right. Such a person is on inquiry notice even if he does not in fact make the investigation. (But the purchaser is responsible only for those facts which the investigation would have disclosed.) [369-371]

a. **Possession:** Thus if the parcel is *possessed* by a person who is *not the record owner*, this will place a subsequent purchaser on inquiry notice. That is, the purchaser must: (1) *view* the property, to see whether it is in the possession of someone other than the record owner; and (2) if there is such a possessor, he must *inquire as to the source of the possessor's rights* in the property.

Example: *O* conveys a house to *A* as a gift. *A* doesn't record, but takes possession and lives in the house. *O* then conveys the house to *B*. *B* pays fair value, and at the time of closing does not have actual knowledge of *A*'s unrecorded deed (or of the fact that *A* is in possession of the premises). After the closing, *B* discovers *A*'s deed and possession.

In a contest between *A* and *B*, *A* will win if the court concludes (as it probably would) that *A*'s possession put *B* on inquiry notice of *A*'s interest. That is, the court would likely conclude that if *B* had inspected the premises before closing, he would have discovered *A*'s presence, and would have asked questions that would have led him to learn of *A*'s paramount title. In this scenario, *B* would not be a subsequent purchaser "without notice," and would therefore lose the protection of the recording act. [370]

4. **Purchaser from one without notice:** If a purchaser who takes without notice of a prior unrecorded instrument *resells* the property, the *new* purchaser is treated as one who may claim the benefit of the recording act, even if *he* buys *with* actual notice. This is done to protect the earlier (innocent) purchaser's market for the property. [371]

> **Example:** In a jurisdiction with a race-notice statute, *O* conveys to *A*. *A* does not record. *O* conveys to *B* for value; *B* does not know of the conveyance to *A*. *B* records. *A* then finally records. *B* gifts the property to *C*, who at the time he takes knows of the late-recorded deed to *A*.
>
> In a contest between *A* and *C*, *C* wins because *B*'s act of taking without notice of the grant to *A*, and for value, plus her prompt recording, cut off all rights of *A*. Therefore, *B* can and does pass fee simple to *C*, regardless of the fact that *C* didn't take for value and didn't take without notice of the late-recorded deed to *A*. [371-371]

III. TITLE REGISTRATION (THE TORRENS SYSTEM)

A. **How the system works:** In some parts of the U.S., the *"title registration"* system or *"Torrens"* system is available as an *option*. This system enables the owner of a parcel to obtain a *certificate of title*, similar to an automobile certificate of title. When the holder of the certificate wishes to sell, his prospective purchaser merely has to inspect the certificate itself (on which nearly all encumbrances must be noted) — a lengthy title examination is unnecessary. [371]

1. **How it works:** The registration process begins with an *application* by a person claiming ownership of a parcel to have it registered. Notice is given to anyone shown on the ordinary land records as having an interest in the property. Then, a court hears any claims regarding the property, and if satisfied that the applicant indeed has good title, orders a certificate of title to be issued. [371]

B. **Where used:** The Torrens system is never required, but is available as an option in 11 states. In only a few areas does the system account for a significant portion of the land area (e.g., Hawaii, Boston, parts of Minnesota and parts of Ohio.) [371]

IV. TITLE ASSURANCE

A. **Examination by lawyer:** One way the purchaser sometimes assures himself that he is getting valid title is to have a title examination performed by his *lawyer*. Usually, the lawyer does not directly search the records; instead, he orders an *"abstract"* of title from an abstract company and reviews that abstract. The lawyer then gives his client a written opinion as to the state of the title. The lawyer is liable for his own negligence in rendering an opinion on the title as presented in the abstract (but not liable for any mistake in the abstract itself — here, the abstract company might be liable). [375]

B. **Title insurance:** The leading means by which a buyer of property can assure himself of a good title is *title insurance*. [376-378]

1. **Covers matters not shown in title search:** Title insurance will protect the buyer against many risks that would *not* be disclosed even by the most careful title search. For instance, the buyer would be covered if title turns out to be bad because of forgery of an instrument in the chain, fraudulent misrepresentation of marital status by a grantor (so that the spouse's inchoate right of dower persevered), defects in a prior grant due to lack of delivery, etc. Also, the policy usually covers the insured's *litigation costs* in defending his title even if the defense is successful.

2. **Scope:** But title policies usually contain a number of *exceptions*, including the following: [377-377]

   a. **Facts which survey would show:** Policies usually exclude facts which an *accurate survey* of the property would disclose. Thus *encroachments* (either by the insured onto adjacent property or vice versa) and violations of set-back rules are generally not covered.

   b. **Adverse possession:** Also, the title policy does not protect against a claim of *adverse possession*, at least if the physical possession exists at the time the policy is written. Therefore, the buyer must still *inspect* the property.

C A P S U L E S U M M A R Y

CHAPTER 13
RIGHTS INCIDENT TO LAND

I. NUISANCE

A. Defined: A landowner may sue another person for *"private nuisance."* Private nuisance is an interference with a landowner's *use and enjoyment of his land*. [385]

1. **Substantial interference:** The interference with the plaintiff's use and enjoyment must be *substantial*. Thus if P's damage consists of his being *inconvenienced* or subjected to unpleasant smells, noises, etc., this will be "substantial" damage only if a person of *normal sensitivity* would be seriously bothered.

2. **Defendant's mental state:** There is *no* rule of *"strict liability"* in nuisance. P must show that D's conduct was *negligent*, *intentional* or *abnormally dangerous*.

   a. **Intentional:** If P wants to show that D's conduct was "intentional," P does not have to show that D *desired* to interfere with P's use and enjoyment of his land. P merely has to show that D *knew with substantial certainty* that such interference would occur.

   Example: D, a factory owner, knows that his plant is spewing pollutants and smoke into the air over P's property. P can sue D for "intentional" nuisance so long as P can show that D was on notice of what was happening, even if D did not "desire" this result to occur.

3. **Unreasonableness:** Even if D's conduct is intentional, P will not win in nuisance unless he shows that D's actions were *"unreasonable."* In determining what is reasonable, the *nature of the neighborhood* is likely to be quite significant.

   Example: A steel mill located in an otherwise completely residential area is much more likely to be found an "unreasonable" interference than is a steel mill in the middle of an industrial park.

B. Remedies: P has a chance at either or both of the following remedies: [386]

1. **Damages:** If the harm has already occurred, P can recover *compensatory damages*.

2. **Injunction:** If P can show that damages would not be a sufficient remedy, he may be entitled to an *injunction* against continuation of the nuisance. To get an injunction, P must show that the harm to him actually *outweighs* the social utility of D's conduct.

> **Example:** D operates a large cement plant employing hundreds of people. The Ps sue D for nuisance because of dirt, smoke and vibrations, which interfere with their nearby property. A court might not issue an injunction even though nuisance occurred, because the harm to the Ps may be found not to outweigh the job-creation and other economic utility of D's plant. But in that event, D would still have to pay money damages for the harm, no matter how socially useful D's conduct.

II. LATERAL AND SUBJACENT SUPPORT

A. Generally: Every landowner is entitled to have his land receive the necessary *physical support* from adjacent and underlying soil. The right to support from adjoining soil is called the right of *"lateral"* support. The right to support from underneath the surface is known as the right to *"subjacent"* support. [387]

B. Lateral support: The right to *lateral* support is *absolute*. That is, once support has been withdrawn and injury occurs, the responsible person is liable *even if he used utmost care* in his operation. [388]

> **Example:** A and B are adjoining landowners. A very carefully constructs a large excavation extending almost to the edge of his property. This causes B's soil to run into A's excavation, impairing the surface of B's property. B's right to lateral support has been violated, and he may recover damages.

1. **Building:** But the absolute right to lateral support exists only with respect to land in its *natural state*. If the owner has constructed a *building*, and the soil under the building subsides in part due to the adjacent owner's acts, but also in part because of the weight of the building itself, the adjacent owner is *not liable* unless he has been *negligent*. (If P's building is damaged, and he can show that his land would have been damaged even with no building on it, courts are split as to whether D is liable in the absence of negligence.)

C. Subjacent support: The right to *subjacent* support arises only where sub-surface rights (i.e., *mineral rights*) are *severed* from the surface rights. When such a severance has taken place, the owner of the surface interest has the right not to have the surface subside or otherwise be damaged by the carrying out of the mining. [388]

1. **Structures existing:** The surface owner has the absolute right to support, not only of the unimproved land, but also support of *all structures existing* on the date when the severance took place.

III. WATER RIGHTS

A. Drainage: Courts are split as to the rights of an owner to *drain surface water* from his property onto the property of others. In general, courts seem to be moving to a rule that an owner may do this only if his conduct is *"reasonable"* under all the circumstances. [389]

B. Streams and lakes: States are sharply split as to when and how a landowner may make use of waterfront *streams and lakes* that abut his property. [389-392]

1. **Common-law approach:** In all parts of the country except for about 17 western states, courts apply the common-law *"riparian rights"* theory. Under this theory, *no advantage is gained by priority of use*. Instead, each riparian owner is entitled to only so much of the water as he can put to *beneficial use* upon his land, with due regard for the equal rights of the other riparian owners, and without regard to how long the owner has been using the water.

Example: *A* and *B* each own property that abuts a river. *A* is upstream from *B*. Under the common-law "riparian rights" theory, A may make "reasonable use" of the water — for instance, to irrigate his crops — but reasonableness will be determined by reference to *B*'s reasonable needs as well as *A*'s. The fact that A has been using the river for a particular use longer than *B*, or vice versa, is irrelevant.

    a. **Riparian only:** *Only riparian owners* are entitled to make use of the water, under this doctrine. That is, the owner's land must *abut* the stream or lake, at least in part. So one whose land is not contiguous with the water may not carry the water by pipe or ditch to his property.

  2. **Prior appropriation doctrine:** Seventeen *arid* states (all west of the Mississippi) adopt a completely different theory, called the *prior appropriation* doctrine. In many of these states (e.g., California), an owner must apply for a *permit* to use the water; if the application is accepted by the government, the user's priority dates from the time of the application.

    a. **Riparian ownership not required:** Under the prior appropriation system, water may be appropriated by a *non-riparian owner*.

C. **Ground water:** In most American states, an owner may make only *"reasonable use"* of *ground water* drawn from under his property. For instance, he may generally use as much of the water as he wishes for applications on the parcel which sits on top of the pool, but he may *not divert* the water to other properties which he may own. [392-392]

IV.   AIR RIGHTS

A. **Airplane flights:** [392]

  1. **Direct overflights:** If an airport permits flights to occur *directly over* an owner's property, and within the *"immediate reaches"* of his land, the landowner may sue in *trespass*. But flights beyond a certain height are not deemed to be in the "immediate reaches," so no trespass suit may be brought.

  2. **Adjacent areas:** If flights occur at low altitude on property *adjacent* to P's property, some states may permit him to bring a suit for *nuisance* if the flights are low enough, frequent enough and noisy enough to substantially interfere with his use and enjoyment of his land. Also, a court may let such an owner bring a suit in "inverse condemnation," to establish that the interference is so great that it amounts to a "taking" for which compensation must be given under the U.S. Constitution.

B. **Other air-rights issues:** [393-394]

  1. **Tall buildings:** An owner generally has the right to build as *high a building as he wishes* (assuming that it satisfies all applicable zoning requirements and building restrictions). Thus if two owners are adjacent to each other, one cannot object to the other's tall building on the grounds, say, that it ruins the quality of radio and television signals.

  2. **Right to sunlight:** Generally, a landowner has *no right to sunlight*. For instance, an owner almost never acquires an easement of "light and air" by implication or even by necessity. So if *A* and *B* are adjoining owners, *B* can, without liability, build in such a way that *A*'s sunlight is blocked. (But if *A* uses sunlight as a source of *solar energy*, it is possible that he might have a claim — perhaps in nuisance — against *B* for blocking that energy source by a tall building.)

CHAPTER 1

INTRODUCTION

I. "PROPERTY" GENERALLY

A. General definition: A person may be said to hold a property interest, in the broadest sense, if he has any *right* which the *law will protect* against *infringement by others*. In addition to *tangible* property (land and chattels), courts have increasingly recognized broad categories of *intangible* property interests. For instance, a teacher with tenure in a public school system may be found to have a constitutionally-protected property interest in continued employment.

    1. Real and personal property: In this book, we are concerned almost exclusively with rights in tangible property, i.e., all *real* property and tangible *personal* property. "Real" property includes land and any structures built upon it. "Personal" property includes all other kinds of property; while our discussion of personal property concentrates on tangible property (e.g., an automobile), a few types of intangible property (e.g., bank accounts) are considered. The bulk of the treatment of personal property is in the following chapter, so that the remainder of the book concentrates heavily on real property.

B. Possession vs. title: Perhaps the most important distinction which will appear throughout the course of this outline is the distinction between *possession* and *title*.

    1. Possession: There is no precise definition of the term "possession", and its use varies according to the context. However, a person may generally be said to have possession of land or personal property if he has *dominion and control* over it.

    2. Title: Title, on the other hand, is roughly synonymous with what the layman thinks of as "ownership." Thus a tenant in a residential apartment building has possession of the apartment, but the landlord has title to it.

        a. Divided title: A unique feature of Anglo-American property law is that title to a parcel of real estate can be spread among numerous owners and in several different ways. The chapters on future interests, marital estates and concurrent interests are all illustrations of this fact.

C. Law and equity: Another frequently-drawn distinction is between *law* and *equity*. The difference between courts of law and courts of equity is discussed more fully *infra*, p. 87. The basic idea is that a law court awards *money damages*, and an equity court awards other sorts of relief, usually *injunctions*.

D. Bundle of rights: The non-lawyer thinks of property as a single right: one either "owns" personal or real property, or one does not. But in fact, ownership consists of a number of different rights, often called a *"bundle"*: the right to *possess* the object; the right to *use* it; the right to *exclude* others from possessing or using it, and the right to *transfer* it. Even the right of transfer has two distinct aspects, the right to make a *gift*, and the right to *sell*. See D&K, p. 86.

    1. Splitting up: Frequently, an "owner" of real or personal property will be found to have some but not all of these rights. For instance, one who "owns" a vacant downtown acre in "fee simple" (the broadest form of ownership known to American law — see *infra*, p. 50) does not have the right to erect a 150 story building on the site, if buildings of that height are forbidden by the local zoning code. Similarly, a person "owns" his kidneys in the sense that government cannot remove a kidney without his consent, yet one may not make a for-profit sale of one's kidney to be transplanted into another. (See *infra*, p. 6.)

2. **The right to exclude others:** Even the right to *exclude* others, which goes to the core of what it means to "own" property, is subject to limits imposed by society. Most obviously, a property owner must allow fire and police officials on his property in certain circumstances. Some courts have cut back even further on the owner's right to exclude. For instance, one court has held that the owner of a farm may not use trespass statutes to keep out private citizens who are trying to furnish medical or legal services to migrant workers living on the farm. See *State v. Shack*, 277 A.2d 369 (N.J. 1971). As the court said in *Shack*, "title to real property cannot include dominion over the destiny of persons the owner permits to come upon the premises."

II. SOURCES OF PROPERTY LAW

A. **Cases:** The principal source of property law is *case law*, i.e., opinions by judges. Property case law is largely the product of decisions by the appellate courts of the individual *states*. In contrast to many other areas of the law (e.g., constitutional law), the state courts are more or less free to develop their own property case law without interference by the U.S. Supreme Court. (However, in a few situations, e.g., zoning, constitutional issues will arise, and as to these the U.S. Supreme Court has the final word.)

B. **Statutes:** Another large body of law is *state statutes*. The law of property has been heavily subjected to statutory modification of the old common-law principles and there are few property questions that can be answered wholly without reference to any statute.

C. **Restatements and model acts:** A third source of authority consists of secondary materials prepared by law professors and other experts. Foremost among these are the various Restatements: (1) the *First Restatement of Property* (published beginning in 1936); (2) the *Second Restatement of Property* (published in 1976, and dealing only with landlord-tenant law and selected topics under the general title of "Donative Transfers"); and (3) the *Third Restatement of Property* (published in the late 1990s and early 2000s, and dealing only with "servitudes" and mortgages).

1. **Model acts:** Also, a number of *model statutes* have been drafted (e.g., the Uniform Residential Landlord-Tenant Act.) These have been enacted in some states, and are sometimes looked to (on a non-binding basis) by the courts of other states.

CHAPTER 2

TWO TYPES OF NON-REAL PROPERTY: PERSONAL PROPERTY AND INTELLECTUAL PROPERTY

Introductory note: This chapter considers two types of non-real property: personal property and intellectual property. With respect to personal property, we consider: (1) the rights of finders of lost chattels; (2) the rights of *bona fide* purchasers of goods; (3) bailments; and (4) gifts. With respect to intellectual property, we discuss briefly copyrights, trademarks, patents and the right of publicity.

I. RIGHTS OF POSSESSORS

A. Rights from possession generally: Normally, one obtains title to goods by acquiring them from, and with the consent of, their prior owners (e.g., a purchase or gift transaction). There are a few situations, however, in which one may obtain title, or its rough equivalent, by the mere fact of *possessing* the article. The best examples of title from possession are: (1) *wild animals*; (2) the *finding* of *lost articles*; and (3) *adverse possession*.

B. Wild Animals (*ferae naturae*): Wild animals (often referred to in court decisions by their Latin name, *ferae naturae*) are normally not owned by anyone, of course. Therefore, it is not surprising that the courts have held that once a person has *gained possession* of such an animal, he has rights in that animal superior to those of the rest of the world.

 1. **What constitutes "possession":** However, it is not always easy to tell when a person has obtained "possession" of a wild animal. Obviously, the *capture* of such an animal is sufficient. But where less than outright capture has occurred, the line between possession and non-possession becomes blurry.

   a. **Chasing:** The mere fact that one has *spotted* and *chased* an animal is not sufficient to constitute possession. Thus in the classic case of *Pierson v. Post*, 3 Cai. R 175 (Sup. Ct. N.Y. 1805), P found and chased a fox as part of a hunt; D then stepped in, killed the fox, and carried it away. The court held that "mere pursuit" gave P no legal right to the fox, and that D thus had the right to interfere.

   b. **Trapping or wounding:** One who *mortally wounds* an animal or fish, so that capture is almost certain, is deemed to have possession. Brown, pp. 15-16. Similarly, the catching of an animal or fish in a *trap* is sufficient.

   c. **Business competition:** The courts are more likely to be sympathetic to the interfering defendant if he acts out of *business competition* with the plaintiff, rather than out of spite or malice.

   Example: P claims that after he set some decoys on his own pond to lure ducks in order to hunt them, D fired guns nearby to drive the ducks away. *Held*, P is entitled to recovery, because D's act was a violent and malicious interference with P's livelihood. But if the ducks had been lured away from P's pond by D's use of the same type of decoys for his own business purposes, P would *not* have been entitled to recover. *Keeble v. Hickeringill*, 103 Eng. Rep. 1127 (K.B. 1707),

- **d. Custom:** In a close case, the court may look to the *"customs"* or *"usages"* prevailing in the activity or trade involved. For instance, the custom among American *whalers* was that the ship or company which lanced the whale and thereby killed it was the owner, even though the whale immediately sank, floated to the surface several days later, and was found by another. In *Ghen v. Rich*, 8 F. 159 (D.Mass. 1881), the court applied this usage, and thus granted the company which killed the whale recovery against D, who had bought the whale at an auction from the person who found it on a beach. (The court ignored the fact that D had already paid the fair value for the whale, and was thus required to pay twice; it is possible that a modern court would recognize a defense by D that he was a "*bona fide* purchaser." See *infra*, p. 9.)

- **2. Return to natural state:** If a wild animal is captured, and then escapes to *return to its natural state*, the courts have generally held that the finder's ownership is *extinguished*. The animal then becomes the property of whoever recaptures him. Brown, p. 18.

- **C. Finders of lost articles:** The saying "finders keepers, losers weepers" is *not accurate*. The finder of lost property holds it, at least for a certain time, *in trust* for the benefit of the true owner; thus he is a custodian, or "bailee" (see *infra*, p. 12) for the true owner. What is important for our purposes here, however, is that the finder has rights *superior to those of everyone except the true owner*. Brown, p. 24.

  Example: P, a chimney sweep, finds a jewel, and carries it to the shop of D, a goldsmith. He asks D's apprentice to examine it and tell him what it is. The apprentice takes out the stones, and refuses to return them. P sues for the value of the stones.

  Held, for P. The finder of an object, although he does not by finding acquire absolute ownership, is entitled to possess it as against anyone but the true owner. *Armory v. Delamirie*, 1 Strange 505 (K.B. 1722).

  - **1. Possession derived from trespass:** The rights of finders are an example of the broader principle that a possessor of personal property has rights superior to those of anyone except the true owner. Thus even if the possessor has obtained his possession *wrongfully*, he will be entitled to recover from a third person who interferes with that possession.

  - **2. Measure of damages:** Most courts allow the possessor the right to recover the *full value* of the object from the third party who has taken it. That is, the old common-law action of *trover* (which entitles the plaintiff to the object's value, and lets the defendant keep the object) is allowed.

  - **3. Article lost by possessor:** As a corollary of the rule that a possessor has rights superior to those of everyone except the true owner, the courts hold that a possessor who *loses* the property after finding it or otherwise acquiring it may nonetheless recover it from the third person who subsequently finds or takes it.

  - **4. What constitutes acquisition:** For the finder to gain these special rights, he must do more than merely discover the property, he must take it into his *possession*. Just as in the case of wild animals, the existence of "possession" is sometimes hard to determine. The finder must have: (1) *physical control* over the goods; and (2) an *intent* to assume *dominion* over them. Brown, p. 24.

5. **Conflict with the owner of real estate:** When the person who finds the item is not the owner of the real estate on which it is found, a conflict between the *finder* and the *real-estate owner* is likely to develop. The courts have not devised very clear rules for resolving such conflicts.

   a. **Trespasser:** If the finder is a *trespasser*, the owner of the real estate where the object is found will be preferred. Brown, p. 26.

   b. **Other cases:** But if the finder is on the property with the owner's implied or express *consent*, the cases are divided and confused. In general, the English courts tend to award possession to the property owner, and the American courts tend to grant possession to the finder. But these are by no means hard-and-fast rules, and the presence of other factors will often be dispositive.

   c. **"Lost" vs. "mislaid" property:** Courts have frequently distinguished between *"lost"* and *"mislaid"* property.

      i. **Mislaid:** An object has been *"mislaid"* rather than lost when it was *intentionally put in a certain place*, and then forgotten by its owner. Such mislaid objects are usually held to have been, in effect, placed in the *"custody" of the landowner*; therefore, the *finder does not obtain the right to possession*.

      Example: P, a customer in D's barbershop, finds a pocketbook that has been left there by some other customer. *Held*, possession goes to D, because the owner (whoever it is) intentionally placed the pocketbook on D's table, and thus entrusted it to D's care. Therefore, P is a finder of mislaid property (not lost property) and isn't entitled to possession. *McAvoy v. Medina*, 11 Allen 548 (Mass. 1866).

      ii. **"Lost property":** Conversely, property that has clearly *not* been intentionally deposited by the owner (i.e., is *"lost"* rather than "mislaid" property) is likely to be *awarded to the finder*.

   d. **Public vs. private portion of premises:** Courts have frequently distinguished between objects found in a *private* portion of the landowner's premises, and objects found in a portion of the premises *open to the public*. The landowner has a better chance of prevailing against the finder if the object is found in a private area, usually on the rationale that the owner of the premises not open to the public has an intent to possess the place and whatever may be located within it. Brown, p. 26.

      i. **Public place:** Conversely, the finder, rather than the landowner, is more likely to prevail if the object is found in the portion of the premises which is held *open to the public*.

   e. **Underlying equities:** However, a court's decision on whether the goods are "lost" or merely "mislaid", or whether they have been found upon "private" as opposed to "public" premises, is likely to be heavily influenced by the court's perhaps unconscious sense of the *equities*. For instance, in *Hannah v. Peel*, 1 K.B. 509 (Eng. 1945),

P was a soldier who was billeted during the war in a house owned by D. P discovered a brooch on the windowsill of his room, which the court found him to be entitled to in preference to D. The court relied on the fact that D had never actually lived in the house, and that he had therefore never been "physically in possession" of the premises. Probably the decision can best be explained on the grounds that it simply seemed *fairer* to the court to award possession to the soldier than to the homeowner who had never lived in the house.

f. Statutory solutions: Many states have enacted *statutes* governing the disposition of lost and mislaid property. These statutes, sometimes called "estray" statutes, typically require the finder of lost or mislaid property to notify a designated government official who enters a description of the item in a registry. These statutes have often rendered less significant the distinction between property found in a "public" place and that found in a "private" place.

D. Ownership of bodily tissues: Does a person "own" her own organs, blood and other *bodily tissues*? To the extent that by "ownership" we mean the right to *sell* the object, the answer under present American law is mixed — some bodily tissues may be sold, for some purposes, but for the most part a person is not permitted to sell her organs or other tissues.

1. Transplant: The question arises most commonly in the case of *organ transplants*. Here, American law is clear: a person may *not* sell his organ to be used in a transplant. A federal statute, 42 U.S.C. §274(e), makes it "unlawful for any person to knowingly acquire, receive, or otherwise transfer any human organ for valuable consideration for use in human transplantation if the transfer affects interstate commerce" (as virtually any organ transfer would be found to do). This ban applies even to direct donor-donee deals, so you commit a federal crime if you sell, say, your kidney directly to a donee who desperately needs it.

a. Policy determination: In essence, Congress has made a policy determination that a person should not have the right to sell her organs for transplantation.

b. Other sales allowed: But other types of tissue sales are implicitly allowed, both by the federal statute and by most states. For instance, most states allow a person to sell his *blood* to a *blood bank*.

2. Use of cells in research: The other "hot topic" relating to ownership of bodily tissues is this: When a person's tissues are extracted as part of a medical procedure, does the patient continue to "own" the extracted materials, so as to control how they are used for *scientific and commercial purposes*? The main case to have considered the issue so far, *Moore v. Regents of the University of California*, 793 P.2d 479 (Cal. 1990), has answered *"no"* to this question.

a. Facts: The plaintiff in *Moore* was John Moore, who had been a leukemia patient at the UCLA Medical Center. The defendants were the Center, and UCLA, which owns the Center. The defendants, in the course of treating P, removed his spleen with his consent. They then used cells from P's spleen to establish a "cell line," which they patented. The cell line turned out to have great medical and commercial value — products derived from the cell line are expected to have sales in the billions of dollars, and at the time of suit, UCLA had already earned hundreds of thousands of dollars in royalties. P sued the Ds on a number of theories, including conversion — he asserted that by taking his spleen, without telling him that his cells had commercial value or that they would be used for commercial purposes, the Ds had converted P's "property."

b. Claim rejected: A majority of the California Supreme Court *rejected* P's conversion claim. The court held that once P's cells had been removed from his body, he simply *did not retain any ownership interest in them*. Under existing law, the majority wrote, human biological materials are not viewed as "belonging" to the person from whom they have been taken. Furthermore, to extend conversion liability to bodily tissues that have been removed from a patient would "threaten with disabling civil liability innocent parties who are engaged in socially useful activities, such as researchers who have no reason to believe that their use of a particular cell sample is, or may be, against a donor's wishes." (Even a "bona fide purchaser" who buys from a thief or other wrongful taker of property does not get good title, as is discussed *infra*, p. 9, so an innocent researcher who bought a product derived from P's cells without knowledge of P's ownership interest would nonetheless face civil liability if P's conversion claim had been upheld by the court.)

    i. Breach of fiduciary duty claim upheld: The majority did, however, hold that P could sue the attending physician who removed his spleen, for *breach of fiduciary duty* or *lack of informed consent*, if P could show that the physician did not tell him that his cells had commercial value that the physician intended to exploit. However, this was a Pyrrhic victory for P, since this claim would be good only against the physician, not against richer defendants such as UCLA.

c. Dissents: Two members of the court dissented from the majority's conclusion that P did not "own" his cells and thus could not recover in conversion. One of them argued that P should be found to have had, at the time his spleen was removed, "at least . . . the right to do with his own tissue whatever the defendants did with it" (i.e., contract with researchers and drug companies to exploit its commercial potential), even if society properly prevents the sale of, say, organs for transplantation. The majority's ruling simply unjustly enriched UCLA at P's expense.

E. Adverse possession: In every jurisdiction, there exist *statutes of limitations*, which place limits upon the time within which the owner of real or personal property must bring a suit to recover possession, or for damages for the loss of possession. After the statutory period (and any extensions of it) have passed, the actual possessor of the goods or real estate is immune from any suit by the rightful owner. He is said to have gained title by *adverse possession*. The rules of adverse possession are discussed extensively in the next chapter, in a real estate context; here we touch briefly upon several elements relating to adverse possession of personalty.

1. Same rules traditionally applied: Traditionally, the *same rules* have been applied to adverse possession of personalty as to the adverse possession of real property. Most importantly, the possession has been required to be *adverse* or "*hostile*" to the rights of the true owner, rather than being in subordination to his rights. (See *infra*, p. 33.)

Example: Suppose that a painting is stolen from Owner, and the thief sells it to an art dealer, who sells it to Possessor. Possessor and his heirs hold the painting for 100 years, during which time none of them has the slightest reason to believe that the painting is stolen. However, Possessor and his heirs keep the painting in the family vault during the entire time.

Under the traditional rule, Owner or his heirs could come along, even at the end of the 100-year period, and recover the painting, because the statute of limitations would never have run. (Possessor would never have been an "adverse possessor," since his possession was not "open" or "hostile" due to the fact that the painting was never displayed.) This would be true even if Owner and his heirs never made reasonable efforts to find out what had become of the painting.

2. **Modern trend:** But a number of modern courts have rejected this traditional rule, in favor of a *"discovery"* rule. By this rule, the true owner's cause of action accrues "when she *first knew*, or reasonably *should have known* through the exercise of due diligence, of the *cause of action, including the identity of the possessor. . . ."* *O'Keeffe v. Snyder*, 416 A.2d 862 (N.J. 1980).

    a. **Distinction:** Under the discovery rule, if the true owner, immediately after the loss, fails to use reasonable diligence to find the possessor, and the use of such diligence would have identified the possessor, *the statute of limitations will begin to run immediately*, even if the possessor keeps the property hidden. Conversely, even if the possessor displays the property openly, if the owners fails to learn that the possessor has it (and this failure is not due to the owner's lack of diligence), the statute of limitations will *never* start to run.

    b. **Rationale:** The principal reason for the modern use of the "discovery" rule for personal property is that, in contrast to the possession of real estate, "open and visible possession of personal property . . . may not be sufficient to put the original owner on actual or constructive notice of the identity of the possessor." *O'Keeffe, supra*. "For instance, if jewelry is stolen from a municipality in one county in New Jersey, it is unlikely that the owner would learn that someone is openly wearing that jewelry in another county or even in the same municipality." *Id*.

    c. **Tacking:** What if the first possessor transfers the property to a second, thence to third, etc.? Courts applying the discovery rule have generally held that the statute of limitations does *not* begin anew with each change of possession. Therefore, if an owner knows or should know the identity of the first possessor, and the statutory period passes during the first possession, the owner does not get another bite at the apple if the first possessor transfers to a second possessor, whose identity remains unknowable to the owner.

        i. **Criticism:** This rule has been criticized as making it "relatively more easy for the receiver or possessor of an art work with a 'checkered background' to gain security and title than for the artist or true owner to reacquire it." *O'Keeffe, supra*, (dissent).

3. **Nature of title acquired:** Once the statutory period has passed, the possessor becomes, for all practical purposes, the *owner* of the property. Thus not only can the true owner no longer sue to regain possession, but he is not entitled to use *self-help* to recover possession.

II. ACCESSION

A. Concept of accession generally: It may happen that a person *improves the property of another* by mistake. This is known as *accession*. Most situations of accession involve the use of *labor* to improve another's property, and it is on this sort of accession that we focus.

    1. Traditional rule: The traditional rule was that the owner of the original materials had title to the finished product, unless that product was so different from the original materials that essentially a *new species* of object had been created. If a wholly new product were created (e.g., wine made from another's grapes), the maker, not the owner of the materials, had title.

    2. "Disproportionate value" test: But most modern decisions have abandoned the "different species" test, and instead look at the extent to which the maker has *added value* to the other person's materials. If the value added is *wholly disproportionate* to the value of the original materials, the maker gains title; otherwise, the owner of the original materials has title to the finished product.

        a. Good Faith requirement: Virtually all of the cases which have granted title to the person who improved another's property have imposed a requirement of *good faith*. A *willful trespasser* upon another's property will probably not be entitled to recover, no matter how much he has increased the value of the materials by his labor.

III. *BONA FIDE* PURCHASERS

A. Nature of problem: Suppose that one who is in wrongful possession of goods (e.g., a thief, a defrauder, a finder, etc.) *sells them* to a *"bona fide purchaser"*, i.e., one who buys for value and without knowledge that the seller is without title. It might be thought that the seller cannot convey better title than he himself holds; courts frequently so state, and sometimes this statement is true. But there are a number of situations in which the holder of a less-than-good title can indeed convey better title than he holds.

    1. General rule: As noted, the general rule is that *a seller cannot convey better title than that which he holds.* This rule is universally applied, for instance, where the seller has *stolen* the property.

    Example: A car is stolen from P, a car rental agency. The car is ultimately purchased by Consumer from a car dealer in another state. Consumer pays fair value for the car, and has no idea that the car is stolen.

      Held, P may recover the car: "[A] possessor of stolen goods, no matter how innocently acquired, can never convey good title . . . . For a sale of such merchandise, though to a *bona fide* purchaser for value, does not divest the person from whom stolen, of title." *Schrier v. Home Indem. Co.*, 273 A.2d 248 (App. Ct. D.C. 1971).

    2. Exceptions: But where the goods are acquired from the original owner not by outright theft, but by less blatant forms of dishonesty and/or crime, a *bona fide* purchaser may be *protected*. The two principal areas where the *bona fide* purchaser receives better title than his seller are: (1) where the seller has a *"voidable"* rather than a "void" title; and (2) where the true owner has been *estopped* from denying that the possessor/seller has good title (e.g., the owner *entrusts* the goods to a *merchant*).

a.   "Voidable" title: Whereas the thief, and anyone holding under him, has an absolutely "void" title, courts have recognized something called a *"voidable"* title. If goods pass from the owner to one with a voidable title, the owner may recover the goods as long as they are still in the hands of the person with the voidable title; but once the voidable-titleholder transfers them to a *bona fide* purchaser, the true owner's right are *extinguished*. The voidable title thus becomes "firm" in the hands of the *bona fide* purchaser. This principle of voidable title is incorporated in §2-403(1) of the *Uniform Commercial Code*, which is binding in all states on sales of goods and in certain other transactions; §2-403(1) states that "A person with voidable title has power to transfer a good title to a *good faith purchaser for value.*"

   i.   Fraud: One who takes from the true owner gains a voidable title even if the taking was *fraudulent*. Thus if *A* sells goods to *B* and *B* pays in counterfeit money, or a bad check, *B* has nonetheless obtained voidable title, and if he immediately resells the goods to *C*, *A* cannot get them back from *C*.

b.   Estoppel: A second way in which the true owner of a chattel may lose his right to recover it from a *bona fide* purchaser who took it from a person with less-than-good title, is through the principle of *estoppel*. If the owner, by his words or conduct, has expressly or impliedly represented that the possessor of the goods is the owner of them, or that he has the authority to sell them, the owner is "estopped" (i.e., precluded) from denying the truth of these representations to one who buys in good-faith reliance on the representation. Brown, p. 202.

   i.   Entrusting to merchant: Estoppel usually arises in cases where the true owner *entrusts the goods* to a *merchant*, who then (in violation of his agreement with the true owner) sells them to a good-faith purchaser. At common law, the mere fact that the true owner entrusted the goods to a merchant was never enough to estop him from recovering them from the good-faith purchaser; some *additional conduct* by the true owner inducing reliance on the part of the good-faith purchaser had to be shown.

   ii.   UCC expands doctrine: The *UCC* goes further in protecting the good-faith purchaser against an owner who has entrusted good to a merchant. Under UCC §2-403(2), "*Any entrusting* of possession of goods to a merchant who deals in goods of that kind gives him power to transfer all rights of the entruster to a buyer in ordinary course of business." Thus in contrast to the common-law rule, the mere act of entrusting the goods is sufficient to estop the true owner from recovering them, once they have passed to a good-faith purchaser.

   Example: Consumer leaves his watch with Jeweler for repairs. Jeweler is in the business of not only repairing watches, but of selling used and new watches. Jeweler sells the watch to Purchaser, who pays fair market value, and who has no suspicion that the watch belongs to Consumer. Under UCC §2-403(2), Consumer may not recover from Purchaser!

iii. Rationale: The result in the above example seems harsh, and one may wonder why the UCC expanded the common-law doctrine of estoppel so substantially. One commentator has explained that "the need to expedite sales of inventory by protecting buyers in the ordinary course of business is a widely felt commercial reality, while the risk to original owners such as those who bring watches to a retail jeweler for repair is more theoretical than real." Brown, p. 205.

IV. BAILMENTS

A. **What constitutes a bailment:** A *bailment* can be defined as the *rightful possession* of goods by one who is *not their owner*. Brown, p. 209. The bailee (the person holding the goods), by virtue of his possession, owes a duty of care to the bailor (the owner). This duty, which varies depending on the circumstances, is discussed *infra*, p. 12.

B. **Creation of bailment:** Some cases state that a bailment only arises where the parties make a valid *contract* for it to exist. However, most courts agree that no formal contract is actually necessary; for instance, *consideration* is not a requirement. Brown, p. 210. Nonetheless, there are two requirements which must be met before a bailment arises: (1) the bailee must have actual *physical control* over the object; and (2) he must *intend* to assume custody and control over it. *Id.* at 213-23.

1. **Physical control:** The bailee must come into *actual physical control* of the bailed property.

   a. **Parking lot cases:** The issue of actual control arises frequently in *parking lot cases*. If the parking is done by the parking-lot attendant, and the car owner turns over the key, actual control will almost always be found. But in a *"park-and-lock"* lot, where the car owner parks himself and keeps his own key, most courts have found that the lot never obtains actual control of the car.

      i. **Presence of attendants:** But even in the park-and-lock case, if the lot provides substantial *attendant presence*, and makes implied or express *assurances* that security will be maintained, the court may conclude that control has passed to the lot.

2. **Intent to possess:** The bailee must also have an *intent* to possess the bailed goods, i.e., to assume custody and control over them. The issue usually arises where the person alleged to be a bailee has not expressly consented to assume custody, but has by words or action arguably induced the owner of the item to place it under the former's control.

   a. **Presence of attendant:** Where the owner merely *puts down* a coat or other item in a commercial establishment, and does not entrust it directly to an attendant, the courts have frequently found that no bailment was created.

      i. **Contrary intent:** But by conduct or words, one may impliedly represent to another that objects will be cared for. If so, presence of an attendant, or any other kind of knowledge on the part of the bailee, may not be necessary. For instance, if a store contained a sign saying "coat rack for customers' use," there might be a bailment even if the store's employees never learned that O was actually using the rack.

C. Rights and duties of bailee: The precise duties owed by the bailee depend upon a number of factors, including who is benefitted by the bailment, how the damage to the bailed property arises, and the presence of any contractual limitations.

1. **Duty during custody:**   During the time that the bailee has the object in his possession, he is *not an insurer* of it. He is liable for loss or damage occurring to the object only if he is shown to have exercised some *lack of care*. The precise degree of carelessness which will be required before the bailee is liable, however, traditionally has turned upon *who is benefitted* by the bailment.

    a. **Mutual benefit:**   If the bailment is *mutually beneficial to both parties*, the bailee must use *ordinary diligence* to protect the bailed object from damage or loss. Brown, p. 258.

        i.   **What is "mutual benefit":**   There is usually not much question about whether the bailment is for the bailor's benefit. As to the benefit to the bailee, such benefit of course exists when the bailee makes a *charge* for the bailment itself. But even beyond this, courts have been quick to find benefit to the bailee if the bailment is done as part of *other services* being rendered to the bailor, for which the bailor is paying (e.g., a hotel that stores jewelry for hotel guests).

    b. **Sole benefit of bailor:**   If the benefit is found to be *solely for the bailor's benefit*, the bailee is generally held to be liable *only for gross negligence*. Brown, p. 265.

    c. **Sole benefit of bailee:**   Conversely, if the bailment is *solely for the benefit of the bailee* (i.e., the bailor lends the object to the bailee for the latter's use), the bailee is required to use *extraordinary care* in protecting the goods from loss or damage. *Id.*, at 264-65. (But even in this situation, the bailee is not an insurer, and some degree of fault must be shown before he will be liable.)

2. **Duty to redeliver:**   The discussion above concerns the loss or damage to the goods while they are still in the bailee's possession. A different problem arises when the bailee *turns them over* to a third person, perhaps one who claims to be the true owner. As to misdelivery, most courts hold that the bailee is *strictly liable*. That is, even if he uses reasonable care, but nonetheless delivers the goods to a clever imposter, the bailee is liable to the bailor for the true value of the goods. Brown, pp. 282-83. Similarly, if the bailee simply *keeps the goods*, he will be liable for their full value, under the tort doctrine of conversion.

    a. **Involuntary bailee:**   One exception to the rule of strict liability for misdelivery is applied to cases of *involuntary bailment*. The involuntary bailee is generally liable for misdelivery only if it arises from his *negligence*. *Id.* at 327.

3. **Contractual limitations on liability:**   Bailees, particularly those operating in a commercial context, frequently attempt to modify their duty of care, or the extent of their liability, by *contractual provision*.

    a. **Modification of duty of care:**   Many courts have refused to allow a bailee to contract to *exempt* himself from liability for his own negligence. Brown, p. 273. But other courts, and the Restatement 2d of Contracts § 195, allow such agreements as long as they do not relieve the bailee from liability for "**gross** negligence" or "**willful** and wanton" carelessness. *Id.* at 273.

b. **Limitation of liability:** Virtually all courts allow the parties to place a **contractual limit** on the **extent** of the bailee's financial liability if he does violate the relevant standard of care. However the limitation must be reasonable under the circumstances, and, again, it must not protect the bailee from liability for his willful or gross negligence. *Id.* at 273.

c. **What constitutes a contract:** Both modification of the standard of care and limitation of liability can only be accomplished by a **contract**, which of course requires the mutual assent of bailor and bailee. This means that the bailee cannot accomplish either of these goals merely by **posting a sign** limiting his liability; he must show that the bailor **saw and accepted** the terms of the sign. Brown, p. 270.

   i. **Ticket or claim check:** Frequently, the bailee prints terms limiting his liability on the **claim check**, **receipt** or **ticket** which is given to the bailor. If the bailee can show that the bailor either was, or reasonably should have been, **aware** of the terms on the document, the printed terms will be binding. However, it is generally difficult for the bailee to show actual knowledge on the bailor's part, and most American courts have held that one in the bailor's position might reasonably have regarded the document as a **mere token for identification purposes**, not as a contract. *Id.*, 272-73. In that event, the terms are not binding, and usual principles of liability apply.

V. GIFTS

A. **Definition of gift:** A *gift* is the voluntary transfer of property by one person to another **without any consideration** or compensation.

1. **Present transfer:** A gift is a **present transfer** of property. If the gift is to take effect only in the future, it is a mere **promise** to make a gift, and is unenforceable as a contract because of its lack of consideration. (However as noted *infra*, p. 17, the courts have striven to find a present, rather than future, gift where the situation is ambiguous.)

2. **Inter vivos vs. causa mortis gift:** We do not discuss gifts of property **by will** in this chapter. The gifts that we consider here fall into two categories: (1) gifts "*inter vivos*" and (2) gifts "*causa mortis*". An **inter vivos** gift is an ordinary one in which the donor is not responding to any threat of death. A gift *causa mortis* is one made in contemplation of immediate approaching death. Brown p. 77. Most of the rules governing the two classes of gifts are the same, but where there are differences, these are noted below. The principal difference is that an ordinary gift *inter vivos* is **not revocable** once made (i.e., the donor cannot "take back" the gift, as a matter of law) but the gift *causa mortis* is automatically revoked if the donor escapes from the peril of death which prompted the gift. For more about gifts causa mortis, see *infra*, p. 15.

3. **Requirements:** There are three requirements for the making of a valid gift (whether *inter vivos* or *causa mortis*): (1) there must be a **delivery** from the donor to the donee either of the subject matter of the gift, or of a written instrument embodying the terms of the gift;

(2) the donor must possess an *intent* to make a gift; and (3) the donee must *accept* the gift. Brown, pp. 77-78.

B. Delivery: The essence of the requirement of delivery is that *control* of the subject matter of the gift must pass from the donor to the donee.

1. **Rationale:** The main rationale for the requirement of delivery is that without such a requirement, gifts would be enforceable even if the only evidence showing they had been made was an *oral statement* on the part of the alleged donor. This would leave people open to ill-founded and fraudulent claims of gift. Therefore, courts require delivery as additional proof that a gift was really intended and made. Brown, p. 78.

2. **Delivery through third person:** Suppose the donor puts the property into the hands of a *third person* rather than giving it directly to the donee. If the third person re-transfers the property to the donee, no difficulty of delivery arises. But if this re-delivery from third person to donee does not occur (or occurs only after the donor's death) the transfer to the third person is *not necessarily adequate delivery*.

   a. **Agency test:** The general rule is that transfer to a third person will constitute valid delivery only if the third party is acting as an *independent* agent, or as the agent of the *donee*. If the third party is the *donor's agent*, no delivery has occurred. The rationale for this is that if transfer has merely been made to the donor's agent, the donor has not parted with dominion and control, the basic test for delivery. Brown, p. 87.

3. **Symbolic and constructive delivery:** There are some types of personal property which because of their nature cannot be physically delivered (e.g. certain intangibles, such as the right to collect a debt from another person). There are other types of personal property which, while theoretically capable of manual delivery, would be highly inconvenient to deliver (e.g. heavy furniture.) Yet to dispense with the requirement of delivery altogether in such cases would leave alleged donors open to false claims that a gift had been made. Accordingly, the courts have adopted a middle position in such cases, and permit *"symbolic"* or *"constructive"* delivery. (A delivery is symbolic if, instead of the thing itself, some other object is handed over in its place. A delivery is constructive if the donor delivers the means of obtaining possession and control of the subject matter, rather than making a manual transfer of the subject matter itself. Brown, p. 92.)

   a. **Difficult or impossible to make manual transfer:** Constructive or symbolic delivery will not be allowed unless delivery of the actual subject matter would be *impossible* or *impractical*. *Id.* at 93.

   b. **Dominion must be surrendered:** Also, a symbolic or constructive delivery will not be effective unless the donor has *parted with dominion* and *control* of the property.

   c. **Use of key:** The delivery of a *key* to a locked receptacle will often constitute adequate constructive delivery of the receptacle's contents. Use of the key will be upheld whenever the manual transfer of the contents would be impractical or inconvenient.

   Example: O is paralyzed and confined to his bed. O gives various keys to P (his housekeeper), telling her that everything in the house is hers. The keys unlock several items of heavy furniture, including a bureau in which a life insurance policy on O's life is found.

Held, the delivery of the keys constituted constructive delivery of the items of furniture themselves, since the weight and bulk of these items made actual manual delivery nearly impossible. But the keys did not constitute constructive delivery of the insurance policy, because the policy could have been manually delivered (e.g., by O's telling his nurse to hand the policy to O, who could have then handed it to P). *Newman v. Bost*, 29 S.E. 848 (N.C. 1898).

d. Intangibles: Often the subject matter of a gift is an *intangible*, i.e., a claim of some sort against another person. Since the claim itself cannot be physically transferred, the courts are compelled to recognize constructive or symbolic delivery.

i. Document as embodiment of claim: Some types of intangibles have a *document* so closely associated with them that the document is treated as the *embodiment* of the claim. The business custom is to assign the obligation by transferring the document, and by surrendering the document to the obligor when the obligation has been satisfied. Any *negotiable* instrument falls within this class (e.g., promissory notes, bonds, bills of lading, etc.). Also usually considered within this class are *stock certificates*, insurance policies and savings bank account passbooks (discussed *infra*, p. 18). Therefore, as to all these items, courts hold that *delivery of the document* is sufficient to constitute delivery of the intangible claim represented by it. Brown, pp. 156, 162.

ii. Savings accounts: In some situations, a gift of the contents of a savings account may be made even without delivery of physical possession of the savings passbook to the donee; the issue of bank accounts is discussed further *infra*, p. 18.

4. Written instrument: Virtually all courts hold that delivery to the donee of a *written instrument under seal* stating the particulars of the gift constitutes sufficient delivery.

a. Unsealed instrument: Where a written instrument is given to the donee, but it is *not under seal*, the courts are split. Most courts hold that *even an unsealed instrument* is a *valid substitute for physical delivery* of the subject matter of the gift, assuming the instrument is a clear symbol of the right to possess the subject matter.

Example: O writes to his son, P, that O wishes to give P his valuable Klimt painting, but that O wishes to retain possession of the painting for his lifetime.

Held, this letter (together with other correspondence between O and P) sufficed to meet the delivery requirement, and physical delivery of the painting itself was therefore not required. *Gruen v. Gruen*, 496 N.E.2d 869 (N.Y. 1986), discussed more extensively *infra*, p. 17.

5. Gifts *causa mortis*: Courts are generally hostile to gifts *causa mortis,* i.e., *made in contemplation of the donor's death.* Therefore, they frequently impose *stricter requirements for delivery* in such cases than where the gift is made *inter vivos* with no expectation of death. Brown, pp. 132-33. Courts have been more likely to require *actual physical delivery* in such cases, at least if the property is capable of readily physical delivery.

a. Revocation: One essential feature of a gift that's determined to be *causa mortis* is that if the donor *does not die of the contemplated peril*, the gift may be *revoked*. In fact, most courts hold that the failure of the donor to die from the contemplated peril *automatically* revokes the gift, even if the donor indicates a desire that the gift remain valid.

b. Contemplation of death: The gift *causa mortis*, as noted, is one made in contemplation of death. In any case where the donor *dies shortly after making the gift*, the court will *presume* that the gift is *causa mortis*, unless the donee comes forward with evidence that the donor was *not* acting in contemplation of death. And, as noted, once the court decides the gift is *causa mortis*, the court is likely to impose strict physical-delivery requirements.

     i. Rationale: Why do courts impose stricter delivery requirements for gifts *causa mortis* than other gifts? Because courts worry that if they don't do this, such gifts will interfere with statutes requiring that *wills meet certain formalities* (e.g., attestation) to *reduce fraud*. That is, the fear is that a claimant will falsely say, "He gave me a gift of [item X] just before he died, but he told me I couldn't take possession until after his death." Since oral gifts (unlike oral wills) are valid, if there's no requirement of physical delivery the opportunity for false claims is large.

     ii. Portable: Courts are especially skeptical of the validity of a gift *causa mortis* without physical delivery where the item is *portable* (e.g., a document), so that the donor/decedent could easily have made physical delivery if she had wanted to.

     Example: Test dies intestate. He leaves behind a heavy desk, and a life insurance policy in the desk. Fred, Test's friend, claims that two days before Test died (while Test was gravely ill and knew it), Test said to him, "I'm giving you right now the desk over there, and also the proceeds of the life insurance policy that's in the upper drawer of the desk." Donna, his daughter, is Test's only heir at law. In the ensuing litigation between Fred and Donna about who gets the items, Fred shows only the above facts.

     Donna will probably get the insurance policy, because: (1) the fact that Test died soon after making the alleged gift makes the gift *causa mortis* in the absence of any evidence by Fred showing that it wasn't *causa mortis* (i.e., wasn't intended to be revocable if Test recovered); and (2) where the gift is causa mortis, the court will insist on physical delivery to make the gift effective, as long as physical delivery was feasible (which was the case with the very-portable insurance policy).

     On the other hand, Fred will have a better chance of getting the desk (i.e., convincing the court that Test intended an immediate gift of the desk), since immediate physical delivery of the desk would have been difficult or impossible for Test to make given the desk's large weight.

6. Declaration of trust: One situation in which delivery is not really required is where the owner of the property *declares a trust* for the benefit of another, with *himself as trustee*. While a discussion of the law of trusts is beyond the scope of this outline, a few principles may be stated:

     a. Unless statute so requires, the declaration of trust does *not* have to be in *writing* (Brown, p. 147).

b. Proof that the trust was indeed created must be "complete, certain, and unequivocal." *Id.*

c. In most courts, the declaration of trust is valid even though the settlor (the owner of the property) has ***reserved the power to revoke***. *Id.* at 149.

d. If the owner attempts to make an ordinary gift by delivery, and fails, the court will not sustain it as a trust. *Id.* at 149.

C. Donor's intent to give: In addition to a delivery, there must be an *intent* on the part of the donor to make a gift. Obviously, if *A* hands *B* *A*'s diamond ring and says "Take care of this for me until I ask for it back," there has been no gift even though there has been a delivery.

1. Intent to make present gift: Furthermore, the intent must be to make a ***present*** transfer, not one to take effect in the future. (As noted *supra*, p. 13, a promise to make a future gift is not enforceable because of lack of consideration.)

2. Present gift of future enjoyment: However, courts generally go out of their way to find that there has been a present gift of the ***right*** to the subject matter, with only the ***enjoyment*** postponed to a later date. In the case of personal property (as with real property; see *infra*, p. 69), there may be a present transfer of title, with the right of enjoyment postponed until a future date.

a. Gift subject to life estate: For instance, most courts hold that a donor may make a valid gift of a ***future interest*** in personal property, subject to the donor's ***life estate***. In this situation, even though the donor does not immediately deliver the subject matter of the gift to the donee, the intent to make a present gift will usually be found to have been satisfied.

Example: In 1963, O writes a letter to his son, P, saying that O is giving P his valuable Gustav Klimt painting for P's birthday. The letter says, however, that O wishes to retain possession of the painting for O's lifetime. A subsequent letter by O to P similarly refers to O's intent to make a present gift of the painting to P, subject to O's right to lifetime possession. The painting remains in O's possession until his death in 1980, at which time D, P's stepmother, refuses to turn the painting over to P. D contends that: (1) O never intended to make an ownership transfer in 1963, but only expressed the intent that P would get the painting on O's death; and (2) if physical delivery of the subject of the gift is possible, such delivery (rather than delivery of a written instrument) must take place for the gift to be valid.

Held, for P. As to argument (1), it is true that the donor must intend a present gift (not a future gift), but here there was clear evidence of O's intent to make a present transfer of a remainder interest in the painting (subject to O's life interest). As to argument (2), the very purpose of the remainder-subject-to-a-life-interest structure used by O was to permit O to keep possession of the painting during his lifetime, so it would be illogical (and therefore not required) for O to deliver the painting to P; therefore, a written instrument was enough to meet the delivery requirement. *Gruen v. Gruen*, 496 N.E.2d 869 (N.Y. 1986).

D. Acceptance: Courts usually hold that the giving of a gift is a *bilateral* transaction requiring an *acceptance* of the gift on the part of the donee. Brown, p. 127. However, at least if the gift is a beneficial one, the court will *presume* that the donee intended to accept.

1. Donee unaware: The issue usually arises where the donor gives the property to a *third person* to be held until it is given to the donee; if the donor dies before the donee ever learns of the gift, it can be argued that the gift was invalid for lack of acceptance (since the gift could obviously not have been made after the donor died.) However, the courts have usually held that the gift took effect *immediately* upon its execution by the donor, subject to the donee's right to repudiate it subsequently. So long as no repudiation occurs after the donor's death, the gift is valid. *Id*, at 128.

E. Special problems of bank accounts: A common and troublesome class of gifts is that involving *bank accounts*, particularly savings accounts. Where the depositor of funds wishes to give another person either present or future rights in the funds, he may set up the account in any of four basic ways:

[1] by opening the account in the *other person's name* (e.g., A deposits the funds in an account bearing *B*'s name);

[2] by acting as *trustee* for the other person (e.g., A deposits funds in an account bearing the designation "*A* in trust for *B*" — this is the so-called *"Totten Trust"*);

[3] by having the account *jointly* in his own name and that of the other, subject to withdrawal by either (e.g., A deposits funds in an account denominated "*A* and *B* jointly, with right of survivorship" — this is the usual form for a joint savings or checking account); and

[4] by depositing in his own name, but with a clause stating *"payable on death"* to the other person — this is the so-called "P.O.D. account."

The comments below apply to *each* of these types of two-party accounts, unless otherwise noted.

1. Right of survivor: Most litigation arises when the depositor *dies* before the other person. In most states, so-called "bank protection" statutes exist which permit the bank to pay over the funds to the survivor; the bank is assured by the statute that it will not be liable to the decedent's estate if it does so. However, the existence of such a statute does not necessarily establish, as between the decedent's estate and the survivor, who is entitled to the money.

a. Right of withdrawal: The person depositing the funds frequently maintains (either as a practical or legal matter) the right to control and *withdraw* the funds during his lifetime.

i. Modern view: Modern cases tend to hold that the depositor's right to withdraw or control the funds during his lifetime does *not* prevent a valid gift from arising as to the balance remaining at the depositor's death. In fact, the so-called *"Totten Trust"* (A deposits in a account denominated "*A* in trust for *B*") derives its name from the case of *In re Totten*, 71 N.E. 748 (N.Y. 1904), holding that the depositor's right to withdraw the funds and thereby revoke the arrangement does not invalidate the gift of the balance remaining at death. Modern courts usually agree with the result in *In re Totten*, sometimes on the grounds that such "in trust" accounts serve as *"the poor man's will."*

b. **Donative intent required:** Even if the jurisdiction is one which recognizes the survivorship features of the various types of two-party accounts, the survivor in a particular case is not *necessarily* entitled to the balance. Rather, he is entitled to the balance only where a *donative intent* on the part of the depositor existed.

For more about joint bank accounts, see *infra*, p. 139.

c. **Revocation by will:** As long as the depositor held the exclusive right to control and withdraw the funds during his lifetime, the courts uniformly hold that *no gift occurs until the moment of death.* At that point, if the will gives the contents to a third person, that bequest is effective (i.e., the still-living co-account-holder takes nothing).

2. **Rights of parties *inter vivos*:** Disputes between two parties to a bank account may also arise while *both* are still *alive*.

a. **Totten and P.O.D. accounts:** In the case of a Totten trust or P.O.D. account, the courts generally *presume* that during the depositor's lifetime, he has the right to withdraw all funds. (However, a contrary showing may be made, at least in the case of the Totten Trust, by the beneficiary, to the effect that an immediate gift was intended by the depositor.)

b. **Joint account:** Similarly, in the case of a *joint account*, most courts presume that during the lifetime of the parties, the contents belong to the parties *in proportion to the net contributions of each*, unless there is clear and convincing evidence of a different intent. For more about this, see *infra*, p. 139.

Quiz Yourself on
PERSONAL PROPERTY

1. Oscar was the owner of a very valuable painting, "Rosewood." In 1980, Rosewood was stolen from Oscar's home. Oscar reported the theft to the police, collected insurance proceeds, and made no further efforts to locate the painting. (For example, he did not report the theft to a national information bank that lists stolen paintings, nor did he notify local art dealers.) In 1983, unbeknownst to Oscar, Anita, an art collector, "bought" Rosewood from a private gallery for $10,000. (This price was approximately the fair market value of the painting at the time, on the assumption that there was clear title.) The galley showed Anita documents indicating that the gallery had the right to sell the painting, and Anita had no reason to believe the painting to be stolen.

Anita proudly displayed the painting at her house for the next 25 years. Even though Anita and Oscar lived in the same town, Oscar did not learn of Anita's possession of the painting until 2012, when a friend happened to mention it to him. The local statute of limitations on actions to recover personal property is 10 years. Assuming that the state follows the "modern" rule regarding when the statute of limitations on stolen personal property begins to run, if Oscar sues Anita in 2012, may he recover the painting from her?

---

2. Olivia's 2005 Suburu was stolen one day while parked on the street in front of her house. Six months later,

Arnold purchased from Dealer a used 2005 Suburu to which Dealer appeared to have good title. Arnold paid the full fair market value for the car. In fact, the car was the one which had been stolen from Olivia, though there was no way Arnold could reasonably have known that the car was stolen property. Through a random check of Vehicle Identification Numbers by local police, the police discovered that the car being driven by Arnold was stolen property, and so notified Olivia. Olivia has now sued Arnold in 2009 for return of the car. Arnold defends on the grounds that he is a bona fide purchaser for fair value. Assume that there are no relevant statutes. May Olivia recover the car? _____

3. In 1990, Sidney, a wealthy industrialist, said to his son Norman, "I am hereby giving you my valuable Monet painting, 'Ballerinas.' " Sidney did not, however, at any time give Norman possession of the painting, nor did he give him any document indicating any transfer. The painting continued to hang on Sidney's wall for the next 20 years. In 2010, Sidney died. His will bequeathed all of his personal property to his daughter, Denise. Who owns the painting, Norman or Denise? _____

4. Albert, an elderly widower, placed $100,000 in a bank savings account bearing the designation, "Albert in trust for Bertha." Bertha was Albert's girlfriend. During the next two years, Albert made no withdrawals, nor did Bertha. Albert then died, leaving all of his personal property by will to his son Steven. Steven and Bertha each now claim the proceeds of the bank account. Neither produces any evidence of Albert's intent in creating the bank account. What part, if any, of the proceeds should be awarded to Bertha? _____

Answers

1. **No.** To begin with, anyone whose chain of title includes a thief cannot prevail over the "true" owner. But the true owner's right to recover the property can become time-barred. The modern rule on the running of the statute of limitations is sometimes called the *"discovery"* rule; by that rule, the statute of limitations on an action to recover stolen property normally does not begin to run against the record owner until the owner knows, or should know, the identity of the possessor. But the rule assumes that the owner has made prompt **reasonable efforts** to find the possessor or to put the world on notice of the stolen property. Here, Oscar did not do this; for instance, he failed to list the painting in the information bank, a step that a reasonably diligent owner would normally take. Therefore, a court will probably hold that the statute began to run against him immediately. In that event, Anita became the owner by adverse possession in 1990.

2. **Yes.** As a general rule, *a seller cannot convey better title than that which he holds*. This is true of the unknown thief. Therefore, Dealer never got good title (regardless of whether he thought he did), and could not in turn give good title to Arnold. Consequently, even though Arnold paid full value and was completely innocent, he will lose the car. (Statutes in most states set up a certificate of title program, which would have protected Arnold in this situation.)

3. **Denise.** There are three requirements for the making of a valid gift: (1) delivery; (2) intent to make a gift; and (3) acceptance by the donee. Here, the delivery requirement was not satisfied, since Sidney did not give Norman either physical possession of the painting or possession of any symbolic or written instrument representing the gift.

4. **All, probably.** The account here is a "Totten Trust" (the name commonly used to describe an account of the form "A in trust for B"). Most courts, and the Uniform Probate Code, hold that where the trustee of a Totten Trust (here, Albert) dies before the beneficiary (here, Bertha), the beneficiary is *presumed* to be entitled to all funds left in the account. This presumption is rebuttable by a showing that the trustee intended a different result, but there is no such evidence here.

VI. INTELLECTUAL AND OTHER INTANGIBLE PROPERTY

A. Property in ideas and expressions: Real property and personal property are both "tangible" types of property — you can see them and touch them. But various forms of *in*tangible property are becoming ever more important to our economy and our legal system. In particular, so-called *"intellectual property law"* — the regulation of products of intellectual work — forms a major area of law with which every lawyer needs at least some familiarity. Here, we provide an extremely superficial overview of intellectual property law, really just a roadmap to the subject. You will likely take one or more upper-year courses dedicated to this area.

    1. Three core types of IP: There are three core types of intellectual property ("IP"): *copyrights, patents* and *trademarks*. Copyrights and patents are almost exclusively the product of federal statutory law. Trademarks are a mixture of federal and state law. After our treatment of these three core types of IP, we briefly consider "publicity rights," which are almost solely a creature of state law.

    2. Conflicts: All four of these domains pose a similar type of quandary for the legal system: what is the optimal degree of "ownership" to be given to the creator of the idea? If *too little* ownership is given, people will *not have adequate incentives to invest time and money* in creating and exploiting the idea. But if *too much* private property is created in ideas, this would *"limit our autonomy* and block desirable economic activity by creating *insuperable transaction costs."* Singer, § 4.1.

B. Copyrights: *Copyright* law is regulated by a federal statute, the Copyright Act, that essentially preempts state law. The Act, 17 U.S.C. § 101 et seq, protects the *expression of ideas*, whether embodied in books, articles, musical forms, works of painting and sculpture, motion pictures, or the like.

    1. Rights given to copyright holder: The Copyright Act gives certain rights to owners of *"original works of authorship"* that are *"fixed in any tangible medium of expression."* A partial list of the copyright owner's exclusive rights includes:

        [1] the right to *reproduce* the copyrighted work (e.g., to print books or make sound recordings).

        [2] the right to prepare *"derivative works"* based on the copyrighted work (i.e., to create works that start from the original work and vary it; thus the owner of the copyright to *Gone With the Wind* has the right to create a sequel using the same characters).

        [3] the right to *sell, rent or lease copies* of the copyrighted work to the public.

        [4] the right to *perform* the copyrighted work publicly (in the case of literary, musical, dramatic, motion-picture, and other types of work that are capable of performance).

        [5] the right to *display* the copyrighted work publicly (e.g., the right to display a painting or sculpture, or a motion picture).

    See 17 U.S.C. § 106.

2. **Material must be "original" but not necessarily "novel":** To be protected by copyright, the material must be "*original*" in the sense that it was created by the author rather than copied from someone else. But the material does not have to be "*novel*," in the sense that it never existed before. (That makes copyright law quite different from patent law, where only novel inventions may be patented.)

   Example: As the Supreme Court put it in a leading case, "originality does not signify novelty; a work may be original even though it closely resembles other works so long as the similarity is *fortuitous*, not the result of *copying*. To illustrate, assume that two poets, each ignorant of the other, compose identical poems. Neither work is novel, yet both are original and, hence, copyrightable." *Feist Publications, Inc. v. Rural Telephone Service Co.*, 499 U.S. 340 (1991). See also DKA&S, p. 65.

3. **Ideas and facts not copyrightable:** *Ideas* and *facts* narrated by an author are *not* protected by copyright — only original *"expressions"* of ideas or facts can be protected. Singer, § 4.4.1.

   a. **Compilations:** On the other hand, *compilations* of facts are protected, but only if the compilation represents some *"minimal degree of creativity." Feist, supra.* Typically, for a compilation of uncopyrightable facts to possess the minimum required creative element, the author must *select, coordinate or arrange the facts* in a somewhat *original* way. *Id.*

   Example: Rural Co. (P) is a local telephone company that serves a small rural population. It prints a telephone directory listing every individual subscriber by name and phone number, arranged alphabetically by last name. Feist (D) is a publishing company that specializes in publishing phone directories for areas bigger than the small area covered by P's directory. D takes 1,309 subscriber listings from P's directory and exactly reproduces the listings in D's directory, mixed in with subscriber names licensed from other local phone companies. P asserts that D has violated P's copyright in its compilation of subscriber names.

   Held, for D. Facts are not copyrightable, because they don't meet the requirement of "originality" — facts don't owe their origin to an act of authorship, which is what the Copyright Act requires. But *compilations* of facts *can* be sufficiently original, if the selection and arrangement of the included facts entails a "minimal degree of creativity." However, *mere "sweat of the brow"* — i.e., *hard work* in compiling the facts — does *not* meet the originality requirement; only the selection, coordination and arrangement of facts in an original way can do that. Here, P merely took the data provided by its subscribers and listed it alphabetically by surname. Such a listing "is not only unoriginal, it is practically inevitable." Since P's white pages lacked the required originality, D's use of the listings cannot constitute copyright infringement. *Feist Publications, supra.*

4. **When copyright protection begins:** Copyright protection in a work begins as *soon as the work is created* in a tangible medium (e.g., writing on a page). That's true *whether or not there is a copyright notice* on the work.

   Example: Author writes an unpublished novel, with no copyright notice on it. He then puts the typed manuscript in his drawer. The manuscript is protected under copyright laws from the first moment it existed on paper. If a thief sneaks in and makes a copy, the thief has violated Author's copyright.

5. **Registration:** The Copyright Act provides a mechanism for *registering* copyrights. The owner deposits material (including a copy of the work) with the federal Copyright Office. The Office reviews the material, and decides whether to issue a registration certificate. Registration is not required in order to gain copyright protection (just as putting a copyright notice on the work is not required). However, at least if the work originated in the United States, the owner *cannot bring a copyright infringement action* without first registering. 17 U.S.C. § 411. See generally RKK&A, p. 1302

6. **Duration of protection:** The *duration* of copyright protection depends on what type of person owns the copyright.

   a. **Owned by author:** Normally, the human *"author"* of the work owns the copyright. In that case, the copyright lasts for the *life of the author plus 70 years*, after which the work enters the public domain and may be used by anyone.

   b. **Works for hire:** But the Copyright Act recognizes the special category of a *"work for hire."* A work is a "work for hire" if either: (1) the work was prepared by an *employee* within the scope of his or her employment;[1] or (2) in certain circumstances (e.g., collective works and movies), the work was specially ordered or commissioned. 17 U.S.C. § 101. In either case, where the work is for hire, the *"author"* is normally deemed to be the *employer or commissioning person*, *not* the person doing the act of creation.

      i. **Different duration:** If the work is a work for hire, the copyright lasts for *95 years from the year of its first publication*, or *120 years from the year of its creation*, whichever comes *first*. So normally, the work for hire will enter the public domain 95 years after its first publication.

7. **Fair use:** Even if the defendant' work is shown to have been copied from, and is substantially similar to, the plaintiff's copyrighted work, the defendant has an important affirmative defense: *fair use*. The Copyright Act says that "the fair use of a copyrighted work ... for purposes such as *criticism, comment, news reporting, teaching ... scholarship* or *research*, is *not an infringement of copyright*." 17 U.S.C. § 107.

   a. **Multi-factor test:** The Copyright Act lists *four factors* that the court is to consider in determining whether the use qualifies for the fair use exemption:

      "(1) the *purpose and character* of the use, including whether such use is of a *commercial nature* or is for nonprofit *educational* purposes;

      (2) the *nature* of the copyrighted work;

      (3) the *amount and substantiality of the portion used* in relation to the copyrighted work

---

1. Whether someone is an "employee" is determined by a multi-factor test drawn from common-law principles. An "employee" is distinguished from an "independent contractor." The label used by the employer is not dispositive. One important factor is the employer's degree of *control* over the details of how, when and where the work is to be created: the greater the degree of control, the more likely the author is to be found to be an employee rather than independent contractor.

as a whole; and

(4) the effect of the use upon the ***potential market for or value of*** the copyrighted work."

17 U.S.C. § 107.

b. Use as parody: One type of use that is often found to constitute fair use is ***parody***. The original copyrighted use usually cannot be parodied successfully without taking a substantial portion of the original (which under factor (3) above militates against a finding of fair use). But in parody cases, the fact that the parody usually does not materially ***decrease the market for or value of*** the original copyrighted work weighs heavily towards a finding that the use is fair.

Example: Alice Randall writes a fictional work called *The Wind Done Gone* ("TWDG"), a parody of *Gone With the Wind* ("GWTW"). P (the trustee for the Mitchell Trust that owns the copyright to GWTW) sues D (the prospective publisher of TWDG) for an injunction against publication, alleging that TWDG violates the copyright on GWTW. P shows that TWDG uses many characters from the original novel, as well as many plot points. D raises a fair use defense, arguing (accurately) that Randall's novel is a critique of GWTW's depiction of slavery and the civil-war era American South, by "flip[ping] GWTW's traditional race roles, portray[ing] powerful whites as stupid or feckless, and generally set[ting] out to demystify GWTW and strip the romanticism from Mitchell's [story]."

Held, for D. Based on the preliminary record at this point, D is likely to qualify for the fair use defense. The fact that substantial elements of GWTW have been incorporated in D's parody will not disqualify the work from the fair use defense, as long as the allegedly infringing work's "overriding purpose and character is to parody the original [rather than] serv[ing] as a market substitute for the original." Here, the evidence is that TWDG is essentially a parody, and is unlikely to displace many sales of GWTW or of licensed derivative works made from GWTW. *Suntrust Bank v. Houghton Mifflin Co.*, 268 F.3d 1257 (11th Cir. 2001).

8. Contributory infringement: The Copyright Act itself does not expressly provide for liability for ***"contributory infringement."*** But under general common-law principles, one who ***intentionally induces or encourages another to infringe*** a copyright can be civilly liable for contributory infringement. In a number of cases, book publishers, movie studios and record studios have brought contributory-infringement suits against makers of ***hardware and software*** that can be and is used to ***copy*** copyrighted works.

a. Results mixed: The copyright owners have had mixed success with these contributory-infrinement suits. Here is a brief summary of the two major rulings by the U.S. Supreme Court in the contributory-infringement area:

[1]**Capable of non-infringing uses:** The fact that the product made by the defendant *can* be used (and often *is* used) by end-users to infringe the plaintiff's works is ***not sufficient*** to make the defendant liable for contributory infringement, as long as the defendant ***does not overtly promote*** infringing use, and the product is capable of ***substantial non-infringing*** uses.

Thus in *Sony Corp. v. Universal City Studios*, 464 U.S. 417 (1984), Sony, the maker of a video cassette recorder (VCR), was found not liable for contributory copyright infringement, because the product was capable of (and used for) substantial non-infringing uses like time-shifting. The fact that the product was also used for substantial infringing uses didn't matter, since Sony hadn't encouraged those uses.

[2]Purpose of promoting infringement: On the other hand, someone who distributes a device with the clear *purpose* of *promoting its use* to infringe copyright *will* be contributorily liable for the resulting infringement by end-users.

Thus in *Metro-Goldwyn-Mayer Studios Inc. v. Grokster, Ltd.*, 545 U.S. 913 (2005), the defendants were two software companies that made and distributed free software that allowed users to share files over peer-to-peer networks. The vast majority of filesharing acts by users were acts of infringement. Furthermore, each of the defendants had actively encouraged infringement (e.g., they each advertised themselves as the "best alternative to Napster," a copyright-infringing Internet service that had previously been put out of business). Therefore, the Supreme Court said, the defendants were liable for contributory infringement, even though some of the uses to which the software was put were non-infringing.

C. Patents: The U.S. *patent* system is so complex and specialized that we cannot really even summarize it here. Here are a few of the most superficial points about patent law:

1. **Inventions:** Patent law protects, in essence, *inventions and discoveries*. In the language of the Patent Act, what is protected are inventions and discoveries of *"processes,"* *"machines,"* *"manufactures"* and *"compositions of matter."* 35 U.S.C. § 101.

2. **Novel, useful and nonobvious:** To be patentable, an invention must be: (1) *novel*; (2) *nonobvious*; and (3) *useful*.

   a. **Novelty:** The requirement of *novelty* means, in essence, that the invention must be *"new,"* i.e., *not previously invented or discovered* anywhere. Patent law is different from copyright law in this respect. In copyright law, if two people independently create substantially the same work, both have copyrights in what they did. But under U.S. patent law, only the first to invent or discover the process, machine, etc., can receive a patent. 35 U.S.C. § 102.[2]

   b. **Nonobviousness:** The requirement of *nonobviousness* means essentially what it says. As the statute puts it, the invention is not patentable "if the differences between the subject matter sought to be patented and the *prior art* are such that the *subject matter as a whole would have been obvious* at the time the invention was made to a *person*

---

2. But the U.S. is in the process of *changing* from a "first-to-invent" system to a *"first-to-file"* system. Under an amendment to the Patent Act signed into law in late 2011, starting in 2013 the first person to file a patent application for an invention, regardless of the date of invention, gets the patent. This will bring the U.S. into conformity with the patent systems of most of the world. It will remain the case, however, that only one applicant can receive the patent for any given invention.

having ordinary skill in the art to which said subject matter pertains." 35 U.S.C. § 103.

    c. **Usefulness:** The requirement of *usefulness* is embedded in the definition of what is patentable: any "new and useful" process, machine or composition of matter. 35 U.S.C. § 101. The statute does not define "useful," and the term is not often the subject of litigation. But an invention that could never "work" (e.g., a perpetual-motion machine) would not be deemed useful.

  3. **Application process:** The inventor applies to the U.S. Patent and Trademark Office for a patent. The application must follow a prescribed format, including a written description of the invention and a set of "claims." 35 U.S.C. §§ 112, 192.

    a. **"Claims":** The *"claims"* in the application describe in detail the *scope of protection* that the applicant is seeking, i.e., the aspects that make the invention novel and non-obvious. (*Example of a claim:* "A mousetrap mechanism ... comprising a spring-based striking element comprising a striker bar and a cocking bar, the cocking bar projecting at an angle with respect to the striker bar ...").

    b. **Search of prior art:** A Patent Examiner conducts a search of prior art to determine whether the requirements of novelty, nonobviousness, etc., are satisfied. Often, the Examiner requires that the claims be narrowed, or their number reduced, to account for prior art.

  4. **Duration:** Once the patent is granted, the patent term is **20 years** from the earliest *filing date* of the patent application. 35 U.S.C. § 154.

D. **Trademarks:** A *trademark*, in the broad sense of the term, is a name, symbol, type of packaging or other means of *identifying the producer of a good or service.* Singer, § 4.3. Trademarks are protected under both federal and state law. We concentrate here on federal protection. The federal statute protecting trademarks is called the *Lanham Act*, 15 U.S.C. §§ 1051-1127.

  1. **Definition of "trademark":** Under the Lanham Act, a "trademark" applies only to goods (not services). A trademark can consist of "any *word, name, symbol,* or device, or any combination thereof," when used to *"identify and distinguish"* a person's goods from those produced by others, and to "indicate the *source*" of the goods. 15 U.S.C. § 1127.

    a. **"Service mark":** A *"service mark,"* under the Lanham Act, is the same as a trademark, except that it is used to identify a service rather than a good. *Id.*[3]

  2. **Function:** Trademark law gives the owner of a "mark" the *exclusive* right to *use that mark* in connection with the sale of a particular good or service in a particular *geographic area.* Singer, § 4.3. The main purpose of trademark law is to protect *consumers* from being *confused* by the fact that two companies are using the same or similar names for their products.

    Example: In recent years, Jordache has been using the trademark "Jordache Basics 101" to describe jeans that it manufactures and sells. Levi Strauss has long held the

---

3. We'll use the term "trademark" here in a broad sense, to refer to both "trademarks" on goods and "service marks" on services.

federal trademark for "501" as a trademark for jeans it makes and sells. Jordache sues Levi for a declaratory judgment that "Jordache Basics 101" is not likely to cause the public to be confused between those jeans and the "501" jeans made by Levi. *Held,* Levi has made an initial showing that there is enough likelihood of consumer confusion that the case must go to trial. *Jordache Enterprises, Inc. v. Levi Strauss & Co.,* 841 F.Supp. 506 (S.D.N.Y. 1993).

a. **Suit by owner of mark:** Although protection of consumers against confusion is the principal purpose of the trademark laws, consumers do not have standing to bring trademark enforcement actions. Instead, the owner of a trademark has the right to sue infringers, i.e., people who are either selling goods that contain a *counterfeit* of the owner's trademark or are marketing goods under a *confusingly-similar name.* So, for instance, on the facts of *Jordache, supra,* instead of a suit for declaratory judgment of non-infringement brought by Jordache, the litigation could have consisted of an action by Levi Strauss to establish that Jordache was violating Levi Strauss's trademark by selling goods with a confusingly similar name, and to *enjoin* Jordache from continuing to do so.

3. **Federal and state law:** Much of federal trademark law derives from state law prohibiting a merchant from *"passing off"* or "palming off" her own goods as having been made by someone else. It is very common for plaintiffs (owners of marks) to join a federal Lanham Act infringement claim together with a claim for violation of state trademark laws. Unlike suits for patent and copyright infringement (over which the federal courts have *exclusive* jurisdiction), a suit for federal Lanham Act violations may be brought in *either* state or federal court.

4. **Trademark Register:** An important aspect of the federal trademark-regulation scheme is that federal law gives the owner of a trademark a way to *put the world on notice* that it is the owner and is claiming the mark for a particular use. The U.S. Patent and Trademark Office (PTO) maintains two *registers* that list trademarks, the more important of which is the "Principal Register." A mark that appears on the Principal Register is known as a "registered trademark" (indicated by the "®" symbol). A newcomer can then consult these registers to avoid using a mark that is already taken. RKK&A, p. 1264. Having a registered trademark not only allows the owner to put the world on constructive notice of the mark, but entitles her to get an *injunction* against anyone else who adopts the same or a confusingly-similar mark. 15 U.S.C. §§ 1116, 1117.

a. **Procedure for registration:** A merchant who would like to register her mark submits an application to the PTO. The mark is reviewed by an examiner. If the mark appears to satisfy requirements for a registered trademark, the PTO publishes the mark in its Official Gazette. Anyone who believes he would be injured by registration of the mark (e.g., someone who already has a registered mark that is similar) has 30 days to oppose the registration. RRK&A, p. 1264. If there is no opposition, what happens next depends on whether the mark is already being used.

i. **Requirement that mark be used or intended to be used:** The applicant must say, in her application, *either:*

[1] that she is *already using* the mark in interstate commerce, or

[2] that she has a bona fide *intent to use the mark* in commerce in the future.

(1) Already in use: If the mark is *already* in use (an *"actual use"* application), the PTO issues a *certificate of registration*, and registers the mark on the Principal Register. The owner is then immediately entitled to use the "®" symbol in connection with the mark, and to enjoin others from using the mark.

(2) Intent to use: But if the applicant merely *intends* to use the mark in the future (an *"intent to use"* application), the PTO issues a "Notice of Allowance." Then, the applicant must begin to use the mark in interstate commerce, and must file a verified statement that this has occurred. The applicant has at most 36 months from the issuance of the Notice of Allowance to file this statement of actual use. Only after the filing of this statement will the PTO issue the certificate of registration and place the mark on the Principal Register. RRK&A, p. 1264.

5. **"Distinctive" vs. "generic" marks:** A mark must be *"distinctive"* in order to be registrable. That is, the mark must tend to *identify the precise source* of the goods or services. Therefore, designations that are merely *"generic"* — i.e., that are common names for the products or services in question — may not be registered.

> **Example:** A maker of candies would not be permitted to register "Candy" as a trademark for the candies — the term "candy" is a generic term used to describe the whole category, so it must be kept available for other manufacturers to refer to their products without infringement.

a. **Descriptive terms:** Similarly, terms that are *"descriptive"* of the type of goods or services in question generally may not be trademarked. For instance, *geographical* words or phrases that merely indicate the place of origin of the product or service generally cannot be trademarked.

> **Example:** An importer of feta cheese from Greece would not be allowed to trademark the term "Greek Feta," because a consumer encountering the mark would likely assume that it merely described the origin of the goods.

b. **Secondary meaning:** Even if a mark is not *inherently* distinctive, it may *become distinctive* through the way it is *used in the marketplace*. In that event, the mark is said to have developed *"secondary meaning."* To say a mark has developed secondary meaning is to say that in the mind of the consuming public, the primary significance of the mark is now to indicate the precise source of the product, rather than to describe the product.

> **Example:** Initially, the mark "Kool," used on cigarettes, would likely have been unregistrable, on the grounds that it was merely descriptive of the "cool," mentholated, taste of a category of cigarettes. But over the years, a particular cigarette company, R.J. Reynolds, has, through its advertising, conditioned the public to regard "Kool" cigarettes as mainly referring to a particular brand of mentholated cigarette made by Reynolds. Therefore, the mark "Kool" has developed a secondary meaning, and has become registrable. After registration, Reynolds can now prevent anyone else from selling cigarettes under the "Kool" mark.

6. **Anti-cybersquatting statute:**　An important modern use of trademarks is the right to use one's mark in e-commerce, including on websites. This has raised the problem of *"cybersquatting,"* in which a person uses another's trademark, typically as part of a website's name, and then in effect holds the domain registration for that name hostage so that it can be sold at a profit to the trademark owner. Congress dealt with this problem by passing, in 1999, the *Anticybersquatting Consumer Protection Act (ACPA)*, 15 U.S.C. § 1125(d).

   a. **What the Act does:** The ACPA prohibits registering or using an Internet domain name that is identical to or confusingly similar to a trademark, if the person "has a *bad faith intent to profit from that mark.*" If the Act is violated, the court can impose civil liability, and can also order the domain name to be *transferred* to the owner of the mark.

      Example: The Ds (two individuals) own a company called Virtual Works. They register the domain name *www.vw.net*. Evidence shows that at the time of registration, (1) the Ds were aware that the public might associate the "vw" in the domain name with Volkswagen (P), and (2) the Ds hoped to profit by selling the domain name back to P.

      Held, for P. The Ds acted with a bad-faith intent to profit from a protected mark, and thus violated the ACPA. Therefore, they are ordered to transfer the domain name to P. *Virtual Works, Inc. v. Wolkswagen of America, Inc.*, 238 F.3d 264 (4th Cir. 2001).

   b. **"Gripe" websites:**　Suppose that someone uses another's trademark in a domain name not in order to profit by confusing potential customers, but instead to *complain* about the mark owner's behavior. These are often called *"gripe"* websites. Typically, the domain name combines a trademark with derogatory words like "sucks" or "iHate" or "fraud."

      i. **Use is protected:** Usually, courts have found that as long as the gripe website is used for criticism rather than for commercial profit, the domain name is *protected by the First Amendment* and does *not* violate the ACPA. See, e.g., *Taubman Co. v. Webfeats*, 319 F.3d 770 (6th Cir. 2003) (*www.taubmansucks.com* does not violate the ACPA rights of mall operator Taubman Co., because D is "free to shout 'Taubman Sucks' from the rooftops [and] essentially that is what he has done in his domain name.")

E. **The right of "publicity":**　Most states today recognize, either by common law or statute, a *"right of publicity."* In those states recognizing the right, in theory every individual, famous or not, possesses the right. But as a practical matter, the right is only of economic value to *celebrities*.

   1. **Right to exclusive use of name and likeness:**　The right of publicity is usually defined as a person's right to the *exclusive use of her name and likeness.* In its most basic form, the right entitles a celebrity to prevent others from using the celebrity's name or photograph for *commercial purposes*, including the advertising of products.

   2. **Right during lifetime:** Where the right is recognized, it always extends throughout the *lifetime* of the celebrity.

3. Right after death: In most states that recognize the right of publicity, the right *persists after the celebrity's death*, generally for a period *between 20 and 100 years*. DKA&S, p. 70. The right is usually held to *descend by will or by intestacy. Id.*

> **Example:** After Dr. Martin Luther King's death, D manufactures and sells a plastic bust of Dr. King. The Ps are Dr. King's heirs. The Ps sue D in federal court, contending that Dr. King had a common-law right of publicity under Georgia law, that that right passed to them at his death, and that D's sales of the bust infringe this right. The federal court certifies to the Georgia Supreme Court several questions concerning the right of publicity under Georgia law.
>
> *Held* (by the Georgia Supreme Court), all the certified questions are answered in favor of the Ps. Both public and private figures have a common-law right under Georgia law not to have their names and photographs used for the financial gain of the user without their consent. Furthermore, "we hold that [this] right of publicity survives the death of its owner and is inheritable and devisable." Lastly, the right of publicity need not have been exploited during the person's lifetime in order for it to pass by will or intestacy at his death. *Martin Luther King, Jr. Center for Social Change v. American Heritage Products*, 296 S.E.2d 697 (Ga. 1982).

a. Evoking a celebrity: Suppose all the defendant has done is to *"evoke"* the identity of a *celebrity*. Should the defendant be liable for the tort of misappropriation of identity, in those states where the tort is recognized? Several courts have answered *"yes"* — even though the celebrity's name or "likeness" is not used, if advertising causes the reader to think that the celebrity is being *referred to* for the advertiser's financial benefit, that's enough to constitute common-law appropriation.

> **Example:** D, a manufacturer of VCRs, runs an ad depicting a robot, dressed in a wig, gown and jewelry, which D has consciously selected to resemble the hair and clothing of P (TV personality Vanna White). The robot is posed next to a game board, which is recognizable as the *Wheel of Fortune* game show set. D refers to this ad internally as the "Vanna White ad." P does not consent to the ad, nor is she paid. She sues for, among other things, violation of her common-law right of publicity.
>
> *Held*, for P. D has violated P's common-law right of publicity, by appropriating P's "identity." It does not matter that D has not appropriated P's name or "likeness." The right of publicity will be deemed to have been violated whenever a person's *"celebrity value"* is *exploited* by the defendant, regardless of the means by which this is done.
>
> But a dissent argues that the majority's opinion is a "classic case of overprotection," and that courts should not make it tortious to simply "remind the public of a celebrity" or to simply "evoke the celebrity's image in the public's mind." The majority's decision "impoverishes the public domain." Furthermore, giving P the power to keep others from invoking her image in the public's mind cannot be squared with the First Amendment. "Where does White get this right to control our thoughts? ... [N]ot allowing any means of reminding people of someone [is] a speech restriction unparalleled in First Amendment law." *White v. Samsung Electronics America, Inc.*, 971 F.2d 1395 (9th Cir. 1992).

CHAPTER 3

ADVERSE POSSESSION

I. INTRODUCTION

A. Ejectment actions: Just as there are Statutes of Limitation that bar the bringing of criminal prosecutions or suits for breach of contract after a certain period of time, so there are Statutes of Limitations that eventually bar the owner of property from suing to *recover possession* from one who has wrongfully entered the property. A property owner's cause of action against a wrongful possessor of it is known as the action of *ejectment*. In virtually all states, the owner must bring his ejectment action within 20 years of the time the wrongdoer enters the land; some states allow only a shorter period, e.g., 10 years. (See *infra*, p. 38.)

    1. Barring of stale claims: One reason, of course, for the existence of a time limit on the bringing of an ejectment action is to *bar stale claims*. With the passage of time, witnesses' memories grow dim and unreliable, and the reliance interest of the defendant (the wrongful possessor) in not having to face a lawsuit becomes stronger. Therefore, it is not unfair to have a cut-off point after which no further ejectment action may be brought.

B. Gaining title by adverse possession: But a statute of limitations on actions to recover real property has an additional major effect, not shared by other Statutes of Limitations: once the limitations period has passed, the wrongful possessor now in reality has *title to the land*, since the original owner can no longer recover it from him. This title is said to have been gained by *adverse possession* (or *"AP"*).

    1. Clearing titles to land: The doctrine of adverse possession thus furnishes the additional benefit of *clearing titles to land*.

        Example: A state has a 20-year statute of limitations on ejectment actions. X claims that he holds title to Blackacre, and wants to sell it to Y. Y will only have to check the land records going back 20 years — plus perhaps some additional period to cover the possibility that the running of the statute of limitations might have been "tolled" for some reason — in order to check X's claim of ownership. The fact that, say, 100 years ago X's alleged "predecessor in title" took the property by wrongfully entering on it, is irrelevant, since the right of the rightful possessor to regain possession has long since been barred by the statute of limitations.

C. Scope of this chapter: Most of this chapter is devoted to a discussion of how one becomes the owner of property by adverse possession. A final section at the end of the chapter (*infra*, p. 39) discusses the kind of title which one gets by adverse possession, including the boundaries of the property acquired.

D. Components of adverse possession: To obtain title by adverse possession, the possessor must satisfy *five main requirements*:

    [1] the possession must be *"open, notorious and visible"*;

    [2] the possession must be *"actual"*;

[3] the possession must be *"hostile,"* i.e., without the owner's consent;

[4] the possession must be *continuous*; and

[5] the possession must be for at least the length of the *statutory period* (perhaps longer if the owner was under a disability).

We consider the first two requirements in "II. Physical Requirements" (*infra*, p. 32), the third in "III. Mental Requirements" (p. 33); the fourth in "IV. Continuity of Possession" (p.36); and the fifth in "V. Length of Time Required" (p. 38).

II. PHYSICAL REQUIREMENTS

A. **Summary of physical requirements:** The concept of gaining title by adverse possession requires, of course, that the person entering the land actually physically *"possess"* it. However, the concept of possession is a vague one. Accordingly, courts have developed a number of catch-words by which to determine whether the requisite physical possession exists. The precise wording varies from state to state, but typically the physical possession must meet these three requirements:

[1] It must be *"open, notorious, and visible"*;

[2] It must be *"actual"*; and

[3] It must be *"exclusive"* (a minor requirement discussed briefly *infra*, p. 33).

B. **"Open, notorious and visible":** One of the functions of a statute of limitations is to penalize a claimant who "sleeps on his rights". The owner of real property who fails to bring an action for ejectment should be penalized (by the drastic step of taking his title away from him) only if he could reasonably be *expected to know* that another person has entered the property, and was asserting a claim to it. Therefore, nearly all courts require that the adverse possessor's use of the land be *"open, notorious and visible."*

1. **Effect of actual notice by owner:** If the possessor can show that the owner had *actual* notice that the former was in possession of the land and asserting a claim to it, the "open, notorious, and visible" requirement is met. Powell, Par. 1013, p. 1089.

2. **Measured against typical owner's conduct:** Where actual knowledge by the true owner cannot be shown, the "open, notorious, and visible" test is met if the adverse possessor's use of the property is similar to that which a *typical owner* of *similar property* would make of it.

   a. **Nature of land taken into account:** Thus the *nature of the land* is taken into account. A more noticeable possession would be required for land within a city or town (e.g., the building of a structure) than for land in a sparsely settled area or wilderness.

   b. **Effect of fence or other enclosure:** The necessary possession will often be shown by the fact that the possessor has put up a *fence* or otherwise enclosed the land. The existence of such an enclosure is not likely to be sufficient in a densely populated and built-up area, but in rural areas this will often be dispositive. A few states have statutes *requiring* enclosure for adverse possession. See Burby, p. 271, fn. 31.

C. Actual possession: Courts often say that the possession must be *"actual."* This term, however, largely overlaps with the requirement that possession be "open, notorious and visible."

1. **Percentage of land used:** At least a *reasonable percentage* of the land claimed by the adverse possessor must be actually used. Again, however, the precise percentage of use required will vary depending upon the nature and utility of the property. For instance, if a mine or quarry were located on a one-acre plot, use of the mine without use of any other land might constitute sufficient possession; use of a similar mine on a tract of 1,000 acres, on the other hand, would not be enough for possession of the entire plot.

2. **Occupation by tenant of adverse possessor:** The adverse possessor does not necessarily have to be in possession of the property *personally*. For instance, if he leases his possessory interest to a *tenant*, the tenant's possession may suffice for meeting the "actual possession" requirement. Burby, p. 272.

   a. **Important point:** This is an important point, because you will encounter scenarios in which the adverse possessor purports to rent the property out to a tenant and collects rent from her rather than physically occupying the property directly. In this scenario, the "landlord" typically *meets* the "actual possession" requirement.

      Example: *O* owns Blackacre. *A* physically occupies the property for a short while. *A* then purports to lease the property to *T*. *A* collects rents from *T* for the statutory period, and does not remit any of this rent to *O* or otherwise acknowledge that *O* is the record owner. *T*'s possession will be imputed to *A*, and *A* will therefore become the owner by AP at the end of the statutory period. That's because although *T*'s possession was not hostile as to *A* (see *infra*, p. 33, for the requirement of hostility), *A*'s constructive possession (via *T*) was hostile as to *O*.

3. **Distinguished from constructive possession:** The concept of "actual" possession should be distinguished from that of *"constructive"* possession. The latter, discussed *infra*, p. 40, applies where one holds a defective, but written, title to a described parcel of land, and takes actual possession of only a small portion of it; by doing so, he may be held to have "constructive" possession of the entire parcel. But except in this defective-instrument situation (often called holding "color of title"), actual possession of the entire parcel is necessary for obtaining title by adverse possession to it.

D. Exclusive possession: The adverse possessor must be in *exclusive* control of the property. This really only means that he must not be sharing control of the property with the true owner, and the property must not be available to the public generally. However, it is possible for two persons (neither of them the record owner) to be in joint possession of property, in which case they would eventually gain joint title to the property by adverse possession. Burby, p. 273.

III. MENTAL REQUIREMENTS

A. "Hostile" possession: Most courts require that the adverse possession be *"hostile."* However, this does not mean that the possession must be characterized by ill-will towards the true owner. Rather, it refers to the fact that the possession must be inconsistent with the true owner's rights and *without the owner's consent*.

1. **Possession by tenant:** A prime example of a possession that is *not* "hostile" is possession by a *tenant* under a valid lease. The tenant's possession is obviously with the landlord's permission, so the tenant does not become the owner of the property by adverse possession merely because he has been there under a lease for more than the statutory period. (However, if the tenant repudiates the lease, or in some states if the lease term ends and the tenant stays in possession, his possession may be transformed into a "hostile" possession; see *infra*, pp. 36 and 161.)

2. **Measured by objective evidence:** In determining whether the necessary hostility exists, courts generally do not attempt to delve deeply into the subjective thoughts of the adverse possessor. Instead hostility is determined by looking at the possessor's *actions*, and his *statements* to the owner and to others.

   a. **Offer to buy property:** An *offer* by the possessor to *buy* the property from the owner may sometimes indicate that the possessor acknowledges that he has no lawful claim to the property. But such an offer may merely represent the possessor's attempt to avoid litigation in such a matter where he believes that he has a valid claim to the property.

B. **"Claim of right":** Some courts insist that the possession must be pursuant to a *"claim of right"* by the possessor. However, such courts vary in the meaning they attach to the phrase "claim of right."

   1. **Majority usage is synonymous with "hostile":** Most courts hold that the requirement that the possessor have a "claim of right" merely means that his possession must be hostile, i.e., *not with the owner's permission.*

      Example: In most jurisdictions, a *squatter* who takes possession of land while acknowledging he has no right to be there may gain title by adverse possession.

      a. **Minority rules out bad faith possessor:** But a *minority* of courts hold that the possessor must have a *bona fide belief* that he has *title to the property*. Under this view, a squatter would never gain title by adverse possession, no matter how long his occupancy of the land was undisturbed.

   2. **Color of title:** One may possess property under a *written instrument* purporting to give him title to that property. If the instrument is invalid for some reason (e.g., because the property described in the deed does not match the property occupied), the possession is said to be under *"color of title."* Such "color of title" is virtually always *sufficient* to meet the hostility requirement.

   3. **Starts as permissive and then becomes hostile:** A possession that *starts as a non-hostile* one can *become hostile.* When this happens, the period of possession starts running at the moment the possession turns hostile. So, for instance, if the possessor holds a valid possessory interest that is *less than a fee simple*, and the interest *terminates*, the possessor's period of hostile possession will begin right afterward, as long as the possessor somehow indicates that his occupancy is inconsistent with the record owner's rights.

    a. Life estate *per autre vie* or fee simple determinable: For instance, the possessor might be someone who holds a *life estate per autre vie*, or a *fee simple determinable* — if the holder continues in possession after the end of the life estate or fee simple determinable, this period of additional possession will typically count for adverse-possession purposes.

C. Boundary disputes and other mistakes: The layman's notion of the utility of adverse possession is that it validates claims by squatters. But in the vast majority of cases where the doctrine applies, the possessor is operating under the ***mistaken, but honest belief***, that he has title to the property in question. Such a situation most commonly involves a mistake as to the location of a ***boundary line***.

    1. Majority view: The majority view is that one who possesses an adjoining landowner's land, under the mistaken belief that he has only possessed up to the boundary of his own land, ***meets the requirement of "hostile" possession***, and will become an owner by adverse possession.

        Example: O is the true owner of Blackacre. A is the true owner of Whiteacre. When A moves onto Whiteacre, he mistakenly believes his land goes all the way up to a creek, which is in fact 15 yards into Blackacre. Accordingly, he builds a fence up to the creek, and uses the enclosed portion of Blackacre for farming. At the end of the statutory period, according to most courts, A becomes the owner of that portion by adverse possession, even though he would not have used it had he known the true boundaries.

        a. Minority view: But a minority of courts holds that the possessor in this kind of "mistaken boundary" situation does ***not*** hold "hostilely," if it can be shown that he would not have held the land had he known that he lacked title to it.

    2. Agreement on boundaries: It often happens that the two adjoining landowners realize that there is some uncertainty about where the true boundary lies, and therefore make an ***agreement*** fixing the boundary. If this agreement turns out to be wrong, when measured against the true state of title, can the party who has gotten the better end of the agreement gain title up to the agreed boundary by adverse possession?

        a. Majority view allows adverse possession: Most courts hold that in this situation, a claim of adverse possession may be made. 3 A.L.P. 790. This is not really a situation in which the encroached-upon landowner "consents" that the other party occupy his land. Rather, it is a case of mistake, and under the majority view would presumably be dealt with like any other mistaken possession (so that the requisite "hostility" is present).

D. Co-tenants: Suppose that A and B hold title to Blackacre as ***co-tenants***. If A has sole possession of the property for the statutory period, does he thereby take title by adverse possession to B's one-half interest (thereby becoming sole owner)?

    1. Other co-tenant must be on notice: The answer is, "not necessarily." In a co-tenancy, each party is entitled to occupy the premises, and one cannot exclude the other. Thus unless A has ***actively blocked*** B from taking joint possession, or has otherwise put B on notice that he is repudiating B's one-half interest, the requisite hostility as to B does not exist.

Example: The Ps and Ds are all co-tenants of Blackacre. The Ps (or their predecessors in interest) occupy and farm the property for the statutory period, pay the taxes, and execute leases and mortgages concerning the land. The Ds never occupy the premises.

Held, these facts are not enough to give the Ps full possession by adverse possession. There must be a showing that the Ds were actually put on notice that the Ps claimed the full property, which could have been done by refusing to allow the Ds to enter. The payment of taxes, execution of leases and mortgages, etc., were not inconsistent with joint ownership, since a co-tenant can take these actions on behalf of the other co-tenants. *Mercer v. Wayman*, 137 N.E.2d 815 (Ill. 1956).

2. **Conveyance of fee simple by one tenant:** If one co-tenant purports to *make a conveyance in fee simple* to a third person, and the other co-tenant knows of the conveyance, the conveyance will be held to represent the necessary declaration of hostility. (Then, possession by the third party purchaser would also be adverse to the non-conveying co-tenant. Burby, p. 278.)

E. **Tenant's hostility to landlord:** Where one occupies property as a *tenant* of the true owner, this possession is not hostile, since it is with the owner's (the landlord's) permission. But there are at least two situations in which possession begun as a tenant can turn into the sort of hostile possession required for the adverse-possession doctrine.

1. **Repudiation or disclaimer:** First, if the tenant *repudiates or disclaims* the lease, hostile possession will begin.

   Example: Tenant tells Landlord that in Tenant's opinion the lease is invalid because it fails to meet the Statute of Frauds. This is sufficient to make his possession thereafter hostile. If Tenant then keeps the property for the statutory period following the disclaimer, he will be the owner by adverse possession. 3 A.L.P. 792-3.

2. **Holdover tenant:** Secondly, the tenant may become an adverse possessor if he *holds over* at the end of the lease term. In most states, the landlord faced with a holdover tenant may *elect* either to eject the tenant, or to treat him as a "tenant at sufferance" (one who is allowed to remain only as long as the landlord wishes.) If ejectment proceedings are started, this is sufficient to make the tenant's further possession adverse. But if the landlord does nothing, thus creating a tenancy at sufferance, this would probably be treated as "permissive" possession, and therefore the adverse-possession doctrine does not apply.

IV. CONTINUITY OF POSSESSION

A. **The continuity requirement generally:** The adverse possession must be *"continuous"* throughout the statutory period. However, this requirement does not mean that the possessor must occupy the property every day throughout the statutory period, or else begin all over again. A number of special rules, discussed below, may permit him to use even time when he is not in actual occupancy towards the statutory period, or at least prevent him from having to start all over again following an interruption.

1. **Abandonment:** However, it is clear that if the possessor *abandons* the property, his possession is deemed to end. Then, if he returns, the statutory period starts all over again.

B. Seasonal possession: Suppose the possessor occupies the property only *seasonally* (e.g., during the summers). If the property is such that this kind of seasonal use is ***all that most owners of similar property would make***, the possession is deemed to be continuous, and the entire twelve months of the year will be counted towards the statute of limitations.

> **Example:** Suppose the property consists solely of forest. An adverse possessor, X, who each year comes onto the land and cuts the timber during the standard timber-cutting season for that region would probably meet the continuity-of-possession requirement, because notwithstanding the gaps in his presence on the land he has behaved as an average owner of such forested land would behave. Therefore, the entire 12 months of the year would count towards X's adverse possession.

    1. Intermittent activities like hunting: But intermittent activities that are ***not the sort of activities done only by true owners*** — like occasional ***hunting*** on the property — are generally ***not*** enough to constitute continuous possession.

C. Interruption by non-owner: An entry onto the property ***by a third person*** may interrupt the adverse possessor's possession.

    1. Ouster by second adverse possessor: For instance, suppose *A* adversely possesses property owned by O, and is then ***ousted*** by *B*, who starts his own adverse possession of the property. If *B* in this situation continues to hold the property, *A*'s possession has obviously been interrupted. Nor will *B* be allowed to "tack" *A*'s time of possession onto his own possession (see *infra*, p. 38).

D. Tacking: Possession by two adverse possessors, one after the other, may be ***"tacked"*** if the two are in ***"privity"*** with each other. That is, their periods of ownership can be ***added together*** for purposes of meeting the statutory period.

    1. Meaning of "privity": "Privity" in this context means that the two parties have ***some direct relationship*** with each other, usually either a familial or economic one. So, for instance, if *A* purports to ***sell or give*** the property to *B*, *B*'s holding period may be tacked on to *A*'s for purposes of reaching the statutory holding period.

> **Example:** *A*, who owns Whiteacre, adversely possesses a small strip of the adjacent Blackacre, due to confusion about boundaries. *A* adversely possesses that piece of Blackacre for 15 years; he then sells Whiteacre to *P*, who holds for another seven years (and who adversely possesses the same strip). *A*'s 15 years of possession can be "tacked" to *P*'s seven years, so that *P* meets a 20-year limitations period. (In most courts, this is true whether *A*'s deed to *P* recited the false boundary lines that *A* and *P* believed to be correct, or recited the true boundary lines that do not include part of Blackacre.)

    2. No privity: But if the two successive adverse possessors are ***not*** in ***"privity,"*** i.e., do not have some ***continuity of interest***, then ***tacking will not be allowed***.

> **Example:** *A* adversely possesses Blackacre for 15 years. He then abandons the property. *B* then enters and adversely possesses for another seven years. *B* cannot "tack" his holding period to *A*'s holding period, since they had no continuity of interest. But if *A* had purported to give *B* his interest by oral gift, deed, bequest or inheritance, then *B* could tack.

3. Tacking on owner's side: An "inverse" tacking problem is presented where the ***true owner*** of the property ***conveys*** it during the time an adverse possessor holds it. This problem is discussed *infra*, p. 38.

V. LENGTH OF TIME REQUIRED

A. Statutory period: The basic length of time for which the property must be adversely possessed varies from state to state. Two-thirds of the states require fifteen years or longer. Powell, Par. 1019, p. 1098. In some states, the period becomes shorter if one pays taxes, or if one has "color of title" (i.e., a defective written instrument purporting to give title).

B. Disabilities: If the true owner of property is under a ***disability***, in nearly all states he is given ***extra time*** within which to bring an ejectment action, and the adverse-possession period is correspondingly lengthened.

1. Disability must exist at time adverse possession began: Most disability statutes apply only to ***disabilities existing at the time the adverse possession began.***

a. No tacking: Thus there can be no "tacking of disabilities," either in the case of successive disabilities in the same owner, or disabilities in each of two successive owners. Burby, p. 277.

2. Types of disability: Disability statutes typically cover ***infancy*** (i.e., anything less than the age of majority), insanity, imprisonment, and occasionally, being outside the jurisdiction. Powell, Par. 1022, p. 1102.

3. Statutes giving grace period: One common kind of statute provides that where a disability exists at the time adverse possession begins, the true owner may bring his action anytime within some stated ***"grace period,"*** i.e., some specified period of time (usually ten years) after the lifting of the disability.

C. Tacking on owner's side: Suppose that after an adverse possession has begun, the true owner conveys his record title to another, either by deed, will, or inheritance. Does the time of possession against the first owner get added to the time against the subsequent owner? The answer is ***"yes."*** This might be termed ***"tacking"*** on the ***owner's side***. See Cribbet, pp. 335-36.

Example: O is the owner of Blackacre in 1980, when A enters and begins to adversely possess. In 2000, O conveys the property to X. Under a 21-year statute of limitations, A gains title by adverse possession in 2001, even though by then he has not held for 21 years against either O or X separately.

VI. RIGHTS OF ADVERSE POSSESSOR

A. Rights before end of statutory period: Prior to the end of the statutory period, the adverse possessor has, of course, not yet obtained title to the property. But he does have some rights, at least against persons other than the true owner.

1. Suit against third person: Thus the adverse possessor is entitled to bring a ***trespass*** action against one who enters the land; this is because trespass is an action that vindicates possessory, rather than ownership, interest in the land. (To put it another way, the trespasser may not raise the defense that the plaintiff lacks title). Burby, p. 270. However, the measure of damages is likely to be reduced to take into account the fact that the adverse possessor does not yet have a permanent interest in the land.

2. **Relations with owner:** The adverse possessor does not, however, yet have any meaningful rights as against the ***true owner*** of the land. In fact, if the owner brings suit before expiration of the statutory period, he can recover ***mesne profits***, an amount equal to the reasonable rental value of the land for the period that the adverse possessor has held it. Burby, p. 270.

B. Rights after expiration of statutory period: Once the statutory period has expired, so that the adverse possessor gains title, his position is of course improved.

1. **Possessor gains good title:** In fact, a title gained by adverse possession is almost as good, as a legal matter, as one obtained by a deed from the record owner.

2. **Easements may not be extinguished:** If an adjoining landowner has an ***easement*** against the adversely-possessed property, this easement will probably not be extinguished by the passage of the statutory period. This is because the holder of an easement normally does not have a right of action against a mere possessor, so there is nothing for the statute of limitations to run against. 3 A.L.P. 825-26.

3. **Not valid against interest of government:** Generally, it is not possible to gain title by adverse possession to land owned by the ***federal government***, or by a ***state*** or city. 3 A.L.P. 827.

4. **Not recordable:** It is usually not possible to ***record*** a title gained by adverse possession, since there is no deed. However, if a judicial determination is made that title by adverse possession has vested, then the decision can be recorded. 3 A.L.P. 830.

    a. **No need to record:** As a corollary, there is no penalty for failing to record a title gained by adverse possession. This means that one who wishes to purchase property from its record owner ***cannot be sure*** that title has not passed to someone else by adverse possession, unless he makes a ***physical inspection*** of the property. In fact, even if he finds that the record owner is currently in possession, he cannot negate the possibility that title by adverse possession vested in someone else, and that the record owner is himself now an adverse possessor who has not yet held long enough to re-acquire title! However, such a sequence of events is so unlikely that it is, for practical purposes, disregarded by title examiners.

5. **Hard to prove marketability:** Although one who holds title by adverse possession theoretically holds a title as good as record ownership, he will find it difficult to sell the property. His contract of sale will usually require him to convey ***"marketable"*** title (*infra*, p. 310). It will often be impossible to prove that there is no person who could assert a valid claim, since a claimant's time to sue may have been extended, under many statutes, due to disabilities, the non-possessory status of the remainder interests, etc.

    a. **Modern view:** However, modern courts will generally find a title to be "marketable" once the statutory period and another ten or so years have passed, even though there is some remote possibility that the record owner's claim may still be alive.

6. **Transferred like any other title:**   A title gained by adverse possession is transferred in the same way as any other title. The transfer must thus be *in writing*, in accordance with the Statute of Frauds. This means that an *oral transfer*, or a *disclaimer of interest* in the property, or an *abandonment* of it, will not by itself suffice to strip the adverse possessor of his title.

> **Example:** O owns Blackacre. X owns Whiteacre, the adjacent parcel. X constructs a garage on what X believes is entirely Whiteacre land, but which in fact occupies a 10-foot-by-20-foot strip of Blackacre as well. The garage sits there for the 21-year statutory period, which expires in 2003. In 2004, X tears down the garage intending to build a new one, does a survey, realizes that the old garage was encroaching, and builds the new one entirely on Whiteacre. At the same time, X tells O orally, "I never intended to build on your property, and I hereby renounce any rights I may have gotten by doing so."
>
> X is still the owner (by adverse possession) of the 10 x 20-foot strip of Blackacre. Once title to that strip vested in X in 2003, it was a title like any other. That title could not be divested or abandoned by X's cessation of possession (i.e., tearing down of the old garage) or by X's oral attempt to renounce his rights. If X wants to surrender the rights to the strip, the only way for him to do so is by making a formal, written conveyance of it, just as if he had originally obtained the strip by conveyance.

   a. **Compare with transfer made before title passes:**   Contrast this with a transfer made *before* the statutory period has expired. Before the end of the statutory period, the adverse possessor may convey his possessory interest *orally*, since the Statute of Frauds does not cover such a transfer. Similarly, he may lose his interest by *abandoning* it, or by *permitting the true owner to enter*. Thus on the facts of the above Example, X's renunciation of any intent to encroach, or his tearing down of the garage, would each have ended his adverse possession if it had occurred before the statutory period expired in 2003.

C. **Scope of property obtained:**   By hypothesis, there will never be a valid, enforceable deed describing the property obtained by adverse possession. (If there were, the adverse-possession doctrine would not be necessary). Consequently, there will often be a serious question about exactly what land the adverse possessor acquires.

   1. **Property actually occupied:**   Normally, he acquires title only to that property *"actually"* occupied. The amount of property so occupied by a particular act of dominion will vary with the nature of the property. Thus where property is not suitable for cultivation, fencing in a large area, and hunting over a portion of it, may suffice to occupy the whole enclosed area. Conversely, in more densely populated areas, direct use and occupancy of each portion of land may be necessary. See the discussion of the "actual possession" requirement *supra*, p. 33.

   2. **Constructive adverse possession:**   There is, however, one important exception to this rule requiring "actual" possession. By the doctrine of *"constructive"* adverse possession, one who enters property under *"color of title"* (i.e., a written instrument that is defective for some reason) will gain title to the *entire area described in the instrument*, even if he "actually" possesses only a portion of it.

Example: X conveys to P a deed to a parcel of rural property. The metes and bounds description in the deed covers 100 precisely-defined acres, which as it happens are enclosed by a fence. P physically occupies 3 acres, where he builds a house and garden. X turns out (unbeknownst to P) never to have owned the property at all. P occupies the 3 acres for the statutory period. Because the entire tract was included within P's deed, he will be deemed to have been in possession of the entire tract, even though he occupied only part of it.

a. **Must be recognized as unit:** The parcel of land claimed to be constructively possessed must be one which is recognized in the community as a *single parcel* likely to be owned by a single owner. In a farming area where most farms are small, for example, it would be difficult to establish constructive possession of a huge tract of woodlands. (That's why, in the above Example, it makes a difference that the entire parcel was enclosed by a single fence.) 3 A.L.P. 820.

   i. **Must be contiguous:** This means that, at the very least, the part actually occupied and the part constructively claimed must be *contiguous*.

      Example: O is the record owner of lot X in Boston and lot Y in Chicago. *A* executes a deed of both lots to *B*. *B* takes actual occupancy of lot X, and holds it for the statutory period. He has not gained title to lot Y by constructive adverse possession, since the two lots are not contiguous, or recognized in the community as being a single parcel.

VII. CONFLICTS BETWEEN POSSESSORS

A. **Nature of problem:** Up to now, we have been concerned with conflicts between the adverse possessor and the "true" owner. Now we consider conflicts between two persons whose interests are solely possessory, where one has ousted the other from possession.

B. **"First in time, first in right":** The general rule is that the *first possessor has priority over the subsequent one*.

   Example: O owns Blackacre. P moves on to the land, claiming he is the rightful owner. Before expiration of the statutory period, D forces him off the land, and occupies it himself. P can successfully sue to regain possession of the land (by use of an action called "ejectment"). See *Tapscott v. Cobbs*, 52 Va. 172 (1854). See also Boyer, pp. 235-36.

   1. **Passage by gift or will:** The prior possessor can also pass along his possessory interest by gift or will, so that the person who takes by that gift or will can recover the property from the dispossessor.

C. **Remedy of ejectment:** As the above example indicates, a person who has the right to possess land, and who is ousted from that possession by another, may bring an action of *ejectment* to regain possession.

Figure 3-1
Adverse Possession

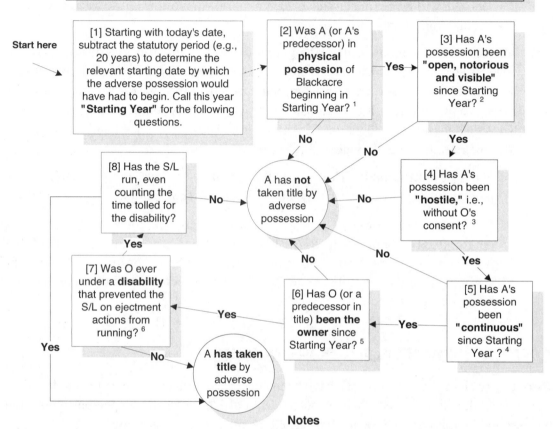

Use this chart to determine whether "A," the potential adverse possessor, has acquired title to Blackacre by adverse possession from "O," the record owner. ("S/L" = "statute of limitations.")

Start here

[1] Starting with today's date, subtract the statutory period (e.g., 20 years) to determine the relevant starting date by which the adverse possession would have had to begin. Call this year **"Starting Year"** for the following questions.

[2] Was A (or A's predecessor) in **physical possession** of Blackacre beginning in Starting Year?[1]

[3] Has A's possession been **"open, notorious and visible"** since Starting Year?[2]

A has **not** taken title by adverse possession

[4] Has A's possession been **"hostile,"** i.e., without O's consent?[3]

[8] Has the S/L run, even counting the time tolled for the disability?

[7] Was O ever under a **disability** that prevented the S/L on ejectment actions from running?[6]

[6] Has O (or a predecessor in title) **been the owner** since Starting Year?[5]

[5] Has A's possession been **"continuous"** since Starting Year?[4]

A **has taken title** by adverse possession

Notes

[1] Courts often say that the possession must be "<u>actual</u>." Most important: At least a reasonable percentage of the land claimed by the adverse possessor must be actually used.

In one instance "<u>constructive</u>" rather than "actual" possession will suffice: If A is record owner of an adjacent parcel and is confused about the boundaries (so that A believes he owns a strip that's actually owned of record by O), A's actual ownership of the adjacent piece plus "constructive" ownership of O's strip will suffice -- here, A just needs to show that he regarded the strip as his own (e.g., he fenced it in).

[2] The idea is that A must behave in such a way towards the property that O would realize that A is asserting a claim. If O has actual notice of A's claim, that's enough. If O does not have actual notice, then the question is whether A's use is similar to that which a typical owner of similar property would make.

[3] The idea is that A's possession must be inconsistent with O's rights, and <u>without O's consent</u>.

Most important: If A is O's <u>tenant</u>, A's possession is not hostile, unless A repudiates the lease and says he's claiming ownership.

If A claims under a grant of title from someone other than O -- even if the grant is invalid -- that's enough to meet the hostility requirement. For instance, in the case of a <u>boundary dispute</u>, if A honestly but mistakenly believes that he has received title to a "strip" that really belongs to adjacent owner O, A meets the "hostile possession" requirement.

[4] Keep in mind that on the adverse side, "<u>tacking</u>" is allowed for purposes of the continuity requirement -- as long as A and A's "predecessors in title," so to speak, have occupied for the whole period, that's enough.

<u>Example</u>: A1 owns Whiteacre, adjacent to Blackacre, owned by O. Due to a mistake in A1's deed, A1 thinks that he owns a 20-foot-wide strip between the two parcels that really belongs to O. A1 holds for 10 years. A1 then sells to A2, with a deed that (falsely) recites that the strip is part of Whiteacre. A2 holds for 10 more years. Assuming a 20-year statutory period,

A2 now owns the strip (assuming the other requirements like "open, notorious" are met) -- his 10 years get "tacked" to A1's 10 years.

For "<u>seasonal</u>" property, the continuity-of-possession requirement is met as long as A makes the same seasonal use each year that a real owner would be likely to make.

[5] There is in effect "<u>tacking</u>" on the <u>owner's</u> side as well -- so an owner's time to sue can be used up by possession that was adverse to the prior owner.

<u>Example</u>: O1 owns Blackacre beginning in 1980, the same time that A comes into hostile possession of the property. O1 sells to O2 in 1990. Assuming a 20-year limitations period, A owns the property in 2000, because O2 is charged with the time A possessed hostilely to O2's predecessor in title (O1) just as with the time A possessed hostilely to O2.

[6] <u>Infancy</u> is the most common disability you should look out for. (The time when O was an infant doesn't count for running of the statute.)

Quiz Yourself on
ADVERSE POSSESSION

5. In 1960, Beck purchased valid title to Blackacre, located in Ames. That same year, Warren purchased valid title to Whiteacre, the adjoining parcel. Both parties reasonably but mistakenly believed that the boundary line between Blackacre and Whiteacre was a large oak tree, so in 1961 both fenced their property accordingly. In reality, the proper boundary between the two parcels is 30 yards to the south of the oak tree, so that the existing fencing has been depriving Warren of the use of land which belongs to him. In 2008, Warren discovered the error, and has brought an action to recover the 30-yard strip. May Warren recover the strip? (Assume a 20-year statute of limitations for this and Q. 6-7). _____

6. In 1960, Osmond, the owner of Blackacre, left the property "to my son Steve and my daughter Deborah in equal shares." Steve moved onto the property and lived there for the next 40 years. Deborah never liked the property, and made no attempt to live there at any time. In 2008, Deborah died, leaving all of her personal and real property to her son Frank. If Frank now seeks a judicial declaration that he is the owner of a one-half interest in Blackacre, will he succeed? _____

7. Orlando acquired Blackacre in 1960. In 1970, Alice acquired Whiteacre, the adjacent parcel. Alice built a fence on what she thought was the border between the two properties. In fact, her fence encroached 40 yards into Orlando's property. Alice actively, openly and continuously occupied this 40-yard strip for the next 35 years. In 2005, Orlando discovered the error, and informed Alice that she had been using his property. Alice said, "O.K., I now recognize that this strip is your property." She also moved the fence. Shortly thereafter, Alice died, leaving Whiteacre to her son Stokes. Who owns the strip, Stokes or Orlando? _____

Answers

5. No, probably. Beck obtained title to the 30 yard strip by the doctrine of ***adverse possession***, 20 years after he first fenced in the property (i.e., in 1981). One of the requirements for adverse possession is that the possession be ***"hostile."*** But most courts hold that one who possesses an adjoining landowner's land, under the mistaken belief that he has only possessed up to the boundary of his own land, meets the requirement of hostile possession. (But a minority of courts would disagree with the result, and would hold that Warren may recover possession because Beck's possession was not hostile.)

6. Yes. Steve and Deborah held the property as co-tenants. As a general rule, co-tenants each have equal access to the premises. If Steve had refused Deborah's attempt to live on the premises, then Steve's occupancy for the statutory period would have been "hostile," and Steve would have taken Deborah's half interest by adverse possession. But since Deborah never asked to live on the premises, and Steve never said that she couldn't, Steve's occupancy was not hostile, so he does not take her interest by adverse possession even though he was in sole occupancy for more than the statutory period. Consequently, Deborah still owned her one-half interest at the time of her death, and that interest passed to Frank.

7. Stokes. In 1990, Alice became the owner of the strip by adverse possession. Once she gained title by adverse possession, her title was of the same quality, and subject to the same rules, as if she had gotten title by deed. Therefore, she could not convey that title to anyone else except by compliance with the Statute of Frauds. Her oral "grant" to Orlando was ineffective because it was not in writing as required by the Statute of Frauds. Therefore, Alice owned the strip at her death, and it passed to Stokes.

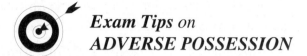 *Exam Tips on*
ADVERSE POSSESSION

Whenever it appears that a person has *encroached on another's property*, check to see whether the encroacher may have taken title by adverse possession. Adverse possession questions are favorites of profs, in part because an adverse-possession issue can be well-hidden inside an essay fact pattern involving other topics.

Note: In the examples in this section, we assume a 20-year adverse-possession statute unless otherwise noted.

Adverse possession generally

Remember to list and discuss *all* the requisite elements even if they are obvious. In your analysis, discuss in greater detail the elements that are less clear. Also, note the *state statutory period*. If one isn't mentioned, write that you're assuming the occupation has occurred for the requisite length of time.

☛ **Hostility requirement:** Make sure the occupation is *hostile*. If the rightful owner *assents* to the occupation (e.g., by giving *verbal permission* to the occupier, or by *accepting rent* from the occupier, then this requirement has *not* been met).

   ☞   **Owner's knowledge:** The rightful owner's *knowledge of the encroachment,* coupled with his *lack of response* to it, will likely be viewed as **assent**.

   Example: The occupier, AP, tells the rightful owner, O, that AP knows he is encroaching and he will remove the encroachment if O so requests. O remains silent. O's silence will be construed as permission. Therefore, AP is not holding with the required hostility, and his holding won't count toward the statutory period.

   ☞   **Co-tenancy:** If the contest is between two co-tenants (call them *A* and *B*), and *A* claims to have taken sole title by adverse possession, look for clear actions indicating the *ouster* of B, the other cotenant. If there's no ouster — no sign that A kept *B* from the premises — A won't take *B*'s share by adverse possession.

   Example: A and *B* inherit Blackacre as co-tenants. A decides to live on the property; *B* continues to live far away. A pays all taxes and insurance, and makes all repairs on the property. A pays nothing to *B* for imputed rent. At the end of the statutory period, has A taken *B*'s one-half interest by adverse possession? No. If there is no evidence that A prevented *B* from using the premises and thus ousted her, the court will presume that *B* consented to the arrangement. Therefore, A won't take *B*'s interest by adverse possession.

☛ **Physical requirements:** Look in your fact pattern for, and note in your answer, the *physical actions* that would reasonably *give notice* to a rightful owner that her land is being hostilely occupied. (*Examples:* AP builds a fence around O's property, or plants and harvests crops, or pays property taxes — any of these would put O on notice that AP is occupying the property.)

- ☛ **Continuity requirement:** Remember that the claimant must possess the property *continuously* for the statutory period. Be careful to note when the occupier's possession is interrupted.

  - ☞ **Exception:** But if the interruptions are *consistent* with the appropriate use of the property, then the occupier's claim is *not* affected. (*Example:* A summer cabin need only be occupied during the summer months.)

- ☛ **Requirement of actual possession:** The occupier must *"actually possess"* the property. But possession does not necessarily require that the occupier be physically present on the property.

  - ☞ **Lease:** For instance, if the occupier *leases* her interest to another, the lessee's time on the premises will count toward the occupier's holding period.

    Example: AP moves onto Blackacre, which belongs to O. AP remains there for 10 years, then purports to lease his interest to T. T remains for another 10 years. At the end (assuming a 20-year statute), AP owns by adverse possession — the time T was in possession under claim of right from T will be credited to AP. (But these 10 years won't count towards any claim of adverse possession by *T* against either AP or O, because T is there with AP's permission.)

  - ☞ **Possession under color of title:** Also, look for a situation where a party receives a *defective deed* and is therefore not in legal possession of the property. In that situation, she is entering the property under *color of title* (which meets the "hostility" requirement in most states), and she will be deemed to have gained possession of the *entire area described in the deed,* even if she *does not use part of the described land.*

    Example: AP purchases realty at a foreclosure sale, unaware of the fact that O purchased it six months earlier and has not defaulted on any payments. AP records her deed, constructs a house on part of the property, and encloses the house and a small area around it with a fence, but does not use any of the other land around it. At the end of the requisite period of time, AP can claim title by adverse possession of the *entire plot* that is described in the deed.

- ☛ **Future interest:** Be on the lookout for a possessor who is claiming against the holder of a *future interest* in the property — profs love to test this, because it's tricky. You have to check whether the future interest existed at the moment the adverse possession began, because the solution depends on this.

  - ☞ **Interest exists when possession starts:** If the future interest *already exists* at the time the adverse possessor enters, the statutory period does *not* begin to run against the holder of the future interest until the future interest *becomes possessory*.

    Example: Z makes a will leaving Blackacre "to *B* for twenty years; the remainder to *C*. However, if *C* is not alive at the termination of *B*'s estate, *C*'s oldest child at the death of Z shall take the remainder." When Z dies, in 1975, *B* and *C* are alive and D, a minor, is *C*'s oldest child alive. AP moves on to the property in 1976 and *C* dies in 1984. Twenty years after Z's death (in 1995) D discovers that AP has been in possession of the realty for 19 years. However, D attempts to have AP ejected from the realty only after two more years have passed (in 1997), at a time when AP has been in possession for 21 years. Nonetheless, D will succeed in his action because the statute of limitations began to run against him only two years previously — since D's future interest existed at the time AP began his possession, AP's possession began to count against D only when D's interest became possessory (at the termination of *B*'s 20-year interest, in 1995), so only two years had elapsed by the time D brought his ejectment suit.

☞   **Successor in interest:** But don't confuse the above situation with a situation where there is a *successor in interest* to the property (i.e. where the owner conveys his interest to another after the adverse possession has already begun). In that case, *tacking* is *allowed*. In other words, the time against the first owner gets added to the time against the subsequent owner.

CHAPTER 4

FREEHOLD ESTATES

I. INTRODUCTION

A. Feudalism in brief: American property law is in large part derived from English land law. English land law, in turn, is in important part a product of English society as it existed during the Middle Ages. In particular, it is helpful to understand a little bit about *feudalism*, which was the economic structure of England during at least the 13th through the 15th Centuries.

   1. Nature of feudalism: In feudal times, all land was treated as owned, in the first instance, *by the king*. He then in turn gave possession (but not what we would consider untrammeled ownership) of various parcels to his lords and barons, who had a corresponding obligation to provide the king with a certain number of soldiers (knights).

   a. Subinfeudation: Each lord then had the right to give possession of a parcel to an underling, in return for either production of a certain number of soldiers, or for other services (e.g., farming of the parcel). The party receiving possession was said to be a *vassal*. His holding of the land was said to be in *tenure*. He could in turn give possession of this land to someone else, creating a new tenure. This process of tenures within tenures was called *subinfeudation*.

   b. No substitution: The key aspect of subinfeudation was that each person in the chain who at one point held possession *kept his place* in the chain. Thus if *A* held Blackacre "of the king" (i.e., the grant of the land by the king was directly to *A*), and *A* wished to give possession to *B*, he made sure that *B* held in tenure from him, not from the king. That is, *B* had to render his services (e.g., production of knights) directly to *A*, not to the king.

   c. Incidents of tenure: A tenant (one who had possession) owed certain *duties to his lord*, and had certain *liabilities* to him. These duties and liabilities were known as the *"incidents of tenure."* For instance, under the incident of "wardship," if a tenant died leaving an heir under 21, the lord automatically got to be the heir's guardian, and was entitled to possess the land (and collect its rents and profits) until the heir turned 21. Similarly, under the incident of "relief," when a tenant died, his heir had to pay the lord a sum (e.g., a year's rent) to gain possession of his inheritance. See generally DKA&S, pp. 187-89.

   d. Tax evasion, and combatting it: Many of the rules we will encounter during this chapter were responses by the king and the high-level lords to attempts by rich land-possessors to evade the feudal incidents of tenure, and thereby in effect to evade taxes. *Id*. at 189-190. For instance, the Statute of Uses (*infra*, p. 88) was such an anti-tax-evasion measure.

   2. The Statute *Quia Emptores:* The Statute *Quia Emptores,* enacted in 1250, gave tenants (i.e., persons who held in tenure from another) the right to convey their interest in the property without penalty. However, the statute *forbade "subinfeudation."*

Example: Suppose that *A* held Blackacre "of the king." Then suppose that prior to 1290, he granted tenure to *B*. After 1290, *B* could convey his interest in the property to *C* without penalty. However, *C* would not then hold his tenure from *B*, but rather, from *A*. *C* was simply substituted for *B* in the chain of ownership.

    a. Gradual abandonment of tenure: *Quia Emptores* thus prevented new tenures from being created. Other aspects of the feudal system also gave way through the centuries, until the last vestiges of the tenurial system that were of any practical importance were abolished in England in 1925.

3. Tenure in the United States: The system of tenure existed in many of the thirteen colonies. Moynihan, p. 25. Furthermore, since the king had the right to waive the effect of the Statute *Quia Emptores*, persons receiving colonial lands from him were free to subinfeudate (as did the family of William Penn in Pennsylvania). Again, however, as in England, statutory reforms have removed the present-day importance of tenure in the U.S.

    a. Shaped historical events: However, many of the rules and statutes which are discussed elsewhere in this book represent responses to the system of tenure.

B. The concept of "estate": The system of tenure has contributed to our modern-day Anglo-American notion of an *"estate"* in land. As we shall see, it is never really correct to say that X "owns" Blackacre. Instead, one owns an "estate in Blackacre", which may either be an extensive one (e.g., a fee simple absolute) or a more limited one (e.g., a term of years).

1. "Estate" defined: An estate is an interest in land which has two characteristics: (a) it is or may become *"possessory"*; and (b) it is measured in "terms of *duration.*" Restatement, §9.

    a. Distinguished from easements and equitable servitudes: Requirement (a) means that neither an *easement* (*infra*, p. 203) nor an *equitable servitude* (*infra*, p. 237) is an "estate," since these cannot become possessory. Powell, Par. 172, p. 12.

    b. Meaning of duration: The key aspect of our concept of estates is that of *duration*. Ownership of a given parcel of land may be split into two or more time periods. For instance, suppose that O, the outright owner (the owner in "fee simple") of Blackacre bequeaths it "to *A* for life, remainder to *B*, but if *B* dies without issue, then to *C*." As soon as O dies, *A*, *B*, and *C* all acquire estates; *A*'s is present, and *B*'s and *C*'s are future in the sense that they are not now possessory. Thus the ownership of Blackacre is divided into three temporal portions.

2. Freehold and non-freehold estates: Estates in land are traditionally divided into *freehold* and *non-freehold*. The distinction is essentially historical; to understand the distinction, one must first understand a little about the mysterious feudal concept of *seisin*.

    a. Meaning of "seisin": We will discuss the concept of seisin more thoroughly *infra*, p. 83, in connection with the treatment of springing and shifting future interests. For the moment, it suffices to say that a person had seisin of Blackacre (or, in the terminology of the Middle Ages, was "seized of Blackacre") if he had: (1) possession and (2) one of certain types of claims to what might roughly be termed "ownership" of the property.

  i. **Seisin and freehold estates:** In particular, the requisite claim of "ownership" was that associated with several estates, called the *freehold estates*. Thus one who had both a freehold estate, and possession, had seisin of the land; one who had a non-freehold estate could not have seisin.

3. **The freehold estates:** Three freehold estates have been recognized since the Middle Ages:

   [a] **Fee simple:** The *fee simple* (which may be either absolute or defeasible);

   [b] **Fee tail:** The *fee tail*; and

   [c] **Life estate:** The *life estate*.

4. **Non-freehold estates:** The non-freehold estates (i.e., those to which seisin does not attach) are:

   [a] **Estate for years:** The *estate for years* (e.g., a 20-year lease);

   [b] **Periodic estate:** The *periodic estate* (e.g., a month-to-month tenancy);

   [c] **Estate at will:** The *estate at will*; and

   [d] **Estate at sufferance:** The *estate at sufferance*.

   The non-freehold estates are discussed *infra*, p. 157.

5. **Example of seisin:** To see the relationship between seisin and the freehold estates, consider the following example: O has a fee simple absolute interest in Blackacre. Since the fee simple is a freehold estate, O has seisin of Blackacre. Suppose O now grants *A* a life interest in Blackacre, and keeps a reversion (i.e., the right to regain possession of Blackacre after A's death) in himself. Since a life estate is a freehold estate, *A* gains seisin as soon as he enters the property. But now, suppose that *A* gives *B* a 20-year lease on Blackacre. Even if *B* enters, he does not obtain seisin, since his lease is an estate for years, which is a non-freehold estate. The seisin remains in A; he is also treated as being constructively in possession of the land.

6. **No new estates creatable:** Apart form the recognized freehold and non-freehold estates listed above, ***no new estate may be created***. That is, one who wishes to convey property either by deed or will may convey only one (or more) of these estates; he may not make up a new kind of estate. If he tries to do so, the courts will generally treat the conveyance as establishing one of the conventional estates. This is one of several ways in which courts have attempted to prevent undue restraints on the alienation of the land. Moynihan, p. 34.

   Example: O bequeaths Blackacre to "my grand-daughter Sarah and her heirs on her father's side." Sarah then conveys Blackacre to "Albin Johnson and his heirs."

   Held, O's bequest to Sarah, since it attempts to restrict intestate descent of the property to her paternal side, is not one of the traditional estates and is therefore invalid. Accordingly, Sarah will be deemed to have received a fee simple absolute, which she has conveyed to Johnson. *Johnson v. Whiton*, 34 N.E. 542 (Mass. 1893).

C. **Chain of title:** One of the central concepts in property law is *"chain of title."* Chain of title refers to the sequential links between the various owners of a parcel: *A* conveys to *B*, who conveys to C, etc. As we examine the freehold estates in this chapter (and the future estates in the next chapter), we will be tracing a parcel's chain of title from one grantor to the next. Chain of title problems are discussed in more detail in our treatment of the recording system, beginning *infra*, p. 367.

1. **Grant from U.S. Government:** For most parcels in America, the chain of title traces back to a grant by the ***U.S. Government***. D&K, p. 11. (Actually, when the U.S. Government conveys public lands to a private person, the grant is referred to by the special term ***"patent."***) The federal government in turn traces its title back to the original "discovery" (and conquest) of America by white European explorers. *Id.*

    a. **Effect of Indian titles:** Obviously, Native Americans were here before whites arrived. However, American courts have held that although Native Americans had "possession" of the land on which they lived, they did not have "title" to it, and could thus not convey title. Therefore, a title derived from the federal government, or from one of the states or colonies, has priority over an earlier purported "grant" from an Indian tribe. See *Johnson v. M'Intosh*, 21 U.S. (8 Wheat) 543 (1823).

II. FEE SIMPLE

A. **Fee simple absolute:** The *fee simple absolute* is the most unrestricted estate, and that of longest duration, known to Anglo-American law.

    1. **Restrictions on use:** Even a fee simple absolute, however, is subject to certain limitations. For instance, the holder of such a fee cannot use the property in violation of valid zoning rules (*infra*, p. 261). Similarly, he cannot use the property in a way constituting a nuisance to an adjoining landowner (*infra*, p. 385). But the fee simple absolute, unlike all the other estates (both freehold and non-freehold) is of ***infinite duration***.

    2. **Inheritability:** One important attribute of the fee simple is that it is ***inheritable***, under intestacy statutes. In fact, under the statutes of nearly all states, if the owner of a fee simple absolute dies without any direct descendants (i.e., children or grandchildren), and without a will, then his ***collateral relatives*** (e.g. brothers and sisters) will inherit the property.

        Example: O, a New York resident, holds a fee simple absolute in Blackacre. He dies without a will, and without issue (i.e., without children, grandchildren or great-grandchildren). He also has no surviving spouse or parent. However, he is survived by a brother and a sister. Under N.Y. Est., Powers and Trusts Law sc4-1.1(a) (7), the brother and sister will each take a one-half interest in Blackacre by intestate succession.

    3. **Words needed to create:** The common law was extremely restrictive with respect to the words needed to create a fee simple absolute. Such an interest could be ***conveyed*** (i.e., transferred "*inter vivos*," or between living persons) only by use of the magic words "***and his heirs***." Thus a conveyance "to *A* and his heirs" gave *A* a fee simple absolute, but a conveyance "to *A*" or "to *A* forever" or "to *A* and his assigns" or even "to *A* in fee simple" merely gave *A* a life estate! Moynihan, p. 32. However, a grant "to *A* **or** his heirs" was acceptable; see Powell, Par. 180, p. 21.

a. Meaning of "and his heirs": The common-law requirement that the conveyance be to *A* "and his heirs" does not mean that *A*'s heirs obtain any interest from the conveyance. For once the conveyance is made, *A* could turn around and transfer the property to *B*, and upon *A*'s death, his heirs would get nothing.

b. Modern states abolish requirement: In the substantial majority of states, statutes now *abolish* the requirements that the phrase "and his heirs" be used. Some other states have reached a similar result by case law. So a conveyance *"to A"* is *sufficient* to convey a fee simple absolute in nearly all states today.

B. Fee simple defeasible: In contrast to the fee simple absolute, the fee simple *defeasible* has *"strings attached."* That is, although one who holds a fee simple defeasible may use and hold the property forever, or convey it, or have it be inherited by his heirs, he must use it *subject to a restriction.* Fees simple defeasible fall into three categories:

[1] the fee simple *determinable*, which lapses automatically if an impermissible event occurs;

[2] the fee simple *subject to a condition subsequent*, which gives the grantor a right to reenter the property and terminate the estate if the impermissible event occurs; and

[3] the fee simple *subject to an executory limitation*, which provides for the transfer of the property to a third person (one other than the grantor) if the impermissible event occurs.

We consider each of these below.

1. Fee simple determinable: A fee simple *determinable* is a fee simple which *automatically* comes to an end when a stated event occurs (or, perhaps, fails to occur).

a. Restriction on uses: The most common function of the fee simple determinable is to *prevent the property from being put to a certain use* which the grantor opposes. The limitation gives the grantor control over the use of the property, even after it has changed hands several times.

Example: O holds a fee simple absolute in Blackacre. He is a staunch teetotaler, and is determined that Blackacre will never be used for the sale of liquor. He therefore sells the property "to *A* and his heirs so long as the premises are not used for the sale of alcoholic beverages, and if they are so used, then the premises shall revert to O." *A* then purports to convey a fee simple absolute to *B*, who builds a bar on the premises. When the first alcoholic beverage is sold, *B*'s interest automatically ends, and the property reverts to O.

i. Possibility of reverter: By definition, the creator of a fee simple determinable is left with an interest, i.e., the right to regain title if the stated event occurs. This right is called a *possibility of reverter.* Thus in the above example, O, following the conveyance, is left with a possibility of reverter if alcohol is sold. The possibility of reverter is discussed more extensively *infra*, p. 69.

b. Words needed for creating: Words with a *"durational aspect"* typically signal a fee simple determinable. DKA&S, p. 207. That is, the words used to create a fee simple determinable are generally ones that make it clear the estate is to have a particular duration, and is then to end *automatically* upon the occurrence of the stated event.

i. **"So long as":** Most commonly, the fee simple determinable is created by use of the phrase *"so long as"* (or "as long as"). The above Example — where *A* takes "so long as the premises are not used for the sale of alcoholic beverage" — is a good illustration.

ii. **"Until or "during":** Other common formulations are *"until* [event X happens]," *"during* [the time when Event X has *not* yet happened]," or "*while* [Event X has not yet happened]."

iii. **Mention of "reverting":** If the grant mentions that the property will *"revert"* to the grantor on the happening of the stated event, that term will usually indicate a fee simple determinable.

Example: The Os convey property (later known as the Hutton School grounds) to the Ds, a school district. The deed provides that "this land to be used for school purpose only; *otherwise to revert to Grantors herein."* The Os die intestate, leaving S as their only heir. The Ds stop holding classes on the property in 1973, and begin using it for storage purposes only. In 1977, S, without having taken any legal steps to re-enter the land, conveys to the Ps all of his interest in the Hutton School grounds. The Ps bring suit to acquire title to the property. They argue that the deed from the Os to the Ds created a fee simple determinable, that title therefore reverted to S (as the Ds' heir) automatically when the Ds stopped using the property for school purposes, and that S's conveyance of his interest in the property to the Ps was therefore effective to give the Ps a fee simple absolute.

Held, for the Ps. The original deed from the Os to the Ds created a fee simple determinable in the Ds, leaving a possibility of a reverter in the Os and their heirs. The use of the word "only" immediately following the grant demonstrates that the Os wanted to give the land to the school district only as long as it was needed and no longer (thus suggesting a limited grant, rather than a full grant subject to a condition). Also, the phrase "otherwise to revert to grantors herein" suggests a *mandatory return* rather than a permissive return. Therefore, when there came a time when the property was no longer used for school purposes, it reverted to S *without any formal action on his part. Mahrenholz v. County Board of School Trustees*, 417 N.E.2d 138 (Ill. 1981).

iv. **Statement of motive or purpose not enough:** On the other hand, a mere statement of the transferor's *motive or purpose* in making the transfer is *not* usually enough to create a fee simple determinable — typically, a fee simple absolute results from such a statement. DKA&S, p. 207.

Example: Suppose O conveys Blackacre "to City for the purpose of operating a public library." O's statement of purpose/motive won't turn the conveyance into a fee simple determinable — City will receive a fee simple absolute, and will thus have the right to do with the property as it pleases at any time.

c. **Not subject to Rule Against Perpetuities:** Why do you have to distinguish between a fee simple determinable (which we're discussing here) and the other two types of fee simple defeasibles (f.s. subject to condition subsequent and f.s. subject to executory limitation)? One big reason has to do with the *Rule Against Perpetuities*.

i. **RAP not applicable to possibility of reverter:** In order to prevent undue restraints on alienation of land, the Rule Against Perpetuities prevents most estates from taking effect after a certain period following their creation. (*Infra*, p. 96.) However, the Rule is usually held ***not to apply to a possibility of reverter following a fee simple determinable.*** But it *does* apply to an executory interest following a fee simple subject to executory limitation (discussed *infra*, p. 55). The following two examples illustrate the startlingly different consequences that can flow from the distinction between the two estates.

Example 1: *O* conveys a building "to City so long as the premises are used as a public school." City has a fee simple determinable, and *O* has a reversion. Now, suppose that 100 years after this grant, City stops using the building as a school, and instead uses it as a library.

The common-law Rule Against Perpetuities does *not* apply to *O*'s reversion. Therefore, the heirs of *O* (perhaps four or five generations following *O*'s death) automatically own the property. And since there may be many such heirs (some of whom may not even be traceable), it will be hard or impossible for City to clear its title — and get a fee simple absolute — even if it's willing to pay off the heirs.

Example 2: Now, by contrast, assume that *O* in Example 1 conveyed the building "to City, but if City ceases to use the building as a public school, to *A* and his heirs." City has a fee simple subject to executory limitation (see *infra*, p. 55), and *A* has an executory interest. Because executory interests are subject to the Rule Against Perpetuities (see *infra*, p. 98), *A*'s interest is subject to the Rule. Since the (purported) executory interest in *A* or his successors might not vest until after all lives in being at the time *O* conveyed plus 21 years, the executory interest is *void* as a violation of the RAP. Consequently, City has a fee simple absolute. Cf. DKA&S, p. 250.

(1) **Significance:** So it's especially vital to distinguish the fee simple determinable (where the grantor has a reversion, to which the RAP *doesn't* apply) from the fee simple subject to an executory limitation (where, as discussed *infra*, p. 98, the future interest is held by someone other than the grantor, and as to which future interest the RAP *does* apply).

ii. **Statute of Limitations:** Because of the risk of having a fee simple determinable tying up land titles for hundreds of years, many states have enacted ***statutes of limitations*** which bar a possibility of reverter after a certain period. Many of these statutes bar the possibility of reverter after a certain period following the ***creation*** of the fee simple determinable (e.g., 40 years).

Example: On the facts of Example 1 above, suppose the state had a 40-year statute of limitations on possibilities of reverter, running from the moment of their creation. Forty years after O conveyed to City, the limitation would in effect disappear, and City's fee simple determinable would be transformed into a fee simple absolute.

2. **Fee simple subject to condition subsequent:** A close relative of the fee simple determinable is the fee simple ***subject to a condition subsequent***. The latter is also geared to

the happening of a particular event, but unlike the fee simple determinable, the fee simple subject to a condition subsequent *does not automatically end* when the event occurs. Instead the grantor has a *right* to take back the property, but nothing happens until he *affirmatively exercises that right*.

a. Words used: In most jurisdictions, the language of the grant must meet two requirements before it will be found to establish a fee simple subject to a condition subsequent:

   i. Words of condition: First, it must indicate that the grant is *subject to a condition* by such phrases as "upon express condition that", "upon condition that", or "provided that", etc. Restatement, §45.

   ii. Right of re-entry: Second, there must generally be a provision that if the stated event occurs, the grantor may *re-enter the property*, and terminate the estate. *Id.*

   Example: O conveys Blackacre to *A* in fee simple, "but upon condition that no alcohol is ever served upon the premises. If alcohol is served, grantor or his heirs may re-enter the property and terminate the estate." *A* then sells the property to *B*, who builds a tavern. The mere sale of alcohol by *B* will not bring the estate to an end. Instead, O (or, if he is dead, one or more of his descendants) must re-enter the property or (under modern procedures) bring suit. Only when this happens will the estate terminate. Thus if O and his heirs do nothing, the condition is not enforced.

b. Absence of re-entry clause: If the conveyance contains the appropriate phrase "upon condition that. . .," but does *not* have a re-entry clause, most modern courts will not treat it as a condition subsequent. Powell, Par. 188, p. 32. Instead, the court is likely to treat the condition as simply establishing a *covenant* on the part of the grantee to obey the restriction. If he does not, all the grantor can get is *money damages*.

c. Terminology: Where a fee simple subject to a condition subsequent does exist, the grantor (the person creating the condition) is traditionally said to have a *"right of entry for condition broken."* The modern tendency is to call this a *"power of termination."* See 1 A.L.P. 418. The right of entry/power of termination is discussed more fully *infra*, p. 70.

d. Perpetuities: Traditionally, the right of re-entry has *not* been subject to the *Rule Against Perpetuities*, so that it can theoretically go on forever. However, many states have set a *time limit* on the use of the right, just as with possibilities of reverter. (*Supra*, p. 52.) Cribbet, pp. 45-46.

3. Condition subsequent distinguished from fee simple determinable: It may sometimes make a great deal of difference whether something is a fee simple determinable or a fee simple subject to condition subsequent. (In the case of the former, as noted, the estate ends *automatically* on the happening of the stated event; in the case of the latter, a grantor or his heirs must *actually re-enter or bring suit*, which in a particular case they may not bother to do.)

a. Statute of limitations: One reason why it can be important to distinguish between a fee simple subject to condition subsequent and a fee simple determinable relates to the *statute of limitations*. Where a fee simple determinable is involved, the holders of the possibility of reverter (the grantor or his heirs) in some states have an *unlimited* time in which to sue; in other states, a *very long* statute of limitations exists (e.g., 40 years from the grant). By contrast, in the case of a fee simple subject to a condition subsequent, the statute usually starts to run *upon the occurrence of the stated event*, and is usually for a relatively *short period*. That means that the holder of a right of re-entry after a fee subject to condition subsequent is much more likely to be found time-barred than is the holder of a reversion following a fee simple determinable.

    i. **Different result in *Mahrenholz*:** For instance, suppose the court in *Mahrenholz, supra*, p. 52, had held that the grant to the Ds created a fee simple subject to a condition subsequent, rather than a fee simple determinable. Then, when the Ds stopped using the premises for a school in 1973, they would not have been found to have lost title automatically, and S would later have conveyed to the Ps a mere right of re-entry. The statute of limitations on the Ps' right of re-entry would probably have been relatively short, and would probably have begun to run as soon as the Ds stopped using the property for a school. If the Ps did not bring suit until after this short limitations period had run, the Ps would have been time-barred, and the result would have been opposite the actual result in *Mahrenholz*.

  b. **Courts prefer condition subsequent:** Courts *dislike forfeitures*, particularly *automatic* ones such as those involved in fees simple determinable. Therefore, when there is some doubt about whether a conveyance establishes a fee simple determinable or a fee simple subject to a condition subsequent, the court will interpret it as the *latter*. It may do this even though the words used in the conveyance are those traditionally associated with a fee simple determinable.

4. **Fee simple subject to executory limitation:** A third kind of defeasible fee simple is called a fee simple *subject to an executory limitation*. The fee simple determinable, and the fee simple subject to a condition subsequent, exist by definition only when the estate will return to the *grantor* (or his heirs) when the stated event occurs. An executory limitation, by contrast, provides for the estate to pass to a *third person* (one other than the grantor) upon the happening of the stated event.

Example: O conveys Blackacre "to *A* and his heirs, but if the property is used for other than residential purposes, then to *B* and his heirs." *A* holds a fee simple subject to an executory limitation in favor of *B*. If either A, or one who receives the property from him, uses the property for commercial purposes, then title automatically passes to *B* or (if *B* is dead) his heirs.

  a. **Death without issue:** One common kind of fee simple subject to executory limitation centers around the *death without issue* of the original grantee.

    Example: O conveys "to *A* and his heirs, but if *A* dies without children surviving him then to *B* and his heirs." *A* has a fee simple subject to executory limitation, and *B* has an executory interest (which will become possessory only if *A* dies without surviving children).

  b. **Not allowed at early common law:** At early common law, the only estates that could follow a fee simple were the possibility of reverter (which follows a fee simple determinable) and the right of entry for condition broken (which follows a fee simple subject to a condition subsequent). Both of these, as noted, are for the benefit of the grantor or his heirs. The fee simple subject to an executory limitation, insofar as it would cause seisin to shift to a ***third person***, was an ***illegal "shifting" interest***.

  i. Statute of Uses: However, the Statute of Uses (enacted in 1535) made such shifting interest feasible. Therefore, executory limitations are analyzed further *infra*, p. 89, in connection with the discussion of the Statute of Uses. See Cribbet, p. 46.

  c. Perpetuities: The ***Rule Against Perpetuities (RAP) applies*** to executory interests. Therefore, if such an interest might vest more than 21 years plus lives in being from the time the interest was created, the interest will be ***void***, a big difference from a reversion following a fee simple determinable, and from a right of re-entry following a fee simple subject to condition subsequent. Compare Example 1 on p. 53 (fee simple determinable followed by reversion, so the RAP does not apply to the reversion) and Example 2 on p. 53 (fee simple subject to executory limitation followed by purported executory interest, where the RAP applies to make the executory interest invalid, making the fee simple absolute). See also *infra*, p. 98, for our main discussion of the RAP as it applies to executory interests.

5. Defeasible estates other than fee simple: The fee simple is not the only estate that may be defeasible. For instance, it is possible to have a ***defeasible life estate***. Defeasible life estates are discussed *infra*, p. 58.

6. Preference for outright grant: When you're interpreting an ambiguous grant, keep in mind that courts have a strong preference for an interpretation that results in the grantor's conveying her ***entire interest in the property*** (rather than some sort of fee simple defeasible or restrictive covenant). This preference is parallel to courts' dislike of restraints on alienation. So in an ambiguous situation, the court would prefer to find that a conveyance created a fee simple ***absolute*** rather than that it created some sort of fee simple defeasible.

  a. "For the purpose of" clause: A clause saying that the property is to be used ***"for the purpose of"*** thus-and-such, but without stating the consequences if the property is used for some other purpose, is a good example. As is discussed *supra*, p. 52, such a clause will probably be interpreted to impose no restriction at all, i.e., to create a fee simple absolute, rather than to create a fee simple determinable or fee simple subject to condition subsequent.

III. THE FEE TAIL

  A. Keeping property in the family: Suppose that O, the owner of a fee simple in Blackacre, wished to ensure that the property would ***remain within his family*** indefinitely. If O had a son, A, he would attempt to reach his objective by making a conveyance or bequest "to A ***and the heirs of his body***". If this bequest were given effect as intended, then upon A's death the property would go to A's heirs (who under the English system of primogeniture would be limited to A's ***oldest surviving son***), then to the heirs of that person, and so on through the centuries. It ***could not be conveyed to someone outside of the family***.

1. **The "fee tail":** This form of bequest — "to *A* and the heirs of his body" — is known as the *"fee tail."* (The term probably derives from the French "tailler," which means to "cut down" or carve, indicating an estate cut down to the grantor's liking.)

B. **Modern U.S. treatment of the fee tail:** The fee tail, as a method for insuring that property will descend along blood lines and will not be conveyed outside the family tree, is completely *dead* in the U.S. (as it is in England). A few states still recognize the fee tail, but permit a "disentailing conveyance" to be made. Other states have a variety of ways of treating a conveyance which at common law would have created a fee tail. Some of the various treatments (usually by statute) are as follows:

   1. **Fee simple absolute:** In 27 states, a grant or bequest that would be a fee tail at common law is simply *converted by statute to a fee simple absolute*. Thus a grant "to *A* and the heirs of his body" gives *A* a fee simple absolute. Moynihan, pp. 41-2. Thus in a majority of states, the fee tail is *completely without consequence*, at least in the case of a present-day conveyance.

      a. **Remainder following fee tail:** If the conveyance or devise was intended so that there would be a *remainder* to follow the fee tail, about half of these states treat the grantee's interest as being a fee simple *subject to an executory limitation*. For instance, suppose O leaves Blackacre "to *A* and the heirs of his body, remainder to *B* and his heirs". In roughly 13 states *A* gets a fee simple, but if he dies without surviving issue, the property passes to *B* in fee simple. Powell, Par. 198, p. 52.

   2. **Disentailable fee tail:** Four states, Delaware, Maine, Massachusetts, and Rhode Island (as to deeds only) continue to *recognize* the common-law fee tail. However, each of these states permits a simple *"disentailing conveyance"* to a third party, so that the latter may receive a fee simple.

   3. **Fee tail for one generation:** A few other states (e.g., Connecticut and Ohio) have statutes providing that *only the grantee* gets a fee tail, and his issue get the property in *fee simple absolute*.

   4. **Life estate in grantee, followed by fee simple:** Eight states (e.g., Florida, Illinois, Missouri, and in some cases Georgia) give the grantee or devisee a *life estate*, with a remainder in fee simple to his issue. This result is functionally quite similar to the kind of provision described in paragraph (3) *supra*.

IV. LIFE ESTATES

A. **General meaning of "life estate":** The *life estate*, unlike the fee tail, retains tremendous practical significance today. As the term indicates, the estate is one which lasts for the lifetime of a person.

   1. **Ordinary life estate and estate *per autre vie*:** Ordinarily, the lifetime by which the life estate is "measured" is that of the holder of the life estate (e.g., O grants a life estate "to *A* for his lifetime, then to *B* in fee simple.") Occasionally, however, the measuring life is that of someone other than the holder of the life estate (e.g., O grants "to *A* for the life of *B*,

then to *C* in fee simple".) This latter type of life estate is called an estate *"per autre vie"*. The estate *per autre vie* is discussed further *infra*, p. 59.

2. Life estate by operation of law: Ordinarily, a life estate is created at the wishes of the grantor or testator. Occasionally, however, a life estate may be created **by operation of law**.

    a. Dower and curtesy: For instance, a surviving spouse at common law gained the right of dower (for a widow) or curtesy (for a widower). Dower and curtesy are in essence life estates, and are discussed *infra*, p. 123.

B. Creation of the ordinary life estate: The most common phrase used for creating a life estate is "to *B* during his life" or "to *B* for life."

    1. Other phrases used to create: However, there are a number of other phrases which may create a life estate.

        a. Until death: For instance, "to *B* until he dies" would create a life estate. See Moynihan, p. 48.

        b. Gift over upon death: Also, a life estate may be inferred from the fact that following the grantor's death, there is a gift over to another. For instance, "to *B* and then at his death to *B*'s children in fee simple" would give *B* a life estate. Moynihan, p. 48.

C. Life estate defeasible: Just as a fee simple may be *defeasible* rather than absolute, so a life estate may be defeasible. For instance, suppose that *A* devises Blackacre "to *B*, for so long as she shall remain my widow, then to my son *C*." This would create a life estate determinable, by analogy to the fee simple determinable. Moynihan, p. 50.

    1. Difficulty of construction: If there is no gift over upon the recipient's death (e.g., in the above example, the bequest read simply "to *B* for so long as she remains my widow"), it may not be clear whether there is a fee simple determinable or a life estate determinable. This issue can be important, since if *B* dies without having remarried, the property can be taken by will or intestacy if it is a fee simple determinable, but will revert to *A*'s heirs if it is a life estate determinable. The modern trend is probably towards treating this as a *fee simple determinable*. Moynihan, p. 51.

D. Estate now of limited utility: A life estate in real property is very *inflexible*, and is therefore of limited utility. For instance, suppose that *A* leaves Blackacre to his widow, *B*, for life, then to their surviving children. As long as *B* is willing to live on the property for the rest of her life, the arrangement works out all right. But suppose that she finds the property too large and expensive to keep up, and wants to move to a Florida condominium. She cannot convey a fee simple interest in the property unless she gets the written consent of the remaindermen (in this case, the children of her marriage with *A*). If even one of the children objects, she is locked in.

    1. Unascertained remaindermen: Even worse, there can be situations where the *identity of the remaindermen* cannot be ascertained until the life estate ends. For instance, suppose *A* devised the property "to my wife *B* for life, then to her surviving issue." No matter how old *B* is, it is always possible that she could have another child (perhaps by adoption). Since it is not possible to obtain the consent of the hypothetical, unborn child, who could take an interest in the property as a surviving issue, the property is effectively unsalable.

2. **Additional power of disposition:** One way around this problem is for the grantor to give the life tenant the power to sell, rent, or mortgage the property. There is still a life estate, since upon the life tenant's death, the property cannot pass by devise or intestacy.

3. **Equitable life estate:** The problem of inflexibility is also avoided by the use of an *equitable* life estate (as distinguished from the "legal" life estate that we have been discussing). An equitable life estate is one in which the legal ownership of the property is given to a *trustee*, and the *use* of the property is the only thing given to the life tenant. The trustee is given the right to sell, rent, mortgage or otherwise administer the property as he deems fit. Following the death of the life tenant, the property can either continue under the trustee's administration, for the benefit of other persons (e.g., the surviving issue of the testator and his widow) or the trust can end with legal title vesting directly in a third person. See the discussion of equitable estates, and modern trusts, *infra*, p. 83.

E. **Life estate *per autre vie*:** Usually, a life estate is measured in terms of the life of the grantee. However, it is possible to create a life estate that is measured by the life of *someone other than the grantee*. Such a life estate is called an estate *per autre vie* ("by another's life", *supra*, p. 57).

1. **Death of the life tenant:** The estate *per autre vie* is identical to the ordinary life estate in most respects. However, there is one important difference: where the measuring life is that of the grantee, upon the grantee's death the estate automatically comes to an end, and possession passes to the grantor or to some third person. But in the case of an estate *per autre vie*, upon the death of the life tenant, the estate can *continue*, since the measuring life may still exist. Who gets the estate next has been the subject of great confusion and controversy.

   a. **Modern-day statutes change rule:** Today, this issue is usually resolved by statute. Generally, upon the life tenant's death, the balance of the life estate (until the measuring life ends) is treated as *personal property*, which passes by will or by intestacy. (Some states have intestacy statutes making a distinction between real and personal property so that heirs who would receive real estate will not necessarily be the ones to receive the personalty.)

F. **Duties and powers of life tenant:** Let's talk now about the *powers and duties* of the life tenant.

1. **Powers of life tenant** The life tenant has certain *powers* vis-à-vis the property, but these are more *restricted* than for the holder of a fee simple, because the life tenant cannot act in a way that would damage the remainder or other future interest.

   a. **Right to keep income:** The life tenant has the exclusive right to *lease out* the premises (but not beyond the term of the life tenant's own life), and the exclusive right to *keep all rents.* If there is an *existing lease* on the property at the time the life tenant receives her interest, then unless the conveyance states otherwise, the life tenant is entitled to keep all of the rents under that lease.

      i. **Must pay expenses:** But the life tenant's right to keep all rents is subject to her obligation, discussed below, to pay all current expenses.

Figure 4-1
Freehold Estates

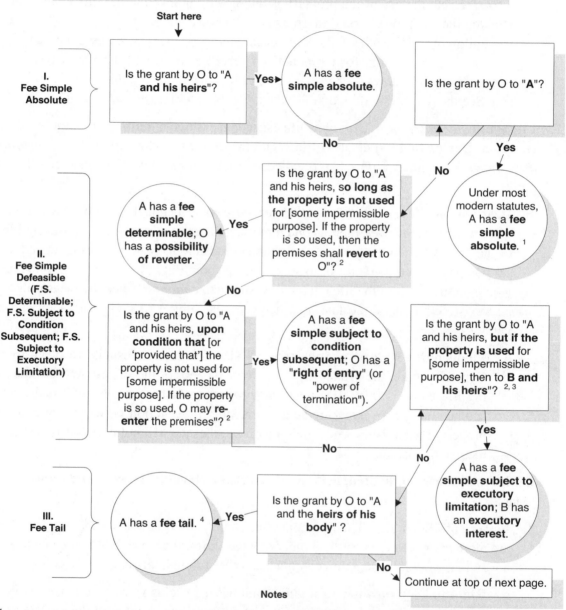

Use this chart to determine what freehold estate is created by particular words of grant. O is the conveyor; A is the recipient of the grant. Where a future interest is also created, B is the recipient of that interest. Unless otherwise noted, the common-law treatment of the grant is all that is discussed.

Start here

I. Fee Simple Absolute

Is the grant by O to "A **and his heirs**"?

Yes▶ A has a **fee simple absolute**.

No

Is the grant by O to "**A**"?

Yes → Under most modern statutes, A has a **fee simple absolute**. [1]

No

II. Fee Simple Defeasible (F.S. Determinable; F.S. Subject to Condition Subsequent; F.S. Subject to Executory Limitation)

Is the grant by O to "A and his heirs, s**o long as the property is not used** for [some impermissible purpose]. If the property is so used, then the premises shall **revert** to O"? [2]

Yes ◀ A has a **fee simple determinable**; O has a **possibility of reverter**.

No

Is the grant by O to "A and his heirs, **upon condition that** [or 'provided that'] the property is not used for [some impermissible purpose]. If the property is so used, O may **re-enter** the premises"? [2]

Yes▶ A has a **fee simple subject to condition subsequent**; O has a **"right of entry"** (or **"power of termination"**).

No

Is the grant by O to "A and his heirs, **but if the property is used** for [some impermissible purpose], then to **B and his heirs**"? [2,3]

Yes → A has a **fee simple subject to executory limitation**; B has an **executory interest**.

No

III. Fee Tail

A has a **fee tail**. [4] **◀Yes** Is the grant by O to "A and the **heirs of his body**"?

No → Continue at top of next page.

Notes

---

[1] In other words, in most states today the language "to A and his heirs" is not necessary for creating a fee simple absolute -- a plain old "to A" suffices.

[2] When you deal with any kind of fee simple defeasible (i.e., a fee simple that is not absolute and can therefore end), your main job is to distinguish between the fee simple determinable (f.s.d.) and the fee simple subject to condition subsequent (f.s.s.c.s.). The distinction is that the f.s.d. ends <u>automatically</u> on the happening of the stated event, whereas the f.s.s.c.s. only ends upon both the happening of the event and some <u>affirmative action</u> by the holder of the reversionary interest (i.e., a suit or an attempt to re-take the

premises). If in doubt, resolve ambiguity in favor of f.s.s.c.s., since courts try to avoid forfeitures.

<u>Example 1 (fee simple determinable)</u>: Grant by O "to A, so long as the premises continue to be used as a house of Islamic worship. If the property ceases to be so used, it shall revert to O." (Note the use of "revert" [not "re-enter"], indicating that the change happens automatically.)

<u>Example 2 (fee simple subject to condition subsequent)</u>: Grant by O "to A, upon condition that the property continues to be used as a house for Islamic worship. If the property ceases to be so used, O or his heirs may re-enter the premises." (Note

Notes continued on next page

Figure 4-1 (cont.)
Freehold Estates

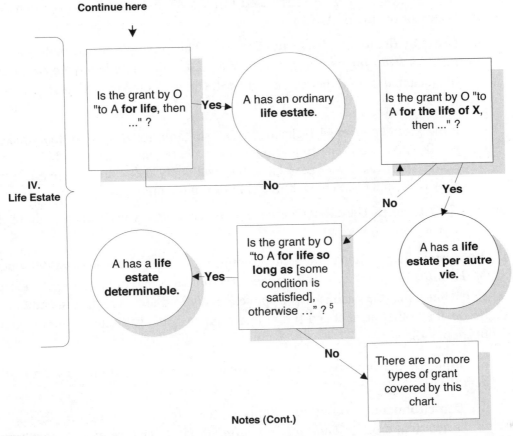

Continue here

IV. Life Estate

Is the grant by O "to A **for life**, then ..." ? → **Yes** → A has an ordinary **life estate**.

Is the grant by O "to A **for the life of X**, then ..." ?

No

A has a **life estate determinable**. ← **Yes** ← Is the grant by O "to A **for life so long as** [some condition is satisfied], otherwise ..." ? [5]

Yes → A has a **life estate per autre vie**.

No → There are no more types of grant covered by this chart.

Notes (Cont.)

that the change happens only if O or his heirs affirmatively takes action to re-enter.)

[3] Apart from "use" restrictions, a common fee simple subject to executory limitation involves A's "<u>death without issue</u>." Assuming (as is likely) that the court interprets this type of bequest to refer to A's death without <u>survivors</u> (not the running out of his line at some future time after his death with survivors), the bequest is a f.s. subject to executory limitation if the gift over is to some third person (not to O or O's heirs).

<u>Example</u>: O grants "to A and his heirs, but if A shall die without issue, then to B and his heirs." Because the court will probably interpret this to refer to a "definite failure of issue" (i.e., A's failure to die with survivors), the state of title is: A has a fee simple subject to executory limitation; B has an executory interest.

[4] Keep in mind that states vary tremendously in how they treat a grant that would, at common law, create a fee tail. For instance, a slight majority of states convert the fee tail into a fee simple absolute.

[5] Use the same rules of interpretation as for fees simple that may be determinable. Thus if the life estate is to be cut off automatically upon the happening of the stated event, it's a life estate determinable; if O's heirs have a right of reentry, it's a life estate subject to condition subsequent; and if title moves to a third person on the stated event, it's a life estate subject to executory limitation.

<u>Example</u>: O grants "to A, my wife, for life, but if A should re-marry, then to my son S." Title is: life estate in A subject to executory limitation; executory interest in S.

---

b. **Conveyance of interest:** The life tenant may *convey* any interest in the property, up to and including the entirety of his own interest.

Example: If *A* holds a life estate, he may convey to *B* either for the life of *A* (in which case *B* has an life estate *per autre vie;* see *supra*, p. 59), or for a term of years.

i. **No greater:** But the life tenant *cannot* convey a *fee simple*, or any other estate *greater than the life estate he holds.* If he does purport to convey a greater interest (e.g., a fee simple), the conveyance will be effective, but only to convey the *entirety of the grantor's life estate*.

Example: *O* conveys a life estate to *A*. *A* purports to convey "to *B* and her heirs." *A*'s conveyance will be interpreted to pass *A*'s life estate to *B* (so that *B* has an estate for the life of *A*).

ii. Lease by life tenant for term of years: This principle means that if a life tenant makes a *lease for a term of years*, that lease will *immediately be cut short* if the life tenant *dies*. And that's true even if the holder of the reversion acquiesced to the lease.

Example: *O* conveys Blackacre "to my son Sam for life." Sam then makes a 15-year lease of the property to Tenant. *O* is aware that the lease is being made, and tacitly approves. Two years later, Sam suddenly dies. Tenant's lease is immediately over, and *O* can have him ejected from the premises.

2. Duties of life tenant: The life tenant has a number of *duties* vis-à-vis the future interest. These include the following:

a. No waste: The life tenant may not commit *waste*, i.e., an *unreasonable impairment of the value* the property will have when the holder of the future interest takes possession. (Since the rule against waste applies to landlord-tenant relations, and to relations between all other present and future interests, the topic is discussed more extensively *infra*, p. 94.)

Example: If the property includes a *structure*, the life tenant may ordinarily *not demolish* it.

i. Demolition and rebuilding: Suppose the life tenant proposes to demolish a structure in order to *build a more valuable (and perhaps bigger) structure* at his own expense. Such a use is often called *"ameliorative waste."* Courts are *split* on whether and when the life tenant is entitled to commit ameliorative waste:

(1) Traditional rule: The traditional (and English) rule has been that the life tenant may *not* commit ameliorative waste, i.e., demolish a structure and build a new one even if this would increase the value of the property.

(2) Modern rule: But most courts in America now seem to have *rejected* the traditional rule and allow at least some ameliorative waste. Under this modern/majority approach, the life tenant may demolish an existing structure and build a new one provided that:

[1] the *value* of the *reversion* is *not decreased* (i.e., the waste really *is* "ameliorative"); and

[2] because of *changes to the neighborhood*, or for other reasons, it is very *unlikely that a rational person* in the position of the future-interest holder would, if she owned the property outright today, want to *continue the prior use*.

Cf. S&W, p. 152.

Example: Suppose that a one-acre parcel contains only one building, a small barn built in 1850 and not modernized since. The neighborhood has now become completely suburban, so that all nearby parcels contain modern houses, and there are no barns. The barn itself has not been used for any purpose in 30 years, since no agricultural activity is conducted on the parcel. L, the life tenant, wants to demolish the barn and build (at L's expense) a conventional suburban house. If L does this, the value of the property will be increased by $200,000. R, the holder of the remainder, opposes L's proposal, arguing that the rural character of the land should be preserved.

A court is very likely to side with L, and permit the demolition and building. Clearly the waste would be "ameliorative," since the value of the property would be increased by $200,000. Furthermore, on these facts few owners of the land would maintain the barn in its present form, since it cannot readily be used. Therefore, condition [2] above (change in neighborhood that makes the present use irrational) is satisfied.

b. Current operating expenses: The life tenant must *pay all current operating expenses* of the property.

   i. Repairs: Thus the life tenant must *make (and pay for) reasonable "maintenance-style" repairs* (though probably not major structural repairs like a new roof).

   ii. Taxes: The life tenant must *pay all property taxes.*

   iii. Limited to rental or occupancy value: In the case of a dispute between the life tenant and the holder of the future interest, the life tenant's responsibility for current operating expenses like repairs and taxes applies *only* to the extent the life tenant *received rents* from the property, or the extent of the property's *fair rental value* if the life tenant herself occupies it. That is, the life tenant has *no personal liability for current operating expenses* beyond the *net financial benefits* she has received.

   So, for instance, suppose the property consists of *vacant land*, and the life tenant does not pay taxes, so the holder of the future interest steps in to pay them. That future holder will have the right to be repaid out of any proceeds of the property's sale, and to foreclose on the life tenant's interest to ensure repayment, but *not to get a money judgment against the life tenant* — the obligation *runs only against the property*. (But if the life tenant *collects rents* and then doesn't pay the taxes, then the life tenant *is* personally liable to the future-interest holder for the unpaid taxes up to the amount of rents collected).

c. Payment of mortgage: When a *mortgage* is put on the property before the life tenancy is created, most courts *allocate* the duty to pay mortgage interest and principal *between the life estate and the future interest.* Usually the allocation of both interest and principal is done more or less *in ratio to the present value* of the life estate versus the present value of the future interests (so that if the life estate and remainder have approximately equal net present values, the life tenant and the remainderman will each be obligated to pay half of each installment of interest and principal).

i. **No personal obligation:** However, as with repairs or taxes, neither the holder of the life estate nor the holder of the future interest is ***personally liable*** for his or her allocated share of the mortgage, except to the extent that the share is more than covered by the net operating income of the property. Therefore, when a property does not earn enough in any given year to cover the life tenant's fairly-allocated share of mortgage interest and principal, the remainderman is ***not entitled to an order compelling the life tenant to make up the shortfall;*** instead, the remainder-man's sole remedy is to lay out the money and then get it back "off the top" if the property is sold while the life estate is still in force.

A consequence of this rule is that the remainderman may have to ***choose*** between (1) letting the entire value of the remainder interest be ***lost*** through nonpayment of the mortgage and foreclosure and (2) ***making up*** any shortfall between operating profits and the life tenant's fairly-allocated share of mortgage interest and principal (and waiting for an eventual sale to get the money back).

Quiz Yourself on
FREEHOLD ESTATES

8. O'Malley was the owner in fee simple of Blackacre. As a gift, O'Malley delivered to Abel a deed to Blackacre; the deed read, "to Abel and his heirs." Abel recorded the deed as required by local statutes. Abel then delivered a deed to Blackacre to Barbara, who recorded it. Abel then died, leaving as his sole heir his son, Callaway. Who owns Blackacre? _____

9. In the State of Ames, there is a one-year statute of limitations on actions to enforce a right of entry for condition broken. Ames also has a statute barring any possibility of reverter 50 years following the cre-ation of a fee simple determinable. In Ames, O held a fee simple absolute in Blackacre. Because O had watched his daughter's marital prospects be ruined by her early involvement as a pornography star, O sold Blackacre to A, a nightclub operator, under a conveyance, "To A and his heirs so long as the premises are not used for topless or erotic dancing, and if they are so used, then the premises shall revert to O." This conveyance took place in 1980. A complied with this restriction. In 1988, O died, leaving all his real and personal property to his son S. In 1990, A conveyed, "To B and his heirs, in fee simple absolute." That same year, B began to use the premises as a topless bar, and continued doing so for the next 19 years. In 2012, S asks the court for a determination that the property now belongs to him because of B's operation of the topless club. Should the court grant S's request? _____

10. Same facts as the prior question. Now, however, assume that the deed from O to A stated, "To A and his heirs, provided that no topless or other obscene dancing ever takes place on the premises. If such dancing does take place, Grantor or his heirs may re-enter the property." All other facts remain the same, except that in 2012, S files suit for a decree authorizing him to re-enter the property. Should the court grant S's request? _____

11. O conveyed Blackacre "to A for life, remainder to B." One year later, A quitclaimed all of his interest in Blackacre to C. After this quitclaim deed, what is the state of title? _____

Answers

8. Barbara. The gift "to Abel and his heirs" does not mean "to Abel for life then to his heirs." Instead, "to Abel and his heirs" means "to Abel in *fee simple*." Therefore, Abel had the right to do whatever he wished with the property, and his deed of it to Barbara was effective. Thus when Abel died, he had no interest in Blackacre to leave to his son and heir.

9. Yes. The original grant from O to A was a *fee simple determinable*. We know this because of the phrase "so long as…," and the word "revert." Therefore, after the conveyance, O was left with a *possibility of reverter*. When O died, his possibility of reverter passed to his son S. When A purported to convey a fee simple absolute to B, he really conveyed only a fee simple determinable subject to S's possibility of reverter. When B began using the premises for the forbidden purpose in 1990, title *automatically* reverted to S, without S taking any formal action. Therefore, S remained the owner of the property in 2012, and is entitled to a judicial decree to that effect. (If more than 50 years passed after O's original creation of the fee simple determinable, then S or his successors would lose their right to this decree, since they would be barred by the 50-year statute of limitations on possibilities of reverter.)

10. No. Now, the O-to-A conveyance established a *fee simple subject to a condition subsequent*. (The words "upon condition that" or "provided that," when taken with a clause providing for re-entry, establish that a fee simple subject to condition subsequent, rather than a fee simple determinable, was created.) This left O (and, after his death, S) with a right of entry, not a possibility of reverter. By the statute of limitations, S was required to bring his suit for re-entry within one year of B's commencement of the illegal use, i.e., by 1991. When S did not do so, his right of entry was extinguished. So by comparing this question with the prior one, you can see the importance of distinguishing between a fee simple determinable and a fee simple subject to a condition subsequent.

11. Life estate *per autre vie* in C, remainder in fee simple in B. After the initial conveyance by O, A was a life tenant. In all states, a life tenant may convey the interest which he holds, or a lesser one (but not a greater one). Therefore, A was capable of conveying his life estate to C; once that conveyance took place, C had a life estate *per autre vie* (life estate measured by another person's life), since C's interest would end when A died, not when C died. B continued to hold the fee simple remainder that he got when O made the initial conveyance.

Exam Tips *on*
FREEHOLD ESTATES

Defeasible fees

This is a frequently tested area. Your success in tackling this subject will depend heavily on your ability to dissect the language used.

☛ **Key phrases:** When analyzing a fee simple defeasible to determine whether it is determinable or subject to a condition subsequent, look for key words.

☞ **Determinable phrases:** "So long as," "during," "until" indicate that it is *determin-*

able and ends *automatically* upon the occurrence of the event.

☞ **Condition-subsequent phrases:** When a fee simple is subject to a *condition subsequent,* the grant will usually contain a phrase like "upon condition that," "but if," or "provided that," and also a clause providing for *re-entry* when the condition is broken.

☛ **Restraints on alienation disliked:** Remember that courts *dislike restraints on alienation.* This attitude manifests itself in several ways:

☞ **Defeasible vs. absolute:** If there is a doubt whether a defeasible fee or a fee simple absolute is indicated, courts will *prefer* finding that a grant is a *fee simple absolute.*

Example: A deed contains the following provision: "To have and to hold the described tract of land in fee simple, subject to the understanding that within one year from the date of the instrument said grantee shall construct and thereafter maintain and operate on said premises a public health center." Because the language "subject to the understanding that" does not clearly indicate a defeasible fee, a court would probably interpret the conveyance as a *fee simple absolute* with the imposition of a *personal contractual obligation* on the grantee. (So if the grantee fails to construct, the grantor gets damages but doesn't get back the property.)

☞ **Condition subsequent vs. determinable:** If there is a doubt, courts will *usually,* but not always, interpret a defeasible fee as *subject to a condition subsequent* rather than determinable, because courts disfavor forfeitures.

☞ **Automatic end:** But if the language indicates that the estate is to come to an end *automatically* on the happening of the stated event (i.e., *without any action* by the grantor or his heirs), this will make the grant a fee *determinable,* even if there is some other ambiguity in the language.

Example: O's grant provides: "To A and B, exclusively, as joint tenants, with right of survivorship, to be used as a parking lot, but if said premises should ever be used for a different purpose, then this conveyance shall immediately become void." Because of the clear language indicating that the estate is to end *immediately* (without action by O or his heirs), a court would probably determine that this grant is determinable despite use of the "but if" language (which would otherwise usually suggest a condition subsequent).

Fee tails

☛ **Fee tail generally:** Look for the language *"and the heirs of his body."* This language of course always indicates that at common law, the grant was a fee tail (could only pass to the grantee's direct line, and would revert to the grantor if the grantee's line ran out).

☞ **Note modern consequences:** But if your fact pattern does not tell you to assume that common-law rules are in effect, you should say in your analysis that although this would be a fee tail at common law, modern statutes may change its effects — you might want to note, for instance, that in a slight majority of states a fee tail is converted by statute to a fee simple absolute.

☞ **"If A dies without issue...":** Sometimes the fee tail is accompanied by language stating what happens if the grantee *dies without issue.* If so, note in your answer that in some states (though just a minority), the fee tail is treated as a fee simple subject to executory limitation, with the remainder passing in fee simple.

Example: O grants "to A and the heirs of his body, but if A dies without issue, then to B." Note that while in a slight majority of states A gets a fee simple absolute, in some states A gets a fee simple subject to an executory limitation — in that event, if A dies without issue, B gets the property in fee simple absolute.

Life estates

☛ **Duties of tenant and remainderman:** Questions regarding the life tenancy most frequently involve distinguishing between the *duties* of the *life tenant* and the duties of the *remainderman*.

    ☞ **Duties:** Remember that the *life tenant* is required to pay *real estate taxes* that become due during the life tenancy. The life tenant is also responsible for mortgage *interest* to the extent that it does not exceed the reasonable rental value of the realty. However, the *remainderman* is responsible for payment of *principal*.

        ☞ **Trick:** Don't be tricked by a fact pattern that indicates that the reasonable rental value of the realty exceeds the sum necessary to pay *both* the principal and the interest on a loan. The life tenant's responsibility still will not extend to payment of principal.

☛ **Waste:** Profs love to test for *waste.* Look for a fact pattern where the life tenant does an affirmative act that causes *unreasonable, permanent damage* to the holder of the future interest.

    ☞ **Cutting timber:** Questions often involve the *cutting of timber.* If the life tenant is making reasonable use of the wood for the purpose of *maintaining* the realty (e.g., to repair the fences surrounding livestock pastures), then she will not be liable for waste. But if she's cutting the timber to sell it, and timber cultivation is not the sole reasonable use of the property, then the cutting *will* usually be waste.

    ☞ **Earth and minerals:** The life tenant may not *remove minerals* unless: (i) the property was used for mining prior to the commencement of the life estate ("open mines" doctrine) or (ii) mining is the only way of accomplishing the purpose of the lease (because mining is the only use for which the property is suitable or because mining is necessary for the agricultural use of the property that was intended).

    Example: X dies, leaving his farm to his son Y for life, remainder to Z charity. Y tries farming the land for awhile because his father was a farmer, but he loses interest. Instead, he finds that mining gravel from the land is very lucrative. Y is liable to Z for voluntary waste because gravel was never removed from the land previously and the property was fit for farming, its intended purpose.

☛ **Conveyance:** A life tenant can *convey* the interest which she holds, but may not convey one that is larger.

    Example: X conveys a parcel of realty "to Y for Y's life, and the remainder to my children." Y may convey his estate to Z, but only one that terminates on Y's death.

☞ **Lease by life tenant:** Be on the lookout for a life tenant who makes a *"lease"* for a term of years. If the life tenant dies, the lease is over, even if the remainder-holder approved of the lease (but didn't sign as landlord) before it was made.

Example: O conveys Blackacre "to my daughter Jean for life." Jean is 30. O learns that Jean is about to lease the property for 20 years to A. O makes no objection, and Jean makes the lease. Two years later, Jean dies in a car accident. At that moment, A's lease ends automatically, since it can't be for longer than the landlord's interest in the property.

CHAPTER 5

FUTURE INTERESTS

I. INTRODUCTION

A. Future estates: The estates discussed in the previous chapter are ones which are *possessory*, or present. The common law also recognizes, however, a number of estates that are non-possessory. Since these estates may or will become possessory in the future, they are commonly referred to as *future estates*.

  1. Estate exists in present even though not now possessory: These future estates, even though they are not possessory, nonetheless exist in the present. For instance, suppose *A* conveys Blackacre "to *B* for life, remainder in fee simple to *C* and his heirs". At the time of conveyance, *C* has a remainder in fee simple; it is only the aspect of possession that is future.

B. Five estates: There are five kinds of future estates, each of which will be discussed in this chapter:

  [1] The *possibility of reverter*, which follows the fee simple determinable (*infra*);

  [2] The *right of entry*, which follows an interest (fee simple or other) subject to a condition subsequent (*infra*, p. 70);

  [3] The *reversion*, which is left in a grantor after he makes a conveyance of a lesser estate (*infra*, p. 71);

  [4] The *remainder*, which is a future interest in one other than the grantor, and which takes effect after the termination of an earlier estate (*infra*, p. 72); and

  [5] The *executory interest*, which like the remainder is a future interest in one other than the grantor, but which generally takes effect by cutting short a prior interest (*infra*, p. 88).

II. THE POSSIBILITY OF REVERTER AND THE RIGHT OF ENTRY

A. Reversionary interests: We have seen that under the Anglo-American system of estates, ownership of a given parcel of land may be split among a present interest and one or more future interests. One way such a split can occur is if the owner of a present estate (either a possessory fee simple absolute or some lesser present interest, such as a life estate) transfers possession, but not the full interest he owns. Where this happens, the grantor is left with one of several kinds of *reversionary interests:* (1) the *possibility of reverter;* (2) the *right of entry;* and (3) the *reversion.*

B. Possibility of reverter: Suppose the owner of a fee simple absolute transfers a *fee simple determinable* (*supra*, pp. 51-54). The grantor is said to retain a *possibility of reverter*. That is, if the fee simple determinable comes to an end, possession reverts to the grantor; since it is not certain that this will ever occur, the word "possibility" is used.

Example: O owns a fee simple absolute in Blackacre. He conveys "to A and his heirs, so long as no liquor is sold on the premises, and if liquor is sold thereon, title to revert to O and his heirs". After the transfer, O has a possibility of reverter; he will automatically regain possession if A or anyone holding under him sells liquor.

1. **Distinguish from reversion:** The possibility of reverter should be distinguished from the *reversion* (discussed *infra*, p. 71), which is a non-contingent prospect of getting the property back, Thus, if in the above example, O's conveyance had been "to A for life," with nothing more, O would have a reversion, not a possibility of reverter, since A's life is sure to come to an end.

2. **Alienability of possibility of reverter:** All states agree that a possibility of reverter is *inheritable* under the intestacy statute, and devisable by will. However, the states are in dispute about whether such a possibility of reverter may be *conveyed inter vivos*; the modern trend is to *allow* such conveyances. B,C&S, p. 226.

C. **Right of entry:** If the holder of an interest in land conveys all or part of his interest and attaches a *condition subsequent* to the transferee's interest, the transferor is said to have a *right of entry* (or as it is sometimes called, a right of entry for condition broken). This right gives the transferor ability to take back the estate if the condition subsequent occurs.

Example: O owns Blackacre in fee simple. He conveys "to A and his heirs, on condition that liquor never be sold on the premises; if liquor is sold thereon, O or his heirs may re-enter the premises." The conveyance to A has been made subject to a condition subsequent, and O therefore reserves a right of entry.

1. **Not incident to reversion:** Sometimes, the *only* interest retained by a grantor is this right of entry for condition broken. This is the case in the above example, since O conveyed all his other interest in the land (his fee simple).

   a. **Incident to reversion:** Much more commonly, however, a transferor who holds a right of entry *also holds a reversion*. For instance, nearly every *lease* contains several right of entry clauses, by which the landlord may re-enter if the tenant breaches a covenant (e.g., the covenant to pay rent). Such a right of entry is incident to the landlord's reversion at the end of the lease term.

2. **Alienability:** The distinction between a right of entry incident to a reversion and one that is not so incident is important with respect to *alienability*.

   a. **Incident to reversion:** Where the right of entry is incident to a reversion the general rule today is that it *passes with the reversion*. Thus if a landlord sells his interest in property, and assigns the leases he holds, the assignee may retake the premises in situations where the original landlord could have done so. Moynihan, p. 108.

   b. **Not incident to reversion:** Where a right of entry is not incident to any reversion, however, alienability may be somewhat more restricted.

      i. *Inter vivos* **transfer:** At common law, such a right of entry could *not be conveyed inter vivos*.

      ii. **Present-day split:** Today, most states continue to treat a right of entry unaccompanied by a reversion as *not transferable inter vivos*. A minority, however, have enacted statutes permitting such a transfer, either in all cases or at least where a breach of the condition has already occurred. Powell, Par. 282, pp. 249-52.

    iii. Devise and descent: On the other hand, in most states a right of entry without a reversion is *devisable* and *descendible*. Moynihan, p. 109. See Rest., §164, Comment a; §165. A minority of states maintain the traditional rule that the right of entry is neither descendible nor devisable.

D. Executory interests: The possibility of reverter and the right of entry are both defined as to belong to the *grantor*, rather than a third person. However, under modern law, an interest similar to a fee simple determinable, or to a fee simple subject to a condition subsequent, can be created that gives a third person an interest comparable to a possibility of reverter or to a right of entry. In such a case, the present interest is called a "fee simple subject to an executory interest," and the third party has an *executory interest*. See the further discussion of this topic *infra*, p. 89.

III. REVERSIONS

A. Reversions generally: A *reversion* is created when the holder of a vested estate transfers to another a *smaller estate*; the reversion is the interest which *remains in the grantor*. See Rest. 2d (Donative Transfers) §1.4, Comment c.

Example: *A* holds a fee simple absolute in Blackacre. He conveys "to *B* for life." *A* has retained a reversion, which will become possessory in *A* (or his heirs) upon *B*'s death.

    1. No reservation needed: It is not necessary that the grantor specifically reserve a reversion in himself. As long as the estate conveyed is legally smaller than the grantor's original estate, he retains a reversion. Thus in the above example, *A* retained a reversion even though nothing to this effect was stated in the grant, since a life estate is smaller than a fee simple.

    2. Holder of less-than-fee-simple: Even when *A* holds a *less-than-fee-simple interest*, he can create a reversion in himself by transferring a still smaller estate. Thus if *A* held a fee tail, and conveyed "to *B* for life," *A* would have a reversion in fee tail.

        a. Two life estates: Similarly, under the modern view, if *A* owns a life estate, and conveys to *B* for *B*'s life, *A* has a reversion. In this situation, although it can be argued that one life estate can't be smaller than another, the fact is that *B*'s life estate can terminate before *A*'s, whereas *A*'s cannot terminate before *B*'s. See Moynihan, p. 94, n. 2.

    3. Transfer of term of years: At common law, if an owner of a freehold estate created a *leasehold interest* (i.e., a term of years) in another, the grantor was not said to retain a reversion. Instead, he was regarded as continuing to hold the seisin in the land, and his freehold was merely subject to the terms of years. But in modern parlance, the landlord is said to have a reversion subject to the lease term. C&L, p. 290.

B. Will not necessarily become possessory: A reversion will *not necessarily ever become possessory*. If events occur in such a way that it becomes certain that the reversion can never become possessory, it is said to have been *divested*.

Example: O conveys Blackacre "to A for life, and then to B and his heirs if B survives A." O has a reversion which will become possessory when A dies, if B has predeceased A. But if A dies before B, the reversion is divested, since B now holds a fee simple absolute.

C. Distinguishing from possibility of reverter: It will sometimes be important to distinguish between a reversion and a possibility of reverter (particularly in the context of the doctrine of merger, *infra*, p. 80). To do this, one must examine the interest given away by the grantor; if he has given away a fee simple determinable, he retains only a possibility of reverter. If he has given away something less than a fee simple, he retains a reversion.

D. Alienability: Reversions have always been viewed as *alienable inter vivos*. Moynihan, p. 95. Furthermore, they are *devisable* and *descendible*.

   1. Possibility of divestment: However, remember that a reversion may be subject to divestment. Thus suppose that A, who holds a fee simple, conveys to B for life, than to C and his heirs if C survives B. A is free to transfer or devise his reversion to X. But if, following such a transfer or bequest, B dies while C is still living, X takes nothing.

IV. REMAINDERS

A. Definition: A *remainder* is a future interest in *someone other than the grantor or the grantee of a possessory interest*, if the interest can become possessory only upon the *expiration* of the *prior possessory interest*, created by the *same instrument*. That is, for a remainder to exist, the following requirements must be met:

   [1] A grantor must convey a *present possessory estate* (called the "particular" estate) to one transferee;

   [2] He must create a *non-possessory* estate in *another* transferee, by the *same instrument*; and

   [3] The second, non-possessory, estate (the remainder) must be capable of becoming possessory only on the *"natural" expiration* (as opposed to the *cutting short*) of the prior estate.

   Example: *O* conveys "to A for life, then to B and his heirs." *B* has a remainder because: (1) a present interest has been created; (2) a future interest has been created in a different person by the same instrument; and (3) the second interest will become possessory only after the natural expiration of the first one (i.e., after A's death).

B. Following a term of years: In modern parlance, one can refer to an estate following a *term of years* as a remainder. Thus if O conveys "to A for 10 years, then to B and his heirs," B would today be said to have a remainder.

   1. Common-law view: But at common law, B would be said to have not a remainder, but a *present freehold*, subject to A's less-than-freehold term of years. C&L, p. 294. That is, at the time of the conveyance the seisin was deemed to pass from O directly B (since by definition the holder of a non-freehold estate could not hold seisin).

   2. Following life estate: The main time you as a student should be worrying about whether a future interest is a remainder is when the prior interest is a *life estate* (rather than, say, a term of years).

C. Remainders distinguished from reversions: It is usually not difficult to distinguish a remainder from a reversion.

    1. Created in one other than the grantor: The remainder is by definition created in *someone other than the transferor*. The reversion, by contrast, is an interest left in the transferor after he has conveyed an interest to someone else.

        a. Reversion may be transferred: However, keep in mind that a reversion may be transferred from the transferor to a third person. What determines whether something is a remainder is its *original* status.

        Example: O conveys "to A for life, then to B and his heirs." B then conveys his interest back to O. O holds a remainder, not a reversion, since the interest was originally created in a third party (B), not the transferor (O).

D. Successive remainders: It is possible to have *successive remainders*, with no limit.

    Example: O conveys "to A for life, then to B for life, then to C for life, then to D and his heirs." B, C, and D all have remainders. See Moynihan, p. 110.

E. No remainder following fee simple: At common law, a fee simple was regarded as the maximum estate that may be created. Furthermore, all types of fee simple (absolute, determinable, and subject to condition subsequent) were regarded as being of equal size. The result was that, under the common-law view, there could be *no remainder after any kind of fee simple*.

    1. No remainder after fee simple determinable: Most significantly, this means that at common law there could not be a remainder following a *fee simple determinable*.

F. Two kinds of remainders: Remainders are usually divided into two main classes: *vested* and *contingent*.

    1. The distinction summarized: We'll be talking immediately below in detail about how you can distinguish vested remainders from contingent ones. But the basic idea is that:

        ❑ **Vested:** A *vested remainder* is one that is *certain to become possessory* whenever and however the prior estate terminates, and we can say at the moment of creation who will take possession; whereas ...

        ❑ **Contingent:** A *contingent remainder* is one that is *not certain* to become possessory. The uncertainty can be caused either (a) by the fact that the remainder's ever becoming possessory is subject to the *occurrence of a condition precedent* that might not occur by the time the prior estate terminates; or (b) by the fact that the remainder has been created in favor of a person who is at the time of creation either *unborn or unascertained.*

    2. Why it makes a difference: Why do we have to worry about distinguishing between vested and contingent remainders? At common law, there were three main consequences to the distinction, though only one of these has major practical importance today.

        a. Rule Against Perpetuities: The consequence that most significantly lives on today relates to the *Rule Against Perpetuities* (*infra*, p. 96). *Contingent remainders are subject to the Rule Against Perpetuities, but vested remainders are not.* See DKA&S, p. 232. Thus a particular bequest or conveyance creating a remainder may turn out to be completely enforceable or completely unenforceable, depending solely on whether the remainder is contingent or vested. See *infra*, p. 97.

b. Transferability: At common law, the two types of remainders differed sharply with respect to *transferability*. Vested remainders have always been transferable *inter vivos*. Contingent remainders, on the other hand, were basically *not transferable inter vivos* (though there were major exceptions).

  i. Modern law: Today, in most states, contingent remainders *are transferable inter vivos*, so the vested/contingent distinction is not important with respect to transferability. *Id*. See *infra*, p. 82.

c. Destruction: Finally, at common law a contingent remainder was *destroyed* if it did not vest upon termination of the proceeding life estate. This is the doctrine of "destruction of contingent remainders," discussed *infra*, p. 79. There was no comparable doctrine destroying vested remainders. But again, this distinction is not very significant today, because most states have abolished the doctrine of destruction of contingent remainders. *Id*. See *infra*, p. 80.

G. Vested remainders: A remainder is *vested* if the following two conditions are met: (1) *No condition precedent* is attached to it; and (2) the person holding it has already been *born*, and his identity is *ascertained*.

Example: O conveys Blackacre "to *A* for life, remainder to *B* and his heirs." *B* has a vested remainder, since his identity is ascertained, and there is no condition precedent which must be satisfied in order for his interest to become possessory. (It is true that *A* must die in order for *B* to take possession, but this is not the fulfillment of a condition precedent; it is simply the natural expiration of the prior estate.)

Note: Our discussion of exactly what constitutes a condition precedent is postponed until the treatment of contingent remainders, *infra*, p. 76. For the moment, it suffices to state that as long as the remainder will become possessory *whenever and however the prior estate terminates*, no condition precedent exists. Thus in the above example, no matter however and whenever *A*'s life estate ends, *B*'s estate will immediately become possessory; therefore *B*'s remainder is vested.

1. Three types: Within the class of vested remainders, there are three sub-classes: (1) remainders *indefeasibly vested*; (2) remainders *vested subject to open*; and (3) remainders *vested subject to complete defeasance*.

2. Remainder indefeasibly vested: A remainder *indefeasibly vested* is one which is *certain to become possessory* at some future time.

  a. Possession in heirs or devisees: For the remainder to be indefeasibly vested, it is not necessary that the remainderman himself is certain to come into possession in the future; it will suffice that either the remainderman or his successors in interest (e.g., his devisees or grantees) will someday take possession.

  Example: O conveys Blackacre "to *A* for life, remainder to *B* and his heirs." It is not certain that *B* himself will ever take possession, since he may die before *A*. But it *is* certain that either *B* or someone who acquires *B*'s interest through conveyance, bequest, etc., will someday take possession. Therefore, *B*'s remainder is indefeasibly vested.

3. **Vested remainder subject to open:** The vested remainder *subject to open* exists when it is possible to point to one or more persons and say that they (or their successors) are certain to have a possessory interest someday, but there remains a chance that *others will share this interest*. That is, a remainder is subject to open when, in addition to the persons now vested, others may also gain a vested portion.

   a. **After-born children:** The principal situation in which a remainder vested subject to open is likely to exist is where a gift is made to the "*children*" of someone, and the possibility exists that *additional children will be born* subsequently.

   Example: O conveys "to *A* for life, remainder to *B*'s children and their heirs." At the time of conveyance, *B* has only one child, X. Immediately following the conveyance, X is said to have a vested remainder subject to open; if another child, Y, is then born to *B*, X's remainder "opens up" to give Y a half interest in it. (The remainder stays open until either *A* dies, in which case only the then-living children of *B* will take anything, or *B* dies, in which case he can have no further children. See Moynihan, p. 119, fn. 3).

4. **Vested remainder subject to complete defeasance:** Suppose the remainderman exists, his identity is ascertained, and his interest is not subject to a condition precedent. Suppose further, however, that although his interest will become possessory if all prior interests were to end today, it cannot be said with certainty that his interest will ever in fact become possessory. In this situation, the remainder is said to be *vested subject to complete defeasance*. See Rest. §157(c), and Comment o thereto. This defeasance may occur either through natural termination or through "divestment" (i.e., a cutting short of the remainder).

   a. **Possibility of expiring before becoming possessory:** A vested remainder may fail to become possessory because it naturally *expires* before all prior interests end.

   Example: O conveys "to *A* for life, then to *B* for life." *B*'s interest is a vested remainder subject to complete defeasance through expiration, since if *B* dies before *A*, *B*'s remainder will never become possessory. See Rest. §157, Illustration 11.

   b. **Divestment:** The other way in which a remainder subject to defeasance can fail to become possessory is if it is *divested*, i.e., *cut off* prior to its natural termination.

      i. **Executory interest:** The most important way this may happen is that the remainder is subject to divestment by what is called an *executory interest* (described more fully *infra*, p. 89). Such an interest cuts off the remainder (either before or after it becomes possessory) and gives it to someone other than the grantor.

      Example: O conveys "to *A* for life, then to *B* and his heirs, but if *B* dies without issue, then to *C* and his heirs." *B* has a remainder vested subject to divestment. If *A* died immediately, *B*'s interest would become possessory. But if *B* died without issue (either before or after *A*'s death), *B*'s interest would be completely defeated or "divested." *C*'s interest, which cuts short *B*'s vested interest, is called an executory interest. See Moynihan, p. 120.

      ii. Right of entry: Similarly, if the grantor retains a ***right of entry*** if the remainder-man does not meet a certain condition, the remainder is vested subject to divestment.

      Example: O conveys "to A for life, then to B and his heirs, upon condition that the premises always be used for a church; if the premises are not so used, O or his heirs shall have the right to re-enter the premises." B's interest is vested, but the cessation of church activities, plus the re-entry by O or his heirs, would cause the title to return to O. Therefore, B has a remainder subject to divestment, and O has a right of entry for condition broken (*supra*, p. 70).

  c. Distinguished from contingent remainders: The principal difficulty in dealing with vested remainders subject to divestment is that they are often hard to distinguish from ***contingent*** remainders that are subject to a condition precedent. This matter is more fully discussed immediately *infra*.

H. Contingent remainders: All remainders that are not vested are ***contingent***. The remainder will be contingent rather than vested if *either* of two things is true:

[1] the remainder is subject to a ***condition precedent***; or

[2] the remainder is created in favor of a person who at the time of creation is either ***unborn*** or ***unascertained***.

  1. Contingent can become vested: The fact that a remainder is contingent at the time of its creation does not mean that it can never become vested. On the contrary, we will see frequent examples below of remainders which ***become vested*** either through the satisfaction of a condition precedent, through the birth of a child, or through the eventual determination of the identity of a person or class.

  Example: O conveys "to A for life, then to the children of B who survive B." At the time of the conveyance, the remainder in B's children is contingent, since there is no way to know which children will survive B. But if B dies while A is still alive, the remainder immediately becomes vested in those children who have survived B.

  2. Condition precedent: Where a remainder is ***subject to a condition precedent***, it is contingent. That is, the fact that some condition must be met before the remainder could possibly become possessory is by itself enough to make it contingent. See Rest. 2d (Donative Transfers) §1.4, Comment b.

  Example; O conveys "to A for life, then, if B is living at A's death, to B in fee simple." B must meet the condition precedent of surviving A, before his remainder can become possessory. Therefore, his remainder is contingent.

    a. Distinguishing from condition subsequent: Recall that where a remainder is subject to a condition ***subsequent***, it is termed a vested remainder subject to divestment (*supra*, p. 75). It is thus important to be able to distinguish between a condition precedent and a condition subsequent. This is not always an easy thing to do.

    b. Test: The difference between the two is really one of ***words alone***, not of substance. The test is as follows: if the condition is incorporated into the ***clause that gives the gift to the remainderman***, then the remainder is contingent. If, on the other hand, one clause creates the remainder, and a ***subsequent clause*** takes the remainder away, the remainder is vested (subject to divestment). See Moynihan, p. 121. The two examples that follow illustrate the difference.

Example 1 (vested remainder subject to divestment): O conveys "to *A* for life, remainder to *B* and his heirs, but if *B* dies before A, to *C* and his heirs." Although for *B*'s interest ever to become possessory, *B* must live longer than A, *B*'s remainder is vested, not contingent. That's because no condition was attached in the clause giving *B* his interest ("then to *B* and his heirs. . ."), and a second clause was added to take the interest away from *B* if he fails to survive. (The second clause is thus a condition *subsequent*).

Example 2 (contingent remainder): O conveys "to *A* for life, then if *B* survives A, to *B* and his heirs; otherwise to *C* and his heirs." Here, *B* has a *contingent* remainder. That's so because the condition of survivorship is incorporated into the very gift to *B*, making it a condition precedent. See C&L, p. 295, examples 2 and 6.

i.   **Read left to right, and resolve one before starting on the next:**   So when you're deciding whether a remainder is vested or contingent, you're in the business of careful parsing of grammar. As DKA&S put it, "You must classify interests ***in sequence as they are written.*** You start reading to the right, classify the first interest, then move on to the second interest and classify it, and then move to the next interest."

Let's apply this "parsing" rule to the above two Examples. In Example 1, grammatically speaking the first of the remainder interests is created solely by the words "remainder to *B* and his heirs," so the remainder is vested (there's no condition contained in clause itself). Then, moving to the right, the next remainder is created by the words "but if *B* dies before A, to *C* and his heirs," so that next remainder is taking away the first remainder (i.e., divesting it), making the first one "vested subject to divestment."

By contrast, in Example 2, the first remainder is created by the words "then if *B* survives A, to *B* and his heirs," so the condition is part of the remainder (making the remainder contingent).

c.   **Use of the word "but":**   One key phrase you should look for is ***"but if."*** Where the condition occurs following this phrase, it will almost always be an indication that the remainder is being taken away and is therefore subject to a condition subsequent (making the remainder vested subject to divestment). That was the case, for instance, in Example 1 above. By contrast, where the condition follows the phrase "then if . . .," the condition is probably precedent. That was the case in Example 2 above.

d.   **Requirement of survivorship:**   One frequent situation in which a condition precedent occurs is where the remainderman must ***survive*** the holder of the prior interest.

Example: O conveys "to *A* for life, then if *B* survives *A*, to *B* and his heirs; otherwise to *C* and his heirs." *B* has a contingent remainder, because *B*'s estate is subject to the condition precedent that *B* survive *A*.

i. Still necessary to distinguish from condition subsequent: But always remember that a condition of survivorship can be a condition *subsequent* just as easily as a condition precedent. It's just a question of the conveyance's grammatical structure.

Example: O conveys "to *A* for life, then to *B* and his heirs. But if *B* fails to survive *A*, to *B* and his heirs." *B* has a vested remainder subject to divestment by *B*'s failing to survive *A*.

e. Preference for vested construction: Where it is not clear whether the remainder is contingent or vested, most courts show a *preference for the vested construction*.

f. Alternative contingent remainders: A conveyance may create what are usually called *alternative contingent remainders*. These are particularly likely to occur where a condition precedent involves survivorship.

Example: O conveys "to *A* for life, then to *B* and his heirs if *B* survives A, otherwise to *C* and his heirs." *B*'s remainder is contingent upon surviving A; *C*'s remainder is contingent upon *B*'s not surviving A. Therefore, *B* and *C* have alternative contingent remainders. (But suppose the conveyance read "to *A* for life, then to *B* and his heirs; but if *B* dies before A, to *C* and his heirs." *B* would have a vested remainder subject to divestment, and *C* would have an executory interest, cutting off *B*'s remainder. This is another illustration of the fact that the form, rather than the substance, of the words of the conveyance frequently controls.)

3. Unascertained remaindermen: A remainder is also contingent, rather than vested, if it is held by a person who is either: (1) *unborn* or (2) *not yet ascertained*.

a. Unborn: A contingent remainder in favor of an unborn person can arise as follows: O conveys "to *A* for life, then to the children of *B*." At the time of the conveyance, *B* has no children. Therefore, the remainder is contingent in the unborn children. (At common law, if *A* died before *B* had any children, the contingent remainder would be destroyed, and O's reversion would become possessory. See *infra*.)

i. May later vest: But a remainder in favor of unborn children, like any other contingent remainder, may *become vested* due to later events. Thus if, prior to A's death, *B* had a child, X, X would have a vested remainder subject to open (in favor of any other children of *B* born before A's death).

b. Unascertained persons: Similarly, a remainder may be contingent because it is in favor of a person of class whose identity *cannot yet be ascertained*.

i. Heirs of living person: The most common example of this is a remainder in favor of the *heirs of a living person*.

Example: O devises Blackacre "to *A* for life, then to *A*'s heirs." Assuming that the Rule in Shelley's Case is not enforced in the jurisdiction (see *infra*, p. 81), the heirs have a remainder, and it is contingent. The reason for this is, of course, that until *A* dies, it is impossible to say who his heirs are. At *A*'s death, the remainder will both vest and become possessory.

ii. Widow: Similarly, a conveyance in favor of the *widow* of a living person might be held to be contingent. Thus O conveys "to A for life, then to his widow." At the time of the conveyance, A is married to B. If the term "widow" is held to have been used in its literal sense of a surviving spouse, the remainder in the widow is contingent, since there is no way to know whether B will survive A or will still be married to him when A dies. See Moynihan, p. 126.

I. Destructibility of contingent remainders: The common law treated contingent remainders differently from vested ones in several respects, one of which was crucially important: a contingent remainder was deemed "*destroyed*" unless it *vested at or before the termination of the preceding freehold estates*. This rule was usually called the "*destructibility of contingent remainders*."

Example: O conveys "to A for life, remainder to the first son of A who reaches twenty-one." At A's death, he has one son, B, age sixteen. Since B did not meet the contingency (becoming twenty-one) by the time the prior estate (A's life estate) expired, B's contingent remainder is destroyed. Therefore, O's reversion becomes possessory.

1. Reason for rule of destructibility: The basis for the common-law destructibility rule stems from the concept of seisin. One of the common-law rules regarding seisin was that a freehold interest could not "spring" out of the estate of the grantor at some future time. This rule against freeholds commencing *in futuro* is usually called the rule against springing interests; see *infra*, p. 86.

a. Illustration: Now, consider the remainder of B, in the above example. At A's death, B has not yet met the conveyance. Since another of the rules concerning seisin is that it can never be in "abeyance" (i.e., it must always be "in" someone) it must return to O. Then, when B becomes twenty-one, for him to obtain seisin would require that the seisin "spring" out of O's estate. Since this springing would be taking place at a time other than the time when the original conveyance was made, it would seem to violate the rule against springing interests. Since there was no way in which B's interest could legitimately become possessory, it was deemed destroyed. See C&L, p. 299.

2. Ways of destroying a contingent remainder: We will consider the two main ways in which a contingent remainder could be destroyed at common law: (1) *normal expiration* of the supporting freeholds; and (2) *merger* of the supporting freeholds.

3. Normal expiration: One way the contingent remainder could be destroyed is if the preceding freehold estate (typically a life estate) had a *natural termination* before the condition precedent was satisfied.

Example: O conveys "to A for life, remainder to A's oldest son B when B reaches 25." At A's death, B is 23. Since B has failed to satisfy the condition as of the moment when the preceding estate (A's life estate) ended, under the common-law approach B's contingent remainder is deemed destroyed at the moment of A's death. At that moment, O's reversion becomes possessory.

a. Remainder vests at the same time: But if the contingent remainder vests at precisely the *same moment* that the supporting prior freehold terminates, the remainder is *not destroyed*.

Example: O conveys "to A for life, remainder to his surviving children." A dies, survived by a son, B. During A's life estate, B's remainder was contingent, since it was subject to the condition that he survive A. Since that remainder vested at precisely the moment of A's death, the remainder was not destroyed. B therefore takes title.

b. **Equitable remainder:** Also, a contingent remainder that is *equitable* will not be destroyed by termination of the prior freehold.

Example: O conveys "to T and his heirs in trust to pay the income from the land to A for life, then in trust to convey the land to A's first son to reach the age of 21." A dies, leaving an 18-year-old son. Three years later, when the son reaches 21, he should get the land — his contingent remainder was an equitable one (legal title to the land remained in T), so it won't be destroyed. See 1 A.L.P. 514.

4. **Merger:** Secondly, a contingent remainder could be destroyed at common law because the estate preceding it (usually a life estate) was *merged into* another, larger, estate. The smaller estate thus disappears, and the contingent remainder dependent upon it is destroyed.

a. **Basic doctrine of merger:** The basic rule of merger is that whenever *successive vested estates* are owned by the *same person*, the smaller of the two estates is *absorbed* by the larger. See Moynihan, p. 131.

Example: O conveys "to A for life, remainder to A's first son for life if he reaches 21, remainder to B and his heirs." When A has a 19-year-old son, A conveys his life estate to B. Since B now has two successive vested estates (the life estate and B's own vested remainder in fee simple), the smaller estate, the life estate, is merged into the fee simple and disappears. Since the son's remainder has not yet vested at the time A's life estate disappears, the contingent remainder is destroyed. See C&L, p. 300.

b. **Must not be intermediate vested estate:** For the merger doctrine to apply, the two vested estates in question must not be *separated* by a third vested estate in someone else.

Example: O conveys "to A for life, then to B for life, then to C and his heirs." A conveys his life estate to C. A's life estate will not merge into C's remainder in fee simple, because another vested estate (belonging to B) separates the two.

5. **The destructibility rule today:** The destructibility rule obviously defeats the intention of the grantor most of the time. Also, the doctrine depends on the illegality of springing interests, which is no longer much of a factor following the enactment of the Statute of Uses (*infra*, p. 88). Therefore, about *three-quarters* of American states have *abolished the destructibility of contingent remainders,* either by statute or judicial decision. DKA&S, p. 242. The Restatement of Property (§240) also rejects destructibility.

Some review examples on remainders:

Example 1: Owner conveys "to Able for life, remainder to Able's widow for her life, remainder to Baker and his heirs." Able is living and is married to Wanda. Baker is living.

The remainder to Able's widow is contingent, since it is not known whether Wanda will survive Able and still be married to him at Able's death. The remainder to Baker is vested. The contingent remainder to Able's widow will vest, if at all, upon Able's death, since at that time his widow can be ascertained.

Example 2: Owner conveys "to Able for life, remainder to Able's children and their heirs." Able is living, and has one child, C1. Later, another child, C2 is born. Then, C1 dies. One year after that, Able dies.

At the time of conveyance, C1 obtained a vested remainder subject to open. This remainder opened up to admit C2 at the latter's birth. Therefore, each held a one-half interest. When C1 died, his half interest passed to his heirs. C2 maintains the other half interest. Both half interests became possessory on Able's death.

Example 3: Owner conveys "to Able for life, remainder to Able's first son and the heirs of his body, remainder to Baker and his heirs." While Able is still childless, Owner dies without a will, leaving Able as his heir.

Able has a life estate. His unborn first son has a contingent remainder in fee tail. Baker has a vested remainder in fee simple. Owner had no interest left following the conveyance, so Able inherits nothing from him.

J. **Alienability of remainders:**   Historically, one of the principal differences between vested and contingent remainders was that vested ones were more freely *alienable*.

1. **Vested remainders:**   Vested remainders have always been alienable *inter vivos* (i.e., by deed), devisable, and descendible.

   a. **Subject to divestment:**   This is true even if the vested remainder is subject to partial or total divestment or defeasance. However, the remainder is subject to the same possibility of divestment in the hands of the person who acquires it.

      Example: O conveys "to A for life, then to B and his heirs, but if alcohol should ever be sold upon the premises, O or his heirs may re-enter the property." B is free to transfer his vested remainder (in fee simple subject to condition subsequent) to X. But if, after the transfer to X, alcohol is sold on the premises, O or his heirs still has the right to re-enter.

2. **Contingent remainders:**   Contingent remainders, on the other hand, were largely *inalienable* at *common law*. Thus there could be no *inter vivos* conveyance, nor any involuntary transfer (e.g., in bankruptcy, or by attachment of creditors).

   a. **Modern American view:**   But in most American states, the present view is that a contingent remainder is *alienable, devisable,* and *descendible*, just as a vested remainder is. See Moynihan, pp. 136-37. In a few states, there are some limits on *inter vivos* transfers, but contingent remainders are apparently devisable and descendible in every jurisdiction. See 1 A.L.P. 533, 535.

V.   THE RULE IN SHELLEY'S CASE

A. **The Rule summarized:**   Feudal property law produced several strange rules. One of the most bizarre of these was known as the ***Rule in Shelley's Case***, which was designed to thwart certain medieval tax-evasion schemes. The Rule provides as follows: ***if a will or conveyance creates a life estate in A, and purports to create a remainder in A's heirs*** (or in the heirs of

A's body) and the estates are ***both legal or both equitable, the remainder becomes a fee simple*** (or fee tail) ***in A.*** C&L, p. 302.

Example: O conveys "to A for life, remainder to A's heirs." If there were no Rule in Shelley's Case, the state of the title would be: life estate in A, contingent remainder in A's heirs, reversion in O. But by operation of the Rule in Shelley's Case, the state of the title is this: life estate in A, remainder in A (not A's heirs). Then, by the doctrine of merger, A's life estate will merge into his remainder in fee simple, and A simply holds a present fee simple.

B. Step-by-step approach: Here's a ***step-by-step approach*** to deciding whether the Rule in Shelley's Case applies, and for carrying it out if it does apply:

[1] Is there a ***single instrument*** that creates: (a) a ***life estate*** in land in A (with A being the "ancestor"); and (b) a ***remainder*** in persons described in the instrument as "***A's heirs***" (or a remainder in "the heirs of A's body")? (If the answer is "no," the Rule in Shelley's Case can't apply, so no need to go further.)

[2] If the answer to [1] is "yes," are the life estate in A and the remainder in A's heirs (or in the heirs of A's body) either ***both legal*** or ***both equitable***?

[3] If the answer to [2] is "yes," the Rule in Shelley's case ***applies***, to make the remainder in "A's heirs" a remainder in fee simple in A. (Or, if the instrument gave a remainder in "the heirs of A's body," the Rule makes the remainder into a remainder in fee tail in A.)

[4] If the Rule applies, then the doctrine of ***merger*** (see *supra*, p. 80) will usually apply — but that's a separate operation, not part of the Rule. Thus in the above Example, all the Rule does is to make the title be life estate in A, remainder in A (rather than in A's heirs). Now, by separate operation of the merger doctrine, A's life estate merges into his remainder in fee simple, leaving A with a present fee simple.

See DKA&S, p. 243.

C. The Rule under modern law: The Rule in Shelley's Case serves no useful purpose today. It is often a trap for the unwary, and virtually always thwarts the will of the grantor.

1. Abolished: For these reasons, the Rule has been ***abolished*** in "the ***overwhelming majority***" of American states. DKA&S, p. 243. "Only in Arkansas and perhaps in two or three other states is it reasonably certain the [R]ule still lives." *Id.*

VI. DOCTRINE OF WORTHIER TITLE

A. General statement of rule: Another wierd common-law rule is the "***Doctrine of Worthier Title***." The Doctrine provides that ***one cannot, either by conveyance or will, give a remainder to his own heirs***. See Moynihan, p. 149. Actually, the "Doctrine" is really two fairly distinct rules having a common origin, one involving wills, and the other involving *inter vivos* conveyances. Only the *inter vivos* rule is of importance today; therefore, when we refer to the Doctrine, we'll be talking solely about the *inter vivos* branch.

B. The *inter vivos* branch: The Doctrine of Worthier Title is still very much alive in some jurisdictions, and when it applies it can have important practical consequences. Cf. DKA&S, p. 244.

1. **Common-law statement of rule:**   The Doctrine, in its common-law form, provides that if the owner of a fee simple attempts to create a life estate or fee tail estate, with a ***remainder to his own heirs***, the ***remainder is void***. Thus the grantor ***keeps a reversion***. C&L, pp. 310-11.

   Example: O conveys "to A for life, remainder to O's heirs." The Doctrine of Worthier Title makes the remainder void. Consequently, O is left with a reversion. He is thus free to convey the reversion to a third party; if he does so, his heirs will get nothing when he dies, even if he dies intestate.

   a. **Alternate name is "rule forbidding remainder to grantors' heirs":**   The Doctrine is sometimes called the *"rule forbidding remainders to grantors' heirs."*

2. **Practical effect of rule:**   The Doctrine often has an important practical impact. If the Doctrine did not exist, the grantor's heirs would have a contingent remainder, which would not be affected by any later conveyance made by O or any later devise made in O's will. But when the Doctrine applies, the remainder is completely nullified, and an *inter vivos* conveyance by O of his reversion, or a devise of it in his will, will prevent the heirs from taking anything.

   Example: In 2006, O conveys "to A for life, remainder to O's heirs." In 2007, O conveys "to B and his heirs." In 2008, O dies, leaving C as his sole heir and devisee. In 2009, A dies. Assume that the Doctrine of Worthier Title applies in the jurisdiction. After A's death, what's the state of the title?

   Because the Doctrine applies, the 2006 remainder in "O's heirs" was invalid. O therefore kept a reversion following the 2006 conveyance. He conveyed that reversion to B. When O died, his heir/devisee, C, took nothing. Once A's life estate ended in 2009, B became the owner in fee simple absolute. (But if the Doctrine did *not* apply in the jurisdiction, C would have a contingent remainder, which would then vest and became possessory as a fee simple once A died; B would take nothing.)

3. **Originally rule of law, not construction:**   In its common-law form, the Doctrine of Worthier Title is a ***rule of law, not of construction***. Thus even if, in the above example, the trust document makes it clear that O intends to give a remainder to his heirs, the Doctrine will apply.

   a. **Now generally rule of construction:**   The common-law version (i.e., the "mandatory rule of law" version) of the Doctrine is still in force in a few states. But in most states, the rule has been ***transformed into one of construction***. That is, the Doctrine applies only where the grantor's language, and the surrounding circumstances, indicate that he ***intended to keep a reversion***; in a sense, the Doctrine merely establishes a ***presumption that a reversion rather than a remainder is really intended***.

VII. THE STATUTE OF USES AND EXECUTORY INTERESTS

A. **Concept of "seisin":**   Before we explore the mysteries of the "Statute of Uses," you must first understand a little bit about the concept of *"seisin"*. A person was said to have seisin of a parcel of land (or to be "seised of it") if he had ***possession of it under a claim of freehold***.

Table 5-1
***CHECKLIST*: Present- and Future-Interest Pairs**

Use this chart to see what present interests go with what future
interests. "*O*" is the grantor; "*A*" receives the present interest; "*B*" is
the third party (if there is one) who receives the future interest.

Grant of Present Interest in *A*	Matching Grant of Future Interest in *B* or *O*	Example	Notes
[1] *O* grants **fee simple determinable** to *A*.	*O* has **possibility of reverter.**	*O* conveys "to *A* and his heirs, *for so long as* no commercial serving of liquor occurs on the premises; after which title is to *revert* to *O* and his heirs."	The reverter becomes possessory *automatically* on the happening of the forbidden event (commercial serving of liquor).
[2] *O* grants **fee simple subject to condition subsequent** to *A*.	*O* retains **right of entry.**	*O* conveys "to *A* and his heirs, on condition that no liquor is commercially served on the premises; *but if* liquor is commercially served, *O* or his heirs may re-enter the premises."	Right of entry does not happen automatically; grantor must affirmatively take back the premises.
[3] *O* grants *A* **something less than a fee simple** (e.g., life estate or estate of years); no other grant listed.	*O* retains **reversion** following *A*'s interest.	*Example 1: O* conveys "to *A* for life." *Example 2: O* conveys "to *A* for a term of 20 years." In either case, *O* has a reversion following *A*'s interest.	*O*'s reversion is created automatically; no special language is needed.
[4a] In a single instrument, *O* grants a possessory **less-than-fee-simple interest** to *A*, followed, only on the natural termination of *A*'s interest, by an interest in someone other than *O* (i.e., *B*).	*B* has a **vested remainder**, if (i) there is *no condition precedent* to *B*'s interest becoming possessory; and (ii) *B* has already *been born* and his *identity ascertained*.	*O* conveys "to *A* for life, then to *B* [an existing person] and his heirs." *B* has a vested remainder in fee simple. It's a remainder because it was created in the same instrument as the prior less-than-fee-simple interest in *A*. At creation, it's a vested remainder because (i) there's no condition precedent (no matter how or when *A* dies, *B* or his heirs will take possession); and (ii) we know who *B* is.	1. For the remainder to be vested: (a) there must not be a condition precedent to *B*'s interest; that is, the interest must become possessory "whenever and however the prior estate terminates" (see Example 1 in [4b] below) *and* (b) we have to know, at the moment in question, exactly who *B* is (see Example 2 in [4b] below, where we *don't* know). 2. A remainder may *start* by being contingent, then *later vest* (see Note 1 in [4b] below). 3. Vested remainders are of several types (*indefeasibly* vested, vested *subject to open*, and vested *subject to divestment*). For more about this, see section IV(G) in this chapter.

Table 5-1 (cont.)
CHECKLIST: **Present- and Future-Interest Pairs**

Grant of Present Interest in *A*	Matching Grant of Future Interest in *B* or *O*	Example	Notes
[4b] Same as [4a] above. That is, in a single instrument, *O* grants a possessory **less-than-fee-simple interest** to *A*, followed, only on the natural termination of *A*'s interest, by an interest in someone other than *O* (i.e., *B*).	*B* has a **contingent remainder**, if *either* (i) there is a **condition precedent** to *B*'s interest's becoming possessory; or (ii) *B* doesn't yet *exist* or his *identity* is not yet known.	*Example 1 (remainder is contingent because of a condition precedent): O* conveys "to *A* for life, then, if *B* survives *A*, to *B* and his heirs. Otherwise, to *O* and his heirs." *B* has to meet the condition precedent of surviving *A* for his remainder to become possessory, making it contingent. *Example 2 (remainder is contingent because holder isn't known): O* conveys "to *A* for life, then to the first-born child of *X*." If at the time in question, *X* has no children, the remainder in the oldest child is contingent.	1. A remainder that's contingent when it comes into existence *can later become vested.* For instance, in Example 2 at left, the remainder is contingent at the time *O* conveys, because X has no children. As soon as X has a child, the remainder is vested. 2. Distinguish between a *contingent* remainder and a *vested* remainder *subject to divestment.* The difference is *solely linguistic.* Thus "to *A* for life, then to *B* and his heirs; but if *B* doesn't survive *A*, property reverts to *O* and his heirs" is functionally the same as Example 1 at left, but the "but if" language makes it a vested remainder subject to divestment.
[5] *O* **bargains and sells** to *A*, with the possibility that *A*'s interest can be cut short (so that *B* takes). *A* has a fee simple **subject to an executory limitation.**	*B* has a **shifting executory interest.**	*O* bargains and sells "to *A* and his heirs, but if liquor is ever sold commercially, then to *B* and his heirs." *A* has a fee simple subject to executory limitation, and *B* has a shifting executory interest. (For bargain & sale deeds, see section VII(E) in this chapter.)	This differs from a possibility of reverter (see box [1]) only because if the divesting event occurs, the property goes to a *third party* (*B*) rather than back to the grantor (*O*).
[6] *O* bargains and sells to *B*, possession to occur at some point after the conveyance. *O* still has seisin.	*B* has a **springing executory interest.**	*O* bargains and sells "to *B* and her heirs, from and after the date that *B* graduates from an ABA-approved lawschool." *B* has a springing executory interest.	This is an executory interest (it benefits someone other than the grantor). And it's a springing interest because seisin doesn't pass immediately; it "springs out" of *O* when the future event (law school graduation) occurs, if it ever does.

That is, he had to meet two requirements: (1) he had to be in *possession* (though this could be done for him by a tenant); and (2) he had to own a *freehold estate* in the property, i.e., either a *fee simple*, a *fee tail* or a *life estate*.

1. **Transfer of present freehold:** The deed as we know it today did not exist at common law (at least where the estate being transferred was a present, possessory, freehold). Instead, a freehold was generally transferred by the *"livery of seisin"* (sometimes called a *"feoffment"*). This was accomplished by having the transferor and the transferee *go onto the land*, at which point the transferor handed the transferee a twig, stating that he was transferring seisin. It was required that the transferee *immediately take possession* after the livery of seisin (so that O could not enfeoff A today, the feoffment to take effect on, say, A's death or the passage of one year).

B. **Common-law restrictions:** The common law imposed several very important *restrictions* on the types of estates that could be created:

1. **No "springing" interests:** A freehold estate could not be created to *commence in futuro*. This was a direct consequence of the requirement that seisin be delivered by a present transfer of possession. Such an estate was known as an illegal *"springing interest,"* because the estate would take effect in the future by springing out of its present owner.

   Example: O is the owner of Blackacre. His daughter, D, is engaged to marry A. O wishes to ensure A that A will receive a fee simple in Blackacre when he marries D. But the rule against "springing" interests, or interests to begin *in futuro*, means that at common law, O could not convey "to A and his heirs from and after A's marriage to D."

   a. **Freehold following lease term:** But the owner of a freehold estate could create a freehold to commence after a term of years. Thus O could convey "to A for 10 years, then to B and his heirs."

2. **No "shifting" interests:** A grantor could not give to any grantee an estate which would *cut another estate short*. This prohibition is frequently referred to as the ban on *"shifting" interests*. Like the rule against springing interests, the ban on shifting interests seems to derive from the requirement that a livery of seisin take effect immediately rather than in the future.

   a. **Interest in stranger can't follow fee simple determinable:** One consequence of the ban on shifting interests is that a *fee simple determinable* could be followed only by a possibility of reverter in the grantor, and *not by a shifting interest to a third person*.

      i. **Common-law view:** Recall that the common law took the view that a fee simple (even a determinable one) could not be followed by a remainder. (See *supra*, p. 73.) Since the remainder was the only type of estate in a third person recognized by the common law, any interest in one other than the grantor purporting to follow a fee simple determinable was treated as void.

         Example: O conveys "to A and his heirs as long as the property is used during the next twenty years for agricultural purposes, and then to B and his heirs." The gift to A and his heirs is a fee simple determinable (to last forever, unless the land is used for non-agricultural purposes at some point during the first twenty years). Therefore at common law the interest in B and his heirs cannot be a remainder. The only way to construe the gift to B is as a shifting interest (which would cut off A's interest) and such an interest is not valid at common law. Consequently, at common law O has a possibility of reverter.

b. No gift in stranger following fee simple subject to condition subsequent: The ban on shifting interests also meant that there could be no interest in a third party after a fee simple *subject to a condition subsequent*.

Example: O conveys "to A for life, then to B and his heirs, but if B marries C before A's estate ends, then to D and his heirs." B has a remainder in fee simple subject to divestment if the condition subsequent is met. Since D's interest can become possessory only by cutting short B's interest, D's interest is not a remainder, but a shifting interest that is invalid.

3. No gap between estates: There could be no *gap* between the *end* of an estate and the *start* of a succeeding remainder. If there was such a gap, the remainder was void.

Example: O conveys "to A for life, then one day after A's death, to B and his heirs." At common law, the interest in B is not a valid remainder, since it does not follow immediately upon the expiration of the preceding estate. Therefore, the interest in B is void.

C. Uses before the Statute of Uses: Until now, everything we have said about estates in land has referred to *legal* title, i.e., title that would be enforced by a court of law. But the law courts were not the only source of judicial relief in England; a separate court, called the Court of Chancery, gave relief if: (1) the rigid rules of the common law did not provide it and (2) fairness required. The relief given by the chancellor was known as *equitable* relief, and the court system that grew up around the chancellor was known as *equity*.

1. Equity enforces the use: In the case of land law, the jurisdiction of the equity courts applied to cases where a *use* was established. Thus O, the owner of a legal fee simple in Blackacre, might transfer legal title to T as Trustee, for the use of O. If T failed to use the property for O's benefit (e.g., he failed to pay over the rents, or he sold the property), the court of equity could intercede, to force T to use the property for O's benefit. The court had no power to affect the legal title, which would remain in T.

a. *Cestui que use*: The person in whose favor a use is created is commonly called the *cestui que use* (i.e., beneficiary).

2. Flexibility: Prior to 1536, landowners found that the system of uses gave them much flexibility in dealing with their lands, which would not be available if only legal estates were considered.

a. Springing and shifting interests: Most importantly, uses could be employed to create *shifting* and *springing* interests, which were not available at common law. Thus O could convey "to T and his heirs for life, for the use of A and his heirs, but if A or his heirs should fail to live on the property, then to the use of B and his heirs." If A or his heirs failed to live on the property, the equitable title would "shift" to B, whereas such a shifting estate was not valid with respect to the legal title.

3. Bargain and sale: There were several ways in which a use could be created. Most important was the *bargain and sale*. A bargain and sale was an *agreement* by which the owner of land promised in writing to sell the land to another, or to hold it for the other's use. The existence of the bargain and sale deed gave the beneficiary equitable title to the property, just as, under modern law, the vendee under a land sale contract may obtain specific performance of the contract (an equitable remedy).

D. Enactment of the Statute of Uses: In addition to the ability of uses to allow shifting and springing interests, uses had another virtue (from the landowner's point of view): uses could be employed to *escape the feudal incidents of tenure* (*supra*, p. 47). Since these incidents passed directly or indirectly to the king, the rise of uses meant the fall of the public treasury. Therefore, in 1536, Parliament enacted the *Statute of Uses*, generally considered to be the most important statute ever passed dealing with English land law.

1. **Meaning of Statute:**   The Statute of Uses provided that *where one person is seised of land to the use of another person, the latter shall be seised of the same size estate as he had in use*. That is, the *equitable estate is converted into the corresponding legal estate*.

   Example: O conveys Blackacre "to T and his heirs, to the use of A and his heirs." The requirement for application of the Statute of Uses are met, since T stands seised of a fee simple estate, to the use of A. Therefore, the Statute transforms A's equitable fee simple into a legal fee simple. T's legal estate is, consequently, nullified. The state of the title is simply: legal fee simple in A. (The Statute of Uses is said to "*execute*" the use in A, i.e., transform it into the corresponding legal estate.)

E. Conveyancing after the Statute: The Statute of Uses completely changed the patterns of land conveyancing. As noted, prior to the Statute, uses were much more flexible than legal estates; enactment of the Statute gave the conveyancer the ability to obtain the same flexibility in a legal estate.

1. **Other kinds of conveyancing:**   The principal effect of the Statute was to allow the types of conveyancing that had previously been employed to create uses, to be utilized now for the purpose of *creating legal estates*.

   a. **Bargain and sale:**   For instance, recall that the *bargain and sale* could be used, before the Statute of Uses, to raise a use in another. After the Statute was enacted, the bargain and sale became a very powerful way of transferring a legal estate.

      i. **No livery of seisin necessary:**   The key feature of the bargain and sale was that it *did not require any livery of seisin*. It did not require the parties to visit the land, nor did it require an immediate change in possession. The entire transaction could be done in secret, far from the property.

         Example: O, the fee simple owner of Blackacre, wishes to transfer legal title to A; he wants to do this secretly, in his lawyer's office. O executes a bargain and sale deed which states that O "bargains and sells Blackacre to A and his heirs." The deed raises a use in A, which is immediately executed by the Statute of Uses, transforming A's interest from an equitable into a legal fee simple.

F. Future interests after the Statute (executory interests):   The Statute of Uses virtually nullified the impact of the common-law restrictions on future interests (summarized *supra*, p. 86). Although these restrictions still applied to a conveyance that was strictly common-law (e.g., a formal livery of seisin), these restrictions *did not apply to a use which was transformed by the Statute into a legal estate*. Thus the Statute facilitated *"executory interests."*

1. **Springing executory interest:**   Recall that a use could be of the "*springing*" variety, i.e., one that is to take effect at some point after the date of the conveyance. Such a springing use could now be executed, i.e., transformed into the corresponding legal estate. This type

of interest, created by action of the Statute upon a springing use, became known as a *springing executory interest*.

Example: O is the fee simple owner of Blackacre. He wishes to convey title to his prospective son-in-law A, but only from the time that A actually marries O's daughter B, yet he also wishes to convince A right now that A will definitely get the land if he goes through with the marriage. O therefore bargains and sells the property "to A and his heirs from and after the date of A's marriage to B." The bargain and sale raises a use in A, which is executed under the Statute, becoming a fee simple in A to commence upon the marriage date. A's interest is a springing executory interest.

2. **Shifting executory interest:** Prior to the Statute, a *shifting* use could be created, i.e., one which cut short a prior equitable interest that had not yet naturally terminated. After the Statute, this shifting use would be executed, becoming a *shifting executory interest*.

Example: O, who owns Blackacre in fee simple, bargains and sells it "to A and his heirs, but if the premises are ever used for other than residential purposes, then to B and his heirs." The bargain and sale raises a use in A in fee simple subject to condition subsequent, and a use in B. The Statute executes both of these uses, so that the state of title becomes: fee simple in A subject to an executory limitation, and shifting executory interest in fee simple in B. If A or his heirs fail to use the property for residential purposes, the gift over to B will take effect.

Note: Observe that the legal fee simple created in A in the above example is not called a fee simple subject to condition subsequent, but rather, a fee simple *subject to an executory limitation*. Similarly, what would be a fee simple determinable if it were followed by a reversion in the grantor, is called a fee simple subject to an executory limitation where the gift over is to a third person. (See *infra*.)

3. **Gap in seisin:** The Statute of Uses also made it possible to create legal interests in such a way that there could be a "gap" between two interests. The interest following the gap can be thought of as another type of springing executory interest.

Example: O bargains and sells Blackacre "to A for life, and one day after A's death, to B and his heirs." The bargain and sale raises an equitable life estate in A, an equitable reversion for one day in O, and an equitable fee simple in B. The Statute executes the uses, so that the title is: legal life estate in A, legal reversion in O, springing executory interest in B in fee simple.

4. **Contingent remainder following term of years:** Prior to the Statute, an equitable contingent remainder could be created following a term of years. After the Statute, it became possible to create a *legal contingent remainder after a term of years*.

Example: O bargains and sells Blackacre "to A for ten years, then to A's oldest son then living." The bargain and sale deed creates an equitable leasehold interest in A, and an equitable contingent fee simple in A's oldest son. The Statute executes these uses, so that the state of title is: legal leasehold in A, contingent remainder in fee simple in A's oldest son.

5. **Interest in stranger after fee simple determinable:** Recall that prior to 1536, the only interest that could be created following a *fee simple determinable* was a possibility of reverter. (*Supra*, p. 86.) But by means of the Statute, an *executory interest* could be cre-

ated in a ***third person*** following a fee simple determinable (or, more properly, a fee simple subject to an executory limitation.)

Example: O bargains and sells Blackacre "to *A* and his heirs, for as long as no alcohol is sold on the premises; then to *B* and his heirs." The bargain and sale deed raises a use in fee simple determinable in *A* and his heirs, and a remaining use in fee simple in *B* and his heirs. The Statute executes these uses, so that the state of title is: legal fee simple in *A* subject to an executory limitation, executory interest in *B*.

6. **Outwitting the Rule in Shelley's Case:** The Statute of Uses provided a convenient way of avoiding the ***Rule in Shelley's Case***.

Example: In the year 1600, O bargains and sells "to *A* for life and one day after *A*'s death to *A*'s heirs." The bargain and sale raises a use in *A* for life and a springing use in *A*'s heirs. The Statute of Uses executes these uses, so that the legal title becomes: life estate in *A*, springing executory interest in *A*'s heirs. The Rule in Shelley's Case does not apply, because the heirs take by executory interest rather than by remainder. (See *supra*, p. 82.)

G. **Identifying executory interests:** The following rules will help you identify executory interests:

1. **Use required:** An executory interest, by definition, can be created only by a conveyance that raises a use (usually, a ***bargain and sale deed***). Thus where a conveyance is accomplished by means of a common-law feoffment (i.e., livery of seisin), there can be no executory interest created.

2. **Cannot be created in grantor:** By definition, an executory interest cannot be created in the original grantor; executory interests are always created in ***third persons***. Thus there should be no difficulty in distinguishing between an executory interest on the one hand, and a reversion, possibility of reverter and right of entry on the other.

3. **Distinguishing between executory interest and remainder:** But it is not always so easy to distinguish between an executory interest and a ***remainder***, since both are created in persons other than the grantor. The difference is essentially that a remainder ***never cuts off*** a prior interest, but merely awaits the prior interests's ***natural termination***. An executory interest, on the other hand, is generally one which ***divests***, or ***cuts off***, a prior interest before that prior interest's natural termination.

   a. **Test:** To determine whether the second interest is cutting short the first, or merely awaiting the natural termination of the first, use the "read from left to right" test described *supra*, pp. 76-77, in connection with conditions precedent and subsequent.

   Example: O is the fee simple owner of Blackacre. He bargains and sells "to *A* for life, then to *B* and his heirs if *B* survives *A*, otherwise to *C* and his heirs." Because the limitation on *B*'s interest is stated in the same clause as the gift to *B*, *B* and *C* each have equitable contingent remainders that are executed by the Statute of Uses into alternate legal contingent remainders. But suppose that the bargain and sale had been "to *A* for life, then to *B* and his heirs, but if *B* should die before *A*, to *C* and his heirs." Now *B*'s interest would be vested subject to divestment, because the divesting language ("but if. . .") comes in a separate clause following the clause giving the gift to *B*. *C*'s interest would then be an executory interest, divesting *B*'s interest. See Moynihan, p. 198.

H. Active trust: The Statute of Uses was directed at the situation where the legal title was a sham, and actual possession of the property was in the hands of the equitable owner. Thus where the holder of the legal title took a more *active* interest in the property, the Statute has always been held *not to apply.* For instance, if the legal titleholder occupies the premises and pays rent to the equitable owner, or actively rents out the premises and pays the rents over to the equitable owner, this will be considered an *active trust* to which the Statute is inapplicable.

> **Example 1:** Owner, the fee simple owner of Blackacre, devises "to Trustee and his heirs to the use of Able for life and then to the use of Able's heirs." The will states that Trustee is to collect the income during Able's life and pay it over to Able quarterly.
>
> The use during Able's life is an active one, since Trustee is required to collect the income and pay it over to Able. Therefore, the Statute does not execute Able's equitable life estate. But the use in Able's heirs is not active, since no management duties are imposed on Trustee. This use is therefore executed. Thus the state of the title is: legal life estate *per autre vie* in Trustee, equitable life estate in Able, legal contingent remainder in fee simple in Able's heirs. (The Rule in Shelley's Case cannot apply, since the estate in the ancestor is equitable and the estate in the heirs is legal; see *supra*, p. 82.)

> **Example 2:** Owner, the fee simple owner of Blackacre, devises "to Trustee and his heirs to the use of Able for life and then to the use of Able's heirs." Trustee is then to collect the income during Able's life and pay it over to Able quarterly, and on Able's death is too con-vey the premises to Able's heirs.
>
> The analysis of Able's interest is the same as in Example 1: the use during Able's life is an active one; therefore, the Statute does not execute Able's equitable life estate. But the analysis of Able's *heirs'* interest is different than in Example 1. Now, Trustee has active duties with respect to the heirs as well as with respect to Able, by virtue of the duty to con-vey the premises. This means that the heirs' use is not executed either. Thus Trustee has a legal fee simple, Able has an equitable life estate and Able's heirs have an equitable con-tingent remainder in fee simple; the Rule in Shelley's Case then applies, so that the remainder in the heirs becomes an equitable remainder in Able. Able's equitable life estate then merges into this remainder, giving Able a present equitable fee simple.

> **a. Foundation of modern trust:** The recognition that the Statute of Uses does *not* apply to an active use was the foundation of the *modern trust*. The "trust" as we now know it is an *active* one, with substantial duties of management given to the trustee. Thus even where the Statute of Uses is still in force (see *infra*), the modern trust is not affected.

I. The Statute of Uses today: In many states, the Statute of Uses is considered to be part of the common law, and is thus *in force unless repealed.* Only a few states (e.g., New York) have expressly repealed the Statute, so that in many states it is *still in force*. In other states (e.g., Illinois), statutes have been explicitly enacted containing provisions similar to those of the Statutes of Uses. C&L, p. 334.

J. Alienability: In nearly all jurisdictions, *executory interests* are *completely alienable*. That is, they may be transferred *inter vivos*, devised by will, and passed under the intestacy statutes. Moynihan, p. 206-07. Thus they are no different from remainders (either contingent or vested) with respect to transfer.

Figure 5-1
Future Interests

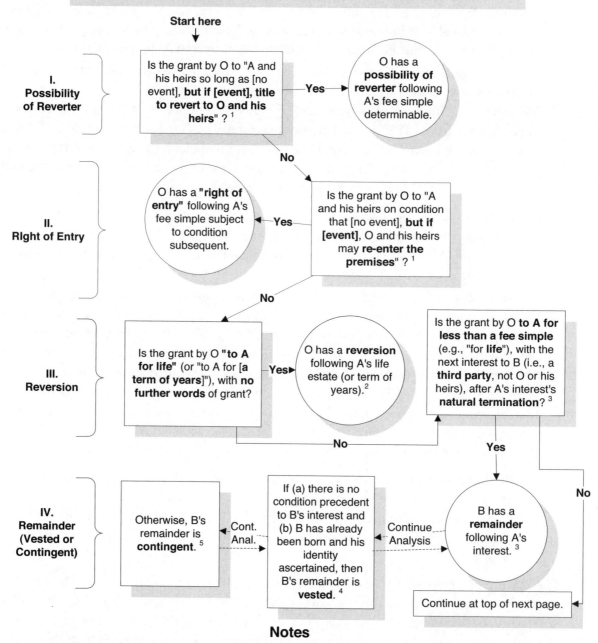

Use this chart to determine what future estate is created by particular words of grant. O is the conveyor (holder of a vested estate, usually a fee simple); A is the recipient of a freehold interest; B is the third-party recipient of the future interest, if any. Unless otherwise noted, the common-law treatment of the grant is all that is discussed.

Start here

I. Possibility of Reverter

Is the grant by O to "A and his heirs so long as [no event], **but if [event], title to revert to O and his heirs**" ?[1]

Yes → O has a **possibility of reverter** following A's fee simple determinable.

No

II. Right of Entry

O has a **"right of entry"** following A's fee simple subject to condition subsequent.

← **Yes** — Is the grant by O to "A and his heirs on condition that [no event], **but if [event]**, O and his heirs may **re-enter the premises**" ?[1]

No

III. Reversion

Is the grant by O **"to A for life"** (or "to A for [a term of years]"), with **no further words** of grant?

Yes ► O has a **reversion** following A's life estate (or term of years).[2]

No

Is the grant by O **to A for less than a fee simple** (e.g., "for life"), with the next interest to B (i.e., a **third party**, not O or his heirs), after A's interest's **natural termination**?[3]

Yes

No

IV. Remainder (Vested or Contingent)

Otherwise, B's remainder is **contingent**.[5]

← **Cont. Anal.** — If (a) there is no condition precedent to B's interest and (b) B has already been born and his identity ascertained, then B's remainder is **vested**.[4]

◄ **Continue Analysis** ·· B has a **remainder** following A's interest.[3]

Continue at top of next page. ◄

Notes

[1] Your main job is to <u>distinguish</u> between a <u>possibility of reverter</u> and a <u>right of entry</u>, since the two are quite similar. Both are reversionary interests -- that is, they vest in the original grantor and his heirs (O in our chart), not in some third person. The <u>possibility of reverter</u> follows a <u>fee simple determinable</u>. The <u>right of entry</u> follows a <u>fee simple subject to condition</u>

<u>subsequent</u>. For examples of the f.s.d. and the f.s.s.c.s., see note 2 to Figure 4-1.

[2] A <u>reversion</u> is the estate that's created when the holder of a vested estate (most often, a fee simple) <u>transfers to another a smaller estate</u>. The reversion is the interest which remains in the grantor.

Notes continued on next page

Figure 5-1 (cont.)
Future Interests

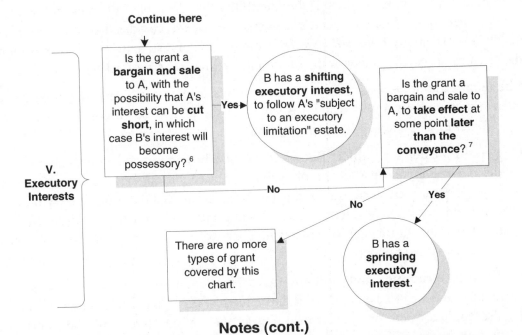

Notes (cont.)

[3] For a <u>remainder</u> to exist, <u>three requirements</u> must be satisfied: (1) a grantor (O) must <u>convey a present possessory estate</u> to one transferee (A); (2) the grantor (O) must <u>create a non-possessory estate in another transferee</u> (B) by the <u>same instrument</u>; and (C) the second, non-possessory estate must be capable of becoming possessory only on the "natural" expiration (as opposed to the cutting short) of the prior estate.

<u>Example</u>: O conveys "to A for life, then to B and his heirs." B has a remainder, because: (1) O conveyed a present possessory interest to A (the life estate); (2) by the same instrument O created a non-possessory estate in a third person (B); and (3) B's estate will automatically become possessory when A's estate naturally expires.

[4] For there not to be a condition precedent, the remainder must become possessory "whenever and however the prior estate terminates."

<u>Example</u>: O conveys "to A for A's life, remainder to B and his heirs." Assuming that B is a named individual who is alive on the date of the conveyance, this is a vested remainder, because: (1) there's no condition precedent attached to B's interest (it will become possessory no matter how or when A's life interest ends); and (2) the person holding it, B, has already been born and is clearly identified in the instrument.

[5] All remainders that are not vested are contingent. So you are looking for a remainder where either: (1) there's a <u>condition precedent</u> to the interest's becoming possessory; or (2) the holder has either not yet <u>come into existence</u> or not yet <u>been identified</u>.

<u>Example 1 (remainder that's contingent because of a condition precedent)</u>: O conveys "to A for life, then, if B is living at A's death, to B in fee simple." B must meet the condition of surviving A for his remainder to become possessory; therefore, the remainder is contingent.

<u>Example 2 (remainder that's contingent because the holder is not yet in existence or identified)</u>: O conveys "to A for life, then to the children of B." At the time of conveyance, B has no children. (Once B has a child, the remainder becomes vested subject to open.)

Note that a remainder that's contingent when it comes into existence can (and often does) <u>later become vested</u>. For instance, in Example 2 above, while B has no children the remainder is contingent, but once the first child is born, the remainder becomes vested (though subject to "open" in favor of later-born children).

[6] <u>Example</u>: O bargains and sells land "to A and his heirs, but if liquor is ever sold on the premises, then to B and his heirs." The "but if" clause cuts A's interest short. Since the estate then goes to a third person (i.e., not to O and his heirs), that third-party interest is called an executory interest, of the "<u>shifting</u>" variety.

[7] <u>Example</u>: O wants to reassure his prospective son-in-law A that if A marries O's daughter, D, A will get Blackacre. Therefore, O bargains and sells Blackacre "to A and his heirs from and after the date of A's marriage to D." This is an executory interest of the "<u>springing</u>" variety, since: (1) it benefits a third party (not the grantor), and (2) it will take effect at some point after the grant (i.e., seisin will "spring" out of O).

VIII. WASTE

A. The concept of waste generally: Whenever ownership of property is divided between a present and future interest, there is the possibility that the acts of the present holder will be to the detriment of the future interest. The doctrine of *waste* provides that if the present interest's acts: (1) substantially *reduce the value* of the future interest; and (2) are *unreasonable* under the circumstances, the holder of the future interest has a cause of action.

B. Life tenant and tenant for years: A claim of waste can arise against any holder of a present interest that amounts to less than a fee simple absolute. Most commonly, waste is committed by a *life tenant*, or a tenant for a *term of years*.

    1. Fee simple determinable: But waste can also be committed by one who holds a fee simple *determinable*, or a fee simple subject to a condition subsequent or to an executory interest. However, since usually it is far from certain that these interests will ever end, the courts are much more reluctant to find that a given act constitutes waste. In general, the less likely the future interest is to become possessory, or the further away the date of likely possession, the stronger a showing will be required to establish a case of waste.

    2. Tenants in common and joint tenants: The common-law concept of waste, as noted, requires damage to the holder of a future interest. In a few states, however, the doctrine is also applied where one holder of a present interest interferes with the rights of *another present interest*. Thus one tenant in common might be liable to another tenant in common for acts which diminish the value of the latter's interests. See Burby, pp. 33-34.

C. Types of waste: Waste is usually divided into three general categories: (1) voluntary waste; (2) permissive waste; and (3) equitable waste.

    1. Voluntary waste: *Voluntary waste* exists where an *affirmative act* causes unreasonable, permanent damage to the holder of a future interest.

    Example: T has a 20-year lease on Blackacre, owned by O. The premises include a residential structure. T demolishes the structure to use the property as a parking lot. Assuming that T's action was unreasonable, he has committed voluntary waste (even though the value of the property may actually have been increased by his action; see *supra*, p. 62).

        a. Act by third person: If the damage is committed not by the holder of the present interest, but by a *third person*, the present holder will not be liable for waste, if he was without fault. Burby, p. 34.

            i. Negligence: If, however, the third person's act was facilitated by the *negligence* of the present holder, the latter is liable for waste.

        b. Act of God: If the premises are damaged by an *act of God* (e.g., a fire or a hurricane), the present holder will not be liable, again assuming that his negligence did not contribute to the damage. Nor will he have the duty to rebuild.

        c. Ameliorative: Voluntary waste may exist even where the value of the property *increases* as a result. See *supra*, p. 62. Such waste is sometimes called *ameliorative* waste.

2. Permissive waste: *Permissive waste* results not from an affirmative act, but from ***omission*** by the present holder to ***care for the property adequately***. The present holder has an obligation to keep the land and buildings in a ***reasonable state of repair***. Thus a failure to keep a building ***painted*** so that the wood does not deteriorate, or to fix small ***leaks***, is waste.

   a. Act of God: But, as noted, there is no duty to repair major damage done by force of nature or by the acts of a third person. Thus if a roof is severely damaged by a hurricane, it is probably not waste to fail to repair it. See Rest.§146.

3. Equitable waste: The holder of a ***legal fee simple*** (even one that is subject to an executory interest) is immune from legal liability for waste. But a court of ***equity*** will grant relief if his conduct will damage the prospects of the holder of an executory interest, possibility of reverter, etc. The equity court may enjoin this conduct under the doctrine of ***equitable waste***.

D. Acts constituting waste: Decisions about what constitutes waste are necessarily on mostly a case-by-case basis, since no two fact patterns are exactly the same. However, the courts have evolved fairly specific rules dealing with several common types of cases.

1. Cutting up timber: As a general rule, a life tenant or a tenant for a term of years commits waste if he ***cuts timber*** on the land. There are, however, a number of exceptions:

   a. Estovers: Under the common-law doctrine of ***estovers***, the tenant may cut timber needed for repairs, fencing, and fuel, so long as the wood is used on the property in question.

   b. Commercial use: If the only ***commercially-feasible*** use of the property is for commercial timber-cutting, the tenant may use it for this purpose.

   c. Prior use: Similarly, if the property was used for commercial harvesting of timber ***prior*** to the life estate of term of years, the tenant may continue this use.

   d. Agricultural purposes: Finally, if the land is clearly of an ***agricultural*** nature, the tenant may clear the timber so as to be able to farm. Burby, p. 38.

2. Earth and minerals: The tenant may normally not remove ***earth and minerals*** from the property. Again, however, there are exceptions:

   a. "Open mines" doctrine: First, if the property was used for mining ***prior*** to the commencement of the life estate or term of years, the tenant may ***continue*** this use.

   b. Accomplishing purpose of tenancy: Secondly, the tenant may mine if this is the only way of accomplishing the purpose of the lease or life estate. This would be the case where mining is the only use for which the property is suitable. Similarly, if removal of earth and stones was necessary to permit the agricultural use that the grantor or landlord intended, this could be done. Burby, p. 38.

3. Structural changes: Traditionally, ***any structural change***, even one that improved the value of the property, was deemed waste. Thus ***removal of a building***, or major ***alterations*** to one, were automatically considered waste. But present-day courts generally do not hold that any structural alteration is automatically waste. Modern rules on structural changes are summarized *supra*, p. 62.

E. Remedies for waste: There are several possible remedies for waste:

1. **Damages:**   If the future interest is *sure to become possessory* (e.g., a landlord's interest, or a reversion or remainder vested absolutely), the court will generally award *damages*. The damages will be based upon the *diminution in value* of the future interest stemming from the waste.

2. **Injunction:**   An *injunction* issued by a court of equity is also frequently available. If the future interest is *not certain* to become possessory (e.g., a contingent remainder, or an executory interest following a fee simple determinable), an injunction may be the only relief that the court may award (since damages for an interest not sure to become possessory are highly speculative). The acts being enjoined are referred to as *"equitable waste"*.

   a. **Injunction with damages:**   Occasionally, the court will award an injunction together with money damages, even though the usual rule is that equitable relief is not available where money damages will suffice.

3. **Sale by judicial order:**   Where a tenant wishes to alter the property substantially, and has not yet done so, another alternative is open to the court: it may, in some states, *order the property sold*.

IX. THE RULE AGAINST PERPETUITIES

A. Historical development of Rule: The rise of executory interests meant that it was possible to tie up the ownership of the land for long periods. For instance, it would be possible for O to convey by bargain and sale deed "to A for life, then to such of A's lineal descendants who are alive 100 years after A's death." The interest in the descendants is not subject to destruction, since it is a springing executory interest, not a contingent remainder. This conveyance would mean that no disposition of the property could be made for A's life plus 100 years, during which time it might be highly desirable, from a social viewpoint, for the land to be transferred to someone else. It was in recognition of the undesirability of permitting title to be tied up for long periods that the courts developed the *Rule Against Perpetuities* (the "Rule" or "RAP").

Note: A detailed treatment of the Rule, including its many exceptions and exceptions to exceptions, is beyond the scope of this outline. This subject is usually treated in detail in the course on wills and trusts or estate planning.

B. Statement of Rule: The Rule Against Perpetuities is generally stated as follows: *"no interest is good unless it must vest, if at all, not later than 21 years after some life in being at the creation of the interest."* See B,C&S, p. 246.

1. **Paraphrase of Rule:**   To paraphrase this statement, an interest is invalid unless it can be said, with absolute certainty, that it will either *vest or fail to vest*, before the end of the period equal to: (1) a life in existence at the time the interest is created plus (2) an additional 21 years.

   Example: O conveys his fee simple interest in Blackacre "to A for life, remainder to the first son of A whenever born who becomes a clergyman." At the date of the conveyance, A has no son who is presently a clergyman. Viewing the matter from the date of the convey- ance, it is possible to imagine a situation in which the remainder to the son could vest later than lives in being plus 21 years. Thus *A*'s son could be born to *A* after the date of the conveyance, and this son could become a clergyman more than 21 years after the death of *A* and of any sons born before the conveyance. Since this remote vesting is possible (even though somewhat unlikely) *the contingent remainder is invalid*. This is so even though it *actually turns out* that *A* has a son alive before the date of the conveyance who ultimately becomes a clergyman. See B,C&S, p. 248.

2. **Judged in advance:** As the above example makes clear, the common-law version of the Rule Against Perpetuities requires that the validity of the interest be judged *at the time it is created*, not at the time the interest actually vests. If, at the time the interest is created, it is *theoretically possible* (even though very unlikely) that the interest will vest later than 21 years after the expiration of lives in being, the interest is invalid. This is so even if it actually turns out that the interest vests before the end of lives in being plus 21 years. (But the Restatement 2d and a number of states have adopted "wait and see" statutes changing this common-law rule; see *infra*, p. 105.)

3. **"Rule of logical proof":** The *burden* is on the person seeking to uphold the validity of the interest to *prove logically that it could not possibly vest remotely*. As DKA&S put it, "The essential thing to grasp about the Rule is that it is a *rule of logical proof.* You must prove that a contingent interest is certain to *vest or terminate* no later than 21 years after the death of some person alive at the creation of the interest. If you cannot prove that, then the contingent interest is void from the outset." DKA&S, pp. 246-47.

4. **Effect of Rule when it applies:** What happens when the Rule applies to make the interest invalid? "When an interest violates the Rule ... it is *struck out* and the *remaining valid interests stand.* Take out a pencil and line out the void [interest]." DKA&S, p. 250.

   a. **Effect on prior interest:** If the interest that is invalidated by the rule is the last interest in the sequence, the effect of the Rule's application will often be to *"upgrade"* the immediately-prior interest to a *fee simple absolute*.

   Example: O conveys Blackacre "to *A* and his heirs, but if *A* or his heirs shall ever use the premises for a non-residential purpose, then to *B* and his heirs." As written, *A* has a fee simple subject to an executory interest, and *B* has a (purported) executory interest. But *B*'s interest might vest later than lives in being plus 21 years. (See the Example on p. 98 for how this might occur.) Therefore, *B*'s executory interest is invalid. The court will re-write the document so as to strike the language "then to *B* and his heirs." The effect will be to leave *A* with a fee simple absolute.

C. **Interests to which the Rule applies:** For the Rule to have any force, the interest must be one that is *contingent*, i.e., not automatically vested at the time it is created.

   1. **Contingent remainders:** The Rule applies to *contingent remainders*. In fact, one of the principal reasons why it is still necessary to be able to distinguish between vested and contingent remainders is precisely because a vested remainder is vested from the moment of its creation, whereas a contingent remainder violates the Rule if it might not vest or fail before the end of lives in being plus 21 years.

   Example: O conveys "to *A* for life, remainder to the first son of *A* to reach the age of 25 and his heirs." At the time of the conveyance, *A* does not have a son who has reached the age of 25. The remainder in the son is contingent, rather than vested, since it is not known which son, if any, will reach the age of 25. It is possible that the first son to reach 25 will be one who has not yet been born as of the date of the conveyance; such a son's interest would vest later than lives in being plus 21 years, if *A* has no other sons, or if all his sons die within four years of the conveyance. Since there is a possibility of remote vesting, the gift to the oldest son violates the Rule Against Perpetuities and is invalid. See B,C&S, p. 248.

2. **Vested remainders:** A *vested* remainder, by contrast, can *never* violate the Rule Against Perpetuities. A vested remainder, by definition, vests at the moment it is created. This is true even if *possession* is not to occur until the future; the important thing is that the remainder vests "in interest"', not possession, immediately.

    Example: O conveys "to *A* for life, remainder to *A*'s children for life, remainder to *B* and his heirs." It is possible that *A*'s last surviving child will be one who has not been born as of the date of the conveyance, and who will live more than 21 years longer than any of *A*'s other children born before the date of the conveyance. It is also possible that, following the last child's death, possession will go not to *B* (who may already be dead) but to an heir or devisee of *B* not yet living at the time of the conveyance. Nonetheless, the gift to *B* and his heirs does not violate the Rule Against Perpetuities, because that gift is a vested remainder, which vested in interest (though not in possession) on the date of the conveyance. Burby, p. 419.

3. **Reversionary interests not within Rule:** The Rule does *not* apply to *reversionary interests* (i.e., *possibilities of reverter, rights of entry* and *reversions*; see *supra,* pp. 69, 70, and 71, respectively). This is because these interests, like vested remainders, are deemed to *vest as soon as they are created*.

4. **Executory interests:** An *executory interest* is *not vested at its creation*. Thus such an interest *may* violate the Rule. DKA&S, p. 250.

    Example: In 2004, O conveys a building to City, "so long as City continues to use the property as an animal shelter, then to Able and his heirs." In 2006, while O is still alive, the City stops using the building as an animal shelter, and leases it to an insurance company as office space. Assuming the common-law Rule applies, what's the state of the title?

    City has a fee simple. By the terms of the conveyance, City received a fee simple subject to an executory limitation (see *supra,* p. 55), and Able received an executory interest. But viewed as of the moment of the conveyance in 2004, it was theoretically possible that City might use the building as an animal shelter for, say, 200 years, then stop using it for that purpose. At that moment, by the terms of the conveyance, the executory interest in Able's heirs would vest (i.e., become possessory). Since that would or could be happening at a moment in which no "measuring life" (i.e., no person related to the interests created in the 2004 conveyance; see *infra,* p. 102) would still be alive, that theoretical possibility is enough to invalidate the executory interest in Able. Consequently, the court will "take a pencil and [cross] out the void gift" (DKA&S, p. 250), leaving City with a fee simple.

5. Options to purchase land: An *option* to *purchase land* will often be subject to the Rule Against Perpetuities.

   a. Option as part of lease: If an option to purchase property is part of a *lease* of that property and is exercisable only during the lease term, then the option is (at least in the United States) *not* treated as being subject to the Rule. The theory behind this exclusion is that the option gives the lessee an incentive to improve the property, and does not really restrict alienability very much. See C,S&W, p. 132.

   Example: Tenant leases Blackacre from Landlord. The lease runs for 50 years. The lease provides that at any time until the end of the lease, Tenant may purchase the property for $200,000. Since the purchase option is part of a lease, it need not satisfy the Rule Against Perpetuities. Therefore, even though no measuring life is listed and the option is exercisable more than 21 years after its creation (so that the option would be a violation of the Rule if the Rule applied), the option is valid.

   b. Options "in gross": But if the option is *not* part of a lease or other property interest, most states hold that the Rule *does* apply. (Such unattached options are called options *"in gross."*) Thus under the majority rule an option in gross will be unenforceable if by its terms it could be exercised beyond the end of the Perpetuities period, even though the optionee paid real money for it in the belief that it would be exercisable. DKA&S, p. 261. And that's true even if the optionee attempts to exercise before the end of the Perpetuities period.

   Example: Broadwest owns a building, which includes a small amount of commercial space and a large theater that Broadwest has never been able to regularly rent. In late 1978, Broadwest conveys the building to Symphony Space (a nonprofit theater group) for a very below-market price of $10,010, and receives in return an option to repurchase the building for $1. (Broadwest also leases back the commercial space from Symphony Space.) The option clause says that the option may be exercised at any time, with the closing to take place in any of the years 1987, 1993, 1998 and 2003, whichever the exerciser chooses. Broadwest's purpose in doing this cheap-sale-plus-buyback-option transaction is to get the property's property tax bill eliminated (since the property will now be owned by a non-profit, and thus exempt from tax), but with Broadwest never surrendering real economic ownership, including the right to profit from any increase in the building's value.

   In 1985, Broadwest's successor in interest notifies Symphony Space that it is exercising the option, with the closing to occur in 1987. Symphony Space refuses to convey, arguing that the option is void under the Rule against Perpetuities.

   Held, for Symphony Space — the option is subject to the Rule against Perpetuities, and void under it. The court declines to recognize any "commercial transactions" exception to the general rule that options fall within the Rule against Perpetuities, as that rule has been codified by the New York State Legislature. Nor does the "option as part of a lease" exception apply, because although the transaction here included a small lease (of the commercial space), the lease exception applies only where the *entire property* subject to the option is being leased, which is not the case here.

Since the option here was between two corporations, and no human measuring lives were mentioned, the option would be void if it could be exercised more than 21 years after the option was created. Since the option by its terms could be exercised in 2003 (24 years after its creation in late 1978), it could be exercised more than 21 years after creation, and is thus void. (Nor is the court willing to adopt the "wait and see" approach [see *infra*, p. 105], since the legislature clearly did not contemplate that approach when it codified the Rule. So the fact that the attempted exercise — the "vesting" of the interest — is in fact occurring within the 21-year period doesn't save the interest.) *The Symphony Space, Inc. v. Pergola Properties, Inc.*, 669 N.E.2d 799 (N.Y. 1996).

Note: *Symphony Space* is fascinating not just for its demonstration that options will be subject to the Rule against Perpetuities, but also for its demonstration of just how costly an extra word (or, in this case, date) can be when dealing with the Rule. Had the drafter for Broadwest been content with an option that had to be exercised no later than 1998, there would have been no perpetuities problem, since the "vesting" (exercise) of the option would have occurred, if at all, less than 21 years after the option's 1978 creation. But because the drafter added that exercise could occur in 2003, that extra date caused the entire option to be invalid! And, by the way, according to an appraisal done in 1988 during the litigation, that was a $21.5 million error — the difference between the $5.5 million value of the leaseback of the commercial space, and the value of the entire building if the option was valid. So be careful how you draft options and other interests in real estate!

    i.   **Third Restatement changes rule:** The Third Restatement of Property (Servitudes) *changes* the common-law rule: *options* (even in gross) *are not subject to the Rule.* See §3.3, and Comment a thereto. So on the facts of *Symphony Space*, *supra*, Broadwest's successor *would* have been entitled to exercise the option, under the Third Restatement's approach.

6. **Right of first refusal (RAP may apply):** Courts are *split* about whether a *right of first refusal* to purchase or re-purchase the property is subject to the Rule.

    Example: *A* conveys Blackacre to *B*. The deed says that if *B* or his heirs or assigns at any time desires to sell the property on particular terms and conditions, the property must first be offered to *A* or his heirs and assigns on those same terms and conditions.

    Of those jurisdictions applying the RAP, some, but not all, will apply the Rule to *A*'s right of first refusal here. If the jurisdiction applies the RAP to *A*'s right of first refusal, the right will be invalid. That's because the right could be exercised later than all measuring lives (here, *A*'s and *B*'s) plus 21 years. For instance, *B*'s heirs might own the property for 150 years, then try to sell it, at which point all lives in being at the time of *A*'s conveyance have long ended. But if the clause's effectiveness was limited to, say, "No later than 20 years after the death of *A*," the clause would *not* violate the Rule and would therefore be enforceable.

7. **Land-use restrictions (RAP doesn't apply):** *Land-use restrictions,* such as *equitable servitudes* (p. 238 *infra*), are *not covered* by the RAP.

Example: O owns both Whiteacre and Blackacre, two adjacent parcels. O sells White-acre to "*A* and his heirs." In the deed, O and *A* agree that neither will ever use their property for anything other than single-family residential use, and that this "equitable servitude" will apply to O's and *A*'s successors in interest. The deed to *A* is properly recorded.

These restrictions are not only enforceable against *A* and his assigns (see *infra*, p. 238), they are not subject to the RAP. Therefore, if *A*'s descendants or assigns use the property for non-residential uses 200 years from now, the court will issue an injunction against the use (assuming that the neighborhood hasn't changed in such a way as to make the restriction obsolete; see *infra*, p. 247).

D. Table: The table below summarizes when the Rule Against Perpetuities does and doesn't apply.

Table 5-2

CHECKLIST: **Interests to Which the RAP Does or Doesn't Apply**

Future Interest	Does the RAP Apply?	Example of Gift that Violates or Doesn't Violate the RAP
Contingent Remainder	Yes	*O* "to *A* for life, remainder to his first son to turn 30, " made when no son of *A* has turned 30. Remainder violates RAP even if son turns 30 one year later.
Vested Remainder	No (vests at creation)	*O* "to *A* for life, then to *A*'s last surviving child for life, then to *C* and his heirs." Remainder in *C* is vested (since subject to no contingency), and thus doesn't violate the RAP, even though it may not become possessory for 100 years, in hands of *C*'s successors.
Reversion	No (vests at creation)	*O* "to *A* for life." *O*'s reversion doesn't violate the RAP.
Possibility of Reverter	No (vests at creation)	*O* "to *A* and his heirs so long as property is used as a church." *O* has a possibility of reverter that cannot violate the RAP even though it might become possessory in 200 years.
Right of Re-Entry	No (vests at creation)	*O* "to *A* and his heirs, but if property ceases to be used as church, grantor and his heirs may re-enter." *O* has a right of re-entry that cannot violate the RAP even though it might become exercisable in 200 years
Executory Interest	Yes	*O* "to *A* and his heirs so long as property is used for a church, then to *B* and his heirs." Executory interest in *B* violates the RAP, even if *A* stops using as a church one year later.

CHECKLIST: **Interests to Which the RAP Does or Doesn't Apply**

Future Interest	Does the RAP Apply?	Example of Gift that Violates or Doesn't Violate the RAP
Option to Purchase, in lease	**No**	*O* rents to Corp, Corp gets right to purchase during lease-term. Corp's right can't violate the RAP even if lease lasts 99 years.
Option to Purchase, in gross (i.e., not in lease)	**Yes**, in some but not all courts	*O* sells *A* "right to purchase property for $100,000 at any time." Some courts say this violates the RAP even if *A* tries to exercise 1 year later.
Right of First Refusal	**Yes**, in some but not all courts	*O* gives *A* right to match any offer at any time. Some courts say this violates the RAP even if *A* asserts it means it's only exercisable by him during his lifetime (not by his successors).
Land-Use Restriction (e.g., Equitable Servitude)	**No**	*O* conveys Lot 1 to *A* while keeping Lot 2; *O* and *A* agree that each lot will have a single-family-use restriction, binding on their "assigns." Neither restriction will ever violate the RAP, so each can bind for 200 years.

E. Meaning of "lives in being" ("measuring lives"): Recall that the RAP requires that the interest vest within "lives in being" plus 21 years. What lives count as "lives in being" for this purpose? (Or, as the concept is often phrased, what lives count as *"measuring lives"* or *"validating lives"*?)

1. Persons causally connected: A measuring life is any life that is found among "persons whose lives are *somehow causally connected with the vesting or termination* of the interest[.] ... These include the preceding *life tenant*, the *taker* or takers of the *contingent interest*, anyone who can *affect the identity of the takers* (such as *A* in a gift to *A*'s children), and anyone else who can *affect events relevant to the condition precedent*." DKA&S, p. 246.

   a. Person named in document: Normally, the measuring life will be a person *named or directly referred to* in the document that creates the interest.

   Example: O conveys "to my daughter D for life, then to her first child to reach the age of 21." D is childless at the date of the conveyance. D is the "life in being" or "measuring life." The contingent remainder to D's oldest child is valid, because we know that any child D may eventually have will reach 21 within 21 years after D's death.

   i. Person not named: But there is *no logical requirement* that to be a measuring life, the person must be mentioned in the document. Sometimes the measuring life will be a person (or a group) that the document *doesn't mention,* but whose life is nonetheless *causally related* to vesting or termination of the interest. For instance, if a person's **grandchild** is referred to, this will likely mean that the parent of that grandchild (even if not mentioned) can be a measuring life.

Example: O devises "to the first of my grandchildren to reach the age of 21." O is survived by two sons and one daughter (none of whom is mentioned in the will), as well as by four grandchildren.

The measuring life is the survivor of O's three children. That is, we know that any grandchild will have to turn 21 no more than 21 years after the last of O's three children dies.[1] Consequently, even though we don't know precisely *which* child of O will serve as the measuring life, and even though none of O's children is mentioned in the will, we know that the gift to the "first grandchild to reach 21" will inevitably vest or fail within *some* life-in-being-plus-21-years (i.e., within the life of O's last surviving child plus 21 years). Therefore, the gift to the first-grand-child-to-turn-21 is valid. Cf. DKA&S, p. 247, including Example 25.

F. Special situations: The common-law Rule requires, as noted, that there be **no possibility** that the interest in question might vest after lives in being plus 21 years. There are a number of special sub-rules that have evolved to deal with certain possibilities.

1. **Fertile octogenarian:** There is a **conclusive presumption** that **any person, regardless of age** or physical condition, is capable of **having children**. This presumption is often derisively referred to as the "**fertile octogenarian**" rule. When coupled with the rule that a gift to a class is invalid if the gift to any member of the class is invalid (*infra*, p. 104), the fertile octogenarian rule can have a devastating effect.

   Example: T devises property "to A for life, then to A's surviving children for life, then to the surviving children of B." At the time of T's death, B has three children, and B herself is 80 years old. It is conceivable that B could now have another child, and that that child would take after lives in being plus 21 years (for instance, if all of A's children were born after T's death, and died more than 21 years after T's death). Therefore, B's three now-living children will not take anything, since their interest violates the Rule. It is irrelevant that, as a medical matter, B could not possibly have any further children. Burby, p. 415. See also *Jee v. Audley*, 1 Cox 324 (Ch. 1787).

2. **Unborn widow:** Similarly, if an interest is created which will flow through the "**widow**" of X (by naming and relying on her in determining when the interest will vest), the common-law view is that the interest **must fail.** The "widow" is not necessarily the person who is married to X when the interest is created; X could later marry someone born after the interest was created, who would not be a relevant life-in-being for the purposes of the vesting of the interest in question. Since the "unborn widow" might live longer than 21 years after the death of X, the only life in being, the interest **might** not vest within 21 years of X's death and is therefore invalid under the Rule Against Perpetuities. This is often

---

1. Even if all the grandchildren already living at O's death die before 21, and then all O's children die except the younger son, and it ends up that the only grandchild to turn 21 was in the womb of O's daughter-in-law (the one married to the younger son) at the time the younger son dies, this won't violate the Rule. That's because for purposes of the RAP, a child is "considered as in being from the time of conception if later born alive." DKA&S, p. 246, n. 18. So the only-grandchild-to-turn-21 would be deemed to be in being at the moment of O's younger son's death, and the gift would vest within 21 years after that death.

called the *"unborn widow"* rule. (The rule developed in a less gender-equal time; it would, of course, apply equally to widowers.)

Example: In 2010, T bequeaths Blackacre "to *A* for life, then to *A*'s widow, then to the issue of *A* and *A*'s widow who survive them." At the time of T's death, *A* is married to *B*. It is possible that *B* will either predecease or divorce *A*, and *A* will then marry someone born after 2010 (we'll call her *C*.) *C* would not be a life-in-being in 2010, the time of the bequest. So the contingent remainder to the issue is not logically certain to vest within 21 years of some life that was in being *at the time the remainder was created* (*C* might live longer than 21 years after the death of *A*). Therefore, the contingent remainder to the issue of *A* and "*A*'s widow" must fail.

a. **Problem is less severe:** Several factors make the unborn widow problem *less severe* today than you might imagine:

   i. **Applies only to widow of non-testator:** First, note that in a bequest scenario you never have to worry about the unborn-widow problem if the bequest is to take effect upon the death of *the testator's own widow* — that's because the testator's widow will have to qualify as a measuring life (a grantor obviously can't leave a widow who hasn't been born yet). Only when the interest is to become possessory upon the death of the widow of *someone other than the testator* can there be an unborn-widow problem. So typically, the unborn-widow rule will apply where the reference is to the testator's *child's* widow, and there is a further gift over to the testator's *grandchildren* that is invalid because of the unborn-widow problem. That's the case in the above Example, where the gift over might be to the surviving child of *A*'s widow, not the surviving widow of T (the testator).

   ii. **Existing spouse intended:** Second, most courts will accept evidence that by the term "widow," the grantor intended to refer to an existing spouse (in the above example, *A*'s spouse in 2010, *B*). If this evidence is accepted, then the existing spouse will be a relevant life in being, and the remainder will be valid (since it will vest immediately after the existing spouse's death.)

   iii. **Problem solved by "wait and see" statutes:** Finally, the "unborn widow" rule only applies where the validity of the interests is judged at the time the conveyance was created. In those states that have adopted *"wait and see"* statutes (see *infra*, p. 105), the conveyance will be valid so long as the "widow" turns out to be a person born before the conveyance or bequest.

3. **Class gift:** If a gift is made to all members of a *class*, the entire gift fails unless it can be said that *each member of the class* must have his interest vest or fail within the lives in being plus 21 year period. The problem usually arises where the class obtains new members following a testator's death.

    Example: T bequeaths property "to *A*, then to *A*'s surviving children who attain the age of 25." At the time of the bequest, *A* has two children, *B* and *C*. It is possible that another child (whom we shall hypothetically call "D"), will be born after T's death; since *A*, *B*, and *C* might all die prior to D's fourth birthday, D's interest would then vest too remotely (more than 21 years after the deaths of *A*, *B* and *C*, the measuring lives). Because of this theoretical possibility, not only is the gift invalid as to children born after T's death, but it is also invalid as to the rest of the class of children, i.e., *B* and *C*. See Burby, p. 422.

Note: But a court might avoid the result in the above example by construing the class refer only to those members who could take without violating the Rule Against Perpetuities. Alternately, the court might view the class as closing at the time of T's death. Finally, if the bequest referred not to "the children" but specifically to "*B*", "*C*", etc., then each gift would be evaluated on its own, and would be valid. See Burby, pp. 423-24.

G. "Wait-and-see" approach: Under the common-law Rule as noted, the validity of an interest is to be measured as of the time it is created; if a scenario could be imagined whereby the interest might vest too remotely, it is invalid regardless of how things actually turn out. But the Restatement 2d and a number of jurisdictions have now adopted some type of *"wait-and-see"* rule, by which the validity of an instrument is determined *at the time it vests*. See, e.g., Rest. 2d (Donative Transfers) §1.4.

1. **Explanation:** In other words, under the "wait-and-see" approach the interest fails if it *"does not vest"* with the period of the Rule; the approach rejects the common-law view that the interest fails "if it 'might not vest', if it ever vests, within the period of the rule." Rest. 2d (Donative Transfers) §1.4, Comment a. So *if the interest actually vests within lives in being at the time of creation plus 21 years, the fact that things might have worked out differently is irrelevant* — the interest is valid.

   Example: O, who owns Blackacre in fee simple, conveys "to *A* and his heirs, but if *A* or his heirs ever use Blackacre for other than residential purposes, to *B* and his heirs." Under the traditional what-might-happen view, the gift over to *B* is void, since the premises might stop being used for residential purposes more than lives in being plus 21 years following the conveyance. But under a wait-and-see test, if the property ceases to be used for residential purposes within 21 years after the death of the survivor of O, *A* and *B*, the gift over to *B* and his heirs is valid. That is, the interest in *B* has actually vested within the required period, so it is valid even though things might have worked out in such a way that vesting was too remote. See Rest. 2d (Donative Transfers) §1.4, Illustr. 17.

2. **Effect on fertile octogenarian and unborn widow cases:** Observe that the "wait-and-see" rule renders the "fertile octogenarian" and "unborn widow" cases almost impossible to occur. So long as the octogenarian does not in fact have a child, or the widow referred to in the instrument in fact turns out to be someone born prior to the instrument, the Rule Against Perpetuities cannot be violated. See Rest. 2d (Donative Transfers) §1.4, Comments h and §i, §Illustr. 8 and § 9.

3. **Effect on class gifts:** The "wait-and-see" approach provides that in most cases involving transfers to a class of persons, "the interest of each class member will in fact vest in time," thereby allowing those members of the class whose interests have not yet vested to have a valid interest under the Rule. Rest. 2d (Donative Transfers) §1.4, Comment k.

4. **Uniform Rule:** The *Uniform Statutory Rule Against Perpetuities (USRAP),* drafted in 1986, has now been adopted by 24 states.[2] The USRAP *dramatically weakens* the common-law Rule.

   a. **What the USRAP does:** This weakening is due to the USRAP's use of a *special kind of "wait-and-see"* approach: *No interest may be held void* on account of the

Rule *until 90 years have passed from its creation*. After 90 years, the court looks to see whether the interest actually vested beyond the Perpetuities period. If so, the court invalidates it; but if the interest vested within the 90 years, it's valid. DKA&S, p. 265.

    i. Consequence: Since no interest can be invalidated for at least 90 years after it was created, the USRAP makes the Rule even less likely to result in the invalidation of an interest than does the typical wait-and-see statute. (Under the typical statute, an interest that vests beyond the period of the Rule can be *immediately* invalidated.)

X. RESTRAINTS UPON ALIENATION

A. General problem: There is another respect to which one who conveys land might attempt to tie it up for future generations. He might explicitly provide that the grantee *may not alienate* (i.e., transfer) the property. Such a restriction is known as a *restraint on alienation*.

    1. Generally void: A detailed discussion of restraints on alienation is beyond the scope of this outline. However, the general principle is that restraints upon the alienation of a *fee simple* are *void*. See generally Rest. 2d (Donative Transfers), Part II.

        Example: *O* conveys Blackacre "to *A* and his heirs, but no conveyance by *A* to any third party shall be valid." Since this restricts the alienation of a fee simple, the restriction will be void, and *A* may convey to whomever he wishes.

        a. Bans on will or intestacy transfers: Direct restraints upon the grantee's right to dispose of the property *by will* or *by intestacy* also come within the ban upon restraints upon alienation.

    2. Life estate: A *life estate*, however, may be subjected to restraints. Thus O might convey "to *A* for life, but *A* shall have no right to convey his interest; then to *B* and his heirs." The restraint upon *A* is justified by the need to protect *B*'s future claim interest. Burby, p. 428.

    3. Indirect restraint: Certain types of *indirect* restraints on the use or disposition of property are *upheld* by the courts. *Use restrictions* fall within this category. For instance, O might convey "to *A* and his heirs, provided that the property not be used for non-residential purposes." Such a restriction will not be invalid as a restraint on alienation. Such restrictions are discussed in the chapter on land-use controls, beginning *infra*, p. 261.

        a. Defeasible estates: Also, the defeasible estates (e.g., the fee simple determinable) can be viewed as permissible restraints on alienation. See *supra*, p. 51. For instance, O may convey to *A* and his heirs, but if the property shall ever be used for purposes of the sale of alcohol, grantor or his heirs may re-enter."

---

2. These states are Arizona, California, Colorado, Connecticut, Florida, Georgia, Hawaii, Indiana, Kansas, Massachusetts, Michigan, Minnesota, Montana, Nebraska, Nevada, New Mexico, North Carolina, North Dakota, Oregon, South Carolina, Tennessee, Utah, Virginia, and West Virginia (plus the District of Columbia). DKA&S, p. 265.

Quiz Yourself on

FUTURE INTERESTS

12. O held a fee simple absolute in Blackacre. He conveyed "to A for life." After this conveyance, what interest, if any, does O hold in Blackacre? _____

13. O conveyed Blackacre "to A for life, then to B and his heirs." Immediately after the conveyance, what interest, if any, does B have in Blackacre? _____

14. O conveyed Blackacre "to A for life, then to B's children and their heirs." At the time of this conveyance, B had one child, C. Immediately following the conveyance, what interest, if any, does C have in Blackacre? _____

15. O conveyed Blackacre "to A for life, then to B and his heirs. However, if B dies without issue, then to C and his heirs." Immediately following this conveyance, what interest, if any, does B have in Blackacre? _____

16. O conveyed Blackacre "to A for life, then, if B is living at A's death, to B in fee simple." Immediately after this conveyance, what interest, if any, does B have in Blackacre? _____

17. O conveyed Blackacre "to A for life, then to B and his heirs, but if B dies before A, to O and his heirs." Immediately after this conveyance, what interest, if any, does B have in Blackacre? _____

18. O conveyed Blackacre "to A for life, remainder to the first daughter of A who produces a child while married." A then died. At A's death, he has one daughter, D, who has not yet married or had a child. O is still alive. Immediately after A's death, what is the state of title to Blackacre? Assume that all common-law doctrines are in force without statutory modification. _____

19. O conveyed Blackacre "to A for life, remainder to A's oldest daughter for life if she has a child while married, remainder to B and his heirs." At a time when A's oldest daughter, D, had not yet married, A conveyed his life estate to B. After that conveyance, what is the state of title? Assume that all common-law doctrines are in force without statutory modification. _____

20. O, in his will, left Blackacre "to A for life, remainder to A's heirs." A then issued a quitclaim deed (giving whatever interest A had, without specifying or warranting what that interest was) to B. Two years later, A died, leaving as his sole heir at law S, a son. What is the state of title to Blackacre? _____

21. In a state with no statutes modifying the relevant common-law rules, O conveyed Blackacre "to A for life, remainder to O's heirs." Shortly thereafter, O quitclaimed any interest he might have in Blackacre to B. O then died, leaving as his sole heir a son, S. A then died. What is the state of title? _____

22. The same facts as the prior question. Now, however, assume that all transactions occurred in the early 21st century, in a state that follows the usual 21st-century approach to conveyances of the ones described in the question. Assume further that in O's initial conveyance to A, he added the sentence, "I mean for this gift to take effect in exactly the manner that I have expressed." What is the probable state of title? _____

23. O owned Blackacre in fee simple. He bargained and sold it "to A and his heirs, but if liquor is ever served on the premises, then to B and his heirs." Immediately after this conveyance, what is the state of title? _____

24. O conveyed Blackacre "to A for life." At the time of the conveyance, Blackacre had always been used as farm land, and O knew that A was a farmer. However, the parties made no agreement concerning the use to which A would put the property. A took possession, and began farming. Shortly thereafter, oil was discovered on an adjacent parcel. A immediately drilled an oil well on the property, and struck a gusher. A sold the resulting oil and put the proceeds of the sale in his bank account. Has A's conduct violated O's rights? _____

For questions 25-30, assume that the common-law Rule Against Perpetuities is in effect.

25. O has just conveyed "to A for life, remainder to A's oldest son who survives A for life, remainder to B and his heirs." A and B were alive at the time of the conveyance, but A does not yet have a son. Is the remainder to B and his heirs valid? _____

26. In 1980, O conveyed "to A for life, remainder in fee simple to the first son of A who has a child while married." At the time of this conveyance, A has no son who has had a child while married, but did have an unmarried childless son, B. In 1985, B had a child while married. In 2005, A died. Is the remainder to B valid? _____

27. In 1980, O, the owner of Greenacre, gave to A Corporation (in return for a payment of $20,000) the following document: "I, O, hereby grant to A Corp. an option to purchase Greenacre at any time during the next 30 years for a price equal to $100,000 plus an additional sum equal to the compounded interest, at 10%, on $100,000 from the date of this option." O died in 1990, leaving all his real and personal property to B. In 2012, A Corp. seeks to exercise its option. The state follows the majority approach to all relevant issues. Does A Corp. have a right to exercise the option? _____

28. In 1970, O bequeathed Blackacre "to A for life, then to A's widow for life, then in equal parts to A's widow's surviving children who attain the age of 21." At the time of this bequest, A was not yet married. In 1975, A married B, a 30-year-old woman. A died in 1988, leaving B as his widow. B died last year, leaving one child, C, aged 22. Does C get Blackacre? _____

29. In 1970, O bequeathed Whiteacre "to A for life, then in equal shares to those of A's children who survive him, but only when each attains the age of 30. I want to be sure that children born to A after my death are included in this bequest." In 1970, A had one child, B, who was 10. In 2012, A died, without ever having had any other children, and with B still alive. Does B take the property? _____

30. Same facts as prior question. In a state following the most common statutory modification to the Rule Against Perpetuities, would the gift to B be valid? _____

Answers

12. **A reversion.** When the holder of a vested estate transfers to another a smaller estate, we call the interest which remains in the grantor a "reversion." Since the estate created by O is smaller than the one he held (i.e., a life estate is smaller than a fee simple absolute), what O was left with was a reversion.

13. **Indefeasibly vested remainder.** A remainder is a future interest which can become possessory only upon the expiration of a prior possessory interest created by the same instrument. Since B's interest was created by the same instrument that created A's life estate, and since B's interest will become possessory when that prior life interest expires, B has a remainder. This remainder is a vested remainder, because it is not subject to any condition precedent, and an identified already-born person (B) holds the remainder. The remainder is "indefeasibly" vested because it is certain to become possessory at some future time (even if B dies before A does, the remainder will pass by will or intestacy to B's heirs, and there is certain to be

somebody who will be there to take possession when A dies).

14. **Vested remainder subject to open.** For an explanation of why C's interest is some sort of vested remainder, see the answer to the prior question. The vested remainder is "subject to open" because if another child (let's call him D) is born to B, C's remainder "opens up" to give D a half interest in it. The remainder will stay open until either A dies (in which case only the then-living children of B will take anything), or B dies, in which case he can have no further children.

15. **Vested remainder subject to divestment.** B has a remainder vested subject to divestment. If A died immediately, B's interest would become possessory. But if B died without issue (either before or after A's death), B's interest would be completely defeated or "divested." (C's interest, which cuts short B's vested interest, is called an executory interest.)

16. **Contingent remainder.** A remainder is contingent rather than vested if it is either subject to a condition precedent, or created in favor of a person who is unborn or unascertained. Here, the remainder to B is subject to a condition precedent (the condition that B survive A in order for his remainder to become possessory). If B does survive A, his remainder will become vested at the same time it becomes possessory.

17. **Vested remainder subject to divestment.** Notice that the grant here is functionally indistinguishable from that in the prior question, yet the remainder here is vested (subject to divestment), whereas the one in the prior question is contingent. This relates solely to the words: here the clause creating the remainder in B does not contain any limit, and the limit is introduced by a separate clause containing the phrase, "but if." As a matter of interpretation, the separate clause beginning with "but if" indicates that the remainder is being "taken away," and this indicates a condition subsequent rather than a condition precedent (thus a remainder subject to divestment rather than a contingent remainder).

18. **Fee simple in O.** After the initial conveyance by O, D had a contingent remainder. But at the time A died, D did not meet the contingency (having had a child while being married). By the common law doctrine of ***destructibility of contingent remainders***, a contingent remainder was deemed "destroyed" unless it vested at or before the termination of the preceding freehold estates. Since D had not met the contingency by the time the prior estate (A's life estate) expired, D's contingent remainder was destroyed. Therefore, O's reversion became possessory, giving him a fee simple absolute. (Today, most states have, by case law or statute, abolished the doctrine of destructibility of contingent remainders.)

19. **Fee simple in B.** By the doctrine of ***"merger,"*** whenever ***successive vested estates are owned by the same person***, the smaller of the two estates is absorbed by the larger. When A conveyed his life estate to B, B then had two successive vested estates (the life estate and the previously-received vested remainder in fee simple). Consequently, the smaller estate (A's life estate) was merged into the fee simple, and disappeared. Then, by the doctrine of destructibility of contingent remainders (see prior question), the destruction-by-merger of A's life estate caused D's contingent remainder dependent upon it to also be destroyed, since that contingent remainder did not vest at or before the termination of the preceding freehold estates.

20. **Fee simple absolute in B.** Under the ***Rule in Shelley's Case***, if a will or conveyance creates a freehold in A, and purports to create a remainder in A's heirs, and the estates are both legal or both equitable, the remainder becomes a fee simple in A. Thus by operation of the Rule, A received both a life estate and a remainder in fee simple. Then, by the doctrine of merger, A's life estate merged into his remainder in fee simple, and A simply held a present fee simple. A's quitclaim deed to B transferred this fee simple to B. A had nothing left at the time of his death, therefore, so S took nothing.

21. **Fee simple absolute in B.** The ***Doctrine of Worthier Title*** provides that if the owner of a fee simple

attempts to create a life estate (or fee tail estate), followed by a remainder to his own heirs, the remainder is void. The grantor thus keeps a reversion. So after the initial conveyance by O, A had a life estate and O had a reversion (with the remainder to O's heirs being void). Therefore, O's quitclaim deed to B was effective to pass O's reversion to B. Once A died, the reversion held by B became a possessory fee simple absolute. Since the initial remainder to O's heirs never took effect, S (O's heir) took nothing.

22. **Fee simple absolute in S.** Today, most states make the Doctrine of Worthier Title a rule of construction, rather than an absolute rule of law as it was at common law. In other words, the Doctrine applies only where the grantor's language and surrounding circumstances indicate that he intended to keep a reversion. Here, O's statement that he wants the gift to take effect exactly as written rebuts the presumption that a reversion rather than remainder was intended. Consequently, the gift will take effect as written, which means that O's quitclaim deed to B was of no effect. Consequently, O's heirs held a contingent remainder before O's death, and that remainder vested in S when O died. When A died, S's remainder became possessory.

23. **Fee simple in A subject to an executory limitation, and a shifting executory interest in fee simple in B.** The bargain and sale raises a use in A in fee simple subject to condition subsequent, and a use in B. The Statute of Uses executes both of these uses. The net result is that if A or his heirs serves liquor on the property, then the gift over to B will take effect.

24. **(a) Yes.** A life tenant may not normally remove earth or minerals from the property. (There are two exceptions: (1) if the property was used for mining prior to the commencement of the life estate, the tenant may continue this use; and (2) the tenant may mine if this is the only way of accomplishing the purpose of the life estate. But neither of these exceptions applies here.)

   (b) Sue for waste. If the holder of the present interest substantially reduces the value of the future interest, and acts unreasonably under the circumstances, the holder of the future interest has a cause of action for waste. Here, by removing valuable oil, A has reduced the value of O's reversion. The court will certainly award damages, and might also award an injunction against future pumping.

25. **Yes.** The remainder to B is a vested remainder, which vested in interest (though not in possession) on the day of the original conveyance by O. Therefore, the remainder to B vested less than 21 years after some life in being at the creation of the interest (e.g., A's life).

26. **No.** We always analyze the Rule Against Perpetuities as of the date of the conveyance, not by reference to how things actually work out. Viewing the matter from the date of the conveyance, it is possible to imagine a situation in which B would die, an additional son — call him C — would be born to A after the conveyance, A would die, and C would marry and have a child more than 21 years after the death of A and B. Under this scenario, however unlikely it is, the remainder would vest in C more than 21 years after all named lives in being at the creation of the interest.

   Because of this possibility, the gift to B (which is a contingent remainder) will fail, ***even if it actually turns out that B marries and has a child***. Observe that the key difference between this question and the prior question is that here, the remainder to B is contingent (we don't know at the time of the conveyance which child, if any, of A will marry and have a child), whereas in the prior question, the gift to B and his heirs was a vested remainder. Since the contingent remainder won't vest until it becomes possessory, and this might (however unlikely) be more than 21 years after lives in being at the time of the conveyance, the gift to B fails (whereas the gift to B in the prior question succeeds because it is a vested remainder, which vests at the moment of creation).

27. No. What A Corp. has purchased here is an option "in gross." (That is, the option is not granted in connection with a present lease of the property.) In most states, an option in gross is subject to the Rule Against Perpetuities — it will be unenforceable if it could be exercised beyond the end of the Perpetuities period, even if the optionee paid real money for it in the belief that it would be exercisable. Since there is no measuring life in being at the time of the option's creation (A Corp. is a corporation, not an individual), the option violated the Rule by being scheduled to last more than 21 years. (But a judge might order B to refund A Corp.'s $20,000 option purchase price.)

28. No. As of 1970, it was possible that A would live a long time more, would marry someone born after 1970 (call this hypothetical person "X"), and would then die after 1991. X would thus be a life not yet in being at the time of O's bequest, and anyone taking after X's death would be taking more than "lives in being plus 21 years" after 1970 (since the only relevant "life in being," i.e., "measuring life," would be A). Thus the bequest to "the widow's surviving children" is invalid. This is true (at least at common law) even though the person who actually takes (here, B) was someone who was in fact born by 1970. This is the **"unborn widow"** rule. (But again, a modern "wait and see statute" would cause the gift to be valid, since the widow, B, turns out to be a valid measuring life, making the gift valid as long as it vests in B's children less than 21 years after her death, as it did here.)

29. No. It was possible, viewed as of 1970, that another child (let's call him hypothetically C) would be born to A after 1970. It was also possible that A and B might also die prior to C's ninth birthday. If both of these events happened, C's interest would then vest too remotely (more than 21 years after the deaths of the measuring lives, i.e., A and B). Because of this theoretical possibility, not only was the gift invalid as to children born after 1970, but it was also invalid as to the rest of the *class* of children, i.e., B. (If O had not included the remark about specifically covering later-born children of A, then the court might have saved the bequest by viewing the class as closing at the time of O's death, or by viewing the class as referring only to those members who could take without violating the Rule Against Perpetuities. But with the bequest as written, the common-law approach would be that since there might be a member of the class who could not take without violating the Rule, no member of the class may take.)

30. Yes. The most common statutory modification today is the **"wait and see"** approach, by which if the interest *actually* vests within lives in being at the time of creation plus 21 years, the fact that things might have worked out differently is irrelevant. Since here, B was a life in being at the time of O's bequest, the gift to him is valid even though it might have turned out that the hypothetical later-born C took later than lives in being plus 21 years.

 *Exam Tips on* **FUTURE INTERESTS**

Spend a lot of time reviewing the material in this chapter, especially the Rule against Perpetuities (RAP); and read the complex fact patterns carefully. On an exam, allocate a lot of time to solve a Future Interests or RAP problem — they take a lot of analysis.

Grantor's Interests

☞ **Grantor's interests, generally:** Always identify what type of interest the grantor retains, if she retains something. Memorize the following pairings (all assume that the grantor starts with a fee simple absolute):

o   If grantee gets a *life estate* or an *estate for years* (and grantor keeps the rest), then grantor retains a *"reversion"*;

o   If grantee's interest is *determinable* (i.e., is to *terminate automatically* on the stated event), then grantor has a *"possibility of reverter"*;

o   If grantee's interest is *subject to condition subsequent* (i.e., interest won't terminate automatically, but needs some action by grantor), then grantor has a *"right of re-entry"*.

Remainders

Remember that a remainder is an interest that is: (1) created in one other than the grantor, and (2) follows an estate (created by the same instrument) that is certain to terminate.

> *Example:* O conveys "to A for life, then to B and his heirs." B has a remainder in fee simple (a type of vested remainder).

☛ **Distinguishing between vested and contingent:** Read the language of the conveyance or bequest carefully to distinguish between the two main types of remainders (*vested* and *contingent*). This will be vital to solve Rule against Perpetuities problems.

    ☞   **Contingent:** A remainder will be contingent if it meets either of two conditions: (1) it won't become *possessory until the fulfillment of a condition; or (2) it's in favor of an unborn or unascertained* person.

> *Example:* M has a son, A. A has one child, B, who has no children. M conveys realty "to A for life, with the remainder to B's children." At the time of the conveyance, B's children, because they are not yet born, have a contingent remainder.

        ☞   **Alternative contingent remainders:** Where a condition precedent involves survivorship, it is likely you will find an alternate party who is to take if the condition is not met. In such a fact pattern, you will have "alternative contingent remainders."

> *Example:* T's will bequeaths her realty "to my nephew, A for twenty years, remainder to my niece B if she is living at that time; but if B is not living at the termination of A's estate, to the oldest child of B at the time of my death." T dies, survived by A, B and B's two children, E, age 14 and F, age 7. B and E have alternative contingent remainders.

    ☞   **Vested:** If there are no conditions precedent to a person's taking, then the remainder is vested. Don't get misled by conditional language in another part of the grant.

> *Example:* O conveys realty "to A for life, but if A should ever use liquor on the premises to B for life; then to C." C's remainder is vested, since he will take either on the death of A or on the death of B, events that are certain to occur. The "liquor" contingency is a "red herring" when it comes to C's interest.

        ☞   **Vested subject to divestment:** If a condition exists which could destroy the interest *after* it has vested (and maybe even after it has become possessory), the interest is "vested *subject to divestment.*" It is easy to confuse a vested remainder subject to divestment with a contingent remainder. A clue to the former is language granting an unconditional grant followed by a "but if" clause.

Example: Testator's will devises realty "to A for life; and upon the death of A: a one-third interest to the children of A, a one-third interest to the children of B, and a one-third interest to the children of C, but if any of C's children should fail to survive to the age of 25 years, then the interest of such child or children of C shall pass to all grandchildren of C equally, share and share alike." Several years after Testator dies, while A is still alive, C gives birth to Z. After Z's birth, Z's interest is a vested remainder subject to divestment — that's so because: (1) it's vested, because if A were to die today, Z would take, but (2) it's subject to being divested if C should die at an age of less than 25 while A was still alive.

☞ **Vested subject to open:** Some remainders are "vested *subject to open.*" Look for a situation where a holder of a vested interest may have to *share the interest* with others in his class who do not yet have vested interests. The most common example of this is a remainder to the children of a living person.

Example: T's will devises realty "to B for life, remainder to be divided equally among B's children, share and share alike." At T's death, B is still alive, and has one child, X. X has a "vested remainder subject to open," since he may have to share his interest with others if B has any more children.

Executory interests

☞ **Executory interests generally:** An interest that follows an estate which may, but will *not necessarily* terminate, is an executory interest. The most commonly tested is the shifting executory interest, a subsequent estate which can possibly cut off a prior estate.

Example: T bargains and sells realty: "to my children, but if my friend F is still alive 30 years after this conveyance, to F." The children's estate may be cut off if F lives another thirty years. Therefore, the children have a fee simple determinable, and F has a shifting executory interest.

☞ **Perpetuities problem:** If your problem has an executory interest, always be on the lookout for a violation of the *Rule against Perpetuities* — such violations are common in exam questions containing executory interests.

Example: O devises realty "to my niece A and her heirs for as long as the property is not used for the sale of alcohol; but if the property is ever used for the sale of alcohol, to the National Cancer Association." The Association's interest is a void executory interest because its interest will not vest until alcohol is sold on the property, an event which might occur outside of the perpetuities period.

Rule against Perpetuities (RAP)

Remember the core statement of the rule: *"No interest is good unless it must vest, if at all, not later than 21 years after some life in being at the creation of the interest."*

Example: O conveys: "to A, her heirs and assigns, so long as the premises are used as a working farm, then to B and his heirs." A and her heirs have a fee simple determinable. Notice that the property might be used for residential purposes for 200 years, longer than any life in being at the time of the conveyance. Then, if the property stopped being used as a farm, the shifting executory interest to B and his heirs would vest. Since that vesting would be more than 21 years after any life in being at the time of the conveyance, the vesting would not be within the Perpetuities period. Therefore, the interest in B is deemed invalid from the beginning (even though it might in fact vest while, say, A or B was still alive — the mere *possibility* of a too-late vesting ruins the interest, at common law).

Concentrate on the following issues concerning the RAP:

☛ **Step 1 — Does the RAP apply:** First, check to see whether the RAP applies. There are several important *exceptions*:

 ☞ **Shifting executory interest:** The RAP normally applies to shifting executory interests (as in the above example), but ***not*** where the shifting interest is in favor of a ***charity***, and follows a valid interest in favor of a ***different charity***. This is a frequently-tested point.

  Example: A devise provides: "To Senior Center, for so long as the realty shall be used as a home for the elderly, but if racial discrimination is practiced in the admission of residents to said home, to Senior Life for as long as the realty shall be used as a home for the elderly." The fact pattern indicates that Senior Center and Senior Life are both charitable institutions. The devise to Senior Life is a valid executory interest and not void under the RAP, because it follows a prior interest that was also held by a charity.

 ☞ **Vested remainder:** The Rule doesn't apply to an interest that is ***vested***. Don't mistake a vested remainder ***subject to a condition subsequent*** (not subject to the Rule) for a ***contingent remainder*** (subject to the Rule). (This is the main reason you have to determine whether a remainder is vested or contingent.)

  Example: T's will devises realty "to A for life; and upon the death of A: a one-third interest to the children of A, a one-third interest to the children of B, and a one-third interest to the children of C, but if any of C's children should fail to survive to the age of 25 years, then the interest of such child or children of C shall pass to all grandchildren of C equally, share and share alike." Several years after T dies, C gives birth to Z. Z's interest is a vested remainder subject to divestment on account of a condition subsequent (survival). Therefore, it is not subject to the Rule.

 ☞ **Grantor's interests:** The Rule does not apply to interests maintained by the grantor. Thus it doesn't apply to ***reversions***, ***possibilities of reverter*** and ***rights of re-entry***. That's true even though these might be held by a descendant of the grantor by the time they take effect, several generations in the future.

 ☞ **Land-use restrictions:** The Rule doesn't apply to ***land-use restrictions,*** such as ***equitable servitudes***.

  Example: Neighboring landowners, *A* and *B*, each agree in writing on behalf of themselves and their assigns that neither property will ever be used for non-residential purposes. Even though this restriction (an "equitable servitude") will by its terms remain in force for hundreds of years, the RAP doesn't apply. Therefore, at common law a successor in interest to *A* gains the benefit of the restriction, and can sue a successor to *B* for an injunction if the latter tries to build an office building.

But the RAP *does* apply to some interests where you might not think it does.

☞ **Options:** For instance, in most states the Rule applies to *options to purchase realty* unless they are *attached to a lease* or other interest in the realty. This is one that profs like to test, because it's tricky.

> *Example 1:* X and Y enter into an option agreement whereby Y pays for the right to purchase realty at a fixed price thirty years from the date of the agreement. One year later, X sells the land to Z. Y protests that the sale to Z violated the option. Y will lose, because Y's option agreement is void under the Rule.

> *Example 2:* Same basic facts. Now, however, assume that Y *leases* the property from X for 99 years, and the option to buy is only to be effective while the lease is in force. Now, the option will *not* be void under the Rule, because it's appurtenant to a lease or other interest in the real estate (so the Rule doesn't apply at all).

☞ **Right of first refusal:** In some (but not all) courts, *a right of first refusal* is subject to the Rule.

> *Example:* O conveys Blackacre to A. The deed says that "Before A or his assigns shall re-sell the property, the seller shall give O or his assigns 30 days in which to buy the property on the same terms and conditions." In some courts, O's right of first refusal is subject to (and violates) the RAP, since it might not become an actual right to buy until after all lives in being plus 21 years had passed. If so, the right would be void even if O himself attempted to exercise it.

☛ **Step 2 — Measuring each interest:** Once you have determined that the Rule applies, measure *each* of the interests to determine their validity.

☞ **Life in being:** Always identify (and note in your answer) the life (or lives) in being. Don't skip this step. And be careful to resist the temptation to classify the interest merely based on the number of years mentioned in the grant.

> *Example:* X conveys realty "to Y, his heirs and assigns; but if Z shall be living thirty years from the date of this deed, then to Z, his heirs and assigns." Z is the relevant life in being, and the 30-year condition is irrelevant. Z's and Z's heirs' interests are valid because the interests will vest or fail within Z's lifetime. (If Z lives another 30 years it will vest; if he dies before 30 years it will fail).

☞ **Bequest v. *inter vivos* gift:** Remember to measure the interests at the time they are effective. Remember that in the case of a *will*, the interests are considered created from the date of the testator's death.

☞ **Gift to grandchildren:** Be on the lookout for gifts to unborn *grandchildren*: the validity of the gift will frequently turn on whether it was created in a will or a conveyance. If it is an *inter vivos* gift, there is always the chance of the conveyor having children after the conveyance has been made. These after-born children cannot be lives in being. Therefore, their own children's interests could possibly vest outside the perpetuities period, even if the gift must vest before that child turns 21. However, if the gift is a *bequest*, then each of the children of the devisor can serve as the "life in being" for their respective children (the testator's grandchildren), and the gift to them will be valid as long as they take effect before the child turns 21.

Example: By will, X devises realty "to such of my grandchildren who shall reach the age of 21; and by this provision I intend to include all grandchildren whenever born." At the time of his death, X has three children and two grandchildren. At X's death all his children are lives in being, since he can't have more children once he's dead. Thus, X can't have grandchildren who can turn 21 more than 21 years after the measuring lives, and the gift to those grandchildren is valid.

☞ *Must* **vest if at all:** Determine whether it is *logically possible* for the interest to vest outside of the perpetuities period. If it is, the interest is *void*. Don't be misled by a fact pattern that indicates that an interest *did in fact vest* within the period — this won't save the bequest, under the common-law approach. (But many states today have "wait and see" statutes which change this result.)

Example: X leaves Blackacre in his will "to my wife for life, remainder to those of my children who achieve the age of twenty-one years. If any child of mine shall predecease me, or if any child of mine shall survive me but shall die before achieving the age of twenty-one years, that child's share shall be distributed equally among any of that child's children who shall marry…" At his death, X has three children, A, B, and C, ages 18, 19, and 22. Two years after X's death, A gives birth to Z, and dies one week later at the age of twenty. Z marries at the age of eighteen. Since Z's marriage *might* have taken place more than 21 years after the deaths of X's three children (the lives in being), her interest *might* have vested outside of the perpetuities period. Therefore, the gift to Z is void at common law; it is irrelevant that Z in fact married within the period of lives in being + 21 years. (But the gift to Z would be valid under a "wait and see" statute, since it in fact vested within a life in being at X's death + 21 years.)

☞ **Class gifts:** Generally, a *class* must *close within the perpetuities period* and all conditions precedent for every member of the class must be satisfied, if at all, within the period.

☞ **Per capita gift:** When there is a gift of a *fixed sum* to each class member, the amount of the gift is not dependent upon the number of children or grandchildren who fulfill the condition of survival. Each gift is tested separately under the Rule, and some may be valid while others are invalid.

Example: G's will provides: "I further direct that my realty be sold, and that the proceeds of such sale be given to a charity…, provided, however, that out of said proceeds two thousand dollars shall first be given to each of my children and grandchildren who survive to the age of twenty-two years." At the time of G's death, his children A, B, and C are 18, 19, and 22 years old, respectively. Two years after G's death A gives birth to Z. A dies a week later at the age of 20. After the property is sold, C demands payment of two thousand dollars from the executor. Because the disposition provided that the members of the class must survive to age 22, the Rule is violated as to some possible bequests (e.g., as to Z), because it is possible that interests of certain members of the class will vest outside of the perpetuities period. However, since the gift was a per capita disposition, C's interest vested immediately upon G's death and is valid.

☞ **Partially void grant:** Separately evaluate *each clause* of a grant. Just because one part is void under the Rule does not mean that all other interests are void. In your answer, say which parts are void and which are valid.

Example 1: C conveys a parcel of land "to D and his heirs until the U.S. goes to war with the Republic of Z. In that event the land is to go to E." E's interest is void under the Rule because his interest might vest hundreds of years after the conveyance. However, D's interest is a valid fee simple determinable because it vested immediately.

☞ **Consequences of void grant:** Be prepared to figure out and explain the *consequences* of a grant that's void because of the RAP — you'll want to explain who took the interest(s) that remained after the failure.

Example: O conveys Blackacre by deed: "to A and his heirs as long as it is used exclusively for residential purposes, but if it is ever used for other than residential purposes, to the American Red Cross." Several years later, O dies, leaving a will by which he devises all his real estate to his brother, B. Several years after O's death A contracts to sell Blackacre to X in fee simple. X refuses to perform because he claims that A cannot give good title.

A will lose if he sues to have the contract specifically performed. Explanation: Because the shifting executory interest to the American Red Cross was void under the Rule, A retained a fee simple determinable and O retained a possibility of reverter, which he devised to B in his will. Therefore, B must join in any conveyance of the property.

CHAPTER 6

MARITAL ESTATES

Introductory Note: In this chapter, we examine the special property problems raised by the fact that two people having an interest in property are married. Any discussion of property rights during marriage must be divided into the common-law system (followed in most states) on the one hand, and the system of community property (followed in eight states) on the other hand. Therefore, our first three sections treat three different aspects of the common-law system: property rights during marriage, property rights upon divorce, and property rights on death of one spouse. Then, we treat the community-property system. Next, we treat various non-traditional approaches to marriage, including domestic partnerships and same-sex marriage. Finally, we discuss briefly homestead laws, which protect the family residence from seizure by creditors.

I. THE COMMON-LAW SYSTEM — RIGHTS DURING MARRIAGE

A. Introduction: All but eight states govern marital property in a way that is derived from traditional common-law principles. The common-law system of marital estates, as it existed in, say, the England of the 1500s, has been so changed by modern statutes that it is almost unrecognizeable. However, because a few vestiges of the traditional system survive, you must have some sense of how the common-law approach to marital property worked.

B. The feudal system: The feudal era granted the husband extreme dominion over his wife's property — the husband received virtually unfettered ownership of his wife's property during their joint lives.

    1. Coverture and jure uxoris: This complete dominance was carried out in part by two doctrines, coverture and *jure uxoris*.

        a. Personal property (coverture): At the moment of marriage, the wife ceased to be a separate person for legal purposes — "husband and wife were regarded as one, and that one was the husband." D&K, p. 367. Under the doctrine of ***"coverture," all personal property owned by the wife at the time of the marriage became the property of the husband.***

        b. Real property (*jure uxoris*): The husband's dominion over his wife's ***real estate*** was almost as complete. The husband did not gain formal legal title to lands owned by his wife at the moment of marriage. But under the doctrine of ***"jure uxoris"***, the husband had the right to ***possess*** all his wife's lands during marriage, including land acquired by the wife after the marriage. D&K, p. 368. Two practical consequences of the *jure uxoris* were that the husband could ***spend*** the rents and profits of the land as he wished, even if the wife protested, and he could ***sell*** his right (e.g., assign to another person the right to rents and profits).

c. **Abolished today:**   The doctrines of coverture and *jure uxoris* do not exist anywhere at present, due to the enactment of Married Women's Property Acts, discussed below.

C. **Tenancy by the entirety:**   A second doctrine which was of great importance during the feudal era was the *"tenancy by the entirety."* Since husband and wife were viewed as one person in the eyes of the law, any ***conveyance*** to two people who were in fact married created a tenancy by the entirety. We will discuss the tenancy by the entirety in much greater detail beginning *infra*, p. 145. For now, understand two main things about the tenancy by the entirety, as it stood under the feudal-era common law: (1) it was the only way that two people who were in fact married could receive a conveyance of property (so that even if a conveyance stated that H and W were to take as "joint tenants" or as "tenants in common," the tenancy by the entirety was created); and (2) neither spouse, acting alone, could ***terminate*** the tenancy by the entirety (unlike the "tenancy in common," which could be "severed" by either party's unilateral action).

D. **Married Women's Property Acts:**   Beginning in 1839, all states enacted Married Women's Property Acts, designed to give the woman legal equality, and to protect her property from her husband's creditors. D&K, p. 368.

1. **Effect on coverture and *jure uxoris*:**   These Married Women's Acts have almost completely abolished the doctrines of coverture and *jure uxoris*. For instance, if a woman holds title to real estate at the moment of her marriage, or receives sole title by gift or bequest after marriage, she ***controls the management*** of that property herself. Similarly, any property held by a married woman in her own name is ***immune from the claims of her husband's creditors***.

2. **Effect on tenancy by the entirety:**   The effect of Married Women's Acts on the tenancy by the entirety is less clear. Many of these Acts have had the effect of abolishing the tenancy by the entirety, which now exists in only about half of the common-law states (see *infra*, p. 145). All states hold that the husband's creditors today cannot get at the wife's interest in the tenancy by the entirety, and most seem to hold that while the marriage and the tenancy by the entirety exist, one spouse's creditors cannot even separately attach or sell that spouse's interest. The topic is discussed more fully *infra*, p. 146.

II. THE COMMON-LAW SYSTEM — EFFECT OF DIVORCE

A. **The traditional "title" view:**   Under traditional common-law principles, if the parties were *divorced*, the division of their property depended heavily on who held formal legal *"title"* to the property.

1. **Title in husband's name:**   Most significantly, if the legal title to property was held by one spouse alone, that spouse ***retained title upon divorce***. Since the husband was usually the sole wage earner, property was far more often in his sole name than in the wife's sole name, so this principle benefitted husbands.

2. **Co-tenancy:**   If the property was held in one of the three forms of co-tenancy, this arrangement generally persisted after the divorce. Thus property held by the spouses as tenants in common (see *infra*, p. 143) continued as such after the divorce, so each could sell or keep his or her undivided one-half interest. If the spouses held the property as joint

tenants (a form that gives full ownership to whichever spouse survives; see *infra*, p. 137), the joint tenancy continued after divorce. If the property was held in a tenancy by the entirety (see *infra*, p. 147), the divorce acted as a "severance," converting ownership into a tenancy in common. D&K, p. 382.

3. **Alimony:** Since the wife was not entitled to any share of property as to which the husband held sole legal title, the common law needed some way to make sure that the wife would not be left destitute. The answer was to require the husband to continue ***supporting*** the wife, by payment of *"alimony."*

B. **The modern doctrine of "equitable distribution":** Today, every state that follows the common-law (rather than community-property) approach to property has ***abolished*** the doctrine that legal title controls the division of property upon divorce. Instead, all of the common-law states have substituted, by statute, a doctrine called *"equitable distribution."* Under the equitable distribution approach, property is divided by the court according to principles of "equity" or "fairness," not according to legal title.

1. **Move towards equality of split:** When the court divides the property according to equitable principles, the modern trend is towards an ***equality*** of division. Some states *require* an equal division, others institute a *presumption* of equality, and others merely use equality as a *starting point* at which individual factors are then considered. D&K, p. 384. In all states, the equitable distribution principles reflect the view that marriage should be looked upon as an ***economic partnership***, and that a wife who has served as a homemaker rather than wage earner should be regarded as having contributed to that partnership just as heavily as the wage earning husband did.

2. **Factors governing split:** In those states that allow the judge to consider individual circumstances of the marriage in deciding how the property should be split, a number of factors are usually considered. Here are some of the common ones:

   a. The ***duration*** of the marriage (so that the longer the marriage, the more likely the court is to award an equal distribution);

   b. The ***age***, ***health***, ***occupation***, ***income sources*** and ***employability*** of each spouse. (Thus a wife who is elderly and without job skills is likely to be awarded a higher percentage of the marital assets than a young wife who has already established a career.)

   c. The contribution of each party to the ***acquisition*** or ***appreciation in value*** of the marital property. (Thus a husband who mismanages the marital property would get a lesser division than a husband who, through great effort and skill, caused the marital assets to appreciate.)

   d. The contribution of a spouse as a ***homemaker*** or to the family unit. (Thus a wife who has stayed home and reared children might get a larger portion than the wife in a childless marriage, all other factors being equal.)

   Most of these factors, as well as several others, are listed in §307 (alternative A) of the Uniform Marriage and Divorce Act, which is representative of the equitable distribution principles applied by most states.

3. **What property is covered:** Most states allow the court to divide only *"marital property"* under equitable distribution principles. Usually, marital property is defined to

include only property *acquired during the marriage from the earnings of the parties*. So property acquired by a spouse *before marriage*, or acquired by one spouse through a *gift or bequest* to that spouse, is not included in the pile of assets that may be distributed. The most frequently-litigated question is whether the value of a *professional degree* earned by one spouse during the marriage may be counted as marital property, and thus subject to equitable distribution.

   a. Majority view: Most courts have concluded that a professional degree should *not* be treated as marital property, and thus should not be subject to equitable distribution. See, e.g., *In re Marriage of Graham*, 574 P.2d 75 (Col. 1978), holding that H's MBA was not marital property, because it did not have an exchange value, could not be assigned or sold, could not be acquired by the mere expenditure of money, would terminate on the death of the holder, and thus had none of the attributes usually associated with the concept of "property."

       i. Reimbursement theory: Although most courts, as noted, refuse to find a professional degree to be marital property, some states, most notably New Jersey, allow the other spouse to obtain *reimbursement* for that spouse's contribution to the acquisition of the degree. Under this reimbursement theory, if H's medical or other professional degree had a "cost" of, say, $200,000 (measured by both the cost of tuition and the earnings that the couple forewent by having H study rather than earn), the non-degreed spouse could receive a reimbursement of half this amount (on the assumption that H and W each contributed half the cost or "sacrifice" for the acquisition of the degree). See D&K, pp. 391-92.

   b. Minority (New York view): One of the very few states that recognizes a professional degree as marital property is New York. See *O'Brien v. O'Brien*, 489 N.E.2d 712 (N.Y. 1985), holding that H's medical license was marital property for equitable distribution purposes, and refusing to allow mere reimbursement of expenses as a remedy. The result in New York seems to be due mostly to that state's unusual language in its equitable distribution statute, by which the court is directed to consider each party's "direct or indirect contribution . . . *to the career or career potential* of the other party. . . ." N.Y. Dom. Rel. L. §236.

       i. Celebrity status: In fact, the New York courts have treated as marital property not just professional degrees but also one spouse's *celebrity status* or other enhanced earning power. Most strikingly, in *Elkus v. Elkus*, 572 N.Y.S.2d 901 (1st Dept. 1991), an intermediate trial court held that the career and celebrity status of W (opera star Frederica von Stade) were a marital asset, which she could be required to share with H, who had served as W's vocal coach and travelling companion during their marriage while W rose from unknown to star.

   c. Professional good will: Even in the majority of courts that do not treat a professional degree as a marital asset, *"professional good will" is* a marital asset that may be equitably distributed. By "professional good will," the courts mean the enhanced earning capacity that comes from a professional's *reputation* and *client or customer list*. For instance, whereas a newly-graduated neurosurgeon in most states has no career-related prospects that are to be treated as marital property, a neurosurgeon who has built up a practice and reputation and who has been earning large sums from that practice will usually be found to hold an asset — the practice — that can be valued and subject to distribution. See, e.g., *Dugan v. Dugan*, 457 A.2d 1 (N.J. 1983).

III. THE COMMON-LAW SYSTEM — DEATH OF A SPOUSE

A. The traditional common-law approach (dower and curtesy): At common law during the feudal era, a wife who survived her husband did not normally inherit his property, nor did a husband who survived his wife. Instead, the surviving spouse was provided for by the doctrines of "dower" and "curtesy."

1. Dower: At common law, a widow was not the heir of her deceased husband; that is, if he died without a will, she took nothing. Instead, under the doctrine of primogeniture, all property went to the oldest son. Therefore, to provide for the widow (as well as to provide for her younger sons and all of her daughters, who similarly got nothing), the estate of *dower* was established.

    a. What constitutes dower: The estate of dower entitled a widow, on her husband's death, to a *life estate* in *one-third* of the lands of which he was seised at any time during their marriage, provided that the husband's interest was *inheritable by the issue* of the marriage (if any). So any land owned in *fee simple* by the husband alone, or in fee simple by the husband and a third person as tenants in common, qualified for dower.

        i. No dower in life estate: The requirement that the husband's interest had to be one which would be inheritable by the issue of the marriage meant that there could be no dower in a *life estate* held by the husband, even one *per autre vie*.

    b. Dower inchoate: While the husband was still alive, the wife got a right of *dower inchoate* as soon as the husband became seised of any eligible freehold.

        i. Effect on conveyances: One of the key features of common-law dower was that a conveyance of the freehold by the husband to a third party did *not affect the right of dower inchoate*. So the husband could not, by conveying property during his life, defeat the right of dower. If he purported to make such a conveyance, and then died, his widow could subsequently make her claim for dower against the holder of the property. (However, the wife could, during the marriage, consent to release her inchoate dower interest in property so that the husband could transfer it free and clear.)

        ii. Effect on creditors: Similarly, *creditors* of the husband's estate were subordinate to the dower rights — if the husband owned land, but died deeply in debt, dower rights were the widow's only chance of receiving anything.

2. Curtesy: At common law, a *widower* was entitled to a *life estate* in *each piece of real property* in which the wife held a freehold interest during their marriage, provided the freehold was inheritable by the issue of the husband and the wife. This was known as the right of *"curtesy."*

    a. Issue born alive: Curtesy was similar to dower in most respects. The biggest difference was that the right of curtesy attached only where *issue of the marriage* were *born alive*. So if H and W were childless, and W predeceased H, H would have no right of curtesy.

   b. Applies to all land, not one-third: Also, whereas dower entitled the widow to a life interest in only one-third of her husband's inheritable freeholds, curtesy gave a life estate in *all* the wife's inheritable freeholds.

3. Abolished in most jurisdictions: Dower and curtesy have both been completely *abolished* in all but *five* American jurisdictions (Arkansas, Kentucky, Ohio, Michigan and Iowa). DKA&S, p. 336. Of these five states, three have abolished curtesy and extended dower to husbands. *Id.*

4. Practical importance: In those states where dower or curtesy still exist, the main practical consequence is that *both husband and wife* must *sign any deed* if the recipient is to take free and clear of the right, even though only one spouse holds title. *Id.*

   a. Elective share available: The five states in which dower and/or curtesy still exist also give the surviving spouse the right to an "elective share" (see *infra*). The elective share is usually more generous than dower or curtesy. Therefore, the survivor almost always takes the elective share rather instead.

B. Modern "elective share" statutes: The modern substitute for dower and curtesy is the *"elective share."* Under an elective share statute, the surviving spouse has the right to *renounce (or "take against") the will*, and instead receive a portion (set by statute) of the estate. All states following the common-law approach to property have a forced elective share statute, except for Georgia. DKA&S, p. 337.

1. Effect: Since in community-property states the surviving spouse is deemed to own half the marital property (see *infra*, p. 125), and since all common-law property states except Georgia now have forced elective shares, it is now virtually everywhere the case that *one spouse cannot "disinherit" the other*.

2. Personal as well as real property: Forced elective share statutes virtually always apply to *personal property* as well as *real property*. (Contrast this with dower and curtesy, which apply only to real property.)

3. Size of share: The elective share is usually expressed as a *fraction* of the property owned by the decedent at his or her death, not as a dollar amount. Most commonly, the fraction is *one-half* or *one-third*. DKA&S, p. 337. Usually, the elective share is somewhat less generous than the intestate share, giving the decedent some ability to disfavor the surviving spouse.

4. Property to which share applies: The elective share generally applies only to property owned by the decedent *at death*. This is quite different from dower and curtesy, which attach to property owned at any time during the marriage.

   a. Non-probate assets not included: Only *probate assets* are typically included in the elective share. Thus assets passing outside of probate are generally *not* covered, including:

   [1] *life insurance proceeds*; and

   [2] property held by the decedent and a third person as *joint tenants*.

b. Right to set aside certain transfers: However, many states "call back" into the elective share certain assets that were transferred by the decedent before his death. For instance, many states count in the elective share gifts made by the decedent to third persons during the last few years of life (or gifts made with the apparent intent to defeat the elective share).

   i. Assets controlled but not owned: Similarly, many states count assets that the decedent didn't "own" at death, but that he or she *controlled*. For instance, assets in a revocable trust set up by the decedent are frequently treated as part of the elective share. D&K, 402.

5. Length of marriage irrelevant: Most elective share statutes treat the *length of the marriage* as *irrelevant* — a woman widowed after one day of marriage gets the same fraction of her husband's estate as one married for 50 years.

   a. Contrast with community property: Contrast this with a community-property system (see *infra*, below), in which there is no elective share but property acquired by either party during the marriage, and wages earned by either party, are deemed owned 50/50 — under such a system, the longer the marriage, usually the larger the amount of marital property.

   b. Uniform Probate Code's sliding scale: Some non-community-property jurisdictions have come to believe that the community-property approach is better in this respect, and that the elective share should get larger the longer the marriage lasts. Thus the Uniform Probate Code was amended in 1990 to incorporate a *"sliding scale"* for the elective share — the longer the marriage, the larger the fractional share. The scale ranges from 3% for marriages of less than a year to 50% for marriages of 15 years or more. See UPC §2-201.

IV. COMMUNITY PROPERTY

A. Introduction: In eight states, the system of marital property rights has long been completely different from the common-law system derived from dower and curtesy. The system of *community property* has traditionally been in force in Arizona, California, Idaho, Louisiana, Nevada, New Mexico, Texas, and Washington. The system derives from European *civil-law* jurisprudence, not from the Anglo-American common law.

1. Wisconsin and Alaska: *Wisconsin* and *Alaska* have also, to varying degrees, now joined this list of community-property states. Wisconsin has enacted a statute — the Uniform Marital Property Act; see *infra*, p. 128 — that applies community-property principles (even though the statute uses the phrase "marital property" instead of "community property"). And in Alaska, spouses may (but need not) agree to hold their property as community property, making Alaska an *"elective"* community-property state. DKA&S, p. 338.

B. Basic theory: The basic premise of the community-property system is that property acquired during a marriage results from the joint efforts of husband and wife. Implicitly, the system recognizes that a wife, even one who stays at home and does only housework and childbearing, contributes as much to the economic well-being of the marriage as does the husband who is the actual wage earner.

1. **Consequence:** Consequently, the property acquired during the marriage (with certain exceptions discussed briefly below) belongs *jointly* to husband and wife from the moment it is acquired. This joint ownership has its most significant consequences when property is disposed of, or when the marriage terminates by divorce or death.

2. **Not a detailed treatment:** Community property is an extremely complex subject, which is often treated as a separate course in schools located in community-property states. Furthermore, since community-property systems are almost completely statutory, they vary substantially among the eight community-property states. Therefore, our discussion below treats only a few major issues, and then only in an extremely general fashion.

C. **What is community property:** The biggest single issue in most community-property disputes is whether the property at issue constitutes *community* property, or *separate* property. There is a *presumption* that all property acquired during the course of the marriage is *community* property, but this may be rebutted by a showing that the property is part of a class treated as separate property.

1. **Acquired before marriage:** All property acquired by either spouse *before marriage* is separate, not community, property.

2. **Acquired by gift or inheritance:** Property acquired by *gift, inheritance* or *bequest*, even after marriage, is separate property.

3. **Income from separate property:** *Income from separate property* is, in most states, separate property itself. Thus if H owns a bond before marrying W, not only is the bond separate, but any interest received on the bond after marriage is also, in most states, separate property.

4. **Income and proceeds from community property:** *Income* that is earned from *community* property is itself community property. Furthermore, if community property is sold, and new assets are purchased with the sale proceeds, the assets are community property.

   a. **Title irrelevant:** Keep in mind that the *title* recited on a deed, stock certificate or other form of property is *irrelevant*. If H sells a bond that is community property, and uses the cash proceeds to buy a car, the car is community property even if the bill of sale and certificate of title are in his name alone.

5. **Earnings:** A key feature of the system is that income produced by either spouse's *labor* is *community property*. Thus if H is an employee, his salary is community property. Furthermore, if he receives stock in his employer, pension rights or insurance, these would be treated as fruits of his labor, and therefore community property.

6. **Purchases made on credit:** When property is bought on *credit*, it will frequently not be clear whether the property is community or separate property. If the note or obligation is signed by only one spouse, and is secured by separate property belonging to that spouse, the asset is separate property. But in most other situations (e.g., note signed by the husband, but no security given), courts are likely to find that the asset is a community one. See 2 A.L.P. 151-55.

   a. **Down payment made before marriage:** A similar problem arises when a down payment is made out of separate property (e.g., H supplies the down payment to buy a house, and then marries W), and community funds are then used to finish paying for the purchase. There are at least three ways of handling this; perhaps the most reasonable is to treat the property as part separate and part community, in proportion to the separate and community funds used to pay for it. See B,C&S, p. 326.

7. **Conflict of laws:** Complications arise when the parties live in one state and acquire property located in another. Similarly, the effect of a *change of domicile* from one state to another is sometimes complicated.

   a. **Domicile in community-property state at time of acquisition:** If the parties live in a community-property state at the time they acquire property, the property's status depends on whether it is realty or personalty.

      i. **Realty:** If *real estate* is acquired, the law of the state *where the land is situated* determines whether the land is community or separate property. Thus if H and W are residents of California (a community-property state), and they use money saved from the husband's salary to buy land in New York (not a community-property state), the law of New York applies. The property is therefore separate property, belonging to either H or W or both, depending on how the deed is drafted. B,C&S, p. 327.

      ii. **Personalty:** But any *personal property* the couple acquire is measured by the law of the *state of domicile*. Thus if H and W live in California, and buy a car in New York while on vacation, California law applies. If the car is purchased with savings from the husband's salary, it is community property.

      iii. **Move to non-community state:** If the parties *then* move to a non-community-property state, the property keeps whatever status it had as of the time of its acquisition. Thus community assets acquired in California remain such if the parties move to New York. C&L, p. 240-44.

   b. **Property acquired before move to community state:** But if the parties live first in a non-community-property state, *buy assets,* and then *move* to a community-property state, the law is less clear.

      i. **Real estate:** Certainly *real estate* is evaluated by the laws of the state *where the land is located*, just as if the parties had lived in a community-property state when they bought the land.

      ii. **Personal property:** Where *personal property* is concerned, most states apply the law of the *domicile* at the time of acquisition. Thus a car bought while the parties reside in New York would remain the separate property of whomever held formal title to it, even if the parties moved to, say, Texas.

         (1) **California "quasi-community property" rule:** But California has made such personal property "*quasi*-community property." The property is separate property in the sense that the non-owner spouse has no testamentary rights in it, and has no right of control, management or disposition. But when a divorce occurs, or the owner dies, the property is *treated as if it were community property*; thus the divorce court may assign one-half (or in certain cases even more) to the non-owner, and the non-owner gets a one-half interest as survivor. Burby, p. 242.

8. **Transformation of status:** Property which starts out as being separate property can be *transformed* into community property by act of the owning spouse. Thus if H owns a house when he marries W, he may be found to have made either a written or oral agreement to treat the house as belonging jointly to H and W.

D. **Management:** The right to *manage and control* community property has been subject to great change in recent years.

1. **Traditional view:** Traditionally, the right to manage and control the property was given exclusively to the husband; his role was that of a fiduciary, who was required to act with due regard to his wife's interests as well as his own.

    a. **Personal property:** This meant that the husband could convey personal property to a third person, even without adequate consideration, and the third person would take free and clear of the wife's interest. (However, the husband, as fiduciary, would be liable to the wife if he misused his authority by giving the property away or receiving too little money for it.)

    b. **Real property:** But a *conveyance or mortgage of real property*, or a lease for more than a year, have generally not been allowable unless the *wife joins*.

2. **Greater role for women:** Most of the community-property states have changed their statutes in the last ten years, to give the spouses roughly *equal management and control rights*. For instance, the California Code is now sexually neutral with respect to control; either spouse may manage and control any item of community property, but most conveyances of personal as well as real property require the written consent of both spouses. See Cal. Civil Code §§5125, 5127.

E. **Divorce:** In most states, and in most circumstances, when *divorce* occurs the community property is *evenly divided*. However, some states allow the court to divide the community property as it sees fit, if the divorce is granted on grounds of adultery or extreme cruelty; the court may thus award more than half to the innocent spouse. Burby, p. 261. If the divorce is given to *both* parties, an even division of community property is always required.

F. **Death:** Upon the *death* of one of the parties, the community property is treated as having belonged half to the deceased spouse and half to the surviving spouse. The half belonging to the deceased spouse is thus subject to his right to devise it by will to whomever he wishes. If no testamentary disposition is made, the property passes in some states to the surviving spouse (who now owns the entire interest), and in other states to the issue or heirs. Burby, p. 263.

V. DOMESTIC PARTNERSHIPS, SAME-SEX MARRIAGES, AND OTHER VARIATIONS ON TRADITIONAL MARRIAGE

A. **Generally:** So far in this chapter, we have assumed that it is clear who is "married" and thus covered by the special rules governing marital property we've just discussed. But modern American life is not so simple: there are various forms of "quasi-marriage" or non-traditional marriage that at least some states are now recognizing. We consider several types of variations on traditional marriage: (1) old-fashioned *"common-law* marriage"; (2) *"domestic partner-*

ships" (sometimes called *"civil unions"*); and (3) *same-sex* arrangements, including same-sex marriage.

B. Common-law marriage: Many states recognized *"common-law marriage"* in the 19th century, in part because it was often difficult for couples to make a long trip to the county courthouse to get a marriage license. DKA&S, p. 344. Today, there are still 11 states that recognize such marriages (Alabama, Colorado, Iowa, Kansas, Montana, Oklahoma, Pennsylvania, Rhode Island, South Carolina, Texas and Utah, plus the District of Columbia). *Id.*

   1. Definition: The concept of common-law marriage was (and is) that if two people *cohabit*, and *hold themselves out to the public as being husband and wife*, they should be *treated as married. Id.*

   2. Consequence: In states still recognizing common-law marriage, a couple that is deemed to be common-law married is *treated exactly the same as a couple married pursuant to a marriage license. Id.* For example, if one member of the couple dies without a will, the other will take by intestate succession.

C. Cohabitation and domestic partnerships: Beginning in the 1960's, many couples began to *live together,* without holding themselves out to the community as being married. DKA&S, p. 345. Even in the 11 states recognizing common-law marriage, the common-law doctrine would not apply to such cohabitation, since it requires a holding out. On the other hand, after many years or even decades of living together, it can be economically harsh for one member of the couple (usually the woman) to be deprived of any of the wealth that the couple has accumulated during their time together, but as to which title is held in the other member's name. Consequently, courts and legislatures have evolved several methods of dealing with the economic issues posed by cohabitation.

   1. Contract law as a solution: A few courts have used the tools of *contract law* to give some share of the assets to the non-titled member of the couple.

      a. California approach: Most dramatically, California, in *Marvin v. Marvin*, 557 P.2d 106 (Cal. 1976), held that where a couple cohabits, a contract to divide their wealth equitably can be *implied from the conduct of the parties* — in other words, no express contract is necessary. The idea, according to *Marvin*, was that the court could *"presume ... that the parties intended to deal fairly* with each other." If such fair dealing meant that the spouse who had acquired legal ownership of the assets during the cohabitation would share some of the wealth with the other spouse, then the court would enforce that "implied contract" to share.

      b. Rejected elsewhere: But the implied-contract theory of *Marvin* has been *rejected* nearly everywhere outside of California. For instance, in New York, "only a written or oral *express* contract to share earnings and assets between unmarried partners is enforceable." DKA&S, p. 345, citing *Morone v. Morone*, 407 N.E.2d (N.Y. 1980).

D. Same-sex marriage, civil unions and domestic partnerships: *Same-sex couples* have long sought the right to marry, in part to obtain the benefits that accrue to married couples under both federal and state law. As of this writing (April 2012), federal recognition of same-sex marriage still seems far away. But there is a groundswell of *state recognition* of the right of same-sex couples to marry, or at least to enter civil unions and domestic partnerships that yield state-law legal consequences that are the same or nearly the same as marriage.

1. **State-law incidents of marriage:** There are of course many property-related *state-law consequences* to being married. A partial list includes:

  ❏ the *surviving spouse's rights* if the other spouse *dies intestate*;

  ❏ the surviving spouse's right to *take against the decedent's will*, i.e. to receive an *elective share* (see *supra*, p. 124);

  ❏ the surviving spouse's right to *receive pension and retirement benefits* under both private and public plans; and

  ❏ the right to *get a divorce*, and thereby receive an interest in marital assets (e.g., *equitable distribution*).[1]

  Cf. DKA&S, p. 357.

2. **State law on same-sex marriages:** Here is a brief (and inevitably soon-to-be-very-out-of-date) summary, as of April, 2012, of state law on the right of same-sex couples to marry or otherwise receive marriage-like treatment.

  a. **Right to marry:** *Six states* currently allow same-sex couples to *marry*: *Connecticut, Iowa, Massachusetts, New Hampshire, New York and Vermont,* plus *Washington D.C.* Two additional states, Washington and Maryland, have passed laws to begin granting marriage licenses in 2012.[2] See http://en.wikipedia.org/wiki/Same-sex_marriage_in_the_united_states, "Same-sex marriage in the United States," last accessed April 13, 2012.

  b. **Decisions based on state constitutions:** Of the six states mentioned above that now allow same-sex marriages, three — Connecticut, Massachusetts and Iowa — reached that result directly or indirectly as a result of *judicial decisions* finding that the state's prior ban on same-sex marriages *violated the state constitution.*

    i. **Iowa decision:** For example, in a widely-followed decision, *Varnum v. Brien*, 763 N.W.2d 862 (Iowa 2009), the Iowa Supreme Court held that the state's ban on same-sex marriage violated the state constitution's *equal protection clause.*

      (1) **Heightened scrutiny:** First, the court decided that the ban on same-sex marriages should be subjected to at least an *intermediate level of scrutiny*, under which a legislative classification will be struck down unless it is *"substantially related"* to the achievement of an *"important"* government objective. In deciding that the sexual-orientation classification at the heart of the law should

---

1. There are of course major *federal-law* consequences of marriage, as well — the ability to file a joint tax return, to receive the federal estate tax marital deduction, and to receive Social Security survivor benefits are just a few major examples. However, since federal recognition of any variant of same-sex marriage or civil union has not occurred, we concentrate here on state law.

2. In these two states, the same-sex-marriage statute is subject to a voter referendum in November, 2012 that may delay or cancel the right.

be subjected to intermediate-level review (rather than to the easy-to-satisfy rational-relation review), the court relied on four factors:

[1] The disadvantaged class (gay and lesbian people) have suffered a *history of purposeful discrimination;*

[2] The characteristic at issue — sexual orientation — *was not related* to the class members' *ability to contribute to society*, and was instead based on *"irrelevant stereotypes and prejudice"*;

[3] The characteristic in question was, if not completely "immutable or unresponsive to attempt to change," at least *"highly resistant to change"* and *"forms a significant part of a person's identity"*; and

[4] The affected class had historically been *politically powerless*, or at least not sufficiently politically powerful to bring a prompt end to the discrimination against them.

(2) Not "substantially related" to state's objectives: The court then concluded that while the state was arguably pursuing some important governmental objectives in banning same-sex marriages, the ban was *not "substantially related"* to the achievement of any of these objectives. For example, whereas the government argued that the ban advanced the goal of promoting *"child-rearing by a father and a mother* in a marital relationship which social scientists say ... is the optimal milieu for child rearing," the court decided that the ban was *both under-inclusive and over-inclusive* as a means of achieving this objective. The state's ban on same-sex marriages, while allowing virtually any opposite-sex adults to wed, was *underinclusive* because "it does *not exclude from marriage* other groups of parents — such as child abusers, sexual predators, parents neglecting to provide child support, and violent felons — that are *undeniably less than optimal parents*." Conversely, the ban was *overinclusive*, in that it did not prohibit same-sex couples from *raising children*, something that many unmarried same-sex couples in Iowa do. The court then concluded that "[a] law *so simultaneously over-inclusive and under-inclusive is not substantially related* to the government's objective."

c. **Statutes:** Other states have legalized same-sex marriage by purely *legislative* means. For instance, in early 2009 Vermont became the first state to pass a statute legalizing same-sex marriage without being effectively required to do so by litigation.

3. **Civil unions and domestic partnerships:** Other states have not gone so far as to legalize same-sex marriage, but have passed statutes giving gay couples the right to elect to enter into a *"civil union"* or a *"domestic partnership,"* by which electing couples get some or all of the same state-law rights and responsibilities that they would have if they were married. Civil unions and domestic partnerships vary widely from state to state in their effects.

a. **Near-equivalent to marriage:** At one end of the spectrum, some civil unions and domestic partnerships are *virtually identical to marriage* under state law.

i. **New Jersey:** For instance, in 2006 New Jersey by statute gave same-sex couples the right to enter into a civil union that gives "all of the same benefits, protections and responsibilities" as state law gives to married couples.

ii. California: Similarly, in California gay couples (and opposite-sex couples in which one person is above the age of 62) can enter into a domestic partnership, under a statute that the California Supreme Court has described as giving them "virtually all of the benefits and responsibilities afforded by California law to married opposite-sex couples." *In Re Marriage Cases*, 183 P.3d 384 (Cal. 2008). That's true despite the present uncertainty about whether California voters' decision to outlaw true same-sex marriage will ultimately pass federal constitutional muster (see *Perry v. San Francisco, infra*, p. 132). The domestic-partnership statute means, for instance, that *California community-property law applies* to domestic partners both during the partnership and after its dissolution.

b. Smaller subset of rights: At the other extreme, some states give electing same-sex couples a much smaller subset of the rights given to married couples. For instance, Colorado C.R.S. 15-22-105, enacted in 2009, lets two people (same-sex or otherwise) enter into a "designated beneficiary agreement," whereby one member can become a beneficiary of the other's public pension rights, health- and life-insurance policies, etc.

4. Bans on same-sex marriage: On the other hand, more than 40 states have either statutes or constitutional provisions explicitly *restricting marriage to two persons of opposite sex.* This roster includes some states that allow civil unions or domestic partnerships that confer some or most of the rights and responsibilities of marriage.

a. State constitutional-law rulings: Although as noted three state supreme courts have held that state bans on same-sex marriage violate the state constitution, a number of state supreme courts have reached the *opposite* result, *upholding their bans* against state-constitutional attack. For instance, the highest court of New York held, in *Hernandez v. Robles*, 855 N.E.2d 1 (N.Y. 2006) that New York's statute limiting marriage to opposite-sex couples did *not* violate the due process or equal protection clauses of the state constitution. (But this result was nullified by the New York Legislature's passage in 2011 of a statute legalizing same-sex marriage.)

b. California Proposition 8: Even when a state recognizes same-sex marriage, that recognition may not be final. In several states, voter referendums have *reversed* a state's judicial grant of same-sex marriage rights. Most famously, in early 2008 the California constitution was interpreted by the California Supreme Court as guaranteeing the right of same-sex couples to marry, but a voter referendum later that year, "*Proposition 8*," amended the state constitution to take away that right.

i. Proposition struck down: But the federal Ninth Circuit has ruled that Proposition 8 *violates* the federal *Equal Protection rights* of same-sex couples. *Perry v. San Francisco*, Nos. 10–16696, 11–16577 (9th Cir. Feb. 7, 2012). The court reasoned that just prior to Proposition 8, same-sex couples could marry in California (because of the California Supreme Court's 2008 opinion so holding), but that Proposition 8 singled out same-sex couples and improperly took from them a right of marriage that they previously shared with every other California citizen.

(1) *Romer v. Evans*: The Ninth Circuit in *Perry* relied on a U.S. Supreme Court case, *Romer v. Evans*, 517 U.S. 620 (1996). *Romer* had struck down a Colorado state constitutional amendment that barred any state or local law from giving protection against discrimination based on sexual orientation. Under the Fourteenth Amendment's Equal Protection clause, such a governmental action, since it treated one group of citizens (gays) less-favorably than all others, had to pursue a "legitimate" objective. The motivation for the amendment in *Romer*, the Supreme Court said there, consisted solely of "animosity towards the class of persons affected," which was not a legitimate objective.

(2) **Same reasoning applies here:** The Ninth Circuit concluded that the *Romer* reasoning applied to Proposition 8: when the voters changed California law by removing, only from same-sex couples, a right of marriage that they had previously enjoyed with all other couples, the change was not made in pursuit of a "legitimate" interest, but was merely an expression of *moral disapproval* of gays and lesbians, an illegitimate interest. Therefore, the stripping of the marriage right violated the federal Equal Protection clause even under the easiest-to-satisfy test ever used in Equal Protection cases, the test requiring merely that the government action be reasonably related to the achievement of a legitimate governmental objective.

(3) **Status:** *Perry v. San Francisco* seems to be headed inevitably to the U.S. Supreme Court.

5. **Divorce or dissolution:** Now that same-sex marriages and marriage-like civil unions have begun to spread, courts are starting to face the problems of whether and how to *dissolve* such marriages or unions. Where the marriage was contracted in a state recognizing same-sex marriages, and the parties continue to reside in that state, the solution is easy — the usual rules of divorce apply. Similarly, if a state allows civil unions, and the parties still live in that state at the time the relationship breaks up, the civil union statute typically provides for divorce-like termination-of-status proceedings.[3]

a. **Migration:** But suppose the same-sex couple marry in State *A*, and then *move* to State *B* (a state that *doesn't allow* gay marriage), where the relationship breaks up. It's uncertain how the courts of State *B* should handle the breakup. The problem is most acute in a state that does not itself allow same-sex couples to marry in-state, but that recognizes same-sex marriages if they were *valid in the state where contracted*. In such a state, presumably the state will allow a couple residing in the state to divorce under that state's laws, even though they could not have been married in the state.

VI. HOMESTEAD EXEMPTIONS

A. **Purpose of homestead exemptions:** Most states have enacted so-called "*homestead exemptions*." The purpose of these homestead laws is to ensure that *general creditors of a homeowner cannot have the property sold to satisfy a money judgement*; thus the ability of the homeowner and his family to keep the residence is maintained, if they haven't signed a mortgage.

---

3. Thus in California, for instance, parties to a civil union, who have rights and responsibilities virtually identical to marriage, are bound by the state's community-property rules, including the rules applicable to property division after the marriage is dissolved.

1. **Usually limited dollar amount:** The homestead statutes almost never provide that the homestead is immune from creditors regardless of its size or cost. Instead, most states establish a dollar limit (e.g., $50,000 in New York; see N.Y. C.P.L.R. §5206(a)); if the home is worth more than that, it may be sold at the behest of creditors, but the homeowner gets to keep the statutory dollar amount. Other states place a limit on the acreage of the real estate.

2. **Subject to purchase-money mortgages:** In all states, the exemption does ***not apply*** to a ***purchase-money mortgage***, i.e., a mortgage given as security for a loan used to buy the property in the first place. Powell, Par. 263, p. 193.

3. **Right of surviving spouse:** Where title to homestead property is held by one spouse, if that spouse dies first the ***surviving spouse*** usually continues to have some degree of protection against creditors of the other's estate. Also, some states limit the extent to which the spouse who has title may ***devise*** the property. See generally B,C&S, p. 277 and C&J, pp. 336.

B. Bankruptcy Law: The Federal Bankruptcy Act grants a homestead exemption of its own, in ***bankruptcy cases***. The bankrupt's property used as a residence is exempt up to a value (as of 2012) of $21,625. (If an exemption in a residence is not claimed up to this amount, the amount not claimed, up to about $11,000, may be applied to any other assets, such as bank accounts, stocks and bonds, etc.) See 11 U.S.C. §522(d)(1), (5).

1. **State alternative:** Alternatively, the bankrupt may take advantage of the ***state exemption*** given by the state of his domicile, if he feels this is more advantageous. §522(b)(2).

2. **State may forbid federal exemption:** But the Act gives each state the right to enact a statute ***preventing*** its citizens from claiming the federal exemption. In that case, the bankrupt is forced to use the state exemption. §522(b)(2).

Note: In addition to the real property homestead exemption discussed above, nearly all states, and the federal Bankruptcy Act, also provide certain exemptions for various items of personal property (e.g., prescription drugs, farm implements, the family Bible, etc.).

Quiz Yourself on
MARITAL ESTATES

31. In 1980, O conveyed Blueacre, a 900-acre farm, to H. In 1985, H married W. In 1990, H, in return for reasonable consideration, delivered to A a deed in fee simple for Blueacre. In 2012, H died. What is the state of title in Blueacre? (Assume that the common law is in force in all relevant particulars.)

_____

32. H and W live in a community-property state. If H and W are divorced, which of the following items will be community property? (Assume that H and W's divorce is no-fault.) _____

(a) Blackacre, which W bought before the marriage, and which has remained in her name before the divorce.

(b) Whiteacre, which W inherited from her father after the marriage, and which has remained in her name until the divorce.

(c) $20,000 in a bank account entitled "H and W jointly," representing net rental proceeds paid by a tenant of Whiteacre; all of these payments were made after W inherited the property as described in (b) above.

(d) $100,000 in a bank account in H's name alone; this represents money earned by H from his salary during the years following the marriage, while working for ABC Corp., a large company.

(e) Stock in ABC Corp. held in H's name, which he received as part of ABC Corp.'s stock ownership plan.

(f) A summer home purchased by H, in his own name, from which the down payment and all subsequent mortgage payments have been made out of H's earnings.

Answers

31. **Fee simple in A for 600 acres; life estate in W for 300 acres, with remainder in A.** The common-law estate of *dower* entitles a widow, on her husband's death, to a life estate in one-third of the lands of which he was seised at any time during their marriage, provided that the husband's interest was inheritable by the issue of the marriage (if any). Since H was seised of Blueacre at some point during the marriage (from 1985 through 1990), W held the estate of dower inchoate. On H's death, this became the estate of dower consummate. The husband cannot, by conveying his property during his life, defeat the right of dower. If he purports to make such a conveyance, his widow may subsequently make her claim for dower against the present holder of the property. So W is entitled to have 300 acres set aside for her for life by A; after her death, A can once again take possession of them. (Observe that A's lawyer should have had W join in the deed from H before allowing A pay money for the property.)

32. **(d), (e) and (f) are all community property.** They are all either H's earnings during the marriage, or things purchased from those earnings. (a), (b), and (c) are separate property, because property received by a spouse before marriage, and property received by gift, inheritance or bequest after marriage, are separate, and income from separate property is separate property.

CHAPTER 7

CONCURRENT OWNERSHIP

Introductory note: This chapter examines various ways in which two or more persons may own present possessory interests in the same property. The three varieties of co-tenancy are: (1) *joint tenancy* (which includes the right of survivorship; (2) *tenancy in common* (which does not have the right of survivorship); and (3) *tenancy by the entirety*, which exists only between husband and wife, and which includes not only survivorship but indestructibility, in the sense that neither party can convey his interest or otherwise destroy the right of survivorship. After we discuss these three types of co-ownership, we treat various issues involving the relation between parties (e.g., the right to possession of the premises, the duty to account for rents received from third persons, etc.).

I. JOINT TENANCY

A. Each tenant owns whole interest: In a *joint tenancy*, two or more people own a *single, unified*, interest in real or personal property. Each joint tenant has exactly the same rights in the property; thus one cannot have a greater interest than the other.

    1. Right of survivorship: The most significant feature of the joint tenancy is that each joint tenant has a *right of survivorship*. That is, if there are two joint tenants, and one dies, the other becomes sole survivor of the interest that the two of them had previously held jointly. Survivorship is discussed more fully *infra*, p. 139.

    2. Right of possession: In a sense, each of the joint tenants owns the "entire" interest, subject only to the rights of the other(s). While this may sound somewhat metaphysical, it has one clear consequence: each joint tenant is entitled to *occupy* the *entire* premises, subject only to the same right of occupancy by the other tenants. Thus the parties are not required to divide up the premises for occupancy, though they are free to do this if all agree. Relations between joint tenants (and between other types of co-tenants, including tenants in common and tenants by the entirety) are discussed *infra*, p. 147.

B. Four unities: Under the traditional common-law view, a joint tenancy exists only where the so-called "*four unities*" exist: (1) the unity of "interest," (2) the unity of "title," (3) the unity of "time" and (4) the unity of "possession." See Moynihan, p. 217.

    1. Unity of interest: Unity of *interest* means that the joint tenants must have *identical interests*, both as to their share, and as to the *duration* of their interest. Thus one joint tenant *cannot* have a *one-fourth* interest and the other a *three-fourths* interest. Similarly, if one person has a one-half interest for life, and the other has a one-half interest in fee simple, the two are not joint tenants because the durations are not identical. See 2 A.L.P. 6.

    2. Unity of title: Unity of *title* means that the joint tenants must each acquire title by the *same deed or will*.

3. **Unity of time:**   The unity of *time* means that each joint tenant's interest must *vest at the same time*.

> **Example:** *O* owns Blackacre in fee simple. In 2005, she conveys "one-half of my interest in Blackacre" to "my son *S*, to hold jointly with me." In 2006, she conveys "my remaining interest in Blackacre" to "my daughter *D*." *S* and *D* own as tenants in common, *not* as joint tenants with right of survivorship, because *S*'s and *D*'s interests were not created by a single instrument at the same time, making a joint tenancy impossible. (That's true even if *S* and *O* were found to have held as joint tenants prior to *O*'s conveyance to *D*.)

4. **Unity of possession:**   Unity of *possession* means that all the joint tenants have a right to possess and enjoy the entire property. (This unity, unlike the other three, also exists as to tenants in common.)

C. **Creation of joint tenancies:**   At common law, there was a *presumption* that any co-tenancy was a joint tenancy, unless a clear intention to create a tenancy in common was shown. (The presumption did not apply where the co-tenants were husband and wife; here there was a presumption that a tenancy by the entirety was intended; see *infra*, p. 145.)

1. **Modern statutes reverse presumption:**   Today, all states have *reversed* the common-law presumption, and now *presume* that a co-tenancy is a *tenancy in common* unless there is a clear intent to establish a joint tenancy. Most states have done this by statute; some have done it by case law.

2. **Standard language:**   The usual (and clearest) phrasing used to create a joint tenancy is "*to A and B as joint tenants with right of survivorship, and not as tenants in common*."

3. **Conveyance by *A* to *A* and *B*:**   Frequently the holder of a fee simple interest will wish to establish a joint tenancy between *himself and another*. The most direct way to do this, of course, would be to convey to himself and that other person as joint tenants; thus *A* would convey his fee simple "to *A* and *B* as joint tenants."

   a. **Common-law view prohibits:**   But this could not be done at common law. Recall that two of the "four unities" were those of *time* and *title*. (*Supra*, p. 137.) Because of the common-law rule that no person could convey to himself, a conveyance that purported to be from *A* to "*A* and *B* as joint tenants" really conveyed only a one-half interest to *B*. Both the unity of time and the unity of title were therefore broken, and *A* and *B* took as tenants in common.

      i. **Conveyance to "straw man":**   Therefore, if *A* wished to create a joint tenancy in himself and *B*, he had to convey to a "*straw man*." He would thus convey to *C* and *C* would in turn convey to *A* and *B* as joint tenants.

   b. **Modern view allows direct creation:**   But many states have enacted *statutes* explicitly authorizing the holder of a fee simple to create a joint tenancy in himself and another. Other states have reached this result by *case law*.

4. **Personal property:**   Joint tenancies may also be created in *personal property*. But the statutes establishing a presumption in favor of tenancies in common apply to personal property as well as real property.

a. **Bank accounts:**   One common example of a possible joint tenancy in personal property is the *joint bank account*, either checking, savings, or safe deposit.

   i. **Ambiguous "joint account":**   Banks, to protect themselves, usually insist that if the account has two names on it (i.e., it's in some sense a "joint account"), the depositor(s) must sign paperwork that says that upon the death of one holder, the *survivor gets the balance.* Yet this paperwork may not reflect the *intent of the depositor*; for instance, the depositor may merely intend to create a *"convenience account,"* so that the other named holder (e.g., the elderly depositor's child) can pay the depositor's bills. When the depositor dies, if the bank pays over the proceeds to the surviving joint account-holder, the decedent's heirs may claim that the estate, not the surviving joint holder, is entitled to the account balance, so as to further the decedent's intent in creating the account.

   (1) Majority rule: In most states, the account paperwork described above (saying that the survivor gets the proceeds) is viewed as *not controlling*, so that the *intent of the depositor* is what determines whether there is a right of survivorship or not. On the other hand, most states put the *burden of proof* on the person *challenging* the right of survivorship: "The surviving joint tenant takes the sum remaining on deposit ... unless there is *clear and convincing evidence* that a convenience account was intended." DKA&S, p. 290.

   (2) During holders' joint lifetimes: What about withdrawals from a "joint account" made while *both account holders are alive*? Again, the bank will likely insist on paperwork saying that either account holder may withdraw all contents at any time. But as with the survivorship issue discussed above, regardless of what the bank's paperwork says, in most states "the *presumption* is that the joint account belongs to the parties *in proportion to the net contribution of each party.*" DKA&S, p. 290. So if *A* deposits the entire sum into an account on which *A* and *B* are both listed, and *B* then withdraws sums without *A*'s permission (or later ratification), *B* can be required to repay the funds. *Id.* However, this presumption that the depositor does not intend to make a gift to the other holder can (as in the payment-on-death scenario described above) be *rebutted* by clear and convincing evidence to the contrary. *Id.* (For more about bank accounts, see *supra*, p. 18.)

D. **Right of survivorship:**   As noted, the principal distinguishing feature of the joint tenancy is that the *surviving* tenant has the *entire interest* in the property. The deceased tenant does not have the ability to *leave his interest by will*, nor is there anything to pass by intestacy to his heirs. Strictly speaking, what happens is that there are two joint tenants each of whom owns a complete interest, and when one of them dies, the other has an interest that is no longer subject to the former's rights. But, loosely speaking, the survivor is said to receive the other's interest under a *"right of survivorship."*

   1. **Heirs and devisees take nothing:**   When a joint tenant dies, her *heirs* (if she dies intestate) or her *devisees* (if she leaves a will that purports to leave her joint tenancy interest) *take nothing* — the interest is *extinguished* at the moment of the decedent / joint tenant's death, so there is nothing to pass by will or intestacy.

a.   **Signing a will is not a severance:**   Also, the mere *execution of a will* by a joint tenant purporting to leave the joint tenancy interest to a third person does *not* act as a severance — since the will provision has not yet taken effect (and never will take effect, since the interest will be extinguished at the moment the testator dies), courts do not treat the signing of the will as a conveyance.

2.   **Creditors:**   An unsecured or judgment-lien *creditor* of *one* joint tenant *does not have rights* against the interest of the *other joint tenant.* Therefore, if the debtor joint tenant dies first, the surviving joint tenant usually takes the property *free and clear* of the deceased tenant's creditor — the decedent's interest (and thus the creditor's "interest in that interest") simply *ceases to exist* at the moment of the debtor/joint-tenant's death. Moynihan, p. 220.

> **Example:** *A* and *B* own Blackacre as joint tenants. Finance Co., which has lent money to *A* unsecured, gets a judgment against *A*, which under local law becomes a lien against all of *A*'s real property. *A* dies. In most states, Finance Co. has no rights against Blackacre — at *A*'s death, his joint tenancy interest was simply extinguished, resulting in an unencumbered fee simple in *B*.

a.   **Statutes:** However, some states have statutes preserving an attachment, mortgage, or other lien on a joint tenant's interest after his death. Moynihan, p. 220, n. 2.

b.   **Mortgage creditors:** As to *mortgage* creditors of a joint tenant, courts are split; see *infra*, p. 142.

E.   **Severance:**   There are a number of ways in which a joint tenancy may be *severed*; severance will normally result in the creation of a *tenancy in common*.

1.   **Conveyance by one joint tenant:**   A *conveyance* by one joint tenant to a *third party* will cause a severance, and thereby create a tenancy in common. That's because the third party does not have unity of time or title (*supra*, p. 138) with the remaining original joint tenant, so that the joint tenancy relationship has been destroyed.

> **Example:** *A* and *B* hold Blackacre as joint tenants. *A* conveys his interest to *C*. This conveyance automatically severs the joint tenancy. Therefore, *B* and *C* are *tenants in common*, not joint tenants.

a.   **Motive irrelevant:**   This principle that any conveyance by either joint tenant immediately severs the joint tenancy and replaces it with a tenancy in common applies even where a joint tenant is acting for the *sole purpose* of severing the tenancy, and even where the recipient of the conveyance *immediately reconveys back* to the severing joint tenant. In other words, the *motive* of the conveying joint tenant is irrelevant.

> **Example:** *A* and *B* are joint tenants in Blackacre. *A* learns he is about to die. Therefore, and for the sole purpose of severing the joint tenancy, he conveys "all my interest" in Blackacre to his wife *W*. Title is now: *B* and *W* as tenants in common. *W* then immediately reconveys "all my interest" back to *A*. At that moment, *A* and *B* are tenants in common. Now, when *A* dies (leaving all his estate to *W*), title is: *B* and *W* as tenants in common. *A* has thereby avoided having *B* become the sole owner on *A*'s death.

b. **Where three or more joint tenants:** Suppose that there are *three* or more original joint tenants. A conveyance by one of them to a *stranger* will produce a *tenancy in common* as between the *stranger and the remaining original joint tenants*, but the *joint tenancy will continue* as between the *original members*.

Example: *A*, *B*, and *C* hold Blackacre as joint tenants. *A* conveys his interest to X. The conveyance by *A* severs the joint tenancy as between *A* and the other two. Thus X holds an undivided one-third interest in the property as a tenant in common with *B* and *C*. *B* and *C* hold a two-thirds interest, but they hold this interest as joint tenants with each other, not as tenants in common. Thus if X dies, his interest goes to his heirs or devisees. But if *B* dies, his interest goes to *C*.

   i. **Conveyance between joint tenants:** Essentially the same analysis applies if there are three joint tenants, and one conveys to *another of the joint tenants*. As to the interest conveyed, the grantee becomes a tenant in common. But as to the interest not conveyed, the joint tenancy survives.

c. **Conveyance to one's self:** Suppose a joint tenant tries to terminate the joint tenant's fee by conveying his interest to *himself*. Since the joint tenant could terminate the joint tenancy by conveying to third person, and that third person could then re-convey to the original joint tenant (thus leaving the original joint tenant with a tenancy in common), why shouldn't the joint tenant be able to accomplish the same objective without all the hocus-pocus of a "straw man"? At least one court (in the case set forth in the following example) has held that a conveyance by a joint tenant to himself, made for the purpose of terminating the joint tenancy, does indeed have that effect.

Example: T learns that certain property is held by herself and P (her husband) as joint tenants. She wants to be able to bequeath the property to someone other than P. She therefore executes a deed in which she grants to herself an undivided one-half interest in the property; the deed states that its purpose is to terminate the joint tenancy. Simultaneously, she executes a will leaving her one-half interest in the property to someone else. She then dies.

Held, the deed by T to herself was effective to terminate the joint tenancy. A transfer by T to X, followed by a re-transfer by X to T, would have sufficed to terminate the joint tenancy. Therefore, there is no reason that T could not accomplish the same result without use of a straw-man intermediary. Since T always had the power to sever the tenancy, allowing her to do this by grant to herself does not enlarge her powers. Therefore, T's undivided one-half interest in the property passes by her will, not by right of survivorship to P. *Riddle v. Harmon*, 162 Cal. Rptr. 530 (Cal. Ct. App. 1980).

Note: Observe that P, in *Riddle*, would not necessarily ever have learned about the termination until T died and her will was read — P could have gone for years thinking that he held a joint tenancy when he did not. Allowing T to terminate the joint tenancy without giving notice to P can therefore be criticized as unfairly violating P's reliance interest. Also, allowing the joint tenant to break the tenancy by transferring to herself can be criticized as an invitation to *fraud* — for instance, the deed executed by T to herself in *Riddle* was never recorded and did not have to meet any sort of formalities, so it could have been forged after T's death by a beneficiary under her will. See DKA&S, p. 284.

2. **Granting of mortgage:**   Jurisdictions are not in agreement as to whether the ***granting of a mortgage*** by one joint tenant severs the joint tenancy. The answer in a particular state depends principally upon whether the state treats a mortgage as representing a transfer of title, or as merely being a lien to secure repayment.

   a. **Title theory states:**   In some states, the mortgagor, by granting the mortgage, is deemed to transfer title to the property to the mortgagee. In such a state, called a ***"title theory"*** state, the mortgage is, not surprisingly, a severance since it is a conveyance. Moynihan, p. 222. If the mortgage is defaulted upon, the mortgagee ***can foreclose on the undivided one-half interest of the mortgagor***, and have this auctioned at the foreclosure sale. The interest of the other party is not affected.

   b. **Lien theory state:**   Most states, however, follow the ***"lien theory"*** of mortgages, by which a mortgage is deemed to be merely a security for repayment, and not a transfer of title. In such states, the mortgage ***does not act as a severance***, at least in the sense that the right of survivorship is not destroyed. However, in lien theory states, the key issue becomes: Is the mortgage enforceable if the mortgagor ***dies*** before the other tenant? Courts in lien theory states are ***split*** on this issue.

      i. **Mortgage remains effective:**   Some states, either by case-law or statute, hold that the mortgage can be ***enforced*** against the decedent's interest. Under this approach, the case is treated basically as if the state were a title theory state — the foreclosing mortgagee auctions off the decedent's one-half interest, with the survivor given the right to pay off the mortgage if he chooses. C,S&W, pp. 201-02.

      ii. **Mortgage not effective:**   But other states take the view that the mortgage is ***not enforceable*** if the mortgagor dies before the other tenant.

         Example: P and his brother, *B*, own property as joint tenants. Without P's knowledge, *B* and his friend D1 sign a note in favor of D2, and *B* gives a mortgage on the joint property to D2 to secure this note. *B* dies before the note is paid. *B* bequeaths all his property to D1. P brings suit to have the court declare that P takes the entire property by right of survivorship, and that D2's mortgage was extinguished on *B*'s death.

         Held, for P. Illinois is a lien theory state, so P's execution of a mortgage did not sever the joint tenancy. Upon *B*'s death, P therefore became the sole owner of the property. Furthermore, the mortgage was merely a lien on *B*'s interest in the joint tenancy; since *B*'s interest ceased to exist the moment he died, so did the lien on his interest. Therefore, P holds sole title to the property, and D2's lien is extinguished. *Harms v. Sprague*, 473 N.E.2d 930 (Ill. 1984).

3. **Lease:**   If one joint tenant executes a ***lease***, the courts are similarly split about whether the joint tenancy is severed. Most courts probably hold that such a lease (which applies only to the lessor's interest in the property) is ***not*** a severance. See, e.g., *Swartzbaugh v. Sampson*, 54 P.2d 73 (D.C. App. Cal. 1936), holding that where the lessee was in sole possession of the premises, the non-lessor joint tenant could not have the lease judicially rescinded.

4. Partition: The joint tenancy can be severed by *partition*, i.e., the dividing up and distribution of the land (partition "in kind") or the sale of the land and distribution of the proceeds. This can be done either by agreement of the parties, or by court order at the request of one party. See *infra*, p. 150.

   a. Contract to sever: Similarly, the parties may make an *agreement* to sever the joint tenancy, even without partitioning the property.

   Note: Observe that the doctrine of severance, insofar as it results in a termination of the right of survivorship, applies only to joint tenancies, and not to joint *life estates* with a contingent *remainder* in fee to the survivor. In the latter case, the right of survivorship is more or less indestructible.

F. Abolition in a few states: In at least two states, Georgia and Oregon, joint tenancies have been completely *abolished*. In a number of other states, joint tenancies continue to exist, but the *right of survivorship* has been either abolished or required to be expressly provided for in the creating instrument. Arizona, Illinois, Kentucky, North Carolina, Tennessee, Texas, and Washington are among the states that have done this. See 2 A.L.P. 14, n. 12, and A.L.P., 1976 Supp., p. 163, n. 12. Insofar as such a statute has the effect, in a particular case, of eliminating the right of survivorship, the joint tenancy is for practical purposes transformed into a tenancy in common, even though it may still be called a joint tenancy.

II. TENANCY IN COMMON

A. Nature of tenancy in common: The tenancy in common, like the joint tenancy, is an estate shared by two or more people in the same property at the same time. But whereas in a joint tenancy each party has an equal interest in the whole, each tenant in common has a *separate* "undivided" interest. The most important practical difference between the tenancy in common and the joint tenancy is that there is *no right of survivorship* between tenants in common.

   1. Only one unity required: Recall that a joint tenancy must have four "unities"; see *supra*, p. 137. The tenancy in common, by contrast, requires only *one unity*, the unity of *possession*. That is, each tenant in common is entitled to possession of the *whole property*, subject to the same rights in the other tenants. But since the unities of time, title, and interest are not required, the tenants may receive their interests at *different times* and by *different conveyances*.

   a. May have unequal shares: Even more importantly, the tenants in common may have *unequal shares*. Thus *A* and *B* may hold as tenants in common, with *A* holding an "undivided one-quarter interest" and *B* an "undivided three-quarters interest". Similarly, *A* may hold an undivided one-half life estate, and *B* an undivided one-half fee simple; the two could still be tenants in common with respect to each other. See Moynihan, p. 224.

   i. Presumption as to size of interest: If the conveyance does not state the size of the interest of each tenant in common, there is a *presumption* that the shares are *equal*. But this presumption may be *rebutted* by evidence, drawn from surrounding circumstances, that unequal shares were intended. For instance, suppose that *A* and *B* (not husband and wife) take title to Blackacre as tenants in common, and that *A* puts up one-third of the money and *B* two-thirds; if *B* can show that there was no intent by him to make a gift to *A*, he will be held to have a two-thirds interest. See 2 A.L.P. 20.

B. No right of survivorship: Each tenant in common takes his share as an individual; this is in contrast to the joint tenancy, where the joint tenants take as a single "unit." As a consequence, each tenant in common has the right to make a ***testamentary transfer*** of his interest, and if he dies intestate, his interest will ***pass under the statutes of descent***. In other words, there is ***no right of survivorship***.

Example: *A* and *B* take title to Blackacre as tenants in common. They have equal shares. *A* dies, without a will, leaving only one relative, a son S. Title to Blackacre is now: a one-half undivided interest in S, and a one-half undivided interest in *B*.

  1. **Right to convey or lease:**   Similarly, the tenant in common may convey his undivided interest, or lease it to a third party. If he leases it, he may have the duty to share the rents with his co-tenants; see *infra*, p. 148.

C. Presumption favoring tenancy in common: As noted, most states now have either a statutory or case law ***presumption*** in favor of tenancies in common rather than joint tenancies, as long as the co-tenants are not husband and wife. See *supra*, p. 138.

D. Heirs: A tenancy in common can, of course, be created by action of the parties (e.g., O conveys "to *A* and *B* as tenants in common.") But such a tenancy can also result from ***operation of law***; one common way is through ***intestacy***. Where the intestacy statute specifies that two persons are to take an equal interest as co-heirs, they take as tenants in common.

Example: *A*, the fee simple owner of Blackacre, dies without a will. His sole surviving relatives are a son, S, and a daughter, D. Under the local intestacy statute, where a person is survived by two or more children and not by a spouse, the children share equally. S and D will therefore take title to Blackacre as tenants in common, each holding an undivided one-half interest.

E. Conveyance by one co-tenant: One tenant in common may ***convey*** his interest to a third person without the consent of the other tenant in common. After the conveyance, the grantee simply ***steps into the conveying co-tenant's shoes***, and holds as tenant in common with the non-conveying co-tenant.

  Example: *A* and *B* hold Blackacre as tenants in common with equal shares. *A* conveys his interest to *C*. *C* and *B* are now tenants in common with equal shares.

  1. **Can't bind absent co-tenant:** But a tenant in common may ***not*** make a conveyance that in any way ***binds another tenant in common*** who does not participate in that conveyance.

    Example: *A* and *B* hold Blackacre as tenants in common with equal shares. *A* purports to convey the entire fee simple to Blackacre to *C*. This conveyance has no effect on *B*'s tenancy in common. And that's true even if *B* knew of the conveyance and did not object. Therefore, the conveyance is effective to pass *A*'s interest to *C*, but not to pass *B*'s interest to *C*. Consequently, *B* and *C* now hold as tenants in common.

  2. **Grant of mortgage or judgment lien:**   Similarly, if one tenant in common purports to grant a ***mortgage*** on the property, or allows a ***judgment*** to be entered against him that is a

lien on his property, the mortgage or lien will be *effective only against that tenant's own undivided interest*, not the interests of the other co-tenant. Then, if the property is eventually sold or partitioned (see *infra*, p. 150), the mortgage or lien will be effective only against the first co-tenant's proceeds.

> **Example:** *A* and *B* own Blackacre, a house and lot, as tenants in common. *A* grants to Bank a mortgage on "Blackacre." Since *B* has not joined in granting the mortgage, Bank's mortgage is good only against *A*'s undivided one-half interest in Blackacre. Therefore, if Blackacre is sold, Bank's mortgage entitles it to be satisfied only out of *A*'s one-half interest in the proceeds. The same is true if Blackacre is sold in a partition action.

3. **Creation of easement or settlement of boundary dispute:** The same rule is true of attempts by one tenant in common to grant an *easement*, *settle a boundary dispute* with a neighbor, or do anything else that would affect title — the action does not affect the legal rights of any other tenant(s) in common who does not sign the grant or agreement. And that is true even where one tenant in common has *sole occupancy* of the premises, and the attempt to change title by grant of an easement, settlement of a boundary dispute, etc., is done by that occupying tenant in common.

III. TENANCY BY THE ENTIRETY

A. **Common-law concept of entirety:** At common law, the husband and wife were regarded as *one person*. (See *supra*, p. 120.) As a consequence, there was a special form of co-ownership between husband and wife, the *tenancy by the entirety*.

1. **Four unities required:** The same four unities required in the case of joint tenancy (*supra*, p. 137) must be met for a common-law tenancy by the entirety.

2. **Right of survivorship:** Similarly, the surviving spouse has a *right of survivorship*.

3. **No severance:** The critical difference between the tenancy by the entirety and the joint tenancy is that as to the former, there is *no doctrine of severance*, i.e., *no way to terminate the tenancy* while husband and wife are both still alive and still married. The indestructibility of the tenancy by the entirety is discussed further *infra*, p. 146.

B. **Creation of estate:** At common law, *any conveyance* to two persons who were in fact husband and wife *necessarily* resulted in a tenancy by the entirety. 2 A.L.P. 24.

1. **Modern view:** The modern view universally treats husband and wife as two individuals. Consequently, *only twenty-two states* retain the tenancy by the entirety at all. (The eight community-property states never had it in the first place, and twenty states have abolished it). See Moynihan, p. 231.

2. **Presumption favoring entirety:** In those states where the tenancy by the entirety survives, there is usually a *presumption* that a conveyance to persons who are actually husband and wife is intended to create a tenancy by the entirety. 2 A.L.P. 25. However, in most of these states the presumption is a *rebuttable* one, so that if there is outside evidence that a tenancy in common or a joint tenancy was intended, or if the deed itself contains the words "joint tenants" or "tenants in common," the grantor's intention will be respected.

a. Exception in few states: But in a few states, the presumption in favor of the tenancy by the entirety remains so strong that even the use of the words "joint tenancy" or "tenancy in common" in the deed will *not* be sufficient to rebut it.

3. Personal property: At common law, there could not be a tenancy by the entirety in *personal property*. But most states that now allow such tenancies at all allow them in personal as well as real property.

C. Indestructibility:

As noted, the key feature of the tenancy by the entirety is that it is *not subject to severance*. So long as both parties are alive, and remain husband and wife, neither one can break the tenancy.

1. Right of survivorship: This means that if H and W take property as tenants by the entirety, they know that the survivor of them is assured of a complete interest in the property.

2. No partition: Thus neither party may obtain a *judicial partition* of the property.

a. Termination by agreement: However, if *both spouses* are so inclined, they may agree to terminate the tenancy by the entirety, replacing it by a tenancy in common or joint tenancy.

3. Conveyance: In some (but not all) states one spouse may *convey* his interest in the tenancy. But this conveyance cannot affect the other spouse's right to the entire estate if the latter survives. Thus even if a state permits, say, H to convey his interest to X, if H predeceases W, W will own the property outright and X will get nothing. (But conversely, if W dies before H, X will own the property outright). See Moynihan, p. 234. Thus a buyer in a state where tenancies by the entirety exist must be sure to have his deed signed by both H and W; otherwise, he may not even end up with a one-half interest.

4. Rights of creditors: Courts are in dispute about whether a *creditor* of one of the spouses may attach or levy on that spouse's interest in the tenancy by the entirety.

a. Majority view does not allow claim: Most states do *not allow* a creditor to attach or force a sale of the debtor's interest in the entirety while the other spouse is still alive. See, e.g., *Sawada v. Endo*, 561 P.2d 1291 (Hawaii 1977), holding that this result follows from the indivisibility of tenancies by the entirety.

5. Divorce: If the parties are *divorced*, the tenancy by the entirety *ends*. In some states, the property is then deemed to be held in joint tenancy. But in most states, the property is held as tenants in common, so that if one tenant dies before there has been a sale of the property, there is no right of survivorship in the ex-spouse.

a. Equal shares: Where the property is deemed to be held in joint tenancy following a divorce, the shares are by hypothesis equal, since that is the nature of a joint tenancy. (*Supra*, p. 137.) Where the property is held in a tenancy in common, most courts *presume* that the shares are also equal.

D. Management of the property:

Recall that at common law, the husband had the exclusive right to use and manage the property in which his wife had an interest. (*Supra*, p. 119.) This was, not surprisingly, as true of property held as tenants by the entirety as it was of property to which title was solely in the wife. The husband could *convey a fee simple* without the wife's consent, and his creditors could attach and sell the entire estate if the wife died first. 2 A.L.P. 28.

1. **Married Women's Acts:** The enactment of Married Women's Acts has changed this result in virtually all states. Most states hold that *neither spouse* may *convey* his or her interest in the property. Nor may a creditor of just one spouse attach or levy against the debtor's interest in the property. 2 A.L.P. 29.

IV. RELATIONS BETWEEN CO-TENANTS

A. **Few distinctions among tenancies:** The rights and duties of each co-tenant during the co-tenancy are more or less the same regardless of whether a joint tenancy, tenancy in common or tenancy by the entirety is involved. Therefore, the following discussion is applicable to all types unless otherwise noted.

1. **Some differences:** Some differences among types have been discussed above; for instance, under the common-law view the husband has sole right of management and use in a tenancy by the entirety, whereas each party to a joint tenancy or tenancy in common has an equal right of management and use. However, the following discussion assumes that where tenancy by the entirety is involved, the modern view (equal rights of management for both spouses) is in force.

B. **Possession by one tenant:** Each co-tenant has the *right to occupy the entire premises*, subject only to a similar right in the other co-tenants. Moynihan, p. 225.

1. **Agreement regarding possession:** The parties are always free to change this equal right by *agreement*. For instance, co-tenants might agree that each will exclusively occupy one-half of the premises.

2. **Normally no duty to account:** Suppose property held in co-tenancy is solely occupied by *one tenant*. With certain exceptions, that occupying tenant has *no duty to account* for the value of his exclusive possession. That is, he has no duty to calculate the reasonable rental value of his sole possession, and pay one-half of it to the other tenant. Nor is he normally liable for any profits he makes from his use of the land.

   a. **Rationale:** This rule follows from the notion that each tenant is entitled to occupy the entire premises subject to the same right in the other. If the sole occupant were required to account for the reasonable value of his occupancy, then the non-occupying co-owner would be able, merely by refusing to exercise *his* right to possession, to "convert the status of the occupying tenant from that of co-owner to rent-paying tenant." Moynihan, p. 226.

3. **Ouster:** But if the occupying tenant *refuses to permit* the other tenant equal occupancy, then he must account to his co-tenant for the latter's share of the fair rental value of the premises. In this situation, there is said to be an *ouster* of the tenant who has been refused occupancy.

   a. **What constitutes ouster:** What constitutes "ouster" for these purposes? Most courts holds that ouster occurs *only* when the out-of-possession tenant *physically attempts* to occupy the premises, and the occupying tenant refuses to allow this access. Most courts hold that ouster does *not* occur where the out-of-possession tenant merely demands that the occupying tenant either *pay rent or vacate*. So in the common situation where one co-tenant has a use for the property and the other does not, the former *can effectively occupy the premises without paying rent*, a situation that many commentators think is unfair.

Example: Spiller, Mackereth and others own a building as tenants in common. The lessee of the building vacates. Spiller then enters and begins using the building as a warehouse. Mackereth writes to Spiller demanding that Spiller either vacate half the building or pay rent. Spiller does neither. Mackereth brings suit for half the fair rental value of the premises.

Held, Spiller owes nothing. To start with, "in [the] absence of an agreement to pay rent or an ouster of a co-tenant, a co-tenant in possession is not liable to his co-tenants for his use and occupation of the property." Ouster will be deemed to occur only when the occupying co-tenant refuses a demand by the other co-tenants that the latter be allowed in to use and enjoy the land. Mackereth's demand letter, and Spiller's refusal to agree to pay rent or move out, was not enough to oust Mackereth, because Mackereth was not demanding equal use/enjoyment of the premises, merely rent. Nor did Spiller's placement of locks on the building act as an ouster of Mackereth, since the evidence was that Spiller was trying to protect goods he was storing in the building, not trying to keep Mackereth or the other co-tenants out. *Spiller v. Mackereth*, 334 So.2d 859 (Ala. 1976).

4. Depletion: A second situation in which the occupying tenant will have a duty to account is if he *depletes the land*, or otherwise lessens its value. For instance, if he takes away and sells its mineral resources, such as oil, gas or coal, he will be liable to his co-tenants for their share of the profits he has made. Moynihan, p. 227.

C. Premises rented to third party: Although a co-tenant is normally entitled to occupy the premises himself without accounting for their reasonable rental value, the same is not true if he *leases the premises* to a third person. Once he does this, and collects rents, he is required to *share* these rents with his co-tenants.

1. Statute of Anne: This duty to account for rents received derives from an English statute, the Statute of 4 and 5 Anne. A majority of states have enacted similar statutes, and nearly all the remainder hold as a matter of case law that there is a duty to account for such rents. Moynihan, p. 226. But these statutes and decisions generally apply only to rent received from third persons, *not to the rental value of occupancy* by a co-tenant himself.

D. Payments made by one tenant: Sometimes, one co-tenant will make certain payments, and then wish to recover from the other co-tenants their share of the expenditures. Or, he may wish to deduct such expenditures before paying his co-tenants their share of rents he has collected from a third person. Finally, he may wish to have the expenditures credited to him before the proceeds are distributed in a partition proceeding (*infra*, p. 150).

1. Taxes and mortgage payments: One tenant may make *property tax* or *mortgage* payments on the property. Generally, such payments are viewed as being *made for the benefit of all the co-tenants*, since their interest in the property is protected. Therefore, the tenant making the payment will be allowed to *deduct* the payment from the rents he has collected from third persons, and he will be reimbursed for the payments "off the top" before any proceeds from a partition sale are distributed. If the other co-tenants are personally liable for the indebtedness (e.g., if they have assumed the mortgage), in some states the tenant who has made the payment may bring a *direct suit* against them for contribution. 2 A.L.P. 73-75.

    a. Mortgage completely paid off: If a mortgage is completely paid off by one co-tenant, he becomes "subrogated" to the mortgagee's interest, and thus holds an "equitable lien" against the property. He can therefore usually have the property sold and recover his overpayment from the proceeds.

2. Repairs: The cost of *repairs* is handled in a similar way. If one tenant pays these costs, and the others have not agreed to help him, most courts do not allow him to make a direct recovery against his co-tenants for their share. But he may deduct their portion of the repairs before turning over any rents received from third persons, and he may receive credit for his expenditures before any partition proceeds are distributed.

    a. Right of contribution where possession shared: Where *possession is shared* between the tenant who makes the payment for repairs and another tenant, a number of courts will allow a direct action for contribution. Moynihan, p. 228.

3. Improvements: If one tenant pays for *improvements* to the property, which the other tenants have not agreed to, the former is *never* permitted to recover contribution in a direct suit. And he is not normally permitted to deduct the cost of improvements from rents that he collects from a third person. However, if the rents he collects are *increased* as a result of the improvements, he may collect just the increase, up to the cost of the improvement.

    a. Rationale: The reason for these rules is that it would be unfair to allow the non-paying tenant to be "improved out of his estate"; for instance, if an automatic deduction from third-party rents were allowed, a tenant who counted on receiving his share of the rents would be deprived of them. 2 A.L.P. 81. Yet where a tenant, by paying for improvements, has increased the cash flow of the property, it is fair to allow him to recoup his payment from the increase.

    b. Partition: The party who pays for an improvement is always free to seek *partition* from the court, and except in the case of a tenancy by the entirety, he will get it. (*Infra*, p. 150.) If the property can be divided "in kind" in such a way that the parcel containing the improvement can be given to the person who paid for it, the court will do so. Otherwise, it will order the property sold and the person who paid for the improvement will get, off the top, any increase in value from the improvement up to its cost.

4. Acquisition of outstanding interest: Co-tenants are required to act towards each other in *good faith*. If they receive their interests at the same time (e.g., from the same will, or by the same conveyance), they will usually be held to be in a *fiduciary relationship*. One important consequence is that if one of them *buys an outstanding interest*, he *holds that interest on behalf of all of them.*

    a. Buying at foreclosure or tax sale: The same principle generally applies to a co-tenant who buys the property at a *foreclosure sale* or *tax sale*. The foreclosure or tax title is not automatically held for the benefit of the other tenants, but they have a *right to* *elect to contribute* within a reasonable time after the sale; if they do so, they maintain their ownership interest.

Example: *A* and *B* inherit from *O* Blackacre, a lot with a house on it; they take as equal tenants in common. At the time they inherit, the property is already subject to an outstanding mortgage of $100,000 held by Bank. Shortly after they inherit, the mortgage falls into default, and Bank starts foreclosure proceedings, notice of which Bank gives to both *A* and *B*. *A* (but not *B*) bids at the foreclosure sale, and is the winner bidder at $100,000, all of which goes to Bank.

A court will almost certainly hold that in bidding, *A* owed a fiduciary duty to his co-tenant *B*. Therefore, post-foreclosure-sale, *B* will have the right to elect to participate equally in the purchase. Consequently, provided that *B* so elects within a reasonable time after the foreclosure, and pays *A* $50,000, *B* will be restored to his pre-foreclosure position as equal co-tenant.

E. Partition: Any tenant in common or joint tenant (but not a tenant by the entirety) may bring an equitable action for *partition*. By this means, the court will either *divide the property*, or *order it sold* and the *proceeds distributed*. Normally, each tenant has an absolute right to partition.

1. Partition in kind: In some cases, there is a fair way to divide the property, so that each tenant can be given a parcel proportional to his interest. For instance, a large farm, all of whose acreage is roughly comparable, might be subdivided. This is known as partition "*in kind*." Even if a precise apportionment is impossible, the court may order partition to another, to reflect the disparities in the physical division.

2. Partition by sale: Where partition in kind is not possible, or would be unfair to one party, the court will order the property sold, and the proceeds divided. This is a partition *"by sale."*

3. Preference for partition in kind: Most courts state a preference for partitioning the property *in kind* rather than by sale, and say that they will approve a partition by sale if and only if the *physical characteristics* of the property prevent division of the property in kind, or if division in kind would be *extremely unfair* to one party.

Example: The property is in a residential zone, and requires 100 feet of street frontage for any house. The property is vacant now, and has 150 feet of frontage. *A* owns two-thirds and *B* one-third, as tenants in common. *A* proposes to divide the property so that he gets two-thirds of the square footage, and so that he gets 100 feet of frontage. The court probably won't order partition in kind, because this would leave *B* with 50 feet of frontage, too little to build a house on. Therefore, the court will probably order the land sold.

a. Where opponent of partition lives or works on the property: Where the party who is opposing partition by sale *lives on the property* or *uses it for a business*, courts are especially *reluctant* to in effect evict that party by requiring that the entire parcel be sold.

Example: The Ps own 99/144ths of a 20-acre parcel, and D owns the remaining 45/144ths. D lives in a house at one edge of the property, and operates a rubbish and garbage removal business from part of the property. The remainder of the property is unused, and the Ps are not in possession of any part. The Ps want to convert the entire parcel into a residential development (and do not want the property partitioned in kind, since the residential parcel would be less valuable per acre with D's older house and garbage business adjacent to it than if the whole parcel became a development). D resists partition by sale, because she does not want to move her home or relocate her garbage business.

Held, D wins, and the property will be partitioned in kind, not by sale. Under Connecticut law, partition by sale will only be ordered if the physical attributes of the land are such that partition in kind would be impractical or inequitable, and the interests of the owners would be better promoted by partition by sale. The burden is on the party requesting partition by sale to demonstrate that these requirements are met. Here, the Ps have failed to meet either requirement. The property could certainly be partitioned in kind, with the Ps left to convert their roughly 2/3 portion to residential use. Furthermore, it is the interests of *all* the tenants in common, not merely the economic gain of one tenant or group of tenants, that the court must consider. Here, the lower court failed to give adequate weight to the fact that D would lose both her home and her livelihood if she were forced to participate in a sale of the entire property. *Delfino v. Vealencis*, 436 A.2d 27 (Conn. 1980).

Note: Courts continue to say that partition in kind is preferred over partition by sale. But in most cases where the parties disagree about which type of partition should be used, the court ends up decreeing partition by sale. DKA&S, pp. 296-97. One reason is that courts usually conclude that a sale is the fairest for all parties (though in a case in which only one party lives or works on the property, such as in *Delfino*, the fairness of a sale is harder to see). Probably *economic efficiency* will be better served in most instances by a *sale*; for instance, the plaintiffs in *Delfino* were probably right in arguing that any gain to D in being able to continue to live and operate her business on the property would be outweighed by the loss of the ability to develop the whole parcel as residential real estate — in any event, if D's use of the property was really more valuable than the lost residential development use, D should in theory be able to be the highest bidder for the property at the partition sale.

  b. **Accounting for rents and profits:** As noted above, before the proceeds from a partition sale are distributed, a tenant who has paid more than his share for repairs, mortgages, taxes, or improvements, will be repaid from the proceeds. Conversely, if one co-tenant has received more than his share of third-party rents, the other tenants will receive a matching share of the partition proceeds off the top. Thus an *accounting* for rents and profits is often part of a partition proceeding.

4. **Agreement not to partition:** The parties are always free to *agree* that they will *not partition* the property in the future. However, since partition is an equitable action, the court may *disregard* the agreement, and order partition, if the agreement is for an unreasonably long period of time, or if circumstances have changed.

Quiz Yourself on

CONCURRENT OWNERSHIP

33. O conveyed Blackacre "to A and B as co-tenants." A then died, bequeathing all of his real and personal property to his son, S. B is still alive. What is the state of title to Blackacre? _____

34. O conveyed Blackacre "to A and B as joint tenants." B then conveyed to C, by a quitclaim deed (conveying whatever interest B had in the property). Subsequently, A died, bequeathing all of his real and personal property to his son, S. What is the state of title? _____

35. O, the fee simple owner of Whiteacre, died, leaving the property by will to his three children, A, B, and C, "as tenants in common." A purchased C's interest. The property is a single-family home. A moved in, and used the property as his principal residence. B, a bachelor, has now demanded to live in the home as well. If A refuses, will a judge order A to share the house with B? _____

36. Henry and Wanda were husband and wife. Using funds supplied entirely by Henry, the two purchased Blackacre from Oscar. (The deed from Oscar to Henry and Wanda read, "To Henry and Wanda in fee simple," without further elaboration.) Shortly thereafter, Henry became infatuated with a younger woman, Georgia. To celebrate the six-month anniversary of their affair, Henry conveyed to Georgia his interest in Blackacre. (Assume that the land is located in a state that permits such a conveyance.) For the next five years, Henry continued to be married to Wanda, but carried on his affair with Georgia. Then, Wanda died, leaving all of her real and personal property to her and Henry's daughter, Denise. Shortly thereafter, Henry died. What is the state of title? (Assume that the common-law approach to all relevant matters is in force, unmodified by statute or case law.) _____

37. Herb and Wendy, husband and wife, were the owners of Blackacre, which they held by tenancy of the entirety. In 2011, Herb and Wendy were divorced. They intended to sell the property, but before they could do so, Herb died suddenly in 2012. Herb's will leaves all his real and personal property to his son by a prior marriage, Stan. What is the state of the title to Blackacre? _____

38. Arthur and Bertha, after inheriting Blackacre from their father, held it as tenants in common. Originally, Arthur lived in the premises, and Bertha had no interest in doing so. After a few years, Arthur moved out, and sent Bertha the following letter: "I am moving out of Blackacre. You have the right to live on the property. If you do not do so, I will rent it out." Bertha made no response. Arthur, after advertising for a tenant, rented the property to Xavier, who responded to the ad. Xavier paid $20,000 of rent during the first year. (Xavier paid all operating costs, such as utilities.) At the end of the first year of this rental, Bertha learned of the arrangement and sent Arthur a letter stating, "You owe me one-half of the rents paid by Xavier." Is Bertha correct? _____

39. Omar, the owner of Whiteacre, left the property to his daughter Carol and his son Dan, in equal parts. The will said nothing about who should occupy the property. The property was a single-family home. Dan already had a home of his own, suitable for his family. Carol did not. Therefore, Carol moved into the house, and has since occupied it. The estimated fair market rental value of the house is $18,000 per year. Dan has demanded that Carol pay him one-half of this amount, to compensate for her use of the premises. Carol has responded, "You are free to live here with me, but I'm not paying you any money for my use of the premises." If Dan sues for one-half of the fair market rent represented by Carol's occupancy of the premises, will Dan prevail? _____

40. Edward and Felicia, brother and sister, received Whiteacre as a bequest in their mother's will. Edward,

who had been living on the property while his mother was still alive, continued to do so after her death. Felicia has never had any interest in living on the property. The property is presently worth approximately $800,000, and has a rental value of $50,000 per year. However, Edward has rejected all suggestions by Felicia that the property be sold or rented out to third parties (though Edward has always indicated that Felicia is welcome to live on the property with him). What sort of action, if any, may Felicia bring to accomplish her goals? _____

Answers

33. B and S hold as tenants in common. Today, all states establish a presumption that an ambiguous conveyance creates a tenancy in common rather than a joint tenancy. Therefore, O's ambiguous conveyance made A and B hold as tenants in common. Consequently, when A died, there was no right of survivorship on the part of B. Instead, A's undivided one-half interest in Blackacre passed to S. S and B now hold as tenants in common.

34. S and C as tenants in common. When B conveyed to C, this had the effect of *severing* the joint tenancy between A and B. Therefore, A and C held as tenants in common, not joint tenants, immediately after the conveyance by B to C. Therefore, when A died, C had no right of survivorship. S inherited A's share of the tenancy in common.

35. Yes. Each tenant in common is entitled to *possession of the whole property*, subject to the same rights in the other tenants. It does not make any difference that one of the tenants in common has a larger undivided interest than the other — the relative size of the interests matters only when the property is sold and the proceeds are allocated.

36. Fee simple absolute in Georgia. Oscar's original conveyance to Henry and Wanda created a tenancy by the entirety in them, since at common law any conveyance to two persons who are in fact husband and wife necessarily results in such a tenancy. (In fact, in the 22 states that retain tenancy by the entirety, there remains a presumption that a husband and wife who take property take it by the entirety.) When Henry conveyed his interest to Georgia, this did not have the effect of destroying the tenancy by the entirety, since such a tenancy is *indestructible* while both parties are alive and remain husband and wife. But the conveyance did have the effect of passing to Georgia whatever Henry's rights were. When Wanda died before Henry, her interest was extinguished, and there was nothing for her to pass to Denise. Since Henry would have taken the entire property had he kept his interest, Georgia steps into his shoes, and takes the entire property.

37. Wendy and Stan each have an undivided one-half interest as tenants in common. Where husband and wife are divorced, the tenancy by the entirety automatically ends. In most states, the property is then deemed to be held as tenants in common (i.e., without right of survivorship). Thus when Herb died, his undivided one-half interest as tenant in common passed to Stan.

38. Yes. Although a co-tenant is normally entitled to occupy the premises himself without accounting for their reasonable rental value, the same is not true if he leases the premises to a third person. Once he does this, and collects rents, he is required to share these rents with his co-tenant.

39. No. Each co-tenant is entitled to occupy the entire premises, subject only to the same right on the part of the other tenant. But the occupying tenant has, in general, no duty to account for the value of his exclusive possession. If Carol refused to let Dan live in the property, then Carol would be liable to pay Dan one-half of the rental value of the premises. But as long as Carol holds the premises open to Dan, she does not have to pay Dan any part of the imputed value of her own occupancy.

40. She should bring an action for partition. Any tenant in common or joint tenant (but not a tenant by the entirety) may bring an equitable action for partition. By this means, the court will either divide the property, or order it sold and the proceeds distributed. Normally, each tenant has an absolute right to partition, even over the objection of the other. Here, since the property probably cannot be readily divided, the court will order it sold. Felicia will get half of the sale proceeds.

Exam Tips on
CONCURRENT OWNERSHIP

Joint Tenancy

☛ **Joint tenancy vs. tenancy in common:** Generally, a tenancy in common, ***not*** a joint tenancy, is presumed unless there is a ***clear intent*** to establish a joint tenancy.

☞ **Identify interest:** First look at the grantor's language. A joint tenancy is clearly indicated by a grant which provides: "To A and B as joint tenants with right of survivorship."

☞ **Ambiguity:** Watch for language that does ***not*** clearly indicate a joint tenancy; when this happens, lean in favor of a tenancy in common.

Example: O grants realty "to A and B, to be held by them jointly." Most courts would find a tenancy in common because of the ambiguous language. However, in your answer, analyze the surrounding circumstances which may influence a court to decide differently. For instance, if A and B are related to each other and to O, and the property is a single-family residence, you can argue that O intended to keep the property in the family and that he would not have created a situation where one cotenant might possibly be forced to share a home with a stranger (which could happen with a tenancy in common).

☞ **Survivorship:** Remember that the unique characteristic of a joint tenancy is that upon a cotenant's death, her share ***passes to the surviving cotenants in equal shares***; the remaining cotenants are then in joint tenancy with each other.

Example: A, B and C are in joint tenancy with each other. Each holds an undivided one-third interest in the property. If A dies, her interest passes to the other two. Therefore, B and C will each hold an undivided one-half interest in the property, as joint tenants.

☞ **Severance:** The most frequently-tested issue regarding a joint tenancy is the issue of ***severance***. Often fact patterns will be complicated, with several transfers having occurred, and you will be asked to determine the rights of the various parties to the property; to do this, you'll have to recognize where severance of the joint tenancy has occurred.

☞ **Sale or other conveyance:** Look for a ***conveyance*** by one cotenant to another party. This *effects a severance* as to that interest but *not* as to the interests of the other joint tenants.

Example: A, B, and C are joint tenants in a parcel of land. B sells her share to Z. The result is that A and C hold equal shares of a two-thirds interest in the land as joint tenants with each other, and Z holds a one-third interest in the land as a tenant in common vis a vis the other two.

☞ **Devise:** Don't be fooled when a cotenant devises her share of a joint tenancy in her *will*. This does *not* effect a severance, nor does it pass the share on to the devisee. The decedent's share automatically passes to the other cotenant(s).

Example 1: O conveys realty "to my brothers A and B, their heirs and assigns as joint tenants with right of survivorship." A dies, devising his interest to his only child, "C for life, and then to C's son, S, for life, and then to S's children, their heirs and assigns." B dies and devises his interest "to my friend, F, his heirs and assigns." F later conveys by quitclaim deed "to P, his heirs and assigns."

P owns the realty in fee simple because: (1) A's interest went to B when A died (despite the fact that A tried to devise it by will), leaving the whole parcel in B; (2) B devised the whole parcel to F; and (3) F conveyed the whole parcel to P.

Example 2: A, B, and C are joint tenants of a parcel. A conveys her interest to D, her daughter. Later, B dies, with a will leaving all B's real estate to S, his son.

When A conveyed her interest to D, D became a tenant in common with a one-third interest, while B and C continued to be joint tenants as to the remaining two-thirds. B's attempted devise to S was ineffective and C received B's interest, leaving C with an undivided two-thirds interest and D with an undivided one-third interest as tenants in common.

☞ **Mortgage:** If a joint tenant mortgages his interest in a state that treats a mortgage as a transfer of *title*, then the joint tenancy is *severed*. However, in a state where a mortgage is treated as merely a *lien* to secure repayment, the tenancy is usually *not* deemed *severed*.

☞ **Partition:** Another method of severance that appears in fact patterns is *partition*: the dividing up and distributing of the land or the sale of the land and distribution of the proceeds, which can be done either by agreement of the parties, or by court order at the request of one party. Partition effects a severance — each cotenant is given a share equal in value. If the estate can't be divided equally, the cotenant who receives the land of greater value may be required to make a cash payment to the other cotenant.

Tenancy in common

☞ **T/C generally:** A conveyance to two or more people is presumed to be a tenancy in common unless a contrary intention is shown.

☞ **No ability to affect other co-tenant's rights:** Keep in mind that a tenant in common may not make a conveyance (including a mortgage) that in any way *binds another* *tenant in common who does not join* in the conveyance.

> *Example:* Blackacre is owned by *A* and *B* as tenants in common. *A* borrows money from Bank and signs (but *B* doesn't) a mortgage to Bank on "Blackacre." If *A* doesn't pay the money back, Bank can foreclose on only *A*'s tenancy in common interest, not *B*'s. And that's true even if *B* knew about and approved *A*'s signing of the mortgage (as long as *B* didn't sign the mortgage or explicitly give *A* the right to sign on *B*'s behalf).

Tenancy by the entirety

☞ **Tenancy by the entirety generally:** In jurisdictions which recognize tenancy by the entirety, a conveyance *to a husband and wife* is *presumed* to create a tenancy by the entirety. But the presumption operates only if there's no indication that the parties had a contrary intention.

> *Example:* Bride and Groom receive a wedding gift of a parcel of realty. The deed states: "to Bride and Groom, husband and wife, as joint tenants." Several years later Bride and Groom separate and Bride moves in with another man, Mon. At Mon's request, Bride executes a quitclaim deed conveying her interest in the realty to Mon.
>
> The "as joint tenants" language rebutted the presumption of a tenancy by an entirety, and instead created in Bride and Groom a joint tenancy with right of survivorship. When Bride conveyed to Mon, the joint tenancy was severed, and Groom and Mon became tenants in common.

Ouster

☞ **Ouster generally:** Look for a fact pattern which indicates that a tenant not in possession of the land has attempted to physically occupy the land and the occupying tenant has refused to allow access. When this occurs, point out that the cotenant who has ousted the other cotenant or prevented her from occupying the premises may be required to *account to the other cotenant for rent.* (Each co-tenant normally has a right of *equal access* to the property.)

Partition

☞ **Sale vs. in kind:** If you have a partition problem, you'll need to say whether the court will order partition *"in kind"* (physical division) or instead a partition by *sale.* Point out that courts have a general *preference for partition in kind*, but not where this would be *unfair* to one side.

> *Example:* The property is in a residential zone, and has 1-acre minimum lot sizes for houses. The property is vacant now, and is 1.5 acres. *A* owns two-thirds and *B* one-third, as tenants in common. The court probably won't order partition in kind, because this would leave *B* with .5 acres, too small to meet the 1-acre minimum to build a house on. Therefore, the court will probably order the land sold, and the proceeds divided two-thirds / one-third.

CHAPTER 8

LANDLORD AND TENANT

I. INTRODUCTION

A. Non-freehold estates: This chapter is about the ***non-freehold estates***. (See *supra*, p. 49.) The estates that are non-freehold are: (1) the tenancy for *years*; (2) the *periodic* tenancy; (3) the tenancy at *will*; and (4) the tenancy at *sufferance*. These estates are discussed one at a time beginning *infra*, p. 159.

    1. Landlord-tenant relationship: These non-freehold estates have one particularly important characteristic: each normally includes a duty, on the tenant's part, to ***pay rent***. Thus they involve the ***landlord-tenant*** relationship.

B. Conveyance aspects: The leasehold and the freehold at common law had a key feature in common: they were both ***estates in land***, typically created by a ***conveyance***. Until about the last few decades, the law of landlord-tenant was dominated by these estate, conveyancing, aspects.

    1. Independent covenants: For instance, since a tenant was deemed to receive an estate in land, his rights and duties were treated as ***independent*** of the landlord's rights and duties. Thus if the landlord promised to keep the property in repair (a promise which landlords seldom make), a breach of this promise did not relieve the tenant from the duty of paying rent; the rent was owed as payment for the estate, and the promise to do repairs was merely a collateral promise which could be enforced only by a separate contractual suit brought by the tenant. This doctrine is generally referred to as the ***independence of covenants***.

    2. Destruction of premises: Similarly, if buildings upon the land were completely ***destroyed*** by fire or other act of nature, the tenant still had the duty to pay rent. Again, this stemmed from the idea that the tenant was paying rent for the land itself, not the buildings on it.

    3. Modern tendency: But since the late 20th century, courts have shown a strong tendency to ***move away from the doctrine of independence of covenants***. See, e.g., Rest. 2d, Introduction to Landlord and Tenant, p. vii.

        a. Warranty of habitability: The most striking example is the present willingness of most courts to hold that, at least with respect to residential premises, the landlord makes an ***implied warranty of habitability***, the breach of which entitles the tenant to terminate the lease and move out, withhold rent, or use rent monies to make the repairs himself. See *infra*, p. 169.

        b. Destruction of premises: Similarly, in many states the tenant's duty to pay rent is dependent upon the continued existence of buildings on the property, so that fire or flood will relieve him. This result is often produced by statute, but sometimes by case law. See *infra*, p. 172.

C. Leaseholds distinguished from other interests: One characteristic of the leasehold is that the tenant, for the term of his lease, is entitled to *exclusive possession*. This distinguishes the leasehold from several other types of property interests.

1. Hotel guest: For instance, a *guest in a hotel* is usually held not to have a leasehold interest, but rather, a license. (Licenses are discussed *infra*, p. 230.) The same is true of a *lodger* in a boarding house. Consequently, statutes applicable to landlord-tenant relations may not apply; for instance, the hotel keeper may have the right to use self-help to evict a non-paying guest even though such self-help is forbidden by statute to a landlord. See Reporter's Note to Rest. 2d, §1.2, Item 1.

2. Parking lots, sign easements: Similarly, a spot in a *parking lot* is usually held to confer only a license, not a lease. And the right to put a sign upon another's building is generally merely an easement. 1 A.L.P. 184.

II. THE VARIOUS TENANCIES AND THEIR CREATION

A. Statute of Frauds: The original English Statute of Frauds (1677) provided that any lease for *more than three years* must be in writing (or else have the effect of creating merely an estate at will, discussed *infra*, p. 160). Powell, Par. 222, p. 84.

1. American statutes: The need for a writing is similarly governed by statute in all American states. Most of these statutes, however, require a writing for all leases for *more than one year*. 1 A.L.P. 215.

2. Lease to commence in future: The Statute of Frauds in most states also has a separate *contracts provision* requiring a writing for any contract not to be performed within one year *of the making of the contract*. Since a lease can be viewed as a contract, some courts have applied the contract provision, and have thus required a writing even for a one-year lease (or shorter) where, because of the gap between the making of the lease and its effective date, the *end* of the lease would be *more than one year from its making*.

a. Majority view: But most courts hold that the contract section does *not* apply; thus a one-year lease does not have to be in writing, even if it is to begin in the future. This is the position taken by Rest. 2d, §2.1, Comment f.

3. Option to renew: Where a lease provides for an initial fixed period, plus an *option to renew* by one or both parties, the courts are split as to how the Statute of Frauds applies.

a. Majority rule: The majority of courts hold that the fixed term and the option period are *added together*; if the total exceeds one year (or whatever the statutory period is), a writing is necessary. Rest. 2d, Reporter's Note to §2.1.

b. Minority rule: But some courts hold that as long as the fixed period does not exceed one year, it is *valid* regardless of the existence of an option. Rest. 2d, §2.1, Comment c, takes this minority position. (But the Restatement suggests that, when the validity of the option itself is in question, a writing should be required if the option plus the original period exceed the statutory period; Rest. 2d, §2.5, Comment c.)

4. **Effect of non-compliance with Statute:** If the lease is one that is required to be in writing, and it is not, the lease is not necessarily void. If the tenant takes possession, this fact together with the fact that the invalid lease shows that entry is made with the landlord's permission will probably create a tenancy at will (*infra*, p. 160). If, in addition to taking possession, the tenant pays rent, a *periodic tenancy* is created in most states (*infra*, p. 159). 1 A.L.P. 218.

5. **Recording of lease:** Apart from the Statute of Frauds, nearly all states require that leases beyond a certain length be *recorded* in the public records. (See *infra*, p. 360.) 4 A.L.P. 551. In many cases, the cut-off is seven years. Generally, the effect of a failure to record where recordation is required is that the lease is not binding upon a *subsequent purchaser* from the landlord. Powell, Par. 222, p. 86.

B. **The estate for years:** The most common type of leasehold is the *estate for years*. The estate for years is any estate which is for a *fixed period of time*. Thus the lease does not have to be for one or more years; a six-month lease would qualify.

1. **No notice needed to terminate:** An estate for years, by definition, contains its own termination date. Accordingly, *no additional notice of termination* is required to be given by either party; on the last day, the tenancy simply ends, and the tenant must leave the premises.

2. **Maximum duration:** Most states do not impose any *outer limit* on the length of a tenancy for years; thus a 2,000-year tenancy would be upheld in most states. But a few states have statutorily imposed length limits, at least with respect to certain kinds of leases, such as those for agricultural or mining properties. See 1 A.L.P. 211.

C. **The periodic tenancy:** The *periodic tenancy* is a tenancy which continues from one period to the next automatically, unless either party terminates it at the end of a period by notice. 1 A.L.P. 221-22. Examples are a tenancy from year-to-year, *month-to-month*, or week-to-week.

1. **Distinguished from tenancy for years:** Thus while a tenancy for years automatically expires when it reaches the end of its stated term, the periodic tenancy *continues indefinitely, until terminated by one of the parties* by proper notice.

2. **Creation of periodic tenancy:** It is possible to create a periodic tenancy by *express agreement* (i.e., L and T explicitly agree that T will have a month-to-month tenancy of Blackacre.) Normally, however, a periodic tenancy is created by *inference*.

   a. **Lease with no stated duration:** For instance, the parties may make a lease without setting a duration, and also provide that the rent is to be, say, $400 per month. The fact that the rent is to be payable monthly will probably be enough to make the tenancy a month-to-month periodic one. See Rest. 2d §1.5, Comment d.

   b. **Void lease:** Similarly, the parties may make an *invalid lease*. This would probably be due to a failure to comply with the Statute of Frauds, but might be due to a state's requirement that the lease be notarized or in the form of a deed. When the tenant first enters, a tenancy at will is created (*infra*, p. 161), but as soon as the first *rent payment* is made, a periodic tenancy will generally be deemed to exist.

      i. **Length of period:** However, courts are not in agreement as to how the length of the period is to be determined. Most courts would probably hold that the period is the one that is *used in the void lease* for calculating rent. Thus if the rent in the lease is stated on an annual basis, the tenancy will be year-to-year, even though the rent is payable each month.

c. **Arising from holdover:**   Another way a periodic tenancy can arise is when a tenant *holds over* at the end of a lease. In the holdover situation, the landlord has the choice of either evicting the tenant or permitting him to stay; in the latter event, the tenancy is usually treated as a periodic one. This is discussed more fully *infra*, p. 161.

3. **Termination of tenancy:**   A periodic tenancy will automatically be renewed for a further period unless one party gives a valid *notice of termination*. At common law, *six months* notice was necessary to terminate a year-to-year tenancy, and a *full period's notice* was necessary where the period was less than a year (e.g., thirty days notice for a month-to-month tenancy). Rest. 2d §1.5, Comment f. Today, most states have statutes modifying this rule; many of these statutes require only thirty days notice for any tenancy, even year-to-year. (But the parties are free to agree upon longer or shorter notice.)

a. **Notice must specify end of period:**   At common law, the notice also had to set the *end of a period* as the termination date.

Example: T and L orally agree that T will rent Blackacre from L "at a rent of $2,000 per month." No duration is specified. The parties agree that the lease will start July 1. T moves in on July 1. On Oct. 15, T sends L a letter stating, "I have moved out, and the lease is terminated effective immediately."

At common law, this termination notice would not be effective *at all*, because it failed to specify the end of a period as the termination date. The oral agreement created a month-to-month periodic tenancy by implication (since the lack of a writing meant that the agreement failed to satisfy the Statute of Frauds; see *supra*, p. 158). Therefore, the lease could be terminated only by a notice stating the end of the following period as the time of termination. (By contrast, an Oct. 15 letter setting November 30 as the termination date would have been valid, since that would have set the end of the next complete period as the termination date, as required by the common-law rule.)

i. **Modern view relaxes rule:**   It is *still the rule* almost everywhere that a notice of termination *may only be effective as of the end of a period.* But where a notice is not sufficiently in advance of the end of the current period, most courts now allow it to be automatically effective as of the end of the *following period*. See Rest. 2d §1.5, Comment f. Thus on the facts of the above example, the Oct. 15 letter would still not be sufficient to terminate as of Oct. 15 or Oct. 31st, but it *would* be interpreted to terminate validly as of November 30.

b. **Due process right:**   Although normally either party to a periodic tenancy has a right to terminate *without cause* (assuming the termination was not motivated by a legislatively-forbidden purpose, such as racial discrimination), this may not be the case with *publicly financed or subsidized* housing. As to such housing, the tenant may have a *due process* right not to be evicted without cause.

D. **Tenancy at will:**   A *tenancy at will* is a tenancy which has *no stated duration* and may be *terminated at any time* by either party.

1. **No notice for termination:** At common law, *no prior notice* of termination is required, as it is for periodic tenancies. (However, the tenant has a reasonable time within which to remove his goods if the landlord demands possession.) 1 A.L.P. 229.

   a. **Modern statutes:** But modern statutes in many states give a tenant at will a right to prior notice, similar to that given to a short-term periodic tenant. This has tended to blur the dividing line between tenancies at will and periodic tenancies.

2. **How the at-will tenancy arises:** The parties could create a tenancy at will expressly, by agreeing that either may terminate at any time. But generally, such a tenancy is created by *implication*. For instance, T might take possession with L's permission, with no term stated and no period for paying rent defined. Or, T might take possession under a void lease; his possession would create a tenancy at will, but this would be transformed into a periodic tenancy as soon as he made the first rent payment (*supra*, p. 159). 1 A.L.P. 230-31.

3. **Events causing termination:** Apart from an affirmative notice of termination by either party, a tenancy at will will terminate automatically upon the *death* of either party, or upon a *conveyance* of the reversion by the landlord. An *assignment* by the tenant of his interest also terminates the tenancy, but most courts hold that a *sublease* does *not* terminate. Moynihan, p. 84.

E. **Tenancy at sufferance:** The so-called "*tenancy at sufferance*" exists only in one limited situation: that in which a tenant *holds over* at the end of a valid lease. This "tenancy" is extremely insubstantial; it will end as soon as the landlord exercises his option either to evict the tenant or to hold him to another term. (See immediately below).

   1. **Landlord's right of election:** When a tenant holds over after his lease has ended, the landlord has a *right of election*; he may choose between: (1) *evicting* the tenant, i.e., treating him as a trespasser; and (2) holding him to *another term* as tenant.

      a. **Right of eviction:** The landlord's right to evict a holdover tenant, and the means by which this is accomplished, are discussed *infra*, p. 181.

      b. **Right to elect new term:** The landlord may choose to *bind* the holdover tenant to a *new term*. In nearly all states, the landlord has this right even though the tenant has manifested no desire to remain for an entire additional term. 1 A.L.P. 237-38.

   2. **Common law takes strict view:** The common law took an extremely strict view of holdovers; even a one day holdover, and even one that was virtually unavoidable, generally gave the landlord the right to bind the tenant for an additional term.

      a. **Modern courts more lenient:** But modern courts are considerably more lenient towards the holdover tenant. Although the landlord's right to elect another term is not dependent upon the tenant's assent, the courts recognize *extenuating circumstances*, particularly where only a very short holdover period is involved.

      Example: L and T enter into a one-year written lease for an apartment. The lease provides that if T does not move out at the expiration of the lease, he will be liable for double rent for the holdover period. By midnight of the last day of the lease, everything has been moved out but some rugs and a few pieces of furniture. T and his family sleep in the apartment that night, and the next morning, promptly move everything out. That same morning, L notifies T that it has elected to hold T for an additional year.

A court would likely hold that, given the briefness of the holdover and the lack of intent to hold over by T, L was not entitled to hold T to another term.

    i.   **Sickness:**   Similarly, where T becomes *sick* and is unable to move out, most modern courts would not permit L to elect a new term if the holdover period was reasonably short.

   b.   **Partial holdover:**   If the tenant retains possession of *any portion* of the premises, he will generally be considered to be holding over as to the entire premises. The landlord will thus obtain the right to hold him to a new term for the whole premises.

3.   **How landlord exercises option:**   Where the landlord does have the right to bind the tenant to another term, he may of course exercise this right by written notice. But an *oral notice* will also usually be sufficient. Furthermore, if the tenant *pays rent* for the premises for the time following termination, and the landlord accepts this rent, he will probably be deemed to have elected to hold the tenant for another term. See Rest. 2d §14.4, Comment e and Illustr. 1.

   a.   **Waiver:**   But the landlord may be found to have *waived* his right to treat the tenant as a holdover.

    Example: L and T make a written lease for a one-year term. Just before this year is up, L and T begin negotiations for a new lease. They are still negotiating when the year is up, and T remains in possession. They finally fail to reach agreement, and T moves out as soon as the negotiations terminate. L may not treat T as a holdover, and bind him to another year. In this situation, L has *implicitly consented* to T's holding over for the duration of the negotiations. Therefore, he has no right to change this understanding and bind T to a one-year term. See 1 A.L.P. 214.

4.   **Length and nature of new tenancy:**   Courts disagree as to whether the new tenancy is a term of years or a periodic tenancy. They also disagree about the *length* of the term or period.

   a.   **Way rent calculated:**   Probably the majority view is that a *periodic* tenancy is created, and that the length of the period is determined by the *way rent was computed* under the lease which terminated. Thus if the original lease calculated rentals on an annual basis (even though the rentals may have been payable monthly), the tenancy produced by the landlord's election would be year-to-year. This is the position taken by Rest. 2d §14.4, Comment f.

   b.   **Other provisions of holdover term:**   In all respects except length, the holdover term is governed by the *same provisions* as the original lease. Thus in the absence of an agreement otherwise, the *rent remains the same*, as does the allocation of duties between landlord and tenant (e.g., the duty of repair).

5.   **Election is binding:**   Whichever route the landlord decides to take, termination or renewal, is *binding* upon him. Thus if he says that he is holding the tenant to another term, he cannot thereafter change his mind and evict; similarly, if he starts eviction proceedings, it is too late for him to change his tune and renew the lease. If he fails to take either action within a reasonable period of time, he may be held to have waived his right to elect a new term (though he is unlikely to be found to have waived the right to evict). See Rest. §14.4, Comment c.

III. TENANT'S RIGHT OF POSSESSION AND ENJOYMENT

A. Tenant's right of possession: All courts agree that, unless the lease provides otherwise, the landlord is obligated to deliver *legal right* to possess the premises to the tenant at the commencement of the lease term. That is, the landlord impliedly warrants that he has legal right to give possession to the tenant; he would violate this warranty if, for instance, he had already given a lease for the same period to someone else. (See *infra*, p. 163.) But the courts are sharply split as to whether the landlord also impliedly warrants that he will deliver *actual* possession at the start of the lease term; the question usually arises when a *prior tenant holds over*.

   1. "American" view: The so-called *"American" view* is that the landlord has a duty to deliver *only* legal possession, *not actual possession*. See, e.g., *Hannan v. Dusch*, 153 S.E. 824 (Va. 1930). Despite the designation "American rule," probably at most a *slight majority* of American courts adhere to this view. See Rest. 2d §6.2, Reporter's Note, Item 2.

   2. "English" rule: The contrary position, that the landlord *does* have a duty to deliver actual possession, is usually called the *"English" rule*, since it is followed by all English courts. But notwithstanding this label, almost half of American courts now follow this position.

      a. Tenant's rights for breach: Where the English view is in effect, the lessee generally has the right to *terminate the lease* and recover the damages for the breach. Or, he may continue the lease, and *recover damages* accruing until either he or the landlord succeeds in getting the holdover tenant ousted.

B. Right of quiet enjoyment: The tenant has what is sometimes called the *"right of quiet enjoyment"* of the leased premises. There are two principal ways in which this right can be interfered with:

[1] by a third person's *assertion of a title superior to that of the landlord*, used to evict the tenant (a claim of "paramount title"); and

[2] by *acts of the landlord*, or persons claiming under him, that interfere with the tenant's possession or use of the premises.

(In addition, the landlord's failure to maintain the property in habitable condition, and the destruction of the premises by fire or other cause, are sometimes considered violations of the right of quiet enjoyment; however, for our purposes, these two subjects are treated separately, *infra*, pp. 169 and 172 respectively.)

   1. Claims of paramount title: The landlord, by making the lease, impliedly warrants that he has *legal power* to give possession to the tenant for the term of the lease.

a. **Ways to violate:** There are a number of ways in which this implied warranty might be violated, including the following (assuming in all cases that the consequence of the problem is that the tenant is evicted):

   i. the landlord does not have title to the premises *at all*;

   ii. the landlord has title to the premises, but has *already leased them* to someone else for a period overlapping that of the new lease;

   iii. the landlord has only a *life estate* in the property, which might expire before the end of the lease term; and

   iv. the landlord's title is subject to *termination*.

   > **Example of (iv):** L fails to make mortgage payments. The lender forecloses, takes title at the foreclosure sale, and has T evicted.

   In all of these instances, the third person has a claim of *"paramount title,"* and the tenant's right of quiet enjoyment is violated if and when the third person causes the tenant to be evicted.

b. **Remedies:** Assuming the tenant has taken possession, she tenant may *not* terminate the lease, or refuse to pay rent, merely on the grounds that a third person *holds* a paramount title. Only if that third person then *asserts* his paramount title in such a way that the tenant is *evicted*, may the tenant terminate the lease and recover damages. Rest. 2d §4.3; S&W, §6.31, p. 281. The rule that mere existence of a paramount title (without eviction) may not be used by the tenant as a defense in a rent action or eviction proceeding is sometimes expressed by saying that the tenant is *"estopped to deny his landlord's title"* to the leased property. Rest. 2d §4.3 Comment b.

2. **Interference by landlord or third person:** If the *landlord himself interferes* with the tenant's use of the premises, or *aids someone else* in doing so, this will be a breach of the covenant of quiet enjoyment.

   a. **Acts by landlord:** The clearest breach exists when the landlord himself interferes with the tenant's use of the premises. If the landlord literally takes possession of all or *part* of the leased premises (e.g., he dumps his trash on it, or stores his furniture), it is called *actual eviction*. If, by contrast, he merely interferes with the tenant's *use* or *enjoyment* of the property, there is a *constructive eviction*. (The distinction is discussed in more detail *infra*, p. 165.)

      Example: L leases a house to T. L also owns the property next door, and uses it to give constant loud parties that disturb T in his enjoyment of the house. L may be found to have constructively evicted T, if T moves out of the house because of the noise. Rest. 2d §6.1, Illustr. 5.

      i. **Tenant's remedies:** The tenant's remedies depend in part upon whether the interference amounted to an actual, or just a constructive, eviction. Remedies are discussed *infra*, p. 169.

      ii. **Landlord breaches non-competition clause:** A tenant who plans to use the leased property to run a particular trade or business sometimes obtains a promise from the landlord that the latter will not rent or use any of his nearby property for a purpose *competitive* with the tenant's proposed use. This is commonly called a *non-competition clause*. If the landlord breaches this promise, the tenant will be entitled to sue for damages, or to move out and terminate the lease.

b. Persons holding under landlord: Where T's use of the premises is interfered with by a person *holding under* L, L may be deemed to have breached the covenant of quiet enjoyment. For instance, if L's wife, while running the household she shares with L, throws garbage onto T's premises, this would probably constitute a breach by L.

i. Conduct of other tenants: The most common issue is whether behavior by *other tenants* in the same building violates L's covenant of quiet enjoyment to T.

(1) No general duty: Most cases hold that there is *no general duty* imposed on the landlord to control the conduct of other residential tenants.

(2) Exceptions: But there are two well-established situations where the conduct of other tenants *will* be attributable to the landlord: (1) the other tenants use their portion of the premises for *immoral or lewd purposes*; or (2) the objectionable conduct takes place in the *common areas* under the landlord's control.

(3) Modern tendency where right of control exists: Also, many modern cases show a more general tendency to impute the acts of other tenants to L where these acts are *in violation of the relevant leases*, and L could have prevented the conduct by eviction or otherwise, but hasn't done so. This is the position of Rest. 2d, §6.1, Comment d. This is particularly likely to be the case where L had reason to know, before making a lease with the misbehaving tenant, that a significant chance of inconvenience to others existed.

Example: L rents an apartment to the Ts, and rents the next-door premises to X to run a cocktail lounge. The lease with X explicitly provides that the noise level in the lounge may not disturb neighboring tenants. The noise severely disrupts the Ts. They stop paying rent, and L sues them for back rent. The Ts assert the constructive eviction defense. *Held*, for the Ts. The particular potential for annoyance to the residential tenants, and L's contractual right to control the noise, justify holding L liable for constructive eviction of the Ts. *Blackett v. Olanoff*, 358 N.E.2d 817 (Mass. 1977).

c. Actual vs. constructive eviction: As noted, the courts have distinguished between "*actual*" and "*constructive*" eviction. If the tenant's possession of all or part of the premises is literally taken away from him, the eviction is actual. If it is merely his *use* or *enjoyment* of the property that has been substantially impaired (e.g., excessive noise, terrible odors, nearby premises used for immoral purposes, etc.) the eviction is *constructive*.

i. Complete vs. partial actual eviction: Where the eviction is actual, it can be either *total* or *partial*. Partial eviction might, for instance, occur if the landlord ousted the tenant from a geographical portion of the premises (e.g., by knocking down one of several buildings on the leased property).

(1) Remedies: As one might expect, a tenant who has been totally evicted may regard the lease as *terminated*, and may refuse to pay any rent. Significantly, according to most courts a tenant who has suffered only *partial* actual eviction may also *refuse to pay rent, even though he remains in possession of the rest of the premises*. The courts following this majority view usually defend it by saying that "the landlord *cannot apportion his own wrong*." 1 A.L.P. 284. Rest. 2d §6.1 changes this rule; if the tenant remains on the premises, he is entitled *only* to compensatory damages (though he may elect to terminate the lease and leave the premises, in which case he is relieved from making further rent payments).

ii. **Constructive eviction:** But where the eviction is *constructive* rather than actual, the majority rule is that the tenant is *not* entitled to *terminate the lease*, or to *stop paying rent*, unless he *abandons* the premises.[1] In such a court, if the tenant stays on the premises, his only remedy is to sue for damages. Furthermore, the abandonment must occur within a *reasonable time* following the alleged constructive eviction.

(1) Little use in habitability cases: The defense of constructive eviction has also been used where the tenant claims that the premises were rendered *uninhabitable* due to the landlord's failure to keep them in repair. But the requirement that the tenant promptly leave the premises makes the defense unusable for many tenants, particularly residential slum-dwellers, who lack the funds to find alternative housing. The problems of habitability, including the use of the constructive eviction doctrine, are further discussed in a separate section beginning *infra*, p. 169.

d. **Destruction of premises:** If the premises are *destroyed* by an act of nature (e.g., fire), one might expect that the tenant would be allowed to claim that his right of quiet enjoyment had been disturbed, and that the lease was terminated. However, the common law had special rules, unfavorable to the tenant, governing destruction of the premises. These are discussed separately *infra*, p. 172.

C. **Condemnation:** The government may decide to take all or part of the leased premises by its right of *eminent domain*, or *condemnation*. Special common-law rules have evolved to deal with this situation.

1. **Total vs. partial taking:** The government may *condemn* the entire leased premises or merely a portion.

2. **Total taking:** If the entire premises are taken, the *lease terminates*, and the tenant does not have to pay any further rent.

3. **Partial taking:** But where only a *portion* of the premises is taken (even a majority portion, or a portion necessary to the use that the tenant has been making of the property), the common-law rule is that the lease is *not terminated*. Furthermore, the tenant is required to

---

1. *Blackett v. Olanoff, supra*, p. 165, seems not to have followed the majority rule — the court seems to have let the tenants stay rent-free during the pre-trial period when they were constructively evicted.

continue paying the full rent. (But he may get part of the condemnation award, as discussed *infra*).

    a. Restatement view: Rest. 2d §8.1(2) modifies this rule as to partial takings, in two respects. First, if the condemnation "significantly interferes" with the use contemplated by the parties, the lease terminates (and T is relieved from paying rent). Secondly, even if there is no significant interference, T may be entitled to a *reduction in rent* to reflect whatever small interference with his use has occurred.

4. Damages: Under the state and federal constitutions, the government must pay the *fair value* of any property which it condemns. The common-law approach is to *divide* this award between the tenant and the landlord, in *proportion to the damage* each has sustained from the condemnation.

    a. No rent abatement for partial taking: As noted, whereas a total taking suspends the duty to pay rent entirely, under the common law a partial taking does *not* even *reduce* the tenant's duty to pay rent. Instead, the tenant is required to *wait* for the condemnation award, of which he will receive a portion.

    b. Division of award: In *dividing* the condemnation award between the landlord and tenant, courts have followed conflicting, and sometimes confused, approaches. All courts attempt to divide the award equitably. In nearly all states, the court attempts to set the *overall amount* of the award the *same as if there were no lease*; only the division between the landlord and tenant, not the total given to the two interests, depends upon the existence and terms of the lease.

        i. Tenant's loss of bargain: The principal (and sometimes the sole) component of the tenant's portion of the award will be his *loss of bargain*. That is, he will get an amount equal to the difference between the total rent he would have to pay on the rest of the lease, and the *market value* of that lease, both sums discounted to their present value. Thus suppose the taking is total, the lease calls for ten remaining annual payments of $10,000 each, and the market value of the lease is $11,000 per year; T will get an amount equal to the present value of a $1,000 payment in each of the next ten years. (Conversely, if he made a bad bargain on the lease, so that he would have had to pay higher than fair market rentals, he will get no award).

            (1) No special damages: One important consequence is that the tenant normally does not get *special damages* (e.g., lost profits from the business run on the land), except insofar as these may be evidence of the fair market value of the lease.

D. Illegal use of premises: At the time the lease is signed, it may happen that both parties intend that the tenant will use the premises in a way that is *illegal*. Or, the tenant's intended use may become illegal after the lease is signed. Similarly, his use may be illegal if done without a permit or variance, which he is ultimately unable to obtain. In some, but not all, of these situations, the courts treat the lease as void, so that neither party has any obligation to the other.

1. Both parties intend illegal use: If both parties intend that the tenant will use the premises for a purpose which is *illegal under all circumstances*, all courts agree that the lease is **unenforceable**. Thus if L and T agree that T will run a gambling parlor, a drug-selling operation, or a house of prostitution, the court will not enforce the lease against either L or T. Rest. 2d §§9.1(1), 12.4(1).

2. **Violation of building codes:** Courts have sometimes used an illegality theory to invalidate a lease of residential premises where the property is in serious **violation of building codes** at the time the lease is executed.

    a. **Defense to damages action:** The possibility that the court might hold the lease illegal on account of building-code violations gives the tenant an interesting weapon: The tenant can **withhold** rent, remain in the premises, and raise the illegality as a litigation defense. This tactic probably wouldn't work as a defense to **summary eviction proceedings** (see *infra*, p. 181), since these are expedited proceedings in which most defenses, typically including breach of any warranty of habitability (see *infra*, p. 169), are not allowed. But the tenant *can* wait to be evicted, move out, and then use the illegality defense to avoid being held liable for **back rent** (as well as for post-move-out rent) on account of the illegality. If successful, such a technique means that the tenant lives free for the time until the court orders an eviction. DKA&S, p. 430.

3. **Remedies:** Generally, neither party to an illegal contract is entitled to recover anything from the other; the court **leaves the parties as it finds them**. However, if the court concludes that one party is much more morally culpable than the other (i.e., that the parties are **not "in pari delicto"**), the court may award some kind of recovery to the less guilty party.

    a. **Restitution:** Also, even where the parties are in *pari delicto*, the court may simply decide as a matter of fairness that one is entitled to recover something from the other. Thus where a lease is held illegal for housing code violations, some courts have nonetheless awarded the landlord the **reasonable value** of the leased premises, for the period they were actually occupied by the tenant.

E. **Permitted uses:** In the absence of an agreement otherwise, the tenant is permitted to use the property for **any purpose** that is not illegal. However, the parties are free to agree that the premises be used solely for a particular purpose, or that certain uses will not be permitted. For instance, if the property is designed for residential purposes, the lease will almost certainly restrict the use to non-commercial purposes. Similarly, many business leases set forth with some precision the uses the tenant may make.

1. **Distinguish from mere description:** But such restrictive clauses generally strictly construed against the landlord. Thus if the lease merely **describes** the tenant's use, and does not explicitly require the use, the tenant may usually do as she pleases. 1 A.L.P. 254. Similarly, the fact that both parties intended a particular use will not be dispositive, if the lease does not contain an express restriction.

IV. CONDITION OF THE PREMISES

A. **Common-law view:** The common law applied the principle of *caveat emptor* to the landlord-tenant relationship. Unless the parties explicitly agreed otherwise, the tenant took the premises **as is**. The landlord was **not** deemed to have made any **implied warranty** that the premises were fit or **habitable**, even in the case of residential property. Nor did the landlord have any ***duty to repair*** defects arising during the course of the lease, unless such a duty was explicitly provided for.

1. **Rationale:** This *caveat emptor* approach dated back to an earlier agrarian economy, in which the tenant was interested principally in the land, not the structures on it. If any repairs were necessary, they were usually ones which he could do himself, since: (1) the structures were uncomplicated; and (2) as a farmer, the tenant presumably had some "jack of all trades" handyman abilities.

2. **No longer applicable:** This reasoning is no longer applicable, particularly in urban and suburban areas. Most residential leases are for units in apartment buildings, and tenants in such buildings typically don't want to do (and may well not be permitted under the lease to do) their own repairs. Therefore, the common-law rule that there is no implied warranty of habitability has generally been ***reversed*** today, as least as to residential property; see *infra*, p. 169.

B. **Independent covenants:** The common law placed an additional obstacle in the path of any tenant who wished to hold his landlord accountable for the habitability of the premises. Recall that the common law followed the doctrine of ***independence of covenants*** in leases (*supra*, p. 157), so that the breach of a covenant by one party would not relieve the other party of his duties (though he could sue for damages for the breach). This meant that even where the tenant had the bargaining power to obtain a clause providing that the landlord would make repairs on the premises, and keep them habitable, a breach of this covenant by the landlord ***would not relieve the tenant of the duty to pay rent***. The tenant could, it is true, sue for damages, but this was cold comfort in view of the legal expenses involved, and the fact that the tenant remained in uninhabitable living conditions.

C. **Constructive eviction:** The hardships of the common-law position were somewhat ameliorated by use of the ***constructive eviction*** doctrine (*supra*, p. 165). If the tenant could show that, due to the landlord's failure to make repairs, the premises were rendered virtually uninhabitable, she could claim that she had been constructively evicted; her duty to pay rent would then cease, and she might be able to get damages as well.

1. **Duty to vacate:** But the constructive eviction defense had one huge disadvantage: as noted *supra*, p. 166, it could only be asserted if the tenant ***left the premises***. To a tenant who because of lack of finances, a housing shortage, or whatever reason, could not feasibly find other shelter, this was a fatal obstacle.

D. **Modern implied warranty of habitability generally:** Beginning in the 1960s, there was a dramatic reversal of the general common-law "no implied warranties of habitability" position. State after state changed its position, either through case law or statute. ***Over forty states*** now impose some sort of ***implied warranty of habitability***. C&J, p. 472, note 2.

1. **Restatement view:** The Second Restatement imposes a general duty upon the landlord to keep residential premises in repair during the course of the lease. Rest. 2d, §5.5(1).

a. **Exceptions:** However, the Restatement recognizes an ***exception*** to such a ***duty*** if the defect is:

[1] the ***fault of the tenant***;

[2] caused by a ***sudden non-man-made force*** (in which case the tenant has the right to

terminate but not the right to collect damages or withhold rent; see *infra*, p. 171); or

[3] caused by the conduct of a ***third person*** (e.g., a robber who wrecks the apartment).

2. **Standards for determining "habitability":** In states that impose the implied warranty of habitability, there is disagreement about the *standards* for determining whether premises are habitable.

    a. **Building code violations:** All courts agree that the existence of ***building code violations*** is at least some evidence of uninhabitability. A few courts seem to hold that any non-trivial code violation ***automatically*** constitutes uninhabitability, even without a showing that conditions are unsafe or unhealthy. But most courts seem to require that the conditions not only violate the building code, but are also a ***substantial threat to the tenant's health or safety.*** B,C&S, pp. 438-39, note 1.

    b. **Absence of building code violations:** The big question is whether the converse is true, that is, whether the *absence* of building code violations automatically means that there is no violation of the warranty of habitability. Most courts indicate that presence of a code violation is ***merely one factor***; thus if T shows that there is a substantial danger to his health or safety, the warranty will be held to be breached even if there is no explicit housing code violation. See, e.g., *Hilder v. St. Peter*, 478 A.2d 202 (Vt. 1984).

    c. **Relevance of nature of building:** At least some cases indicate that the ***age of the building*** and the ***amount of rent charged*** may be considered in determining whether the implied warranty of habitability has been breached. This indicates that a condition which might constitute a breach of the warranty in the case of a new, luxury, high-rise, might not be a violation where the building is a 50-year-old low-rent structure occupied by low-rent tenants. See B,C&S, p. 439, note 1.

3. **Kinds of leases to which implied warranty applies:** The courts are split as to the types of leases to which the implied warranty applies.

    a. **Residential leases:** With respect to *residential* leases, some courts hold that there is an implied warranty of habitability in *all* such leases. Others hold that there is such a warranty only where the lease is for a unit in a ***multiple dwelling*** (so that a single-family house, or, in many states, a two-family house would not be included). Still other states cover only ***urban*** residential property, or only property that is explicitly covered by ***housing codes.*** B,C&S, p. 438, note 1.

        i. **Statutes:** Most *statutes* imposing implied warranties are based upon the Uniform Residential Landlord and Tenant Act (URLTA) and the Model Residential Landlord-Tenant Code (Model Code), which are relatively similar to each other. The URLTA covers all residential leases, as does the Second Restatement (see Rest. 2d, §5.1).

    b. **Commercial leases:** Courts are *split* about whether the implied warranty of habitability should be applied to ***commercial*** leases. Most courts do ***not*** apply the warranty in a commercial context. These courts reason that commercial tenants are on average more sophisticated than residential ones, better able to make a pre-lease inspection, and better able to make repairs when needed.

    i. **Statutes:** Most of the *statutes* imposing implied warranties of habitability apply *only to residential leases*. See Rest. 2d, Statutory Note to Chapter 5, Item 1.

4. **Waiver of warranty by tenant:** Where the implied warranty does apply, a crucial issue is whether and when the tenant may *waive* that warranty. In particular, will a clause in the lease *expressly stating that there is no implied warranty* be effective?

    a. **"Boilerplate" clause:** At least where the waiver clause is a standard *"boilerplate"* clause contained in a standard printed lease, most courts have *not honored it*.

    b. **Statutes:** Most statutes have more or less followed the approach of the URLTA. The URLTA provides, in §2.104(d), that a clause shifting the duty of repair onto the tenant is *unenforceable*. However, such a shifting will be allowed if it is "set forth in a *separate writing* signed by the parties and supported by *adequate consideration*," and is made "in good faith and not for the purpose of evading the obligations of the landlord[.]"

        i. **Upgrading can't be required:** Also, under the URLTA the separate agreement must *not* require the *tenant to do work* to bring premises that are now not in compliance with housing codes *into compliance*; thus L could not lease to T a run-down apartment and require him to fix it up to meet code standards. But the URLTA would permit L and T to make a *separate agreement*, not part of the lease, that T would *keep* the premises in repair, assuming that they *already met* code standards at the start of the lease.

5. **Remedies for breach of implied warranty:** Cases and statutes have recognized a variety of *remedies* for a breach by the landlord of his implied warranty of habitability.

    a. **Right to terminate lease:** Where the breach of the warranty is a material one, and the landlord refuses to correct it after *reasonable notice*, the tenant generally has the right to *vacate the premises* and *terminate* the lease.

        i. **Consequence:** If he does so, he is, of course, relieved from the need to make future rent payments. Furthermore, he is entitled to collect *damages* for the breach, either as a set-off against rent which accrued before the termination and was not paid, or as an affirmative recovery from the landlord.

        ii. **Duty to vacate:** Generally, the tenant has the right to terminate the lease only if he has *vacated the premises*. But probably he is not required to vacate "within a reasonable time" after the breach, as he was in the older cases relying upon the constructive eviction defense (*supra*, p. 166). See B,C&S, p. 442. However, the tenant would presumably lose his right to terminate if he had not moved out by the time the landlord *cured* the defects.

    b. **Right to withhold rent:** In those jurisdictions where an implied warranty of habitability is recognized, most courts and/or statutes allow the defendant the significant remedy of *rent withholding*. That is, once the premises fail to be in habitable condition, the tenant may *refuse to pay all or part of the rent to the landlord*, until the defects have been cured.

      i. Deposits required: A few cases, and nearly all statutes on the subject, *require* that the tenant immediately *deposit* the rent in some kind of *escrow account*, as it comes due each month, at least as long as the tenant remains on the premises.

    c. Application of rent for repairs: A number of cases and statutes allow the tenant to *make the repairs* (either personally or by hiring someone to do them), and then to *deduct the reasonable costs* of those repairs from the rent.

6. Retaliatory eviction: A landlord generally has the option to terminate a tenancy at will at any time (*supra*, p. 161), to give notice of the termination of a periodic tenancy (*supra*, p. 160), or to deny the tenant's request for a new lease at the conclusion of a tenancy for years (*supra*, p. 159). But if the landlord is permitted to exercise his right of termination in order to *retaliate* against a tenant who has asserted his right to habitable premises, the warranty of habitability loses much of its value. For this reason, the doctrine of *retaliatory eviction* has been developed, to *prevent the landlord from terminating* as a penalty for certain acts by the defendant.

    a. Complaints about housing violations: The doctrine is most likely to be applied where the landlord attempts to terminate the tenancy in retaliation for *complaints* made by the tenant to a *housing authority* about *code violations* on the premises.

    b. Commercial leases: Nearly all statutes dealing with retaliatory eviction restrict the defense to residential, as opposed to *commercial*, leases. Virtually all cases appear to do the same.

    c. Dissipation of taint: Assuming that the landlord is found to have attempted an illegal retaliatory eviction, is he stuck with the tenant forever? All court which have confronted the issue recognize that public policy should permit the landlord, at some point, to *remove the tenant*. The general approach is that the landlord may subsequently evict if he can show that his *retaliatory motive has been dissipated*, and that he now seeks to evict for other, legitimate, reasons. The question of whether the landlord's motive is no longer retaliatory is a question of fact for the jury.

E. Premises destroyed or suddenly damaged: If the premises are *suddenly destroyed* or damaged by *fire*, flood, lightning, or other natural elements, the common-law view nonetheless required the tenant to *keep paying rent*, and did *not* allow his to *terminate* the lease. The rationale for this position was that the tenant has purchased an estate in land, and assuming that the land itself was not destroyed, he has gotten what he bargained for.

1. Modern statutes relieve tenant: The common-law rule, insofar as it required the tenant to keep paying rent for premises that were no longer usable, was obviously extremely harsh. Furthermore, the landlord, at least in cases of short-term leases, is much more likely to carry *insurance* against destruction of the building than is the tenant. Therefore, during the 20th century about half the states passed *statutes* changing the common-law rule. These statutes typically provide that if the premises are destroyed or so damaged that they are no longer habitable, the tenant may *terminate the lease* and stop paying rent.

    a. Damage must be sudden: The statutes typically apply only to *casualty-type* losses, i.e., ones that are *sudden* and unexpected. Thus if the premises *gradually deteriorate* because of the elements, the statute will not apply. See Rest. 2d, §5.4, Comment f.

b. **Parties may agree otherwise:** Whether or not there is a statute relieving the defendant of liability, the parties are always free to make their *own agreement* governing the effects of sudden destruction. For instance, where such a statute does not exist, a clause in the lease may require the landlord to carry insurance, and also require him either to rebuild the premises within a stated period, or to release the tenant from rent liability.

c. **Case law in accord:** In state where there is no statute, courts have often as a matter of *case law* allowed the tenant to end the lease (and stop paying rent) where the building has been destroyed. See Rest. 2d §5.4, allowing the tenant to terminate the lease if "after the tenant's entry and without fault of the tenant, a change in the condition of the leased property . . . caused suddenly by a non-manmade force, makes the property unsuitable for the use contemplated by the parties. . . ."

   i. **Termination sole remedy:** Most courts would probably *not* allow the tenant to *recover damages,* or to *abate the rent* while remaining in the premises, in this situation. Similarly, the Restatement explicitly makes termination of the lease the tenant's *sole remedy* in the destruction situation; Rest. 2d, §5.4, Comment f.

2. **Duty to repair:** Destruction or sudden damage to the property may also raise issues of whether either party is required to *repair* it. A statute which relieves the tenant of the duty to pay rent will almost certainly also relieve him of the duty to repair, at least where this duty of repair exists only by common-law implication and not by express promise. The duty of repair is discussed further *infra*, p. 177.

V. TORT LIABILITY OF LANDLORD AND TENANT

A. **Tenant's tort liability:** A tenant, during the time he is in possession of the premises, is treated *like an owner*, for purposes of his *tort liability* to others who come onto the property.

1. **Extent of duty:** A full discussion of the tenant's tort liability to others is beyond the scope of this outline. However, here are a few general rules:

   a. **Trespasser:** The tenant has, generally speaking, no tort liability to a *trespasser* on the property (but there are exceptions).

   b. **Licensee:** One who comes on the premises as a *social guest*, but not for a business purpose, has the right to be *warned* by the tenant of dangers that the tenant is aware of. Such a guest is usually called a *licensee*.

   c. **Invitee:** One who comes on the premises for *business purposes*, called an *invitee*, is owed a full duty of *reasonable care* by the tenant. The latter is not only required to warn of dangers of which he is aware, but is also required to make *reasonable inspection* to discover defects, and to take reasonable steps to correct them.

   d. Some courts abolish distinction: Some courts have abolished this three-part distinction, and hold that a tenant, or any other property owner, simply has a general duty to use *reasonable care* for the safety of anyone who comes on the premises.

   For a more detailed discussion of the duties of landowners in general, and tenants in particular, see Emanuel on *Torts*.

B. Liability of landlord: At *common law*, the landlord is generally *not liable* for physical injury to the tenant, or to persons on the leased property with the tenant's consent. Like the absence of an implied warranty of habitability, the rule of no-tort-liability stems from the view that the tenant buys an estate in the land, and takes the premises as they are.

   1. Exceptions: However, the common law has always recognized certain *exceptions* to the general rule that the landlord has no tort liability to his tenant, or to others on the premises with the tenant's consent. The most important situations where the landlord is liable are as follows:

   a. Concealment or failure to disclose: At common law, the landlord will be liable if he *conceals*, or *fails to disclose*, a dangerous defect existing at the start of the lease.

   i. Landlord should know but does not: This rule applies, of course, where the landlord actually knows about the defect, and remains silent. Most courts also apply it where the landlord does not have actual knowledge, but *should know* about the danger, based on facts which he does know. See Rest. 2d §17.1.

   (1) No duty of inspection: But the rule making the landlord liable for concealment is *not* usually interpreted as requiring the lessor to *inspect* the property for hidden defects.

   ii. Liability to persons other than tenant: Nearly all courts hold that if L would be liable to T, he is also liable to *persons on the premises with T's consent*. See Rest. 2d, §17.1(1). But if L has *told* T about the defect (so that it is not a concealed danger), L is not liable to T's guests even if T did not in turn tell them about the danger. Rest. 2d, §17.1, Reporter's Note, Item 7.

   b. Areas kept under landlord's control ("common areas"): In a multi-unit dwelling or office building, certain areas will normally be *retained under the landlord's control*. These may be areas that the tenant is entitled to use (e.g., the *lobby*, *elevator* and *corridor*), or they may be areas to which the tenant normally does not have access (e.g., the *roof*). Regardless of whether the tenant has access, it is universally held that the landlord has a *duty to use reasonable care* to keep these *common areas* safe.

   i. Third persons protected: Anyone who is *on the premises with the consent of the tenant* may recover from the landlord for failure to keep the common areas safe. The fact that the tenant himself may have been aware of the danger, but has forgotten to warn the guest, will not prevent the guest from recovering from the landlord. (And in fact even if the guest knew of the danger, unless he was contributorily negligent, he will be able to recover.) Rest. 2d §17.3, Reporter's Note, Item 11.

   ii. Security against criminal intrusion: Suppose the landlord fails to install adequate *security measures*, so that the criminals are able to enter the building, and rob and assault the tenants. Although courts traditionally have rejected liability in this situation, on the grounds that there is no duty to protect against the criminal acts of a third person, the tide has turned sharply in recent decades. Most courts now require the landlord to use reasonable care in preventing unauthorized access to the building (though what constitutes reasonable care may well depend on the rent level of the building, the nature of the neighborhood, and other factors). See Rest. 2d, §17.3, Comment 1.

   c. **Repairs negligently performed:** If the landlord *attempts to make a repair*, he may incur liability if the repair is done *negligently*.

     i. **Condition made worse or concealed:** All courts agree that the landlord will be liable if his negligence makes the condition *more dangerous*, or lulls the tenant into a *false feeling of security*. This could occur, for instance, if L told T that the danger had been fixed, when in fact it had not.

       (1) Condition not worsened or concealed: Where the landlord is negligent, but does *not* make the condition worse, or make it look deceptively safe, the courts are *split*.

   d. **Landlord contracts to repair:** The landlord may sometimes be under a *contractual duty* to keep the premises safe; for instance, the lease might explicitly impose upon L the duty to make all or certain repairs on the property. If L has such a contractual duty, and fails to use reasonable care to perform it, about *half* the states now permit T to recover for personal injuries that result.

     i. **Only reasonable care required:** Even in these jurisdictions, L does not become liable in tort merely for having failed to perform his contract. Instead, T must show that L *failed to use reasonable care* to perform the contract. Thus L is entitled to *notice* of the danger, and a reasonable time within which to correct it, even though the contract may not explicitly give him this right.

2. **Landlord under legal duty to repair:** Apart from the above traditional common-law exceptions to the general rule that landlords have no tort liability, modern courts impose liability in additional circumstances. One of these arises from the fact that landlords today often have a *legal duty* to keep the premises in *habitable*, and safe, condition. Particularly in the case of *residential* leases, building codes are likely to impose such a duty upon landlords; furthermore, either case law or a statute may impose an *implied warranty of habitability*, whether based upon building codes or on some other standard. (*Supra*, p. 169.)

   a. **Liability:** When the landlord has such a duty (whether imposed by statute or case law) to keep the premises habitable, she will generally be liable in tort for physical injuries caused by a failure to perform that duty.

   Example: Suppose that the jurisdiction imposes on landlords of residential premises an implied warranty of habitability. L, owner of a one-family house, rents it to T. L then negligently fails to maintain the interior staircase of the house. T trips on a broken stair (which was already broken by the start of the lease) and breaks a leg. Most courts will hold L liable in tort for this physical injury that was proximately caused by L's breach of the implied warranty.

b. **Reasonable care standard:**   But as with liability based upon violation of a contractual duty to repair (*supra*, p. 175), any tort liability based upon the implied warranty of habitability is likely to require a showing of *negligence* on the landlord's part. That is, the mere fact that the premises were not maintained in safe and habitable condition will in most courts not be enough; there must be evidence that the landlord *knew*, or *should have known*, of the danger, and had *reasonable time to correct it*.

c. **Third persons:**   Where liability to the tenant would exist, there will be similar liability to *third persons* on the premises with the landlord's consent. See Rest. 2d, §17.6, Reporter's Note, Item 6.

3. **Admission of public:**   If the landlord has reason to believe that the tenant will *hold the premises open to the public*, and he also has reason to believe that this may occur before a condition which the landlord knows is dangerous has been repaired, most states today make the landlord liable for a negligent failure to repair. The rationale for this rule is that where the safety of the public at large is at stake, the landlord has a higher duty than where only casual visitors are expected; the landlord should not be allowed freely to transfer this responsibility onto the tenant.

a. **Duty of inspection:**   In most states, the landlord of such premises has an affirmative *duty to inspect* them to *find and repair* dangerous conditions. See Rest. 2d, §17.2(3).

b. **Defect must exist prior to lease:**   The landlord is only liable only for dangerous conditions existing *at the time the tenant takes possession*. Rest. 2d, §17.2. Thus if the premises are turned over in good condition, and due to the tenant's negligence the structure deteriorates to a dangerous point, the landlord has no liability even if he is aware of the condition.

4. **General "reasonable care" theory:**   A few courts have simply *rejected* the common-law view that a landlord has no general duty to use reasonable care. These courts have usually reached this result as part of an overall change in the common-law treatment of property owners (e.g., an abolition of the distinction between trespassers, licensees and invitees). In landlord-tenant cases, this change means that it is no longer necessary for the plaintiff to fit himself within one of the exceptions discussed above; instead, he need merely show that (1) the landlord has *failed to use reasonable care* with respect to the property and (2) this lack of reasonable care has *proximately caused* the plaintiff's injury.

5. **Exculpatory clauses:**   Courts are divided upon the effect of an *exculpatory clause* in a lease, which purports to relieve the landlord of any tort liability for his negligence. In keeping with the general broadening of landlords' tort liability, most courts today take a *hostile view* of such clauses, particularly in residential leases, and particularly where the clause is part of a standard "boilerplate" fine-print contract, and the clause is not separately bargained for.

a. **Statutes:**   Nearly half the states have *statutes* invalidating exculpatory clauses, in at least some situations. See Statutory Note to Rest. 2d, §17.3. California, Connecticut, Florida, Illinois, Massachusetts, New York and Ohio are among the states with such statutes.

i. **Residential limitation:**   Most of these statutes apply only to *residential leases*.

6. **Transfer of landlord's interest:** If the landlord *transfers his interest* in the property, this may have an impact upon his tort liability, at least for acts and conditions prior to this transfer. This subject is discussed further *infra*, p. 189.

VI. TENANT'S DUTIES

A. **Duty to pay rent:** The tenant normally has a duty, of course, to *pay rent*; this is one of the things that defines the landlord-tenant relationship.

1. **Breach of landlord's duties:** At common law, as noted, covenants were independent, so that even a breach by the landlord of most of his duties did not entitle the tenant to stop paying rent. Most modern courts, particularly those that have recognized the implied warranty of habitability (*supra*, p. 169) have modified this rule, so that a *material breach* by the landlord of his implied or express obligations at least *temporarily relieves the tenant from continuing to pay rent*. Typically, the tenant has the right to withhold rent (which usually has to be paid into a private or public account as it comes due), to make repairs himself and deduct the amount from the rent, or to gain a judicial abatement (i.e., reduction), of rent. These remedies are all discussed beginning *supra*, p. 171.

2. **Termination of lease:** The mere fact that the tenant has *abandoned the premises* will *not* relieve him from the duty to pay rent. But if the landlord has violated his express or implied duty to keep the property in repair, this may entitle the tenant to abandon the premises and also to *terminate the lease*, under the doctrine of constructive eviction. If he does so, no further rent is due. See *supra*, p. 171.

3. **Termination by landlord:** The landlord may be his own actions expressly or impliedly terminate the lease. For instance, if the tenant abandons the premises without cause, and the landlord takes possession for his own purposes, this will probably constitute an acceptance of surrender by the landlord, so that the tenant's further duty to pay rent is nullified. Termination of the lease is discussed more extensively *infra*, p. 181, in the treatment of landlords' remedies.

B. **Duty to repair:** The landlord, at common law, had no general duty to keep the premises in repair. (*Supra*, p. 168.) By contrast, the tenant had an implied duty to make *minor repairs*, an obligation arising from his duty not to commit waste (*supra*, p. 94). As the idea was sometimes put, the tenant was required to keep the buildings *"windtight and watertight."* For instance, he was required to replace a broken window, or to repair a leaking roof.

1. **Modern change in rule:** However, the widespread imposition of an implied warranty of habitability on the part of the landlord (*supra*, p. 169) has resulted in the shifting of the duty of repair from tenant to landlord. In any lease where the landlord is held to have made such a warranty, replacement of a broken window or repair of a leaky roof will probably be his obligation, not the tenant's.

2. **Express promise to repair:** The duty of repair may still be imposed on the tenant by means of an *express promise* to that effect in the lease. However, the courts sometimes refuse to enforce such clauses, particularly in residential leases.

a. **Ordinary wear and tear:** If the clause is simply a general promise to repair, the court will probably hold that there is no duty to overcome the effects of ***ordinary wear and tear***. In any event, many repair clauses contain an explicit exception for such wear and tear.

C. **Fixtures:** The tenant may wish to take a ***chattel***, i.e., an item of personal property, and ***attach*** it to the land. When the attachment has occurred, the chattel is usually called a ***fixture***. There are two principal issues raised by fixtures in landlord-tenant cases: (1) does the tenant have the right to ***make*** the attachment? and (2) does he have the right to ***remove*** it, and if so, when?

1. **Right to affix:** The tenant's right to affix a fixture is generally discussed in terms of the doctrine of ***waste*** (*supra*, p. 94). Thus the tenant is permitted to make the annexation, under the modern view, if this would ***not unfairly interfere with the value of the landlord's reversion***.

    a. **Duty to remove at end:** Even if the annexation is permissible, the landlord always has the right to require the tenant to ***remove*** it at the end of the lease term. (But, as is discussed immediately below, the landlord may also have the right to ***prevent*** the tenant from removing the fixture.)

2. **Removal:** If the tenant has attached an item to the landlord's property so ***tightly*** that it's fair to regard it as ***part of the real estate*** (i.e., it's properly called a "fixture"), as a general rule the ***tenant may not remove it*** at the end of the lease term.

    Examples: Common examples of chattels that are likely to be found to be fixtures (and thus not removable by the tenant) are ***construction materials*** incorporated into the structure (e.g., bricks, nails, or lumber used in repairs), ***electrical wiring and plumbing***, and ***built-in bookcases and cabinets*** specially designed to fit only the particular space they occupy.

    Conversely, items like ***carpeting*** and ***kitchen appliances*** are likely *not* to be deemed fixtures.

    a. **Factors:** The following factors, if present, argue in favor of a finding that the item is a fixture (and thus ***not removable*** at lease-end by the tenant):

        ❑ the item is ***firmly imbedded*** in the real estate;

        ❑ the item is ***peculiarly adapted or fitted*** to the real estate; or

        ❑ the item's removal would ***destroy*** the chattel, or significantly damage the real estate

        Cf. S&W, § 6.48.

        i. **Contrary lease provision:** But L and T are always free to specify, in the lease, a different treatment on this issue of removeability, and if they do so, ***the lease treatment will control***. This can cut either way: a lease might give T the right to remove fixtures that would not otherwise be removable (e.g., because removal would completely destroy the value of the fixture), or it might bar T from removing fixtures that would otherwise be removable (e.g., an item that could be removed without any damage to either the premises or the fixture itself).

b. "Trade fixtures": Where the item is a so-called *"trade fixture"* — an item attached to the real estate by a *commercial tenant* for use in the tenant's *business* — there is a very strong *presumption* that the trade fixture is *removable* as long as the tenant restores the premises to their original condition. In other words, the *"firmly imbedded"* and *"peculiarly adapted or fitted"* factors described above *do not count for much* in the case of trade fixtures.

> **i. Tip:** Therefore, when you see a fact pattern in which the tenant is a *business owner* who installs the items during the lease term for use in the business, you should *presume that the tenant may remove them* if this can be done without major damage to the real estate. And that's true even if the item was *specially adapted* to the real estate and/or *tightly attached* to the real estate. (Of course, this rule presumes that the lease is silent on the issue of removal.)
>
> **Example:** T rents a building from L in which T plans to run a restaurant. T installs (1) specialty lighting in the ceilings, (2) an elaborate bar that is carefully designed to fit a particular alcove, and that is attached to the wall and floor by strong weight-bearing bolts; and (3) a custom refrigeration system that is attached to the building's ductwork. The lease is silent on whether T may remove the items at the end of the lease. 60 days before the end of the lease term, when L learns that T is not planning to renew, L sends T a letter warning T not to remove the items. T removes them anyway, and L sues T for the value of the items.
>
> As long as T has restored the premises to their original condition (e.g., by repairing the ceilings, walls and floors to remove any holes where the items were attached), T will win, because he acted properly. All of the items were "trade fixtures," i.e., items specially adapted for use in the tenant's trade or business. Such trade fixtures may be removed regardless of how embedded they are in the real estate, or how specially adapted to that particular real estate they are, as long as the premises are restored to their original condition.

c. No right to compensation by landlord: If the item is a fixture that therefore cannot be removed by the tenant (or that could be, but is not in fact, removed by him), the landlord has *no duty to compensate the tenant* for the value of the item, unless the lease expressly says otherwise. That's also true of any other kind of improvement on the premises. And it's true even if the lease comes to an *unexpectedly early end.* 1 A.L.P. §1.81, p. 356.

> **Example:** *O* conveys Blackacre, a piece of undeveloped farmland, "to my son Sam for his life." At the time of the conveyance, Sam is 23 years old. Sam immediately leases Blackacre to his friend Fred for 25 years at a monthly rent of $1,000. With the knowledge and approval of *O* and Sam, Fred immediately builds a house on the premises, reasoning that 25 years is a sufficiently long time for him to derive adequate benefit from the house even though he does not hold a fee simple. Fred spends $100,000 to build the house. Two years after the commencement of the lease, Sam dies in a car accident.
>
> Not only is Fred's lease immediately over (see *supra*, p. 62), but *O* is not required to compensate Fred in any way for the fact that the house has increased the value of the property.

D. Duty to behave reasonably: The tenant has an implied duty to *behave reasonably* in his use of the premises.

   1. Disturbing of others: Thus he must not *unreasonably disturb other tenants*. However, the courts have made allowance for the fact that in modern apartment buildings, a certain degree of interference, particularly noise, is inevitable among tenants.

   2. Obey regulations: The tenant is also required to obey *reasonable regulations* promulgated by the landlord. For instance, a reasonable rule might prohibit ballplaying in the building parking lot.

   3. Health and building codes: Also, most *building and health codes* imposes certain duties directly upon tenants. For instance, the tenant will typically be required to dispose of his garbage in a certain way.

   4. Waste: The tenant has a duty *not to commit waste*. The common-law duty to make minor repairs, discussed *supra*, p. 177, in one facet of this duty. For a fuller discussion of waste, as it applies not only to the landlord-tenant relationship but in other situations as well, see *supra*, p. 94.

VII. LANDLORD'S REMEDIES

A. Security deposits: The lease will typically require the tenant to make a *security deposit* with the landlord, usually in an amount equal to one or two months rent. The purpose of the deposit is to secure the landlord against any damages which he may sustain as a consequence of a breach by the tenant. Typically, this security is left to defray damages caused by *abandonment* of the premises by the tenant, or by misuse by him (e.g, excessively large holes left in the walls from nails and tacks).

   1. Interest: In may states, the landlord is required by statute to pay *interest* on the security deposit.

   2. Right to keep deposit: Once the lease terminates, the landlord must return the security to the tenant, after subtracting any damages which he has suffered. Thus if the tenant abandons the premises prematurely, and the landlord relets on his own account (thus terminating the lease; see *infra*, p. 182), the landlord must immediately return the deposit after subtracting his damages; he is not entitled to keep the deposit until the scheduled end of the lease terms. Rest. 2d, §12.1, Reporter's Note, Item 11.

      a. Regulating statutes: Statutes passed in a number of states limit the landlord's right to retain residential security deposits. Such statutes often require the landlord to give the tenant an *itemized list* of claimed damages as well as *receipts* for alleged repairs. Also, the court may award the tenant double or treble damages and/or attorney's fees if the landlord wrongfully withholds a security deposit. C,S&W, pp. 378-79.

      b. Advance rent: Landlords frequently try to establish a right to keep the *entire* security deposit, regardless of the amount of damages actually sustained. To do this, they often call the security deposit by another name. If the lease labels the payment "liquidated damages" it will almost certainly be struck down, or limited to actual damages.

B. Eviction: The landlord may desire to *remove the tenant from the premises*. This may happen either: (1) during the lease term, because the tenant has failed to pay rent or otherwise violated a term of the lease; or (2) after the lease has expired, and the tenant is improperly *holding over*.

1. Termination during the lease term: Prior to the scheduled expiration of the lease, the tenant may *fall behind in the rent*, or materially breach some other promise made by him in the lease (e.g., by making excessive noise and disturbing other tenants).

    a. Express forfeiture clause: Most leases contain a special clause giving the landlord the right to *terminate the lease* if the tenant fails to pay rent or violates any other lease provision. Such clauses are often called *"forfeiture* clauses." These clauses are in principle enforceable in all courts (usually by means of summary proceedings, discussed *infra*, p. 181).

        i. Breach must be material: However, because forfeiture of the right to remain on the premises is a drastic remedy, courts will generally allow it only where the tenant's breach has been *material*. Thus if T is merely a couple of days late with the rent on one or two occasions, the court will probably not allow L to oust him.

        ii. Waiver: Furthermore, the courts will be quick to find that landlord has *waived* the benefit of the forfeiture clause as to a particular breach. For instance, even if T falls three months behind in his rent (enough so that a forfeiture clause would normally be enforced), if L then accepts T's payment of the past-due rent, L waives his right to rely on this default, at least if he remains silent. But L's right to forfeit is lost only as to this one breach; thus if T falls three months behind again, L can forfeit this time.

2. Summary proceedings: If the landlord is entitled to *terminate the lease* before its scheduled expiration (e.g., because the lease gives a right of eviction for non-payment of rent and the tenant doesn't pay), or the tenant is *holding over* after the scheduled expiration, the landlord may resort to judicial proceedings to oust the tenant. Traditionally, this was done by the common-law action of *ejectment*; but this was a terribly slow, cumbersome and expensive procedure. Accordingly, in all states statutes have been enacted, usually called *summary proceedings* statutes, which provide for a *speedy trial* of the landlord's right to immediate possession.

    a. Defenses which must be raised: The speediness of the proceedings is accomplished partly by *restricting the defenses which may be raised*. Thus in many states, the tenant may not raise the defense of an *implied warranty of habitability* to justify his non-payment of rent.

3. Self-help: Despite the existence of judicial summary proceedings, the landlord will sometimes wish to use *self-help* to evict the tenant. That is, he may attempt to *physically oust* the tenant (e.g., by *changing the locks* when the tenant is out).

    a. Common law allows: At common law, the landlord was *permitted* to use self-help, provided that he used no more force than was reasonably necessary to out the defendant.

b. Modern courts split: But at the present time, with summary proceedings available everywhere, the courts are *split* as to whether self-help may be used.

    i. Prohibition: The modern trend is to entirely *prohibit* self-help, so that judicial proceedings are the only solution. This is the implicit position of Rest. 2d, §14.2. See, e.g., *Berg v. Wiley*, 264 N.W.2d 145 (Minn. 1978).

C. Damages for hold-over by tenant: If the tenant *holds over* after the lease terminates, the landlord is entitle to *damages* as well as eviction. This is true whether the tenancy has been terminated before its scheduled end because of a breach by the tenant, or the term has naturally expired and the tenant refuses to leave.

    1. Measure of damages: The landlord is entitled to the *reasonable value* of the tenant's use of the premises. Often, the amount set in the lease will be a good indication of the fair value; but the landlord may prove that the reasonable value was greater, and if he does, he may recover this larger amount. Rest. 2d, §14.5.

    2. Special damages: The landlord is also entitled to *special damages* caused by the hold-over, if the tenant could reasonably have foreseen that these would occur at the time he held over. Thus if T knows that L wishes to move a business from other premises to those now occupied by T, T will be liable for any damages suffered by L (e.g., loss of profits) that his hold-over causes. Rest., §14.6.

D. Abandonment of premises by tenant: If the tenant *abandons* the premises (and defaults on the rent) before the scheduled end of the lease term, the landlord has three basic choices. Each has sharply different consequences, so the landlord's choice is an important strategic decision which must be well thought-out. The three choices are:

[1] to *accept a surrender* of the premises, thus terminating the lease;

[2] to *re-let* on the tenant's behalf; or

[3] to *leave the premises vacant* and *sue for rent as it comes due* (no longer an option in some jurisdictions).

We'll consider each of these in turn.

    1. Accept surrender: L may treat T's abandonment as a *surrender*, and accept it. This has the effect of *terminating* the lease, so that *no further rent becomes due from T*.

        a. How manifested: Such an acceptance of surrender will occur, of course, if L states that he regards the lease as terminated. But more probably, he will simply take possession of the premises himself, or lease them to someone else.

            i. Consequence: If L either takes possession or re-leases to a third person, and does *not notify* T *that he is acting on the latter's behalf*, then L will usually be held to have *impliedly accepted a surrender*. If L is found to have accepted a surrender, L *loses the right to collect* from T *rent* accruing after the surrender. (For this reason, L should generally try instead to re-let the premises "on the tenant's behalf"; see immediately below.)

    2. Re-letting on tenant's account: In most states, the landlord has the right to *inform* the tenant that he is attempting to re-let *on the tenant's behalf*. This is generally a good idea (for the landlord), since there is **no termination** of the original lease, and the tenant will **remain liable** for: (1) all rents coming due, if no new tenant is found, assuming that L searches for one with reasonable diligence; or (2) the difference between the rent paid by the new tenant and the rent reserved in the original lease.

3. **Right to leave vacant:** Perhaps the most important issue concerning landlord's rights in the event of an abandonment is **whether L must make reasonable attempts to re-let**.

   a. **Traditional view:** The traditional view — and probably still the majority one — is that L has **no duty to try to find a new tenant**. He may simply let the property stay vacant, and recover rent from the tenant who has abandoned, even if a perfectly suitable tenant requests the right to lease the premises.

      i. **Rationale:** The reasoning behind this position is that a lease of real property is not a contract, but a conveyance; T has bought the leasehold estate, and L has no obligation to, in effect, re-sell it for him.

   b. **Duty to mitigate:** But an increasing minority of courts now hold that the landlord *does* have a **duty to mitigate**, by attempting to find a suitable replacement tenant.

      i. **Rationale:** The rationale for this view is that a modern lease is an exchange of promises more than it is a conveyance; therefore, there is no reason why the usual contract-law principle of mitigation of damages should not be applied to it. And the rationale for that contract-law principle is itself sensible: no economic or social benefit is served by permitting the landlord to stand idly by while the premises remain vacant.

VIII. TRANSFER AND SALE BY LESSOR; ASSIGNMENT AND SUBLETTING BY LESSEE

A. **Right to transfer generally:** Unless the parties to a lease agree otherwise, either may **transfer** his interest. Thus a landlord may sell his reversion in the property, and the tenant may either **assign** or **sublease** his right to occupy. (The distinction between assignment and sublease is discussed *infra*, p. 184.) For purposes of simplicity, we shall refer to a sale by the landlord of his interest in the reversion as an assignment by him.

   1. **Statute of Frauds:** There is no blanket requirement that an assignment or sublease be **in writing**. But if the duration of the assignment or sublease is such that an original lease of the same duration would have to be in writing, the transfer must be in writing. (See the general discussion of the Statute of Frauds for leases, *supra*, p. 158.) Where the term of the assignment or sublease is less than this, the states differ; a number of states have statutes requiring all transfers, or just all assignments, or just all transfers for longer than a certain period, to be in writing. See Rest. 2d, Statutory Note, to §15.1, Item 7.

   2. **Privity of estate:** The principal significance of an assignment (whether made by landlord or tenant) is that it establishes a **new landlord-tenant-relationship** between the **assignee** and the original party who did not assign. These two people are now said to be in **privity of estate**. Thus if L assigns to L1, L1 and T are now landlord and tenant, and are in

privity of estate. Similarly, if T assigns to T1, L and T1 are in privity of estate. And if both of these things happen, L1 and T1 are in privity of estate.

a. Significance of privity of estate: The significance of privity of estate is this: since an assignee is in privity of estate with the non-assigning original party, the assignee *obtains the benefit*, and *bears the burden*, of any *covenants running with the land*. What covenants run with the land is discussed extensively *infra*, p. 185; the basic idea is that any promise made in the lease which *"touches and concerns"* the land runs with the land, and affects any assignee.

Example: L and T make a lease, in which T promises to pay $1,000 per month rent, and L promises to keep the premises in repair. T then assigns to T1, and L assigns to L1. Both the promise to pay rent and the promise to make repairs run with the land, both as to benefit and burden. Therefore, *L1 may sue T1 if he doesn't pay the rent*, and *T1 may sue L1 if he doesn't make the repairs.*

b. Sublease distinguished: But a *sublease* by a tenant does *not* establish privity of estate between sublessee and lessor. Consequently, the sublessee is *not liable* to the lessor on covenants running with the land. Instead, the *lessee* and the sublessees become in privity of estate; the sublessee is liable to the lessee on covenants running with the land.

Example: L and T sign a lease, in which T promises to pay $2,000 per month rent. T then subleases to S, S promising to pay $1,500 per month rent to T. Since L and S are not in privity of estate, *L may not sue S for the rent* (though he may sue T, who remains liable for it). T may sue S, since they are in privity of estate (and also in privity of contract, discussed below).

3. Privity of contract: *Privity of contract* exists between two parties to a contract. Such privity can serve as a basis for a lawsuit, even where privity of estate is absent. Suppose, for instance, in the above example, that S made a separate contract with L to pay L $1,500 rent every month, but that no landlord-tenant relationship was created between them. L and S would then be in privity of contract, so that L could sue S if he failed to pay the rent.

4. Original parties to lease: The *original parties* to a lease are *both in privity of estate and privity of contract.* If one of them assigns his interest, the privity of estate between them is ended, but *not the privity of contract.* Since *either* privity of estate or privity of contract can serve as the basis for a lawsuit, a party to the original lease will *not* normally be able to *escape liability* by assigning his interest.

Example: L and T sign a lease, in which T agrees to pay monthly rent. T assigns his interest to T1. L may continue to collect the rent from T, because they remain in privity of contract. But L may also recover the rent from T1, since they are in privity of estate. (Of course, he may only recover from one.)

B. Distinguishing sublease from assignment: Because of the difference described above between a sublease and an assignment, it is important to be able to tell whether a given transfer is one or the other.

1. Assignment is transfer for balance: An *assignment* is the transfer by the lessee of his *entire interest* in the leased premises. Therefore, he must transfer for the *entire remaining* *length* of the term of his lease with the lessor. If he transfers something less than that *(even one day less!)*, in nearly all courts he will be held to have made a *sublease*, not an assignment.

2. **Effect of sublease:** As noted, a sublease creates a new landlord-tenant relationship between lessee and sublessee. Therefore, there is *no privity of estate between the lessor and the sublessee*. Since there is also ordinarily no privity of contract between the two, the *lessor cannot sue sublessee for rent*, or for any other covenant running with the land.

   a. **Right to terminate:** However, if the lessee does not pay the rent, or otherwise permit a breach of the lease (e.g., neither he nor the sublessee makes repairs that are required to be made by the original lease), the lessor may, of course, *terminate the lease*, and evict the sublessee. It is only the right to hold the sublessee personally liable for rent or breach of contract that the lessor loses.

   b. **Lessee remains liable:** The *lessee continues to be liable to the lessor* following a sublease, both under privity of contract and privity of estate, since the landlord-tenant relationship between him and the lessor remains.

   c. **No suit by sublessee against lessor:** Conversely, the *sublessee* may *not bring suit* directly against the *lessor* if the lessor breaches a term of the lease (e.g., failure to make required repairs). 1 A.L.P. 313.

3. **Effect of assignment:** Where the lessee assigns, rather than subleases, privity of estate is created between the lessor and the assignee. As noted (*supra*, p. 184), this means that the *assignee will have the benefit and the burden of any covenants* which were made by the original lessee and which run with the land.

C. **Covenants running with the land:** Any promise has, of course, two sides: a *burden* (someone must perform the promise) and a *benefit* (someone will gain from the performance by the other). The *burden* of a promise made in a lease will run with the land (i.e., be enforceable against an assignee of the promisor) if that promise *"touches and concerns"* the *promisor's assignee's interest* in the land. Similarly, the *benefit* of a promise will run with the land (i.e., be enforceable by an assignee of the promisee) if it "touches and concerns" the *promisee's assignee's interest* in the property.

1. **Promises to pay money:** If the lease contains a *promise to pay money*, and the payment relates directly to the land, the promise probably *runs with the land both as to benefit and burden*.

   a. **Covenant to pay rent:** Thus a *promise to pay rent* is treated by *all courts* as *running with the land, both as to benefit and burden*.

     Example: L leases premises to T at a rent of $1000 per month. T assigns his interest to T1, and L assigns his reversion to L1. At least for the length of time that T1 is actually in possession of the premises, L1 may sue him for the $1000 per month rent, since the benefit of the promise went along with L's assignment to L1, and the burden went along with T's assignment to T1. (The liability of T, and the liability of T1 after he assigns to someone else, are discussed *infra*, p. 187.)

b. Promise to pay taxes: Similarly, a promise to pay *taxes* or other assessments on the property runs both as to benefit and burden. 2 A.L.P. 347.

c. Security deposit: Where the landlord has collected a *security deposit*, there is either an express or an implied duty on his part to return it to the tenant at the end of the term, less any damages caused.

   i. Benefit side runs: The *benefit* of such a promise runs with the land, so that an assignee of the tenant will have the right to get the security back.

   ii. Burden side: But courts are *split* as to whether the *burden* runs, so that only some courts require an assignee of a landlord who has not actually received the security deposit to account to the tenant. See 2 A.L.P. 350-51.

2. Promise to make repairs: A promise to *make repairs* on the property runs with the land *both as to benefit and burden.*

   Example: Thus if T covenants to make repairs, this duty is binding upon an assignee from him, and enforceable by an assignee from L.

   a. Warranty of habitability: Similarly, if local law places an *implied warranty of habitability* upon the landlord, this will be *binding* upon subsequent assignees from the landlord. See 2 A.L.P. 346.

3. Covenant not to compete: If the promise is a promise *not to compete* with the other party, whether the burden and benefit run depends on which side — landlord or tenant — makes the promise.

   a. Promise by tenant: A promise *by the tenant* not to compete with the landlord's use of *other property* the landlord owns or rents *runs as to the burden*, since it directly affects the tenant's use of the leased property. But such a promise does not run as to *benefit* — therefore, an assignee from the landlord cannot enforce it.

   Example: L owns an empty storefront (Blackacre), and also owns a liquor store on different property nearby (Whiteacre). L rents Blackacre to T, and T promises in the lease not to compete with L by running a liquor store during the lease. T assigns to T1. If T1 runs a liquor store on Blackacre, L can sue T1 for damages and an injunction (because T's promise directly affected T's use of the subject property, so the burden of the promise ran). Now, suppose that L sells Blackacre to L1. L1 cannot sue T1 (because the benefit of the promise related to Whiteacre, not to the subject property Blackacre, and thus did not run with a transfer of Blackacre).

   b. Promise by landlord: Conversely, a *promise by the landlord* not to use other property to compete with the tenant's use of the leased premises usually *runs as to benefit* (since it helps the tenant's use of the leased property) but *not as to burden*. 2 A.L.P. 346-47. See also Rest. 2d, §16.1, Illustrations 5 and 6.

D. Rights of parties after assignment: We are now in a position to examine in detail the right and liabilities of the *lessor*, the *lessee*, and the *lessee's assignee*, after an assignment has been made by the lessee. (Assignments by lessor are covered *infra*, p. 189.)

1. **Liability of tenant:** The *original tenant*, when he makes a promise in the lease that relates to the leased premises, is bound to keep that promise both by privity of estate and by privity of contract (*supra*, p. 183). If he assigns his interest, his privity of estate terminates. But *his privity of contract remains*; therefore, the *lessor may still sue him* if the promise is not kept. Rest. 2d, §16.1, Comment c.

   a. **Rent:** Thus where a lease sets forth a duty to pay rent (as does virtually every lease), the tenant may not escape his personal contractual liability for that rent by assigning. If L does not receive the rent after the assignment, he has a choice between suing T (on privity of contract) or T's assignee (on privity of estate).

   b. **Release:** The only way T can escape from his privity of contract with L is if, in conjunction with the assignment, he gets a *release* from L of his privity of contract liability. (If L releases T and get contractual rights against the assignee, all in one transaction, this substitution of parties is called a *novation*.)

      i. **Acceptance of rent:** The mere fact that L has consented to the assignment, and has *accepted rent payments* from the assignee, is *not* enough to release T from his contractual liability.

2. **Tenant's rights against assignee:** Although the tenant remains with his privity of contract liability after an assignment, his relationship vis a vis the assignee becomes one of *suretyship*. That is, the assignee is *primarily liable* for the obligation, and the tenant is only *secondarily* liable. This means that if the landlord chooses to sue the tenant rather than the assignee, the tenant can *recover* whatever he has to pay *from the assignee*. This is true even if the assignee does *not expressly assume* the lease duties when the assignment is made.

   Example: L rents premises to T for $2000 per month. T assigns his interest in the premises to T1, but T1 does not make any promise, either to T or to L, that he will make rent payments. He fails to make payments, but remains on the property. L chooses to sue T rather than T1 (he could sue either). After T is forced to pay the past-due rent to L, he may recover that amount from T1. This is because the primary liability is T1's, based on privity of estate. T's liability, based on privity of contract, is a secondary one; T is simply a surety of T1's performance to L. See 2 A.L.P. 355.

3. **Tenant's right to sue on landlord's promise:** Where the *landlord* has made a promise whose burden runs with the land, the tenant will *lose the right to sue* on this promise if he assigns to someone else, and the breach occurs after the assignment. That is, by assigning, T impliedly also assigns his privity-of-contract right to sue for breaches by the landlord *occurring in the future*. See 2 A.L.P. 354.

4. **Liability of assignee:** Assuming that the lessee's assignee does not make any specific promise of performance when he takes the assignment, his liability to the lessor is based upon *privity of estate*. During the time he is in *possession* of the premises, he is liable for performance of promises made by the lessee whose burden *runs with the land*.

   Example: L leases premises to T, for $1000 per month rent. T assigns to T1. During the time T1 is in possession, he is liable to L for the rent, *even if he did not promise either T or L that he would make payments*. This is because the burden of a promise to pay rent runs with the land (*supra*, p. 185), and must therefore be honored by T1 as long as he is in privity of estate with L (i.e., as long as he is in possession of the leased premises).

a. **Assignment by assignee:** But since the assignee's liability is founded upon privity of estate, that liability applies *only for the period* when the assignee is *actually in possession*. He has no liability for breaches by the principal tenant or prior assignees, and he has no liability for breaches by *subsequent assignees*.

> **Example:** L leases an apartment to T for 3 years. After 1 year, T assigns to T1. (Assume that T1 has no dealings with L, and does not make any promise to T about rent that could be interpreted as assuming, i.e., as undertaking personal liability on the lease; see immediately *infra*.) T1 holds for 6 months, then assigns to T2, who holds for the remainder of the lease term. T1 is liable only for back rent during the 6 months he was in possession, not the time T2 was later in possession.

5. **Assumption by assignee:** In the situations discussed thus far, we have assumed that there is an assignment, but that there is no express *assumption* by the assignee, i.e., no promise by him, either to the tenant or the landlord, that he will perform the promises made by the tenant in the lease. But if there *is* such an assumption by the assignee, the assignee is now bound by *privity of contract* as well as by privity of estate.

a. **Promise made to tenant:** If the promise is made to the *tenant* (i.e., the assignee executes a contract with the tenant, in which he gains the tenant's right to the leasehold interest, and promises to fulfill the tenant's obligations), there is privity of contract between the tenant and the assignee. This has at least one, and probably two, important consequences:

   i. **Tenant may sue assignee:** First, the *tenant* may *sue the assignee* if the covenants are not performed. Even if the relationship rested solely upon privity of estate, the tenant would have the right to do this on suretyship principles for a breach occurring while the assignee remained in possession (*supra*, p. 187). But if the assignee has made an explicit promise, his privity of contract liability to the tenant remains *even after a further assignment*.

   > **Example:** L rents premises to T for $2000 per month. T assigns to *A*, and *A* assumes T's obligations, including the duty of rent payment. Two months later, *A* assigns to *B*. If *B* fails to make rent payments, T may sue *A*, not only for the two months that he was actually in possession (which he could do even without an assumption, based upon privity of estate), but for *all subsequent rents* during the occupation of *B* or any other person.

   ii. **Third-party beneficiary rights in landlord:** Secondly, in most states, the *landlord* is a *third-party beneficiary* of the assumption agreement between tenant and assignee. This means that the landlord and the assignee are now *in privity of contract*. So here too, just as in a suit brought by the tenant, the assignee will be liable not only for duties incurred during his actual possession, but also for duties incurred after a further assignment. Thus in the above example, *A* could be sued by L, just as by T, for the rent accruing after he re-assigned to *B*. See 2 A.L.P. 358.

E. Transfer by lessor: Essentially the same rules apply when it is the *lessor*, rather than the lessee, who assigns his interest. That is, the landlord's assignee has the burden of covenants whose burden runs with the land, and has the benefit of covenants whose benefit runs with the land.

Example: L rents premises to T for $300 per month. L then sells his interest in the reversion to P. Since a promise to pay rent is a covenant whose benefit runs with the land (just as the burden does), P may sue T (or T's assignee) for rents falling due after the sale.

1. **Express assignment of contract right:** The above example, since it refers only to rent defaults occurring after the sale by L to P, is accurate even if L did not expressly assign to P the right to receive rents. This right to receive rents falling due after the sale is an attribute of ownership of the land, i.e., it stems from the *privity of estate* between P and T.

   a. **Privity of contract impliedly assigned:** Furthermore, L loses his right to sue for rents falling due after the sale, because his privity of contract rights is impliedly assigned to T. 2 A.L.P. 354.

2. **Burdens upon landlord's assignee:** After a sale of the landlord's interest, the new owner is *liable* for *performance of any promises made by the landlord* whose *burden runs* with the land. Thus if L promised T that he would *keep the premises in repair*, P, who buys the land from L, is liable for making the repairs after the sale. (This is true even if the premises were in disrepair at the time of the sale; but P is entitled to a reasonable time to bring the property back into shape. See Rest. 2d, §16.1, Illustration 30.)

F. Agreements by the parties about transfer: Our entire discussion of transfer thus far assumes that the lease itself contains no provisions restricting transfer. Most leases, however, contain a promise by the *tenant* that he will not *assign or sublease* his interest *without the landlord's consent*.

1. **Generally enforced:** In most jurisdictions, such a clause is *enforced*, even if the landlord is completely *unreasonable* in refusing to consent to the transfer. The rationale is that the landlord has made a personal choice in selecting a particular tenant, and should not be forced to settle for a substitute, however objectively reasonable.

   a. **Strictly construed:** However, such anti-transfer clauses are *strictly construed* against the landlord. Thus if the clause only prohibits assignment, it will not bar a sublease, and vice versa.

   b. **Waiver:** Also, the landlord may, by his words or conduct, *waive* the benefit of the anti-transfer clause. For instance, if the new tenant takes possession (either under an assignment or sublease), and the landlord *knowingly accepts rent directly from him*, this will probably be a waiver of the benefit of the clause.

2. ***Dumpor's Case:*** Suppose the landlord expressly consents to a particular transfer, or otherwise waives his objection to it; does this bar him from objecting to a *subsequent* transfer? In the famous ***Dumpor's Case***, 76 Eng. Rep. 1110 (K.B. 1603), the court held that *L's consent to one assignment destroyed the anti-assignment clause completely*, because the clause could not be "apportioned." Most American courts continue to *follow the rule* of *Dumpor's Case*.

a. Exceptions: Even the courts which apply the rule in *Dumpor's Case* frequently criticize it. Perhaps as a result, the rule is subject to many *exceptions*, which whittle down its importance.

    i. Sublease: For instance, most courts do not apply it to a consent to a *sublease*, as opposed to an assignment.

    ii. "Expressly conditional" language: Furthermore, the landlord is always free to make his consent to a particular assignment *expressly conditional* upon there not being any further assignments; this would certainly seem to be enough to avoid the rule.

    iii. Language in lease: Also, the landlord can put a clause in the lease itself saying that any assignment shall not be a waiver of the right to object to subsequent ones; this, too, would probably avoid the rule.

    See 1 A.L.P. 305.

b. Minority reject rule: Some courts (still a minority, but probably increasing in number) *reject* the rule in *Dumpor's Case* completely. See Rest. 2d, §16.1, Comment g, rejecting the rule.

3. Consent not to be unreasonably withheld: A growing majority of states now hold, either by statute or by case law, that even where the lease prohibits assignment or sublease without the landlord's consent, the *consent may not be unreasonably withheld*. See, e.g., N.Y. Real Prop. L. §226-b, under which L may not unreasonably withhold his consent to a sublease in a multiple dwelling.

Example: L leases aircraft hanger space to T1. The lease provides that written consent by L is required before T1 may assign or sublet his interest. T1 wants to assign the lease to T2. T2 is in all respects a more suitable tenant (e.g., he is in better financial condition than T1), but L refuses to give his consent solely because he wants higher rents than provided in the original L-T1 lease.

Held, L is entitled to withhold his consent only if L has a *commercially reasonable* objection to the assignment. Allowing a landlord to unreasonably refuse consent violates the public policy of prohibiting unreasonable restraints on alienation. It also violates the principle, increasingly recognized, that there is a duty of good faith and fair dealing inherent in every contract. Therefore, L was entitled to refuse consent based on commercially reasonable considerations (e.g., the financial responsibility of the proposed assignee, the suitability and legality of the proposed use, the need for remodeling, etc.), but L was not entitled to withhold consent merely because property values had increased and the lease was now below-market. (But if the lease had expressly provided that L could withhold his consent even unreasonably, such a clause would have been enforced. Here, however, the lease was silent about whether L could unreasonably withhold his consent, and this ambiguity must be resolved against L.) *Kendall v. Ernest Pestana, Inc.*, 709 P.2d 837 (Cal. 1985).

a. Landlord makes deal directly with proposed assignee: In a jurisdiction prohibiting the landlord from unreasonably withholding his consent to a transfer, the landlord can attack the problem by obtaining a lease provision giving him the right to *make his* *own deal* directly with the proposed assignee or subtenant. If he exercises this option, the original lease terminates, and a new lease with the proposed assignee is substituted. Such a clause will probably be enforced in most states, although Rest. 2d, §15.2, Comment i would not permit such a clause unless it were "freely negotiated."

    i.   **Advantage:** One advantage to the landlord of this approach is that if the proposed assignee is willing to pay *more than the original lease amount*, the surplus accrues to the benefit of the *landlord*, not the original tenant.

4. **Waiver by landlord:** Even in situations where the landlord would have the right to consent to the assignment or sublease, his failure to take prompt action when he learns of the attempted assignment or sublease will constitute a *waiver* by him of his right to block it. See Rest. 2d, §15.2, Comment f. To put it another way, the assignment or sublease that takes place in violation of a provision of the lease is not void, but merely *voidable*.

Example: L leases to T; the lease provides that T may not assign or sublease without L's consent, T assigns to T2. L accepts T2's first rent payment without protest. He then decides that he doesn't really want T2 as a tenant, and declare the lease terminated. L will probably not be permitted to terminate the lease, since he waived his right to do so by accepting the rent and by failing to take prompt action once he learned of the transfer. See Rest. 2d, §15.2, Illustr. 5.

IX. SOME IMPORTANT LEGISLATION

A. **Introduction:** We now consider briefly two types of legislation that play an important part in present-day landlord-tenant law, particularly in the residential context.

B. **Fair Housing Laws:** Congress has forbidden many forms of *discrimination* in rental housing, by enacting the Civil Rights Act of 1968, Title VIII of which is commonly called the *Fair Housing Act*. 42 U.S.C. §§3601-3631. The Act prohibits discrimination on the basis of race, color, religion, sex or national origin, in certain real estate transactions. *Rentals* are covered, except that certain rentals of *owner-occupied* dwellings, and of single-family houses whose owner owns no more than three units, are exempted from the Act. Further discussion of the Act is given *infra*, p. 286.

1. **Unintended effect on minorities:** The Fair Housing Act prohibits only *intentional* discrimination on the basis of race, sex, etc. — it does not prohibit policies which have an unintended disparate *effect* on one race. For instance, a landlord's rule that a prospective tenant's net weekly income must be equal to 90% of a month's rent would not violate the Act, even though it may disqualify a higher proportion of blacks than whites, as long as the policy is not adopted for the *purpose* of discriminating against blacks.

2. **State laws:** A number of state have enacted laws similar to the federal Fair Housing Act. In certain situations, a plaintiff is required to use these available state remedies before he may sue under the federal Act.

    a. **Refusal to rent to children:** These state laws have sometimes been interpreted to bar landlords from discriminating against *families with children* (whom landlords often avoid because of noise, mischief and other bother).

C. Rent control laws: Many cities, and a few states, have enacted *rent control statutes*. Usually, these statutes restrict only *residential* rents, not commercial rents.

1. **How statutes work:** Typically, rent control statutes establish a "base rent" for each unit. Often, this is the market rent prevailing at the time the measure is enacted. Then, the landlord may subsequently raise rents beyond the base rent only to the extent needed to give him a *"fair return."* What constitutes a "fair return" is usually determined year-by-year, and typically depends on increases in the landlord's costs (e.g., labor, real estate taxes, etc.), changes in the Consumer Price Index, or both. Often, the landlord is allowed an extra increase if he makes capital improvements to the property.

2. **Constitutionality:** Rent control statutes are generally *constitutional*, so long as they allow the landlord a *reasonable rate of return*. The most important principle relating to fair-rate-of-return is that according to most courts, the landlord must be given the benefit of a *"hardship relief"* provision, whereby he can get an increase above the stated maximum if he can show special facts (e.g., that he paid market value for the building, but that rents in the building at the time he purchased it were way below market).

3. **Restrictions on non-renewal of lease:** Often, rent control restrictions limit the landlord's right to refuse to *renew* a tenant's lease. This is especially true of rent control statutes that give the landlord the right to an extra rent hike when a new tenant arrives — without a provision requiring the landlord to offer the existing tenant a new lease, the landlord would simply refuse to renew, and rent to a new tenant at the higher rate. See D&K, p. 554, n. 65.

4. **Economic criticism of rent control laws:** Most *economists* criticize rent control laws, on the theory that when rents are kept artificially low, landlords *don't build as much housing* as they would if the market for rents were free, and let the *quality* of the stock they already own *decline*. See D&K, pp. 562-65.

Quiz Yourself on
LANDLORD AND TENANT

41. On July 1, 2011, L and T orally agreed that T would lease L's premises for one year, the lease to commence on August 1 of that same year and run until July 31, 2012. T gave a deposit as called for in the oral agreement. On August 1, when T tried to take possession, he discovered that L had rented the premises to someone else. Does T have a valid cause of action against L for breach of the lease? _____

42. L and T agreed that T would rent an apartment from L for $800 per month. No specific term was set. T took occupancy on July 1, and paid the rent for that month.

   (a) What type of tenancy have the parties created? _____

   (b) Suppose that after approximately two years, T wants to terminate the arrangement. If T gives notice of termination on July 15, what is the date on which his termination will be effective, under the common-law view? _____

43. Leonard leased a store to Terry, for a lease term ending August 30, 2009. In July of 2009, Leonard signed a lease with Tina for the premises, to commence September 1, 2009. Leonard knew that Tina planned to operate a new retail store, and that it would be important to Tina to be selling her Fall clothing inventory starting promptly in September. When Terry's lease term ended, he refused to vacate the premises, and was still there on September 20, at which time he moved out. May Tina sue Leonard for damages for failing to make the premises available to her on September 1? _____

44. Lester, the owner of an apartment building, rented a first floor apartment to Tess. Shortly thereafter, Lester rented ground-floor space (immediately below Tess's apartment) to the proprietor of Heavy Metal Heaven, a rock and roll club. The lease between Lester and Heavy Metal provided that Heavy Metal would conduct its activities so as not to materially inconvenience any tenants of the apartment building. But Heavy Metal set its loudspeakers to the maximum level, so that every night, Tess was unable to sleep until the club closed at 2:00 a.m. Tess decided that she could no longer tolerate the noise, and moved out. She then delivered to Lester a notice stating, "I consider our lease at an end." Lester relet the premises at a lower rate. May Lester recover from Tess the difference between the rent paid by Tess and the lower rent he is now receiving? _____

45. Same facts as the prior question. Now, however, assume that it is a tight housing market, and Tess has not been able to find another apartment at the same (relatively affordable) rate she is paying to Lester. Tess has therefore remained a resident in the apartment, but has gone on a rent strike, notifying Lester that she will not pay any rent until he makes the noise stop. Assuming that Tess continues to withhold the rent, may Lester have her evicted? _____

46. Lila, a notorious slum lord, rented a one-bedroom apartment to Terence for $400 per month. The lease made no explicit warranties regarding condition of the premises. Unbeknownst to Terence at the time the lease was signed, the apartment was (and still is) infested with rats, and the toilet did not and does not work. Terence is quite poor, and cannot pay moving expenses or a security deposit to move to a different apartment. He would like to be able to withhold the rent until the rats are exterminated and the toilet fixed. In a jurisdiction following the unmodified common-law rule on relevant issues, may Terence withhold rent on the grounds that the apartment is not habitable? _____

47. Same facts as the above question. Now, assume that the jurisdiction takes an approach towards the relevant issues that is fairly typical of the way most states now approach the issues. May Terence withhold rent? _____

48. Lena is a professional landlord, who owns a number of apartment buildings in the City of Ames. She rented an apartment in one of these buildings to Troy. The lease provided for a one-year term, with no renewal options. After Troy moved in, he discovered that the heat was inadequate, that the locks did not work, and that other things were wrong. He therefore lodged a complaint with the City of Ames Housing Agency, which is in charge of seeing that landlords obey their statutory obligations concerning residential housing. At the Agency's demand, Lena reluctantly fixed the problems. At the end of the one-year lease, Lena notified Troy that she would not renew his lease. Lena customarily renews residential leases, and gave Troy no explanation of why she would not renew his, though he suspects that this is due to his complaint to the Agency. If Troy refuses to move out at the end of the lease term, and Lena sues to evict him, what defense should Troy raise? What is the likely result if he does raise it? _____

49. Lana, a homeowner, rented her home to Tully in 2011 under a one-year lease, since she was to be abroad on an academic sabbatical for that year. The lease said nothing about the parties' obligations in the event of sudden destruction of the premises. Tully agreed to pay a rent of $1,500 per month. (The house had a fair market rental value of $1,000 per month, but Lana charged less because she liked Tully and thought he would take good care of the house.) After Tully had occupied the house for four months, the house was

struck by lightning, and its upper floor (of two) was destroyed. The house is still "habitable" in the sense that Tully could live there, but only under much less pleasant circumstances (including the lack of a formal bedroom) than he had anticipated.

(a) May Tully terminate the lease and stop paying rent? _____

(b) May Tully recover damages from Lana for his "loss of bargain"? If so, in what amount? _____

50. Ludlum rented a suite in an office building he owns to Trotta. As part of the lease, Trotta gave Ludlum a two-month security deposit. The lease was for five years. After three years, Trotta moved out without cause, and stopped paying rent. Because the real estate market was a tight one, Ludlum almost immediately found a new tenant. Ludlum therefore sent Trotta a letter stating, "I am hereby terminating our lease because of your abandonment of the premises. You will be held responsible for all damages I suffer." Ludlum then relet the premises to the new tenant at the same monthly rent, so that his only losses are the loss of one month's rent ($1,000). Ludlum would like to be able to keep the entire security deposit until the expiration of the original five-year Ludlum-Trotta lease term. May he do so? _____

51. Same facts as the prior question. How could the party to whom your answer was unfavorable have altered the result, either by a drafting change or by subsequent conduct? _____

52. Lombard leased office space to Toland, for a two-year term. At the end of the lease term, Toland attempted to renew the lease, but Lombard refused. One week after the lease expired, Toland still had his furnishings on the premises. Summary proceedings were available to Lombard to evict Toland, but these would have taken approximately two months, and Lombard had a tenant who wanted to take occupancy immediately. Therefore, over a weekend, Lombard entered Toland's premises, moved his furniture into the hall, and changed the locks. When Toland arrived Monday morning, he found his furniture in good shape, but he was effectively out of business until he could arrange to move into new quarters; this took him two weeks, during which time he lost $10,000 worth of business. If Toland sues Lombard for $10,000 in damages, will Toland recover? _____

53. Link leased an apartment to Taylor. With two years to go on the lease (which was for $1,000 per month), Taylor moved out and sent Link a letter saying, "I don't want the premises any more." Link allowed the premises to remain vacant, and notified Taylor that he was doing so. Link made no effort to re-let the premises, though he could easily have done so for about the same $1,000 per month that Taylor had been paying. After the term expired (with 24 months of rent unpaid), Link sued Taylor for the cumulative unpaid rent. May Link recover this amount? _____

54. Lillian, the owner of an apartment building, leased an apartment to Tracey, for two years at $1,000 per month. After one year of the lease had expired, Tracey wanted to travel in Europe for 10 months. She therefore transferred to Stuart the right of occupancy for the next 10 months, reserving to herself the right to occupy the premises for the final two months of her lease with Lillian. Rent payments (at the same $1,000 per month) were to be made by Stuart to Tracey, and Tracey would pass them on to Lillian. Tracey went off on her trip, and failed to make any payments to Lillian. Lillian has now learned that Tracey has become insolvent. Meanwhile, Stuart, after occupying the premises for four months, has moved out, and is apparently not sending rent payments to Tracey. The premises are currently unoccupied. Lillian would like to sue Stuart for both the four payments he owes Tracey covering the time he actually occupied the premises, plus the six payments that became due after he left the premises. Which, if any, portion of this money may Lillian recover from Stuart? _____

Questions 55 through 61 below relate to the following fact pattern:

Lloyd, the owner of Blackacre, leased the property to Thelma for a five-year term. In this lease, Thelma promised to pay Lloyd rent of $1,000 per month. Three years into the lease, Thelma assigned her remaining interest in the lease to Tim. In the Thelma-Tim transaction, Tim did not expressly promise Thelma to perform Thelma's obligations under the master lease, but merely accepted from Thelma a document stating, "I hereby assign to you all my rights under my lease with Lloyd." Tim then moved onto the property.

55. After Tim moved in, he made the first six monthly $1,000 payments directly to Lloyd, and Lloyd made no objection. Then, Tim did not make any payments for the next three months. If Lloyd sues Thelma for the three months during which Tim did not make payments, may Lloyd recover? _____

56. Same facts as the prior question. Assume, now, that Lloyd does not sue Thelma for the missed three months, but instead sues Tim for this period. Assume further that Tim was in residence during the three months for which no rent was paid. May Lloyd recover the three months rent from Tim?

_____

57. Same facts as the prior two questions. Now, assume that after missing three months of rent, Tim assigned to Theo any interest that Tim had in the premises. Tim moved out. Theo took possession, and failed to pay the next six months rent. If Lloyd sues Tim for this six-month period, may Lloyd recover?

_____

58. Now, assume that at a time when Tim was in possession (having received an assignment from Thelma of Thelma's rights, but having not made any promises of his own), Lloyd sold the property (and assigned all of his rights in the property) to Leon. In the sale documents, Leon did not make any promises to Lloyd, and merely gave Lloyd the purchase price. Assume further that in the original Lloyd-Thelma lease, Lloyd promised to keep the premises in repair. During Tim's occupancy, Leon has not made required repairs. May Tim sue Leon for damages? _____

59. At a time when Tim was in possession (having taken an assignment from Thelma but not having made any promises), Lloyd sold the property to Leon, as in the prior question. Tim failed to pay rent for six months while he was in possession. Leon has sued Tim for this rent. May Leon recover from Tim?

_____

60. Assume that the original Lloyd-Thelma lease stated, in a negotiated term, that Thelma would not sublet or assign without Lloyd's written consent. Also, assume that when Thelma assigned to Tim, Thelma (as required under the lease) asked Lloyd's consent, and Lloyd consented because he felt that Tim was at least as responsible a tenant as Thelma. Now, Tim seeks to assign to Theo, but Lloyd objects because he feels (reasonably) that Theo is irresponsible. If Theo takes possession, may Lloyd have Theo evicted?

_____

61. Same facts as the prior question. Now, assume that the anti-assignment clause in the Lloyd-Thelma lease was continued in the fine print "boilerplate" of the standard residential lease prepared by Lloyd, and that at the time that lease was signed, the residential housing market was sufficiently tight that nearly all landlords insisted on imposing similar no-assignment provisions. Thelma now wishes to assign her remaining rights to Tim. Tim is willing to assume all of Thelma's obligations, and is a financially responsible and otherwise good tenant. Lloyd refuses to consent to the assignment, solely because he wishes to raise the rent to $2,000 per month (now the prevailing market rent for such an apartment, because of a rise in real estate prices since the Lloyd-Thelma lease was signed). May Lloyd prevent Tim from taking occupancy?

_____

Answers

41. Yes. The issue, of course, is whether the L-T lease must satisfy the ***Statute of Frauds.*** In most states, the Statute of Frauds does not cover a one-year lease, even if the lease is to commence in the future (and thus even if more than one year is to elapse between the date the lease contract is made, and the date on which the lease itself would terminate). So even though more than one year will have elapsed between July 1, 2011 (the date the lease was orally agreed to) and July 31, 2012 (the last day of the lease), the contract here did not need to be in writing, according to the majority view.

42. (a) Periodic tenancy. A periodic tenancy is a tenancy which continues from one period to the next automatically, unless either party terminates it at the end of a period by notice. One way a periodic tenancy is created is where the parties make a lease without setting a duration; in this situation, the period stated for rental payments is usually the period for other purposes. Since L and T stated the rent on a monthly basis, the tenancy will be a month-to-month tenancy.

(b) August 30. When a month-to-month tenancy is terminated, the last date of the lease is generally the end of a period, but not less than one period later than the notice date. Thus T was required to give L 30 days notice, and the lease terminated at the end of the period that was in progress on the 30th day (i.e., the end of the calendar month in which the 30th day after notice occurred).

43. Split of authority. Under the so-called "American" view, the landlord has a duty to deliver only "legal" possession, not actual possession. Under the so-called "English" rule, the landlord does have a duty to deliver actual possession. American jurisdictions are approximately split between the two rules. In a court following the "American" view, Tina would not be able to sue for damages (and probably would not be able to cancel the lease either). In a state following the English rule, Tina would be able to recover damages from Leonard, and would probably also be allowed to cancel the lease. (But Tina's damages would probably be limited to the difference between the amount specified in her lease and the fair market value of the space; she would probably not be able to recover profits she would have made during the holdover period, since she is establishing a new venture whose profits are speculative.)

44. Probably not. Older cases hold that the landlord generally has no duty to control the conduct of other tenants. But the modern trend is to impute the acts of other tenants to L where these acts are in violation of the relevant leases, and L could have prevented the conduct by eviction or otherwise. See Rest. 2d, §6.1, Comment d. Especially where, as here, Lester had reason to know before he made the lease with Heavy Metal that a significant chance of inconvenience to others existed, the court will probably hold against Lester.

45. Yes. Here, Tess can only claim to have been ***"constructively,"*** rather than "actually," evicted. Where the eviction is merely constructive, the tenant is not entitled to terminate the lease, or to stop paying rent, unless she ***abandons*** the premises. If she stays on the premises, her only remedy is to sue for damages (i.e., the amount by which the premises are worth less to her because of the breach). So even assuming that Lester had a contractual duty to prevent Heavy Metal from making excessive noise, Tess did not have the right to remain on the premises without paying rent.

46. No. At common law, the landlord was not deemed to have made any implied warranty that the premises were habitable, even in the case of residential property.

47. Yes. Over 40 states now impose some sort of implied warranty of habitability on residential dwellings. In most or all of these, infestation of rats and/or non-working toilets would render the premises uninhabitable, and in nearly all, the tenant would be justified in not paying the rent (or at least in depositing the rent into a court-administered escrow fund pending the repairs).

48. **The defense of retaliatory eviction, which will probably succeed.** Many courts and statutes (probably a majority) hold that even where the lease term is at an end, the landlord may not refuse to renew the lease when this is done for the purpose of retaliating against a tenant who has asserted his right to habitable premises. The doctrine of retaliatory eviction is most likely to be applied where the landlord attempts to terminate the tenancy in retaliation for complaints made to a housing authority about building code violations. See Rest. 2d, §14.9, recognizing the defense on the facts of this question. The retaliatory eviction doctrine is more likely to be applied where the landlord is a "professional" (i.e., one in the business of renting residential space) than where the landlord is an "amateur" (e.g., one who rents the second floor of his house). See Rest. 2d, §14.8(2).

49. **(a) Yes.** In most states, either by statute or case law, the common-law rule that required the tenant to keep paying rent for premises that were no longer usable, has been reversed. Thus the tenant normally may terminate the lease and stop paying rent, if the damage to the premises is substantial.

(b) No. In most courts, termination and abatement of rent is the *sole* remedy available to the tenant where the premises are destroyed. See Rest. 2d, §5.4, Comment f.

50. **No.** By terminating the lease, and re-letting for his own account, Ludlum also effectively terminated his right to keep the security deposit. Therefore, he must return that deposit to Trotta (less his $1,000 damages).

51. **Ludlum could have re-let for Trotta's account rather than his own.** The event that caused Ludlum to have to return the security deposit was not Trotta's abandonment, but Ludlum's letter of termination and his re-letting of the premises for his own account. Instead, Ludlum should have sent a letter to Trotta stating, "I have no obligation to do so, but I will try to re-let the premises for your account, not mine. I will hold you responsible for any shortfall between what I am able to get on the re-letting and the monthly rent you will owe." By this technique, the Trotta-Ludlum lease would have remained in force, and Ludlum would remain entitled to the security deposit until the expiration of the five years.

52. **Split of authority.** The modern trend is to entirely prohibit a landlord from using self-help, so that the landlord must use judicial proceedings. But other courts, probably still a slight majority, permit the landlord to use at least some degree of self-help to regain the premises (e.g., changing of locks or peaceable removal of furniture, but no touching of another human being). Lombard's conduct was probably acceptable in states following the latter approach.

53. **Yes, probably.** The traditional view is that a landlord has *no "duty to mitigate"*, i.e., no duty to try to find a new tenant, and that he may simply let the property stay vacant, and recover rent from the tenant who has abandoned. But a growing minority of courts hold that the landlord does have a duty to mitigate (especially in residential leases).

54. **None.** Since Tracey transferred to Stuart only the right to occupy the premises for *part* of the time remaining on Tracey's lease with Lillian, the Tracey-Stuart transaction was a *sublease*, not an assignment. A sublease by a tenant does not establish privity of estate between the sublessee (Stuart) and the lessor (Lillian). Consequently, the sublessee here is not liable to the lessor even on covenants running with the land. Thus Stuart is liable only to Tracey, not to Lillian, and Lillian cannot recover anything from Stuart.

55. **Yes.** Thelma, as the original tenant, had both privity of estate and privity of contract with Lloyd. When Thelma assigned to Tim, her privity of estate ended. But her privity of contract remained. Therefore, she was still liable on the original lease. The fact that Lloyd accepted rent payments directly from Tim, with-

out objection, was not sufficient to release Thelma from her contractual liability (even though this acceptance of rent may have constituted an acceptance by Lloyd of the validity of the assignment from Thelma to Tim).

56. **Yes.** Since Tim never promised either Thelma or Lloyd that he would perform Thelma's obligations, he had no contractual liability to pay rent. But by taking possession of the premises Tim entered into ***privity of estate*** with Lloyd. He was therefore liable for performances under the lease whose burden runs with the land. Since the promise to pay rent is such a "running with the land" promise, Tim was liable.

57. **No.** Since Tim never assumed contractual liability for Thelma's promises (see answer to prior question), his obligation was based only on privity of estate. When Tim assigned to Theo, and left the premises, that privity of estate ended. Therefore, there was no basis on which Lloyd could hold Tim liable for the period in which Theo, not Tim, was the occupant.

58. **Yes.** A promise to make repairs runs with the land both as to benefit and burden. Therefore, Tim gets the benefit of that promise, and Leon gets the burden of that promise (even though Leon never promised Lloyd that he would perform Lloyd's repair obligations, and even though Tim had no privity of contract with Thelma).

59. **Yes.** Thelma's original promise to Lloyd to pay rent touched and concerned the land, and therefore ran with the land both as to benefit and burden. Tim, by taking the assignment and moving in, became in privity of estate with Lloyd, and therefore had a non-contractual duty to pay rent for the time of his occupancy (see answer to Question 56 above). Since the benefit of Thelma's promise to pay rent ran with the land, just as the burden did, Leon got the benefit of this running. Therefore, he can recover not just against Thelma, but against Tim.

60. **No, probably.** Most American courts follow the rule in *Dumpor's Case*, by which a landlord's consent to one assignment destroys an anti-assignment clause completely, even though the initial consent was to a particular assignee. (Lloyd could have avoided this problem by making his consent to the original Thelma-Tim assignment "expressly conditional upon there being no further assignments.") A substantial minority of American courts have rejected the rule in *Dumpor's* case; such courts would allow Lloyd to have Theo evicted here.

61. **No, probably.** Most states now hold, either by statute or case law, that even where the lease prohibits assignment or sublease without landlord's consent, the consent ***may not be unreasonably withheld***. This is especially likely to be the case where the anti-assignment provision is a boilerplate clause imposed on a tenant who has little or no bargaining power (as was the case here).

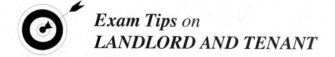

Exam Tips on
LANDLORD AND TENANT

Tenancies — their creation and operation

This is a frequently tested area. Issues to watch for:

☞ **Distinguish:** Distinguish among the various types of tenancies, and be sure to state in your answer which kind is involved. Here are two special kinds (in addition to the ordinary tenancy for a term of years):

☞ **Tenancy at will:** This is a tenancy with no fixed duration. It can therefore be terminated *at any time* by either party.

☞ **Periodic tenancy:** This tenancy continues for a stated period, and *automatically renews* for repeated similar periods unless proper notice of termination is given by either party.

☛ **Tenant's right of possession and enjoyment:** Questions sometimes involve a tenant who is *not given possession* of the premises on time.

☞ **Holdover tenant:** Usually the problem involves a *holdover tenant*, H, who is making it impossible for the new tenant, T, to gain possession of the leased premises. The issue is either: (1) whether T owes rent for the time when T can't get into the premises; or (2) whether T can terminate the lease and recover damages on account of his inability to get entry.

    ☞ **Contrast two rules:** Be prepared to explain that the result on both issues depends on whether the *"American" view* (where the landlord has the duty to deliver *only legal possession*) or the *"English" view* (where the landlord has the duty to deliver *actual possession*) applies. If "American" applies, T owes rent, and can't terminate or recover; if "English" applies, T doesn't owe rent, can terminate, and can recover for breach.

☛ **Condition of premises:** If the premises become *physically damaged* during the course of the tenancy, consider the following:

☞ **Express warranty:** First, consider whether L has made an *express warranty* about the condition of the premises. If so, consider whether that warranty has been breached. Often, the fact pattern will be set up so that there is probably no breach of the express warranty even though there has been some deterioration in, or problem with, the premises.

    Example: A one-year lease between L and T contains a clause allowing T "to give up possession and terminate liability for rent if the premises, through no fault on T's part, are destroyed or damaged so as to be uninhabitable." Several months after coming into possession of the apartment for a monthly rental of $900 a month, T surrenders possession and moves out because of a leaky roof (which leaked from the very beginning). L refuses to accept the surrender, but offers to attempt to re-let the premises on T's account. T declines. T can argue that L has breached his express warranty of habitability. But L has a good argument that (1) the warranty does not cover *deterioration* of the premises due to some latent defect (but only damage by some sudden external force); and (2) the leaky roof did not cause the premises to become completely *uninhabitable*, the only situation covered by the warranty.

☞ **Implied warranty of habitability:** Remember that most states now impose some sort of *implied warranty on landlords* regarding the condition of premises, especially residential ones such as apartments. So if a fact pattern does not indicate whether the common law or statutory law applies, contrast the modern-law implied warranty with the common-law rule (under which L has no duty of repair, and under which because of the independence of covenants even a breach by L would not relieve T of her duty to pay rent). When you talk about the modern implied warranty of habitability, pay attention to these issues:

☞ **Damage by third person:** Courts are split about whether L is liable to repair *damage caused by a third person*; probably most would agree with the Restatement that the warranty does *not* apply in this situation.

Example: Children playing baseball break a windowpane, rain comes in through the broken pane and the living room floor gets warped. L would probably prevail in his argument that because the damage was caused by third persons, L was not required to make the repair.

☞ **Notice:** Make sure that T has *notified* L of the condition which he claims makes the apartment uninhabitable, and has given L a *reasonable amount of time* to make the repair before T has, say, cancelled the lease and moved out.

☞ **Time of departure:** Also, if T has cancelled and moved out, make sure that T did not wait to leave until *after* the condition about which she is complaining no longer exists — if so, T's cancellation is wrongful.

☞ **Substantial impairment required:** Also, remember that there must have been a *substantial* impairment in the use or enjoyment of the property; minor problems won't suffice.

Example: T claims that the apartment is "noisy" because of fights and parties by other tenants. This may not be a sufficiently substantial interference with T's use and enjoyment — it depends on degree. (Also, a given amount of noise may be less damaging if it occurs in daytime or early-evening than if late at night.)

☞ **Commercial vs. residential:** Note that the implied warranty is more likely to apply to a *residential* lease than a *commercial* one. Note in your answer what kind of lease is indicated by the fact pattern.

Fixtures

☛ **Fixtures generally:** Be alert for issues about *fixtures*, whenever a fact pattern indicates that a tenant wishes to remove an item of personal property (originally owned by the tenant) that has somehow become *attached* to the premises. The two main rules to remember about when fixtures may be removed are:

☞ **Damage:** If there will be damage to the real estate from the removal, that cuts in favor of not allowing removal.

☞ **Trade fixtures:** If the fixture is a *"trade fixture"* (i.e., used in the tenant's trade or business), this cuts heavily in favor of allowing removal.

Examples involving fixtures:

(1) If T operates a retail store and puts a prefabricated aluminum structure on the parking lot to be used as an inventory storage shed, this will probably be removable, because it is prefabricated and related to T's business.

(2) Air conditioning units installed by T on the roof of the premises would probably be removable, because they are easily removed without damage to the premises.

(3) If T operates a pizza restaurant and installs specialized gas plumbing in the walls to heat his pizza oven, the plumbing is probably removable as a trade fixture, even though this requires opening the walls (as long as T restores the walls to their pre-lease condition).

L's remedies if T abandons premises

☛ **Landlord's remedies, generally:** Look for a scenario where T *abandons* the premises. The main question to address: Do L's actions indicate the *intent to accept* the surrender? If "yes," then the surrender is deemed accepted and T is off the hook; if "no," then T is still liable for the unpaid balance.

   ☞ **Intent:** So look for particular facts supporting or disputing the finding of intent by L to accept surrender.

      Examples:

      (1) L's silent acceptance of keys from T is probably *not* enough to show intent to accept surrender.

      (2) If L occupies the premises for her own purposes (e.g., for use as a management office for the building) it is probable that a court *would* deem her actions as acceptance of surrender;

      (3) If L re-lets the premises but does not notify T that the re-letting is being done for T's benefit, intent to accept the surrender will be presumed, and L's actions will not be understood as a mere attempt to mitigate damages.

☛ **Duty to mitigate:** Profs sometimes test L's duty to mitigate (by finding an alternative tenant). Distinguish between residential and commercial leases: although an increasing number of courts are imposing upon landlords the duty to try to find a new tenant in the case of residential leases, this is usually *not* the case in *commercial leases*.

Transfer

A number of issues can be tested where there is an *assignment* of a lease.

☛ **Lease prohibits assignment:** Check to see whether the lease itself prohibits assignment. If so, remember that restraints on alienation of estates in land are *strictly construed*. Therefore:

   ☞ **Ban on subletting doesn't ban assignment:** If the lease contains a clause prohibiting *subletting* (where *part* of the remaining leasehold is transferred) then an *assignment* (where there is a transfer of the *entire* remaining interest) would *not* be construed as being prohibited.

   ☞ **Watch for waiver:** Where a landlord reserves the right to terminate a lease in the event of violation of the covenant not to assign, the assignment is *not* automatically void, but merely voidable at the landlord's election. And, according to the "Rule in Dumpor's Case," at common law the landlord's consent to *one* assignment bars him from objecting to *any subsequent transfer* by the assignee.

☞ **Co-tenant's objection:** Notice *who* is objecting to the assignment — a **co-tenant** who objects to an assignment cannot enforce an anti-assignment clause. Such a clause is *for the benefit of the landlord only*.

☛ **Who is liable for unpaid rent:** Assuming that there has been a valid assignment, a common issue is *who is liable* if the assignee does not pay rent.

☞ **Original lessee still liable:** The original tenant *always remains liable* on the lease because she is in *privity of contract* with the landlord (unless she has been released from the obligations of the lease). This point is very frequently tested.

☞ **Assignee is liable on lease only for period of possession:** Generally, the *assignee* of the original lessee can be held liable only for the rent due *during the period of time he was actually in possession* and not for breaches by the original lessee or subsequent assignees.

> *Example:* L enters into a 10-year lease to rent office space to T at $1,000 per month. T occupies the premises for two years and pays rent as it became due. T then assigned the balance of the lease to U, who agrees to be personally liable to L for all obligations under the lease. U assigns the balance of the leasehold to V with several months on the lease remaining. V does not personally assume the obligations of the lease. V takes occupancy for two months but does not pay any rent. V assigns the balance of the lease to W, who does not pay any rent and who abandons the premises at the expiration of the lease five months later. Under these circumstances, V is responsible to L for $2,000 — that is, V is liable for just the amount of rent which was unpaid during his two-month occupancy, not the rent that accrued during W's subsequent five-month occupancy.

☞ **Assignee's assumption is exception:** But there's an important exception to this general rule that the assignee is only liable for rent accruing during her time of occupancy: When the assignee promises the assignor that the assignee will *personally assume the obligations* of a lease there is *privity of contract* between the assignee and the landlord. Therefore, the assignee becomes liable for rent accrued before the assignment went into effect or after it terminates.

> *Example:* After two years of paying rent to L on a five-year lease, T assigns her lease to X, who in the assignment document personally assumes all obligations of the lease. (By this assignment, X will be deemed to be in privity of contract with L.) X, after paying rent for six months, assigns the balance of the lease to Y, who pays rent for two months and then stops paying rent and abandons the premises. X is liable for all rent which accrued during the duration of the lease, including the time when the premises were occupied by Y.

CHAPTER 9

EASEMENTS AND PROMISES CONCERNING LAND

Introductory note: This chapter considers various rights which one may have in the land of *another*. These fall into two broad classes: (1) *easements* (and the related concept of licenses); and (2) *promises concerning land*, which include both covenants that may be enforced at law, and so-called *"equitable servitudes,"* which are enforceable in equity (usually by injunction).

I. EASEMENTS GENERALLY

A. Definition of easement: An *easement* is a privilege to *use the land of another*. Easements can be of either an affirmative or negative nature.

    1. Affirmative easements: An *affirmative* easement is one which entitles its holder to *do a physical act* on the land of another. Most easements are of this variety.

    Example: *A* is the owner of Blackacre. He gives *B* a *right of way* over Blackacre, so that *B* can pass from his own property to a highway which adjoins Blackacre. *B* holds an affirmative easement, since he is permitted to make physical use of *A*'s property (by passing over it).

    2. Negative easement: A *negative* easement is one which enables its holder to *prevent* the owner of land from making certain uses of that land. Such easements are comparatively rare, and do not permit the holder of the easement actually to go upon the property.

    Example: *A* owns Whiteacre, which is right next to the ocean. *B* owns Blackacre, which is separated from the ocean by Whiteacre. *A* gives *B* an easement of "light and air", which assures *B* that *A* will not build any structure on Whiteacre which will block *B*'s view of the ocean. This is a negative easement, since it does not authorize *B* to go on *A*'s property, but allows *B* to restrain *A* from certain uses of *A*'s property. (The negative easement would probably be enforced by an injunction, but might also be enforced by a suit for damages.)

B. Easements appurtenant vs. easements in gross: A second important distinction is between easements that are *appurtenant* to a particular piece of land, and those that are *"in gross."*

    1. Appurtenant easement: An easement *appurtenant* is one which benefits its holders in the use of a *certain piece of land*.

    a. Dominant and servient tenements: The land for whose benefit the appurtenant easement is created is called the *dominant tenement*. The land that is burdened, or used, by the easement is called the *servient tenement*.

    Example: Blackacre, owned by S, stands between Whiteacre, owned by D, and the public road. S gives D the right to pass over a defined portion of Blackacre to get from

Whiteacre to the road. This right of way is an easement that is appurtenant to White-acre. Blackacre is the servient tenement, and Whiteacre is the dominant tenement.

    b. Test for appurtenance: For an easement to be appurtenant, its ***benefit*** must be intimately ***tied to a particular piece of land*** (the dominant tenement). It is not enough that the beneficiary of the easement happens to have an interest in a piece of land that is made more valuable by the easement. Most of the time, in order for the easement to be appurtenant, the dominant tenement will have to be ***adjacent*** to the servient tenement.

2. Easement in gross: An easement ***in gross***, by contrast, is one whose benefit is ***not tied to any particular parcel of land***. The easement is thus ***personal*** to its holder.

    Example: O, the owner of Blackacre, gives his friend E the right to come onto Blackacre anytime he wants and use O's swimming pool. O grants this right purely out of his friendship for E, and without respect to E's ownership of any nearby land. This easement is in gross, and is personal to E, even if E happens to owns a nearby parcel.

    a. Benefit tied to parcel: An easement appurtenant and an easement in gross can usually be distinguished by analyzing the benefit which the easement confers. If it is a benefit which can ***only*** accrue to one who is in possession of a particular parcel (the dominant tenement), the easement must be appurtenant, rather than in gross.

    Example: O owns three lots. Lot 3 is used as a filling station. O conveys Lot 2, but reserves a right of way over Lot 2 (which right of way O intends to use as a driveway to serve Lot 3). When O dies, she devises Lot 3 to her daughter, P. D eventually gains title to Lot 2. P sues for a declaration that she holds a valid easement over Lot 2.

    Held, the easement is appurtenant, since the driveway could only be of use to the possessor of Lot 3. Therefore, the easement was automatically transferred when Lot 3 (the dominant estate) passed by will to P, and P has the full benefits of the easement. *Mitchell v. Castellaw*, 246 S.W.2d 163 (Tex. 1952).

    b. Consequence of distinction: The principal consequence of the distinction between easements appurtenant and easements in gross relates to ***assignments*** and ***division***. Whereas an easement appurtenant passes with ownership of the dominant parcel (as in *Mitchell, supra*), an easement in gross is sometimes not assignable at all, and is frequently not divisible for use by several persons independently of each other. These issues are discussed more fully *infra*, p. 223.

3. Profit: A property interest related to the easement is the ***profit***, sometimes called the ***profit a prendre***. The profit is the right to go onto the land of another and ***remove the soil or a product of it***. Thus the right to mine ***minerals***, drill for ***oil***, or capture wild game or fish, are all traditionally called profits.

    a. Functionally identical: Under American law, the rules governing profits are ***identical*** to those governing easements. Accordingly, all statements made below about easements are applicable to profits, unless the contrary is indicated. See Rest. Special Note to §450, stating that the Restatement does not use the term "profit" at all.

II. CREATION OF EASEMENTS

A. Five ways to create: There are five ways in which an easement may be created:

[1] by an *express* grant (which generally must be in writing);

[2] by *implication*, as part of a land transfer;

[3] by strict *necessity*, to prevent a parcel from being landlocked;

[4] by *prescription*, similar to the obtaining of a possessory estate by adverse possession; and

[5] by *estoppel*.

We'll discuss each of these in turn.

B. Express creation: The most straightforward way of creating an easement is by a ***deed*** or ***will***. Thus *A*, the owner of Blackacre, could give *B*, the owner of Whiteacre, a deed expressly stating that *B* has the right to use a particular strip of Blackacre as a right of way, for a certain period of time.

1. Statute of Frauds: The express grant of an easement must, in all cases, meet the ***Statute of Frauds***, as it applies to the creation of interests in land. This means that there must be a ***writing***, signed by the owner of the servient estate. Also, any ***recording act*** (*infra*, p. 357) will apply, so that if the holder of the easement does not record, he may lose the easement as against a subsequent bona fide purchaser of the servient estate.

a. Short-term easement: Recall that, in most states, a lease for less than one year does not have to be in writing. It could be argued that an easement for less than one year should similarly not have to be in writing. However, a lessee takes actual possession of the leasehold estate, whereas the holder of an easement does not take actual, continuous, possession of the servient tenement. For this reason, most courts require even a very short easement to be in writing; see Burby, p. 68.

i. Restatement rule: But Rest. §467, Comment f, requires a writing only where an estate of the same duration would have to be in writing.

b. Failure to satisfy statute: If the easement is one which must satisfy the Statute of Frauds, and the parties fail to do so, a ***license*** (similar to an easement except that it is revocable at the will of the licensor) will generally be created. See *infra*, p. 230.

2. Reservation in grantor: The owner of land may convey that land to someone else, and ***reserve for himself*** an easement in it. Thus *A* may give *B* a deed for Blackacre, with a statement in the deed that "*A* hereby retains a right of way over the eastern eight feet of the property." This is called an ***easement by reservation***.

a. Statute of Frauds: The Statute of Frauds normally requires a writing signed by the party "to be charged." Since an easement by reservation is enforceable against the grantee, not the grantor, it might be thought that the usual American form of deed (signed only by the grantor) would not be effective as to the reservation. But the courts have held that the grantee, by accepting the deed, and recording it, ***binds himself*** as to the reservation even without a signature. 2. A.L.P. 253.

3. **Creation in stranger to deed:**   At common law, it was ***not*** possible for an owner of land to convey that land to one person, and to establish by the same deed an easement in a ***third person***. As the rule was sometimes stated, an easement could not be created in a ***"stranger to the deed."*** Burby, p. 71.

    a. **Modern view:**   Most modern courts have now ***abandoned*** this rule, and permit an easement to be created by a deed in a person who is neither the grantor nor grantee. Similarly, Rest. 3d (Servitudes), §2.6(2), permits the grantor to create an easement in a third party who is not the grantee.

    b. **Limited exception by other courts:**   Even among courts who pay lip service to the common-law "no easement in a stranger to the deed" rule, an exception is often made for a ***use made*** upon the property ***prior to the conveyance***. See 2 A.L.P. 254-55, n. 2.

        Example: O sells two lots (Lots 19 and 20) to *A*. Lot 19 has a building on it; Lot 20 is vacant, and is used by O's church as a parking lot. O's deed of Lot 20 to *A* is expressly made "subject to an easement for automobile parking during church hours for the benefit of the church. . . ." *A* records the deed to Lot 20, and then sells both lots to *B*. The deed received by *B* does not contain an easement. Several months later, *B* finds out about the easement clause in the first deed, and brings an action to quiet title against the church (i.e., to gain a declaration that the church has no valid easement.) He relies on the common-law rule that an easement may not be created in a stranger.

        Held, for the church. The common-law rule against easements in a "stranger to the deed" is a product of feudal notions that have no relevance today. It not only frustrates the grantor's intent, but is also inequitable because the grantee has presumably paid a reduced price for title to the encumbered property. Here, for instance, O testified that she discounted the price she charged *A* by one-third because of the easement. Nor has *B* relied upon the common-law rule, since he did not even read the deed to *A* until several months after buying the property. Therefore, the easement is valid. *Willard v. First Church of Christ, Scientist, Pacifica*, 498 P.2d 987 (Cal. 1972).

C. **Creation by implication:**   The situation discussed just previously was that in which the owner of land expressly creates an easement. It may happen, however, that two parties are situated in such a way that an easement could be created, but no express language to that effect is used. If certain requirements are met, the court may nonetheless find that an easement has been created ***by implication***.

    1. **Exception to Statute of Frauds:**   Since an easement may normally be created only by compliance with the Statute of Frauds (*supra*, p. 205), creation of an easement by implication is in effect an ***exception to the Statute of Frauds***. For this reason, the requirements for creation of an easement by implication are designed to ensure that there is strong circumstantial evidence that the parties ***did in fact intend*** to create or reserve the easement.

    2. **Summary of requirements:**   For an easement by implication to exist, these three requirements must all be met:

        [1] Land is being ***"severed"*** from its ***common owner***. That is, it's being ***divided up*** so that the owner of a parcel is either selling part and retaining part, or is subdividing the property and selling pieces to different grantees. (See p. 207 for more about this.)

[2] The *use* for which the implied easement is claimed *existed prior to the severance* referred to in [1], and was apparent and continuous prior to that severance. (See p. 208.)

[3] The easement is at least *reasonably necessary* to the enjoyment of what is claimed to be the dominant tenement. (See p. 209.)

3. **Sewers:** One scenario in which an easement by implication can come into existence is where a common owner runs a *sewer line* from one house underneath another parcel to get to the public sewer main. The requirements of severance, prior use and reasonable necessity can be easily met in this scenario.

> **Example:** O owns two vacant side-by-side lots, Blackacre and Whiteacre. Blackacre (but not Whiteacre) adjoins a public street that contains a public sewer main. O constructs a house on Whiteacre, and runs a sewer line from that house underneath Blackacre to the public main. O then sells Whiteacre to *A*, without mentioning the existence of the sewer line either orally or in the deed. Later, *A* sells Whiteacre to *B* and O sells Blackacre to *C*. *C* blocks the sewer line from Whiteacre as it enters Blackacre. *B* sues to have the blockage removed.
>
> *B* will win, because O created an easement by implication, since (1) O owned both parcels simultaneously; (2) the use existed (i.e., the sewer line passed under Blackacre) while O still owned both; and (3) the easement remains reasonably necessary to the owner of Whiteacre.

4. **Severance from common owner:** As noted, an easement by implication constitutes an exception to the Statute of Frauds. To limit this exception, and to guard against false claims, an easement will only be implied where the owner of a parcel *sells part and retains part*, or *sells pieces simultaneously* to more than one grantee. (This is called the requirement of *"severance."*) One of the pieces then becomes the dominant tenement, and the other the servient tenement. This means that an *easement in gross cannot be created by implication*.

Example 1: O owns a two-acre parcel, with a building on each half. The only access from the rear half to the street is by crossing the front half. O sells the rear half to E, and keeps the front half for himself. Provided that the requirements of prior use and reasonable necessity (discussed below) are met, E will gain an easement by implication over the front half, even though the deed from O to E is silent about any easement.

Example 2: *A* and *B* are neighboring landowners. A new street is built adjoining *B*'s property, and the only way *A* can get to it directly is by crossing *B*'s property. He crosses for several years along a particular portion of *B*'s property, and then sells his land to *C*. No easement against *B*'s property could have been created by implication, since there was no conveyance between *A* and *B*. If *A*, or *C* (or one after the other) uses the path long enough, an easement by *prescription* may be created (*infra*, p. 211), but this is a completely different matter. Also, if the new road is the only public way, and at one time in the past the parcels owned by *A* and *C* were under common ownership, an easement by *necessity* (*infra*, p. 210) may exist. But in the absence of a conveyance between *A* and *B*, no easement by implication can exist.

Example 3: O, the owner of Blackacre, conveys the entire parcel to B, There is a swimming pool on the property, and as part of the transfer B promises O orally that O may use the swimming pool whenever he wants. No easement by implication is created, because O is selling his entire parcel, rather than selling part and retaining part. To put it another way, O's easement, if it existed, would be in gross, and no easement in gross may be created by implication. (Nor does O have an express easement, because the Statute of Frauds is not satisfied). O therefore has merely a license, which may be revoked by B whenever he desires. (See *infra*, p. 230.)

a. **Must arise at time of severance:** For an implied easement to be created, it must arise *at the time of severance*, not subsequently.

Example: O owns a parcel, with a house on the rear half and a house on the front half. O conveys the rear half to A, but the deed explicitly provides that A may not use an existing driveway through the front parcel, and must instead use a rear exit to a different road adjoining the rear half. A then sells the property to B, and the deed purports to give B an easement over the front half. At the same time, O orally promises B that B may have an easement over the driveway.

No easement exists, however, either by implication or express grant. This is because an implied easement over the front half could only have been created at the moment the front half was severed from the back half, and the deed from O to A explicitly ruled out such an implied easement. Thereafter, it was too late for creation by implication, and not even O's promise (nor the statement in the deed from A to B) could create an easement. (Nor is O's oral statement sufficient to create an express easement, since it does not meet the Statute of Frauds. B might be able to argue that because of the statement, O is *estopped* to deny that any easement exists; however, this argument is unlikely to succeed.)

b. **Prevented by express clause:** As the above example indicates, an express provision in the deed to the effect that no easement exists will prevent creation of an implied easement, even if the circumstances are such that the easement would otherwise be created. Rest., §476, Comment d.

5. **Prior use:** Most courts require that the use for which the easement is claimed have existed *prior* to the severance of ownership. As the idea is sometimes put, there must have been a *"quasi-easement,"* in favor of one portion of the property and against the other portion, while both were under common ownership. The benefitted portion is called the *quasi-dominant tenement*, and the burdened portion the *quasi-servient tenement*.

Example: O owns two houses side by side on one parcel. To have access to the garage behind house 1 from the street, he builds a driveway which runs between the two houses. To the extent that the driveway runs on the property immediately adjoining house 2, this property is the "quasi-servient tenement"; the property on which house 1 (including the garage) is located is the "quasi-dominant tenement." There is thus a "quasi-easement." If O then conveys house 2, including part of the land and the driveway, to A, an implied easement in favor of house 1 will be reserved (assuming all other requirements of implied easements are met). Or, if O conveys house 1, an implied easement in favor of that house will be granted (again, assuming all other requirements are met).

a. Apparent use: To the extent that a prior use is required, the requirement is met only if the use is *apparent*. That is, the use must be one which the grantee either *in fact* knew about when he received his interest, or *could have learned about* with *reasonable inspection*.

   i. Reasonably discoverable: "Apparent" is *not* the same thing as "visible," however. All that is required is that the existence of the use would be *discovered by a reasonable inspection,* even if not physically apparent to a casual observer.

   Example: Recall (*supra*, p. 207) that a *sewer line* may cross a person's property by virtue of an easement by implication. Suppose that while House 1 and House 2 were under common ownership, a sewer line ran underground from House 1 under House 2 and into the main sewer system. A court would likely hold that at that time, the quasi-easement under House 2 was "apparent" even though not visible, since a plumber could easily have ascertained that the pipes from House 1 ran under House 2. If so, at the moment ownership of House 1 was separated from that of House 2, House 1 received an implied easement for the pipes to run under House 2.

6. Reasonably necessity: According to most courts, an implied easement must be at least *reasonably necessary* to the enjoyment of what is claimed to be the dominant tenement.

   a. Created by grant: Where the implied easement is created by *grant* (i.e., in favor of the grantee), most courts require *only "reasonable"* necessity. Thus the fact that the grantee could use his property to some extent even without the easement will not be fatal to his claim.

   Example: *A* owns both Blackacre and, adjacent and to the east of Blackacre, Whiteacre. A driveway runs from the east side of Blackacre east across Whiteacre, and then to a well-traveled public road. *A* customarily uses this driveway to leave Blackacre. There is a separate much longer driveway running from the south side of Blackacre through a neighbor's land (covered by an express easement) to a much less-well-traveled and less-well-paved public road. *A* conveys Blackacre to *B*. The deed says nothing about any easement across Whiteacre.

   A court would likely hold that *B* has an implied easement over Whiteacre to get to the more-travelled road. That is, the court would likely hold that *B* has a "reasonable necessity" for the easement — the fact that a much less convenient easement exists from the south to a different road probably won't prevent *B*'s necessity from being deemed sufficiently great.

   i. Easement reserved: But where the easement is *reserved* (i.e., created in favor of the *grantor* rather than the grantee), most courts require that it be *"strictly"* or *"absolutely"* necessary.

   Example: Same basic facts as above example. Now, however, assume that *A* sells Whiteacre, while keeping Blackacre; *A* then claims that Whiteacre is now subject to an implied easement in favor of Blackacre. Since the claimed easement was created by "reservation" (in favor of the grantor, *A*) rather than by grant (i.e., in favor of the grantee, *B*), most courts would say that the easement must be "strictly necessary," not just "reasonably" necessary. Since the easement here is not strictly necessary (the owner of Blackacre can use the less-convenient south alternative), a court will likely conclude that the easement by implication does not exist.

7. **Easement of light and air:** A right to have one's *view* remain *unobstructed*, commonly called an easement of *"light and air," cannot, in most states, be created by implication*.

> **Example:** O owns a parcel which contains a house on one half and undeveloped land on the other half. O has intentionally refrained from building anything on the other half, so that he can keep the view from the house (which looks out over the vacant half onto the ocean) unobstructed. O then sells the half with the house to A. Most courts will *not* permit A to argue that he has received an implied easement of light and air over the vacant parcel, such that O may not build a structure on it which would block A's view. To allow such an easement to be implied "would seriously hamper land development." Burby, p. 74-75. (But such an easement of light and air may be created by express grant.)

   a. **Solar energy:** An easement to receive sunlight for the purpose of deriving *solar energy* might more likely be created by implication than an easement merely to "enjoy" sunlight. For instance, if O in the above example had installed solar collectors in the house he sold to A, A might prevail in his claim that O cannot now block the sunlight by building a large structure on the vacant piece.

D. **Easement of necessity:** Two parcels may be so situated that an easement over one is *"strictly necessary"* to the enjoyment of the other. If so, the courts are willing to find an "easement by necessity." Unlike the easement by implication, the easement by necessity does *not require that there have been an actual prior use* before severance. But three requirements must be met:

[1] The necessity must be *"strict"* rather than "reasonable" (the usual standard for implied easements);

[2] the parcels must have been under *common ownership* just before a conveyance; and

[3] the necessity must *come into existence at the time of,* and be *caused by*, the *conveyance* that breaks up the common ownership.

Cf. Rest. 3d (Servitudes), §2.15

1. **Landlocked parcels:** The most common example of such an easement is where a parcel is *"landlocked,"* and access to a public road can only be gained via a right of way over adjoining property.

2. **"Strict" necessity:** While courts say that the necessity must be *"strict,"* they don't mean that the property must have absolutely no use without the access. Instead, they mean that it must be the case that without the easement, the property must not be able to be *"effectively"* used *without "disproportionate effort or expense."* Rest. 3d (Servitudes), §2.15, Comment d. But it's clear that this is a tougher-to-meet standard than the "reasonably necessary" standard for easements by implication created by means of a grant (*supra*, p. 209).

3. **Pre-conveyance actual use not required:** As long as the need for the easement was created by the severance from common ownership, it does not matter that *no actual use* of the claimed right of way occurred before the conveyance.

Example: O owns Blackacre and Whiteacre, two adjacent parcels. Blackacre has a house on it, and abuts the public road. Whiteacre is vacant, and is on the other side of Blackacre from the public road. O conveys Whiteacre to *A*, and the deed says nothing about any access from Whiteacre over Blackacre to get to the road. Since Whiteacre was vacant, while O owned it he had no occasion to create a path or driveway from it across Blackacre to the road. Assume that there is no other public road to which there is access from Whiteacre.

A will have an easement by necessity over Blackacre to get from Whiteacre to the public road. *A* meets the three requirements for such an easement: (1) his need is "strict," not just "reasonable" (since there is truly no other way to get to the road); (2) the dominant parcel (Whiteacre) and the servient one (Blackacre) were under common ownership just before a conveyance; and (3) the cause of *A*'s need for access is the very conveyance by which ownership of the two parcels was separated. Since these three requirements are met, it doesn't matter that prior to the conveyance, the proposed use never actually existed (i.e., O never crossed from Whiteacre to Blackacre).

4. **Need must be caused by conveyance:** For the easement by necessity to exist, the *necessity* must *exist at the moment of the conveyance*, and be *caused by* that conveyance — a necessity that comes into existence *post-conveyance* will *not* suffice. See Rest. 3d (Servitudes), §2.15, Comment c ("Servitudes [by necessity] will be implied only in conveyances that cause the necessity to arise").

    a. **Alternative exists, then disappears:** So if the would-be dominant parcel has some *alternative means of access* at the time of the conveyance, and that alternative means *disappears at some later date*, the dominant holder does not get an easement by necessity.

        Example: *O* owns Blackacre and Whiteacre. The eastern border of Blackacre adjoins the western border of Whiteacre. In 2008, *O* conveys Whiteacre to *A*, with the deed silent as to any right of *A* or his successors to cross Blackacre. At the moment of the conveyance, there are two public roads that serve the parcels: Main Street runs North-South along the western border of Blackacre, and Broadway runs east-west along the northern border of both Whiteacre and Blackacre. (Therefore, prior to the conveyance nobody on Whiteacre ever needed to cross Blackacre to get to Main Street — they would leave the parcel by using Broadway instead.) In 2010, the city unexpectedly closes Broadway completely. *A* now sues *O* for a declaration that *A* has an easement by necessity to cross Blackacre to get to Main Street.

        A will lose. An easement by necessity will only be found to exist when the necessity (1) exists at the *moment of conveyance* by the joint owner of the two properties, and (2) is *caused* by that conveyance. Here, because the necessity did not exist at the moment of the conveyance (due to the availability of access via Broadway), *A* is out of luck. Cf. Rest. 3d (Serv.), §2.15, Illustr. 8.

E. **Easement by prescription:** Recall the a possessory estate in land may be gained by *adverse possession* (*supra*, p. 31). An easement may be created by similar means. Such an easement is called an easement by *prescription*.

1. **Fiction of "lost grant":**   At early common law, courts were reluctant to acknowledge that an easement could be gained without there ever having been consent between the parties. Therefore, they employed the fiction of a *"lost grant"*, by which, in the distant past, it was assumed, the holder of the claimed servient estate granted an easement to the holder of the claimed dormant estate. This "lost grant" could be presumed whenever it would be shown that a particular use had been made from "time immemorial".

2. **Use of statute of limitations by analogy:**   Virtually all states refer to the *statute of limitations* applicable to adverse-possession actions, and apply it *by analogy* to easements.

    Example: In state *X*, the statute of limitations on actions to recover possessions of real estate is 21 years. That is, an owner of record loses his rights to sue an adverse possessor after this time and the latter gains title. *A*, the owner of Lot 1, uses a path over Lot 2, owned by *B*, for 21 years. Assuming that the nature of the use meets the requirements discussed below, after the 21 years *A* has gained an easement by prescription, and may use the path as a right of way forever afterwards.

3. **Use must be adverse, not permissive:**   Just as possession must be adverse in an adverse-possession case, so the *use* must be *adverse* to the rights of the holder of the servient tenement, and not with the latter's *permission*.

    a. **Not in subordination:**   For a use to be adverse, it must not be in *subordination* to the servient owner's rights. Thus if the dominant owner acknowledges that his use is only valid because of the servient owner's consent, the use is not adverse.

        Example: P and D are next-door neighbors. Because he believes in being a good neighbor, and to help P, D agrees that P may use D's driveway to get to P's garage. P thanks D for this, and gives no indication that he is asserting an actual legal right to use the driveway. P's use is clearly in subordination to D's rights, and is therefore not adverse. Even if the usage continues longer than the statute of limitations period, no easement by prescription will be gained. Instead, the use is merely a *license*, which is revocable at will by D.

        i. **Unilateral consent by servient owner:**   But a subordination occurs only if *both* parties agree or appear to agree to it. For instance, assume that in the above example, P claims (even completely without merit) that he has a legal right to use D's driveway. The fact that D agrees to tolerate this use does not convert P's use into a subordinate one. P's use is therefore adverse, and at the end of the statutory period an easement by prescription will be created. This will occur even if D expressly reserves the right to terminate his permission, so long as P does not acknowledge that such a revocation of permission would be binding upon him. This makes sense, since D is at all times free to change his mind, revoke his permission, and start a lawsuit against P if P continues to make his use. If D does not do so during the whole statutory period, it is not unfair to burden him with the use that he has tolerated for so long.

    b. **"Hostility" not required:**   Although the use must be adverse, it does *not* have to be *"hostile."* If the parties make an arrangement which the dominant owner is justified in regarding as permanent, this may be enough to make his use adverse even though there are no ill feelings between the two owners.

Example: Suppose that *A* and *B* are adjoining homeowners. They agree to build a 10-foot-wide driveway between the two houses that will rest half on *A*'s property and half on *B*'s. They split the expenses and create a paved, permanent driveway. Both parties use the driveway continuously. Twenty-five years later, after *A*'s house has been bought by P, and *B*'s house by D, P sues to prevent D from using P's portion of the common driveway.

A court might well hold that, because the driveway was wide and paved, each party intended a more permanent arrangement than simply a license revocable at the will of either. If so, the use by both *A* and *B* would be held to be adverse, and to have ripened into an easement by prescription at the end of the statutory period.

c. **Shift from permissive to adverse:** It is possible for a use to begin as a permissive one (i.e., under a license), and then shift to an adverse one. However, for such a shift to occur, the licensee must openly *renounce* the license and bring home to the licensor that the former's use henceforth is not subordinate.

d. **Shift from adverse to permissive:** Conversely, a use may begin as adverse, and then become permissive if the parties so agree. If the use once again becomes adverse, the statutory period must *elapse all over again*, since the existence of the permissive interval prevents the first and second adverse periods from being "continuous and uninterrupted" (as discussed *infra*).

4. **Open and notorious:** The use must be *"open and notorious"* throughout the statutory period. That is, the use must be such that the owner of the servient tenement is put on notice that the use is occurring. See the analogous open-and-notorious requirement in the context of adverse possession, *supra*, p. 32.

5. **Continuous and uninterrupted:** The use must be *continuous and uninterrupted* throughout the statutory period. A similar requirement exists in the context of adverse possession, but since possession is involved there, the would-be adverse possessor must literally maintain possession continuously. An easement, on the other hand, involves only use, rather than possession; therefore, all that is required is that the *attitude* of *non-subordination* on the part of the user must be continuous, and the use itself must at least be reasonably continuous measured by the needs of the user. Thus in the case of a right of way over a driveway, the continuity requirement would not be violated if the user was out of town for a month, so long as he made reasonably frequent use when he was present.

a. **Occasional use not sufficient:** The continuity requirement serves the same purpose as the "adverse use" requirement, i.e., to prevent a helpful neighbor from unwittingly encumbering his property by tolerating permissive uses or occasional trespasses. Thus if the use is so *infrequent* that *a reasonable landowner would not be likely to protest*, and would view the matter as an occasional minor trespass, the continuity requirement is not satisfied.

b. **Use not necessarily exclusive:** Since an easement is merely a use, rather than a possession, the use does *not* have to be *exclusive*. Thus if *A* uses P's driveway frequently and adversely, the requisite continuity is not destroyed by the fact that *B* also uses the driveway just as often. This stems from the idea that only the attitude of non-subordination, not the physical use, must be continuous. See Rest. §459(1).

c. **Protest by servient owner:** If the servient owner is able to compel the dominant owner to stop the use, either by suit or other means, the requirement of continuity is obviously not satisfied. But if the servient owner merely *protests*, or brings an *unsuccessful lawsuit*, this will *not* be sufficient to interrupt the use. (However, if a lawsuit is brought before the end of the prescriptive period, and the plaintiff ultimately gains a judgment, this will "relate back" to the start of the suit, preventing a prescriptive easement from arising.)

d. **Same person owns dominant and servient estates:** One way the "continuous and uninterrupted" issue can arise is if, at some point during the prescriptive easement period, the *dominant* tenement comes to be *owned by the same person who owns the servient tenement.* In that case, even if a tenant on the dominant property uses the easement, this use will not be "hostile," and the requisite hostile use will therefore be interrupted rather than continuous.

> **Example:** Starting in 1990, O owns Blackacre; *A* owns the next-door parcel Whiteacre. *A* uses a path over Blackacre in an open, hostile and continuous manner for 8 years (the statutory period is 10 years). O then buys Whiteacre and holds it for 1 year. During that year *A* continues to occupy Whiteacre as O's tenant and continues to use the path. Then, O sells Whiteacre to *B*, who uses the path for another 7 years. The issue is whether by 2006, *B* has obtained a prescriptive easement on the path. The answer is "no." That's because, during the 1-year period when O owned Whiteacre (the dominant parcel), *A*'s use was not "hostile" (since it would be deemed to be with the permission of O, now the landlord). Therefore, there will be no tacking from *A* to O to *B*, and *B* will not be deemed to have completed the 10-year continuous-and-hostile-use period by 2006.

6. **Tacking:** Recall that the statute of limitations in adverse-possession cases may be satisfied by combining, or *tacking*, the possession of more than one person, provided that they are in privity with each other. The concept of tacking similarly exists in the context of prescriptive easements. Rest. §464.

a. **Appurtenant easements:** Where the easement is *appurtenant*, the privity required between the users is virtually the same as is required in adverse-possession cases; thus grantor and grantee, landlord and tenant, life tenant and remainderman, or testator and legatee, would all be pairs as to whom tacking would apply.

b. **Easements in gross:** Where the easement is *in gross* (which is possible though unlikely to occur in practice), it is hard to say what kind of privity is required; a caveat to Rest. §463 takes no position on this question.

7. **Difficulty of ascertaining:** How can the lawyer for a purchaser of land tell whether the land her client is about to buy is burdened by any prescriptive easements? There is no easy, sure-fire, way to do this.

a. **Physical inspection:** The lawyer could have her client check the property physically, to see whether there are any indications of an adverse use (e.g., a path cut across the back yard, leading from a neighbor's house to the street). Also, the client could ask nearby residents whether they knew of any use. But since a prescriptive easement, once it has been created, need no longer be actively used (so long as it is not affirmatively abandoned; see *infra*, p. 227), this will not be foolproof.

b. Warranty: Another solution is for the buyer's lawyer to attempt to insert into the deed a warranty by the seller that there are no easements, whether prescriptive or otherwise. Then, if a prescriptive easement does exist, at least the buyer can sue.

F. Easement by estoppel: One last way an easement may be created is by *"estoppel."* An easement by estoppel is created where *A* allows *B* to use *A*'s land under circumstances where *A* should reasonably foresee that *B* will **substantially change position** believing that this permission will not be revoked, and *B* in fact changes position. An easement can come into existence by this method even though the parties never mention the word "easement," or mention the possibility of revocation. See Rest. 3d Property (Servitudes), §2.10 (allowing easements to be created by estoppel, but only if that is the only way to avoid injustice).

> **Example:** O owns Blackacre, which has access to a public road. *A* owns the adjacent Whiteacre, a vacant parcel, which has no such access to any public road. O orally gives *A* permission to use a roadway running across Blackacre in order to get from the public road to Whiteacre. O and *A* don't mention the word "easement" when they work out this arrangement. At the time of this conversation, O knows that *A* plans to build a house on Whiteacre. *A* then indeed builds a house. A court would probably hold that O has given *A* an easement by estoppel. That's because: (1) O should reasonably have foreseen that *A* would substantially change his position in reliance on the belief that O would not revoke his permission; (2) *A* has indeed substantially changed his position in that reliance; and (3) treating the permission as permanent (i.e., making it an easement) is the only way to prevent injustice. See Rest. 3d (Servitudes), §2.10, Illustr. 2.

1. Can be oral: An easement by estoppel may occur **even where there is no writing.** In other words, the usual Statute of Frauds for easements (see *supra*, p. 205) does not apply to easements by estoppel. See Rest. 3d (Servitudes), §2.9. The above Example — in which an easement by estoppel occurs based on O's oral grant to *A* of permission to use the road across Blackacre — is an illustration.

G. Tidelands and the "public trust" doctrine: Apart from the methods described above for creating a formal easement, the *public as a whole* has something like an easement on the *navigable waterways* and on *seashores.* Under the *"public trust"* doctrine, the state holds title to navigable waterways and *tidelands* in trust for the public, and must safeguard the public's interest in these lands. RKK&A, p. 783.

1. Derived from federal law: The public trust doctrine derives from federal law. But it has been left mainly to *state law* to apply the doctrine, so there is variation from state to state.

2. Access to seashore: The most important aspect of the public trust doctrine is that, in states that apply it, the doctrine guarantees to members of the public the right to *use* the "tidelands" portion of the *ocean shore* for *swimming*, *bathing*, and other *recreational purposes*. Tidelands (or the "foreshore") are the shore lands covered by the tides, i.e., the land between the mean high-tide mark and the mean low-tide mark of the ocean. RKK&A, p. 784.

Figure 9-1
Creation of Easements

Use this chart to figure out whether an easement has been created, and if so, what type. For simplicity, the chart assumes that the easement, if any, is an easement appurtenant (i.e., there is a dominant estate which is benefitted by the easement). "S" is the owner of the would-be Servient estate (called "S-acre") and "D" is the owner of the would-be Dominant estate (called "D-acre"). Remember that S-acre (the Servient estate) is the estate that is burdened by the easement, and D-acre (the Dominant estate) is the estate that is benefitted by the easement.

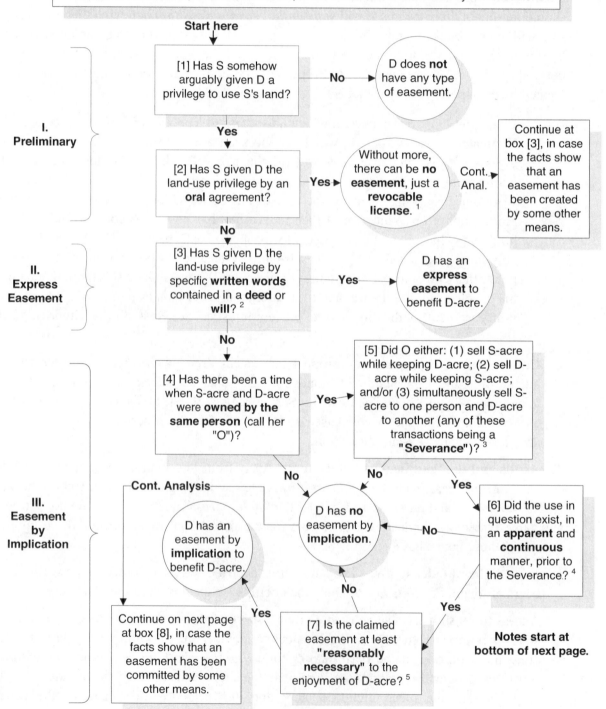

Notes start at bottom of next page.

Figure 9-1 (cont.)
Creation of Easements

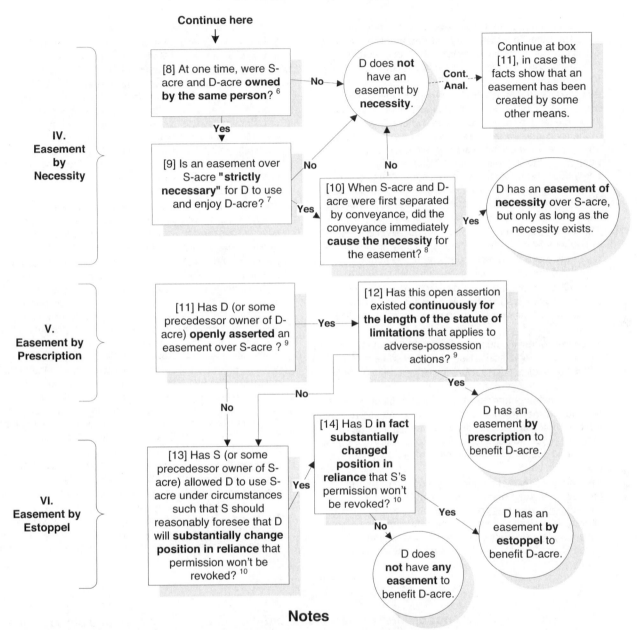

Notes

[1] In other words, there is a <u>Statute of Frauds</u> for express easements. Something that would otherwise be an express easement is turned into a license (i.e., a revocable right to use another's property) by the absence of a writing.

[2] This can happen by either "grant" or "reservation."
<u>Example 1 (grant)</u>: S, owner of S-acre and D, owner of D-acre, are adjacent landowners. S signs a deed (it's a deed even though the only interest it's transferring is an easement) granting D and his assigns the perpetual right to cross S-acre to get to a fishing pond behind S-acre. The deed has created a valid express easement by grant; the benefit of the easement passes with ownership of D-acre, and the burden passes with ownership of S-acre.

<u>Example 2 (reservation)</u>: O owns both S-acre and D-acre, adjacent parcels. There is a pond behind S-acre that O enjoys using. O sells S-acre to S via deed. The deed reserves to O and his assigns (i.e., anyone who comes into ownership of D-acre) the perpetual right to cross S-acre to get to the pond. This deed has created an express easement by reservation.

[3] <u>Example (O sells D-acre while keeping S-acre)</u>: O owns two adjacent one-acre parcels, each with a building on it. The road crosses in front of the front parcel, S-acre. The back parcel, D-acre, is behind S-acre, so that the only way to get from D-acre to the road is to cross along a strip of S-acre. O sells D-acre, the back parcel, to D, while keeping S-acre.

Notes continued on next page

Notes (cont.) to
Figure 9-1 (Creation of Easements)

This arrangement meets the Severance arrangement, and if the two other requirements (boxes [6] and [7]) are met, D will have an easement by implication (enforceable by D's successors in interest as well) to cross S-acre to get to the road.

[4] Example: On the facts of the Example in Note 3, suppose that before O sold S-acre, O's daughter lived in the house in D-acre, and crossed over S-acre (where O lived) to get to the road virtually every day for several years. Since O knew or could easily have discovered that this was happening, the use will meet the "apparent and continuous" requirement. Note that some courts don't even strictly require an actual use prior to Severance, and merely treat such a use as one factor tending to indicate that an implied easement was created.

[5] The required degree of necessity is typically higher when the easement is reserved than when it's by grant -- in the reservation situation, most courts require "strict" or "absolute" necessity, not just "reasonable" necessity.

[6] Notice that although prior co-ownership is required for an easement-of-necessity, there is no requirement of an actual past use, as there is in the easement-by-implication case.

[7] Since the necessity must be "strict" rather than merely "reasonable," the classic illustration of easement of necessity is access from a landlocked parcel to a public road.

Note that although the necessity must be "strict," the dominant owner won't be expected to use an alternative method of access whose cost would be disproportionate to the value of the dominant parcel (e.g., building a bridge that would cost more than the value of the dominant parcel).

[8] The requirement that the severing conveyance be the (immediate) cause of the necessity means that if, immediately after that conveyance, there is a reasonable alternative means of access to the dominant parcel, no easement by necessity exists. And an easement by necessity isn't "retroactively created" if that alternative

method disappears at some time post-conveyance.

Example: O owns Lot 1 and Lot 2, which are adjacent. Lot 1 has direct access to Road 1, and Lot 2 has direct access to Road 2 (but not Road 1). O sells Lot 2 to A, while keeping Lot 1. For 2 years, A leaves Lot 2 by using his access to Road 2. The city then closes Road 2. Even though A's easiest access to a public road is now by crossing Lot 1 to get to Road 1, A does not have an easement by necessity to do this, because the conveyance by O that severed Lot 1 and Lot 2 did not cause the necessity to come into existence (since at that moment of conveyance, an alternate access for Lot 2, via Road 2, existed).

[9] The "open" and "continuous" requirements are interpreted much the same way as they are in the fee-simple-by-adverse-possession scenario. Note, however, that "hostile" use is not a requirement.

Example: D owns D-acre, adjacent to S-acre, owned by S. Beginning in 1980, S allows D and other members of D's household to walk along a dirth path at the edge of S-acre to get from D-acre to a swimming hole on public property adjacent to S-acre. (There is another way for people on D-acre to get to the swimming hole, but it's less convenient.) During each swimming season, D and his family use this path quite frequently. Then, in 2001, S sells his property to X, who immediately blocks the path. If the jurisdiction has a 20-year statute of limitations on ejectment actions (the statute of limitations that would apply to an adverse-possession suit involving actual title to S-acre), D will be found to have obtained an easement by prescription in 2000, and X will not be permitted to block the path.

[10] Example: D owns D-acre and S owns the adjacent S-acre, both vacant lots. Only S-acre has access to the public road. S tells D orally that if D builds a house, D can then use a path across S-acre to get to the road. D builds the house in reliance on this oral promise. Since D has reasonably and foreseeably relied on S's promise, D has a permanent easement by estoppel to use the path to the road.

---

a. **Applies even if property is in private hands:** The state is required to preserve these public trust rights even if the state has transferred the property to *private hands*. Thus even if a municipality were to transfer a particular stretch of ocean tidelands to a private buyer, the public would have a quasi-easement to continue to swim in the tidelands for recreation.

b. **Right of access through private lands:** Most courts applying the public trust doctrine have not just given the public the right to swim in the tidelands, but have held that for this right to be meaningful, the public must have an easement-like *right of access*, *through private dry-sand property,* to *get to* the tidelands. Such courts typically grant the public *both*:

[1] a *"vertical"* right of access (i.e., the right to walk on a path *perpendicular* to the water, running from the street, across the privately-owned dry-sand beach, to the

start of the tidelands); and

[2] a *"horizontal"* right of access (i.e., the right to walk parallel to the ocean on, say, a 3-foot-wide strip of the privately-owned dry sand immediately adjacent to the tidelands, so the public can cross the privately-owned beach to get from one public beach to another).

c. **Right to use beach on private property:** The highest court of at least one state, New Jersey, has gone further. That court gave the public a right to use (not just cross) the *entire dry-sand area* of a privately-owned beach, in *Raleigh Avenue Beach Ass'n. v. Atlantis Beach Club*, 879 A.2d 112 (2005), set forth in the following example.

Example: The Atlantis Beach Club (D) owns Atlantic Ocean beach property in the town of Lower Township, N.J. D has operated the beach as a private club since 1996. (Before that, the beach, though privately owned, was open to the public free of charge.) Only members, who pay an annual membership fee of $700, are permitted anywhere on the beach. Non-members, even ones living immediately adjacent to the beach, are evicted by D, and sometimes charged with trespass, if they enter the beach. The Ps (an Association of nearby residents) sues to establish that under the public trust doctrine, they have the right to access at least some part of the dry-sand portion of D's beach.

Held, for the Ps. Under prior New Jersey case law, "a bather's right in the upland sands [i.e., the dry sand area that is not wet even at high-tide] is not limited to passage ... [and] reasonable enjoyment of the foreshore [the wet portion of the shore] and the sea cannot be realized unless some enjoyment of the dry sand area is also allowed." Just how much of the dry sand portion may be used by the public in any particular case will depend on four factors: (1) location of the dry sand area in relation to the fore-shore; (2) extent and availability of nearby publicly-owned dry sand areas; (3) nature and extent of the public demand for access to the private dry sand area; and (4) the nature of the owner's usage of the dry sand area.

In the present case, all of these factors point towards allowing the public to use the entire dry sand area owned by D. For example, with respect to factor (4) (nature of owner's use), for at least 10 years prior to 1996, perhaps more, D or its predecessor allowed the public access to this beach. Furthermore, a public permit issued to a nearby condominium recited that this beach would have public access. Also, D is operating a "business enterprise" (apparently justifying broader public access than if, say, the beach was used non-commercially and only by individual beachfront land-owners).

Therefore, the Ds must permit public access to the entire dry sand area, under a fee schedule to be approved by the state Department of Environmental Protection. The fees may cover only the costs actually incurred by the Ds in providing services (e.g., lifeguards, trash removal, administration). *Raleigh Avenue Beach Ass'n. v. Atlantis Beach Club, supra*.

III. SCOPE OF EASEMENTS

A. General rules: Once it is established that an easement exists, questions arise as to the *types* of uses to which it may be put by the holder of the easement, and the rights of the owner of the servient tenement. The manner in which the easement was created often has an important bearing on these questions.

    1. Expressly created easement: Where the easement is created by an *express* written conveyance, the terms of that conveyance will normally control. Such a grant will usually spell out not only the physical area involved (e.g., "a ten-foot strip along the entire southern border of the property"), but will also generally spell out the allowable use (e.g, as a right of way for the delivering of coal to the coal chute at the back of *A*'s property"). If the conveyance is ambiguous, the court will look at the circumstances surrounding its making to determine the parties' intent.

    2. Implied easement: If the easement is created by *implication*, the court will look to the use as it existed prior to the conveyance. That use, and any similar use which the parties might reasonably have expected, will be permitted. Burby, p. 83.

    3. Prescriptive easement: When the easement was created by *prescription*, the allowable use is determined by reference to the adverse use that continued during the statutory period and created the easement. The holder of the easement is not restricted to the precise use which occurred during the prescriptive period; he is, however, limited to the same *general pattern* of use. Rest. §478, Comment a. Another way of putting the test is that the present use must be sufficiently similar to the older use that the court may conclude that the property owner *would not have objected* to this new use (just as he did not object to the old one).

        a. Increase in burden: One important factor is whether the new use represents a *greater burden* on the servient tenement than the old use. The bigger the increase in burden, the less likely the court will be to permit the new use.

        Example: A right-of-way easement is created by prescription in favor of the sole house then located on a dominant tenement. After the easement is created, two more houses are built on the dominant property.

        Held, the residents of all three houses may use the right of way, since the basic use (as a pedestrian right of way) remains unchanged, and the increased burden is slight or nil. *Baldwin v. Boston & M.R.R.,* 63 N.E. 428 (Mass. 1902).

    4. Enlargement by prescription: Regardless of the original use, an easement can always be *enlarged by prescription*. For instance, suppose that a conveyance grants an easement as a right of way "solely for pedestrians." If the path is used by an adjoining landowner as an automobile right of way for longer than the statute of limitations period, the use will have been expanded by prescription to include automobiles. See Burby, p. 86. (But the new use must be sufficiently different from the old one that the owner of the servient tenement is placed on notice that an expanded right is being claimed.)

B. Development of dominant estate: It frequently happens that the dominant estate undergoes a general *change in use*. The question then arises whether such a change justifies a corresponding change in the use to which the easement may be put.

1. **Normal development:** The court will usually allow a use that arises from the ***normal, foreseeable, development*** of the dominant estate, where this would ***not impose an unreasonable burden*** on the servient estate. See Rest. §§479 and 484. The *Baldwin* case, *supra,* is an example of this, since it was reasonably foreseeable that the dominant parcel would someday have more than one dwelling on it.

2. **Excessive use:** On the other hand, an increased use that ***unreasonably interferes with the use of the servient estate,*** viewed in light of the parties' original understanding about how the easement would be used, will ***not*** be allowed.

   > **Example:** Suppose Steve owns Whiteacre, and Don owns the adjacent Blackacre. Each has a single-family house located on a 1/4 acre parcel. Both parcels are zoned single family. Steve gives Don a 10-foot wide easement to drive to the public way abutting Whiteacre. Years later, Don's property is re-zoned to allow a 40-story apartment building. Don erects a 39-story building with 300 apartments. Tenants use the easement to cross Steve's property an average of 400 times per day, including late at night. A court would probably hold that the expanded use is so beyond that contemplated by the parties, and so unreasonably interferes with Steve's use of the servient tenement, that it is beyond the scope of the easement.

3. **Remedy for misuse is injunction or damages, not forfeiture:** Even where the holder of the dominant estate misuses the easement (by excessive use, or by a use that is at odds with the purpose of the easement), the servient holder's proper remedy will be an injunction against further misuse, or damages, ***not forfeiture*** of the easement.

C. **Use for benefit of additional property:** An easement appurtenant is, by definition, used for the benefit of a particular dominant estate. The holder of that dominant estate will normally ***not*** be allowed to extend his use of the easement so that ***additional*** property owned by him (or by others) is benefitted. This is true even if the use for the benefit of the additional property does ***not*** increase the ***burden*** on the servient estate.

Example: D owns parcel *A* and P owns parcel *B*. Parcel *A* stands between parcel *B* and the roadway. Parcel *C* is on the other side of parcel *B*, even more landlocked. An easement has long existed across parcel *A* for the benefit of parcel *B*. (Thus parcel *A* is the servient tenement and parcel *B* is the dominant tenement.) P now builds a house that is located partly on parcel *B* and partly on parcel *C*. P also builds a driveway leading from the easement across *B*, then across C, then back to the house:

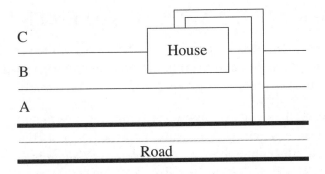

D asserts that P has no right to use the easement for the benefit of parcel C, and therefore blocks the easement. P sues to have the obstruction removed, and D counterclaims for trespass.

Held, for D. "[A]n easement appurtenant to one parcel of land may not be extended by the owner of the dominant estate to other parcels owned by him, whether adjoining or distinct tracts to which the easement is not appurtenant." The express grant of easement from D's predecessor to P's predecessor made it clear that only parcel *B*, not parcel *C*, was to be the dominant tenement. Therefore, when P built the house partly on parcel C, and built the driveway so that it crossed parcel *C* on the way to the house, P was attempting to misuse the easement by extending it to cover another parcel. This amounted to trespass, for which D can recover damages. This is true even though the burden on parcel *A* was not increased by this scheme (since the easement previously served a house located solely on parcel *B*, and that house was replaced by a single house straddling the *B-C* boundary). However, D may not be given an injunction against P's continued use of the easement, because the appellate court will respect the trial court's finding that there was no "actual and substantial injury" to D, one of the requirements for an injunction. (A dissent argues that an injunction should be given to D against trespass, even though the burden to D's property has not been increased by the misuse.) *Brown v. Voss*, 715 P.2d 514 (Wash. 1986).

D. Use of servient estate: To the extent that the holder of the easement gains rights over the servient tenement, the owner of that servient tenement loses the ability to make unrestricted use of his property. However, he may nonetheless make ***any use of the servient tenement*** that does ***not unreasonably interfere*** with the easement. S&W (3d), §8.9, p. 459.

1. No right to relocate easement traditionally: If the easement is for a ***particular portion*** of the servient tenement, the traditional common-law rule has been that the servient owner may ***not relocate*** the easement, by forcing the easement holder to use a ***different*** portion of the servient estate.

   a. Modern view is different: But the traditional rule that the servient owner may not force the easement holder to relocate the easement seems to be ***giving way.*** Thus the Third Restatement (Servitudes), in §4.8, Comment f, says that the servient owner ***may*** change the location if the change ***does not "significantly lessen the utility*** of the easement, ***increase the burdens*** on the holder of the easement in its use or benefit, or ***frustrate the purpose*** for which the easement was created." Cf. DKA&S, p. 725 (the Restatement rule is "gaining adherents").

IV. REPAIR AND MAINTENANCE OF EASEMENTS

A. Servient owner not obligated to maintain: The owner of the ***servient estate*** is ***not required to repair or maintain*** the property used in the easement (e.g., a road or driveway), unless the parties expressly provide otherwise.

   Example: *A*, the owner of Blackacre, grants an easement to *B*, the owner of the adjacent Whiteacre, whereby *B* may use a 10-foot strip of Blackacre to drive his car from Whiteacre to the public road. At the time the easement is granted, there is a bridge that the strip crosses. The easement document is silent about repairs. After the grant of the easement, the bridge washes out. *A* has no obligation to restore the bridge, even if the lack of maintenance means that *B* cannot use the easement as the parties intended. Rest. 3d (Serv.), § 4.13(2).

B. Dominant owner has right to maintain: Conversely, the ***holder of the easement*** has an implied ***right*** to maintain the property used in the easement, if that maintenance is compatible with the intended use of the easement and does not unreasonably interfere with the servient owner's use of the servient estate. Rest. 3d (Serv.), § 4.10, Comm. e.

> **Example:** Same facts as in the above example. *B*, the holder of easement, has a right to rebuild the bridge at his own expense.

1. Limited right to contribution: If the holder of the easement *does* exercise his right to spend money to repair the easement property, normally that holder has the right to ***contribution*** from the holder of the servient estate, but only in an amount that is proportional to the servient holder's ***share of the overall usage benefit*** from the repairs. Thus if all the benefits from using the easement are enjoyed by easement holder, the dominant holder will have no reimbursement obligation. Rest. 3d (Serv.), § 4.13(3).

> **Example:** The same facts as in the above two examples. After *B* (the easement holder) spends $50,000 to repair the bridge, *A* (the servient owner) rarely drives across the restored bridge. *A* has no duty to reimburse *B* for any portion of the repairs. But if *A* uses the bridge as often as *B*, *A* will likely be found to have an obligation to reimburse *B* for half of the $50,000 expenditure.

V. TRANSFER AND SUBDIVISION OF EASEMENTS

A. Transfer of burden: When title to the ***servient estate*** is transferred, the burden of the easement ***remains*** with the property. An easement is just like any other encumbrance upon real estate (e.g., a mortgage) in this respect.

Example: O, the owner of Blackacre, gives *A*, a neighboring landowner, a right of way over Blackacre. O then sells Blackacre to *B*. Following the sale, the easement remains valid against Blackacre; that is, it runs with the land, rather than being personal to O.

1. Subdivision: Similarly, if the servient estate is ***subdivided***, the burden of an easement still attaches to the same parts of the land as before. Of course, the easement may only burden a portion of a larger parcel; after the subdivision, only the portion containing the burdened land will be encumbered. Thus in the above example, if O sold half his property (the half containing the right of way) to *B*, and the other half to C, only *B*'s portion would be subject to the easement.

B. Transfer of benefit: Most of the questions regarding transfer and subdivision involve the *benefit side*.

1. Transfer of easements appurtenant: An easement ***appurtenant*** will normally ***pass with the transfer of the dominant estate***. The new owner of the dominant estate has full rights to the easement, and the transferor loses his rights to the easement. Rest. §487.

a. **Where deed is silent:** This rule — that the easement appurtenant passes with the transfer of the dominant estate — applies even if the deed of transfer *does not mention the easement.*

> **Example:** O owns two adjoining parcels, Lot 1 and Lot 2. He sells Lot 1 to *A*, and in the deed grants *A* the right to use a driveway on Lot 2. *A* then sells Lot 1 to *B*. The deed from *A* to *B* does not mention the easement. Because the easement is appurtenant to Lot 1, the easement automatically passes with the transfer of Lot 1 to *B*.

b. **Exceptions to automatic transfer:** The general rule that an easement appurtenant is automatically transferred together with the dominant estate, applies *unless there is a contrary agreement.* Such a contrary agreement may occur either at the time the easement is created, or at the time the dominant estate is transferred.

> **Example:** Same facts as above example. This time, however, O's deed to *A* expressly provides that this right of way will exist only so long as Lot 1 continues to be owned by *A* himself. When *A* sells Lot 1 to *B*, the easement will be extinguished.

c. **Sub-division:** Similar rules apply to an easement appurtenant where the dominant estate is *sub-divided* into smaller lots, rather than transferred as a whole. That is, if the physical layout of the dominant estate is such that the owners of two or more of the sub-divided lots can take advantage of the easement, each will normally have the right to do so. But if only one part of the dominant estate can benefit, that portion will become the only dominant estate after the subdivision.

> **Example:** *A* owns Lot 1, and X owns adjacent Lot 2. A private road runs from a garage on Lot 1 through Lot 2 to a public road. *A* subdivides Lot 1 into a parcel bought by *B* and a parcel bought by *C*. If the parcels bought by *B* and *C* are laid out such that each one can have access to the private road without going on the other's land, each will have the right to the easement (and there will thus be two dominant tenements). But if *B* can get to the private road only by going over *A*'s portion, he will not have a right to the easement, and *A*'s parcel will be the only dominant tenement.

2. **Easements in gross:** Traditionally, the principal distinction between an easement appurtenant and an easement *in gross* is that whereas the former is assignable, the latter is *not transferable.* Burby, p. 67. The rationale for this distinction is that an easement appurtenant can only be assigned or divided in the same way that the dominant tenement is, a self-limiting feature that is not present in the easement in gross.

    a. **Modern view:** Modern courts are much more *willing* to allow assignment and transfer of easements in gross than were 19th century courts.

        i. **Commercial/personal distinction:** Some modern cases distinguish between easements that are primarily *commercial* (i.e., for economic benefit) and those that are primarily *personal* (for enjoyment rather than personal satisfaction). These courts allow assignment of commercial easements, but not assignment of personal ones.

        ii. **Majority view that all are assignable:** But most modern cases have tended to *reject* this commercial/personal distinction, and hold that easements in gross *are assignable* if that is what the parties intended, *even where the easement is of a* *non-commercial nature.* D&K (2002), p. 830. The Third Restatement (Servitudes) follows this modern approach: all easements in gross are "freely transferable," unless the circumstances indicate that the parties would not reasonably have expected that the benefit would pass to an assignee. §§ 4.6(1)(c) and 4.6(2).

(1) Exception: But even under the liberal Third Restatement rule, if the holder of the easement in gross is a ***close personal friend*** of the servient owner, and/ or the easement is made for ***no compensation,*** a court is likely to conclude that the parties intended that the easement be non-assignable. See Rest. 3d §4.6(2), making easements and other servitudes (whether in gross or not) non-assignable if "the ***relationship*** of the parties, ***consideration paid***, nature of the servitude, or other circumstances indicate that the parties ***should not reasonably have expected*** that the servitude benefit would ***pass to a successor*** to the original beneficiary."

Example: *A* owns property abutting a lake, with a path running from the public road to the lake. *A* gives to his close friend *B*, who lives 10 miles away, a free easement to drive along *A*'s driveway from the road to the lake, and park at the end of the driveway, so that *B* can swim and boat. Even under the more liberal Third Restatement rule — under which easements in gross are generally assignable whether of a commercial nature or not — the close personal relationship between *A* and *B*, and the lack of consideration, would lead to the conclusion that *B* cannot assign his easement to *C*, since *A* and *B* probably intended that the easement would remain personal to *B*. Cf. Rest. 3d, §4.6, Illustr. 2.

b. Divisibility: The traditional view, insofar as it prevented even transfer of easements in gross, necessarily prohibited the ***division*** of such an easement into smaller parts.

i. Restrictions under modern view: Under the modern view, even those easements in gross that *would* be alienable (i.e., typically, commercial ones) are ***not necessarily divisible***. Such an easement may be assigned to more than one person, but they may ***not generally make separate uses***; instead, they must hold ***"as one."***

Example: O holds the exclusive right to fish and boat on the waters of a particular lake. He conveys to his brother, *A*, a one-fourth interest in these rights. O and *A* then set up a partnership, in which they operate boat- and bath-houses, and rent boats to persons wishing to use the lake. After *A*'s death his heirs purport to assign to D (a church group) the right to have its members use the lake. O sues to block D from using the lake.

Held, for O. The easement owned by O was in gross. It was an alienable right (since the conveyance of the rights to O included a reference to his heirs and assigns). But it was not divisible, in the sense that O and *A* each had the right to make separate uses, and grant separate licenses. Therefore, the license to D issued by *A*'s heirs was not valid without the consent of O. *Miller v. Lutheran Conference & Camp Ass'n*, 200 A. 646 (Pa. 1938).

3. Profits in gross: Courts have always been ***willing to permit the assignment*** of most *profits* in gross (i.e., the right to ***remove timber, water, minerals*** or other items from the *soil*). This is perhaps because most profits in gross, unlike most easements in gross, are of a commercial nature, and it is likely to be the parties' intent that they be assignable.

a. Division: But as with the modern view of easements in gross, courts are more reluctant to permit *division* of a profit in gross. If the profit is *non-exclusive*, so that the servient owner may also take the products of the land, division of use by the holder of the profit is likely to be much more burdensome to the servient owner.

    i. Exclusive profit with royalty: If, by contrast, the profit is *exclusive* (i.e., only the dominant owner, not the servient owner, can take the items), and provides for a *royalty* to the servient owner based upon use, the court is quite likely to *allow* apportionment, since this is theoretically to the servient owner's benefit. The right to mine coal from the servient land, for instance, which is to be paid for on a per ton basis, would probably be apportionable, unless there was a clear intent to the contrary. See Rest. §493, Illustration 1.

VI. TERMINATION OF EASEMENTS

A. Introduction: There are a variety of ways in which an easement may terminate. The more important of these are discussed below.

B. Natural expiration: If the term of the easement is not specified, the easement will be for an *unlimited duration* (subject to the exceptions discussed below, such as abandonment).

1. Agreement otherwise: But the parties may always *agree* that an easement is to have a less-than-perpetual duration. Thus O might give A a 20-year easement to use his driveway as a right of way, or the parties might limit the easement to A's lifetime. At the end of this period, the easement would simply cease to exist, and would no longer be an encumbrance.

2. Purpose no longer applies: Or, the easement might be for a certain purpose, and will terminate when that purpose is no longer relevant; thus if O gave A an easement to run his sewer line under O's property, this easement would cease if A was subsequently able to make a direct hookup to the street.

C. Merger: An easement is, by definition, an interest in the land of another. Therefore, if ownership of a servient estate and of the appurtenant dominant estate come into the hands of one person, the easement appurtenant is *destroyed by merger*. This destruction is permanent, even if a severance of the dominant and servient interests subsequently occurs.

Example: O gives a right-of-way easement to A, his next-door neighbor. O then buys A's property. This will cause a merger between the dominant and servient estate, and the easement will be extinguished. Then, if O re-sells what was formerly A's property to B, the easement will not be revived (although a new easement by implication or by prescription might arise). See Rest. §497.

1. Easement in gross: Similarly, if the holder of an easement in gross acquires the servient estate, this will cause an extinguishment of the easement by merger. Rest. §499.

D. Destruction of servient estate: The easement will sometimes involve use not just of the servient land, but of a *structure* on that land. If so, *destruction* of the servient building by fire, other act of God, or the act of a third person, will terminate the easement.

E. Prescription: Just as an easement may be created by *prescription*, so it may be extinguished by this means. That is, the servient owner or a third person may use the servient property in a way inconsistent with the easement, for the statute of limitations period.

Example: O gives A a right of way over O's property, and later builds a fence blocking the right of way. The easement will be destroyed by prescription after the fence has been in place for the statute of limitations period.

F. Release: The easement holder may execute a *release* in writing, surrendering the easement.

G. Estoppel: Even if the holder of the easement does not intend to abandon it (see *infra*, p. 227), his conduct may be such that he is *estopped* from subsequently exercising his easement rights. This will occur if (1) the holder's conduct or words are *reasonably likely to lead the owner of the servient tenement to change his position in reliance*, and (2) the latter in fact does so. See 2 A.L.P. 305.

Example: E holds an easement to use a driveway running over O's land. E then builds his own driveway, and uses it instead of O's driveway for ten years. O, who assumes that E has abandoned his easement of O's driveway, tears up the driveway and plants a lawn. A court will probably find that E should reasonably have foreseen that his building of his own driveway, and his using it instead of O's for ten years, would cause O to think that E was abandoning his easement. Assuming that O's filling in of his own driveway was in direct reliance upon this mistaken impression, the court will hold that E is estopped from demanding his easement rights now.

    1. Extent necessary for protection: But the estoppel will only occur to the *extent necessary to protect* the servient owner's reliance interest. Suppose, for instance, that in the above example, O, after filling in and planting his driveway, later decides that he wants to restore the driveway. Once he rebuilds the driveway, E will probably regain his easement rights. 2 A.L.P. 307.

H. Abandonment: Normally, an estate in land cannot be destroyed by *abandonment*; this is certainly true of the possessory estates. But an easement is merely a use rather than a possessory interest. Accordingly, courts permit it to be terminated by abandonment in certain circumstances.

    1. Words alone insufficient: The easement holder's *words alone* will *never* be sufficient to constitute an abandonment. Thus if O gives A a right of way over O's property, no oral or written statements by A that he doesn't want the easement any longer, or that he abandons it, will be sufficient to destroy it. (However, if the writing is signed by A, it may be a valid release, as distinguished from an abandonment.) Rest. §504, Comment c.

    2. Intent plus conduct: For the easement to be abandoned, there must be an *intent* on the part of the easement holder to abandon it, coupled with *actions* manifesting that intent.

Table 9-1
ISSUES CHECKLIST: Easements

Use this checklist to help you spot issues in analyzing easements. Where the easement is appurtenant, the dominant tenement is "D-acre," and its holder (the beneficiary of the easement) is "D." Whether the easement is appurtenant or in gross, the servient tenement is "S-acre," and its holder is "S." A predecessor who owns both D-acre and S-acre is called "O."

Issue	Rule	Examples
[1] Was an easement *validly created?*	S (or predecessor O) must have somehow given D a *privilege to use S-acre*. The only methods by which an easement could have been created are: 1. **Express** easement (requires: specific words in a deed or will); can be by *grant* or by *reservation*. 2. Easement by **implication** (requires: severance of D-acre from S-acre; use prior to severance; and use that's "reasonably necessary" to the enjoyment of D-acre). 3. Easement by **necessity** (requires: co-ownership of D-acre and S-acre by same person [O] at some past time; easement is "strictly necessary" for D's enjoyment of D-acre; conveyance by O that separated D-acre and S-acre created the necessity). 4. Easement by **prescription** (requires: open assertion by D [or predecessor] of an easement over S-acre; continuously for the length of the adverse-possession statute of limitations). 5. Easement by **estoppel** (requires: S allowed D to use S-acre in such a way that S should reasonably have foreseen D's substantial change of position in reliance on use; D actually substantially changed position in reliance on the permission).	**Examples** **Express (by reservation):** O conveys S-acre to S; deed reserves to O right to cross S-acre to get to D-acre. O then conveys D-acre to D. **Implication:** While O owns both parcels, D-acre has house, and S-acre has underground sewer pipes connecting D-acre's house to public sewer in roadway. O conveys S-acre to S; deed silent about pipes. O then conveys D-acre to D. D has easement to use pipes to get to public sewer. **Necessity:** While O owns both parcels, S-acre has house abutting the road, and D-acre is vacant (on non-road side of S-acre). While O owns both, he never enters D-acre. O conveys D-acre to D. (Deed is silent on access to road.) D builds house that is now land-locked and needs road access across S-acre. Even though there was no road access use across S-acre prior to O's conveyance, D has easement to cross S-acre to get to road. **Prescription:** D-acre and S-acre have always been separately owned. Statute of limitations for adverse possession is 10 years. Starting in 1990, D's family continuously and openly uses a path across S-acre as a quicker way to get to the road (another way is available). S tolerates this. By 2000, D has easement by prescription. **Estoppel:** D-acre and S-acre are separately owned. D-acre is land-locked and vacant. S knows that that D is about to build a house whose inhabitants will need to cross S-acre for road access. S gives oral permission for such crossing. D builds the house. D has easement by estoppel.
[2] Has easement holder *exceeded the proper scope of use?*	General rule on scope depends on type of easement: 1. **Express** easement: Scope controlled by document creating easement. **(cont. on next page)**	**Examples** **Express:** If conveyance gives D the right to "use the path for pedestrian access," D does not have the right to pave the path for vehicular traffic.

Table 9-1 (cont.)
ISSUES CHECKLIST: **Easements**

Issue	Rule	Examples
[2] (cont.) Has easement holder *exceeded the proper scope of use?*	2. **Implied** easement: Scope controlled by use prior to severance (plus similar foreseeable uses). 3. Easement by **necessity**: Scope controlled by the extent of the necessity. 4. Easement by **prescription**: Scope = same general pattern as use occurring during statutory period. 5. Easement by **estoppel**: Scope = use by D that was foreseeable to S at time of estoppel. Special rules on scope: 1. Uses that expand due to *normal development* of D-acre are *OK*, if they don't *unreasonably interfere* with use of S-acre. 2. Use by D to benefit *additional property* owned by D (other than D-acre) is *not allowed*, even if it doesn't materially increase the burden on S-acre.	**Implied:** Easement for sewer pipes. If the house on D-acre expands, probably bigger pipes can be installed across S-acre if reasonably necessary. **Necessity:** Easement for access to public road. If another road is built, allowing access from D-acre to the new road without crossing S-acre, easement across S-acre terminates. **Prescription:** Easement for pedestrian access to get to road (the use that was made during the prescription period). The easement probably cannot now be expanded to cover auto access. **Estoppel:** S foresees that D will build single-family house needing access to road; S gives oral permission. If D builds 100-unit apartment building instead, S is probably not required to give access. **Example:** D-acre has 5 acres, 1 small house. O sells D-acre to D; easement by implication occurs, to let house owners on D-acre cross S-acre to get to road. If 3 more houses are built on D-acre, probably all have right of access, since that's due to normal/foreseeable development of D-acre. **Example:** D owns D-acre, which has express easement to cross S-acre to get to the road. D buys X-acre, located on the opposite side of D-acre from S-acre. Probably D has no easement to cross S-acre to get from X-acre to the road, even if this would not materially burden S-acre.
[3] Who has the burden and/or right to *maintain & repair* the easement?	1. S has *no duty to maintain* easement over S-acre, unless parties have expressly so agreed. 2. D has *implied right to maintain* easement, if this doesn't unreasonably interfere with S's use of S-acre. D has right to *contribution* from S if S also uses the easement.	**Example:** D has easement by implication to cross a driveway on S-acre to get to road. If driveway is damaged in storm, S has no obligation to repair it. D has right to repair it. If S also uses the driveway, D has the right to pro-rata contribution from S for the repair cost. But if S doesn't use the driveway at all, D has no right to contribution from S.
[4] Does a transferee from D *get the benefit* of the easement?	1. If easement is *appurtenant*, it will *automatically pass* with transfer of D-acre, even if deed is silent. 2. If easement is in *gross* (i.e., there's no D-acre, just D's right to access S-acre), modern view is that easement is transferable unless a close personal relationship between D and S suggests that parties didn't intend for D to be able to assign.	**Example (easement in gross):** S gives close friend D (who owns house 2 blocks away) written right to use S's pond in perpetuity. Probably this right is not assignable by D to X, who does not know S, since S and D probably didn't intend for D to have a right of assignment.

a. **Mere non-use not enough:** Mere *non-use* of the easement, even for a long period, is typically *not enough* to show the requisite intent to abandon. However, *affirmative conduct* by the easement holder, *coupled with non-use*, *can* be enough.

Example: *A* conveys to *B* the right to use a strip on *A*'s land as a driveway to get to the public road that abuts *A*'s property. Several years later, a different public road is built adjacent to *B*'s property. *B* stops using the driveway for a period of three years, during which *B* uses only the new public road.

This cessation of use would probably *not* be enough to constitute abandonment, because it does not constitute unequivocal evidence that *B* intended to relinquish the benefits of the servitude. If, however, *B* also built a masonry wall between his property and *A*'s, blocking *B*'s access to the driveway over *A*'s property, this act would be unequivocal enough to constitute abandonment, and the easement would be extinguished. Rest. 3d (Serv.), § 7.4, Illustr. 1 and 2.

I. **Revocation:** An easement is a full-fledged interest in property (albeit, a non-possessory, "incorporeal" one). Therefore, it is *not revocable* at its grantor's will. What would otherwise be an easement will, if it is revocable, generally be a *license* (discussed immediately *infra*).

VII. LICENSES

A. **Nature of license:** A *license* is a right to use the licensor's land that is *revocable* at the will of the licensor. This quality of revocability is the main feature which distinguishes licenses from easements. (But there are two special types of licenses which are not fully revocable; these are discussed *infra*, p. 232.)

B. **How license created:** A license, since it is revocable, is considered a relatively insignificant interest. Therefore, it is *not required* to satisfy the *Statute of Frauds*, and may be created orally.

Example: O, the owner of Blackacre, orally tells *A*, his next-door neighbor, that *A* may use O's pool any time he wishes. O has created a license in *A* to use the pool; O is the licensor and *A* is the licensee. If *A* uses the pool, he is absolved from liability for trespass. But O has the right to revoke the license at any time, and any use of the pool by *A* after that is a trespass.

1. **Attempt to create easement:** One way in which a license may be created is where a landowner gives another a right to use for former's land, which use would be an *easement* if formal requirements (particularly the Statute of Frauds) were satisfied, and these requirements are not.

Example: O orally tells *A* that *A* may use O's driveway as a right of way to get from *A*'s land to the public highway. The parties believe that this oral agreement is sufficient to give rise to an easement, and intend that it be irrevocable. Nonetheless, because the Statute of Frauds, applicable to easements, has not been satisfied, only a license is created. O may revoke the license at any time.

2. **Oral agreement must produce a license, not an easement:** You'll sometimes be called upon to distinguish between a license and an easement. One thing you can rely on that if the understanding is *oral*, it *must be a license rather than an easement* (since

licenses can be oral but easements must meet the Statute of Frauds). Therefore, you can deduce that any oral grant of the right to use the grantor's property must, if it is valid at all, be a license and thus ordinarily be revocable.[1]

3. **License that could never be easement:** Only certain uses of land are capable of being made easements. Other uses are so transitory, or so different from the common-law notion of an easement, that even if they are created in writing, and involve the use of land, they are not easements. These uses will generally (though not always) be licenses, even if they are in writing.

   a. **Ticket:** A *ticket* to a sports event, concert, or other public spectacle, is always considered a *license* rather than an easement. Thus even if the ticket were considered to be a writing of a type sufficient to meet the Statute of Frauds, and stated that the right to attend was irrevocable, it would still only be a license. Thus a ticket will normally be *revocable* at the will of the licensor (though the doctrine of unjust enrichment may require that the licensor refund any money paid by the licensee for the ticket).

   b. **Right to park:** Similarly, the right to use a *parking lot* is generally only a license, not an easement or a lease.

   c. **Right to post sign:** Where the owner of land gives another person the right to *erect a sign* on the former's premises, this right may be either a lease, license, or easement, depending on the wording and intent of the parties.

4. **Intent to make revocable:** An easement, as noted, can never be revocable at the will of the grantor. Therefore, if the parties create what would otherwise be a valid easement, but they provide that the easement is revocable at the grantor's will, a license results. See Rest. §514, Comment c and Illustration 2.

5. **Distinguished from lease:** You may also sometimes have to distinguish between a license and a *lease* (or sublease). The basic distinction is that a license merely confers the *non-exclusive right* to "use" the premises in a particular way, whereas a lease gives the lessee *exclusive possession* of specified premises for a stated time, typically without very narrow limitations on use.

   a. **Particular type of use:** So look to whether the person is getting non-exclusive rights *limited to a particular kind of use* (likely to be a license) or is instead getting the right to occupy defined premises coupled with the right to exclude others from the premises (probably a lease or sublease).

   b. **Tight definition of premises:** Another factor you should look to is whether the "premises" to which the arrangement applies are *tightly defined*: if they are, a lease is more likely, and if they are not, a license is more likely.

   Examples: Thus a right to come onto the property to engage in a recreational activity like hunting will typically constitute only a license, whereas the right to store goods under lock and key in a particular structure will typically rise to the level of a lease or sublease.

---

1. Easements by *estoppel* (*supra*, p. 215) represent a possible exception to this rule, since these can be oral.

C. Exceptions to revocability: As noted, a license is normally revocable at the licensor's wish, even if the parties have agreed otherwise. But there are some situations where the courts restrict or eliminate the revocability of a license.

1. **Oral license acted upon:** The most important case where a license may be irrevocable is that in which the use *would have been an easement* except that it did not meet the Statute of Frauds, and the licensee makes *substantial expenditures* on the land in *reliance* on the licensor's promise that the license will be permanent or of long duration. Most (though not all) courts will give the licensee at least limited protection from revocation. See Rest. §519(4).

    a. **Limited extent:** In the reliance scenario, the license will be irrevocable *only to the extent necessary to protect the licensee's reliance interest*, i.e., his investment in the improvements.

        Example: O orally gives A, an electric company, the right to build whatever power lines it needs over a strip of O's property. A builds one line, and O then revokes. A court might allow A to keep the existing power line as long as it needs it, but would probably not permit A to build any additional lines, even though the license contemplated these; only maintenance of the original line is necessary to protect A's reliance interest. See Rest. §519, Illustration 3.

VIII. COVENANTS RUNNING WITH THE LAND

A. Definition: Like easements, *"covenants"* may under some circumstances run with the land. A covenant running with the land is simply a *contract between two parties* which, because it meets certain technical requirements, has the additional quality that it is *binding against one who later buys the promisor's land*, and/or *enforceable by one who later buys the promisee's land*.

1. **Legal relief:** When we use the term "covenant," we are talking about a promise that is subject to *legal* rather than equitable relief. That is, when a covenant is breached the relief granted is *money damages*, not an injunction or decree of specific performance.

        Example: When members of a *condominium association* or *homeowners association* promise the association that they will *pay maintenance fees*, these promises are covenants running with the land. If the promise is violated, the association's remedy will be a judgment for damages against the member (a "legal" rather than "equitable" remedy).

    a. **Building restrictions:** By contrast, when the promise is that the promisor's land will *not be used in a certain way*, the promisee will generally be interested in gaining an *injunction* from a court of *equity*, not in recovering money damages. For instances, if the promisor covenants that he will *not build a non-residential structure* on his property, the promisee will generally wish to block construction of a commercial building, not merely wait for the building to be built, and recover damages. Such land-use restrictions are called *"equitable servitudes,"* and are discussed *infra*, p. 238.

B. Statute of Frauds: For a covenant to run with the land, it must be *in writing*.

Example: D, a developer, sells a parcel of land to O. As part of the sale transaction, O promises that it will pay D $100 per year for maintenance of a private road and private recreational facilities for the benefit of O's land and other land in the subdivision. If O's promise is to run on the burden side (i.e., be binding upon X, who later buys O's land), the promise must be in writing (though not necessarily signed by O). It is not clear whether the promise is binding on O himself if it is not in writing.

1. **Acceptance of deed poll:** Most property sales are made by a ***deed poll***, i.e., a deed signed by the grantor but not by the grantee. Where the covenant is one that is made by the grantee, nearly all courts hold that the grantee's ***acceptance of the deed poll*** containing the promise satisfies the Statute of Frauds, with respect to any promise made by the grantee that is recited in the deed. 2 A.L.P. 365.

C. **Running with the land:** The main question about covenants is, When do they ***run with the land***?

   1. **Running of burden and benefit:** More specifically, we want to know: (1) When does the ***burden*** run (so that the promisor's assignee is bound)? and (2) When does the ***benefit*** run (so that the promisee's assignee can sue for damages if the covenant is breached)?

      To answer these two questions, we have to worry about: (1) the ***"touch and concern"*** requirement; and (2) the requirement of ***"privity."***

      a. **"Touch and concern":** For the burden to run, under the traditional rule the burden must ***"touch and concern"*** the promisor's land. Similarly, for the benefit to run, under the traditional rule the benefit must "touch and concern" the promisee's land. For our detailed discussion of "touch and concern," see *infra*, p. 236.

         i. **Modern approach abandons requirement:** But the modern approach — as exemplified by the Third Restatement — ***abandons*** the "touch and concern" requirement entirely.

      b. **Privity:** Also, for the burden to run, there must traditionally be ***"privity of estate,"*** which usually means both a land transfer between the promisor and promisee ("horizontal" privity) plus a succession of estate from promisor to promisor's assignee ("vertical" privity). For the benefit to run, horizontal privity is sometimes required, but vertical privity is generally not. (For our detailed discussion of privity, see p. 233-235 below.)

   2. **Diagram:** To aid in our discussion, here is a diagram showing how the terms "horizontal" and "vertical" privity are used:
      On the facts as diagrammed, *B* has promised *A* that *B* and his "assigns" will never use Blackacre in a certain way (e.g., for retail purposes), and that if they do, they'll pay damages. The issues are whether *B*'s assignee, *D*, is burdened by this promise (i.e., can be liable for damages), and whether *A*'s assignee, *C*, is benefitted by it (i.e., can sue for damages).

   3. **Privity between promisor and promisee ("horizontal" privity):** Where a court requires ***"horizontal" privity***, it means that there must be ***some land transfer between the original promisor and the original promisee.***

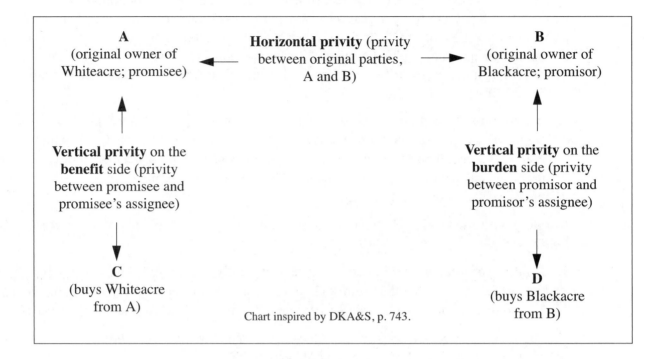

Chart inspired by DKA&S, p. 743.

a. Running of burden, under traditional rule: In America, *horizontal privity is traditionally required in order for the burden to run*. This mainly means that if the original parties are *"strangers to title,"* the burden will not run. Thus traditionally, two *neighboring landowners* could not get together and agree that neither would use his property for a certain purpose, and have this restriction be binding on a subsequent purchaser from either of them.

Example 1: In our diagram, assume that *A* and *B* have never had any land transaction between them other than *B*'s promise to *A* that *B* and his assign won't use Blackacre for retail purposes. *B* sells to *D*, who builds a store on Blackacre. Under the traditional rule, *A* can't sue *D* for damages for breaching the *B-to-A* covenant. This is so because there was never any land transfer between *A* and *B*, and thus no horizontal privity between them.

i. Requirement satisfied: But the horizontal requirement is satisfied (even under the traditional rule) if the original promisor and promisee have some land-transfer relationship.

Example 2: Same basic fact pattern as Example 1 above. Now, however, assume that *A* originally owned both Whiteacre and Blackacre. Then, *A* sold Blackacre to *B*, and the deed recited *B*'s commitment (on behalf of himself and his assigns) not to use Blackacre for retail purposes. Again as above, *B* conveys to *D*, who builds a store. Now, *A can* sue *D* for damages, because there was horizontal privity between *A* and *B*, in the sense of a land transfer between them.

ii. Modern/Restatement approach abandons requirement: But   the   *"modern"* approach — used by the Third Restatement — *abandons* the requirement of horizontal privity entirely. Thus under the Restatement, in Example 1, *A* could recover damages from *D* even though there never was a property transaction between *A* and *B*.

b. Running of benefit: Most courts traditionally hold that there must also be horizontal privity for the *benefit* to run. (Nearly all courts hold that the same privity rule that applies to running of burden applies to running of benefit; since most courts have traditionally required horizontal privity for running of burden, they have also required it for running of benefit.)

Example: In terms of Example 1 above, assume that *A* conveys Whiteacre to *C*, with no prior property transfers having occurred between *A* and *B*. *B* builds a store on Blackacre. If the state follows the traditional rule that horizontal privity is required for the burden to run, the state will probably also require horizontal privity for the benefit to run. In that instance, *C* won't be able to sue *B* for damages, because the benefit won't run due to the lack of horizontal privity between *A* and *B*.

   i. Restatement abandons: Again, the modern/Third Restatement approach is *not* to require horizontal privity for the running of the benefit any more than for the running of the burden. So under the Third Restatement, in the above example, *C can* sue *B* for damages.

4. Privity on promisor side and on promisee side ("vertical" privity): When a court requires *"vertical"* privity, this refers to the relationship between the *promisor* and his *successor* in interest, or the relation between the *promisee* and *his* successor. So in terms of our diagram on p. 233, the issue is whether *A* and *C* are in vertical privity, and whether *B* and *D* are in vertical privity.

   a. Running of burden: For the *burden to run*, the traditional rule is that the party against whom it is to be enforced must succeed to the *entire estate* of the original promisor, in the durational sense.

      i. Usually not a problem: In most law school problems that you will see, vertical privity on the burden side will *not* be a problem. For instance, in our main example/diagram on p. 233, *B* sold his entire interest in Blackacre to *D*, so *B* and *D* were in vertical privity. Therefore, even under the traditional rule there would be no problem with either *A* or *C* (after *C* took Whiteacre from *A*) suing *D* for money damages if *D* built a store on Blackacre. (But if *D* merely *leased* the premises for 20 years from *B*, and built the store, then according to the traditional rule *A* or *C* couldn't sue *D* on the promise, because *D* would not be deemed to be in full vertical privity with *B*.)

      ii. Third Restatement's rule: In any event, many courts today, and the Third Restatement, *abandon the requirement of vertical privity* for the running of the burden as to *negative covenants,* but not generally as to affirmative covenants.

   b. Running of benefit: The vertical privity requirement has even less bite on the *benefit* side. Even under the traditional rule, the benefit may be enforced by anyone who has taken *possession* of the promisee's property with the promisee's permission.

      Example 1: On the facts of our main example on p. 233, if *A* gave a long-term lease to *C*, *C* could sue *B* for damages if *B* built a store on Blackacre.

Example 2: Dev, a developer of a subdivision, causes each buyer to promise in his deed to pay a monthly charge to cover the cost of maintaining common areas of the development. Dev sells a lot to *A* and extracts such a promise. Later, Dev assigns his interest in collecting the common charges to a newly-formed ***Homeowners Association*** (HOA). *A* doesn't pay her common charges, and the HOA sues her to recover the back charges.

The HOA will win, even though the association owns no property in the development. Thus the requirement of vertical privity is almost completely relieved in this instance, even under traditional rules.

5. **"Touch and concern" requirement:** Courts have traditionally required in some circumstances that the promise *"touch and concern"* particular land.

   a. **Running of benefit:** For the ***benefit*** to run, the traditional rule is that the benefit must ***touch and concern*** the promisee's land. But this requirement does not have too much practical bite — most kinds of covenants that have anything to do with real estate (e.g., promises to make repairs, promises not to demolish, promises to pay money to a homeowners association, etc.) are found to "touch and concern" the promisee's land (as well as the promisor's land).

      i. **Burden in gross:** If the benefit touches and concerns the promisee's land, the benefit will run ***even though the burden does not***. That is, ***the benefit can run even if the burden is "in gross,"*** i.e., personal to the promisor.

         Example: *D* sells land containing a restaurant to *P*. As part of the transaction, *D* promises not to operate a competing restaurant within a two mile radius. (Assume that the state holds that a non-compete promise "touches and concerns" the promisee's land.) *P* then conveys the property to *X*. *X* can sue *D* for breach of the promise — since the benefit touches and concerns the *P/X* land, the benefit can run even though the burden is "in gross," i.e., personal to *D* and not tied to any particular land owned by *D*.

   b. **Running of burden:** For the ***burden*** to run, the traditional rule is, again, that the burden must "touch and concern" the promisor's land.

      i. **Running of burden when benefit is in gross:** Furthermore, about half of the courts following the traditional requirement of "touch and concern" impose an additional significant requirement: these courts hold that the burden will not run if the ***benefit*** does not touch and concern the promisee's land. (That is, half the courts say that ***the burden may not run when the benefit is in gross***.)

         Example: *A*, the owner of Blackacre, sells it to *B*. *B* promises not to operate a liquor store on the property so as not to compete with any similar store that may be owned by *A* from time to time anywhere within a 10-mile radius of Blackacre. Assume that the court is one which holds that such a "territorial" non-compete promise does not touch and concern the promisee's land. *B* then sells Blackacre to *C*. About half of such courts would hold that *A* cannot sue *C* for breach, because the burden will not run where the benefit is in gross, i.e., personal to *A*.

    c. Restatement Third eliminates rule: The Third Restatement entirely *eliminates the "touch and concern" requirement,* as to the running of both the burden and the benefit.

        Example: On the facts of the prior example, it won't matter whether *B*'s non-compete promise is deemed to touch or concern the land of *A* (the promisee) — if *B* sells to *D*, and D opens a liquor store on the property, *A* can sue *D*, according to the Third Restatement.

IX. EQUITABLE SERVITUDES / RESTRICTIVE COVENANTS

A. Building restrictions: A suit at law on a covenant running with the land can only culminate in *money damages*, as we have seen. This relief is generally adequate where the covenant is a promise to pay for benefits received on the land (e.g., a promise to pay dues to a homeowners' association) or an affirmative promise to take certain acts on the land (e.g., a promise to maintain a fence). But where the promise is a *negative* one, involving a *restriction on building*, money damages are not usually the desired relief. Rather, an *injunction* against the forbidden construction is the relief generally desired by the promisee.

    1. Technical requirements: Furthermore, as we have seen, the enforcement of a covenant at law, particularly against an assignee of the original promisor, is fraught with technical difficulties. Traditionally, there needed to be privity of estate between the promisor and the promisee (*supra*, p. 233), as well as between the promisor and the latter's successor (*supra*, p. 235). Furthermore, traditionally the covenant had to "touch and concern" the land, at least that of the promisor (*supra*, p. 236). These requirements may prevent the obtaining of money damages against the person now in possession of the promisor's estate, even where money damages would be adequate relief.

B. *Tulk v. Moxhay:* The inadequacy of legal remedies for breach of a building restriction led to the famous English case of ***Tulk v. Moxhay***, 41 Eng. Rep. 1143 (1848).

    1. Facts of *Tulk:* In *Tulk*, P was the owner of an empty piece of ground in Leicester Square, as well as of several houses surrounding it. He sold the vacant ground to Elms; the deed to Elms contained Elms' promise to maintain the vacant ground as a garden, with no structure on it. Title to the ground eventually passed to D, whose deed contained no such promise, but who conceded that he knew of Elms' original covenant. P sued D for an injunction to prevent him from building on the garden.

    2. No remedy at law available: Even if P had wished, he could not have waited until D destroyed the garden, and then sued for monetary damages. The reason for this was that under the English interpretation of the requirement of horizontal privity, there must be a continuing property relationship between promisor and promisee, thus making it impossible for a grantor in fee to impose a running covenant on his grantee.

    3. Equitable relief: English courts prior to *Tulk* had apparently held that if a covenant was not enforceable at law, it could not be enforced at equity either. But the court in *Tulk* *granted P an injunction even though the covenant was not enforceable at law.*

4. Effect of notice: The court stressed that D had had *actual knowledge* of the promise made in the deed to Elms. It seems probable that the restriction would *not* have been binding on D had he taken without actual or constructive knowledge; later cases have indeed imposed a notice restriction (see *infra*, p. 241).

C. Equitable servitudes: Since *Tulk v. Moxhay*, equity courts in both England and America have been willing to enforce land-use agreements as *"equitable servitudes"* against the burdened land, as to subsequent purchasers who took with *actual or constructive notice*. They have done so *whether or not* the agreement constituted a valid *covenant running with the land* at law. (See the discussion *infra*, p. 239 as to privity and the "touch and concern" test where equitable relief is at issue.) See 2 A.L.P. 403.

> **Example:** *A* and *B* own adjacent lots with houses on them, Blackacre and Whiteacre, respectively, which have never been under common ownership. One day, *A* and *B* sign a document in which each promises, on behalf of himself and his assigns, never to permit his property to be used for purposes other than as a single-family residence. They file this document in the land records pertaining to both parties. *A* then sells to *C* and *B* sells to D. D files plans to tear down the house on Whiteacre for the purpose of constructing a medical office building. *C* sues for an injunction against construction of the medical building.
>
> The court will almost certainly grant *C* the requested injunction. *A* and *B* have each agreed to an "equitable servitude" on their property. The burden of each promise would be found to run to any successor who took with actual or constructive notice (as D did here, given that the restriction was shown in the land records for Whiteacre). Even in a state that requires "horizontal privity" for the running of a legal covenant (see *supra*, p. 233),[2] the court would enforce the restriction as an equitable servitude, by granting the injunction.

1. Theory for enforcement: Courts are not completely in agreement on the theory for granting equitable relief (usually an *injunction*). Most courts hold that the agreement creates an *"equitable property interest"* in the burdened land, similar to an easement. As a consequence of this theory, the promisee may enforce the agreement without showing that appreciable damage or injury to his property will occur from a breach (a showing that must be made in the usual suit for specific performance). See 2 A.L.P. 403-04.

D. Statute of Frauds: At least in those courts following the majority view that an equitable servitude is a property interest, the servitude must *satisfy the Statute of Frauds*.

1. Acceptance of deed poll: As with covenants at law, an equitable servitude will meet the Statute of Frauds requirement if it is contained in a *deed poll* that is accepted by the grantee/promisor (but not signed by him). 2 A.L.P. 407.

2. Reference to filed plat: Restrictions on building are frequently contained not in the deed, but in a *plat* of a *subdivision*. (See *infra*, p. 293.) If the plat is recorded, and the deed makes reference to the plat (even if only as a means of identifying the property conveyed), the Statute of Frauds is satisfied as to the restrictions. 2 A.L.P. 408.

3. Implied reciprocal servitude: Suppose that the deed given to a grantee contains a promise by him to obey certain restrictions on use. If the grantor (probably a developer) agrees

---

2. There is no horizontal privity here, because *A* and *B* were "strangers to title," i.e., had no privity of estate with each other. See *supra*, p. 234.

orally that he will *insert similar restrictions in other deeds* given to subsequent buyers, does this oral promise satisfy (or constitute an exception to) the Statute of Frauds? The courts are *split* on this issue, which is discussed further *infra*, p. 243. See particularly *Sanborn v. McLean, infra*, p. 244.

E. Affirmative covenants: Most of the agreements for which equitable enforcement is sought are *negative* in nature; they generally are agreements not to violate certain building restrictions.

1. **American view:** But the *vast majority* of *American* courts are *willing* to grant equitable enforcement of *affirmative* as well as negative agreements.

   Example: At the time *A* sells Blackacre to *B*, *B* promises *A* in writing that *B* and his assigns will maintain a hedge at the edge of the property. *B* then conveys to *C*, who has actual knowledge of *B*'s promise. An American court would almost certainly order *C* to keep the hedge in place.

F. Requirements for running: The requirements for the *running* of an equitable servitude (i.e., enforcement by or against someone other than the original parties) are significantly more *liberal* than the traditional requirements for the running of a covenant at law:[3]

[1] *Privity is not generally required*, either of the horizontal or vertical variety;

[2] Although the *burden* must in most courts *"touch and concern"* the land in order to run, in most courts the *burden can run* even though the *benefit does not "touch and concern"* the land;

[3] For the benefit to run, the original parties must be fairly *specific* about *who may enforce* the promise (i.e., what land was intended to benefit); and

[4] a subsequent purchaser from the promisor will be bound only if he had actual or constructive *notice* prior to taking.

We consider each of these aspects below.

1. **Privity:** The various requirements of *privity*, so important to the enforcement of a covenant at law against and by successors to the original parties, are *not applicable to an equitable servitude*.

   a. **Between original parties (horizontal privity):** The lack of a privity requirement is most significant with respect to the *original parties* to the agreement creating the servitude. Whereas a covenant at law will traditionally run only if the original parties had some sort of property relationship (see *supra*, pp. 234-234), the servitude is binding on successors *even if covenantor and covenantee were strangers to each other's title*.

   Example: *Neighboring landowners* who have not had any other property transactions between them may agree that neither will make a particular type of use of his land; this

---

3. Thus you will notice that of the four items listed here, only [3] and [4] are requirements; [1] and [2] are items that would traditionally be required for running of a covenant at law, but aren't requirements for an equitable servitude.

agreement will create an equitable servitude, enforceable against or by a purchaser from either. The example on p. 238 is an illustration.

2. **The "touch and concern" requirement:** Neither the benefit nor the burden of a restrictive covenant will run unless it can be said to *"touch and concern"* the promisor's (in the case of a running burden) or the promisee's (in the case of a running benefit) land. (This is the same rule as has traditionally applied to covenants at law; see *supra*, p. 236). But the courts' interpretation of what constitutes "touching and concerning" is somewhat more liberal than in the case of a covenant at law.

     a. **Promisor's land:** The vast majority of *restrictions* upon the *promisor's* use of his own land *will* be found to "touch and concern" that land. Since these use-restriction cases are the main situations where equitable relief is sought, the touch and concern requirement will nearly *always be met on the burden side.*

     b. **Promisee's land:** On the *benefit* side, the equity courts are more liberal than courts interpreting a covenant at law have traditionally been.

         i. **Building restrictions:** In the usual case of an agreement that involves a *building restriction* — and in fact any promise that affects the quality of a neighborhood or area — the promise will be held to "touch and concern" the land of *any landowner* in that *neighborhood or area*, not just an immediately adjacent one. 2 A.L.P. 412-13. Thus if a lot owner promises that he will not construct a commercial building on his premises, *any nearby landowner may sue for an injunction*. (But it must also be shown that the original parties *intended* the land of the plaintiff in question to be benefitted; the requirement of intent to benefit specific land is discussed *infra*, p. 241.)

     c. **Third Restatement eliminates requirement:** The Third Restatement, adopted in 2000, completely *abandons the "touch and concern" requirement* for equitable servitudes just as it does for covenants at law. See Rest. 3d Property (Servitudes), §3.2 ("touch and concern" requirement is eliminated for all "servitudes," defined to include equitable servitudes as well as covenants at law.)

     d. **Running of burden where benefit is in gross:** Recall that where the benefit is *in gross*, courts are traditionally in disagreement about whether the burden may run at law (*supra*, p. 236). The courts are similarly in disagreement about whether *equity* will enforce a burden where the benefit is in gross.

         i. **Homeowners' association:** The issue of the running of the burden where the benefit is in gross is most important where a *homeowners' association* sues to enforce building restrictions. Since such an association often owns no property in the development, it could be argued that the restriction should not be enforceable at equity against an assignee of the original lot purchaser. But American courts by and large *permit the association to obtain an injunction* in this situation.

         ii. **No problem under Third Restatement:** Again, the Third Restatement entirely eliminates the issue of whether the burden can run when the benefit is in gross. See Rest. 3d, §2.6 (benefits in gross are valid). So on this classic issue of whether a homeowner's association can sue to enforce building restrictions against an assignee of an original purchaser, the Third Restatement's answer is "yes" — it doesn't make any difference that the association does not itself own land (and thus holds the benefit of the restrictions "in gross").

3. **Intent to benefit particular land:** If the benefit is to run to a particular piece of land (so that its owner may enforce the promise), it is not enough that the agreement "touch and concern" that parcel. It must also be the case that the original parties *intended* to benefit that particular parcel, in a way that would permit later owners of the parcel to enforce the promise. 2 A.L.P. 415-16.

> **Example:** *A* and *B*, next-door neighbors, agree that neither will build an outhouse on his property. *B* begins to build an outhouse, and *C*, his neighbor on the other side, sues for an injunction. Since there is no evidence that *A* and *B* intended their agreement to benefit other nearby parcels of land, *C* will not be able to obtain the injunction.

a. **External evidence about intent:** All states but California permit a showing of an intent to benefit a particular parcel by evidence *external* to the written agreement. Thus the court will hear evidence about the geographical location of the burdened and allegedly benefitted lands, and the physical location of the buildings on them. But evidence of an oral agreement to benefit the particular land, without any other, more tangible, evidence, will probably not be sufficient to overcome the Statute of Frauds.

b. **General development plan:** The intent to benefit particular lands may also be shown from the fact that there was a *general development plan*. The effect of such a plan on the intent requirement is discussed *infra*, p. 242.

4. **Notice to subsequent purchaser:** Equity will not enforce an agreement against a *subsequent purchaser* unless she had *notice* of the restriction before she took.

a. **Significance of recording:** The notice requirement is satisfied not only if the subsequent purchaser has actual knowledge, but also if she has *"constructive"* knowledge. Constructive notice occurs most often where the restriction is *recorded* before the subsequent purchaser takes.

i. **Two questions to ask:** So in analyzing whether a restrictive covenant is binding on a subsequent purchaser of the burdened land, you must ask *two questions*: (a) Did the purchaser have *actual knowledge* of the restriction? and (b) Was the purchaser on *"constructive notice"* of the restriction, perhaps by virtue of the restriction's being embodied in a deed in the purchaser's chain of title? If the answer to both questions is *"no,"* the purchaser *won't be bound by the restriction.*

> **Example:** Devel, a developer, owns a 40-lot subdivision. He intends to file a plat showing that all lots are limited to single-family use, but never gets around to doing so. He sells Lot 1 to *A* with a single-family restriction contained in the deed (and with a reciprocal promise in the deed that he, Devel, will also restrict his other 39 lots). He then sells Lot 2 to *B* without any restriction in the deed (and without *B*'s having an actual knowledge that any lot is burdened or promised to be burdened).
>
> Even though Devel has created a single-family restriction on Lot 2 (and all other lots) by his arrangement with *A*, *B* will not be bound by that restriction,

because he took without "actual" or "constructive" notice (both terms are discussed below) of the restriction on Lot 2.[4]

G. Significance of building plan: A developer will often formulate a *general building plan* or development plan, by which all or most of a subdivision is to be made exclusively residential, with provision for parks, roads, and other common areas. Usually this plan is embodied in a subdivision *plat*, or map, which is recorded, together with the applicable restrictions and covenants. The purpose of such a plan is to assure each prospective purchaser that he will be buying into a planned residential neighborhood. Once the developer has sold off the lots, he typically disappears from the picture, at least as far as enforcing the covenants is concerned. Therefore, it becomes important to know the circumstances under which one lot owner may enforce the restrictions against another. The answer to this question depends upon several factors, particularly the wording of the restrictions, and whether the plaintiff seeking enforcement received his land before or after the party against whom he wishes to enforce the limitation.

1. **Enforcement by developer:** The *developer* himself, of course, will be *able to enforce* the restriction so long as he owns some of the remaining property. Enforcement by him does not involve the running of the benefit, so that he will always be able to enforce either against the original buyer (the promisor) or against an assignee from the promisor who takes with actual or constructive notice.

2. **Enforcement by subsequent purchaser from developer:** When enforcement is sought against a purchaser by a *later purchaser* from the developer, the latter will have to show that the earlier purchaser and the developer *agreed that the benefit would run* to the latter's land. (This is a general requirement for the running of the benefit of a servitude; see *supra*, p. 241.) This showing may be made in one of several ways.

   a. **Express provision in deed:** The deed from the developer to the earlier purchaser may itself *expressly* provide that enforcement may be obtained by any subsequent (or prior) purchaser of a different lot from the developer.

   b. **Existence of building plans:** Even where the deed from the developer to the early purchaser does not say anything about the benefit, the *mere existence of a general building plan* will probably be enough to create a presumption that other purchasers whose lots fall within the terms of the plan were intended to be benefitted.

   Example: Developer devises a residential development plan for the Happy Acres subdivision. He tells each prospective purchaser about the plan, including the fact that it will keep the community entirely residential. He then sells Lot 1 to *A*, with all the restrictions of the plan embodied in the deed. But the deed to *A* does not specifically refer to the plan, and does not indicate who may enforce the restrictions. Developer then sells Lot 2 to *B*. Since *B* can show that a general plan existed at the time of the

---

4. We are assuming that the single-family nature of the development did not put *B* on "inquiry notice" of the possibility that Devel had agreed to a single-family restriction on Lot 2. If the court finds that the single-family nature of the neighborhood would have caused a reasonable buyer in *B*'s position to have done further research to discover whether Devel had agreed to such a restriction, then this "inquiry notice" will be a form of constructive notice, and *B* will be bound by the restriction. *Sanborn v. McLean*, on p. 244, is an illustration of such inquiry notice.

deed to *A*, and that *A* knew of this plan, the court will presume that all subsequent lot purchasers were intended to be benefitted by the restriction in *A*'s deed.

i. Evidence that other lots are restricted: A general plan may be shown by evidence that all *other lots* in the vicinity contain similar restrictions. However, it must be shown that the general plan existed *prior to the sale to the defendant* (or to the defendant's predecessor in title). 2 A.L.P. 418. Therefore, a showing that restrictions were placed in *subsequent* deeds will not be relevant; only restrictions inserted prior to the sale to the defendant will show that a plan existed at the time the defendant bought.

3. Enforcement by prior grantee: Now consider the converse situation: an early grantee from the developer wishes to enforce a restriction against a *later purchaser* from the developer, or that later purchaser's assignee. Unlike the case of enforcement by a subsequent grantee, this is not a matter of the simple running of a benefit; the problem is that the plaintiff has by hypothesis received his land before the restriction against the defendant even existed. Nonetheless, there are several ways in which enforcement by the prior grantee may be available.

a. Express promise of restriction made by developer: The developer may make an *express written promise* that his remaining land is subject to the same restrictions. If so, his retained land becomes immediately burdened, and this burden will simply run with the land when he conveys it to later purchasers. The prior purchaser will thus have no difficulty in enforcing the restrictions against the later buyers.

b. Implied reciprocal servitude: Even if the developer has not expressly and in writing restricted his remaining land, the theory of *"implied reciprocal servitude"* is often used to allow an early purchaser of one lot to enforce against a later purchaser of a different lot. This theory holds that if the early purchaser acquires his land in *expectation* that he will be entitled to the benefit of subsequently created servitudes, there is *immediately* created an "implied reciprocal servitude" *against the developer's remaining land*. 2 A.L.P. 426. (Sometimes the phrase "implied reciprocal *easement*" is used, but it means the same thing.)

i. General plan must exist: Unlike the third-party beneficiary theory, this implied reciprocal servitude theory will usually apply only where it is shown that there was a *general development plan* in existence at the time the prior purchaser bought. Otherwise, there will normally be no way for the prior purchaser to show that he reasonably expected to have the benefit of such restrictions placed in subsequent deeds.

ii. Restrictions not inserted in later deeds: The implied reciprocal servitude theory is applicable if the developer inserts the promised restrictions in later deeds. But the theory's greatest value to the early purchaser is that some courts may apply it *even if the restrictions are not inserted in the later deed*.

iii. No oral promise: If the developer has made an oral promise to the early purchaser that later sales will contain the restriction, the implied reciprocal servitude theory will probably be applied by most courts. But some courts have gone so far as to hold that *even if there is no such oral promise* made to the early purchaser, if that purchaser can show that a general plan of restrictions exists, the implied recip-rocal servitude will arise against the developer's remaining land.

Example: Developer, who owns a large tract, sells numerous lots in it in 1892 and 1893. Each deed limits construction to residences costing more than $2,500. In late 1893, Developer conveys Lot 86 to X, without any restrictions. Part of Lot 86 eventually passes to D, who begins to build a gas station. The Ps, owners of nearby restricted lots, sue for an injunction. There is no evidence that Developer made any explicit promises to the buyers of the restricted lots that he would impose similar restrictions on later purchasers.

Held, for the Ps. The mere fact that all of the earlier deeds contained identical residential-only restrictions, and that the entire neighborhood was residential, is enough to prove that Developer was following a common plan or scheme. There-fore, when he sold the early lots, his remaining land became subject to a reciprocal negative easement, with the same restrictions as those imposed on the lots already sold. Although D's own chain of title did not disclose this restriction, the nature of the neighborhood put him on inquiry notice that a reciprocal negative easement might exist, and he was under the duty to check other deeds from Developer. If he had done so, he would have discovered the restrictions, and therefore the recipro-cal negative easement; consequently D had constructive notice of the restriction, and took subject to it. *Sanborn v. McLean*, 206 N.W. 496 (Mich. 1925).

    iv. Statute of Frauds: Observe that the concept of implied reciprocal servitudes is in a sense an exception to the Statute of Frauds, since the theory is that the restric-tion on the developer's remaining land arises without any reference thereto in the deed. For this reason, many states will not permit the reciprocal servitude to arise without an explicit promise by the developer *in the deed* that he will subject his remaining lots to the same restriction. Note that in such a state, *Sanborn v. McLean* would probably turn out differently.

    v. Plan must be in effect at earlier time: For the implied reciprocal servitude the-ory to apply, the prior purchaser must show that a general building plan existed *at the time he bought*, since it is at that time that the implied reciprocal easement in the grantor's remaining lands must arise, if at all. Similarly, if the developer exacts *stricter* restrictions in later deeds, an earlier purchaser will probably not be able to enforce these more severe restrictions under the implied reciprocal servitude the-ory. 2 A.L.P. 426.

H. Selection of neighbors: Covenants and restrictions are sometimes used not to control land use, but to facilitate the *selection of neighbors*. For instance, each deed executed by a devel-oper may provide that the purchaser must become a member of the homeowners' association, and that he may not sell his land to anyone who is not a member of that association. If the association has untrammeled power to decide who may become a member, existing members (i.e., existing residents of the development) will have the *de facto* right to select their neigh-bors. Such arrangements are theoretically enforceable (either by damages for their breach or by an injunction against the forbidden sale), but they are likely to run up against one or both of the following obstacles to enforcement:

1. **Restraint on alienation:** First, the arrangement may be held to be an illegal ***restraint on alienation***. See the general discussion of restraints on alienation *supra*, p. 106.

   a. **Right of first refusal:** But if the Association has merely a ***right of first refusal***, rather than the outright power to block a transfer, this fact will probably save the arrangement from being an illegal restraint on alienation.

   b. **Co-ops and condos:** In the case of ***cooperative associations*** and ***condominium*** units, share restrictions usually take the form either of a requirement that the owners' association approve any proposed transfer, or a right of first refusal. These restrictions are usually ***upheld***, sometimes on the theory that an owner's board needs to assure that the new member will be financially responsible.

      i. **Reasonableness:** However, most courts hold that condo and co-op transfer restrictions will only be upheld if they are ***reasonable***. For instance, a provision stating that a condo board can veto the proposed deal and instead buy the unit for what the seller originally paid would be likely to be struck down as unreasonable.

      ii. **Preemptive option:** Many co-op and condo associations restrict transfers not by keeping the right of approval, but by instead keeping a ***right of first refusal***. That is, the association has a stated time in which it can match the proposed selling price and acquire the unit itself. Usually such "preemptive options" are upheld. D&K, pp. 933-34.

I. **Restriction to single-family use:** Covenants and restrictions often attempt to preserve the residential quality of a development. Most significantly, covenants and restrictions often prohibit the construction of anything but ***single-family residences***, and prohibit anything but a single family from using each residence.

   1. **Enforceable:** Generally, such restrictions are ***enforced*** by a court. For instance, a restriction limiting properties to single-family uses would generally be enforced to prevent operation of a retail store or a hospital on the premises.

   2. **Broadening definition of "family":** However, courts in recent years have generally broadened the meaning of "family." For instance, an unmarried heterosexual couple, an unmarried same-sex couple, or a married couple caring for a large number of foster children, would all have a good chance of persuading a court that they are living as a "family unit" and thus not violating a single-family restriction.

      a. **Group homes:** The most controversial issue is whether a ***group home*** (e.g., for the mentally retarded, or for persons with AIDS) is a single-family residence for purposes of a restriction or covenant. Here, the courts have split, but the modern trend seems to be in favor of regarding such a group home as a single-family residence. See D&K, pp. 910-11. Alternatively, some courts concede that a group home for the retarded may not be a single-family residence, but then simply refuse to enforce the covenant on the grounds that it is void as against public policy. See the further discussion of group homes and the meaning of "single family residence" in the context of zoning laws, *infra*, p. 287.

J. **Restrictions on activities:** Covenants and restrictions may affect not only the type of dwelling and who lives there, but also may police more narrowly the ***activities*** that take place. For instance, homeowners associations and condominium associations (see *infra*, p. 342) often enact *rules and regulations* governing such items as *pets*, *satellite dishes*, the *parking of vehicles*, and other aspects of everyday life.

1. **Must be reasonable:** Generally, courts *enforce* such restrictions (assuming that they satisfy the requirements for covenants, listed above). However, most courts impose some sort of a requirement of reasonableness on use restrictions. Probably the most common approach is to apply a "mere rationality" standard, under which the restriction will be upheld unless it is *"irrational"* or *"wholly arbitrary."* This is generally a quite difficult standard for the person attacking the restriction to meet.

    > **Example:** Lakeside Village is a large condominium development (530 units in 12 separate three-story buildings). Before the project is built, the developer places certain covenants and restrictions into a declaration recorded in the real estate records. Those restrictions include a pet restriction, under which "no animals (which shall mean dogs and cats) ... shall be kept in any unit." Ten years later, P buys a unit, and moves in with her three cats. D (the Condominium Association) demands that she remove the cats, and fines her. P sues to have the restriction ruled unenforceable as to her.
    >
    > *Held*, for D. A California statute says that a use restriction set out in a recorded declaration is an enforceable equitable servitude "unless unreasonable." This language means that such a restriction shall be enforced unless it is "wholly arbitrary" (or else violates a "fundamental public policy" or "imposes a burden on the use of affected land that far outweighs any benefit.") The restriction here is not "wholly arbitrary," since the restriction is "rationally related to health, sanitation and noise concerns legitimately held by residents of a high-density condominium project...." Many owners may have relied on the pet restriction in deciding to purchase at Lakeside Village. Furthermore, since the restriction could be repealed by a majority vote of owners, its continued existence reflects the majority's desire to keep it. *Nahrstedt v. Lakeside Village Condominium Assoc., Inc.*, 878 P.2d 1275 (Cal. 1994).

    a. **Third Restatement agrees:** The Third Restatement agrees with the California approach, saying that activity restrictions, like other "indirect restraints," will be valid unless they *"lack a rational justification"* (comparable to *Nahrstedt*'s "wholly irrational" standard.) See Rest. 3d, Servitudes, §3.5.

2. **Distinction between recorded restriction and later-enacted regulation:** Notice that the restriction in *Nahrstedt* was contained in the *original* recorded subdivision plan, and was thus to be treated like an equitable servitude of which P had constructive notice. Courts often distinguish between use restrictions contained in this type of recorded servitude, and restrictions that are merely enacted *after the fact* as part of a *property owner association's regulations*.

    a. **"Reasonableness" standard:** In the latter situation, most states apply a *"reasonableness"* rather than "wholly arbitrary" standard, so it is much easier to get the court to strike down the restriction. The Third Restatement agrees with this distinction, holding that an owners' association has the obligation to *"act reasonably in the exercise of its discretionary powers* including rulemaking, enforcement and design-control powers." See Rest. 3d, Servitudes, §6.13(c).

K. Summary of the effect of equity on law: The willingness of courts to grant equitable enforcement (particularly injunctions) for covenants goes a long way towards making the traditional rules for covenants ***at law*** irrelevant.

  1. Third Restatement: In fact, the Third Restatement (Servitudes), adopted in 2000, completely ***eliminates the distinction*** between equitable servitudes and covenants at law — the same rules apply to both types of land restrictions, which the Restatement collectively calls "servitudes." See D&K (2002), p. 869.

X. MODIFICATION AND TERMINATION OF COVENANTS AND SERVITUDES

A. Modification and termination generally: Covenants and servitudes can be modified or terminated under a number of circumstances. (For simplicity, we'll refer to modification or termination of a "servitude," but we mean "covenant or servitude.") We consider only a few of those circumstances here.

  1. Agreement by all parties: The servitude can be ***modified*** or ***terminated*** if all parties to it so ***agree***. But they must do so in a document that satisfies the ***required formalities for creation*** of the servitude in the first place (e.g., it must be in writing, and in most states must be notarized). Typically, this means that an ***oral agreement***, even by all affected parties, to terminate or modify a servitude will ***not*** suffice, because the Statute of Frauds requires that the modification or termination be in writing, just as the original servitude had to be in writing.

  2. Abandonment: The servitude can be extinguished by ***abandonment*** by the benefitted party. But abandonment is hard to establish, and requires unequivocal evidence of an intent to abandon. Mere ***cessation of use*** is typically ***not*** enough.

  3. Changed conditions: The servitude may be modified or terminated by court order when ***conditions have so changed*** that it is ***impossible to accomplish the purposes*** for which the servitude was created.

    Example: Developer owns 10 adjacent parcels, which he sells to 10 separate buyers. In each deed, he inserts a restriction that the property be used only for single-family purposes. Lots 1-8 are condemned for use as a public multilane highway. The resulting noise and traffic make Lots 9 and 10 no longer suitable for residential use. The owner of Lot 9 wants to transform his house into a retail store. The owner of Lot 10 wants both lots to remain residential. A court would be justified in terminating the servitude, because the purposes for which it was created (maintenance of a viable residential neighborhood) can no longer be accomplished. Rest. 3d (Serv.), § 7.10, Illustr. 1.

  4. No expiration from passage of time: But the ***mere passage of time***, without more, will ***not*** cause a covenant or servitude to be extinguished.

    a. Statutory limits on duration: The ***Rule Against Perpetuities*** is generally held to be ***not applicable*** to covenants restricting land use. C&L, p. 1054. Yet such covenants and restrictions clearly fetter the alienability of land. For this reason, just as a number of states have restricted the duration of possibilities of reverter and rights of entry (see *supra*, p. 53), so some of these states have placed **limits on the duration** of covenants running with the land and equitable restrictions.

Quiz Yourself on

EASEMENTS AND PROMISES CONCERNING LAND

62. Orin owned a large country estate, Country Oaks, which contained a trout stream. Orin's friend and neighbor Norman, owner of an adjacent parcel, fished in the stream for several years with Orin's consent. Orin decided to sell Country Oaks to Alfred, but wanted to protect Norman's fishing rights. Therefore, with Alfred's consent, Orin's deed to Alfred contained an easement granting Norman and his successors the right to fish in the stream in perpetuity, as well as the right to get to the stream by a path running through the estate. Five years later, Alfred conveyed Country Oaks to Barbara. The Alfred-to-Barbara deed did not contain any easement for fishing.

 (a) If the jurisdiction follows the traditional common-law approach to relevant issues, may Norman continue to fish in the stream? _____

 (b) In a jurisdiction following a contemporary approach to the relevant issues, may Norman continue to fish in the stream? _____

63. Angela is the owner of Auburnacre. Burt is the owner of Blueacre. The two parcels are adjacent, and have never (at least as far as property records go back, which is 200 years) been under common ownership. A lake, located on public land and open to the public, borders the eastern edge of Auburnacre; the Auburnacre-Blueacre border is on the west side of Auburnacre. For many years, the lake had been useless because it was algae-infested. However, in 1995, the state redredged and reclaimed the lake, so that it is now usable for fishing. Beginning in 1995, Angela allowed Burt to cross Angela's property to get to the lake for boating. (Because the land is out in the country where few roads exist, Burt would have to drive for 25 miles in order to get to the lake if he were not permitted to cross Auburnacre.) No written agreement between Angela and Burt regarding Burt's right to cross Angela's land ever existed.

 In 2011, Burt conveyed Blueacre to Carter. Shortly thereafter, Carter attempted to cross Auburnacre to get to the lake. Angela objected, and thereafter put a roadblock across the path, in the middle of Auburnacre, that Burt had formerly used. May Carter compel Angela to remove the roadblock so that Carter can cross over to use the lake? _____

64. For many years, Daphne owned a 10-acre parcel of waterfront land known as The Overlook. The westernmost five acres of the property (called "West Overlook") contained a house and a driveway leading to Main Street, a public road. The easternmost five acres (called "East Overlook") consisted of a little-used summer house located on a peninsula jutting out into the western side of Lake Moon, a two-mile wide lake; East Overlook had a dock on the lake. The only land-based way to exit East Overlook would have been to use the driveway across West Overlook to get to Main Street. However, Daphne never left East Overlook by crossing West Overlook in this manner. Instead, if she wanted to leave East Overlook she always sailed from her dock in a small motorboat across Lake Moon; at the opposite shore of the lake she used a car she kept adjacent to Smith Avenue, a public street.

 In 2001, Daphne sold East Overlook to Frederika. The deed made no mention of any easement across West Overlook. As Daphne knew, Frederika was buying East Overlook to use it as a waterfront summer house; Frederika was happy with the limitation that to enter and leave, she would have to do so by some sort of boat crossing the lake between Smith Avenue and East Overlook. But then, in 2011, Frederika suffered a stroke that made it extremely dangerous for her to travel the two miles by boat. She asked Daphne to permit her to enter and exit by use of a van that would use the driveway over West Overlook to connect East Overlook with Main Street. Daphne refused. Frederika has now sued for a judicial declaration that she has an easement to cross West Overlook by van. Should the court find for Frederika?

_____

65. Astrid and Ben were adjacent landowners. Astrid's property was valuable beach front property. Ben's property adjoined Astrid's on the side away from the ocean. From 1990 to 2010, Ben and his family continually (at least once a week in nice weather) got to the beach by walking along a beaten path crossing Astrid's side yard. (They could have driven to a public beach four blocks away, but preferred walking directly to the beach area behind Astrid's house.) Astrid never gave permission to Ben to use this path in this way, but she did not voice any objection either. Then, in 2010, Astrid sold her property to Charles. Charles immediately barred the path so that Ben could no longer use it. The statute of limitations for actions to recover real property in the jurisdiction is 15 years. Does Ben have a right to continue using the path to the beach? _____

66. From Dunes Development Co., George purchased a house just off the 16th fairway of Sandy Dunes Country Club. The Club was constructed by Dunes Development Co. The deed from Dunes stated that George would have the right to free use of the Sandy Dunes Golf Course indefinitely, but was silent on whether the golf rights received by George were transferable. Two years later, George sold the house to Henry. The George-to-Henry deed was silent about the existence of any right to use the golf course. By the time of this conveyance, the course was no longer being operated by Dunes Development Co., but rather, by Ian, who bought it from Dunes. When Henry attempted to use the golf course for free, Ian refused. If Henry brings suit against Ian to enforce the free-golf provision of the deed, will Henry prevail?

_____

67. Quince owned a limestone quarry, and a manufacturing plant in which he worked the limestone into gravestones and monuments. A parcel owned by Pierce lay between the quarry and the manufacturing plant. Therefore, Quince purchased from Pierce an easement to drive his trucks along a 10-foot-wide strip of Pierce's land, so the stone could be taken from the quarry to the manufacturing plant. Quince's business grew over the years, and in 2010, Quince shuttered the plant, and built a newer, larger plant some miles away. At the time the old plant was shuttered, Quince told Pierce by telephone, "I won't be needing the easement across your land anymore." Shortly thereafter, Quince sold the quarry, as well as the shuttered plant and the land it stood on, to Raymond. Raymond immediately started driving his trucks from the quarry to the plant. If Pierce brings suit to stop Raymond from crossing Pierce's property, will Pierce be successful? _____

68. Abbott and Bingham were adjacent landowners, and fanatic tennis players. Abbott, the richer of the two, built a clay tennis court on his property. At the time of construction, he said to Bingham, "For as long as you own your property, you are free to use the court whenever you wish, so long as I am not playing on it." Bingham immediately sent Abbott a letter, stating, "I want to thank you for your generosity in allowing me to use your tennis court whenever I want (assuming you are not using it, of course) for as long as I stay in the house. I regard this as significantly enhancing the value of my own property." For 10 years, the arrangement worked well. Then, Abbott discovered one day that Bingham was having an affair with Abbott's wife. Abbott angrily wrote to Bingham, "I am hereby revoking your right to use my tennis court. Never set foot on my property again, under pain of prosecution for trespass." Bingham now sues for a declaratory judgment that he is entitled to use Abbott's court. The state where the land is located has a 25-year statute of limitation on adverse-possession actions.

(a) What property interest, if any, did Abbott grant to Bingham at the time the court was constructed?

_____

(b) Should the court hold that Bingham has the right to use Abbott's court now? _____

69. Allison and Bertrand were neighboring land owners who owned fee simples in adjacent parcels of land. The parcels were separated by a fence which lay on Allison's property. Since proper maintenance of the fence was important to Bertrand's property as well as to Allison's, both parties agreed that when the fence needed repairs and painting from time to time, Allison would cause this to be done, and Bertrand would then reimburse Allison for half the cost. The agreement also provided that if Bertrand did not pay a debt that was properly owing, Allison could get a lien on his land for the unpaid debt. The agreement was embodied in a document signed by both parties, and filed in the local real estate records indexed under both Allison's and Bertrand's names. The document did not specifically give Bertrand any right to come upon Allison's land to make the repairs if Allison declined to do so.

Two years after this agreement, Bertrand conveyed his parcel to his daughter, Claire, in fee simple. Claire never explicitly or implicitly promised to pay for repairs to the fence. Five years after this conveyance, Allison spent $1,000 to have the fence extensively repaired and repainted. (There had been intervening repairs which occurred while Bertrand still owned his parcel, and which he paid for. The $1,000 was for work done to repair wear and tear that occurred after Claire took title.) Allison now seeks to recover $500 from either Bertrand or Claire. If both refuse to pay, will Allison's suit be successful against Claire, assuming that there is no special statute in force relevant to this question, and assuming that the common-law approach applies? _____

70. Same basic fact pattern as prior question. Now, assume that Bertrand never made the conveyance to Claire. Assume further that Allison, five years after her deal with Bertrand, conveyed her parcel to her brother Doug. If Doug sues Bertrand for enforcement of the promise, may Doug recover?

_____

71. Same basic fact pattern as prior two questions. Now, assume that the original Allison-Bertrand document also contained a promise by Allison that she would not replace the wooden fence with a structure made of any other material (because Bertrand liked the look of natural wood). (This promise was contained in the document that was filed in the land records.) Assume that as in the prior question, Allison conveyed the property to Doug, and further assume that Bertrand conveyed his property to Claire. If Doug begins to replace the wooden fence with a shiny metal one, may Claire get an injunction against Doug?

_____

72. Harry and Isadore were adjacent landowners in a residential area. Each believed that swimming pools were "tacky." They therefore agreed, in a writing signed by both and made binding on each one's "heirs and assigns," that neither would ever permit his property to have a swimming pool placed upon it. Three years later, Isadore sold his parcel to James. At the time of purchase, James did not have actual knowledge of the Harry-Isadore agreement. A check by James of the real estate records failed to disclose the Harry-Isadore agreement (because it had never been filed by either party). If James had asked Isadore, Isadore would have told him about the agreement, but James never asked, and Isadore never thought to mention it. James has now begun work to prepare his site to contain a swimming pool. If Harry sues to enjoin the construction by James, should the court grant Harry an injunction? _____

73. Developer, a residential real estate developer, purchased a farm and set about creating "Happy Farms," a planned residential community. Developer prepared a subdivision map (or "plat") for Happy Farms, which showed that all 36 lots on Happy Farms were to be used for residential purposes, showed where

roads and sewers were to run, and contained other details indicating that the property would be a residential community. Developer then sold parcel 1 at Happy Farms to Kathy. In the deed from Developer, Kathy agreed that her parcel would be subject to the restrictions contained in the plat, which was filed in the real estate records. Developer did not state in the deed that other parcels later sold by him would be subject to similar restrictions, though Developer orally told Kathy, "Other buyers will be subject to the same limitations, so you'll be sure that you'll have a purely residential community with high standards."

Developer then sold parcel 2 to Lewis. Due to Developer's administrative negligence, the deed to Lewis omitted the restrictions contained in Kathy's deed. However, there is evidence that Lewis knew that a general residential plan had been prepared by Developer and filed in the real estate records. Several years later, Lewis attempted to open a candy store on part of his property. (This is allowed by local zoning laws, since the area is zoned mixed-use.) If Kathy sues Lewis to enjoin him from using his property for non-residential purposes, will the court grant Kathy's request? _____

Answers

62. (a) No. At common law, it was not possible for an owner of land (Orin) to convey that land to one person, and to establish by the same deed an easement in a third person. This was the rule against creating an easement in a ***"stranger to the deed."***

(b) Yes, probably. Most modern courts (and the Third Restatement of Property) have abandoned the common-law "stranger to the deed" rule, and allow an easement to be created by a deed in a person who is neither the grantor nor the grantee. This is especially likely where the easement relates to a use that existed prior to the conveyance. Since Norman fished in the stream prior to the Orin-to-Alfred conveyance, a modern court would probably uphold the easement in the deed to Alfred. Once that easement is recognized as valid, ***it burdened the land***, and therefore is still in force even though it was omitted from the Alfred-to-Barbara deed.

63. No, probably. Normally, an easement may be created only by compliance with the Statute of Frauds, which did not happen here. Therefore, the only kinds of easement that might have come into existence are (1) an easement "by implication"; (2) one "by necessity"; and (3) one "by estoppel." But an easement by implication will only come into existence if (among other requirements) the owner of a parcel sells part and retains part, or sells pieces simultaneously to multiple grantees (the requirement of ***"severance"***). Here, neither Angela nor her predecessors ever owned what is today Blueacre and thus never sold any part of it; consequently, the requirement of "severance" is not satisfied.

An easement by necessity doesn't exist, because the two parcels, Auburnacre and Blueacre, were never under common ownership, as required for such an easement. And an easement by estoppel doesn't exist because neither Burt nor Carter ever made any substantial or foreseeable reliance on the supposed easement (e.g., they didn't spend money building a boathouse). So Carter has no easement at all.

64. No. Frederika's best hope of establishing an easement is to show that the requirements for an ***"easement of necessity"*** are satisfied. For such an easement, three conditions must be met: (1) The necessity must be "strict" rather than "reasonable"; (2) the parcels must have been under common ownership just before a conveyance; and (3) the necessity must come into existence at the time of, and be ***caused by***, the conveyance that breaks up the common ownership. Here, the first two requirements are satisfied, but the third one is not: Frederika's need to cross West Overlook was not created by the conveyance of East Overlook to her, and indeed did not come into existence until her later stroke. Cf. Rest. 3d (Servitudes), §2.15 and Illustr. 8 thereto (where need arises post-conveyance because government condemns the access road used by the would-be dominant parcel, no easement by necessity exists).

Nor can this be an "easement by estoppel," because such an easement requires substantial and foreseeable *reliance* by the would-be easement holder as of the time the easement came into existence. Since the facts tell us that Frederika was, as of the moment she took, happy to enter and exit by boat, she has not relied on the right to cross West Overlook.

65. Yes. Ben has obtained an easement by *prescription*. When one property owner uses another's property for more than the statute of limitations period applicable to adverse-possession actions, and does so in an adverse manner (see answer to prior question), an easement by prescription results. The requirement of "adverse" use is satisfied here by the fact that Ben never asked Astrid's permission, and Astrid never expressly consented, merely tolerated the use. The use must be reasonably continuous, which was the case here. The use need not be exclusive, since it is only an easement by prescription, not formal title, that is being granted by adverse possession. This easement by prescription, once it came into existence in 2005, became a burden on Astrid's land, so that Charles is bound even though he was not the owner while the easement was ripening.

66. Yes. The original deed from Dunes to George created an easement appurtenant, since the free-golf rights were clearly intended to benefit a purchaser of the house in his capacity as owner of a house adjacent to the course. Both the benefit and burden of an easement appurtenant pass with transfer of the property. (It doesn't matter that the deed to the dominant parcel doesn't mention the easement — when a dominant parcel is conveyed, an easement appurtenant automatically passes unless the parties manifest a different intention.) Thus the benefit passed when George sold the dominant parcel to Henry, and the burden passed when Dunes Development sold the servient parcel to Ian. (This rule that both benefit and burden pass with the land is always subject to a contrary agreement; thus if the original deed from Dunes to George had said that George's rights were not transferable to a subsequent purchaser of a house, Henry would be out of luck. But here, no such provision was present in the deed.)

67. No. An easement is like any other estate in land, in the sense that any extinguishment of it must normally satisfy the Statute of Frauds. Therefore, Quince's oral statement, taken by itself, did not extinguish the easement, and that easement passed to Raymond when the dominant tenement (the quarry and manufacturing plant) were sold to Raymond.

68. (a) A license. A license is a right to use the licensor's land that is revocable at the will of the licensor. A license is not required to satisfy the Statute of Frauds, and thus may be created orally. This is what happened here: Abbott did not sign any writing, and Bingham's confirmatory letter did not satisfy the Statute of Frauds as is normally required for an easement (since it was not signed by Abbott, the only person who could create the easement); nonetheless, a license was created.

(b) No. The feature that distinguishes a license from an easement is that the license is *revocable at the will of the licensor*. Therefore, Abbott had the right at any time to revoke the license, regardless of his motive.

69. No. Since Claire never promised to pay for repairs, the only way Bertrand's promise could be binding on Claire is if that promise was a "covenant running with the land." In particular, Claire will only be bound if the burden of the covenant runs with the land. At common law, there are several requirements in order for the burden to run. One is that the burden "touch and concern" the land. Here, this requirement is satisfied, since non-payment would result in a lien which would touch and concern the land. But a second requirement in most states is that there must be *"horizontal privity"* between promisor and promisee. In particular, it remains the general rule in states following the common-law approach that the *burden of the* *covenant may not run with the land where the original parties to the covenant were "strangers to title,"* i.e., had no property relationship between them at the time of the promise. Here, this rule is not satisfied: Allison and Bertrand were strangers to title, and thus could not create a covenant the burden of which would run with the land (unless Allison gave Bertrand an easement to come onto Allison's land to make repairs if she did not do so herself; the facts say that this did not happen).

70. No, probably. The vast majority of jurisdictions apply the same horizontal privity requirement for the running of a benefit as they do for the running of a burden, whatever that rule is in the particular jurisdiction. Since the burden of the promise here would not run (see the answer to the prior question) nearly all states would refuse to allow the benefit to run either, so that Doug would not be permitted to recover.

71. Yes. Since Allison's promise not to change fences is a negative promise, and the relief sought by Claire is an injunction, the question is whether we have a valid *"equitable servitude"* (not a "covenant at law," as we had in the two prior questions). An equitable servitude is a promise (usually negative in nature) relating to land, that will be enforced by courts against an assignee of the promisor.

The promise here satisfies the requirements for equitable servitudes, which are less stringent than for covenants at law. Most states still say that the promise must "touch and concern" both the promisor's land and the promisee's land; that requirement is satisfied here, since Allison (the promisor) has bound herself with respect to a structure on her property, and the appearance of Bertrand's property is directly affected by the promise. Horizontal privity (privity between Allison and Bertrand, the original promisor and promisee) is *not* required for an equitable servitude; therefore, the fact that Allison and Bertrand had no pre-existing property relationship and were thus "strangers to title" does not prevent Allison's promise from being an enforceable equitable servitude, even though it prevented Bertrand's counter-promise to pay for repairs from being enforceable at law as to Bertrand's successor (see Question 69). Nor is there any vertical privity requirement for equitable servitudes, so Claire could enforce the servitude against Doug even if she only held, say, a lease on the property owned by Bertrand. Courts will not enforce an equitable servitude against an assignee of the promisor unless the assignee was on actual or constructive notice of the servitude at the time he took possession. But the fact that the Allison-Bertrand agreement was filed in the land records put Doug on such constructive notice.

72. No. Harry is trying to enforce an equitable servitude against Isadore's property. But equity will not enforce an agreement against a subsequent purchaser unless the purchaser had *notice* of the restriction at the time he took. This notice can be either actual or "constructive." But the facts make it clear that James did not have actual notice at the time he purchased, and the absence of any valid recordation of the agreement means that James did not have constructive notice either. Therefore, the restriction is not binding against him, and he can build the pool.

73. Yes, probably. Most courts will apply the doctrine of *"implied reciprocal servitude"* in this circumstance. This theory holds that if the earlier of two purchasers (here, Kathy) acquires her land in expectation that she will be entitled to the benefit of subsequently created equitable servitudes, there is immediately created an "implied reciprocal servitude" against the developer's remaining land. For this reciprocality doctrine to apply, a general development plan must be in existence at the time of the first sale, a requirement satisfied here. Courts frequently apply the doctrine even where the restrictions are not inserted in the later deed (here, the one to Lewis).

Exam Tips on
EASEMENTS AND PROMISES CONCERNING LAND

Easements and covenants regarding land are tested more frequently than you might think. Probably that's because it's easy to draft complex questions that have an objectively-correct answer. So you have to study the technical rules in detail and master them — you can't safely rely on your ability to "argue the pros and cons" without technical knowledge.

Easements, generally

☛ **Type of easement:** Identify the *type* of easement and how it was created. Issues that arise:

   ☞ **Easement by implication:** When an easement is not expressly created, you may argue that an easement has been created by *implication*. For an easement by implication, you must find that *all* of the following conditions are met:

     [1] the servient estate was *used* for the purpose for which the easement is now being claimed *before the severance* of the dominant and servient estates;

     [2] the use was *reasonably apparent and continuous* at the time of the severance, and

     [3] the easement is *reasonably necessary* to the enjoyment of the dominant estate.

     Example: B purchases Lot 1 from O. Lot 1 is a plot with a house on it located adjacent to O's Lot 2, which also contains a house. O then sells Lot 2 to C. B razes the house on Lot 1 and discovers on her lot a sewer pipe connecting Lot 2's house with the public sewer. The pipe runs beneath the surface of the land outside where the Lot 1 house was, and then runs above the surface in an accessible crawl space located beneath the first floor of the now-razed house. B demands that C remove the pipe from B's land; C does not want to do this because of the expense of getting a substitute sewer hookup.

     C has an easement by implication for the pipe across Lot 1. Requirement [1] is clearly satisfied, because Lot 1 was used for the pipe before ownership of Lot 1 was severed from Lot 2. As to requirement [2], C will probably prevail with the argument that the part of the pipe that was in the crawl space was visible through inspection to the owner of Lot 1 at all times, so that the easement was "reasonably apparent and continuous" before the severance. Requirement [3] is easily satisfied, since the owner of Lot 2 has reasonable need for a sewer hookup. Therefore, C will be found to have an easement by implication if he can persuade a court that the use of the pipe was reasonably apparent to O at the time O sold Lot 1.

   ☞ **Easement for "light and air" (i.e., view):** A fact pattern will often indicate that construction on a parcel is *blocking the view* from an adjoining lot. Remember that an easement for an unobstructed view — sometimes called an easement of *"light and air"* — generally *cannot be created by implication.* So unless such an easement is created by express grant, you should say that no easement exists.

☞ **Easement by necessity:** The requirements for an *easement by necessity* are different from those for an easement by implication. For the easement-by-necessity, three requirements must be met:

[1] The servient and dominant parcels must have been under **common ownership** at one time (this requirement is the same as for easement-by-implication);

[2] The use must be **"strictly necessary"** (rather than just "reasonably necessary," the standard for easement-by-implication); and

[3] The necessity must **come into existence at the time of,** and be **caused by**, the **conveyance** that breaks up the common ownership.

But there is **no requirement** that the easement have been in **actual use** prior to severance.

Here are some examples that would probably qualify as easements by necessity (always assuming that Lot 1 and Lot 2 were under common ownership before the severance that created the need for the easement):

❑ Lot 2 is inaccessible to the public road except via a right-of-way over Lot 1. (The easement-by-necessity will exist even if the road, and the need for the right-of-way, didn't come into existence until the moment the two lots were severed.)

❑ Lot 2 has a sewer line that passes through Lot 1 on its way to the public sewer, and relocating the line so it doesn't pass beneath Lot 1 would be prohibitively expensive. (In other words, on the facts of the above sewer example on p. 254, *C* would probably win on easement-by-necessity even if for some reason he lost on easement-by-implication).

☞ **Need arises later:** Be on the lookout for a fact pattern where the need arises some time *after the severance.* Requirement [3] above (that the severance must cause the need for the easement) means that if the would-be dominant parcel has some **alternative means of access** at the time of the severance, and that alternative means *disappears at some later date*, the dominant holder does not get an easement by necessity.

Example: O owns Lot 1and Lot 2, adjacent to each other. At the moment *O* sells Lot 2 to *A*, anyone on Lot 2 can get to a public road by crossing *X*'s land to the east of Lot 2, which *X* has always allowed. Two years after *A* buys Lot 2, *X* revokes *A*'s permission to cross his land. Now, the only way to exit Lot 2 to get to a road is through Lot 1. *A* does not have an easement by necessity to cross Lot 1, because *O*'s act of severing ownership of Lot 1 and Lot 2 didn't cause the necessity to arise.

☞ **Easement by prescription:** Remember that there can be an *easement by prescription* — that is, an easement can come into existence by operation of the *adverse-possession* statute.

☞ **Use must be adverse:** Be sure to identify in your answer all the requirements for this kind of easement: that it be (1) *adverse* to the owner of the servient estate; (2)

"open and notorious"; and (3) *"continuous and uninterrupted"* for the full statutory period.

Pay closest attention to the requirement that the use be *adverse* to the rights of the owner of the servient parcel. That is, look at whether the servient owner has *granted permission* to the dominant owner to use the piece of the servient's land that is in dispute — if permission has been granted, then the use is not adverse.

☞ **Express easement:** An *express* easement is one created by the express agreement of the parties. Most important: an express easement must *satisfy the Statute of Frauds* (i.e., be in writing), and must be *recorded* in the same way as any other interest in land. If a right to use land is oral, it therefore cannot be an express easement (and will usually be just a revocable "license" — see below).

☞ **Easement by estoppel:** If one landowner knows that the other is substantially relying on oral permission to use the first one's land, consider the possibility that there is an easement by estoppel, which doesn't have to satisfy the Statute of Frauds.

> *Example:* A, a farmer, wants to pipe irrigation water from a nearby river across B's land to A's own land. B gives oral permission, knowing that A will spend $30,000 on an irrigation pumping system on A's land and on the pipes. A does this. The resulting pipes that run across B's land are visible to the naked eye. Two years later, B sells to C. C revokes permission. A court will likely hold that due to A's foreseeable and substantial reliance, B created an easement by estoppel. This estoppel is binding on C, because he saw or could easily have seen the pipes on B's land before he bought.

Scope and use of easement

☛ **Scope, generally:** Once you've concluded that an easement exists, look for a change in the *use* of the easement from the time it was created. If the new use arises from the normal, *foreseeable*, development of the dominant estate without imposing an *unreasonable burden* on the servient estate, it is permissible. Be especially skeptical of expansions of the scope of express easements (as opposed to easements by implication or prescription).

☛ **Interference by servient owner:** Also look for *interference by the owner of the servient estate* — the servient owner does not have the right to *unreasonably interfere* with the dominant owner's use of the easement.

> *Example:* X holds an easement for a four-foot-wide strip of land on Z's property for an underground sewer line. Z later connects his own sewer line to X's line. This causes X's sewer line to overload and to occasionally back up waste onto X's property. Z's hookup would be considered an *unreasonable interference* with the servient estate.

Transfer of easement

☛ **Transfer of appurtenant easements:** An appurtenant easement is ordinarily *automatically transferred* along with a conveyance of the dominant estate.

☛ **Transfer of easement in gross:** Commercial easements *in gross* are *freely alienable* as long as alienation does not increase the burden on the servient estate.

> *Example:* O, the owner of Blackacre, gives an easement in gross to Telephone Co. for the erection of poles and wires on Blackacre, so Telephone Co. can provide Blackacre and other nearby owners with telephone service. Cable Co., a cable TV company, then contracts with Telephone Co. to be able to transmit cable television signals through the wires. The wear and tear on the wires is not increased as a result, and the burden on the servient estate is not increased. Therefore, the partial transfer of the easement by Telephone Co. to Cable Co. is valid.

☞ **Recording:** If alienable easements are **recorded**, subsequent grantees of the servient estate take the servient estate subject to the easement.

> *Example:* Same facts as prior example. If Telephone Co. records the easement over Blackacre, and A then buys Blackacre from O, A will be bound by the easement.

Termination of easement

☞ **Abandonment and non-use of express easement:** Fact patterns will often indicate that the easement is **no longer being used.** This is usually a trick: it's true that an easement can be extinguished by abandonment, but abandonment will be found only if the easement-holder has a **clear intent to abandon**, as shown by her **actions** (not just her words). Most importantly, the fact that the easement is **no longer needed <u>won't</u>** by itself show abandonment, at least where the easement is express (rather than by necessity or implication, both of which require that the easement continue to be necessary).

> *Example:* X owns six acres of land, which he divides into three lots. He sells two of them and retains ownership of the middle lot, Lot 2. In his deed to A, the new owner of Lot 1, X reserves for himself an easement over a dirt roadway located on that lot which is necessary for ingress and egress to the main road. After five years, a new road is constructed, making X's use of the dirt roadway unnecessary, although X continues to maintain it. If A brings an action to enjoin X from using the dirt roadway, A will fail because X did not show an intent to abandon the easement, and the fact that the easement is no longer necessary will not extinguish it (given that the easement is an express one).

☞ **Merger:** Remember that an easement can be destroyed by **"merger."** Read carefully to determine whether at any time after creation of the easement the dominant and servient estates come to be **owned by the same person** — if so, the easement is **destroyed and must be re-created** in order to be enforceable.

> *Example:* X owns six acres of land, which he divides into three lots. He sells two of them and retains ownership of the middle lot, Lot 2. In his deed to Y, the new owner of Lot 3, X reserves for himself an easement for access to a lake. Two years later, Y sells Lot 3 back to X. One month later, X sells Lot 3 to A by a deed which does not mention the easement. X then sells his Lot 2 to B by a deed granting a right-of-way over Lot 3 for access to the lake. However, A refuses to allow B access over the right-of-way when B attempts to go to the lake.
>
> If B tries to enforce the easement against A, B will lose. The easement was destroyed when the dominant and servient estates came under common ownership, i.e., when Lot 3 was sold back to X. It was not automatically revived later by X's sale of Lot 3 to A, because the X-to-A deed did not mention an easement. And X's sale of Lot 2 to B with a purported reservation of the easement did not re-create the

easement, because at that point *X* had no interest in Lot 3, and thus no power to create an easement over it.

Profits

☛ **Profits generally:** Occasionally, a landowner will give another person a right to go onto the owner's land and remove the soil or a product of it, such as sand, gravel and stone or minerals. When this happens, call the right a *"profit,"* but treat it *as if it were an easement* (since in the U.S. the rules for profits are the same as for easements).

  ☞ **Right to do what's necessary to exploit:** The holder of the easement has the right to *use and modify* the property in any way reasonably required to exploit the right.

    Example: O gives *A* the right to mine ore from Blackacre, an undeveloped parcel. The property has no roads over it. The only commercially-feasible way for *A* to mine the ore is for *A* to build a dirt road to the mine head. *A*'s profit will be interpreted to permit *A* to build this road at *A*'s expense.

Licenses

☛ **License generally:** A *"license"* is merely a personal privilege to enter upon another's land which is *revocable* and is not an interest in land. If you see a permission that's given *orally*, assume that it's a license, and that it's therefore revocable at the licensor's will.

    Example: O owns a lakefront property with a dock. O orally says to *A* (owner of a land-locked parcel 2 miles away), "Whenever you want, you may launch your boat from my dock." 6 months later, O changes his mind, and refuses to allow *A* access.

    O's grant cannot be an easement, because it's not in writing. Therefore, it's a license. Since it's a license, it's revocable at O's discretion at any time.

Covenants and Equitable Servitudes

The most tested area in this section is the *equitable servitude.* But first, some tips on *covenants*.

☛ **Covenants generally:** If one party is trying to get money damages for breach of a promise about land use, and the defendant is a successor to the one who made the promise, discuss whether the promise is a "covenant at law" that runs with the land.

  ☞ **Intent to run:** Check to make sure that the parties intended that the benefit or burden (whichever is in issue on your facts) run with the land.

    ☞ **"Assigns" as clue:** Look for the word *"assigns"* — if present, that will virtually guarantee an intent to have the benefit (or burden) run. (*Example:* "The parties hereto covenant for themselves, their heirs, successors, and assigns…" The reference to "assigns" of both parties means that the benefit and burden will both run.)

  ☞ **Privity:** In your answer, note whether there is both horizontal and vertical privity. In general, at common law *both must exist* if the burden and benefit are to run.

    ☞ **Horizontal privity:** The most important and frequently-tested type of privity is *horizontal*. Assume as a general rule that there *must be horizontal privity for either the benefit or burden to run.* In other words, make sure that at the time of the covenant, between the promisor and promisee there's either a *landlord/tenant* relationship or a *conveyance* from one to the other. Two *"strangers to title"* don't have horizontal privity at common law, and they therefore can't create a covenant whose burden or whose benefit will run.

Example: A owns Lot 1 and B owns Lot 2. There is a strip of land 10 feet by 100 feet which lies half on Lot 1 and half on Lot 2. A and B both want to use the strip of land as a driveway. They exchange covenants, under which each agrees to keep the driveway unbuilt-upon, and to pay half the costs of keeping it paved and cleared of snow. A then sells Lot 1 to C, and B sells Lot 2 to D. At common law, neither C nor D can sue the other for damages for breach of the covenant. That's so because at the time of the covenant, A and B did not have horizontal privity — they were "strangers to title" — so neither the benefit nor burden of the covenant could run with the land after a sale, under the common-law approach. (But you might note in your answer that under the modern / Third Restatement approach, horizontal privity isn't needed, so C and D *could* sue each other.)

☞ **Touches and concerns land:** Remember that the benefit will run only if that benefit *"touches and concerns"* the promisee's land; similarly, the burden will run only if it touches and concerns the promisor's land. (But the benefit can run even if the burden is "in gross," i.e., doesn't touch the promisor's land.)

  ☞ **Homeowner's association fees:** Watch for *homeowner's association fees* to *maintain common areas.* This is a commonly-tested type of real covenant. Even though the obligation is to pay money, it *is* considered to touch and concern the promisor's land.

  Example: Developer, who has developed condos that abut a golf course, puts in the deed to each unit that the owner will pay annually to an Association of home owners a pro rata share of the fees needed to maintain the course. A buys Unit 1, then sells to B, whose deed is silent about the association-fee promise. The fee promise will be deemed to touch and concern Unit 1. Therefore, the Association will be permitted to bring suit against B to recover the fees (i.e., the burden will be found to run).

☛ **Equitable servitude:** On exams, most covenants must be analyzed as equitable servitudes. That is, in the typical exam setting the promise is a negative one — "I won't use the land in a particular way" — and the plaintiff seeks an *injunction*, not damages for monetary loss.

  ☞ **General rules:** Generally, the *burden must touch and concern the land* in order to run with the land. Although the benefit need not always touch and concern the land, the original parties must be fairly specific as to who may enforce the promise. And successors will be bound only if they had *notice*.

  ☞ **Who may enforce promise:** When the words used do not clearly indicate an intent to bind subsequent transferees, look at the surrounding circumstances. If there's no clear evidence of an intent to let, say, the benefit run, it won't run.

  Example: An agreement is entered into by A and B, two neighbors, permitting A, a scientist conducting an experiment, to let his wolves wander freely over B's property. C, a scientist working with A, buys A's land and tries to enforce the promise. A court will probably hold that there was no intent that the benefit of the promise will run with the land because the promise was given specifically to *A* for the purpose of permitting *him* to complete *his* experiment.

☞ **Successor must have notice before taking:** Remember that only a successor in interest who had *actual or constructive notice* of the servitude can be *bound*. This is a very commonly tested point.

> *Example: O* owns Lot 1 and Lot 2, which are adjacent. *O* sells Lot 2 to *A*, and in the deed agrees that both Lot 1 and Lot 2 will always be limited to single-family housing, and that this limit will be binding on *O*'s and *A*'s heirs and assigns (and will be included in any later deed by either). *A* records the deed to Lot 2. *O* later sells Lot 1 to *C*, but omits the promise from the deed. *C* doesn't know about the promise when he buys. Since the neighborhood is mixed-use (including some stores), there's nothing in the nature of the neighborhood to suggest to *C* that Lot 1 may be burdened by a single-family covenant. *C* starts to build a store on Lot 1, and *A* sues to enjoin him.
>
> *A* will lose — the equitable servitude on Lot 1 isn't binding on *C*, because he took without actual notice and without any form of constructive notice (either record or inquiry). He didn't have record notice because the servitude was included only in the deed to Lot 2, and nothing about Lot 2 was in *C*'s chain of title (which involved only Lot 1). He didn't have inquiry notice because nothing about the neighborhood would have indicated that Lot 1 was likely to be burdened by a single-family-use limitation.

☞ **Subdivision plan:** Where a *developer* records a *subdivision plan* with a description of restrictions, this filing will generally accomplish two things: (1) it will indicate that the *burden and benefit* of the restrictions is intended to *run* with the land; and (2) it gives *constructive notice* to subsequent takers (so the requirement of notice is satisfied).

☞ **Zoning laws:** Don't be fooled when a fact pattern indicates that a deed restriction is *more restrictive* than the applicable *zoning* laws. That is permissible.

☞ **Implied reciprocal servitude:** Where a *large tract* of land has been *subdivided* into lots, watch for a subsequent property owner whose deed does not contain a restriction and a prior grantee who wishes to bind him to restrictions found in his own deed. As long as the court can find that (1) there was a general plan of restrictions for the subdivision; and (2) that the owner whose deed doesn't have the restriction had at least constructive notice of the general plan, the court will probably find that an *"implied reciprocal servitude"* came into existence, and will grant the injunction. This type of fact pattern is surprisingly-often tested.

CHAPTER 10

ZONING AND OTHER PUBLIC LAND-USE CONTROLS

Introductory note: This chapter is primarily about the law of zoning. However, we also consider two other types of land-use regulation: (1) regulations on subdivision; and (2) regulations protecting the environment or protecting historical structures. We also consider two problems raised by the U.S. Constitution's "taking" clause: (1) the possibility that a land-use regulation may so interfere with an owner's enjoyment of his property that the regulation is found to be a "taking" for which the government must pay compensation (a topic which we consider at the very start of this chapter); and (2) the laws on "eminent domain," or condemnation (a topic which we consider at the very end of this chapter).

I. THE "TAKING" CLAUSE, AND LAND-USE CONTROLS AS IMPLICIT TAKINGS

A. Fifth Amendment's "taking" clause: Governments, both state and federal, have the right to take private property for public use. This power is known as the right of "eminent domain" (discussed *infra*, p. 298). However, the Fifth Amendment to the U.S. Constitution provides that *"private property [shall not] be taken for public use, without just compensation."* This is the so-called *"taking"* clause. This clause is made binding on the states by means of the Fourteenth Amendment.

B. The taking-regulation distinction: If the court finds that private property has been "taken" by the government, compensation must be paid. But if the state merely *regulates* property use in a manner consistent with the state's "police power," then *no compensation needs to be paid*, even though the owner's use of his property, or even its value, has been substantially diminished. It thus becomes crucial to distinguish between a compensable "taking" and a non-compensable "regulation."

Land-use regulations that may require the court to distinguish between taking and regulation include *zoning* regulations, *environmental protection* rules, *landmark preservation* schemes, and other schemes by which the government does not attempt to take title to a landowner's property but does regulate his use of that property.

1. General principles: The fact that a state or a local government *labels* something a "regulation" does not mean that it will not be found by a court to have amounted to a taking for which compensation must be paid. For a land-use regulation to avoid being a taking, it must satisfy two requirements:

[1] It must *"substantially advance legitimate state interests"*; and

[2] It must *not* "den[y] an owner *economically viable use* of his land."

Agins v. Tiburon, 447 U.S. 255 (1980).

2. **Difficult to apply:**   These two requirements have been very difficult to apply in practice. However, we can say the following about them:

    a. **Legitimate interests:**   A *broad range* of governmental purposes constitute "legitimate state interests" — maintaining residential zoning, preserving landmarks, and protecting the environment, are among the interests that the Supreme Court has found to be adequate.

    b. **Tight means-end fit:**   There must be a relatively *tight fit* between the state interest being promoted and the regulation chosen, as the result of *Nollan v. California Coastal Commission*, discussed *infra*, p. 267, and *Dolan v. Tigard*, *infra*, pp. 267-268. More than a mere "rational relation" between means and end is required where a regulation interferes with land use.

    c. **Deprivation of economically viable:**   Few land-use regulations are likely to be found to deny the owner *economically viable use* of his land. But regulations denying the right to build *any structure* on the land would qualify. See, e.g., *First English Evangelical Lutheran Church*, 482 U.S. 304 (1987) (another aspect of which is discussed *infra*, p. 268) where such a denial of all economically viable use was found to have occurred.

3. **Physical occupation:**   If the government makes or authorizes a *permanent physical occupation* of the property, this will *automatically* be found to constitute a taking, no matter how minor the interference with the owner's use and no matter how important the countervailing governmental interests. In **Loretto v. Teleprompter Manhattan CATV Corp.**, 458 U.S. 419 (1982), the Court formulated this *"per se"* rule, and applied it to invalidate a statute which required landlords to permit cable television companies to install their cable facilities on the landlord's rental property. (The scheme permitted landlords to charge the cable companies what was in most instances a maximum one-time fee of $1.)

    a. **Rationale:**   The Court distinguished between cases where the state merely prescribes how the owner may use his property (in which case a balancing test is applied to determine whether there is a taking) and cases of permanent physical occupation. The latter type of invasion is "qualitatively more intrusive than perhaps any other category of property regulation," and therefore requires compensation regardless of whether the government action achieves an important public benefit, and regardless of whether it has more than a minimal economic impact on the owner. (Here, for instance, compensation was required even though, by the majority's admission, only about 1 1/2 cubic feet were involved.)

    b. **Easement is physical occupation:**   A post-*Loretto* case shows that the Court will take an expansive view of what kind of regulation constitutes a "physical occupation" of the owner's property. In that case the Court held that a state's refusal to grant a building permit except upon the transfer to the public of a permanent *easement* for the public to pass along a strip of the owners' property constituted a "permanent physical occupation" of that property. See *Nollan v. California Coastal Commission*, also discussed *infra*, p. 267. The easement in *Nollan* would simply have permitted members of the public to walk along the owner's sandy strip parallel to the ocean on their way from one public beach to another. Even though this easement would not have permitted any given individual to remain on the owner's land, a physical occupation was found to exist, so that there was a taking of the owners' property.

4. **Diminution in value:** The more drastic the ***reduction in value*** of the owner's property, the more likely a taking is to be found.

   a. ***Mahon* case:** The significance of a large diminution in value is shown by the classic case of ***Pennsylvania Coal Co. v. Mahon***, 260 U.S. 393 (1922).

      i. **Facts:** A landowner had bought the surface rights to land, and the house on it, under a chain of title which reserved to a coal company the right to mine coal from under the property. Thereafter, Pennsylvania enacted a statute preventing subsurface mining where a house might be caused to sink. The effect of the statute was to bar the coal company completely from mining under the owner's land.

      ii. **Holding:** The Supreme Court held that the regulation so utterly impaired the right to mine coal that it was nearly the equivalent of an appropriation or destruction of the coal. Therefore, the regulation was a taking, which could not be carried out without compensation to the coal company. The Court, in a majority opinion by Justice Holmes, noted that "while property may be regulated to a certain extent, if regulation goes too far it will be recognized as a taking."

      iii. **Dissent:** But a dissent, by Justice Brandeis, argued that the regulation was merely "the prohibition of a noxious use," and therefore did not require compensation. (The "noxious use" factor is discussed immediately below.)

      iv. **May no longer be valid:** The precise outcome of *Pennsylvania Coal* would likely be different today. In *Keystone Bituminous Coal Ass'n v. DeBenedictis*, 480 U.S. 470 (1987), the Court by a 5-4 vote upheld a modern (1966) Pennsylvania version of the statute struck down in *Pennsylvania Coal*. The 1966 statute required that 50% of the coal beneath existing public buildings and dwellings be left in place to provide surface support. The majority made some efforts to distinguish *Pennsylvania Coal*, but there is so little difference between the two statutes that it seems likely that *Pennsylvania Coal* would turn out the other way if decided today.

      However, the ***general principle*** for which the case is cited — that the more drastic the reduction in value of the owner's property, the more likely a taking is to be found — remains ***valid***. (*Keystone* also illustrates that where the state is acting to prevent ***harm to the public***, the courts will be very reluctant to invalidate the regulation as a "taking." See the discussion of the "prevention of harm" rationale, *infra*, p. 265.)

5. **Denial of all economically viable use of land:** Since (as just noted) the more drastic the reduction in value of the owner's property, the more likely a taking is to be found, it's not surprising that the Court has imposed a flat rule that a taking occurs where an owner has

been deprived of ***all economically viable use*** of his land. See *Agins v. Tiburon*, 447 U.S. 255 (1980).

a. **Particular use eliminated:** Cases in which such an extreme taking by deprivation of economically viable use is found are very rare. The fact that the ***particular*** use made by the plaintiff has been completely foreclosed ***will not be enough.*** For instance, suppose a parcel contains an aluminum smelter worth $100 million, and the city where the smelter is located then bans all smelting. The fact that P's *particular* land use — operation of the smelter — has been totally foreclosed will not be enough to make the regulation a "taking"; P is still free to convert the smelter to other uses, or even to raze it and put up some other structure (or sell it to someone who will).

b. **Total ban:** On the other hand, a ***total and permanent ban*** on the building of ***any structure*** on property *is* likely to be enough to deny the owner "all economically viable use" of his land, and thus to constitute a taking automatically.

   Example: South Carolina, in order to protect its coastline from continued erosion, enacts the Beachfront Management Act, which defines certain "critical areas" of erosion danger, and bars any owner of a lot in a critical area from building any permanent habitable structure on the parcel. P is the owner of two parcels which, at the time he bought them for nearly $1 million, were allowed to have houses built upon them; passage of the Act has the effect of preventing P from building any permanent structure on either lot. P contends that this "regulation" deprives him of all economic use of his property, and thus constitutes a taking. A lower state court agrees that P has been deprived of all economically viable use, but the South Carolina Supreme Court reverses on the grounds that even if this is true, the state may regulate to preserve its citizens' health and safety, and that such regulation is not a taking.

   Held (by the U.S. Supreme Court), if P has truly been deprived of all economically viable use of his property, a "taking" has occurred. It is up to the South Carolina courts to decide whether P has really been deprived of all economically viable use. If he has been, a taking exists even though the state is trying to protect the health and safety of residents (unless the state already had, under the "background principles of the state's law of property and nuisance," the right to prevent the particular use by P, an issue to be decided by the state courts on remand; this aspect of the case is described *infra*, p. 265). ***Lucas v. South Carolina Coastal Council***, 505 U.S. 1003 (1992).

c. **Temporary moratorium on development:** In *Lucas*, the ban on all economically viable use of P's property purported to be permanent. What happens if the government merely imposes a *temporary* delay on all economically viable use of property, as where a planning board institutes a ***"moratorium"*** on development of certain property — is the government automatically required to pay just compensation for this delay? As a result of a post-*Lucas* case decided in 2002, the answer is ***"not necessarily"*** — the Court will instead consider ***all the surrounding circumstances*** to determine whether the delay of all economically viable use was so severe as to require that compensation be paid. ***Tahoe-Sierra Preservation Council, Inc. v. Tahoe Regional Planning Agency***, 535 U.S. 302 (2002).

i. **Categorical ruling rejected:** The Supreme Court, by a 6-3 vote, *refused* to find a categorical right to compensation for such a temporary delay in the right to make any economically-viable use of one's property. In an opinion by Justice Stevens, the Court said that "the answer to the abstract question whether a temporary [development] moratorium effects a taking is neither 'yes, always' nor 'no, never'; the answer depends upon the *particular circumstances* of the case."

   (1) **Distinction:** The Court distinguished sharply between *physical* takings and *regulatory* takings. Even a temporary physical occupation of P's property entitles him to compensation. But a similar rule for temporary regulatory takings would wreak havoc: "Land-use regulations are ubiquitous and most of them impact property values in some tangential way — often in completely unanticipated ways. Treating them all as *per se* takings would transform government regulation into a *luxury few governments could afford.* By contrast, physical appropriations are relatively rare, easily identified, and usually represent a greater affront to individual property rights."

   (2) ***Lucas* marginalized:** One consequence of *Tahoe-Sierra* is to *marginalize* the *Lucas* decision. As Justice Stevens put it in *Tahoe-Sierra*, "the categorical rule in *Lucas* was carved out for the 'extraordinary case' in which a regulation *permanently* deprives property of all value; the *default rule* remains that, in the regulatory taking context, we require a more *fact specific* inquiry."

ii. **Significance:** *Tahoe-Sierra* does *not* mean that a ban on all economically-viable use of one's property need not be compensated merely because it turns out to be temporary. The case merely means that there is no *automatic* right to compensation — instead, the surrounding circumstances must be considered in deciding whether there has been a taking. For example, if the property actually *increased in value* during the moratorium, that would cut strongly against a finding that there had been a taking.

6. **"Prevention of harm" or "noxious use" rationale:** A regulation rather than a taking is likely to be found where the property use being prevented is one that is *harmful* or "*noxious*" to others. For instance, a zoning ordinance may properly prevent the operation of a steel mill in the middle of a residential neighborhood; in general, anything which the common law would recognize as a public or private *nuisance* may be barred by regulation, without the need for compensation.

   a. **Bar must fall within common-law nuisance principles:** However, the mere fact that the legislature has labeled a certain use as being "harmful" or "noxious" is *not enough* to ensure that the land-use restriction will be found to be a regulation rather than a taking. If a land-use regulation is so severe that it deprives the owner of "all economically beneficial use of his land," then the restrictions must "do no more than duplicate the result that could have been achieved in the courts — by adjacent land owners ... under the State's law of *private nuisance*, or by the State under its complementary power to abate nuisances that affect the public generally. ... " *Lucas, supra,* p. 264. In other words, the legislature cannot suddenly decide that a particular use is so harmful that it should be immediately banned, if the ban will deprive an owner of all economically viable use of his land, and if the common-law principles of nuisance would not allow the state to get the use forbidden by a court.

> **Example:** Recall the *Lucas* case, *supra*, p. 264: South Carolina bans P and similarly-situated coastal land owners from building any permanent habitable structure on their property. *Held* (by the Supreme Court), given that the state courts have decided that this ban deprives P of all economically viable use of his land, P has suffered a "taking" unless, under South Carolina law, the state could have achieved the same total ban on dwellings by use of the common law of nuisance. Furthermore, "it seems unlikely that common-law principles would have prevented the erection of any habitable or productive improvements on [P's] land; they rarely support prohibition of the 'essential use' of land." However, resolution of this issue is up to the South Carolina courts. *Lucas v. South Carolina Coastal Council*, *supra*, p. 264.

C. **Particular types of land-use regulation:** Let's now look at some particular types of land-use regulations, to see whether they are valid regulations or compensable takings. (Sometimes, the court strikes down a regulation on the grounds that it is so broad as to violate the owner's **substantive due process** rights, rather than because it is a compensable "taking." But roughly the same criteria seem to apply for a due process attack as for an attack based on the "taking" clause.)

1. **Zoning regulation:** In cases where **zoning regulations** impair an owner's use of his property, the Court has been especially **reluctant** to find a compensable taking. A zoning ordinance will not be stricken as violative of due process unless it is **"clearly arbitrary and unreasonable**, having no substantial relation to the public health, safety, morals or general welfare." *Moore v. East Cleveland*, 431 U.S. 494 (1977) (also discussed *infra*, p. 272.)

   a. **Moore:** *Moore* itself was an extremely rare invalidation of a zoning ordinance. The ordinance there allowed only members of a "family" to live together, and defined "family" so narrowly that a grandmother was barred from living with her two grandchildren, one by each of two different children.

2. **Environmental regulation:** Regulations designed to protect the **environment** are similarly subjected to only **mild review**, even if the property owner's ability to use his land is substantially circumscribed.

   a. **Ban on gravel mining:** For instance, in *Goldblatt v. Hempstead*, 369 U.S. 590 (1962), the Court upheld a town "safety regulation" preventing a property owner from continuing to mine a sand and gravel pit as he had done for 30 years. The Court found that the ban was a "reasonable" exercise of the "police power." The Court said that the diminution in the value of the property, although relevant, was not conclusive. (But again, remember that if the regulation **completely deprives** an owner of **economically viable use** of his land, and that regulation could not be justified under common-law nuisance principles, a "taking" will occur even if the government's objective is to protect the environment. See *Lucas v. South Carolina Coastal Council*, *supra*, p. 264.)

3. **Landmark preservation:** **Landmark preservation** schemes, like zoning and environmental regulations, will seldom constitute a taking. For instance, in *Penn Central Transportation Co. v. New York City*, 438 U.S. 104 (1978), the Court found that the New York

City Landmarks Preservation Law did not effect a taking of plaintiff's property. The case is discussed further *infra*, pp. 295-296.

D. Tight means-end fit required: The above discussion of regulations involving zoning, environmental protection, landmark preservation, etc., suggests that a variety of governmental objectives will be found to satisfy the requirement that the government pursue a "legitimate state interest" (see *supra*, p. 261). However, the Supreme Court has in the last few decades required a *very close fit* between the *means* chosen by the state (i.e., the particular land-use regulation selected) and the governmental *objective* being pursued. Even a compelling state interest will be to no avail if the means chosen by the government are not quite closely tailored to advance that interest. (This recent approach in land-use regulation cases contrasts quite sharply with the Court's general approach in other economic regulation contexts, where all that is required is that there be a "minimally rational relation" between the means chosen and the end being pursued.) This modern approach to the means-end fit stems from two cases decided since 1987.

1. **The "substantially advance" requirement:** First, in *Nollan v. California Coastal Commission*, 483 U.S. 825 (1987), the Court required that the means chosen by the government (the land-use regulation) *"substantially advance"* the governmental objective being pursued.

2. **The "rough proportionality" requirement:** Then, in a very striking use of rigorous review, the Court held that when a city conditions a building permit on some *"give back"* by the owner, there must be a *"rough proportionality"* between the burdens on the public that the building permit would bring about, and the benefit to the public from the give back. This "rough proportionality" standard was announced in *Dolan v. City of Tigard*, 512 U.S. 374 (1994).

   a. **Facts:** In *Dolan*, P was a property owner who wanted to enlarge the plumbing and electric supply store she ran on the property. D, the city of Tigard, issued her a permit to do this, but conditioned the permit on P's willingness to (among other things) convey a 15-foot strip of land on her property to the city, to be used as a bicycle pathway. (She would have been required to convey approximately 10% of the property.) The city, at the time it asked for the trade-off, asserted two reasons for it: (1) P would be paving over a larger part of her property, thus expanding the "impervious surface" and worsening the danger of flooding from a nearby creek; the unpaved pathway would help soak up some of the flood waters; and (2) P's bigger store would increase automobile traffic to her site; the bike path, by increasing the attractiveness of biking, might result in a countervailing decrease in car traffic.

   b. **P's attack:** P attacked the requirement that she convey the 15-foot strip as an unconstitutional taking of her property without compensation.

   c. **Court agrees:** The Court, by a 5-4 vote, agreed that the trade-off requirement was an unconstitutional taking of P's property. The Court first noted that under *Nollan, supra,* there had to be an "essential nexus" between the permit condition exacted by the city, and the "legitimate state interest" being pursued; the Court found this requirement satisfied here (since there was a nexus between preventing flooding from the creek and limiting development on P's property; similarly, there was a nexus between reducing traffic congestion and providing for an alternative means of transport, biking).

   d. **"Rough proportionality":**   But the novel part of the Court's holding came in the imposition of a *second* requirement that any permit condition must meet: there must be a *"rough proportionality"* between the trade-off demanded by the city and the burden to the public from P's proposed development. The Court found that the city here had not satisfied this requirement. For example, although the city had calculated somewhat precisely the number of additional car trips per day that would be caused by P's expansion, the city had not tried to show how much of this traffic would be reduced by the proposed bikeway — it was not enough for the city to conclude, as it had, that the proposed bikeway *"could"* offset some of the traffic demand (though a finding that the bikeway "would" or "was likely to" offset some of the demand would apparently have sufficed).

   e. **Dissent:**   The four dissenters in *Dolan* objected to the new "rough proportionality" requirement. When a town imposes conditions and exactions on a person who wants to develop a retail business, this is a form of "business regulation," the dissenters argued, that has always been and should continue to be benefitted by a "strong presumption of constitutional validity." To the dissenters, thrusting on the city the burden of showing rough proportionality, on a case-by-case basis, amounted to "the Court's resurrection of a species of *substantive due process* analysis that it firmly rejected decades ago."

   3. Significance: *Nollan* and *Dolan* demonstrate a much harsher review by the Court of land-use regulations. We now have a scheme whereby: (1) the means chosen by the local government unit must *"substantially advance"* a legitimate aim; and (2) any "give up" required of a property owner must be *"roughly proportional"* to the harm caused by the new land use. As the majority put it in *Dolan*, "We see no reason why the Takings Clause of the Fifth Amendment, as much a part of the Bill of Rights as the First Amendment or the Fourth Amendment, should be relegated to the status of a *poor relation. . . .* "

E. Remedies for temporary takings: The issue of whether a "taking" has occurred will usually arise in one of two ways: (1) the landowner sues to *enjoin* a regulation, contending that the regulation is violating his due process rights; or (2) the landowner brings an *"inverse condemnation"* suit, claiming that the government has effectively appropriated his property, and must pay for it. In a suit brought under (1), the court will simply *strike the regulation* if it finds that due process has been violated; it will not order "just compensation" to be paid. But in an inverse condemnation suit, if a taking is found to have occurred, the court will order *just compensation*.

   1. Temporary takings: The Supreme Court has held that if a land-use regulation is so broad that it constitutes a taking, the landowner may bring an inverse condemnation suit and is entitled to receive *damages* for the *temporary* taking (temporary because the regulation is struck down by the Court). This key holding occurred in *First English Evangelical Lutheran Church v. Los Angeles County*, 482 U.S. 304 (1987).

   a. **Rationale:**   In reaching this conclusion, the Court relied heavily on earlier cases holding that the government's appropriation of private property during World War II, though "temporary," nonetheless constituted a taking. Therefore, " 'temporary' takings which, as here, deny a landowner all use of his property, are not different in kind from permanent takings, for which the Constitution clearly requires compensation."

    b. Application to facts: Thus P in *First English* would be entitled to compensation if it could prove what it alleged in its complaint: that an ordinance passed in 1979 forbidding all use of property within a newly-established "interim flood protection area," and not invalidated by the time the suit started in 1985, deprived it of all use of its property during that period.

  2. Scope of decision: *First English* is probably not as far-reaching as it might at first seem. The case does not establish that any time a land-use regulation interferes with an owner's use of his property and is later found to be invalid, compensation must be paid. Instead, the case only holds that where an owner is denied ***all use*** of his property, and for at least a reasonably ***substantial time*** (e.g., the six or more years in *First English*), compensation must be paid. The majority expressly noted that it was *not* dealing with the "quite different questions that would arise in the case of ***normal delays*** in obtaining building permits, changes in zoning ordinances, variances, and the like[.]"

    a. Consequence: But if the owner can show ***extraordinary delays*** — ones that were not due to routine permit-issuance delays or other parts of the usual land-development process — the owner can recover compensation for the delay.

F. Subsequent owner who takes with notice of restriction: Suppose the case is one of those relatively uncommon ones in which the land-use restriction is so great that a taking will be deemed to have occurred. What happens if the person who owns the property at the time the regulation is put into effect does not sue, but a ***subsequent buyer*** — who buys the property ***with knowledge*** of the restriction — then sues on a takings theory?

  1. *Palazzolo* case: The Supreme Court has held that the subsequent buyer ***may proceed*** with the suit just as the original owner could have. A contrary rule, the Court held, would enable the state in effect "to put an expiration date on the Takings Clause." This ought not to be the rule, the Court continued, because "[f]uture generations, too, have a right to challenge unreasonable limitations on the use and value of land." *Palazzolo v. Rhode Island*, 533 U.S. 606 (2001).

II. ZONING — GENERALLY

A. General nature of zoning: The principal type of public land-use regulation existing in America is ***zoning***. Zoning is generally done on the local, municipal level. The municipality's power to zone comes from the state "police power" (discussed further *infra*, p. 274), which is delegated by state statute to the locality.

B. Use zoning: Perhaps the most important kind of zoning is "use zoning", by which the municipality is divided into districts, in each of which ***only certain uses*** of land are permitted.

  1. *Euclid* case: Such a use zoning scheme was approved by the U.S. Supreme Court in ***Village of Euclid v. Ambler Realty Co.***, 272 U.S. 365 (1926).

    a. Facts of *Euclid*: P, a realty company, owned vacant land in the Village of Euclid which it wished to develop for industrial purposes. The land lay in a district that the

Village had zoned solely for residential uses. P claimed that the value of its land was thereby reduced from $10,000 per acre to $2,500 per acre, and that the ordinance was an unconstitutional violation of P's due process and equal protection rights.

b. Holding: The Supreme Court held that a zoning measure would be struck down as unconstitutional only if it was *"clearly arbitrary* and *unreasonable*, having no substantial relation to the public health, safety, morals, or *general welfare."* The use zoning scheme, insofar as it reduced traffic and noise in residential areas, and facilitated fire prevention (by making it possible to keep fire apparatus suitable for each district's particular use) passed muster under this general standard. The court refused to evaluate the wisdom of each minor provision of the ordinance, since the overall reasonableness of the scheme was clear.

2. "Euclidean" zoning: The *Euclid* case, by resolving doubts about the constitutionality of use zoning, gave rise to a rapid spread of similar ordinances across the nation. The division of a municipality into separate use districts is in fact frequently referred to as "Euclidean zoning".

3. Cumulative use scheme: The ordinance in *Euclid*, like most of the ordinances adopted in the early days of zoning, was *cumulative* in nature. That is, each successive district (starting from single-family residential and going through heavy industrial) permitted all the uses allowed in the previous districts, and added some new ones. Thus single-family residential use was allowed in *every district*, even heavy industrial.

   a. Modern trend differs: But recently enacted ordinances have usually departed from this cumulative scheme. In particular, residential use is generally not allowed in a district zoned for industry. Dwellings in industrial areas are undesirable on health and safety grounds; also, the industrial users may be harassed by nuisance suits brought by the residential owners, and the availability of the large tracts often needed by industry may be curtailed by the intermingling of small residences. See 4 Williams §101.13.

C. Density controls: Distinct from restrictions on use are zoning restrictions which regulate, directly or indirectly, the *density* of population or construction. The usual purposes of such regulations are to maintain the community's attractive appearance, to avoid an overburdening of public facilities (e.g., schools, parks, sewers, etc.) and sometimes (though almost never publicly admitted) to exclude undesirable residents (e.g., poor families who will live in apartments). Many of these density regulations are discussed extensively *infra*, p. 284, in the treatment of exclusionary zoning. A few of the more common techniques are:

1. Minimum lot size: The establishment of a *minimum lot size* for single-family homes;

2. Setbacks: *"Setback"* requirements, mandating a certain amount of unbuilt land on some or all sides of the structure;

3. Minimum square footage: Particularly in single-family residential zones, a *minimum square footage* for the dwelling (e.g., no dwelling permitted with fewer than 1,000 square feet of floor space);

4. Height limits: In the case of office towers and apartment buildings, *height limits*.

III. LEGAL LIMITS ON ZONING

A. **Constitutional limits:** Both the federal Constitution and those of the individual states may impose limits on zoning. Furthermore, at least three different constitutional clauses (in the federal Constitution, and in the constitutions of most states) may bear on the zoning problem. These are (1) the *due process* clause (which has both procedural and substantive implications); (2) the *equal protection* clause; and (3) the *"takings"* clause. (The "takings" clause is discussed *supra*, p. 261, so here we consider only the due process and equal protection clauses.) In the discussion which follows, references are to the federal Constitution unless otherwise noted.

B. **Procedural due process:** The Fourteenth Amendment of the U.S. Constitution provides that no state shall "deprive any person of life, liberty, or property, without *due process of law*." The due process clause has been construed to impose certain *procedural requirements* upon the zoning process; that is, putting aside the substantive content of zoning decisions, there are certain restrictions on the *means* by which zoning actions may be taken.

   1. **Administrative action only:** Procedural due process requirements apply only to zoning actions that are *administrative*, rather than *legislative*, in nature. See 91 Harv. L. Rev. 1508. Thus where an entire, general, municipal zoning ordinance is adopted (clearly a legislative act), there are no procedural due process requirements at all. In this situation, there is no requirement that a landowner who will be affected by the new ordinance be given a hearing; nor is there any requirement that the legislative body which passes the ordinance (typically the town council or board of supervisors) be "impartial."

      a. **Distinction between legislative and administrative action:** In the zoning context, it is not always simple to determine whether a given action is administrative or legislative. Generally an act by an *elected body*, that concerns broad *policy* issues, is a legislative act; thus the enactment of a city-wide zoning ordinance, or of a "master plan" (see *infra*, p. 276) will almost always be considered legislative. The granting of a *variance* (*infra*, p. 278) or of a permit for a *special use* (*infra*, p. 280), since it is usually given by a non-elected body (e.g., the board of zoning appeals), and concerns only one or a small number of property owners, is generally considered to be administrative.

   2. **What process is due:** Once it is established that the proceeding is administrative rather than legislative, an affected landowner receives several procedural protections:

      a. **Right to hearing:** He has the right to a *hearing*, at which he may present evidence and make arguments.

      b. **Impartial tribunal:** He has the right to a decision-making body that is *impartial*. Thus the officials making the decision must not have any *pecuniary interest* in the outcome and must not be subject to undue nonpecuniary influences (e.g., violent community sentiment). 91 Harv. L. Rev. 1526.

      c. **Explanation of decision:** The body which makes the decision must *explain its reasons* for its decision; this will usually require it to make *findings of fact* (e.g., that the denial of a variance to O would not cause him "unnecessary hardship" because he brought the need for the variance upon himself; see *infra*, p. 278).

3. **Which owners have property interests:**   Even if a decision is administrative, not every property owner who may be affected by it will have the right of procedural due process. Certainly an owner whose own property will be subject to a change in classification has such a right. Probably neighboring landowners whose own property may change substantially in value because of the decision are also protected. Thus if O sought a variance to put a lumberyard in a residential area, neighboring lot owners would certainly have the procedural protections referred to above. See 91 Harv. L. Rev. 1517.

C. **Substantive due process:**   At one time (particularly during the New Deal), courts were quick to strike down all sorts of legislative measures on the grounds that they violated the *substantive* property rights of individuals. This was done under the doctrine of "substantive due process." The entire substantive due process concept, which rests largely on courts' willingness to strike down legislation which they believe to be unwise, is seldom applied today. In the zoning area, an ordinance or administrative decision is generally held to be violative of substantive due process only if it fails to bear a ***rational relationship*** to a ***permissible state objective***. To put it another way, the zoning action does not violate substantive due process if it is within the government's ***"police power,"*** a term discussed further *infra*, p. 274.

1. **Broad objectives:**   Since under *Village of Euclid v. Ambler Realty Co.*, discussed *supra*, p. 269, permissible state objectives of zoning include "the public health, safety, morals, or general welfare," it is a relatively rare zoning action that does not have a "rational relationship" to one of these extremely broad objectives. See, e.g., the discussion of "aesthetic zoning", *infra*, p. 275, such zoning for aesthetic purposes is generally permitted today.

2. **Family gets special protection:**   One area in zoning law where a substantive due process argument may well succeed is where the ordinance ***substantially interferes with family rights***. For instance, in ***Moore v. City of East Cleveland***, 431 U.S. 494 (1977), the city of East Cleveland zoned a certain area for single-family occupancy. It defined "family" so as to exclude most extended families; a "family" could include a couple, their parents, and their dependent children, but no more than one child with dependent children. The ordinance thus prohibited P from living with her two sons and her two grandsons, one from each son. The city commenced criminal proceedings against P for the violation, and she was convicted (and sentenced to five days in jail!)

    a. **Holding in *Moore*:**   The Supreme Court reversed P's conviction on substantive due process grounds. The majority opinion noted that freedom of choice in matters of family life is one of the liberties protected by the due process clause; the East Cleveland ordinance had the effect of "slicing deeply into the family itself." The Court rejected the idea that only the "nuclear" family is entitled to due process protection: "The tradition of uncles, aunts, cousins, and especially grandparents sharing a household along with parents and children has roots equally venerable and equally deserving of constitutional recognition." In view of the importance of these familial rights, the Court held, the City failed to establish a strong enough connection between the ordinance and its objectives (which the City claimed were to prevent overcrowding, minimize traffic, and avoid a financial burdening of the local schools).

        i. **No "strict scrutiny":**   The Court in *Moore* did ***not*** apply a ***"strict scrutiny"*** standard (as is generally applied in cases where state action discriminates against a racial minority). But it seemed to require more than a mere "rational relation" between the ordinance and the municipality's objectives.

   b. Dissent: Four members of the Court dissented in *Moore*. Justices Stewart and Rehnquist based their dissent on the grounds that although certain family rights are entitled to due process protection, "The interest that the appellant may have in permanently sharing a single kitchen and a suite of contiguous rooms with some of her relatives simply does not rise to that level. . . ." (in contrast to, *inter alia*, the right of parents to send their children to private schools or to have their children instructed in foreign languages.)

3. **Compared with *Belle Terre*:** But the Supreme Court, in granting family relations substantive due process protection against interference from zoning, has limited the idea of "family" to *relatives by blood or marriage*. In the pre-*Moore* case of *Village of Belle Terre v. Boraas*, 416 U.S. 1 (1974), the Village of Belle Terre limited its entire area to single-family dwelling use; the word "family" was defined as "one or more persons related by blood, adoption, or marriage, living and cooking together as a single house-keeping unit. . . ." The ordinance also permitted a household of "a number of persons but *not exceeding two* . . . living and cooking together as a single housekeeping unit though not related by blood, adoption, or marriage. . . ."

   a. Argument in *Belle Terre*: The Ps in *Belle Terre* sought to rent their house to six unrelated college students. The Ps claimed that the ordinance was unconstitutional on a number of grounds, including the fact that it violated the privacy rights of potential newcomers, and interfered with the right to travel.

   b. Holding: The Court found the ordinance to be *constitutional*. It was not troubled by the fact that the ordinance placed no limit on the size of biological families, yet limited households of unrelated persons to two. The Court cited the Village's desire to maintain "A quiet place where yards are wide, people few, and motor vehicles restricted. . . . It is [permissible] to lay out zones where family values, youth values, and the blessings of quiet seclusion and clean air make the area a sanctuary for people." The Village's restrictions were held to be rationally related to these permissible objectives.

      i. Distinction from *Moore*: Thus *Belle Terre* can be seen as holding that zoning *may substantially restrict the rights of people to form households together*, whereas *Moore* indicates that the same zoning power will be substantially *curtailed* if it is used to affect the *traditional (biological) family structure*.

4. **Drastic reduction in value:** A second situation in which a substantive due process attack on a zoning regulation might succeed is where the regulation *almost completely destroys* the pre-existing *economic value* of the property. (Note that a regulation which almost completely destroys the economic value of property is also likely to be found to constitute a "taking" for which compensation must be paid under the "diminution in value" standard often used by courts. See *supra*, p. 263.)

D. **Equal protection:** The *Equal Protection* Clause of the Fourteenth Amendment, preventing any state from depriving a citizen of "equal protection of the laws," may also occasionally come into play in the zoning context. For instance, any zoning ordinance which was adopted for the purpose of *excluding blacks or other racial minorities* would violate the equal protection clause. (But a discriminatory intent, rather than merely a discriminatory effect, is required; see the discussion of *Village of Arlington Heights v. Metropolitan Housing Development Corp., infra*, p. 286.)

1. **"Rational relation" test:**   Normally, a zoning action that differentiates between two classes of people or between two uses does not violate the equal protection clause so long as it bears a *"rational relation"* to a permissible state objective. This is the same test as is used in the substantive due process area (*supra*, p. 272).

2. **"Strict scrutiny":**   However, there are two types of situations where more than a mere "rational relation" between a zoning measure and its objective will be required.

   a. **Suspect classification:**   *"Strict scrutiny"* will be given to any measure which *discriminates* (and is intended to discriminate) on the basis of race, religion, (possibly) sex, or other *"suspect classification."*

   b. **Fundamental interest:**   Alternatively, strict scrutiny will be given to any classification which *affects a "fundamental interest"* (e.g., the right to travel interstate, the right to vote, etc.). However, since the right to housing has been held by the Supreme Court not to be a "fundamental interest," a zoning ordinance will rarely merit strict scrutiny because of the fundamental interest doctrine; the sole exception is likely to be where the rights of individuals to make intimate *family* decisions are involved, such as in the *Moore* case (*supra*, p. 272).

3. **Significance of "strict scrutiny" standard:**   Where the existence of a suspect classification or fundamental interest does trigger a "strict scrutiny" standard, the zoning measure will be struck down unless the state meets the burden of showing that it has a *"compelling interest"* in meeting the objective in question, and that this objective cannot be satisfied by less objectionable means. No recent Supreme Court zoning cases have applied the strict scrutiny standard.

E. **The "police power":**   When courts uphold a particular zoning action, they frequently do so by saying that the action is within the *"police power"* of the municipality. The term "police power" is a shorthand phrase which generally means that the goal being furthered by the municipality is a legitimate objective.

1. **Modern expansion:** The dimensions of the police power have been substantially expanded since the Supreme Court decided the *Euclid* case, *supra*, p. 269. *Euclid's* formulation of the police power was limited to measures substantially related to "public health, safety, morals, or general welfare." As is discussed further below, most courts today regard the police power as extending to measures reasonably related to *aesthetic objectives,* "family values" (explicitly approved in the *Belle Terre* case), and perhaps even such values as "preserving [the] 'charm' of the New England small town" (see *Steel Hill Dev., Inc. v. Town of Sanbornton*, 469 F.2d 956 (1st Cir. 1972).)

F. **Burden of proof:**   Regardless of the grounds upon which a zoning regulation is attacked, the attacker has the *burden of proof*. The municipality's action is presumed to be valid until the challenger comes forward with evidence showing a violation of substantive due process, equal protection, the takings clause, etc.

G. Aesthetic zoning: As the *Euclid* case made clear, the permissible objectives of zoning include protection of the "public health, safety, morals, [and] general welfare." This formulation left unanswered a question that became increasingly important following *Euclid*: may the zoning power be used for the purpose of pursuing *aesthetic* objectives?

    1. Traditional reluctance to allow: During the early days of zoning (before about 1930), the vast majority of courts refused to allow aesthetic considerations as a basis for zoning regulations. These decisions relied principally on the arguments that: (1) it is unfair to allow the majority to *impose its tastes* upon everyone; and (2) it is impossible to formulate standards that are *sufficiently precise* to avoid discrimination and corruption in enforcement.

    2. Allowable as one (but not sole) objective: Since the 1930's, most courts have come to hold that aesthetic considerations may constitute *one factor* in the municipality's zoning decision, but that such considerations may not be the *sole factor*. This view, like the earlier complete prohibition on aesthetic considerations, seems founded upon fears of tyranny by the majority and discriminatory application. By requiring non-aesthetic factors (presumably more "objective") to be present, courts will be able to guard against these dangers.

        a. Architectural review boards: A number of municipalities have established *architectural review boards*, which have a right or approval over the plans for any proposed building. Such ordinances have generally been upheld.

    3. Allowed as sole objective: Some states, though not most, now hold that aesthetic considerations may even constitute the *sole criterion* for a particular zoning regulation. See, e.g., *People v. Stover*, 191 N.E.2d 272 (N.Y. 1963), upholding a prohibition upon the use of a clothesline in a front or side yard abutting the street.

    4. Exclusionary zoning: Some recent cases have held that a municipality may not exclude all multi-family or low-income housing. An architectural review ordinance, and perhaps other kinds of aesthetically-based zoning, might run afoul of these cases if they have the effect of barring multi-family or low-income housing. See the discussion of exclusionary zoning beginning *infra*, p. 284.

IV. ZONING — ADMINISTRATION

    A. Zoning administration generally: Zoning regulations are almost invariably promulgated at the local, municipal, level. The municipality's power to zone is delegated to it by the state, pursuant to a *zoning enabling statute*.

        1. Standard Enabling Act: Nearly all states have passed a version of the Standard State Zoning Act (referred to henceforth as the Standard Act), which was promulgated in 1923 by the U.S. Department of Commerce.

            a. Permissible goals: §1 of the Standard Act provides that zoning may be used "for the purpose of promoting health, safety, morals, or the general welfare of the community. . . ." Since this is the same formula as used by the Supreme Court in *Euclid*, *supra*, p. 269, in delineating the constitutional bounds of the police power, courts have usually not needed to distinguish between the statutory limits upon a municipality's zoning power and the constitutional limits on that power.

B. Bodies involved in zoning: There are a number of different governmental entities involved in the zoning process.

   1. Local legislature: The zoning code and amendments to it, are enacted by the *local legislature*. At the municipal level, this means the town council, Board of Supervisors, or other popularly elected body.

   2. Buildings department: Day-to-day enforcement of the zoning scheme is usually handled by a local *administrative* agency, typically the buildings department. This department usually has inspectors who investigate complaints that zoning violations exist. It is also this department that generally issues permits for new construction, and which therefore determines in the first instance whether a proposed structure satisfies the zoning requirements.

   3. Board of adjustment: A *board of adjustment* or *board of zoning appeals* is usually appointed. This board hears appeals from the denial of building permits, and from the building department's enforcement of zoning laws. However, its primary function is to award or deny *variances* (see *infra*, p. 278) and *special use exceptions* (*infra*, p. 280).

   4. Planning or zoning commission: The local governing body will generally appoint a *planning commission or zoning commission*. This body is generally composed of local residents who have an interest in land use, including developers, contractors, architects, real estate brokers, etc. See Land Use Nutshell, pp. 62-63. The commission proposes to the local legislature a master plan (if there is to be one; see *infra*), as well as the test of the contemplated zoning ordinance and any amendments. The commission's role is purely *advisory*; all enactments are made by the local legislature.

C. The master plan and its effect: In the early days of zoning, zoning ordinances were often adopted without a great deal of study, and without much thought about future development of the community. Increasingly, however, communities have adopted a so-called *"master plan"* or *"comprehensive plan,"* which analyzes long-range population and employment prospects for the community, and contains general standards for present and future development. A master plan might, for instance, recommend that a particular undeveloped area on the outskirts of the community be presently zoned for agricultural purposes, with the expectation that in perhaps ten years the town will have developed sufficiently to make this area desirable for residential use.

   1. Who prepares: The plan is generally prepared by the planning commission and its technical staff. It becomes effective when it is adopted by the local legislature.

   2. Conflict between plan and ordinance: Particularly where a community has had a zoning scheme before it has adopted a master plan, the plan and the ordinance may come into conflict.

      a. Prior ordinance: Where the ordinance exists *prior* to the adoption of the master plan, most courts hold that the *master plan controls*. Therefore, the prior inconsistent ordinance must be conformed.

b. Post-plan ordinance: Where a zoning ordinance is passed *after* a master plan has been enacted, courts similarly require that the ordinance be at least generally consistent with the plan.

   i. Plan not binding in all details: However a comprehensive plan is necessarily general in nature, and is designed so that it will remain applicable over a substantial period of time, even as conditions change. Accordingly, courts will generally not require that every zoning action taken after adoption of a master plan conform in every precise detail to the plan itself.

3. Adoption of plan not required: Most states do *not* require that a master plan *in fact be adopted*.

   a. Some states now require: But a few states (e.g., California, Florida, Oregon, Washington) now *require* municipalities to enact a master plan.

4. Regional and state-wide planning: Since the early days of zoning, the zoning power, including comprehensive planning of development, has been almost completely in the hands of local municipalities. Not surprisingly, neighboring towns have often failed to coordinate their strategies, so that one town may allow, say, a large industrial development which will adversely impact a residential area in an adjacent town. A few states have therefore attempted to reserve zoning and planning powers at the *state level*. These states include Hawaii, Oregon, and Florida. See B,C&S, pp. 1226-31. In these jurisdictions, the state is given the ability to *override* municipal land-use decisions in certain circumstances, typically including large development proposals (for instance, the creation of a "new town," i.e., a large residential community to be created from scratch).

D. Zoning amendments: A zoning ordinance may be *amended* only by the body which enacted it, i.e., the local legislature. Depending on the circumstances, the amendment may be either of a large portion of the ordinance, or of a relatively small aspect (e.g., the zoning of a particular parcel).

1. Must not be arbitrary or discriminatory: A zoning amendment, like an original ordinance, must not be *arbitrary* or *discriminatory*. This requirement is at the base of the decision involving "spot zoning," discussed *infra*.

2. Must conform to plan: If a master plan has been adopted, zoning amendments must be in conformity with that plan.

3. "Spot zoning" invalid: Courts have always insisted that a zoning scheme be reasonably uniform, rather than arbitrary and discriminatory. This does not mean of course, that all parcels must be zoned for the same uses; it means that like parcels must be treated in the same way, and that the government must have a valid reason for zoning two similar parcels differently. When courts find that like parcels have been treated differently, they frequently strike down the offending portion of the ordinance as *"spot zoning."* The issue of "spot zoning" generally arises in the context of an amendment to an existing plan, rather than in the original adoption of the plan.

   a. Relation to "comprehensive plan" rule: The "spot zoning" rule is thus really a restatement of the universal requirement (stemming from the Standard Act) that zoning be "in accordance with a comprehensive plan." Where a master plan has been adopted, the court may point to the fact that the zoning amendment deviates from the master plan as one of the reasons why the amendment constitutes "spot zoning". Even in the absence of a master plan, the fact that a particular amendment is not consistent with the rest of the overall ordinance will make it "spot zoning."

b. Tests for "spot zoning": There are three fairly specific factors which must usually be present before an amendment is struck down as "spot zoning":

i. Very different use: First, the use permitted by the rezoning must generally be *very different* from the prevailing uses in the surrounding area. Generally, this will mean a business or industrial use in the middle of a residential area. A less jarring juxtaposition (e.g., multi-family dwellings surrounded by single-family ones) will probably not be sufficient.

ii. Small area: Secondly, the area rezoned must generally be *rather small*. In many cases, it will be *one parcel*, and it will rarely be more than a few.

iii. Benefit of one or few owners: Thirdly, the rezoning will generally be considered "spot zoning" only if it is for the *benefit* of the sole or few owners whose property has been rezoned, rather than for the benefit of the community at large.

E. Variances: If a zoning ordinance were inflexibly administered, so that no deviations were ever permitted, great hardship might result to a particular landowner. For instance, if an ordinance prevented the building of a residence on a lot having a street frontage of less than 100 feet, the owner of a irregularly shaped, 98-foot frontage parcel, would have to bear an extreme hardship. Virtually all zoning ordinances therefore have a provision for the granting of *variances*, i.e., relief in a particular case from the enforcement of an ordinance.

1. Standard Act's test: Most states, in their enabling acts, have used the test stated in the Standard Act: variances will be allowed where "owing to special conditions, a literal enforcement of the provisions of the ordinance will result in unnecessary hardship." However, the variance must be such that "the spirit of the ordinance shall be observed and substantial justice done."

2. Summary of requirements: Most states impose three specific requirements for the granting of a variance: (1) denial would result in *"unnecessary hardship"* to the owner; (2) the need for the variance is caused by a problem *unique to the owner's lot*, and not one shared generally by lots in the area; and (3) the variance would not be inconsistent with the *overall purpose* of the ordinance, and would not be inconsistent with the general welfare of the area.

3. "Unnecessary hardship": The landowner must show that literal enforcement of the ordinance would result in *"unnecessary hardship"* to him.

a. Lower value not enough: Courts vary in the degree of hardship which they require to be shown. Virtually all courts agree that the mere fact that the property would be *worth more* if the variance were allowed is *not* by itself sufficient to meet the "unnecessary hardship" standard.

i. Minority view: Some courts go even further, and hold that the owner must show that there is *no reasonable conforming use* which he can make of that property.

    b. Self-induced hardship: The hardship may not be *"self-induced"* on the part of the property owner. This means, for instance, that if the owner of a parcel divides it and sells parts of it in such a way that he is left with an irregularly-shaped parcel that cannot conform to the ordinance, he will probably not be given a variance. Similarly, if the owner knows of the ordinance and ***willfully builds in violation of it***, he will generally not be entitled to a variance if he is later caught, even though redoing the construction work might be extremely expensive and the damage to neighbors trivial. See 5 Williams §146.02.

        i. Purchase with notice: But the courts are split as to whether the acquisition of land, with ***knowledge*** of the zoning restrictions, prevents the purchaser from obtaining a variance because of the self-created hardship rule.

            (1) Fatal to claim: Some courts, including those of New York and Pennsylvania, have held that knowledge of the restriction is fatal to the purchaser's claim of unnecessary hardship.

            (2) Not fatal: But other courts hold that knowledge by the purchaser of the zoning restriction is not by itself enough to defeat his claim of unnecessary hardship.

4. Unique to particular lot: Most courts (and in fact most ordinances), permit a variance to be issued only where the hardship complained of is ***unique*** to the particular lot in question, or at most to a few nearby lots. If the hardship is one that is shared by many similarly-situated lots, the appropriate remedy is a ***zoning amendment***, not a variance.

    a. Rationale: Otherwise, the result will be that only one of numerous similarly-situated landowners will have procured relief, and the uniformity that is a *sine qua non* of every zoning ordinance will be destroyed.

5. No harm to surrounding neighborhood: The variance may not be issued if ***harm would result*** to the ***surrounding neighborhood***. For instance, construction of a medical office building in a residential area might increase traffic and harm the residential appearance of the neighborhood; even if the landowner met the "unnecessary hardship" and "unique difficulty" tests, the variance would be denied for this reason.

6. Distinction between use and area variance: A number of courts have distinguished between ***use*** and ***area*** variances. A use variance is one which permits the property to be put to a use not permitted by the ordinance. An area variance, by contrast, merely relaxes a regulation governing the physical layout of the structure; thus relief might be given from a minimum frontage, minimum floor area, maximum height, or other requirement. Since a use variance is likely to have a greater impact upon the surrounding neighborhood, courts have often been stricter in reviewing such variances than area ones.

    a. Outright prohibition: Some states, including California, Connecticut, North Carolina, Missouri and Texas, have ***flatly prohibited use variances***. 5 Williams §132.02. This has been done both by statute and by case-law.

7. Variances granted too freely: The almost universal evidence is that zoning boards grant variances ***too freely***, with sufficient concern for the statutory requirements. For this reason, courts have become increasingly strict in their scrutiny of variances; some have taken the view that if there is any real doubt about whether a variance was justified, it should not be given.

F. The "special use" or "special exception":   Most zoning ordinances provide for the issuance of so-called *"special use"* permits, or, as they are sometimes called, *"special exceptions"*. (Here, we use the more descriptive of the two phrases "special use.")

1. **Nature and purpose:**   There are certain uses which are, in the abstract, beneficial to the community. Yet, because they typically serve fairly large numbers of people, and create traffic congestion and other problems, it is not desirable to make these uses available *as of right* in any particular zone. On the other hand, it is not desirable to exclude them entirely. The "special use" concept is an attempt to solve this dilemma; the zoning ordinance provides that a specified use is permissible in some (or all) zones, but *only upon the express approval* of the board of adjustment (or other entity).

   a. **Approval of particular use:**   The board of adjustment thus has the opportunity to make sure that the special use is located where it will not cause hardship to surrounding property owners. For instance, the board will often insist that the use be placed so that there is easy access to a major street, thus avoiding traffic tie-ups in otherwise quiet residential neighborhoods.

2. **Typical uses:**   As noted, the special uses are invariably expressly enumerated in the zoning ordinances. Typically, the listed uses include *private schools, clubs, hospitals and churches*, all uses which serve a considerable number of people. Occasionally, certain types of businesses open to the public at large (e.g., gasoline stations) are also included.

3. **Who makes decisions:**   The zoning ordinance, as noted, usually grants the power of deciding on a special use application to the local board of zoning adjustment (or board of zoning appeals, as the board is sometimes called). However, in some states the *local legislature* reserves the power to *itself* to pass on such applications. Finally, in a very few instances, the planning commission is the body which passes upon the application.

4. **Distinguished from variance:**   Some courts have muddled the distinction between a special use permit and a variance. However, the two are fundamentally different. The variance is generally available only in cases of "unnecessary hardship" (see *supra*, p. 278), and is not usually for a use that will serve large numbers of people. The special use, by contrast, is available only for use types specifically listed in the ordinance, which are chosen because of their public benefit function; no showing of hardship on the part of the owner is required.

5. **Standards for granting permits:**   Most litigation on special use permits has centered upon whether the *standards* set forth in the ordinance to guide the administrative agency are *sufficiently definite*. Insufficiently precise standards pose the danger of arbitrary action and favoritism.

   a. **No standards:**   If the ordinance simply says that the administrative agency may issue special permits "as it sees fit" or "within its discretion," with no standards at all, the ordinance will likely be struck down as an improper delegation of legislative power to an administrative agency. 5 Williams §150.02.

b. General welfare: Many ordinances merely state that the special use may be granted only where it is in accordance with the *"general welfare"* of the community, or some similarly vague standard. Although a standard this imprecise makes it very difficult for an owner who has been denied a special use permit to challenge the decision judicially, such standards have generally (but not always) been upheld. See 5 Williams §150.05.

G. Two modern discretionary techniques: In traditional Euclidean zoning, control of building *density* is implemented on a lot-by-lot basis. For instance, a Euclidean ordinance may provide that a district shall be used solely for single-family residence purposes, that each lot shall be at least one-fourth of an acre, and that front and side yards shall be of a certain minimum area. Such a scheme has the desired result of preventing overbuilding, and a consequent strain on schools, sewers and other public facilities. However, it often makes for boring architecture and land use, with each house and each block looking almost the same.

  1. Solutions: Therefore, community planners have devised a number of modern techniques which help prevent this boring sameness, while maintaining the same overall proportion of unbuilt space as in a comparable straight Euclidean scheme. The two principal devices used today to produce these results are: (1) *cluster zoning*; and (2) *Planned Unit Developments (PUDs)*.

  2. Cluster zoning: Under the *"cluster zoning"* concept, the size and width of individual residential lots in a development may be reduced, *provided that the overall density of the whole tract remains constant*. In effect, an area equal to the total of the areas 'saved" from each individual lot is pooled and used as common open spaces (e.g., a private park or swimming complex). 2 Williams §47.01. Cluster zoning may be accomplished not only by building single-family houses on smaller detached lots, but also by building garden apartments or "town houses."

    a. No major legal issues: Cluster zoning ordinances do not raise any major legal or constitutional issues. Therefore, as long as the ordinance is clearly drawn and does not discriminate against certain owners in an unfair way, it should withstand legal challenge.

  3. Planned Unit Development (PUDs): A newer and broader device serving similar aims is the *Planned Unit Development (PUD)*. Whereas cluster zoning ordinances generally allow only residential use, in a PUD, commercial (and occasionally industrial) facilities will frequently be allowed to be intermingled with residential uses.

    a. How it works: The idea behind the PUD is that the developer submits a proposal for a development containing both residential (probably a mixture of single-family and multi-family) and commercial uses, designed in such a way that the overall population and building density is no higher than under a comparable single-use district.

      i. Advantages: As with cluster zoning, one advantage is that more usable common open space is preserved without increasing population density. Another advantage, not shared by cluster zoning, is that *stores and other supporting commercial uses* can be planned so as to be *convenient to the residences*. The PUD is thus often a small community in its own right, complete with commercial areas, schools, recreational facilities, etc.

b. Legal challenge: Most states that have considered the question have **upheld** the legality of the PUD concept.

H. Other discretionary techniques: Two other modern techniques, while not directed at the problem of maintaining density controls without monotony or unnecessary expense, are based upon the same desire for flexibility as the cluster zoning and PUD concepts.

1. Floating zones: A *"floating zone"* is a zone which is established by zoning ordinance, with specified uses, but which is **not mapped in any particular location** at the time the ordinance is passed. Instead, the scheme contemplates that a developer will later apply to have the floating zone made applicable to his land. The zone is thus said to "float" over the entire land in the community, until it is subsequently *"anchored"* on a particular site.

  a. Advantage: The key advantage of the floating zone technique is, of course, **flexibility**. The town can agree that a certain type of use (i.e., a light industrial park) is in theory desirable, and can postpone the question of exactly where this use should be permitted until a particular proposal is put forward. The danger of permitting the use as of right over a large area (which might lead to too many such uses, e.g., too many industrial parks) is avoided.

  b. Criticism of floating zones: Floating zones are criticized for the same reasons as are PUDs. Since the initiative is left with the developer (usually without very precise standards as to when an application should be granted), there is great opportunity for arbitrariness and *"backroom" deals*.

2. Conditional or "contract" zoning: Another device used to preserve flexibility is often called *"conditional"* zoning (if it is upheld) or sometimes *"contract"* zoning (usually when it is struck down). By this device, the rezoning of a particular parcel is made **subject to the developer's promise to comply with certain conditions**, which will presumably better protect neighbors. For instance, a parcel in a residential area might be rezoned for light industry, but only if the developer agreed to **large set-backs** and a **low floor-space-to-land-area ratio**.

  a. Some courts allow: About half of present-day courts **allow** some form of conditional or contract zoning. 1 Williams §29.01. These courts have generally looked to whether the conditions imposed are for the benefit of nearby property owners; if so, the scheme is valid, even though it represents a private "deal" applicable to one parcel only.

I. Non-conforming uses: When a zoning scheme is adopted for the first time, or when an existing zone is changed to a stricter use, there are likely to be existing uses that are not in conformity with the new rules. These are called **non-conforming uses**.

1. Constitutional issue: An ordinance could theoretically be drafted in such a way as to outlaw all non-conforming uses immediately upon the enactment of the ordinance. However, such an ordinance would almost certainly be invalid as an unconstitutional violation of due process. Therefore, virtually all ordinances either (1) grant a non-conforming user a **substantial period within which he may continue his use** (see discussion of the amortization technique *infra*, p. 283); or else (2) let her continue that use indefinitely.

a. **Significant problem:** When the first zoning ordinances were enacted, it was thought that non-conforming uses would fade from the scene rather quickly. However, this has not turned out to be the case. Particularly where the non-conforming use is a commercial one in what has now been zoned as a residential area, the use will probably have a *monopoly* on that kind of business in the neighborhood, and this will tend to increase the value and prolong the existence of the use. (Thus one who had a neighborhood grocery store in what is now a residential-only zone might well have an incentive to continue that use indefinitely.) For this reason, there is a substantial body of litigation concerning exactly what constitutes a non-conforming use, and what terminates that use.

2. **Degree of use necessary:** The relevant date for determining the existence of a non-conforming use is the *effective date of the ordinance*. By this date, the use must be a *reasonably substantial one*. Mere *preparation* for the use is generally *not* enough. Thus suppose one wished to run a commercial laundry in a residential area; the mere fact that one had quit one's job and borrowed money from a bank in order to set up a laundry on a particular site would not be sufficient; actual operation of the laundry would have to be commenced prior to enactment of the ordinance.

3. **Change of use:** A non-conforming user may wish to *change* the particular use to a different, but also non-conforming, one. Most courts have not allowed him to make a significant change in the non-conforming use. Thus in most jurisdictions a non-confirming laundry could not be changed to a non-conforming grocery store. (But a few states have permitted a change in the use where it constituted an *"upgrading,"* i.e., where the new use is more desirable than the old.)

   a. **Change of ownership:** But a *change of ownership* is not considered a change in use. The non-conforming use thus has the opportunity to *transfer his interest at will*. This factor has contributed greatly to the tendency of non-conforming uses to continue for long periods of time.

4. **Expansion of use:** A similar issue is present where the non-conforming user wishes to *expand* her present operation, without changing to a different use.

   a. **Change of building or lot size:** Where she sought to do this by *enlarging her building or lot size*, the courts have generally *not* allowed her to do so.

   b. **Increase in volume:** But if the expansion takes the form only of an *increased volume of activity* without an enlargement of the physical facilities, it will generally be allowed. Thus an expansion, even a dramatic one, in the number of customers patronizing a beauty parlor would not prevent the beauty parlor from continuing to be a valid non-confirming use.

5. **Amortization:** As noted, non-conforming uses have not tended to disappear by themselves. Many municipalities have responded to this problem by so-called *amortization* provisions, by which the non-conforming use may continue *only for a certain length of time* following enactment of the zoning restriction. The theory behind such provisions is that the owner will have had time to recover (i.e., amortize) his investment, and to make plans to continue the use somewhere else if he wishes.

a. **Generally upheld:** Early cases generally disallowed the amortization technique on constitutional due process grounds. But since about 1960, the substantial majority of cases that have considered the issue have *upheld* such provisions, provided that the amortization period is indeed sufficiently long for the owner to recover his costs and to arrange an alternative location.

b. **Minority view:** But a minority of states (including Pennsylvania, Missouri, Arkansas, Idaho, Indiana, Ohio and Delaware) hold that amortization amounts to an *improper taking of private property*. Often, these minority states have concluded that the federal or state *Constitution* prohibits the amortization technique, because it amounts to a taking without due process of law.

Example: The Moon Township zoning ordinance provides that any pre-existing use which would be a violation of a newly-enacted zoning restriction has 90 days from enactment of the restriction to come into compliance. This amortization rule would force P, the owner of an adult bookstore, to close the bookstore and relocate it to a small area elsewhere in the town which allows adult bookstores. P asserts that this constitutes a taking of his property without compensation.

Held, for P. The Pennsylvania Constitution guarantees the "inherent and indefeasible" right of its citizens to possess and protect property, and to be paid compensation if their private property is taken. Any amortization and discontinuance of a lawful pre-existing non-conforming use is *per se* confiscatory and violative of the Pennsylvania Constitution. Also, if municipalities were free to amortize non-conforming uses out of existence, future economic development would be seriously compromised, because the possibility that the municipality could enact zoning changes to force a cessation of business might deter investors. (A concurrence argues that a reasonably long amortization period should be found valid, but agrees that 90 days is in any case much too short to be reasonable.) *P.A. Northwestern Distributors, Inc. v. Zoning Hearing Board*, 584 A.2d 1372 (Pa. 1991).

V. EXCLUSIONARY ZONING

A. **Meaning of "exclusionary" zoning:** Euclidean zoning, when it first began to be practiced, was in theory designed principally to separate the various potential land uses within a particular community, so that industry would not interfere with residential use, etc. It soon became apparent, however, that zoning could furnish a means of keeping certain groups and uses *completely out of the community*. The use of zoning laws to exclude certain types of persons and uses, particularly *racial and ethnic minorities*, and *low-income persons*, is now generally referred to as *"exclusionary zoning."* Another term sometimes used is *"snob zoning."*

1. **Examples of exclusion:** A town could theoretically enact an ordinance completely barring, say, all blacks from residing within the town. Such an ordinance, however, would be instantly struck down as unconstitutional. Therefore, exclusionary zoning techniques are generally much more subtle and indirect. Most exclusion takes the form of restrictions on the *types of allowable residential uses*, so that those uses likely to be of special interest to racial minorities or low-income groups are either not permitted at all or severely circumscribed.

a. **Minimum acre single-family zoning:**   For instance, a municipality could reserve all of its residential land for single-family detached homes on one-half acre minimum lots. Since this would render impossible the construction of conventional apartments, garden apartments, town houses or even inexpensive small single-family houses, virtually no low-income families, and probably relatively few blacks or Hispanics, would be able to move into the town.

b. **Other devices:**   Other devices which might be used to exclude racial and ethnic minorities and the poor, include:

   i.   A *ban on multiple dwellings*;

   ii. If apartment buildings are allowed, a *minimum floor area* for each living unit;

   iii. A prohibition on *publicly-subsidized housing*;

   iv. If apartments are allowed, a *maximum on the number of bedrooms* allowed per living unit (to prevent large families from burdening the school system); and

   v.   A ban on *mobile homes*.

2. **Federal versus state case law:**   Substantial litigation on exclusionary zoning has taken place in both the federal and state court systems. For a number of reasons which are discussed below, federal courts have been relatively reluctant to strike down zoning schemes that have an exclusionary purpose, or effect, or both. State-court decisions, by contrast, which are frequently reached on the basis of the interpretation of the state constitution rather than the federal one, have been much quicker to limit municipalities' right to exclude particular racial, ethnic and economic groups. Because the federal and state patterns have diverged so sharply, each is considered separately.

B. **Federal case-law:**   Where a zoning scheme is attacked in *federal court* as being exclusionary, the attack may be based upon either constitutional or statutory principles.

1. **Constitutional argument:**   A constitutional attack on a zoning scheme alleged to be exclusionary would probably have to be based upon the *equal protection clause* of the Fourteenth Amendment. (See *supra*, p. 273, for a brief discussion of this clause.) Recall that where government action discriminates either on the basis of a "suspect classification" or with respect to a "fundamental interest", the action is subjected to "strict judicial scrutiny," and the state must show a *compelling interest* in the scheme. By contrast, where neither a suspect classification nor a fundamental interest is involved, the government action will violate the equal protection clause only if it bears *no rational relation* to a permissible state objective.

   a. **Suspect classification:**   In the zoning context, virtually any scheme has a rational relation to the permissible state objective of protection the "general welfare." Therefore, as a practical matter, unless the plaintiff can invoke strict scrutiny by showing either that the zoning action involves a suspect classification, or that it affects a fundamental interest, the constitutional attack is almost certain to fail. To make matters even more difficult for a federal plaintiff, the Supreme Court has held that the right to housing is not a "fundamental interest." (See *Lindsey v. Normet*, discussed *supra*, p. 181.) Consequently, an equal protection attack in the zoning area will generally be based upon a theory that a *"suspect classification"* is at issue.

2. **"Effect" versus "purpose":**   The best chance for showing that an ordinance is based upon a suspect classification is to demonstrate that it has *racial* implications. Originally, it was not clear whether a racially discriminatory *effect* was all that had to be shown, or whether a racially discriminatory *purpose* on the part of the government had to be demonstrated.

   a. **Discriminatory purpose required:** Then, in *Village of Arlington Heights v. Metropolitan Housing Development Corp.*, 429 U.S. 252 (1977), the U.S. Supreme Court explicitly held that a racially discriminatory *purpose, not merely effect,* needed to be shown before an ordinance would be subject to strict equal protection scrutiny.

3. **Economic discrimination:**   Where the zoning scheme has a discriminatory effect of intent with respect to the *poor*, a successful equal protection attack is even more difficult. Even if the plaintiff can show that the *intent* (not just the effect) is to discriminate against the poor, strict scrutiny will not be triggered; the Supreme Court has shown no sign that it is willing to treat wealth classifications as inherently suspect. Where a discriminatory effect is all that is shown, the plaintiff virtually never prevails.

4. **Impact on family:**   If the challenged ordinance has a sharp impact upon the *family*, an equal protection attack, or a due process one, may have a reasonable chance of success. The Supreme Court has repeatedly held that the right to make decisions in the raising of one's family is a fundamental right, and that government action infringing upon that right must be subjected to strict scrutiny both from an equal protection and due process standpoint. See, e.g., *Moore v. City of East Cleveland*, discussed *supra*, p. 272, where the Court held that an ordinance restricting the rights of certain relatives to live together was a violation of due process. (But cf. *Village of Belle Terre v. Boraas*, discussed *supra*, p. 273, holding that this right did not extend to unrelated persons desiring to share a household.)

5. **Effect on mentally retarded:**   If a zoning ordinance affects the *mentally retarded*, a successful equal protection attack is difficult, because mental retardation has been held not to be a suspect, or even quasi-suspect, classification. *City of Cleburne, Texas v. Cleburne Living Center*, 473 U.S. 432 (1985).

   a. **Successful suit:**   However, even though zoning ordinances directly affecting the mentally retarded are judged under the very forgiving rational-relation standard, an attack on such an ordinance can nonetheless be occasionally sustained. In *City of Cleburne, supra*, for instance, a city ordinance required that any group home for the mentally retarded obtain a special use permit, and the city declined to issue the permit to the plaintiffs. The Supreme Court, although it left the ordinance on the books, invalidated it as it applied to the group home. The Court concluded that "requiring the permit . . . appears to rest on an *irrational prejudice* against the mentally retarded," since no special use permit was required for similar uses (e.g., nursing homes, apartment houses, etc.). (See the discussion of special uses, *supra*, p. 280.)

6. **Federal statutory (Fair Housing Act) suits:**   Because of the Supreme Court's hostility to constitutionally-based attacks on exclusionary zoning, most federal court plaintiffs have relied on federal *statutory* law in support of their anti-exclusionary zoning battles. In particular, plaintiffs have invoked the *Fair Housing* Title of the Civil Rights Act of 1968, 42 U.S.C. §§3601-3619 (also discussed *supra*, p. 191).

a. **Operative language:** Plaintiffs have generally relied on a provision of the Fair Housing Act which makes it unlawful to "make unavailable or deny, a dwelling to any person because of race, color, religion, sex or national origin." 42 U.S.C. §3604(a). Nearly all federal courts which have considered the matter concede at least that zoning enacted for the purpose of limiting access by racial or ethnic minorities would violate §3604(a).

   i. **Discrimination against the handicapped:** Congress amended the Fair Housing Act in 1988 to prohibit discrimination against the *handicapped*. So zoning restrictions enacted for the purpose of limiting access by, say, developmentally delayed or physically disabled persons would violate the Act.

b. **Discriminatory effect versus purpose:** Recall that a discriminatory *purpose*, not just effect, is required for a *constitutional* attack on exclusionary zoning under the Supreme Court's *Arlington Heights* decision. (See *supra*, p. 286.) But the Supreme Court has never decided whether a discriminatory purpose must also be shown for a Fair Housing Act violation. Most lower federal courts, however, have held that the plaintiff in a Fair Housing Act suit need *not* show that the defendant had a discriminatory intent.

   i. *Prima facie* **case:** Instead, most federal courts hold that the plaintiff merely has to prove that the defendant's land-use controls merely have a *disparate effect* upon blacks or other racial minorities. Once the plaintiff makes the showing, the *burden* then *shifts* to the defendant municipality to show that it was acting in pursuit of a legitimate governmental interest, and that there was no less-discriminatory way of achieving that same interest.

c. **Group homes and anti-rooming-house ordinances:** Non-profit organizations frequently seek to set up *"group homes,"* that is, "small, decentralized treatment facilities housing foster children, the mentally ill, the developmentally disabled, juvenile offenders, ex-drug addicts, alcoholics, and so on." D&K, p. 1102. Since the residents of a proposed group home would generally be handicapped persons, and since the Fair Housing Act prohibits discrimination against the handicapped (see *supra*, p. 287), the home's proponents often try to show that a zoning regulation has a disparate effect on the handicapped.

   i. **Occupancy limits:** The most common zoning impediment to group homes is that a city places a limit on the *maximum number* of unrelated persons that may live together, and this number is low enough to make the proposed home infeasible. However, the Fair Housing Act expressly allows the use of *"reasonable* local, state, or federal restrictions regarding the maximum number of occupants permitted to occupy a dwelling." Often, towns have been able to keep out larger group homes by showing that their maximum-occupant regulation was "reasonable." For instance, limiting a group home to no more than four unrelated persons has often been sustained.

   ii. **State statutes:** About half the states have *statutes* dealing with the group-home problem, typically by *preempting* the application of local zoning ordinances to group homes and setting state-wide rules on such homes instead. D&K, p. 1104, n. 3.

C. State case-law: The highest courts of several states, most notably New Jersey, have taken a radically different view of the legality of exclusionary zoning from that taken by the federal court cases discussed above. Whereas even zoning having a distinct racially discriminatory effect is difficult to attack in federal courts, these states have invalidated ordinances which exclude primarily on the basis of *economic status*.

1. **Traditional views:** Traditionally, state courts were reluctant to invalidate exclusionary zoning devices, and granted municipalities a great deal of latitude in furthering the *"general welfare."*

2. **New cases:** The more-recent group of state court cases invalidating zoning ordinances as exclusionary still typically focus on the "general welfare." Now, however, it is not merely the general welfare of the *present residents* of the *particular community* that is at issue; instead, the welfare of the *entire region* is the relevant criterion. A municipality whose zoning practices fail to advance the general welfare of the region may violate both the *state constitution* and the *state enabling act*.

3. ***Mt. Laurel* case:** The landmark state-court exclusionary zoning case is *Southern Burlington County NAACP v. Township of Mt. Laurel*, 336 A.2d 713 (N.J. 1975).

   a. **Facts of *Mt. Laurel:*** The Ps represented Black and Hispanic persons living in or near Mt. Laurel, who claimed that the town's zoning policies prevented them from finding low- or moderate-income housing. (The court treated the case as one involving principally economic, rather than racial, exclusions.) The Mt. Laurel zoning scheme contained two principal exclusionary features: (1) all areas zoned for residential use required *single-family detached dwellings* with substantial minimum lot-size and floor-area restrictions; and (2) nearly 30% of the town's land area was zoned for industrial use, even though less than 1% of this area was actually used by industry (the rest remaining vacant). (Several PUD's had been built, but these were designed to contain upper-income apartments, principally one-bedroom ones so that families with school-aged children would not be attracted.)

   b. **State constitution and statute violated:** The New Jersey Supreme Court concluded that the Mt. Laurel zoning scheme violated the substantive due process and equal protection rights guaranteed by the *state constitution* (the requirements of which, the court noted, "may be more demanding than those of the federal Constitution"). Also, the court held, the scheme failed to serve the *general welfare of the region as a whole*, and thus violated the state enabling statute.

   c. **"Fair share" requirement:** The key element of the court's holding was that a municipality *may not foreclose opportunities for low- and moderate-income housing*, and must offer an opportunity for such housing "at least to the extent of the municipality's *fair share* of the present and prospective *regional need* therefor." Here, there was evidence that a substantial number of residents of Camden (a decaying older city) and other nearby towns would have moved to Mt. Laurel if low- and moderate-income housing had been available.

d. **Property tax rationale unacceptable:** There was no evidence that the Mt. Laurel City Council had desired to discriminate against low- and middle-income families as such. Instead, the town claimed (and the court accepted) that the town simply desired to make sure that any new housing would "pay its own governmental way." Thus families with school-aged children were discouraged, since schooling of such children placed a large fiscal burden on the town. Similarly, a large portion of the undeveloped land was allocated for industrial and commercial purposes because such uses produce attractive tax ratables. The court flatly ***rejected*** (apparently for all circumstances) ***fiscal considerations*** as a defense for exclusionary zoning; "municipalities must zone primarily for the living welfare of people and not for the benefit of the local tax rate."

e. **Intent not necessary:** The court stated (in footnote 8) that its holding was not dependent upon whether Mt. Laurel ***intended*** to limit low- and moderate-income housing. So long as Mt. Laurel's zoning policies had this ***effect***, the presence or absence of intent was irrelevant. (This was in sharp distinction to the U.S. Supreme Court's *Arlington Heights* decision, *supra*, p. 286, where the equal protection clause was held to proscribe only those action taken with racially discriminatory intent.)

f. **Remedy:** The court declined to strike down the entire Mt. Laurel zoning scheme as invalid. Instead, the town was ordered to redraft those portions of its zoning scheme which served as barriers to low- and middle-income housing. The court indicated that at a minimum this would require:

   i. **Multi-family housing:** The permitting of ***multi-family housing***, without restrictions on the number of bedrooms;

   ii. **Small dwellings:** The allowing of ***small dwellings*** on ***very small lots***;

   iii. **PUD's:** If PUD's are to be used, a "reasonable amount of low- and moderate-income housing" in each PUD, unless opportunity for such housing had already realistically have been provided for elsewhere in the town;

   iv. **Industrial land:** A reservation of land for industrial of land for industrial and commercial purposes not exceeding the amount "reasonably related to the present and future potential" for such uses (clearly not the present 4,121 acres, of which only 100 had been actually used); and

   v. **High density zoning:** In general, ***high density zoning***, "without artificial and unjustifiable minimum requirements as to lot size, building size, and the like. . . ."

4. **Cases from other states:** Cases in several other states (e.g., New York and Pennsylvania) have followed at least some aspects of the *Mt. Laurel* decision.

5. **Statutes in other states:** Still other states have enacted ***statutes*** which may serve to reduce exclusionary zoning.

   a. **California:** For instance, an amendment to the California Planning Enabling Act, Cal. Gov't Code §65302(c), requires every municipal master plan to contain a "housing element," which "shall make adequate provision for the housing needs of ***all economic segments of the community.***"

6. ***Mt. Laurel II:*** Back in New Jersey, the *Mt. Laurel* decision did not produce the result the court expected: eight years later, Mt. Laurel still had an exclusionary zoning code, and no low- or middle-income housing had been built in the town. The New Jersey Supreme Court then decided *Southern Burlington NAACP v. Township of Mt. Laurel*, 456 A.2d 390 (N.J. 1983), popularly known as ***"Mt. Laurel II."*** Here are some of the important aspects of that decision, in which the court tried to put some muscle behind its prior pronouncement that communities may not zone so as to keep out their fair share of the region's poor and middle-income families:

a. **Mature towns:** *Every* community, not just those that are still "developing", must bear its fair share of the region's low- and middle-income housing needs. The fact that a community is *"mature"* will not prevent it from having a "fair share" obligation, so long as the community has at least *some* undeveloped land.

b. **Affirmative devices:** A community will not meet its "fair share" obligation merely by removing exclusionary provisions from its zoning code. Each town has an ***affirmative obligation*** to do everything in its power to cause a fair share of low- and middle-income housing to be built. If because of high land prices, political pressure, or other reasons, removing the exclusionary provisions is not enough to bring about actual construction, then the community must do more. Possible affirmative steps a city could take include: (1) granting ***"density bonuses"*** (i.e., the right to build extra housing beyond what would normally be allowed by the zoning ordinance) if the builder promises to make some of the units be low-income ones; (2) cooperating with the developer in obtaining ***federal subsidies*** for low-income housing; and (3) eliminating bans on ***mobile homes***.

c. **Builder's remedy:** The courts should be free to impose a so-called ***"builder's remedy"*** where appropriate. If the plaintiff who brings a *Mt. Laurel*-type suit is a builder who wants permission to build low- or middle-income housing on property he owns, and the court concludes that the defendant town has not met its fair share obligation, then the trial court is free to ***allow the builder to build his project*** even though the town has never given a permit for it. This will give the builder an inducement to bear the legal expense and wait of lengthy litigation. (Without a builder's remedy, a builder might fight a long lawsuit, have the ordinance struck down, but then watch the town rezone in a way that complies with the court's order, yet not have his own property be part of the new rezoned area. This possibility would discourage builders from bringing *Mt. Laurel*-type suits.)

d. **Legislature reacts:** But the New Jersey legislature has subsequently ***undermined*** much of what the Supreme Court was trying to do in the two *Mt. Laurel* cases. The New Jersey Fair Housing Act of 1985, for instance: (1) put a moratorium on the builder's remedy; and (2) allowed suburban towns (with the approval of a state Council on Affordable Housing) to get out of up to half of their fair share obligation by compensating *cities* (including, presumably, depressed inner cities like Camden and Newark) to rehabilitate *their* housing stock. This "transfer option" has been criticized as turning *Mt. Laurel* upside down, by keeping the poor in the inner cities instead of letting them move into the richer suburbs. See D&K, p. 1127.

D. Statutory protection against religious discrimination: Zoning and other land-use controls have sometimes made it more difficult for property to be used for *religious purposes* than for other purposes. A town might, for example, allow single-family housing to be built "as of right," while requiring churches to gain a special use permit that turns out to be hard to get because of neighbors' opposition.

1. Federal statutory protection (RLUIPA): To protect religious institutions against burdensome or discriminatory land-use regulation, Congress has enacted a series of statutes. The one currently in force, enacted in 2000, is the *Religious Land Use and Institutionalized Persons Act ("RLUIPA")*, 42 U.S.C. § 2000CC *et seq.* While RLUIPA also protects the religious rights of prisoners, we are interested here in that portion of the act that applies to land-use regulations.

    a. What the statute says: RLUIPA prohibits governments from "impos[ing] or implement[ing] a land-use regulation in a manner that *imposes a substantial burden* on the *religious exercise* of a person, including a religious assembly or institution," unless the government carries the burden of proving that the imposition of this burden:

        [1] "is in furtherance of a *compelling governmental interest*"; and

        [2] "is the *least restrictive means of furthering* that compelling governmental interest."

    42 U.S.C. §2000CC(a)(1). So once the person asserting the RLUIPA claim shows that his religious rights have been substantially burdened by the land-use regulation, the court must *apply strict scrutiny*, and will almost invariably *invalidate* the regulation as applied to him.

    b. Nature of statute: Notice that the provision quoted above is *not* based on an *anti-discrimination* rationale: even if government treats religious and non-uses *identically*, if the restriction on a proposed use would substantially burden religious exercise, the restriction must be subjected to strict scrutiny.[1]

    c. The *Guru Nanak* case: The leading case so far on RLUIPA's land-use provisions is *Guru Nanak Sikh Society of Yuba City v. County of Sutter*, 456 F.3d 978 (9th Cir. 2006).

        i. Facts: Guru Nanak was a non-profit organization that wanted to build a Sikh temple in Yuba City, California. Under the relevant County zoning laws, churches could not be built as a matter of right anywhere; a group that wanted to build a church had to apply for a Conditional Use Permit (CUP), and that CUP had to be approved by the County.

            (1) First attempt: First, Guru Nanak applied for a CUP for a two-acre parcel in an area zoned mainly for low intensity residential use. The County's Planning Division (consisting of employees who were professional city planners) rec-

---

1. A separate provision in RLUIPA, 42 U.S.C. §2000CC(b), prohibits land-use regulations that discriminate on the basis of religion, or that totally exclude, or unreasonably limit, religious assemblies in the jurisdiction. However, most litigation on the land-use aspect of RLUIPA involves claims that religious groups have been "substantially burdened," rather than discriminated against.

ommended approval of the CUP. But the County Planning Commission, a public body that had the ultimate say, denied the application based on citizens' complaints that the resulting noise and traffic would interfere with the neighborhood.

(2) Second attempt: Guru Nanak then found a second site, a somewhat-remote 29-acre parcel located in a district zoned for agriculture. A variety of administrative departments suggested several conditions to minimize the temple's environmental impact (e.g., a 25-foot "no development" offer on one edge of the property, and a requirement that all ceremonies take place indoors). Guru Nanak readily agreed to these conditions. As with the first site, various potential neighbors opposed the permit, complaining that the temple would increase traffic and noise; they also claimed that the use would interfere with the agricultural use of their own land. This time, the Planning Commission approved the permit, but in an appeal brought by various neighbors, the County Board of Supervisors, an elected body, rejected the permit, on the grounds that the temple was too far from the city and from other churches, and represented "leap-frog development" rather than orderly growth. It was the denial of this second permit that was litigated before the Ninth Circuit.

ii. **Ninth Circuit's decision:** The Ninth Circuit found that the County had violated Guru Nanak's RLUIPA rights, by imposing a "substantial burden" on the organization's religious exercise.

(1) "Individualized assessment": The court had to first deal with whether RLUIPA even applied. With a few exceptions, RLUIPA applies only where the government is making "*individualized assessments* of the proposed uses for the property involved."[2] The court concluded that such an individualized assessment was present here, because the statutory procedure for issuing a CUP depended on the Planning Commission's evaluation of whether "*under the circumstances of the particular case,*" the use would or would not be detrimental to the health, safety and general welfare of neighbors and the community.

(2) "Substantial burden": The court next had to decide whether the denial of the second permit "*substantially burdened*" Guru Nanak's exercise of religion. RLUIPA does not define "substantial burden." The court applied a definition from a prior case: to be a substantial burden on religious exercise, the government restriction must be "*oppressive* to a significantly great extent."

(3) Satisfied: The court found that the religious burden here was substantial. Most significantly, the court took into account not just the denial of the second

---

2. The "individualized assessments" requirement means that most RLUIPA land-use regulation arises in cases where the local government body is deciding, based on the *facts of the particular case,* whether to grant a special-use or conditional permit. So, for instance, if a municipality decided that churches could be built of right in one zoning category but not in certain others, the absence of an individualized assessment as part of the permitting process would probably prevent the plaintiffs from bringing a RLUIPA challenge claiming that their religious exercise was being substantially burdened.

permit, but the ***entire two-application process***, including the ***reasons given*** for both denials. The ultimate issue was whether Guru Nanak was likely to be successful in ***future applications*** for a CUP. The court concluded that the answer was no, for two reasons: (1) first, the reasons given by the County for denying the first two applications were very ***broad***, and "could easily ***apply to all future applications***" by the group; and (2) the group had readily ***agreed to every mitigation measure*** suggested by the bureaucrats, but the County had nonetheless, without explanation, found that this promise of cooperation was insufficient. So the County was in effect "***shrink[ing]*** the large amount of land theoretically available to Guru Nanak under the zoning code to several ***scattered parcels*** that the [C]ounty ***may or may not ultimately approve.***" That winnowing of choices was enough to constitute a substantial burden.

   (4) Strict scrutiny failed: Once the court found a substantial burden on Guru Nanak's religious exercise, the rest of the case was easy. RLUIPA requires ***strict scrutiny*** of any regulation that constitutes a substantial burden on the applicant's religious exercise. The County had conceded that it had no compelling interest in denying the permit, and thus did not even get to the point of arguing that it had narrowly tailored its restrictions to carry out such an interest. So it was easy for the court to conclude that the County had violated RLUIPA. The court ordered the County to immediately approve the second CUP application.

   d. Significance: *Guru Nanak* demonstrates that if a religious group can show that its land-use application turned on an "individualized assessment" of the proposed use, and that the denial of the application "substantially burdens" the group's religious exercise, the group will almost always win the case under RLUIPA. Rarely, if ever, will the government be able to survive strict scrutiny, which requires a showing that denial of the application was narrowly tailored to the achievement of some compelling governmental purpose.

VI. REGULATION OF THE SUBDIVISION PROCESS

   A. Subdivision generally: The principal process by which vacant land is developed for residential purposes is known as ***subdivision***. Subdivision is usually defined as the dividing of a parcel into two or more ***smaller*** ones, for resale to different purchasers.

   B. Mechanics of subdivision: Generally, subdivision is performed by a professional developer, who buys a large parcel for the purpose of building ***single-family residences*** on the subdivided parcels.

   1. Filing of plat: To begin the subdivision process, the developer usually records a ***subdivision map***, or ***plat***. The plat shows the entire parcel, and indicates the boundaries of each lot that the developer proposes to carve out and sell. Once the plat has been recorded and approved by the municipality, the developer can sell lots simply by reference to the lot number as shown on the plat, rather than by a complex "metes and bounds" description. (Also, the municipality can collect taxes based on these lots as shown on the plat.)

C. Municipal regulation: It is not surprising that most municipalities have exercised their power to *regulate* the subdivision process rather closely. It is at the moment of subdivision that the layout of streets, availability of parks, suitability of water mains and sewers, etc., are all likely to be determined for better or worse. Therefore, most municipalities require a developer to *gain municipal approval* of her *subdivision plans* before the plat may be recorded (and before sales of lots, or construction of dwellings on them, may be made).

D. Dedication of land: The developer will almost always be required to *dedicate*, i.e., *donate* to the municipality, the land allocated on his plat for *streets, sewer mains,* and the like.

   1. Installation of facilities: Furthermore, the subdivider will generally be required to *perform the work* for various facilities himself. He will thus generally be required to *pave the streets, install sidewalks*, and *install water mains, sewers, and other drainage facilities* at his own expense, according to the town's specifications. See B,C&S, p. 1318.

   2. Acceptance by city: Once these developer-installed facilities are complete, however, and meet with the city's approval, *maintenance* of them becomes the city's responsibility (to be financed out of property taxes).

   3. Upheld by courts: Subdividers have sometimes attacked the required dedication of streets and construction of improvements as being a *"taking"* of private property without compensation. However, the courts have generally sustained such requirements as a *reasonable exercise of the police power. Id.*

   4. Park and school sites: Towns also often require the developer to dedicate land for *parks* and *school sites*.

VII. HISTORICAL AND ENVIRONMENTAL PRESERVATION

A. Historical preservation: Certain buildings, or an entire district, may be of great *historical* or *architectural* interest. A number of municipalities have therefore sought to protect such buildings from demolition or radical alteration, or such districts from an incompatible mixing of old and modern styles.

B. Historic districts: A *historic district* is a group of buildings or a neighborhood exhibiting a *common style* of historical or architectural interest. It may be the case that none of the buildings in the district, taken individually, would have great historical or architectural interest; but taken as a whole, the area is worth maintaining because it reflects the life style or architecture of a given period.

   1. No alterations allowed without permit: It is generally impractical for a city to acquire every building within a historic district and make them all museums. Therefore, the usual method of preserving historic districts is to designate the district, and then provide that *no alterations, demolition* or *new construction* may take place within it without the approval of a special district board.

   2. Legal challenges: These historic district ordinances have been subjected to two main types of legal attack: (1) that they are *arbitrary* and *discriminatory* (either in general or as applied in a particular case) because they lack sufficiently precise standards to guide the board in issuing construction permits; and (2) that they constitute a *"taking"* without compensation, because they prevent the owner from making a profitable use of his property. In general, the courts have leaned over backwards to find the ordinances *valid* against these types of attacks.

C. Individual landmarks: Alternatively, a municipality may designate *individual buildings* as *landmarks*, because of their unusually historical or architectural importance. The courts have gone out of their way, as in the case of historic district laws, to *uphold* such landmark preservation laws both in general and as applied in specific cases.

1. How the laws work: The typical landmark preservation ordinance, like most historic district laws, prevents the alteration or destruction of a designated landmark without *approval* of a *specifically-appointed board or commission*.

2. The *Penn Central* case: Landmark preservation ordinances are generally *valid*, at least for federal constitutional purposes, by virtue of the U.S. Supreme Court's decision in the *Penn Central* case.

> **a. Facts of *Penn Central* case:** The Ps, the owners of Grand Central Terminal, sought to build a large modern office building on top of the Terminal. The New York City Landmarks Preservation Commission, relying on the Terminal's status as a landmark, refused to approve any of the Ps' proposals. One of the proposed schemes would have destroyed the southern facade of the terminal (the Beaux Arts facade which resulted in the landmark designation), and the other would have rested a fifty-story office building on the roof of the terminal (a result which the Landmarks Commission referred to as "an aesthetic joke").

>> **i. Theory of suit:** The Ps sued to invalidate the landmark preservation provisions, on the grounds that they prevented the Ps from obtaining a reasonable return on their investment in the terminal, and therefore amounted to a *taking* without compensation.

> **b. Supreme Court affirms:** The U.S. Supreme Court disagreed with the plaintiffs, and *upheld* the landmark-preservative regulations. *Penn Central Transportation Co. v. City of New York*, 438 U.S. 104 (1978). In doing so, the Court made several points:

>> **i. Landmark preservation valid state objective:** The preservation of buildings and areas with special historic, architectural, or cultural significance is an *"entirely permissible governmental goal."*

>> **ii. Not arbitrary or discriminatory:** The Ps had argued that landmark designation statutes are fundamentally different from zoning or historic-district legislation, because they allow the municipality to single out owners of particular buildings to bear the entire burden of the program, and that this selection is potentially arbitrary and highly subjective. But the Court disagreed, noting that zoning and historic-district legislation, too, frequently places an uneven burden. Also, the New York City landmarks law was part of a *"comprehensive plan"* of preservation, and over 400 landmarks had been designated, a strong indication that arbitrariness was lacking.

>> **iii. Reasonable return present:** Apart from their "arbitrary and discriminatory" argument, the Ps also claimed that their ability to use the property was so dimin-

ished that a *taking* had occurred. The Court *rejected* this claim. First, it noted that the landmarks law did not interfere in any way with the *present uses* of the Terminal (as a railroad terminal containing office space); this present use must, the Court said, be regarded as the Ps' *"primary expectation* concerning the use of the parcel." Also, there was no evidence that *all* development of the air space would be prohibited, merely that a structure in excess of fifty stories would be; thus a much smaller building might be permitted, and would contribute to a reasonable rate of return on the parcel.

  iv. Value of TDRs counted: Finally, the Court addressed the status of the Ps' *"Transferable Development Rights" (TDRs)*.

  (1) What TDRs are: Under the landmark preservation law, New York City had given the Ps the ability to *transfer* their development rights above the terminal to *other parcels of land in the vicinity*.

  (2) Value of TDRs must be counted: Particularly since the Ps themselves owned eight such parcels (including four hotels), the value of the TDRs here was significant, the Court said, and was to be counted in determining whether a reasonable return was possible. The Ps had failed to carry their burden of demonstrating that even when the value of these TDRs was counted, a reasonable return was not possible.

  c. Rehnquist dissent: A dissent by Justice Rehnquist contended that a taking had occurred. According to the dissent, any substantial interference with property rights constitutes a taking unless: (1) the use being prohibited is a nuisance; or (2) the prohibition applies over a *broad cross-section of land* and thereby "secures an average reciprocity of advantage," whereby each owner whose use is restricted gains substantial advantages in return. Factor (1) was clearly not present; nor was factor (2), since the loss of revenue suffered by the Ps was infinitely greater than any advantage which they obtained from the landmark preservation scheme. Since neither of these two factors was present, the dissent said, there was a taking even though a reasonable return on investment may be available to the Ps.

D. Federal and state environmental policy statues: Apart from land-use regulations that are motivated by a concern for the environment, there is now a separate body of federal and statute statutory law directed at broader environmental concerns. A detailed consideration of environmental law is beyond the scope of this outline.

 1. CERCLA and hazardous waste sites: One federal statute of special interest to landowners (and their lawyers) is *CERCLA*, the Comprehensive Environmental Response, Compensation and Liability Act, 42 U.S.C. §§ 9601-9675. CERCLA, also known as the *"Superfund"* law, lets the federal Environmental Protection Agency (EPA) *clean up abandoned hazardous waste sites.*

  a. Who can be liable: Once the EPA identifies a hazardous waste site and classifies it as a Superfund site, the Agency may hold various private parties *liable for cleanup costs.*

For our purposes, the most important categories of people who can be held liable include:

[1] the *current owner or operator* of the site; and

[2] the person who owned or operated the site *at the time any disposal of hazardous waste onto the site occurred*.

42 U.S.C. §9607(a)(1) and (2).

b. Successor liability: Category [1] above means that if you *buy a site* that turns out (even *unbeknownst* to you) to contain hazardous waste due to the actions of *prior owners, you can be liable for possibly-massive cleanup costs even though you had nothing to do with the original contamination!* To be sure, you get the right to sue your seller for contribution, and to sue the parties who originally caused the contamination for full indemnity; but these parties may no longer exist or be judgment-proof, so that you can easily be left holding the bag for a sum far in excess of either the present value of the property or the amount you paid.

   i. "Bona fide prospective purchaser" defense: However, CERCLA gives buyers of already-contaminated property a *"bona fide prospective purchaser" (BFPP)* defense. To be a BFPP, you must do two things:

     [a] *Before* you acquire the property, you must carry out *"all appropriate inquiries* into the *previous ownership and uses* of the facility in accordance with generally accepted good commercial and customary standards and practices."

     [b] *After* you acquire the property, you must take reasonable steps to *stop any further contamination* and to limit environmental damage from *past* contamination.

   See 42 U.S.C. §9601(40)(B) and (D).

     (1) "Appropriate inquiries" (non-residential property): As you can see, step [a] above means that before you buy property that could conceivably have had hazardous waste dumped on it sometime in the past, you must make *"appropriate inquiries"* into this possibility. In the case of property that is, at the time you purchase it, *not in residential use* (e.g., a factory or vacant land), this duty of inquiry means that you will need to *hire an environmental expert* to do a so-called *"Phase I environmental study."* In such a study, the environmental expert researches all prior owners of the property, the uses to which they put the property, and anything else that might bear on the existence and scope of hazardous waste on the site.

     If you discover that the site is contaminated, you can still buy it without necessarily having Superfund liability. But if you buy it, step [b] above means that you must closely manage the existing contamination to prevent further harm, a risky obligation that causes many buyers to walk away if they discover contamination.

     (2) "Appropriate inquiries" (residential property): If at the time of your purchase the property is being used for *residential* purposes, then the inquiry you have to do is much simpler; "a *facility inspection* and *title search* that reveal *no basis for further investigation*" are enough to shield you from liability, even if it later turns out that there's hidden contamination. 42 U.S.C. §9601(40)(B)(iii).

VIII. EMINENT DOMAIN

A. Eminent domain generally: The power of *eminent domain* is the power of government (either federal or state) to take private property for public use. The confines of the power of eminent domain are set by the Fifth Amendment to the U.S. Constitution, which provides: "[N]or shall private property be taken for public use without just compensation." This is, of course, the *"taking clause,"* which we've discussed at length *supra*, pp. 261-269.

    1. Condemnation proceedings: Generally, the power of eminent domain is invoked through *condemnation proceedings*. The government decides that a certain parcel is necessary for public use, and (assuming that private negotiations with the owner do not lead to a sale) brings a judicial proceeding to obtain title to the land. As part of this proceeding, the court decides upon the "just compensation" due to the owner.

    2. Inverse condemnation: Occasionally, however, the government will simply make *use* of a landowner's property, without bringing formal commencement proceedings. In this situation, the landowner may bring a so-called *"inverse condemnation"* action, in which he seeks a judicial declaration that his property has been taken by the government. In an inverse condemnation action, the landowner seeks, in effect, a *forced sale*, not merely damages.

B. Requirement of "public" use: Recall that the taking clause says that private property shall not be taken *"for public use"* unless just compensation is paid. This language has been interpreted by the Supreme Court as prohibiting the taking of private property for *private use, even if just compensation is made*. Thus the federal government (and, under an analogous interpretation of the Fourteenth Amendment, a state government) cannot simply take private property from one person, and give it to another, without any public purpose.

    1. "Public use" construed broadly: However, the Supreme Court has construed the requirement of a "public use" quite *broadly*. Here are two principles illustrating just how broadly the Court stretches the phrase:

        ❏ So long as the state's use of its eminent domain power is *"rationally related* to a *conceivable public purpose,"* the public use requirement is satisfied. *Hawaii Housing Authority v. Midkiff*, 467 U.S. 229 (1984).

        ❏ The property *need not be open to the general public after the taking.* As the first rule above suggests, all that "public use" means is that the property be used for a *"public purpose." Kelo v. New London* (discussed immediately *infra*). Therefore, the fact that the property is *turned over to some private user* does not prevent the use from being a public one as long as the public can be expected to derive some benefit (e.g., economic development) from the use.

2. **Urban renewal and economic development (the *"Kelo"* case):** The requirement of a public use can be met even though the government is pursuing the diffuse goal of *"economic development,"* and even if it is doing so by condemning parcels in *non-blighted* areas. This was the controversial result in a 5-4 decision in the 2005 case of ***Kelo v. New London***, 545 U.S. 469 (2005).

   a. **Facts:** In *Kelo*, the long-struggling city of New London, Connecticut, wanted to revitalize itself economically by carrying out a redevelopment plan that included building a $300 million research facility for the Pfizer pharmaceutical company, plus an adjacent conference hotel, residences and pedestrian "riverwalk" along the Thames River. The city believed that the development plan would create jobs, generate tax revenue, and revitalize the downtown. The plaintiffs were the owners of about 15 properties condemned by the city. These properties were mostly owner-occupied houses; none was in poor condition, but all were in the development area.

   b. **Ps' claim:** The plaintiffs claimed that a city's decision to take non-blighted property for the purpose of economic development was not a "public use."

   c. **Majority upholds taking:** By a 5-4 vote, the Supreme Court disagreed with the plaintiffs and *upheld* the condemnation. Justice Stevens wrote for the majority.

      i. **Only a "public purpose" is required:** Stevens began by saying that the requirement of public use did *not mean that the property had to be made open to, or used by, the public at large.* All that was required was that there be a *"public purpose"* behind the taking. Furthermore, the concept of "public purpose" was to be broadly defined, reflecting the Court's "longstanding policy of *deference to legislative judgments* in this field."

      ii. **Application:** Stevens then quickly concluded that New London's plan here met the requirement of public purpose. The city's economic development plan was "carefully formulated," and "comprehensive in character." The city believed that the plan would create new jobs and increased tax revenue. Therefore, Stevens concluded, it easily met the requirement that it serve a public purpose.

   d. **Dissent:** Justice O'Connor *dissented*, joined by Chief Justice Rehnquist and Justices Scalia and Thomas. She would have held that takings for the purpose of *economic development* are simply *not constitutional*, because they are *not for public use.* "Under the banner of economic development, all private property is now vulnerable to being taken and transferred to another private owner, so long as it might be upgraded — i.e., given to an owner who will use it in a way that the legislature deems more beneficial to the public[.]" Indeed, O'Connor could not see *any logical limit* on government's power under the majority's approach: "For who among us can say she already makes the most productive or attractive possible use of her property? *The specter of condemnation hangs over all property.* Nothing is to prevent the State from replacing any Motel 6 with a Ritz-Carlton, any home with a shopping mall, or any farm with a factory."

   e. **Raw transfer to the politically favored:** After *Kelo*, does the "public use" requirement have any bite at all? The answer seems to be "very little." One sliver of continuing significance is hinted at by a concurrence by Justice Kennedy, in supplying the fifth vote to uphold New London's plan. Kennedy asserted that if a taking were clearly shown to have been ***"intended to favor a particular private party***, with only ***incidental or pretextual public benefits,"*** it would be invalid. (That obviously hadn't happened in *Kelo*, since New London's plan was a comprehensive one, and since the identity of most of the private beneficiaries was unknown at the time the plan was formulated.)

C. Measuring "just compensation":   The most frequently litigated issue in eminent domain proceedings is the ***value of the property***. The Constitution requires that ***"just compensation"*** be paid, but this is of course an ambiguous term. The courts have generally held that the ***fair market value at the time of taking*** is what must be paid.

   1. Measuring "market value":   The fair market value, in turn, is based upon the ***"highest and best use"*** that may be made of the property (at least under current zoning regulations). Thus if a vacant parcel is zoned for subdivision, the value that must be paid is the value the land would have to a subdivider (even though the owner himself may never have contemplated subdividing the property). Land Use Nutshell, pp. 287-89.

   2. "Substitution cost" not required: Suppose that because of the unusual needs of the property owner, the cost to ***replace*** the condemned parcel is greater than the market value of that parcel. The condemnee is usually entitled to receive only the market value, not the higher "substitution value" of the land in this situation.

Quiz Yourself on
ZONING AND OTHER PUBLIC LAND-USE CONTROLS

74. For 20 years, Dexter has operated a private dump in the town of Hampshire. The dump now receives approximately 500 tons of garbage per year, about the same annual amount that it has always received. The only negative environmental effect from operation of the dump is odor, and the odors are no more serious than they have always been, i.e., a mildly disturbing garbage smell that depending on wind condition can be perceived as far as one-half mile away from the dump. As the town has become more affluent, the citizens have become increasingly unhappy about the dump. Finally, the Hampshire Town Council recently passed a zoning ordinance providing that no dump may be operated within the town, and further providing that any existing dump must be discontinued within two years following passage of the ordinance. Because Dexter's property now has a huge pile of unsightly garbage on it, its value has declined to $200,000 (versus an approximately $1 million value as an operating dump). Dexter has brought an inverse condemnation suit against Hampshire, arguing that the ordinance amounts to a "taking" of his property and that he must therefore be compensated for the $1 million value it has (though he is willing to give the town a credit for the $200,000 that the property will be worth after it is no longer a dump). Should the court award Dexter the $800,000 relief he seeks? _____

75. Jones operates a car dealership along a highway located in the town of Nordstom. For 20 years, Jones has had a billboard on the edge of his property extolling his dealership's virtues to passersby on the highway. Then, the Nordstrom Town Council enacted a comprehensive zoning ordinance, which among other things bars all billboards anywhere in the town. The "pre-existing uses" section of the ordinance provides that any non-conforming use must be phased out within five years of the ordinance. Jones has sued to overturn the ordinance as applied to him, arguing that while Nordstrom has the right to ban billboards prospectively, it may not require him to remove an existing billboard because this constitutes a taking of his property without due process. Will Jones prevail? _____

76. The town of Twin Peaks is a long-established wealthy community whose residents include almost no blacks or other minorities, and almost no poor people. Twin Peaks never had a comprehensive zoning ordinance until 2010. That year, it enacted an ordinance which, among other aspects, provided that no home may be built on a parcel of land containing less than two acres. Prosser, a local developer, acquired a 10-acre parcel on a quiet street in Twin Peaks. He proposed to build 20 single-family residences on the parcel. Prosser realized, of course, that he would not be permitted to build the development unless he could either have the two-acre minimum removed from the ordinance, or obtain a variance for his development. The Town Council refused to do either. Prosser is reluctant to sue the town, because he does not want to alienate it.

However, Twin Peaks has been sued by Prince, a black resident of nearby Glendale, who argues that if the two-acre minimum were lifted, he would be able to afford, and would choose, to live on Prosser's development. Prince contends that Twin Peaks' refusal to lift the minimum violates his equal protection rights. At trial, Prince has been able to prove that the two-acre minimum has the effect of dramatically reducing the number of black residents in Twin Peaks, since most nearby blacks are insufficiently wealthy to afford the two acre parcels. However, neither side has produced any evidence as to whether the Town Council of Twin Peaks was motivated by a desire to keep out blacks, either at the time the ordinance was originally enacted or at the more recent time when the Council refused to lift the two-acre minimum. On these facts, should the court find that Twin Peaks has violated Prince's equal protection rights? _____

77. Same facts as prior question.

   (a) What statutory action, if any, could Prince bring that would have a good probability of success? _____

   (b) Will Prince succeed with such an action? _____

78. Same facts as prior two questions. Now, however, assume that there is convincing evidence that the Town Council of Twin Peaks was *not* motivated by any racially-discriminatory intent, and that the two-acre minimum zoning rule was enacted for the purpose of maintaining the "uncrowded" and "pastoral" nature of the town. Assume that Twin Peaks is located in the state of New Jersey. No relevant statutes have been enacted.

   (a) What theory might Prosser (the developer, see Question 76) use to attack the two-acre rule? _____

   (b) If the court agreed with Prosser's suit, what remedy would the court be likely to award? _____

Answers

74. **No, probably.** Occasionally, a land-use control is sufficiently draconian that a court will conclude that it amounts to a "taking" for Fourteenth Amendment purposes, for which compensation must be given. But this is extremely rare, especially in the environmental regulation area. A land-use regulation is valid as long as the means chosen "substantially advance" a legitimate state interest, and do not "deny an owner economically viable use of his land." *Nollan v. California Coastal Commission*, 483 U.S. 825 (1987). Here, the town is certainly advancing its legitimate interest in not suffering the noxious odors associated with a dump. Furthermore, Dexter is not being deprived of all economically viable use of his property, but

merely the most "valuable" use. So a court is extremely unlikely to hold that the ordinance constitutes a taking.

75. **No, probably.** The vast majority of states hold that such an "amortization" provision does not violate due process or constitute a taking, as long as the amortization period is sufficiently long for the owner to recover most of his costs and to arrange an alternative use or location. Here, Jones has already had the billboard for 20 years (plus the five-year phase-out), so he has had plenty of time to recoup its costs. Also, he can continue to run his business without the billboard, so the injury to him is not extreme. (But about five states hold, either as a matter of state statutory law or federal constitutional law, that non-conforming uses must be permitted indefinitely, rather than being "amortized.")

76. **No.** Prince probably has standing to assert his claim, since he has been directly affected by the allegedly illegal zoning. However, the Supreme Court has held that a racially discriminatory ***purpose***, not merely effect, needs to be shown before an ordinance will be subjected to strict equal protection scrutiny. Without strict scrutiny, the ordinance here merely has to be rationally related to a legitimate state purpose, which is almost certainly the case. So unless Prince is able to bear the burden of showing that the town's ordinance was enacted (or maintained) for racially discriminatory purposes, the fact that the ordinance has a disparate negative effect on minorities is irrelevant to the equal protection claim. See *Arlington Heights v. Metropolitan Housing Development Corp.*, 429 U.S. 252 (1977).

77. **(a) A federal Fair Housing Act suit.** The Fair Housing title of the 1968 Civil Rights Act makes it unlawful to "make unavailable, or deny, a dwelling to any person because of race, color, religion, sex or national origin."

(b) Yes, probably. If Prince had been able to show that Twin Peaks intentionally tried to limit access by blacks, this would be a clear violation of the Housing Act. The Supreme Court has never decided whether a discriminatory purpose (rather than mere disparate effect) must be shown for a violation of the act, but most lower federal courts have held that the plaintiff in such a suit does ***not*** need to show that the defendant had a discriminatory intent. Instead, plaintiff merely has to prove that the defendant's land-use controls had a disparate effect on blacks or other racial minorities. The burden then shifts to the defendant town to show that it was acting in pursuit of a legitimate governmental interest, and that there was no less-discriminatory way of achieving that same interest. Probably Twin Peaks could not meet this burden, so probably Prince would win his suit on this theory. See, e.g., *Huntington Branch NAACP v. Town of Huntington*, 844 F.2d 926 (2d Cir. 1988).

78. **(a) A *Mount Laurel* "fair share" suit.** In *Southern Burlington County NAACP v. Township of Mount Laurel*, 336 A.2d 713 (N.J. 1975), the New Jersey Supreme Court held that exclusionary zoning practices that fail to serve the general welfare of the region as a whole violate statutory law and the state constitution. The court held that a municipality may not foreclose opportunities for low- and moderate-income housing, and must allow at least that town's "fair share" of the present and prospective regional need for such housing. Since the two-acre minimum prevents even middle-class housing, let alone lower-class housing, from being constructed, the scheme would almost certainly be a *Mount Laurel* violation.

(b) Grant a re-zoning of the parcel. *Mount Laurel* (and a successor case, *"Mount Laurel II"*) hold that where the trial court concludes that the project sought to be built by the developer is suitable for that specific site, the court may order the municipality to rezone the particular project. This is the so-called "builder's remedy." This would permit Prosser to go ahead with his project immediately, rather than merely watch as the town meets its "fair share" obligation by other means, such as allowing an apartment complex to be built in some other part of town. (But the New Jersey legislature has subsequently put a moratorium on the builder's remedy.)

Exam Tips on
ZONING AND OTHER PUBLIC LAND-USE CONTROLS

The topics in this chapter are not very likely to be treated as the major issues in an exam question, but will nevertheless appear as sub-issues. Common topics include:

☛ **Aesthetic zoning:** Remember that most courts will not allow ***aesthetic considerations*** to be the ***sole factor*** supporting the zoning ordinance. Therefore, look for another factor justifying the municipality's decision, and if there isn't one, argue that the decision may well be invalid.

> *Example:* A zoning ordinance prohibits free-standing signs more than fifteen feet high. The owner of a parcel of land wants to erect a fifty-foot sign on her property for commercial reasons. The municipality can argue that, aside from aesthetics, the ordinance is a safety measure because it will reduce the risk of vehicular accidents caused by distracted drivers.

☛ **Spot zoning:** When like parcels are treated differently under an ***amendment*** to a zoning scheme, discuss the issue of "***spot zoning***." Point out that if the court believes that one or a few small parcels have been singled out for treatment favorable to the owner(s), the court may conclude that this constitutes illegal spot zoning, in which case the amendment will be struck down.

> *Example:* A zoning ordinance is enacted designating Lots numbered 1-12 as Single Family Residential. At the time, a nightclub is located on Lot 6 (and is grandfathered in as a non-conforming use). Fifteen months later Lot 6 is rezoned as Commercial, the County Commissioners stating that it is a likely site for a shopping center. The other landowners attack the reclassification of Lot 6. There is a good chance that the court will hold that singling out Lot 6 for special favorable treatment constituted illegal spot zoning.

☛ **Abandonment of "non-conforming uses":** Fact patterns will sometimes involve an owner who has a pre-existing ***non-conforming use*** (i.e., a use that predates the zoning ordinance that makes it non-conforming, but that is permitted to continue for some length of time as a *"grandfathered"* use). When this happens, look for the possibility that the use has been ***abandoned*** by that owner — if so, it ***can't be restarted*** under the grandfathering clause.

☞ **Mere cessation not enough:** But mere ***cessation*** of the use for some period of time does ***not*** constitute abandonment — the owner must be shown to have had an ***intent*** to abandon the use, plus to have made an ***overt act*** demonstrating that intent.

☛ **Taking:** An owner will sometimes argue that land-use regulation of her parcel is so extensive that it amounts to a *"taking"* which, under the Fifth and Fourteenth Amendments, may not occur without compensation. However, no taking will occur unless the restriction fails to *"substantially advance"* a legitimate governmental objective. In the case of zoning, as long as the owner is left with some *economically viable use of his land*, there will be no taking unless the regulation is completely arbitrary (an extremely hard-to-satisfy requirement). So you should lean heavily against a conclusion that a particular zoning restriction constitutes a taking.

> *Example:* A zoning ordinance prohibits free-standing signs more than fifteen feet high. This prevents O from effectively operating a service station on his land near a highway, since he won't be able to signal his existence to motorists. However, since parcel can be used for other economically-viable purposes (e.g., a small shopping center), and since the regulation substantially advances a legitimate governmental objective (fighting visual blight), a court will almost certainly find that there has been no taking.

☞ **Moratorium as taking:** Be alert for a *moratorium on development*. Even if the moratorium is temporary, it may have such an impact on an owner's investment that it rises to the level of a taking for which compensation must be paid.

> *Example:* P owns vacant land in City. City enacts a multi-year moratorium on building any structure on the land, while City prepares a master plan. A court may well hold that even though the ban is temporary, its impact on P is big enough that it's a taking the fair value of which must be paid by City. The court will consider all surrounding circumstances (including length of moratorium, P's income from the vacant land, and whether his land increased in value during the delay) in deciding whether there's been a taking. [Cite to *Tahoe-Sierra v. Tahoe Regional Planning Agency*]

> ☞ **Routine development delays:** Keep in mind that *routine delays* in being able to develop one's property — such as government's ordinary delays in *issuing permits* — *won't* by themselves constitute a taking.

☛ **Eminent domain:** If government is compulsorily acquiring P's property under *eminent domain*, focus on whether government has violated the constitutional requirement that any use of eminent domain be "for *public use*."

☞ **Easy to satisfy:** But point out that the public-use requirement is *very easy to satisfy.* For instance, City can take private property that's non-blighted, and turn it over to a private developer, as long as City reasonably believes that increased tax revenues or economic growth will result. It doesn't matter that the resulting development won't even be open to the public (e.g., a corporate research center). [*Kelo v. New London*]

CHAPTER 11

LAND SALE CONTRACTS, MORTGAGES AND DEEDS

Introductory note: This chapter examines the various steps in the process of transferring (or "conveyancing") land. We examine, in sequence (1) contracts for the sale of land; (2) mortgages (which secure the repayment of loans); and (3) deeds, which are the instruments by which a freehold interest in land is transferred.

I. LAND SALE CONTRACTS

A. Function of a contract: It is theoretically possible for the parties to a commercial land transfer to accomplish the entire transfer in one step. The seller could simply tender his deed, and the buyer could simultaneously hand over the purchase price. If the transaction were handled this way, no *contract* to sell land would be necessary.

   1. The gap: However, in practice, it is almost always desirable for there to be a *gap* (usually a month or more) between the time when the parties agree on a deal, and the time when the title actually passes. During this gap, the buyer typically: (1) arranges financing; and (2) checks the seller's title. For the parties to be bound during this gap, there must be an enforceable agreement between them; this is the purpose of a land sale contract.

B. Statute of Frauds: The *Statute of Frauds* is applicable in all states to any contract for the sale of land, or for the sale of any interest in land. Therefore, either the contract itself, or a memorandum of it, must be *in writing*.

   1. Memorandum satisfying: Normally, the contract itself will be in writing, so that the entire agreement of the parties is documented. However, a *memorandum* of the parties' agreement, specifying some terms but not the entire oral agreement, may also satisfy the Statute.

      a. Elements of memorandum: Generally, the memorandum must state with reasonable certainty the following elements: (1) the *name* of each party to the contract; (2) the land to be conveyed; and (3) the *essential terms and conditions*. 3 A.L.P. 16.

         i. Price: Usually, the memorandum must list the *purchase price*. However, if the party seeking to enforce the contract can show that the parties did not set a price, and instead agreed that a "reasonable price" would be paid, no statement about the purchase price need appear in the memorandum. 3 A.L.P. 20.

         ii. Signature: The *signature* of the *party to be charged* (i.e., the party against whom enforcement is sought) must appear on the contract. Thus if Seller writes a letter to Buyer, confirming the provisions of their oral contract, this letter can constitute a sufficient memorandum if Buyer seeks to enforce the contract against Seller, but not if Seller seeks to enforce it against Buyer.

b. Intent to make subsequent writing: The parties may sometimes prepare a *preliminary, informal*, document, while intending to execute a more complete and formal document later on. The fact that the parties intend to execute a later writing does not make the first writing insufficient as a memorandum. However, the intent to make a later writing may constitute *evidence* that the parties did *not intend to be bound* until they had done so.

c. Broker's contract as memorandum: A document may satisfy the memorandum requirement even if it was prepared for an entirely different purpose. For instance, a contract between the seller and a *real estate broker*, authorizing the broker to sell the property on certain terms, might be held sufficient to bind the seller.

2. Contract for brokerage commission: In many states, a contract between an owner and a *real estate broker* is brought within the Statute of Frauds. In such states, the broker cannot collect his commission unless he has a written agreement.

3. The part performance exception: There is one major exception to the Statute of Frauds for land sale contracts. Under the doctrine of *part performance*, a party (either the buyer or seller) who has taken action in *reliance* on the contract may be able to gain at least limited enforcement of it at *equity*.

a. Acts by vendor: If the vendor *makes a conveyance* under the contract, he will then be able to sue for the agreed-upon price, even if the agreement to pay that price was only oral. 3 A.L.P. 26. This can be thought of as use of the part performance doctrine, though technically what has happened is that once the conveyance is made, the promise to pay is no longer within the Statute.

    i. Price is land interest: However, this exception does not apply if the price is *itself* an interest in land (i.e., the deal is an exchange of one parcel for another). 3 A.L.P. 26.

b. Acts by purchaser: The courts are in sharp dispute as to what acts *by the purchaser* constitute part performance entitling him to specific performance. Here are some of the acts that some courts have deemed to be sufficient part performance:

    i. Possession alone: In a number of states, it is sufficient that the purchaser has *taken possession* of the property, even if the purchaser has done nothing else.

    ii. Possession and payments: In some states, possession alone is not enough, but possession coupled with *payment by the purchaser* is enough.

    iii. Possession and improvements: In some states, possession accompanied by the making of valuable and lasting *improvements* (e.g., construction of a house or garage) is sufficient. This is true in some of the states which also recognize possession-with-payment as sufficient.

    iv. Change of position: In some states, the fact that the purchaser has *changed his position* in *reliance* on the agreement is a factor. In some of these states, this change of position must be accompanied by the taking of possession. In other states, a change in position alone (without taking of possession) suffices, at least where the seller agrees that the oral agreement was in fact made.

Example: Seller and Purchaser orally agree on the sale of Blackacre for $15,000. Purchaser gives Seller a deposit check for $500, but Seller merely keeps the check, without ever endorsing it or depositing it. Neither party contemplates a subsequent written agreement. Purchaser immediately enters into a binding contract to sell his existing house. Seller then reneges, after receiving a higher offer from someone else. Purchaser sues for specific performance. Seller defends on the ground of Statute of Frauds, but agrees that the oral agreement was in fact made.

Held, Purchaser wins, and specific performance is ordered. Under Rest. 2d of Contracts, §129, "a contract for the transfer of an interest in land may be specifically enforced notwithstanding failure to comply with the Statute of Frauds if it is established that the party seeking enforcement, in *reasonable reliance* on the contract and on the continuing assent of the party against whom enforcement is sought, has *so changed his position* that injustice can be avoided only by specific enforcement." The facts here satisfy this standard, which the court accepts. *Hickey v. Green*, 442 N.E.2d 37 (Mass. App. 1982).

   v. No act suffices: In a few states, there is *no act of part performance* that is sufficient to make the oral contract enforceable.

See C&J, p. 989, note 3.

  c. "Unequivocally referable" requirement: Courts generally require that the part performance be *"unequivocally referable"* to the alleged contract. That is, the person seeking enforcement must show that the part performance was clearly *in response* to the oral contract, and not explainable by some other facet of the parties' relationship. This is usually so even though great hardship may result from the court's decision not to enforce the contract.

Example: Suppose that D, an elderly widower, promises P, his adult daughter (or so P alleges), that if P will give up her rented apartment across town, and move in with him to care for him for a wage of $300 per week plus room and board, he will sell P the house for $100,000 (half its true value) in three years. P moves in with D and cares for him for the next two years. D then tells P that he won't be selling her the house at the end of the three years — he denies ever having made the promise. P sues for specific performance of the alleged promise.

A court is likely to find for D, because what P did was not "unequivocally referable" to the alleged contract. That is, while P is claiming that she "partly performed" (by giving up her apartment, moving in with D and caring for him), her "performance" could plausibly have been in response to other aspects of her relationship with D, rather than to the alleged contract. For instance, P has been receiving a current salary and room and board, so it's plausible that P did what she did for these benefits alone. Cf. *Burns v. McCormick*, 135 N.E. 273 (N.Y. 1922).

   i. Some flexibility: Although courts generally recite the "unequivocal referability" requirement, they usually don't enforce it stringently. After all, virtually every act or combination of acts by the person seeking enforcement could be explained by some reason other than an oral contract of sale (e.g., an oral lease). What courts really require is that the acts *"point with reasonable clarity* to the presence of a contract." C,S&W, p. 666.

ii. **Defendant admits contract:**   Furthermore, if the defendant *admits* that the oral agreement took place, but nonetheless tries to plead the Statute of Frauds, courts will not generally apply the "unequivocally referable" requirement at all. Thus in *Hickey v. Green* (*supra,* p. 307), the court ordered specific performance even though the plaintiff's act (sale of his house) could have been very plausibly explained by any of a number of other possible reasons apart from the oral deal — the court was heavily influenced by the fact that the seller admitted that the oral agreement had been reached.

4. **Oral modification and rescission:**   Where an enforceable land sale contract exists, the courts are split as to whether it may be orally *rescinded* or *modified*.

   a. **Rescission:**   A slight majority of jurisdictions hold that a land sale contract may be *orally rescinded*.

      i. **Minority view:**   But a substantial minority of states hold that the *rescission must be in writing*.

   b. **Modification:**   The courts are less willing to permit an oral *modification* (as opposed to rescission) of a contract. Most courts reason that a contract is the sum of its terms, and that enforcement of a land sale contract some of whose terms are oral (the modified terms) contravenes the policy of the Statute of Frauds. See Rest., Contracts, §223.

      i. **Estoppel or waiver:**   Even where the oral agreement to modify is held unenforceable, the *action* of one or both parties may constitute an *estoppel* or *waiver*. If a party's oral promise of a modification leads the other party to *change his position in reliance*, the former likely to be estopped from denying the enforceability of the modification (or, what amounts to the same thing, held to have waived the term of the original contract claimed to have been modified).

         (1) **Retraction:**   One important difference between a binding modification and an estoppel or waiver, is that an estoppel or waiver (but not a modification) can be *retracted*, so long as the other party has not yet *changed his position in reliance*.

C. **Time for performance:**   The sale contract will normally provide a *"settlement date,"* i.e., a date upon which the closing, or passing of title, is to occur. If one party fails to complete the closing on the appointed day, the question arises whether she is liable for breach of contract, and whether she has lost her rights under the contract.

1. **Suit for damages:**   In a suite for *damages* (i.e., a suit brought at law rather than in equity), the time stated in the contract will be deemed to be *of the essence*, unless a contrary intention appears. 3 A.L.P. 118. Thus if Seller refuses to close on the appointed day, Buyer may bring a suit for damages for the delay, even if it is only a few days. Conversely, Seller may sue Buyer if the latter delays; in this case, the recovery would presumably be for the interest which Seller could have gotten on Buyer's money had the closing taken place as scheduled.

2. Suit at equity: But in a suit *in equity* (i.e., a suit for specific performance), the general rule is that *time is not of the essence*, unless either:

[1] there is an *express provision* in the contract making time of the essence; or

[2] such a provision may be fairly *inferred* from the *nature of the property* or of the *surrounding circumstances*.

3 A.L.P. 118.

a. Right to close late: The default rule that time is not of the essence means that generally, even though the contract specifies a particular date for the closing, either party may obtain *specific performance* although he is unable to close on the appointed day. (However, the defaulting party must be ready to perform within a *reasonable time* after the scheduled date.)

   i. Can benefit either buyer or seller: This rule — that a party doesn't lose the right to specific performance for delay if time is not of the essence — can benefit *either* a buyer or a seller. Thus a *buyer* who is unable to procure the necessary financing until several days after the scheduled closing date may obtain a court decree ordering a sale to him; conversely a *seller* who is unable to clear his title until several days late may gain a decree ordering the purchaser to go through with the transaction.

b. Surrounding circumstances: The *surrounding circumstances* may indicate that the parties intend time to be of the essence. For instance, in a period when prices are fluctuating widely, a court may conclude that, although the contract is absent on the issue, the parties intended time to be of the essence. Such intent may also be found when one party is very concerned about a prompt closing and the other party knows of this concern. C,S&W, p. 704.

c. Unilateral action: Some courts hold that where the contract does not explicitly make time of the essence, *either party*, by a *unilateral notification* to the other that it will insist upon strict adherence to the contracted-for settlement date, may make time of the essence. However, the notification must be given at least a reasonable time before the scheduled closing date.

d. Waiver: Even where time would otherwise be of the essence, a party may *waive* his right to assert that fact. For instance, if a party agrees (even orally) to adjourn the closing, he will not be allowed to claim, after the original settlement date, that the other party has defaulted. But such a waiver may be *retracted* as long as the other party has not yet relied to his detriment. See 3 A.L.P. 122-23.

e. "Time of the essence" clause: The parties are free to change the above default rules governing when time is of the essence by *specifying* whether time should or should not be of the essence. Thus a clause stating that "time is of the essence" will normally be *enforced*, both at law and in equity.

f. Consequences: Where time *is* of the essence (either because of contractual language or circumstances), that fact will be damaging to a party — whether buyer or seller — who is not ready and able to perform on time.

i.   Consequences to late seller: A *seller* who does not tender timely performance faces several bad consequences if time is of the essence:

[1] the seller *loses the right to obtain specific performance* against the buyer (assuming that specific performance would otherwise be granted; see *infra*, p. 315);

[2] the *buyer can cancel the contract* and recover his earnest money deposit;

[3] the buyer probably can *elect to get specific performance* against the seller; and

[4] the buyer can *recover money damages* to the extent that the delay caused monetary loss to the buyer (a consequence that would occur even if time was *not* of the essence).

ii.   Consequences to late buyer: Conversely, if it is the *buyer* who does not tender timely performance (i.e., does not timely tender the purchase price) in a deal in which time is of the essence, the buyer faces these consequences:

[1] the *seller can cancel* the contract and refuse to convey even if the buyer is now willing to close;

[2] the seller will probably be able to *get specific performance* ordering the buyer to tender the purchase price;

[3] the buyer *loses his right to compel specific performance*; and

[4] the seller *can recover money damages* against the buyer for the delay, and/or *keep the deposit.*

g.   No margin for error: Where time is of the essence, the standard is an extremely harsh one: even a delay of a *single day* may well be held to be a breach of a time-is-of-the-essence provision. Certainly the court will *not* consider whether the delay has risen to the level of "unreasonable," because the idea behind time-of-the-essence is that either party is entitled to insist on *strict compliance* with the time limit.

D.   Marketable title: In the vast majority of cases, the contract will require the vendor to convey a *marketable*, or *merchantable, title*. However, the courts are not in agreement as to the circumstances in which this obligation arises, or on what exactly a marketable title *is*.

1.   Implied in contract: If the contract is *silent* on the issue of the kind of title to be conveyed by the vendor, an obligation to convey a marketable title will be *implied*.

a.   Quitclaim deed: The parties, are, of course, free to provide that something less than a marketable title will suffice. For instance, if they call for a *"quitclaim deed,"*[1] this will typically indicate an intent not to require marketable title.

2.   General definition of "marketable title": Although courts may disagree as to whether a title is marketable on a particular set of facts, most courts agree on the general *standard* for determining marketability. As one court has put it, a marketable title is one which is

---

1. A quitclaim deed, described more fully *infra*, p. 332, is one which does not purport to do anything more than convey whatever interest the grantor has, if any.

"free from reasonable doubt both as to matters of law and fact, a title which a *reasonable purchaser*, well informed as to the facts and their legal bearings and willing and ready to perform his contract, would, in the exercise of that prudence which businessmen ordinarily bring to bear upon such transactions, *be willing to accept* and ought to accept." *Robinson v. Bressler*, 240 N.W. 564 (Nev. 1932).

a. **Reasonable person standard:** Thus it is *not* sufficient that a court would probably hold the title good in a *litigation*. The title must be *free from reasonable doubt* so that the buyer will be able to resell in the future. If, in the particular community, title examiners have set certain informal standards (e.g., that no title is good so long as there is a recorded mortgage without a recorded discharge), a court is likely to hold that a title failing to meet these informal standards is not marketable, even though the court might well decide in the vendor's favor if he brought a quiet title action effective against the whole world.

   i. **Need not "buy a lawsuit":** As the idea is often put, the purchaser should not be required to *"buy a lawsuit"*.

3. **Deducible of record:** In most courts, the validity of the title must be apparent *from the record*, without resort to unrecorded documents or other external evidence. Again, the rationale for this is that when the purchaser wants to resell, he should not have to present unrecorded documents, or procure testimony, to show that what appears on the record to be bad title is in fact good title. Thus in most courts the vendor may not establish marketability by an unrecorded deed, or by showing that title vested in a predecessor by adverse possession.

4. **Insurability:** The fact that a title company is willing to *insure* the title is *not* by itself sufficient to make the title marketable. (For one thing, a title company will insure almost any title so long as the policy excepts listed defects as found in the title company's search.) However, the parties are free to specify in their contract that all that is required is a title which is insurable by a designated company with designated exceptions.

5. **Defects making title unmarketable:** There are a large number of different defects which might make a title unmarketable, and it is not feasible to list them all here. However, some of the more important types of defects may be summarized. These can be divided into broad classes: (1) defects in the record chain of title; and (2) encumbrances.

   a. **Defects in the record chain of title:** Anything in the prior chain of title indicating that the vendor does not have the *full interest* which he purports to convey may be a defect.

      i. **Variation of names:** Thus a substantial variation between the *name* of the grantee of record in one link and the name of the grantor in the following link is a defect.

      ii. **Misdescription:** A substantial variation in the *description of the land* between one deed and the next may be a defect.

      iii. **Not suitable for recordation:** If one of the deeds was *defectively executed*, so that it was not eligible for recording (even though it was in fact recorded), this will be a defect. Thus an *unnotarized or unwitnessed deed*, in many states, renders title unmerchantable. (But so-called "curative acts" in many states make such technical defects irrelevant after a short number of years following filing; see *infra*, p. 365.)

    iv. Adverse possession: Where the title is required to be marketable of record, the title will usually be insufficient if it is based on *adverse possession*.

b. Encumbrances: Even though the vendor may have valid title to the property, it may be subject to *encumbrances*, a class which includes such things as mortgages, liens, easements, equitable restrictions and encroachments.

    i. Mortgage: An outstanding *mortgage*, of course, constitutes an encumbrance making the title unmarketable.

        (1) Right to pay off at closing: However, the vendor has the right to *pay off the mortgage at the closing*, out of the sale proceeds (though the purchaser has the right to insist that this be done simultaneously with the closing, rather than subsequently). So the fact that a mortgage exists — at least where it's for *less than the anticipated purchase price* — won't render title unmarketable prior to the closing date, if the seller credibly indicates that he'll pay the mortgage off at the closing. (As to the special problems of mortgages where the contract is an installment contract, see *infra*, p. 313.)

    ii. Liens: *Liens* against the property are likely to constitute an encumbrance. For instance, *unpaid taxes*, judgments obtained by creditors, or mechanic's liens filed by persons who have done work on the property, may all constitute defects. (Again, however, the vendor has the right to pay these off at the closing.)

    iii. Easements: An *easement* will be a defect, if it reduces the *"full enjoyment"* of the premises. (But if the easement was notorious and visible, the purchaser will probably be deemed to have seen it, and to have agreed to take subject to it, when he signed the contract. See 3 A.L.P. 137.)

    iv. Use restrictions: Similarly, a privately-negotiated *use* restriction (e.g., a covenant whose burden runs with the land, to the effect that only residential structures will be built) can be a defect. However, courts generally regard title as defective only if the use restriction is *already being violated* before the sale, or if the use that the seller knows the buyer is proposing to make would violate a use restriction.

    Example: All deeds in Blackacre Village, which consists of 20 homes, contain a legally-enforceable covenant that each lot will be used only for single-family residential purposes. Sell, the owner of one such house, signs a contract to sell the property to Purch, with Sell promising to deliver marketable title. Since the covenant is in accordance with the present single-family use of the house, and since Sell has no reason to believe that Purch is planning to use the property for something other than single-family purposes, the existence of the covenant will *not* be deemed to render Sell's title unmarketable.

    v. Encroachments: An *encroachment* by a neighboring landowner (e.g., a driveway or part of a building running onto the vendor's own land) will constitute a defect, if it interferes seriously with the use and enjoyment of the premises. 3 A.L.P. 140. Conversely, if one of the structures on the vendor's land seriously encroaches onto a neighbor's property, title will also be unmarketable. *Id.*

> **vi. Land-use and zoning violations:** A violation of land-use restrictions that are imposed by *law* (as opposed to restrictions privately-agreed upon) may or may not be treated as encumbrances.
>
>> **(1) Building codes:** Most courts hold that violations of *building codes* are *not* encumbrances on title. C,S&W, p. 729.
>>
>> **(2) Zoning violations:** But a violation of a *zoning ordinance* usually *is* treated as an encumbrance. C,S&W, p. 730.

6. Time when title must be marketable: Unless the contract specifies otherwise, the vendor's title is not required to be marketable *until the date set for the closing*. Thus the vendor may sign a contract to sell property which he does not yet own, and the purchaser cannot cancel the contract prior to the closing date because of this fact. 3 A.L.P. 141.

> **a. Outstanding mortgage:** Similarly, the fact that there is an *outstanding mortgage* on the property is not an encumbrance — as long as the mortgage is not in default (and the contract price is greater than the amount of the mortgage), so that the owner has the right and probable ability to pay off the mortgage at the closing, the mortgage's existence does not prevent title from being marketable.
>
>> **i. Installment contracts:** Suppose that the contract is an *installment agreement*, by which the vendor is required to convey title only after all installments of the purchase price have been paid. Unless the buyer can carry the burden of showing *reasonable and serious doubt* about whether the seller will be *able and willing to make the mortgage payments while the contract is in force*, the fact that there is an outstanding mortgage won't render title unmarketable. So, for instance, if the outstanding mortgage principal is considerably less than the present value of the property, and the seller has never missed mortgage payments in the past, the buyer probably won't persuade the court that the seller's title is not marketable. Cf. S&W, p. 784.

E. The closing: At the *closing*, the seller tenders his deed, and any other documents required by the contract or by local custom (e.g., a bill of sale for any personal property involved in the transaction, a satisfaction of mortgage indicating that the mortgage has just been paid off, etc.). The buyer checks each of the proffered documents, and when he is satisfied that everything is in order, tenders payment.

1. Tender: In the usual transaction, the seller's duty to deliver the deed and the buyer's duty to pay the money are *concurrent*. Therefore, if one party is expected to default, the other party must be sure to *tender his own performance*, in order to be able to hold the other party in default, and sue for damages and/or specific performance. The party who tenders must also make a formal *demand* that the other party *perform*. If the non-defaulting party *doesn't* tender performance, she is likely to be found to have waived her right to claim damages for the default (and may lose her right to reclaim any deposit).

Example: Seller and Buyer contract for the sale of Blackacre, closing to occur April 1, for $300,000. The contract requires Seller to deliver marketable title, and time is of the essence. On March 30, Buyer notifies Seller (accurately) that Seller's garage encroaches 2 feet onto Neighbor's property, and that Buyer will not close on April 1 because of the lack of marketable title. (Buyer knew about the defect as early as March 1, but said nothing to Seller until March 30. If Seller had been notified of the encroachment by, say, March 10, there is a good chance he could have purchased the 2-foot strip from Neighbor for a nominal amount, and thus cured the problem.) On April 1, Buyer does not show that he has the $300,000 purchase price available.

If Buyer sues for damages for Seller's failure to deliver marketable title, Buyer will probably lose. That's because (1) Buyer failed to tender performance on the closing date; and (2) Buyer's failure to tender cannot be excused as a futile act, because had Buyer given reasonable notice of the encroachment problem, Seller could likely have cured it before the closing date. Conversely, if Seller can show that he could have cured the defect with reasonable notice, Seller may have a claim for default against Buyer, since Buyer didn't tender performance.

    a. Effect of other party's repudiation: But a tender is necessary only where there is some chance that it would be effective. Thus if the other party has *repudiated*, or if the other party's inability to perform is *incurable* (as would have been the case in the above Example if it was clear that Neighbor wouldn't sell Seller the strip for a plausible price), no tender and demand for performance is necessary. See 3 A.L.P. 148.

F. Remedies for failure to perform: Where one party fails to perform a land sale contract, there are two distinct remedies which may be available to the other party: (1) a suit for *damages*; and (2) a suit for *specific performance*. (Both of these types of relief may generally be sought in the same proceeding, although sometimes an actual award of one will preclude the other.)

    1. Damages: In nearly all situations, when one party breaches a land sale contract, the other may sue for *money damages*.

        a. Measure for damages: In most American jurisdictions, the *measure of damages* for breach of a land sale contract is the *difference between the market price and the contract price* (sometimes called the *"benefit of the bargain"* rule). Thus if the seller breaches, the buyer can recover the amount by which the market value exceeded the contract price; conversely, the seller can recover from a defaulting buyer the amount by which the contract price exceeded the market value. See 3 A.L.P. 170-72.

            i. Time for measuring: As of *what time* does the difference between the market price and the contract price get calculated? The prevailing answer is, *"at the time of the breach."* So where the buyer breaches, and the seller doesn't make a "covering" sale of the property until considerably later, the price eventually received by the seller may not be a good indication of market value at the time of the breach. See, e.g., *Jones v. Lee*, 971 P.2d 858 (Ct. App. New Mex. 1998) (price received by the non-breaching seller at some unknown time after the buyer's breach was merely non-binding evidence as to market value at the time of the breach, which is the time that mattered).

b. **Liquidated damages:** The parties are always free to agree, in the contract, upon *liquidated damages* in the event of a breach. The most common example of such a clause is one providing that if the buyer defaults, the seller may *keep the buyer's deposit*, or earnest money.

2. **Specific performance:** In the vast majority of cases, an action for *specific performance* may be brought against the defaulting party, whether she be vendor or purchaser. A decree of specific performance is a court order requiring the defendant to go through with the transaction (to convey the land, if the defendant is the vendor, or to pay the purchase price, if the defendant is the purchaser).

   a. **Equitable remedy:** Specific performance is an *equitable remedy*. However, whereas equitable remedies (especially injunction) in other contexts are allowed only where a damage action would be inadequate, a less strict rule is followed in real estate specific performance cases. Courts reason that the buyer should not be relegated to a damage claim because *each piece of land is "unique"*; conversely, the seller should not be limited to a damage action because this leaves him with the burdens of owning and maintaining the land (e.g., paying taxes). 3 A.L.P. 173.

   b. **Where not allowed:** However, there are a few circumstances in which all or some courts *refuse to allow specific performance*.

      i. **Hardship on one party:** Since specific performance is an equitable doctrine, it will not be granted where this would result in *undue hardship* or unfairness to one party. This might be the case, for instance, if the *circumstances changed* substantially between the time the contract was signed and the closing date (e.g., zoning of the parcel changed, so that the buyer's proposed use became illegal).

      ii. **Unmerchantable title:** If the seller's title is unmarketable (and the defect cannot be cured by a simple application of the sale proceeds), the court will not, of course, grant the seller a specific performance decree against the buyer for the entire purchase price.

         (1) **Deduction:** But the court may, if the defect is not too grave, grant such a decree with a *deduction for the defect*. 3 A.L.P. 178.

      iii. **Suit by buyer:** If the seller's title is defective, and it is the *buyer* who brings the suit for specific performance, it will generally be granted to him (probably with an abatement of the purchase price to reflect the defect). If the defect is one which could easily be cleared up, the court may, as part of its decree, order the seller to do this.

3. **Two measures not always inconsistent:** Obviously a party to a breached contract is not entitled to be made more than whole. This means that he may obtain specific performance or damages for the difference between market price and contract price, but not both. However, a party who obtains specific performance may nonetheless be entitle to *incidental* damages (e.g., losses directly resulting from the delay in obtaining possession). 3 A.L.P. 182.

4. **Purchaser's rights to recover deposit:** Suppose the purchaser has paid an earnest money *deposit*; may he recover this sum? Obviously if the seller is in default, the buyer

can get his money back as part of his damage or specific performance action. But suppose the seller is not in default, time is of the essence, and the buyer fails to pay the balance on time.

a. **Where contract doesn't contain liquidated damages clause:** First, let's assume that the contract does not contain a liquidated damages clause — in other words, the contract does not say what happens to the deposit in the event of a breach by the buyer. In this scenario, most modern courts seem to allow the breaching buyer to *recover that part of his deposit that is in excess of the seller's actual damages.* See, e.g., *Kutzin v. Pirnie*, 591 A.2d 932 (N.J. 1991), so holding.

   i. **Restatement rule:** This is also the rule imposed by §374(1) of the Second Restatement of Contracts. Under that section, the breaching buyer is "entitled to restitution for any benefit that he has conferred by way of part performance or reliance in excess of the loss that he has caused by his own breach."

   ii. **Rationale:** Why should the breaching buyer get part of his deposit back? Professor Williston answered the question this way: "[T]o deny recovery [in this situation] often gives the [seller] *more than fair compensation* for the injury he has sustained and *imposes a forfeiture* (which the law abhors) on the [breaching buyer]." (Quoted in *Kutzin, supra.*)

b. **Contract contains liquidated damages clause:** But in the vast majority of sale contracts today, the deposit functions like an advanced-paid *liquidated damages clause*. That is, the contract typically says that in the event of a breach by the buyer, the seller can keep the deposit. The question is whether such a forfeiture clause is enforceable, or is instead unenforceable as a penalty. The answer mostly turns on the reasonableness of the deposit as an *estimate* of the seller's likely damages.

   i. **Reasonable estimate:** If the deposit is a *reasonable estimate* (viewed *either* as of the time the contract was made or at the time of suit) of the damages that the seller would likely incur if the buyer breached, most courts will hold that it is *not a penalty*, and will allow the seller to *keep* the full amount. That's true even if, by the time of suit on the deposit, it's known that the seller suffered smaller damages than the amount of the deposit, or even no damages at all.

   ii. **Unreasonable estimate:** But if the deposit is so *large* that it is *neither* a reasonable estimate of seller's actual damages viewed as of the moment of the contract signing nor a reasonable estimate of his actual damages viewed as of the time of the suit, nearly all courts will *refuse to enforce it*, on the grounds that it is a *penalty*.

      (1) **10% down payment:** The most common deposit amount in residential-real-estate contracts is *10%*, so a liquidated damages clause that calls for the seller to keep the 10% if the buyer defaults is likely to be *upheld* as a reasonable estimate.

G. **The equitable conversion doctrine:** During the gap between the signing of the contract and the delivery of the deed, important questions about the rights of the parties may arise. For instance, the property may be *destroyed* during the gap, one of the parties may die, or either party's assets may be subject to collection attempts by creditors. Issues raised by these situations have traditionally been dealt with by reference to the doctrine of *equitable conversion*.

1. **General meaning of doctrine:** As we saw previously, courts of equity will grant either party to most land sale contracts the relief of *specific performance* of the contract. The doctrine of equitable conversion builds on this rule, on the theory that "if there is a specifically enforceable contract for the sale of land, equity regards as done that which ought to be done." DKA&S, p. 483. Therefore, "the buyer is viewed in equity as the *owner from the date of the contract* (thus having the *"equitable title"*); the seller has a claim for money secured by a *vendor's lien* on the land." *Id.*

2. **Effect of party's death:** The equitable conversion doctrine is often applied to resolve questions of how property passes upon the *death* of either the vendor or vendee.

   a. **Vendor dies testate:** For instance, if the *vendor* dies *with a will*, and leaves his real property to one person and his personal property to another, the equitable conversion doctrine is likely to have an important effect. If the will was drawn *prior to the making of the contract*, and the contract was still executory at the moment of the vendor's death, then the equitable conversion doctrine applies so that: (1) *the purchase price goes to the person to whom the personal property was bequeathed*; and (2) *the person to whom the real estate was bequeathed gets nothing.*

   b. **Death of purchaser:** If the *purchaser* dies while the contract is still executory, the equitable conversion doctrine applies so that: (1) the person entitled to receive the decedent's real estate (either under the will or under the intestacy statute) is entitled to the land; and (2) the recipients of the personal property not only do not receive the land, but must pay any remaining portion of the purchase price out of their shares of the estate. See Cribbet, p. 191.

3. **Risk of loss:** The most important, and difficult, issue regarding equitable conversion involves the *risk of loss*, i.e., the risk that the property will be injured or destroyed between the signing of the contract and the delivery of the deed. Courts have followed three main approaches to this problem:

   a. **Loss always on vendee:** A majority of states have adopted the traditional English view that, since the vendee acquires equitable ownership of the land as soon as the contract is signed, *the risk of loss immediately shifts to him*. This is true even though the vendee *never takes possession* prior to the casualty.

   Example: D contracts to sell land to P. Prior to the delivery of the deed, and while D is still in possession, an ice storm damages all the pecan trees on the property, reducing its market value by $32,000.

   Held, the loss falls on P (who does not get back his earnest money, and who has to pay damages for refusing to go through with the contract). In Georgia, as in most states, the doctrine of equitable conversion means that the risk of loss passes to the vendee as soon as the contract is signed; no exception is made merely because the vendee has not yet taken possession. *Bleckley v. Langston*, 143 S.E.2d 671 (Ga. 1965).

    i. Exception: But courts applying this majority rule recognize an exception to it: the vendor will bear any loss which results from his *neglect*, default, or unreasonable delay in carrying out the contract.

    ii. Unmerchantable title: Also, the vendor must bear the loss if, at the time it occurred, he was not in a position to convey the title which he had contracted to convey (e.g., because his title was *unmerchantable* due to, say, tax liens). In such a situation, the purchaser is not regarded as the "equitable owner" of the property, since he could not be forced in a specific performance suit to pay full price for the defective title; see B,C&S, p. 978-79, note 2.

  b. "Massachusetts" view: A minority of courts adhere to the so-called *"Massachusetts" rule* (based on an early Massachusetts decision): the burden of loss remains on the vendor *until legal title is conveyed*, and *even though the purchaser is in possession*. These courts more or less ignore the equitable conversion doctrine, and rely upon the idea that continued existence of the subject matter is an implied condition of the contract.

  c. Risk on party in possession: A third view holds that the risk of loss is on the vendor so long as he remains in possession and has title, but that it then *shifts to the purchaser if the purchaser takes possession or title*. This is the approach taken by the Uniform Vendor and Purchaser Risk Act, in force with some variation in eight states (including California, Illinois, Michigan and New York).

  Note: Regardless of which of these approaches a particular jurisdiction follows, the parties are always free to make an *explicit agreement* resolving the issue in any way they wish.

4. Effect of insurance on risk of loss: Our discussion of the risk of loss thus far has ignored any effect which might flow from the fact that one party had *insurance* on the premises. The courts are in dispute on this issue, just as they are on the risk of loss question where no insurance is present.

  a. Vendor takes out insurance: The issue arises most frequently where insurance is carried *by the vendor* in his own name. In a situation where the risk of loss is on the purchaser, most courts *give the purchaser the benefit of the vendor's insurance*.

    i. Rationale: The rationale for this majority rule is that otherwise, the vendor will receive a large *windfall*: he will receive the full purchase price, plus the insurance proceeds. Therefore, the vendor is deemed to hold the insurance proceeds in a *"constructive trust"* for the vendee. Instead of receiving the proceeds, the vendee is simply given an abatement of the purchase price equal to the amount of the insurance.

  b. No duty to insure: Keep in mind that, even in courts following the majority rule, the vendor is *not under any duty* to keep insurance in force on the property. Thus it makes sense for the purchaser to insist on a clause in the contract requiring such insurance to be maintained on the premises for the purchaser's benefit.

H. Assignment of contract rights: Unless the contract provides otherwise, *either party may assign his rights* under it. In this respect, a contract for the sale of land is no different from any other contract. Thus the seller may, prior to the closing, sell the property subject to the outstanding contract rights. Conversely (and more commonly) the purchaser may assign to a third person the right to pay the purchase price and receive the deed.

1. **Prohibition on assignment:** However, the parties to the sale contract sometimes insert a clause purporting to *prohibit assignment*.

   a. **Enforcement at law:** Generally speaking, such an anti-assignment clause will be *enforced by a court of law*. Thus if the contract provides that any assignment will be of no effect, the seller may sue the buyer who has tried to assign, and recover legal damages.

I. **Real estate broker's role:** Most sales of real estate involve a real estate broker. Detailed coverage of the law of real estate brokerage is beyond the scope of this outline. However, we can discuss briefly a few of the common issues in this area.

   1. **What the broker does:** Normally, the broker makes his money by receiving a commission after the buyer and the seller he has brought together consummate a sale. In most instances, it is the *seller who pays the commission*. Also in most instances, the broker does his work pursuant to an exclusive listing arrangement between him and the seller; generally, this agreement entitles him to be paid even if another broker, or the seller himself, finds the eventual buyer. (Note that the seller's liability for the broker's commission can be limited in the brokerage contract by agreement between the broker and the seller.)

   2. **"Ready, willing and able":** If the broker finds a buyer who in fact goes through with the transaction, the seller will clearly be liable. However, the law in nearly all states has traditionally been that the broker is also entitled to his commission merely by finding a buyer who is *"ready, willing and able"* to consummate the transaction — in other words, the broker who finds such a buyer can collect his commission *even if the transaction never goes through*. (All this assumes, of course, that the prospective buyer produced by the broker is willing and able to do the transaction *at the price*, and *on the terms*, that the seller has set.)

      a. **Seller's default:** So if the transaction ultimately fails to go through because the seller has changed his mind prior to a contract, or has defaulted after entering into a contract, all courts continue to hold that the broker may collect his commission. After all, in this instance consummation of the deal was within the seller's own control, so he should clearly not be able to escape his brokerage obligation.

   3. **Scope of broker's duty:** The broker will typically have a *fiduciary duty* to the party on one side of the transaction.

      a. **Two types of brokers:** Before we review what the broker's fiduciary duty is, and to whom, we have to distinguish between two types of brokers, the so-called *"listing broker"* and the *"selling broker."*

         i. **Listing broker:** The *listing broker* is the broker who *contracts directly with the seller* to list the property (e.g., by putting it into a Multiple Listing Service), and to try to get it sold.

         ii. **Selling broker:** The *selling broker* is a broker whose primary day-to-day relationship is *with the buyer*, and whose relationship with the seller is only indirect. The selling broker typically meets with a potential buyer and shows her various potential properties. If the potential buyer makes a purchase, the selling broker typically gets compensated by receiving a ***portion of the listing broker's commission***. DKA&S, p. 466.

b. **Duties of listing broker:** The listing broker's ***sole fiduciary duty is to the seller***. This makes intuitive sense, since the seller has directly hired the listing broker as the seller's agent.

c. **Duties of selling broker:** The more confusing issue — at least to people outside the real estate industry — is the fiduciary duty of the ***selling*** broker. Most buyers think that the selling broker that they are working with has a fiduciary duty to them. But this is not correct — under the standard compensation arrangement, the selling broker, like the listing broker, ***owes a fiduciary duty solely to the seller.*** This duty stems from the fact that the selling broker is, technically speaking, a ***"subagent"*** of the listing broker. Since the listing broker owes a fiduciary duty only to the seller, and since all compensation to the selling broker comes in the form of a portion of the listing broker's commission, the selling broker's fiduciary obligations ought to be, and are, the same as the listing broker's, i.e., entirely to the seller.

Example: The Ps are brothers and sisters who have inherited a family home from their parents. The Ps consult with Schwartz, a local broker, to get advice about marketing the home for sale. Schwartz consults with the Ds, who are two brokers active in the local market. Schwartz and the Ds agree to a "co-broke arrangement," whereby the Ds will receive from Schwartz half of the commission if a client of the Ds buys the property. Schwartz then, at the Ds' request, signs a listing agreement with the Ps giving Schwartz an exclusive 24-hour right to re-sell the house for $125,000. The Ds do not contact any of the potential buyers that the Ds have previously identified as being possibly interested in the property. Nor do the Ds disclose to the Ps how much the Ds think third-party buyers might pay for the property. Instead, within the 24-hour listing period, the Ds' make their own offer of $115,000. The Ps, believing that this represents the market value of the property, contract to sell it to the Ds for that amount. The Ds then (that same day) contract to sell the home to a third-party buyer, X, for $160,000. Six days after the Ds close on their purchase, they "flip" the property to X, making a $45,000 gain on their six-day cash investment of $11,500. (X is a neighbor of the Ps, who had been previously known to the Ps as a potential buyer, but who the Ps had instructed Schwartz not to contact.) When the Ps learn of this profit, they sue the Ds for breach of what the Ps say was the Ds' duty to get the best possible price for the Ps.

Held, for the Ps. "A real estate broker is a fiduciary. ... As such, he ... 'cannot put himself in a position antagonistic to his principal's interest.' " The fact that here the Ds contracted with Schwartz doesn't matter: "A real estate broker acting as a subagent with the express permission of another broker who has the listing of the property to be sold is under the *same duty* as the primary broker to act in the utmost good faith." This fiduciary obligation means that "upon hearing that a more advantageous sale ... can be made, the facts concerning which are unknown to the principal, the broker has the duty to communicate these facts to the principal before making the sale." Therefore, the trial court correctly ordered the Ds to pay the Ps the $45,000 profit they had earned by this breach of fiduciary duty. *Licari v. Blackwelder*, 539 A.2d 609 (Conn. Ct. of App. 1988).

II. MORTGAGES AND INSTALLMENT CONTRACTS

A. Two devices to secure repayment: Normally, the purchaser is not sufficiently liquid to be able to pay the entire purchase price at once. Therefore, it is necessary for him to find some device by which to pay the purchase price over a period of time. Beyond the portion of the money which the purchaser is able to pay right away, the remainder of the price must in effect be lent either by the vendor or by some third party; in either case, the lender will want *security* for repayment. There are two basic approaches to securing repayment: (1) the *mortgage*; and (2) the *installment sale contract*.

B. Nature of a mortgage: If the buyer does her financing via a *mortgage*, she receives a deed to the property immediately. At the same time, she executes the mortgage. In a conventional third-party-mortgage, the buyer gives the mortgage to a commercial or savings bank, and the loan proceeds are paid to the seller at the closing; the seller is thus out of the picture. In the case of a *purchase money mortgage*, by contrast, the financing is being done by the seller; that is, the buyer pays the seller a down payment, and gives him back a mortgage for the remaining price. Regardless of the type of mortgage, the essence of the transaction is that if the buyer fails to make the payments, the lender may *foreclose* on the property itself (and thus is not required to depend on the personal credit of the buyer). Foreclosure is discussed further *infra*, p. 325.

1. Key terms: As a matter of nomenclature, the following are some key terms: (1) the borrower, who gives the mortgage, is called the *"mortgagor"*; (2) the lender, who has the benefit of the mortgage, is the *"mortgagee"*; and (3) the mortgagor is said to retain *"equity"* in the property (an abbreviation for the "equity of redemption," discussed further *infra*, p. 324).

2. Two documents: There are two documents associated with nearly every mortgage: (1) the *note* (or "bond"); and (2) the *mortgage* itself.

a. The note: The *note* is the buyer's personal promise to make the repayments. Since the note is not an interest in land, it is not recorded. But it serves an important function: if there is a foreclosure against the property, and the foreclosure sale does not yield at least an amount equal to the outstanding mortgage debt (including accrued interest), the note will serve as the basis for a *deficiency judgment* against the borrower. This is because the note represents a personal obligation of the borrower, not merely an obligation to be repaid out of the land.

b. Mortgage: The *mortgage itself* is a document which gives the lender a claim against the land for the repayment of the amount loaned. All right of foreclosure comes from this document, not from the note. Since the mortgage in effect gives the mortgagee an interest in the land, the mortgage is *recorded*.

3. Sale or transfer of mortgaged premises: Usually when mortgaged property is sold, the mortgage is *paid off* at the closing. One reason for this is that if the mortgage has previously been partially paid off, or the land has appreciated in value since the mortgage, the mortgage will probably not meet the financial requirements of the new buyer (since it will be for too small an amount relative to the purchase price). The second reason is that the mortgage may contain a "due on sale," or "acceleration" clause (discussed further *infra*, p. 328). Nonetheless, there are times when the property is sold without paying off the mortgage; this can be done either by: (1) having the purchaser take "subject to" the mortgage; or (2) having the purchaser actually "assume" the mortgage.

a. Sale "subject to" mortgage: If the purchaser merely takes *"subject to"* the mortgage, he is *not personally liable* for payment of the mortgage debt. Of course, if he wishes to keep his equity in the property, he will have to make the payments, since otherwise the mortgagee will foreclose. But if the mortgagee does foreclose, and the property does not bring enough in the foreclosure sale to pay off the outstanding mortgage debt, the mortgagee may *not sue the purchaser for the balance*. (The mortgagee may, however, sue the original mortgagor for this balance, since the sale of the mortgaged premises does nothing to the mortgagor's personal liability.)

i. Payments in "subject to" scenario: If the purchaser does not assume the mortgage, the mere fact that the purchaser then *makes several mortgage payments* does *not* change the basic fact that the purchaser is not liable for any deficiency. In other words, only an *express promise* to assume (i.e., to pay the mortgage) will create in the lender the right to get a deficiency judgment against the purchaser.

ii. "Due on sale" clause makes no difference: The fact that a mortgage contains a *"due on sale"* clause *doesn't* mean that one who purchases the property subject to the mortgage becomes personally liable. A "due on sale" clause provides that if the mortgagor sells the mortgaged property, the mortgagee can require that the mortgage debt be *immediately repaid* in full. Due on sale clauses are common, and are fully enforceable. But such a clause does not give the lender a right to seek payment from the purchaser personally (i.e., the right to a deficiency judgment), if the lender did not already have that right because of an assumption of the mortgage debt by the purchaser.

b. Assumption of mortgage: It is usually in the original mortgagor's interest to persuade the new purchaser to *assume* payment of the mortgage. This has the effect of making the purchaser *liable* for payment of the mortgage, both to the original mortgagor, and to the mortgagee (probably as a third-party beneficiary). The advantage to the mortgagor is that the foreclosure mortgagee is likely to seek a deficiency judgment against the assuming purchaser before coming after the mortgagor; also, if the mortgagee does get a deficiency judgment against the original mortgagor, the latter can in turn sue the assuming purchaser.

i. Receipt of deed with assumption clause: The buyer will be deemed to have assumed the mortgage if she *accepts a deed* that contains a statement that the buyer assumes the mortgage. This is true even if the buyer *does not sign the deed*, because agreements to assume a debt are not within the Statute of Frauds and thus can be made orally or by conduct. (But the buyer will be liable only if she *intended* to assume the mortgage debt, so if she can show that she was not aware of the assumption clause in the deed she received, she will not be liable.)

c. **Novation:** Occasionally, the mortgagor may get the mortgagee to *substitute* the new purchaser for the original mortgagor's own personal liability. This means that not only is the new purchaser personally liable for the mortgage, but the original mortgagor is completely *off the hook*. Such a substitution is called a *novation*. (Needless to say, mortgage lenders are generally not overly enthusiastic about such transactions.)

4. **Assignment of mortgage:** The mortgagee will often wish to liquidate his interest by *selling the mortgage* to someone else. Indeed, government-sponsored corporations like "Fannie Mae" (Federal National Mortgage Assoc.) exist for the sole purpose of enabling banks to write mortgages and immediately sell them to the corporation.

   a. **Transfer of mortgage and note:** Normally, the purchaser of the mortgage will insist on receiving an assignment of both the mortgage instrument and the note.

   b. **Transfer of mortgage only:** As noted earlier, the mortgage exists only as security for the debt. Therefore, a mortgage *cannot be transferred independently of the debt*. Any transaction which purports to transfer the mortgage without the note is void.

   c. **Transfer of note alone:** But a transfer of the *note without the mortgage* is not void. Instead, the mortgage is deemed to pass with the note. Thus even if the buyer receives only the note, he will be able to foreclose on the mortgage if the payments are not made. (However, it is desirable for the purchaser to obtain the mortgage, so that he may record it; otherwise there is a chance that subsequent *bona fide* purchasers or mortgagees may cut off his interest.)

5. **No automatic right to prepay:** The mortgagee has the right to have his money earning interest for the entire term of the mortgage, unless the parties agree otherwise. Thus the mortgagor does not automatically have the right to *prepay* the full principal before the maturity date.

   a. **Prepayment clause:** Therefore, the mortgagor should attempt to insert a clause in the mortgage giving him a *right of prepayment*. In many states, the mortgagor is required to be given this right as a matter of law after a certain period (e.g., after the first two years). The matter is frequently handled by charging the mortgagor a prepayment *penalty* (e.g., six-months interest); the penalty often declines the longer the mortgage has been in force.

6. **Mortgage to secure someone else's debt:** A person may grant a mortgage on her own property to secure repayment of *someone else's debt*. Rest. 3d (Mort.), §1.3. In other words, the mortgagor does not need to *receive any direct benefit* for granting a mortgage.

7. **Absolute deed as substitute for mortgage:** Sometimes an arrangement that is really in economic function a loan is cast in the documents as a *sale by the borrower to the lender,* together with some sort of *repurchase right* by the borrower. Where this happens, courts will treat the arrangement as *being a mortgage*, and the lender will *have to use foreclosure procedures*.

   a. **Oral right of repurchase:** That's true even if the borrower's right of re-purchase was granted *orally* rather than in a writing signed by the lender. In other words, in this special situation where there is clear evidence that what was intended was a financing device rather than a sale, the Statute of Frauds will *not be applied* to the borrower's repurchase option, and the repurchase option will instead be treated as a mortgagor's right of redemption (see *infra*, p. 324).

Example: Investor pays Owner $200,000, and Owner simultaneously conveys Blackacre to Investor. The parties intend this as a financing device. They do this by orally agreeing, at the same time as the conveyance, that if before the first anniversary of the conveyance Owner pays Investor $200,000 plus a 10% profit, Investor will re-convey Blackacre to Owner.

If Owner doesn't make the payment on time, the court will treat this as a mortgage. The consequence is that Investor won't be able to just sit on the deed — instead, Investor will have to start state-law foreclosure proceedings, and Owner will have until the end of those proceedings to pay Investor the $100,000 + 10% and get the property back.

8. **Redemption of mortgage:** When the mortgage is paid off, the property is said to have been *"redeemed"* from the mortgage.

   a. **"Equity of redemption":** Before the mortgage has been paid off — up until the moment when a foreclosure sale is completed if the mortgagor defaults — the mortgagor is said to have an *"equity of redemption,"* i.e., the right to pay off the mortgage and own the property outright.

   b. **Who has right:** Any party with an interest in the property has the right to pay off the mortgage, and thus redeem the property. So a *fractional owner* (say, one of three tenants in common) has the right to pay off the entire mortgage, as does a junior mortgagee, the holder of a long-term lease on the property, etc.

      i. **No redemption until entire mortgage paid off:** But a fractional owner does *not* have the right to pay off *just his "fractional portion"* of the mortgage and thereby redeem his equity (i.e., get free-and-clear title to his fractional interest). Instead, the mortgagee (the lender) is entitled to keep a mortgage on the *entire property* for as long as she is owed a single penny. This means if one fractional owner is unwilling or unable to pay his pro rata share of the mortgage, any other fractional owner risks losing his entire interest unless he is prepared to step in and pay off the entire mortgage.

9. **Mortgagee in possession:** There are a few situations in which the mortgagee will be entitled to *take possession of the property* before the mortgage is paid off or the property foreclosed upon. If the mortgagee does so, he is referred to as a *"mortgagee in possession."*

   a. **Abandonment:** The most important scenario in which the mortgagee will have the right to take possession prior to a complete foreclosure proceeding is the *"abandonment"* scenario. That is, if the mortgagor stops paying and *abandons the premises*, the mortgagee is entitled to take possession and administer the property to maintain the value of his security interest.

   b. **Missing payments not enough:** But the mere fact that the mortgagor has *stopped making payments,* standing alone, does *not* entitle the mortgagee to take possession.

Example: Own, owner of a home, borrows $200,000 from Bank, secured by a mortgage. If Own misses several mortgage payments, this will entitle Bank to start foreclosure proceedings, and to declare the whole principal due (assuming, as is likely, that the note contains an acceleration clause). But it will *not* entitle Bank to immediately oust Own and take possession. However, if Own moves out without putting someone else in possession, then this abandonment *will* entitle Bank to take possession immediately, even before completing foreclosure proceedings.

   c. **Duties of mortgagee in possession:** Once the mortgagee takes possession, he has *duties* that are roughly parallel to those of the actual owner. For instance, he must *maintain the property in reasonable condition*, and must credit any rents (less reasonable expenses of managing and repairing the property) against the mortgage debt.

C. **Foreclosure:** *Foreclosure* is the process by which the mortgagee may *reach the land* to satisfy the mortgage debt, if the mortgagor defaults.

   1. **Modern-day foreclosure:** Foreclosure *by sale* has become the standard means of foreclosing mortgages in America. Since it will frequently be the case that the property is worth more than the outstanding mortgage debt (i.e., that the mortgagor has some "equity" in the property), *foreclosure by a public sale preserves the mortgagor's right to receive the excess.* Also, it safeguards him from being unfairly held for a deficiency judgment.

      a. **Judicial foreclosure sale:** In many jurisdictions, a foreclosure sale must be conducted under *judicial supervision*, and is handled by a public official such as a *sheriff*. The court supervises the advertising done to publicize the sale, and supervises the time and place. Such a "judicial foreclosure sale" requires a *costly* and *time-consuming lawsuit* by the mortgagee. On the other hand, the mortgagor usually cannot attack the foreclosure sale after the fact (e.g., on the grounds that it fetched an unfairly low price, and deprived him of his equity) if the judicially-supervised procedure is used.

      b. **Private foreclosure sale:** Some but not all jurisdictions give the lender a second way to foreclose: he may conduct a *private foreclosure sale*, without the need for a formal lawsuit or judicial supervision. In states that allow this method, the lender must usually bargain for it in advance by getting his security in the form of a *"deed of trust"* (rather than a "mortgage"). Under the deed of trust, the borrower conveys title to the property to the lender or to a third party, who holds the title in trust; if the borrower defaults, the trustee can sell the land without going to court.

         i. **Mortgagee's obligation:** To prevent the lender from conducting a private sale that fetches an *unfairly low price* (so that the borrower either has to pay a deficiency or loses some or all of his equity in the property), statutes and courts in some states that allow private foreclosure sales require the lender to use *good faith* and *due diligence* to get the highest possible price at the sale. If the lender does not do this, he may lose his right to a deficiency judgment, and may even have to pay the borrower damages equal to the amount of equity that the borrower would have realized from a properly-conducted sale.

            (1) **Illustration:** For instance, in *Murphy v. Financial Development Corp.*, 495 A.2d 1245 (N.H. 1985), the court held that the low price received at foreclosure, when coupled with the fact that the mortgagee knew or should have

known that the price was low, meant that the mortgagee failed to do the requisite due diligence when it refused to either set a minimum bid or postpone the sale until more bidders could be found. Therefore, the court awarded the borrowers damages equal to "the difference between a fair price for the property and the price obtained at the foreclosure sale."

(2) Unusual result: But *Murphy, supra,* is an unusual case, in that the low price itself, when coupled with the mortgagee's knowledge that it was low, was found to be enough to cause the sale to be invalidated. In most states, a ***mere low price***, even if the mortgagee is aware of it, will ***not be enough*** for the private sale to be invalidated. The borrower/owner must typically show either that the procedures were somehow ***irregular***, or that the bidding was intentionally ***chilled***.

2. **Deed in lieu of foreclosure:** When the mortgagor can't or doesn't want to continue making payments, and the value of the property is less than the outstanding mortgage amount, the mortgagee generally doesn't gain anything by insisting that the lender go through a formal foreclosure process. In such a scenario, the lender and borrower will often agree to an exchange called *"deed in lieu of foreclosure."* That is, the borrower conveys full title to the property to the lender, and the lender in return agrees not to pursue a deficiency judgment against the mortgagor for the difference between the present value of the property and the outstanding mortgage debt. DKA&S, p. 553.

3. **Not binding on senior mortgagee:** *No foreclosure is ever binding on a mortgagee whose interest is senior to the foreclosing creditor's interest.* In other words, if a *junior creditor* forecloses, that foreclosure proceeding can only wipe out the equity and any interest(s) *junior* to that of the foreclosing creditor. See Rest. 3d (Mort.) §7.1 ("Foreclosure does not terminate interests in the foreclosed real estate that are senior to the mortgage being foreclosed").

    Example: On April 1, Bank lends *O* $100,000, secured by a promptly-recorded mortgage on Blackacre. On May 1, Finance Co. lends *O* $200,000 secured by a promptly-recorded mortgage on the same property. On June 1, Cred lends *O* $50,000, also secured by a promptly-recorded mortgage. In November, *O* falls behind on the payments to Finance Co. but not the payments to Bank or Cred. Finance Co. starts a foreclosure proceeding, and purports to join Bank and Cred in that foreclosure.

    Bank will be entitled to have the action dismissed as to it. Therefore, what will be foreclosed is merely *O*'s equity, plus any interest junior to Finance Co.'s, including Cred's interest. Thus if *X* purchases at a foreclosure sale, *X* will own the property, but subject to Bank's mortgage. And, still assuming that Bank elects not to join the foreclosure proceeding, any amounts paid by *X* will go first to pay off Finance Co., then Cred, then *O*.

4. **Priorities (allocation of foreclosure proceeds):** When a foreclosure sale occurs, the proceeds are distributed in descending order of the claimants, with each mortgagee or lien holder entitled to be satisfied in full before any lower-ranking creditor receives anything. The owner of the equity in the foreclosed property *ranks last* — that is, she does not

receive anything until all persons having a lien or security interest in the property have been satisfied.

a. **Judgment lien creditor's status:** You may have to worry about the status in a fore-closure of a *judgment lien creditor* of the mortgagor. A judgment lien creditor is a creditor who gets a judgment against the mortgagor (typically in an action having nothing to do with the mortgage and perhaps not related to the mortgaged property), and who under state law then gets a lien on all the debtor's real property. The two things to remember about the judgment lien creditor's status are:

[1] the creditor gets an interest that is *equivalent to a mortgage*; and

[2] the priority of that lien (i.e., that mortgage-equivalent) *dates from the day the lien is filed*, not the day the underlying debt that is secured by the lien accrued.

b. **"Future advances" clauses:** You should also be aware of *"future advances"* clauses. Under a future advances clause, the borrower and lender agree that the lender at its option may (or in some cases, that contractually it definitely *will*) **make additional loans**, and that these further loans will be covered by the mortgage. Here are the important principles governing such future advances clauses:

[1] the priority of any later advance *dates back to the recording date* of the mortgage;

[2] statement #1 is true *even if no money at all was advanced* on the date the mortgage was signed and recorded; and

[3] both statement #1 and #2 are true even though the lender had *no contractual obligation* to make the future advance.

Rest. 3d (Mort.), §2.1(f), and §2.3 (including Comm. a thereto). A good summary of these rules is that "later-advances clauses are as powerful — as beneficial to the lender — as you can imagine they might be."

Example: Developer owns a parcel, Blackacre, on which she wants to erect an office building, with construction financing from Bank. Therefore, on April 1 Developer and Bank sign a loan agreement in which Bank agrees to make, over time, up to $1 million in total advances to fund the construction of the building; no advance is required to be made by Bank unless Bank, in its sole discretion, is satisfied that Developer has already invested in the construction an amount equal to the requested advance. Simultaneously with this loan agreement, Developer signs a mortgage document, which Bank records on April 1. On May 1, Developer borrows $100,000 from Cred, secured by a mortgage on Blackacre dated and recorded that same day. On June 1, Bank (which is by then aware of Cred's loan and mortgage) makes its first advance, for $100,000, under the April 1 mortgage. Developer defaults on both loans, and both lenders join in a foreclosure proceeding. The property is sold for just $100,000. Who has priority in the proceeds?

Bank has priority. Bank's priority runs from the date its mortgage was recorded (April 1), even though no advance was made until later. Therefore, Bank has priority over the later-made-and-recorded (May 1) Cred mortgage.

c. Mortgagee can't get excess: *No mortgagee can collect more than the amount owed on the mortgage* (plus expenses of foreclosure, accrued interest, etc.). In other words, any "excess" proceeds remaining after a particular mortgagee has been paid off belong entirely to any junior claimants and/or the equity holder, in descending order of priority. '

d. Equitable subrogation: Another doctrine of interest in connection with mortgages is *equitable subrogation.* Under that doctrine, a person other than the mortgagor who pays off a mortgage can *step into the shoes* of the now-paid-off mortgagee, and maintain that mortgage in place for the payor's benefit, as if it hadn't been paid off. This lets the payor keep the priority level of the paid-off mortgage. Cf. Rest. 3d (Mort.), § 7.6(a).

    i. Where relevant: The most common scenario for subrogation is where there are *three creditors* (let's identify them from most senior as #1 down to most junior as #3). #3 pays off the debt held by #1, and the question then becomes who has priority, #3 or #2? By use of the doctrine of equitable subordination, #3 "inherits" the priority of #1 as if the #1 mortgage had never been dissolved; this lets #3 take ahead of #2. So you should only need to worry about equitable subordination when there are at some point *three claimants in the picture*.

5. Acceleration clauses: A mortgage usually provides that in case of a default, the *entire principal sum* shall become immediately due and payable. Such a provision is known as an *acceleration clause*. If the mortgage did not contain such a clause, the mortgagee would have to start a new foreclosure suit upon each default (and have that proceeding rendered moot by payment of just that outstanding installment).

    a. Waivable: Most acceleration clauses are drafted so that they may be *waived* by the mortgagee. If a waiver provision is omitted, the clause in effect allows full prepayment without a penalty if the mortgagor defaults; the mortgagor might therefore intentionally default, pre-pay in full, and refinance elsewhere at lower rates.

D. Subprime mortgages and foreclosure during the Great Recession: Beginning in about 2000, mortgage lenders began making it steadily easier to obtain a home mortgage. The dramatic easing in mortgage credit led in mid-decade to what is usually called the *"subprime mortgage crisis,"* in which foreclosures skyrocketed. The subprime mortgage crisis, and the consequent failures of financial institutions like Lehman Bros. that made or heavily invested in mortgages, were a major cause of the "Great Recession" that began at the end of 2007, the steepest economic downturn since the Great Depression.

1. How credit was loosened: It's worth spending a moment describing how this easing of home-mortgage credit took place. There were several big changes:

    [1] The *credit-worthiness* that a buyer needed to obtain any sort of mortgage was dramatically *lowered*. Most of this easing took place in the category of "subprime borrowers," that is, the group of borrowers with the weakest credit histories. Additional major growth in loans came through so-called "Alt-A" loans, to borrowers whose credit-worthiness was almost but not quite equal to that of traditional "prime" borrowers.

    [2] Buyers in the subprime and Alt-A categories were often not required to *document their income or assets.* Therefore, these borrowers — often with the express or tacit

encouragement of banks and mortgage brokers — often dramatically exaggerated, or even totally falsified, their income and assets on their mortgage applications.

[3] The minimum *"loan-to-value" ratio* required by lenders steadily dropped, again with most of the change occurring in the subprime and Alt-A categories. Subprime and Alt-A loans were often made at down payments of 3% or even less-than-zero (whereby the buyer/borrower could borrow not only the entire purchase price but also something for renovations).

[4] Many mortgages were written as *"negative amortization"* loans, in which the borrower was permitted to make payments of just a portion of the interest due, with the rest accruing and thus being added to the balance due. These were often combined with low introductory *"teaser rates"* that would reset to higher levels after two years. The combination of the negative amortization and the sudden rise in current interest due once the 2-year teaser period was over meant that unless the borrower could refinance at the end of the teaser period, she would likely lose the house to foreclosure.

See generally Mayer *et al*, "The Rise of Mortgage Defaults", 23 J. Econ. Perspectives 27 (2009).

2. **Price spikes:** Nonprime mortgages (subprime and Alt-A) went from 10% of all mortgage originations in 2003 to 32% by 2005. These mortgages helped fuel a massive spike in American home prices: from early 2000 to early 2006 home prices nationally increased by 89%, as measured by the Case-Shiller National Home Price Index.

    a. **Prices plummet and foreclosures spike:** Then, a vicious combination of an economic slowdown, declining home prices and increasing foreclosures began after 2005. From their mid-2006 high, prices fell nationally by 33% to their (apparent) low-point in mid-2009. *Id.* At the same time, mortgage defaults spiked; for instance, by late 2008 over 23% of subprime mortgages were seriously delinquent. Mayer, *op. cit.* at 28. Meanwhile, new mortgage loans became vastly harder to get.

3. **Judicial response:** State and local governments have responded to the subprime crisis and the Great Recession in a number of ways. Of particular interest to us here is that *state courts* have begun *scrutinizing the foreclosure process* much more tightly.

    a. **Packaging of loans:** Before we look at these judicial responses, we need to take a look at the modern *secondary mortgage market.* Typically, after a lender "originates" a mortgage (i.e., disburses the loan once the borrower has signed the documents), the lender d*oes not keep ownership* of the loan. Instead, the lender *sells* the loan to a *"packager"* like Fannie Mae, Freddie Mac or Ginnie Mae.[2] The packager then *pools* many loans together, and sells *bonds backed by the pool* of loans to hundreds of investors. After this, a servicing company services the loan (by sending bills and collecting payments) under a Pooling and Service Agreement (PSA).

        i. **Consequence:** One consequence of this pooling is that *later mortgage renegotiations become difficult or impossible*. Because the servicer does not own the loan, a borrower who hopes to renegotiate the payment terms — something that many

---

2. Fannie Mae and Freddie Mac are currently, as of early 2012, still operating under federal conservatorship, having effectively gone broke as a result of facilitating and buying too many bad mortgage loans.

borrowers, especially those with "negative equity," have tried to do in recent years — will likely find that neither the PSA servicer or nor anyone else has authority to act on behalf of the "lender," who is not an institution or person as in the old days but is instead a collection of hundreds of bondholders.

Now, we're ready to look at a couple of judicial responses to the mortgage crisis.

b. Proof that foreclosing bank owns the mortgage: One response is that courts and other government agencies have begun demanding better *documentary evidence that the foreclosing creditor really owns the mortgage* in question. Often, a lender or investor who has purchased a mortgage — perhaps by buying the pool of which that mortgage is a part — has asserted in foreclosure papers that it is the owner, but has failed to attach accurate documentary proof of the *chain of title* by which ownership of the mortgage passed from the original lender to the person now claiming to own it.

    i. The "robo-signing" scandal: Starting in 2010, many cases emerged of *"robo-signing"* — cases in which the foreclosing mortgagee was shown to have used forged documents to prove that it was the true owner of the mortgage, or affidavits by bank officers falsely certifying they had reviewed the relevant loan documents to determine that the foreclosing party was the true owner. In February, 2012, after suits by the federal government and 49 states, the five biggest mortgage servicers (all of them large banks) agreed to a $25 billion settlement to remedy these foreclosure abuses.

c. Moratorium on foreclosures: A second response is that some courts have sought to *slow down foreclosures* of entire categories of mortgages. For example, in *Commonwealth v. Fremont Investment & Loan*, 897 N.E.2d 548 (Mass. 2008), the highest court in Massachusetts upheld the state Attorney General's attempt to restrict the ability of a particular lender, Fremont, to foreclose on a broad category of subprime loans it had written in the state. The Attorney General identified a category of adjustable rate subprime loans by Fremont whose combination of features made it "almost certain the borrower would not be able to make the necessary loan payments, leading to default and then foreclosure."[3]

    i. Holding: The court agreed with the Attorney General that these loans constituted an *unfair and deceptive trade practice*, outlawed by state law. Therefore, the court upheld the trial court's injunction under which Fremont was *not permitted to foreclose* on any of these loans without first trying to reach agreement with the Attorney General on a non-foreclosure restructuring of the loan, and then, if such an agreement couldn't be reached, obtaining the trial court's approval for foreclosure.

E. Installment contracts: Land, like personal property, can be bought under an *installment contract*. Such a contract provides for a down payment, with the balance of the purchase price to be paid in installments (usually monthly). What makes such an arrangement different from a purchase money mortgage (the other principal means of seller-financing) is that the buyer

---

3. For instance, the loans had an introductory rate of three years or less that was at least 3 percentage points below the "fully indexed" rate that would apply later, and were written to borrowers for whom the debt-to-income ratio would have been more than 50% if the fully-indexed payments had been used in the computation.

does *not receive his deed* until *after* he has paid all, or a substantial portion, of the purchase price.

1. **Why used:** A buyer almost never uses an installment contract when there is some other financing solution. Such contracts, like their counterparts in the personal property area, are typically used by buyers who have poor credit and no ability to make more than a small down payment; for such buyers an installment arrangement is the only hope of someday gaining title to real estate.

2. **Forfeiture:** The most important practical difference between mortgages and installment contracts is the consequences of a *default*. If the mortgagor fails to make his payments, the mortgage must be foreclosed, pursuant to a whole array of statutory and judicial safeguards (involving substantial expense to the mortgagee). Where the installment buyer defaults, on the other hand, the seller generally just exercised his contractual right to declare the contract *forfeited*; no judicial proceedings are necessary, and the buyer ends up forfeiting both the property and any payments he has already made.

   a. **Modern treatment of forfeiture:** Until the last few decades, courts tended to enforce installment contract forfeiture clauses as written (unless the court could find that the seller has *waived* his right to insist on strict performance, e.g., by accepting last payments in the past). But modern courts have frequently refused to enforce such clauses literally.

      i. **Right to foreclosure safeguards:** For instance, many courts have held that where the buyer has paid a *substantial portion* of the purchase price, and the seller would be unjustly enriched by a complete forfeiture, *statutory foreclosure proceedings applicable to mortgages* must be used. This effectively gives the buyer an equity of redemption (*supra*, p. 324), so that the buyer gets extra time — all the way until the actual foreclosure sale — to make up the missing payments.

   b. **Defenses to summary proceeding:** Where an installment seller declares the contract forfeited, his next step is to seek to *evict* the buyer. To do this, he may usually employ *summary proceedings* of the same sort used to evict a tenant (see *supra*, p. 181).

III. DEEDS

A. **Nature of a deed:** The deed is the document which acts to *pass title* from the grantor to a grantee.

   1. **Doctrine of merger:** The deed typically *replaces the contract* as the embodiment of the parties' relationship. Under the doctrine of *merger*, most obligations imposed by the contract of sale are *discharged* unless they are repeated in the deed. See Cribbet, p. 202. Thus if the contract calls for a merchantable title, as embodied in a warranty deed, but the purchaser carelessly accepts a quitclaim deed, the buyer will not be able to sue on the contractual provisions if the title turns to be defective; he is limited to the provisions of his deed. Thus the contract is relevant only during the gap between its signing and the delivery of the deed.

2. The modern deed generally: There are two basic types of deeds: (1) the *quitclaim* deed, in which the grantor makes no covenant that his title is good; and (2) the *warranty* deed, in which the grantor makes one or more promises about the state of the title. (The various covenants for title which might be made in a warranty deed are discussed *infra*, p. 336.)

B. Description of the property: An accurate *description of the property* is clearly one of the most important aspects of the deed. Not only must the description correspond to what the parties actually intend to convey, but it should be worded in such a way that the grantee's title will be merchantable for purposes of a future sale.

1. Types of description: There are several ways of describing land in the deed. Their use varies both according to the part of the country, and according to whether the land is urban/suburban or rural.

    a. Metes and bounds: One common method is the *metes and bounds description*. Such a description begins by establishing a starting point, usually based on a *"monument"*, i.e., a visible landmark, whether artificial or natural. Then, a series of *calls and distances"* is given, each of which represents a line going in a certain direction for a certain distance. Thus a metes and bounds description might, after specifying a beginning point (e.g., the intersection of two particular streets), state "running thence North 50 degrees 26 minutes 36 seconds West for 273 feet, thence North 59 degrees 30 minutes 8 seconds East for 76 and 37/100th feet," etc.

        i. Used in east coast: The metes and bounds description is found most often east of the Mississippi River.

        ii. Must close: The metes and bounds description must *"close."* That is, by following each of the courses and distances, one must eventually be brought back to the starting point. (However, if the failure to enclose is clearly attributable to a particular clerical error, the court may order the deed reformed or interpreted in such a way that the error is rectified.)

    b. The plat method: Another common method is the *"plat"* method. Recall that a developer who wishes to subdivide his property may record a map, or plat, of that property, which shows the location of individual lots. A recorded plat furnishes a convenient means of describing land; the deed merely refers to, e.g., "Lot 2 in Block 5 in Highwood, a subdivision platted on a map filed in the Officer of the Registrar of the County of Westchester on June 13, 1910." Anyone reading this description in the records would then look at the recorded map to see exactly where the boundaries of the lot are located.

2. Inadequate description: If the description is *not sufficiently specific or accurate* to let a court determine what property is meant, the *entire deed* will be found to be *invalid*.

    Example: *O* owns a 100-acre farm. He hands a deed covering "the 15 acres along the creek" to his son. There are 25 acres each of which could be said to be "along the creek." A court is likely to hold that the description is so imprecise (exactly which acres are covered?) that the deed is invalid.

    a. Subsequent actions of parties: But the court will try to resolve ambiguities, so that it can uphold the deed. In resolving ambiguities, the courts will look to the *subsequent* *actions of the parties*. For instance, if either or both have *physically marked the boundaries* in a particular way, the court will treat this as some evidence of their intent (particularly if both have agreed on the marking).

    b. Construction in grantee's favor: One often-cited canon of construction is that the deed will be interpreted in the way which is *most favorable to the grantee*. See Cribbet, p. 210. Since the deed is almost always drafted by the grantor, this amounts to the traditional contract rule that a document will be construed against the draftsman.

C. Various formalities: We consider now several formalities required for the valid *execution* of a deed.

    1. Identification of parties: The deed must correctly *identify the parties* (the grantor and the grantee).

        a. Void if not satisfied: A deed that does not correctly identify the parties is *void*, i.e., of no effect at all.

            i. Imprecise identification: The deed will also be void if it attempts to identify the parties, but does so in such an *imprecise manner* that a court cannot tell with reasonable precision what particular persons or entities were intended. This is most likely to be an issue on the *grantee* side (since circumstantial evidence will usually help identify the grantor).

        b. Deceased grantee: If the grantee listed on the deed is *dead* at the time the deed is "delivered" (see *infra*, p. 334, for a discussion of delivery), the deed is deemed not to identify the parties correctly, and therefore to be *void*.

        c. Non-existent entity: Similarly, if the grantee is a *corporation* or other entity that *does not exist* at the time the deed is delivered, and never comes into existence, the court will likely hold that the deed is void. S&W, §11.1, p. 811.

    2. Signatures: The grantor must place his *signature* on the deed. However, any mark intended to authenticate the document will suffice (e.g, an "X" mark if the grantor is illiterate). The signature of the *grantee* is *not necessary*.

    3. Seal: At one time, a deed had to have a private *seal* affixed to it to be valid. But today, nearly all states have *abolished* the seal requirement.

    4. Attestation: Statutes in some states require a deed to be *attested* to, i.e., *witnessed* by one or more persons not parties to the transaction.

    5. Acknowledgment: Statutes sometimes require that the deed must be *acknowledged*, i.e., *notarized*. It is only the grantor's signature which must be notarized in such cases. (However, many statutes require acknowledgment and/or attestation only as a prerequisite to *recording*, not as a prerequisite to the validity of the deed between the grantor and grantee.)

    6. Consideration not required: But a deed does *not* require *consideration* to be binding. 3 A.L.P. 287-88. So a deed that is given as a *gift*, or a deed that *falsely states* that it is given in exchange for some *specified consideration*, will nonetheless be *valid*.

D. Delivery of deed: For a deed to be valid, it must not only be executed, but also *"delivered."* But this "delivery" requirement does not refer solely to physical delivery. The concept of "delivery" includes two sub-requirements:

[1] that there be a *physical transfer* of the deed by the grantor to someone else (even if only to an agent of the grantee rather than to the grantee herself); and

[2] that the grantor use *words or conduct* evidencing his *intention* to make the deed *presently operative* to vest title in the grantee.

1. Presumption of delivery from physical transfer: *Physical transfer* of the deed by the grantor *to the grantee* will create a *strong presumption* that the "intent to make presently operative" requirement (requirement [2] above) has been satisfied.

a. Must take effect immediately: But never lose sight of the underlying rule: the requirement that the deed be "delivered" is merely an *abbreviated* way of expressing the idea that the conveyance does not occur unless the grantor intends that it *take effect immediately.*

2. Presumption from fact of recording: The fact that the deed has been *recorded* raises a strong *presumption* that the grantor *intended delivery to occur* prior to the moment of recording.

a. Presumption is rebuttable: But this presumption can be *rebutted* by clear evidence of a contrary intent by the grantor.

Example: Grantor hands the deed to Grantee, with a side letter that says, "Don't record this deed now, because I don't want it to take effect until I die." Grantee records anyway. Here, the side letter successfully rebuts the usual presumption that recordation shows the grantor's intent for delivery to have occurred prior to the recording. (Then, if Grantor dies intestate, the deed won't become effective then either, because this sort of "gift conditional on grantor's later death" is not a valid testamentary substitute, under state laws designed to make sure that wills obey certain formalities like being witnessed.)

3. Request not to record: We've just seen that if the deed is *recorded*, this fact raises a presumption of delivery. But the *converse is not true* — as long as the grantor intends that the conveyance be effective immediately (i.e., intends for delivery to occur now), the fact that the grantor asks the grantee *not to record* the deed until some later date *doesn't prevent immediate delivery* from occurring. Again, remember that delivery is always a question of the *grantor's intent,* and the mere fact that the grantor requests the grantee to wait until recording typically will not mean that the grantor intends for there to be a postponement of delivery.

Example: *O* hands his son Sam a deed, saying, "I want you to have Blackacre. You can move in tomorrow. But don't record the deed until I've had a chance to tell your sister that I gave the property to you instead of her." Delivery will be found to have occurred immediately (especially given the strong presumption of present delivery that applies whenever there is a physical transfer of the deed directly to the grantee).

4. **Delivery to agent of grantee:** As long as the grantor intends for delivery to take place immediately, it *does not matter* that he *does not hand the deed physically to the grantee* — any act sufficient to manifest the grantor's *intent that the deed be immediately effective* will suffice for delivery. For example, if the grantor hands the deed to an *agent of the grantee*, with words making it clear that the grantor intends for the transfer to be immediately effective, this will suffice for delivery.

> **Example:** *O* makes out a deed to Blackacre running "to my son Sam and his heirs." *O* then hands the deed to his secretary and says "Take this for Sam, I want him to have the property." *O* dies the next day. The words to the secretary are sufficient to indicate *O*'s intention to make the gift immediately effective; therefore, delivery will be deemed to have occurred, and the gift will be effective.

5. **Promise of later delivery:** A promise by the grantor of *later delivery* typically means that no delivery is meant to occur at the time of the promise. Thus suppose Grantor says something like, "You'll *get the deed later*, when [event X] occurs." Since Grantor is *not intending to make a present delivery* of the deed, *no conveyance occurs* at the time of the conversation. Then, if Grantee somehow comes into possession of the deed without the intent of Grantor, that won't change the fact that no delivery has occurred.

   a. **Event later occurs:** Nor will delivery occur when the event that Grantor originally referred to *eventually occurs* — for delivery to occur, there must be a *single moment* when the grantor (i) makes a *physical transfer* of the deed to some other person; and (ii) has the *present intent* to make the deed *immediately effective*. So if the physical transfer of the deed and the enabling event occur at different times, this requirement of *"simultaneity"* has never been satisfied.

   Example: Dad says to Son, "Here's a deed to our house. You'll get it when your sister, Sis, moves out to get married." Dad then puts the deed (conveying the house to Son) into a drawer. Sis later moves out to get married, and Son removes the deed from Dad's drawer (without Dad knowing) and records it.

   There has been no delivery. At the time Dad made the "You'll get it when ..." remark, the remark showed that Dad had no intent to make the deed presently operative. Then, when the condition occurred (Sis moved out to get married), there was no indication that Dad still had the present intent to make the deed immediately operative, something that's required to exist at the moment claimed to be a delivery. So neither the occurrence of the condition (Sis' move-out), nor Son's act of gaining physical possession of the deed and recording it, had any legal effect, and Dad still owns the house.

6. **Delivery to a third party (escrows):** Suppose physical transfer of the deed is made not to the grantee himself, but to a *third party,* to be re-transferred to the grantee if certain conditions are met. Assuming that the third party is not an agent of either the grantor or grantee, the transaction is referred to as an *escrow*.

   a. **Terminology:** The third party with whom the deed (or any other instrument) is deposited is usually called the *"escrow agent"* or *"escrowee."* The instruments to him are generally called the "escrow agreement."

b. Must be to stranger: The essence of the escrow is that it is held by a party who is a *stranger to the transaction*. Thus a transfer of the deed to the grantee himself cannot be an escrow; since it cannot be an escrow, in nearly all states conditions upon the effectiveness of the delivery will not be respected.

c. When title passes: The deposit of the deed with the escrow agent usually *does not act to transfer legal title*. Thus legal title remains in the grantor until the performance of the stated *conditions* or the happening of the stated *event*. Burby, pp. 301-02. Once the event or condition occurs, title *automatically vests in the grantee*; re-delivery of the deed by the escrow agent to the grantee is not necessary (though this re-delivery, sometimes called the *"second delivery"* is customary).

    i. Unauthorized delivery: Thus if the escrow agent delivers the deed to the grantee before the condition or event has occurred, this delivery is *ineffective to pass title*.

    ii. Bona fide purchaser: What if the grantee in such a case *records the deed*, and then sells to an innocent third person who buys in good faith and for value (i.e., a *bona fide purchaser*)? The courts are split on this question, with most of them holding that the original grantor keeps title, and that the *bona fide* purchaser is out of luck.

7. Subsequent attempt to revoke: If the delivery is valid, title *passes immediately* to the grantee. Thereafter, *return of the deed to the grantor* has *no effect* either to *cancel* the prior delivery or to *reconvey* the title to him. 3 A.L.P. 314-15. The only way the title can get back to the grantor is if a *new, formally satisfactory, conveyance* (with grantor's signature, attestation, etc.) takes place.

    Examples: Steps like the grantee's *handing the deed back to the grantor*, or his *tearing it up*, or his *falsely stating* (even in writing) *that he has destroyed it*, will not undo the deed's effectiveness.

E. Acceptance: Most courts hold that a deed will not transfer title until it is not only delivered, but *accepted* by the grantee. However, such acceptance will be *presumed* if (as is usually the case) the conveyance is beneficial to the grantee.

1. Rights of third party: The only situation in which an acceptance issue is likely to arise is where the grantee does not immediately *learn* of the conveyance, and in the meantime, a third party has obtained rights. For instance, suppose that O executes a deed to A, and that O then puts the deed in a safe deposit box. He does not tell A about the conveyance, and then dies. In a suit between O's heirs and A, the heirs might prevail on the grounds that A could not have accepted the deed prior to O's death, because he did not know about it. 3 A.L.P. 333.

F. Covenants for title: Recall that there are two basic classes of deeds: (1) quitclaim deeds, in which the grantor does not make any representations as to the state of his title, but simply passes on whatever interest he has; and (2) warranty deeds, which contain various representations regarding the state of the grantor's title. In this section, we examine the various representations regarding title which are customarily made in a warranty deed; these representations are referred to as *"covenants for title"* or *"warranties for title."*

1. **Covenants in "warranty deed":** There are six covenants (individually discussed below) which are commonly used. Thus where the contract calls for *"a general warranty deed"* without specifying the covenants to be included in the deed, or where the contract calls for a deed "with the usual covenants," the court is likely to hold that the contract requires a deed with all six of these (although some American courts may not require one, the covenant for further assurance).

2. **Six covenants:** The six commonly used covenants for title are as follows:

   a. **Covenant of seisin:** The *covenant of seisin* usually means that the grantor is warranting that he *owns the estate* he purports to convey. The covenant might be breached, for instance, if the conveyance was of a fee simple, but a third person had an *outstanding remainder*.

   b. **Covenant of right to convey:** The covenant of *right to convey* is considered by most courts to be the *exact equivalent* of the covenant of seisin. 3 A.L.P. 460.

   c. **Covenant against encumbrances:** The covenant *against encumbrances* is exactly what the name implies, i.e., a representation that there are no encumbrances against the property. Encumbrances are those impediments to title which do not affect the fee simple, but which diminish the value of the land. *Mortgages* and *easements* are examples. The various sorts of encumbrances are discussed more extensively *supra*, p. 312, in connection with the definition of marketable title.

   d. **Covenants of quiet enjoyment and warranty:** The covenants of *quiet enjoyment* and *warranty* are virtually identical today. They do not promise that title is perfect (this is the role of the three covenants already discussed); instead, they constitute a *continuing contract* by the covenantor that the grantee's *possession* of the land will be defended against claims by third parties in existence on the date of the conveyance. Since they are in effect covenants for continued possession, they will run to future grantees, as is discussed more fully below. See 3 A.L.P. 467.

   e. **Further assurance:** The covenant for *further assurance* is not widely used in the U.S. The covenant is a promise by the grantor that he will, in the future, make *any conveyance necessary* to give the grantee the full title that was intended to be conveyed. Cribbet, p. 295.

3. **When and how breached:** The six above covenants can be divided into two broad classes: (1) *present* covenants; and (2) *future* covenants.

   a. **Present covenants:** The covenants of seisin, right to convey and against encumbrances are *present covenants*. That is, they are breached, if at all, at the *moment the conveyance is made*. Therefore, a breach can occur *even though there is no eviction*. All the grantee needs to do to recover on the claim is to show that, in fact, title was defective on the date of the conveyance.

   b. **Future covenants:** The covenants of quiet enjoyment, warranty and further assurance, by contrast, are *future covenants*. They are breached *only when an eviction occurs*.

Example: In 1957, P purchases land from D, and receives a warranty deed. In 1974, P grants an option on the land's coal-mining rights to X. Thereafter, P discovers that a prior grantor reserved to himself two-thirds of the land's coal rights in a recorded transaction, so P only owns one-third of the land's coal rights. In 1976, P sues D for breach of the covenant of quiet enjoyment.

Held, for D. To recover for breach of the covenant of quiet enjoyment, P must show actual or constructive eviction. Here, there was neither, since no one holding a paramount title interfered with P's right to possess the coal (e.g, by beginning to mine it). Nor is constructive eviction shown by the fact that P has been required to renegotiate his contract with X for a lesser amount. If the mere existence of a paramount title were enough to constitute constructive eviction, the warranty of quiet enjoyment would be indistinguishable from that of seisin. *Brown v. Lober*, 389 N.E.2d 1188 (Ill. 1979).

  i. **Constructive eviction:** However, *constructive* eviction will suffice for the future covenants. Thus if a third party actively asserts a paramount claim, the grantee is not required to litigate the matter and wait to be forcibly evicted; instead, he may ***purchase the third party's title*** or satisfy the encumbrance in order to avoid eviction.

c. **Statute of limitations:** A key consequence of the distinction between present and future covenants involves the ***statute of limitations***. The statute starts to run on a ***present*** covenant ***at the time the conveyance is made***; the statute starts to run on a ***future*** covenant ***only when an eviction occurs***. Therefore, when a purchaser only discovers a difficulty with title many years after the purchase, she is likely to find that her only hope of relief lies with the future covenants. For instance, in *Brown v. Lober, supra*, P tried desperately to establish a breach of the warranty of quiet enjoyment (a future covenant) because that claim was not time-barred; there clearly had been a breach of warranty of seisin, but that claim had become time-barred long before P discovered the title problem.

4. **No protection against having to defend invalid claim:**   None of the six covenants is deemed breached merely because someone ***files a claim*** against the grantee asserting facts that, if proved, would demonstrate that the grantee has been given imperfect title. This means that if, the day after the grantee takes by warranty deed, someone else claims to be the real owner, and the grantee successfully defends her title, the grantee ***cannot recover the costs of litigation*** from the grantor — ironically, the grantee does worse (at least as far as recovering her costs from the grantor) if she was given good title than if she had been given bad title.

a. **Summary:** So to summarize, no covenant of title gives any protection at all against the grantee's ***costs in having to defend an invalid claim*** by a third party.

5. **Prior knowledge of defect:** Suppose that the grantee, before he takes his deed, is ***aware*** of a defect. Does he thereby waive the protection of the various covenants with respect to this defect? The issue arises most frequently in the case of the covenant against encumbrances.

a. **Ordinary rule:** Ordinarily, the rule is that such knowledge does ***not*** nullify the various covenants.

6. Enforcement by future grantee (running of covenants): The distinction between the present and future covenants is critical to the issue of whether the covenant *runs with the land*, i.e., whether it is *enforceable by subsequent grantees*.

    a. Present covenants: Most courts hold that the *present* covenants (seisin, right to convey and against encumbrances) *do not to run with the land*. Since these covenants are broken at the moment of the conveyance, they immediately become *choses in action* (i.e., a present right to sue). At common law, such choses in action were not assignable, and the rule against the running of present covenants derives from this fact (even though the prohibition on general assignment of choses has itself been abolished).

    b. Future covenants: The *future* covenants (warranty, quiet enjoyment and further assurance) are universally held to *run with the land*. Since these covenants are not breached until there is an actual or constructive eviction, they would be rendered almost useless if a subsequent transfer of the land cut them off.

7. Measure of damages: A defect in the title is likely not to be discovered for a substantial period of time following the original conveyance. If the land has increased in value, what *measure of damages* may be recovered by the covenantee (or by a subsequent grantee in a case where the covenant runs with the land)?

    a. Majority view: A substantial majority of courts hold that, if the title proves completely defective, the covenantee may recover the *purchase price paid*, plus interest. He may *not* recover for any *appreciation* in the value of the land (or even for the value of the land as it was at the time of the conveyance, if this is greater than the purchase price). A contrary rule would mean that the covenantor's liability is virtually unlimited, a result that is almost certainly not the intent of the parties.

    b. Intermediate transaction: Where the party suing is not the original covenantee, but a *remote grantee*, a number of courts have held that this grantee's damages are *limited to the amount he paid to his own grantor*, if this is less than the amount paid by this intermediate grantor to the covenantor. Thus if O sells to A for $10,000, and A sells to B for $5,000, under this view B would be limited to $5,000 damages in a warranty suit against O.

8. Estoppel by deed: Suppose that A conveys Blackacre to B by warranty deed, at a time when A does not own Blackacre. If A *later* acquires Blackacre, many courts hold that title to Blackacre *immediately passes to B* by the doctrine of *estoppel by deed* (also called the doctrine of after-acquired title). Thus in a sense, the estoppel-by-deed doctrine furnishes B with an additional protection growing out of his warranty deed. The subject of estoppel by deed is discussed more extensively in the treatment of recording acts, *infra*, p. 368.

G. Warranty of habitability: Recall that in the landlord-tenant context, the original rule that the landlord makes no implied warranties of *habitability* is now widely giving way to the opposite rule. (*Supra*, p. 169.) A similar reversal is occurring in the area of outright sales of residences.

    1. Common-law rule: At common law, there were no implied warranties of title, let alone of habitability. A home buyer, like any other purchaser of real property, had only the benefit of those covenants which he could induce the seller to place into the deed.

2. **Modern trend:** But beginning in the 1960's, courts began to feel that the old rule of *caveat emptor* was no more appropriate in home-sale cases than in cases involving the sale of personal property (e.g., a car). Today, most states (and nearly all the states that have considered the matter recently) hold that a ***builder/vendor*** makes a warranty of ***quality*** or ***skillful construction*** when it sells a house. D&K, pp. 624-25.

3. **Lender's liability:** Frequently, a developer/builder who sells shoddy homes will go quickly bankrupt. If so, a suit on an implied warranty or on any other theory against him is not likely to be much good. Some courts have held that a ***lender*** who participates closely with a builder may be subject to negligence or implied warranty liability for failing to see that the houses so produced are merchantable.

4. **Used homes:** The courts have thus far almost always refused to allow an implied warranty claim against one who is ***not in the business*** of building or selling homes. As a practical matter, this means that an implied warranty suit generally cannot be brought by the buyer of a ***used home*** against the ***person who sold it to him***.

   a. **Implied warranty suit against builder:** But most courts now allow a purchaser of a used home to sue the ***original builder*** for breach of the implied warranty of habitability, if a defect is latent when the purchaser buys, and appears within a reasonable time after construction. In other words, ***privity of contract*** seems no longer to be generally required for implied warranty of habitability suits. See, e.g., *Lempke v. Dagenais*, 547 A.2d 290 (N.H. 1988), allowing the purchaser of a used home to recover against the builder for pure economic loss, provided that: (1) the defects were ***latent*** at the time the plaintiff purchased, so that they could not have been discovered by a reasonable inspection; and (2) the defect manifested itself within a ***reasonable time*** after construction.

   b. **Concealment:** Also, even a *non*-builder who re-sells a house that he owns may be liable for ***concealing*** a material defect of which he is aware. See *infra*, p. 340.

5. **Commercial buildings:** Courts have thus far almost always ***declined*** to allow recovery based on implied warranty for sales of ***commercial*** structures.

H. **Misrepresentation and concealment:** A seller of property who ***misrepresents*** the condition of the property will normally be liable to the buyer for damages, under the common-law doctrine of ***deceit*** or "fraudulent misrepresentation". Normally, the buyer will have to show: (1) a ***false statement*** concerning a ***material*** fact; (2) ***knowledge*** by the seller that the representation is false; (3) an intent by the seller that the buyer ***rely***; and (4) injury to the buyer (e.g., that the house is worth less than it would be had the facts been as represented). See *Johnson v. Davis*, discussed *infra*.

1. **Non-disclosure:** The common law traditionally has ***not*** made the seller liable for merely ***failing to disclose*** material defects of which he is aware. But this seems to be changing: Many if not most states that have recently considered the question now hold that the seller has an ***affirmative duty*** to disclose material defects that he is aware of, and that he will be liable in damages if he does not do so. California, Illinois, Florida and New Jersey are among the states so holding.

Example: Buyers contract with Sellers to buy their home for $310,000; Buyers put down a $31,000 deposit. Sellers know that the roof leaks, but affirmatively represent to Buyers that the roof is fine. Before closing, Buyers discover a massive leak, and sue for rescission and return of the deposit.

Held, for Buyers. "Where the seller of a home knows of facts materially affecting the value of the property which are *not readily observable* and are not known to the buyer, the seller is under a *duty to disclose them* to the buyer. This duty is equally applicable to all forms of real property, new and used." Therefore, Sellers must refund the deposit plus Buyers' litigation costs. *Johnson v. Davis*, 480 So.2d 625 (Fl. 1985).

a. **Defect could have been found:** Even these modern cases imposing an affirmative duty on the seller to disclose material defects of which he is aware generally find the seller liable only where *the buyer could not reasonably have discovered* the defect by reasonable diligence.

b. **Seller caused the condition:** Courts are especially likely to find the seller liable for mere nondisclosure where the seller has *brought about the defect or condition.* For instance, in perhaps the only case in which a court has held that a seller owes the buyer the duty of disclosing the presence of *ghosts*, the court relied on the fact that the seller had previously encouraged the house's reputation of being haunted (by reporting the ghosts' presence to *Readers' Digest* and to the local press). Therefore, the court concluded, "Defendant is estopped to deny [the ghosts'] existence and, as a matter of law, the house is haunted." The court then allowed the buyer to rescind the purchase contract. *Stambovsky v. Ackley*, 572 N.Y.S.2d 672 (N.Y.App.Div. 1991).

c. **Disclosure statement required:** Some states have enacted *statutes* requiring the seller to give the prospective buyer a *written statement* disclosing facts about the property, including defects.

   i. **California statute:** For instance, Cal. Civ. Code §1102.6 requires disclosure of dozens of facts, including the existence of structural defects, presence of asbestos, radon gas, lead-based paint or other toxics, flooding or drainage problems, and even "neighborhood noise problems or other nuisances." See *Alexander v. McKnight*, 9 Cal.Rptr.2d 453 (Cal.App. 1992), holding that this statute imposes on the seller a duty to warn any buyer about *"problem neighbors,"* such as ones who hold lots of late-night parties, park too many cars on the property, or retaliate against any neighbor who complains.

2. **Doctrine of merger:** Traditionally, sellers were often insulated from liability by the doctrine of *"merger"*. Under the merger doctrine, a contract of sale merges into the deed, and the deed becomes the final expression of the parties' deal. Therefore, even if the seller made representations or gave warranties in the contract, these would be *extinguished* when the buyer closed on the deal and took the deed. (See the fuller discussion of merger *supra*, p. 331.) The merger doctrine would seem to prevent recovery under either an implied warranty of habitability theory or deceit theory. But the merger doctrine has fallen into great disfavor, so that few if any courts would use it to prevent such a recovery on grounds of implied warranty or deceit. See D&K, p. 616.

I. Cooperatives and condominiums: A few words should be said about two forms of real property ownership which are becoming increasingly common, particularly in or near major cities. These are the *cooperative* and the *condominium*.

1. Cooperative: The term *"cooperative"* is usually used to refer to a means of owning a multi-unit dwelling (ordinarily a traditional apartment house). Typically, the building is owned by a cooperative *corporation*. Each resident of the building must be a *shareholder* in the corporation.

    a. Proprietary lease: Ownership of the corporate shares does not directly confer the right to occupy a unit, but each shareholder is entitled to enter into a *"proprietary lease"*, in which the corporation is the lessor and the shareholder is lessee. The lease almost always provide that its continuance depends upon the lessee's continuing to be the holder of the same shares in the corporation.

        i. Charges: The lease will also require the lessee to pay various charges. Typically, these include: (1) a fixed monthly amount to pay off the lessee's fair portion of the building's *mortgage* interest and principal, if any; and (2) an amount adjusted annually by the board of directors to defray the maintenance and operating costs of the building (the so-called *"carrying charges"*).

    b. Board's right of approval: A key feature of the cooperative form of ownership is that the board of directors, or the entire body of shareholders, typically has the right to *approve or reject* any proposed *sale* of shares in the corporation. Since ownership of shares is a prerequisite to obtaining the proprietary lease, this right of approval gives existing residents of the cooperatives the right to *select their neighbors*. Courts have generally held that this right of approval is not an unreasonable restraint upon alienation.

2. Condominium: The *condominium*, by contrast, is a form of ownership in which each individual resident holds a fee simple in a certain physical space or parcel, but all the residents collectively own certain *"common areas."*

    a. High-rise apartment: If the property is a conventional high-rise apartment building, the individual resident might own a fee simple only in a defined vertical space, and would not own any part of the ground surface area. The condominium association (which is really just the individual owners acting as tenants in common) then would own the fee simple to the soil and to the stairways, recreational areas and other common areas.

    b. "Horizontal" management: In a more *"horizontal"* structure (e.g., two-story *townhouses* spread over a large parcel), each individual resident might own the soil upon which his townhouse stands, but he would not own the surrounding lawns, swimming pool, etc.; these would be held by the condominium association.

    c. Charges: In either event, the association sets charges to defray the cost of maintaining the common areas. But maintenance of the interior living unit (probably including plumbing and heating systems, in a townhouse arrangement) is the responsibility of the individual resident.

IV. CONVEYANCING BY WILL: ADEMPTION, EXONERATION AND LAPSE

A. Conveyancing by will generally: There are three common-law doctrines that are specific to conveyances of property by *will*:

❏ *ademption*;

❏ *exoneration*; and

❏ *lapse*

B. Ademption: The common-law doctrine of *"ademption"* deals with those cases in which a testator makes a devise of specific property — personal property or realty — and the specific property is *no longer part of the testator's estate* at the time of death. The ademption doctrine says that the bequest *completely fails* in this situation, and the legatee *gets nothing.* The specific gift is said to have "adeemed," i.e., failed.

> **Example:** At the time Test writes her will, she owns Blackacre. The will recites that Test "hereby bequeaths Blackacre to my daughter Dee." The will gives all other real and personal property to Test's son Sam. One year later, Test sells Blackacre for $400,000, and does not modify the will. Test then dies. At common law, Dee will get nothing, because the gift of Blackacre is adeemed. The $400,000 in proceeds will go to Sam as the residuary legatee.

1. Tip about equitable conversion: Suppose that the specifically-devised property is, at the moment of the testator's death, under a *contract to be sold.* Assuming that there is no relevant statute, then probably by the doctrine of equitable conversion (*supra*, p. 316) the purchase price will be *personal property*, not real estate, and will go to the person identified as the recipient of personal property under the will.

> **Example:** In the above example, if Blackacre is under contract to be sold at the time Test dies, the $400,000 proceeds will go to Sam as legatee of the personal property, not to Dee as recipient of the specific bequest of Blackacre.

C. Exoneration: Under the common-law doctrine of *"exoneration,"* a person who receives a bequest of property that is *subject to a lien or mortgage* is entitled to receive the property *"free and clear,"* if there is no evidence that the testator intended a contrary result. When exoneration applies, the estate's personal property — i.e., its cash — is used to pay off the lien or mortgage.

> **Example:** Test's will bequeaths Blackacre to her son *S*, and all of her other property, real and personal (including $500,000 in cash), to her daughter *D*. At the time of Test's death, Blackacre is subject to a $100,000 mortgage. Assume that all relevant common-law doctrines apply, and that there is no evidence of Test's desires regarding the handling of the mortgage at her death. When *S* takes Blackacre, who is responsible for the mortgage?
>
> *S* takes free-and-clear of the mortgage, under the common-law doctrine of exoneration. By that doctrine, if the testator does not indicate a contrary intent, any specific devise of real or personal property is to made free and clear of any mortgage or lien.

So here, the mortgage on Blackacre will be paid off with some of the cash that would otherwise have gone to *D* as residuary legatee.

1. **Statutes:** Most states have *statutes* altering the common-law exoneration doctrine.

D. **Lapse:** Under the common-law doctrine of *"lapse,"* if a beneficiary named in a will *pre-deceases the testator,* the *bequests fails*, rather than go to that beneficiary's next-of-kin. Instead, the bequeathed property becomes part of the testator's residuary estate.

1. **Statutes:** Most states have enacted *"antilapse"* statutes. These generally have the effect of abolishing the lapse doctrine — and allowing the dead beneficiary's heirs to take — in certain situations, typically where the pre-deceased beneficiary is a *relative* of the testator. (A common definition of "relative" in such antilapse statutes is "a direct descendant of the testator's grandparent.")

    Example: Test writes a will leaving Blackacre to "my good friend Fred," who is not a relative of Test. The will leaves all the rest of Test's estate to a daughter Dee. Fred dies intestate after Test's will is executed; Fred is survived by a single heir at law, a son Sam. One year later, Test dies. Assume that the state has a statute providing that in the case of a bequest to a person who is a lineal descendant of the testator's grandparent, if the beneficiary has pre-deceased the testator then the heirs at law of the beneficiary shall take so long as there is no indication that the testator intended a contrary result. In all other respects, the common law applies. Who takes Blackacre, Sam or Dee?

    Dee takes Blackacre. Since Fred is not a lineal descendent of Test's grandparent (the facts say that Fred and Test are not relatives), the antilapse statute does not apply. Consequently, the common-law lapse rule applies, so as to cause the bequest to Fred to fail because Fred pre-deceased Test. Therefore, Blackacre becomes part of Test's residuary estate, which goes to Dee.

Quiz Yourself on

LAND SALE CONTRACTS, MORTGAGES AND DEEDS

79. By telephone, Simon agreed to sell, and Bryant agreed to buy, Blackacre for a price of $200,000, the closing to take place on April 1. On March 15, the day after this conversation, Simon sent Bryant a letter confirming all of the relevant terms of the agreement. The letter stated, "I will assume that this letter accurately states our arrangement, and will bind us both, unless I hear from you to the contrary by March 20." Bryant received the letter, but sent no response. On April 1, Simon arrived with a marketable deed at the time and place that his letter specified for closing. Bryant did not show up at all. If Simon sues Bryant for breach of contract, may he recover damages? _____

80. Tycoon, a wealthy industrialist, has for many years owned a 100 acre parcel of undeveloped, heavily-wooded land, called Twin Oaks, in the state of Bates. Grandson, Tycoon's daughter's oldest son, wished desperately to become a farmer. Tycoon therefore orally proposed to Grandson the following arrangement: if Grandson would move onto the property, construct a permanent dwelling, and clear at least 50 of the acres, he could keep whatever crops (or their proceeds) he could grow on the property. Furthermore, if Grandson did all this and then continued to farm for at least five years, Tycoon would leave the property to Grandson in Tycoon's will. Grandson moved onto the property, built a small cabin, cleared 75 acres,

and farmed them for the next seven years, keeping all proceeds as agreed. Tycoon then died, and his will made no mention of the arrangement. (Instead, the will left Twin Oaks to Tycoon's niece, Edna.) If Grandson sues Tycoon's estate for an order of specific performance directing the estate to convey Twin Oaks to Grandson, will Grandson prevail? Assume that Bates follows the majority approach to all relevant matters. _____

81. Shelby, the owner of Blackacre, contracted to sell the property to Bennett. The contract document, dated March 1, provided that the closing was to take place on April 1. The contract did not contain a "time is of the essence" clause, and did not specify the consequences if either party was unable or unwilling to close on the appointed day. On March 25, Bennett said by telephone to Shelby, "My bank loan hasn't gone through yet. I won't be able to close on April 1, but I will be ready on April 10." Shelby replied, "Either close on April 1, or the contract is off." On April 1, Shelby showed up at the appointed place with a deed, but Bennett did not appear. Bennett tendered a check for the purchase price on April 10, but Shelby refused to take it. There is evidence that Shelby was trying to get out of the contract not because the delay was material in light of the surrounding circumstances, but because someone had unexpectedly come along and offered Shelby a higher price. If Bennett sues Shelby for a decree ordering Shelby to convey the property to Bennett for the contract price, will a court grant Bennett's request? _____

82. Squires contracted to sell Whiteacre to Brady, the closing to take place on June 1. The purchase price was to be $200,000, in the form of a cashier's or certified check. The contract required Squires to convey a marketable title. On June 1, both Squires and Brady turned up at the appointed place for the closing. Squires tendered a deed, together with an abstract of title showing that Squires had good title. The contract also required Squires to have a Certificate of Occupancy for a newly-constructed deck attached to the house. Brady demanded the Certificate of Occupancy, and Squires said, "I don't have it." Brady responded, "Well, I refuse to close." Squires asked Brady to show him the certified check for the purchase price. Brady said, "I don't have it. I didn't bother going through with my bank loan, because I knew you didn't have the Certificate of Occupancy." (This assertion is true.) Squires refused to return Brady's 10% deposit, paid to Squires at the time the contract was signed. (The deposit is returnable, according to the contract, only if seller is in default and buyer is not, on the closing date.) If Brady sues Squires for the return of his deposit, will Brady win? _____

83. Same basic fact pattern as prior question. Now, however, assume that the abstract of title proffered by Squires on June 1 showed that the house on the property (an important part of the overall value of the property) encroached 10 feet onto the property of Squires' easterly neighbor. If Brady sues Squires for return of his deposit, and Squires asserts the defense that Brady did not tender his own performance (because Brady did not bring a check to the closing), may Brady recover the deposit? _____

84. Sherman contracted to sell Greenacre to Bruce. The contract was signed on June 1, 2012, and called for a closing to occur on August 1, 2012. On July 1, 2012, Sherman died. His will (executed in 2010) left all of Sherman's personal property to his daughter Deirdre, and all of his real estate to his niece Nell. The closing took place as scheduled on August 1, with the sale proceeds paid to Sherman's estate. Who should receive the sale proceeds, Deirdre or Nell? _____

85. Spratt contracted to sell a house to Booth. After the contract was signed, but before the scheduled closing date, the house burned down. Spratt was not at fault. Neither Spratt nor Booth had any insurance in force on the property. On the closing date, is Booth obligated to pay the purchase price to Spratt, in return for a deed to the now-much-less-valuable property? _____

86. Spence sold a house and lot to Bagley under an installment sales contract. The contract provided for the $200,000 purchase price to be paid at the rate of $5,000 per month for 40 consecutive months (with interest on the unpaid balance also being payable each month). The contract further provided that if Bagley ever became more than 30 days in arrears on any payment, Spence could at his sole option declare the contract forfeited, and reclaim the property. Bagley moved in, and made the first 20 payments without incident. He then lost his job, and fell 90 days behind in the payments. The fair rental value of the property is $2,000 per month. Spence sent Bagley a letter stating, "Because you have violated the terms of our agreement, I am hereby exercising my right to declare the agreement terminated. Please vacate immediately." If Spence seeks an order declaring the contract terminated and decreeing that Bagley leave the premises, will Spence succeed? _____

87. Steel contracted to sell Greenacre to Boswell. The contract stated that Steel would convey marketable title to Boswell, and that the deed would be a warranty deed free of all easements and other encumbrances. On the appointed closing date, Steel tendered to Boswell a warranty deed which stated that the property is "subject to an easement on behalf of a parcel located to the northwest of the subject parcel, enabling the beneficiary of the easement to use the subject parcel's driveway." Boswell and Boswell's lawyer did not carefully read the deed. Instead, they accepted it, and paid the purchase price, without realizing that the deed was subject to the easement. Several days later, when Boswell's neighbor used Boswell's driveway, Boswell realized that he had been given a deed which did not conform to the contract. Boswell now sues to recover damages under the contract for breach of the representation concerning lack of easements. Assuming that Boswell shows that the property is less valuable because the easement exists, may Boswell recover under the contract? _____

88. Fred was the owner of Greyacre, located in the state of Cabot. Cabot law requires all deeds for the transfer of real property to be witnessed by two people. Fred, who was getting on in years, decided to make a gift of Greyacre to his son, Stewart. He therefore prepared a deed giving Stewart the property, signed it, and had it witnessed by two people (thus fulfilling all of the requirements for a deed in Cabot). He handed the deed to Stewart, saying, "You are now the owner of Greyacre." The next day, Fred had a change of heart, realizing that he might live another 15 years and wanting the satisfaction of knowing that he was still the owner of Greyacre. He therefore asked Stewart to return or rip up the deed. Stewart was upset, but he was also a dutiful son. He therefore ripped up the deed (first making a photocopy, however), and told Fred that he had done so. Shortly thereafter, Fred died, leaving all of his personal and real property to his daughter, Denise. Who owns Greyacre, Stewart or Denise? _____

89. In 1980, Spitzer conveyed Blackacre to Butler, under a standard warranty deed. In 2012, as Butler was preparing to resell the property, he discovered that Spitzer's predecessor in title had lost his title through adverse possession before ever conveying to Spitzer. The present holder of title by adverse possession is Adolf, who is not in possession of the property (Butler is), and who has never actively asserted rights to the property. Butler realizes that he will not be able to convey a marketable title to any subsequent purchaser because of Adolf's superior title. Butler therefore wishes to sue Spitzer for breach of some or all of the covenants of title. The statutes of limitation on actions for breach of the covenants of seisin, right to convey and against encumbrances are all five years in the jurisdiction. The statutes of limitation on the covenants of quiet enjoyment and warranty are both three years. If Butler brings suit in 2012 against Spitzer for breach of all of these covenants, on which, if any, may he recover? For each covenant on which he may not recover, state the reason. _____

90. Same facts as prior question. Now, assume that Butler, without disclosing the fact that Adolf had a superior title, conveyed the property by warranty deed to Capshaw in 2000. In 2012, while Capshaw was still the record owner of the property and in possession of it, Adolf brought an action for a declaration that he was the legal owner of the property. If Capshaw immediately brought suit against Spitzer for violation by Spitzer of the covenant of quiet enjoyment, could Capshaw recover? (Assume that nothing in the Butler-to-Capshaw deed refers to any covenants made by Butler's predecessor(s) in title.) _____

91. Schneider conveyed a house and lot to Block, under a general warranty deed. The deed did not list any encumbrances or encroachments. At the time Block received (and paid for) the deed, he was aware that a garage built and belonging to Schneider's eastern neighbor, Jones, was located half on Jones' property and half on Schneider's property. (Block closed the transaction anyway, because he thought he was getting a price that was good enough to overlook this problem.) Several years later, Block decided that he had made a mistake in tolerating this state of events. He therefore instituted a suit against Schneider for breach of covenant.

    (a) For breach of which covenant should Block sue? _____

    (b) Will Block be found to have waived the benefit of that covenant by agreeing to close with knowledge of the problem? _____

92. Developer was in the business of buying large parcels, subdividing them, and building new houses on each. Developer sold a newly built house and the lot on which it stood to Benjamin, a would-be homeowner. The transaction was done by warranty deed. Both the sale contract and the deed contained the following statement in capital letters: "DEVELOPER MAKES NO OTHER WARRANTIES, EXPRESS OR IMPLIED, REGARDING THE STATE OF THE LAND OR STRUCTURES BEING TRANSFERRED." Unbeknownst to either Developer or Benjamin, Developer's employees, because of their ignorance, had failed to use the proper mix of sand and gravel in the cement employed for the building's foundation. Hairline cracks began to appear shortly after the closing, and within one year the house was structurally unsafe and unsalable.

    (a) What action, if any, should Benjamin bring against Developer? _____

    (b) What is the probable result of the action you advised bringing in (a)? _____

93. Same facts as prior question. Assume that during his first and only year of ownership, Benjamin did not become aware of the cracks in the foundation. At the end of a year, he sold the house to Carter, and Carter moved in. If Carter sues Benjamin on the same theory as you gave in your answer to part (a) of the prior question, will Carter succeed against Developer? _____

Answers

79. **No.** The *Statute of Frauds* is applicable in all states to any contract for the sale of land, or for the sale of any interest in land. Therefore, either the contract itself, or a memorandum of it, must be in writing. Furthermore, the contract or memorandum must be signed by the "party to be charged." On the facts here, the party to be charged is Bryant, and the contract is not enforceable against him because of the lack of signature.

80. **Yes, probably.** Most (but certainly not all) states recognize the *"part performance"* exception to the Statute of Frauds for land-sale contracts. Under this doctrine, a party (either buyer or seller) who has taken action in reliance on the contract may be able to gain enforcement of it at equity. In most states, if the "purchaser" (here, Grandson, in the sense that he was "purchasing" the farm in exchange for his services) takes possession, makes improvements and changes his position in reliance, this will be the sort of part performance required. Courts generally require that the part performance be *"unequivocally referable"* to

the alleged contract, i.e., that the part performance be clearly in response to the oral contract, and not explainable by some other facet of the parties' relationship. This requirement seems to be met here, since Grandson has made permanent improvements to the property, by building the cabin and cutting down the trees, and these improvements are not readily explainable by the mere Grandfather-Grandson relationship.

81. **Yes, probably.** In a suit for specific performance of a land sale contract, the general rule is that time is *not of the essence* unless the contract expressly so provides or the surrounding circumstances indicate that it is. Thus generally, even though the contract specifies a particular closing date, either party may obtain specific performance although he is unable to close on the appointed day (as long as the defaulting party is able to perform within a reasonable time after the scheduled date). Since the surrounding circumstances do not suggest that time was of the essence from Shelby's perspective, and since Bennett was able to perform within what a court would probably find was a reasonable time of the scheduled closing date (10-day delay), the court will probably grant Bennett a decree of specific performance. (But a few courts, most notably the New York courts, hold that where the contract does not explicitly make time of the essence, either party, by a unilateral notification to the other that it will insist upon strict adherence to the contracted-for settlement date, may make time of the essence. In such a state, Shelby would win.)

82. **No, probably.** The key to solving this question is that where the seller's duty to deliver the deed and the buyer's duty to pay the money are *concurrent*, then each party must be sure to *tender his own performance*, in order to be able to hold the other party in default. Therefore, Brady could hold Squires in default (and get a return of his deposit) only if Brady tendered his own performance. Since Brady did not have the certified check with him, or even have the funds readily available, Brady did not tender his own performance. Consequently, Squires' own "breach" is irrelevant, and Squires will probably be allowed to keep the deposit. (The result might have been different if Squires' failure to comply with the contract stemmed from an incurable problem, such as complete lack of title in Squires; it also would have been different if Squires had repudiated the contract ahead of time. But neither of these events happened here.)

83. **Yes, probably.** The usual rule that each party must tender his own performance in order to hold the other in breach (see prior question) does not generally apply where a defendant's inability to perform is *incurable*. On these facts, Squires' lack of marketable title (due to the encroachment) was so severe, and so impossible to cure, that Brady's failure to tender his own performance would probably be overlooked by the court, and Brady would get his money back.

84. **Deirdre.** "Common sense" would suggest that the answer should be Nell, since Sherman died while still the technical owner of the real estate, so it would seem fair to give Nell the proceeds from the post-death sale of an asset that was earmarked for her. But instead, courts apply the doctrine of *"equitable conversion."* By this doctrine, the signing of the contract is deemed to vest in the purchaser equitable ownership of the land, and the vendor is treated as becoming the equitable owner of the purchase price at that time. As a result of the equitable conversion doctrine, the purchase price goes to the person to whom the personal property was bequeathed, and the person to whom the real estate was devised gets nothing.

85. **Yes, probably.** Most courts adopt the rule that since the vendee acquires equitable ownership of the land as soon as the contract is signed (see answer to prior question), the risk of loss immediately shifts to him. This is true even though the vendee never takes possession prior to the casualty. There is an exception if the vendor caused the loss negligently, but the facts indicate that this was not the case.

86. **No, probably.** When the purchaser under an installment sales contract has paid a substantial percentage of the purchase price, most courts try hard to avoid allowing the seller to make the buyer "forfeit" his rights under the contract. The court might order Spence to use statutory foreclosure proceedings before

evicting Bagley. In that event, Spence would have to put the property up for sale, and would have to pay to Bagley any amount that the property sold for less the $100,000 that Bagley still owes Spence. (In other words, the installment contract would be treated as if it had been a mortgage.) Or, the court might give Bagley the right to make the payments on which he had been in arrears ($15,000), and then continue with the contract. If the $5,000 monthly payments due from Bagley were no more than a fair rental price for the property, the court would probably not use either of these methods, since the situation would be analogous to a tenant who falls behind in his rent. But here, the monthly payments are much more than fair rental value, so the court would, as stated, take steps to avoid forfeiture.

87. **No, probably.** Under the doctrine of ***merger***, obligations imposed by the contract of sale are generally discharged unless they are repeated in the deed. There is an exception where the contract covenant is "collateral" to (i.e., not directly related to) the promise to convey land. But here, the representation in the contract that there were no easements related directly to the transfer of title, and most courts would hold that that representation was merged out of existence when Boswell accepted the deed that did not repeat the obligation. (But the Uniform Land Transactions Act, if in force in the jurisdiction, would prevent merger from happening.)

88. **Stewart.** If a deed is validly executed and delivered, title passes immediately to the grantee. Thereafter, return of the deed to the grantor, or even destruction of the deed, has no effect either to cancel the prior delivery or to reconvey the title to the original grantor. The only way the title can get back to the grantor is if a new, formally satisfactory, conveyance takes place. Since Stewart never executed and delivered a valid deed to Fred, title remains in him.

89. **None.** The covenants of seisin, right to convey and against encumbrances are all "present" covenants. That is, they are breached at the moment the conveyance is made. Therefore, a breach of these can occur even though there was no eviction. Consequently, these were violated by Spitzer at the time of the original conveyance (at least the covenants of seisin and right to convey were breached, though the covenant against encumbrances may not have been). However, Butler's problem is that these covenants are time-barred: the five year statute of limitations on each began to run at the time of conveyance, and the actions became time barred in 1985. The covenants of quiet enjoyment and warranty, by contrast, are "future" covenants. That is, they are breached only when an eviction occurs. The covenants both promise that the grantee's possession will not be challenged. An action on either of these future covenants is not time barred, since they have not yet started to run. However, there is no cause of action on these, either: until Adolf starts eviction proceedings or otherwise actively asserts that his title is superior, Butler has not even been constructively, let alone actually, evicted. Therefore, Butler will have to wait until Adolf actively asserts his title before he may sue Spitzer. To the extent that the uncertainty renders Butler unable to convey a valid title, Butler is simply out of luck.

90. **Yes.** The future covenants (warranty, quiet enjoyment and further assurance) are universally held to ***run with the land***. Since these covenants are not breached until there is an actual or constructive eviction, they would be rendered almost useless if a subsequent transfer of the land cut them off. Therefore, Capshaw can sue Spitzer even though he had no privity of contract with Spitzer.

91. (a) **Covenant against encumbrances.** The covenant against encumbrances is a representation that there are no encumbrances against the property. The encroachment by Jones was such an encumbrance, so this covenant was violated.

(b) **No, probably.** Most courts hold that even where the grantee is aware of a defect, his knowledge does not nullify the relevant covenant.

92. (a) Suit for breach of the implied warranty of habitability. Many courts today allow a home purchaser to sue a professional developer for the breach of this warranty, in a way that is analogous to the landlord-tenant implied warranty recognized in nearly all jurisdictions.

(b) Split of authority. The strong emerging trend is to recognize an action for implied warranty of habitability in sales by professional developers of new homes.

93. No. Courts have nearly always refused to allow an implied warranty claim against one who is not in the business of building or selling homes. The consequence is that the buyer of a used home, such as Carter, cannot sue the person who sold it to him (Benjamin).

Exam Tips on LAND SALE CONTRACTS, MORTGAGES AND DEEDS

The topics in this chapter tend to be very heavily tested.

Land sale contracts

Within the area of contracts for the sale of land, here are the most frequently-tested issues:

☛ **Statute of Frauds:** When a fact pattern indicates that a contract was made *orally*, make sure you discuss the Statute of Frauds issue. Be on the lookout for exceptions to the general requirement of a writing for any transfer of an interest in land.

☞ **Reliance:** The most important exception is that where the purchaser takes action in *reasonable reliance* on the contract's existence, the court will generally grant at least limited enforcement at equity.

☞ **Actions showing reliance:** Common actions showing reliance are *building a structure*, *fencing in*, paying *taxes*, and making other improvements on the land. Remember that in some courts, the reliance or detriment must be *substantial*, so note the cost and extent of the actions.

☞ **"Unequivocably referable":** Don't forget that in most courts, the supposed reliance actions must be shown to have been taken *clearly in response* to the oral contract, and not otherwise explainable. This is the *"unequivocably referable"* requirement (the reliance must be "unequivocably referable" to the alleged oral contract).

Example 1: B leases and operates a gas station owned by *O*. After the lease period ends, *O* and *B* enter into a oral agreement for the sale of the premises to *B* and they agree that no further lease payments are required. Then *B* installs new equipment on the premises at a cost of $18,000. Since it would otherwise be illogical for *B* to make improvements on the premises after the expiration of the lease period, his actions will probably be found to be unequivocally referable to the alleged oral agreement of purchase. That agreement will therefore be enforceable although oral.

Example 2: O orally says to his daughter, D, "I'm giving you the house and lot." D takes possession of the house, makes substantial and expensive improvements and lives in it for six years (without paying anything to O) until she relocates for business purposes. O and D then have a falling out, and O claims that the house still belongs to him. If D was an only child, O can plausibly argue that D's actions were not unequivocally referable to O's transfer of the property to her because she could have been preparing for her likely inheritance of the land and her actions are therefore otherwise explainable. If the court agrees that this explanation is plausible (the court does not even have to believe that the explanation is probably the correct one), the oral agreement will be without effect.

☛ **Equitable conversion:** The issue of equitable conversion arises frequently in the case where property is destroyed and it must be determined who bears the risk of loss.

☞ **Common scenario:** A contract is entered into for the sale of realty. Then a fire partially destroys the realty. Remember that most courts apply the equitable conversion doctrine here: the signing of the contract is deemed to have shifted equitable title to the buyer, so the risk of loss passes to the buyer at that moment.

Example: In May, O and *B* contract for the sale of O's home, title to close in July. *B* is to move into the house in June and to pay rent until the closing. In June, after *B* moves in, he falls asleep while smoking in bed and causes damage to the house. *B* attempts to collect on an insurance policy he purchased in May. In a jurisdiction recognizing equitable conversion, *B* would be deemed to have an insurable interest as of the time of closing, and he could therefore collect on the policy. (On the other hand, *B* won't be able to void the sale contract, or lessen the purchase price, on account of the fire, because the risk of loss will be deemed to have passed to him on the signing of the contract in May.)

☞ **Exceptions:** But remember that even in courts applying equitable conversion, there are some *exceptions*. Most important: if (1) the damage is due to the *vendor's negligence*, or (2) the vendor did not have, and probably wouldn't have been able to get, *marketable title*, the doctrine doesn't apply.

☞ **Parties' right to allocate:** Also, remember that parties can agree as to when risk of loss passes regardless of the rule in their jurisdiction.

☞ **Death:** If the fact pattern mentions the *death* of one of the parties to the contract after the contract has been entered into, apply the doctrine of equitable conversion in enforcing the contract. If the seller dies, the devisees of his personal property collect the proceeds of the sale. And, if the buyer dies, the buyer's estate may specifically enforce the contract against the seller (and vice versa).

☛ **Marketable title:** Generally, a seller must convey *marketable title,* i.e., a title that a reasonable buyer, fully informed of the facts and their legal significance, would be willing to accept. Look for an impending sale of property where there is an ambiguity about title.

☞ **Common scenario:** You'll sometimes see an earlier series of grants and/or devises which do not validly transfer the property because true title to the parcel lies in a different party. In general, these earlier ineffective grants *won't* impair the marketable title of the person who in fact has good title.

Example: O conveys Blackacre to "my sisters S and T as joint tenants." S dies and devises "all my interest in Blackacre to my daughter, D, for life, then to D's daughters, A and B for life, then to all the children of A and B whenever they are born." T dies, and devises "all my interest in Blackacre to my friend, F." F then quitclaims the parcel to Y for $20,000. Y contracts to sell the parcel to Z, promising to convey marketable title. Z claims that the devise to D renders Y's title unmarketable.

Z will lose. When S died, T received S's interest as the surviving joint tenant, rendering S's attempt to devise her property invalid. Therefore, F received an unclouded title from S and transferred an unclouded title to Y, who can transfer an unclouded title to Z.

☞ **Encumbrances:** Because a reasonably prudent purchaser would not be willing to buy a lawsuit, *encumbrances* on the property requiring litigation to clear them up would render title unmarketable and are also considered to be a breach of warranty. (See also the section on deeds, p. 353 below.) Look for these possible encumbrances:

     ☞ **Zoning ordinance:** Any deviation from an applicable zoning ordinance, however slight, should be considered an encumbrance, because it would present the reasonable buyer with fear of litigation.

     Examples of zoning violations that would probably render title unmarketable:

     ❑ Violation of a setback rule, even if only by a fraction of a foot;

     ❑ Proposed sale of a business and property located in an area zoned exclusively for residential use, even though authorities have never tried to shut the business down.

     ☞ **Adverse possession:** Seller's title based on *adverse possession*, unless there has been a judicial determination, is *insufficient* — the buyer shouldn't be required to litigate whether the requirements for adverse possession have been satisfied.

     Example: AP has been in possession of Blackacre for 21 years (the statutory period is 20 years), has never paid any rent to O (the record owner), and has never made any agreement with O. O lives in another city. AP now contracts to sell Blackacre to B. B declines to close on the ground that AP does not have marketable title.

     B will almost certainly win — a title founded upon adverse possession is not marketable, unless there has been an adjudication that the title has passed to the adverse possessor.

☞ **Mortgage:** An outstanding mortgage may be satisfied by the seller — i.e., paid off — at the *closing*, out of the sale proceeds, thereby avoiding a breach of covenant. So the fact that there is a mortgage prior to closing does not mean that the seller has violated the promise to convey marketable title. (But if the mortgage was for more than the proposed selling price, then the mere existence of the mortgage might make title prospectively unmarketable, since the seller wouldn't be able to satisfy the mortgage out of the sale proceeds.)

☞ **Implied:** If the contract is silent about whether there is an obligation to convey marketable title, the requirement of marketable title will be *presumed*.

☞ **Death of either party:** Remember that the *death* of the seller does not prevent the title from being deemed marketable — the seller's estate can make the sale.

Mortgages

☛ **Mortgage assumption:** Pay attention to whether a party takes *"subject to"* a mortgage or *"assumes"* a mortgage. A party who assumes a mortgage agrees to be personally liable for payments on the mortgage note, whereas one who takes subject to the mortgage does not.

  ☞ **Forever liable:** Don't be misled by a fact pattern where there is a series of subsequent sales and the different buyers assume and/or take subject to the mortgage. *All of the parties who assume the mortgage remain liable on the note and can be sued.*

    Example: O sells to A; A assumes the mortgage to Bank. A then sells to B; *B* assumes the mortgage. A is still personally liable to Bank, even though *B* has assumed.

  ☞ **Absolute deed as disguised mortgage:** Be on the lookout for a transaction that's cast as an *absolute sale* of the property, but where the underlying facts show that the parties intended a *financing device*. When this happens, courts will require that mortgage rules (including foreclosure rules) be used.

    Example: O, who owns a house, wants to borrow $200,000 against it for 2 years from Financier. Financier insists that the transaction be done as an outright sale by Financier to O, with O getting a right to re-purchase the house within 2 years for $240,000, a deadline as to which "time is of the essence."

    If O can't come up with the $240,000 by the 2-year deadline, the court will probably treat this as a mortgage, in which case Financier has to use foreclosure proceedings, and O can "redeem" by paying the $240,000 any time up until the foreclosure sale.

  ☞ **Foreclosure not binding on senior mortgagee:** When you encounter a foreclosure fact pattern, remember that *no foreclosure is ever binding* on a mortgagee whose interest is *senior to the foreclosing creditor's interest.*

    Example: Bank lends first to *O*, and takes a mortgage. FinCo lends second, and takes a mortgage. If FinCo forecloses, the foreclosure sale will not wipe out Bank's mortgage — instead, the buyer at the foreclosure will take *subject to Bank's mortgage.* This result occurs even if Bank has notice of FinCo's foreclosure proceeding. (Separately, the foreclosure sale under the FinCo mortgage will cause Bank's mortgage to become immediately due if the Bank mortgage has a "due on sale" clause.)

Deeds

☛ **Deeds generally:** Concentrate on these issues:

  ☞ **Merger:** Remember that if there is a disagreement between the contract and the deed, *the terms of the deed prevail.*

    Example: O owns two adjacent parcels, Whiteacre (where O lives) and Blackacre, a vacant parcel. O and *B* sign a contract under which O agrees to convey Blackacre to B. As O knows, *B* plans to use the property for a factory. The contract is silent about any restrictions on how Blackacre is to be used. At the closing, O hands *B* a deed in which *B* agrees, on behalf of his successors and assigns, to use the property only for residential purposes. *B* reads the deed, pays the sale price, but refuses O's request that *B* sign the deed. O records the deed.

A court will probably hold that *B* (and his successors) may not use the property for non-residential purposes, because in the case of a conflict the deed controls over the contract. (And the fact that *B* refused to sign the deed is irrelevant, because although the Statute of Frauds requires a writing for a land transfer, the recipient's signature on the writing is not considered necessary to satisfy the statute.)

☞ **Identification of property:** Make sure the deed contains an *adequate description* of the realty so that it can be identified.

☞ **Non-traditional descriptions ok:** Don't rule out a description that is not in the traditional form of metes and bounds, markers, or property address as long as the parcel *can be identified with reasonable effort.* (*Example:* Land covered by a grant of "all my land in the state of X..." is easily identifiable, so the grant is adequate.)

☞ **Error in size:** Also, don't void a description that is sufficient to identify the realty, but makes an error as to the *size* of the parcel. (*Example:* X grants "All of my property located on Barrett Road, consisting of four acres of undeveloped land." Even though the realty is a three-acre parcel, the description is adequate.)

☞ **Identification of parties:** Make sure that the parties are adequately described. (*Example:* A deed cannot be made out to "bearer.")

☞ **Error:** Again, though, a less-than-perfect description is not necessarily void — all that's required is that the intended parties be readily identifiable.

Example: A grant of "all my land in the state of X to my niece and nephew Paula and Mark as joint owners." The first names are sufficient if the parties can be accurately identified, i.e., if there are only one niece and one nephew of the grantor with those names.

☛ **Consideration:** Remember that a conveyance can be a gift, so that there is *no* requirement that a deed be *supported by consideration*.

☛ **Delivery:** Delivery issues are the most frequently-tested aspect of deeds.

☞ **Intent to have deed take present effect:** Remember that a deed isn't effective to complete a transfer unless the grantor *intends that the deed be effective immediately.* Therefore, looks for facts showing the grantor's intent to have immediate effect. These may be *words of present intent* (e.g., "I now give..."). Alternatively, present effectiveness may be shown by the fact that the grantor *gives up control over the deed* so that revocation is not possible. It doesn't matter that later on the grantor acts in such a way as to attempt to revoke the grant (by giving a deed to another party).

☞ **Physical delivery to grantee:** *Physical delivery* is a common way of effecting a present transfer. Tricks to watch out for:

☞ **Delivered to cotenant:** Watch for a fact pattern where the deed grants realty in cotenancy and the deed is handed to only one of the tenants. Delivery to one cotenant is usually viewed as *delivery to all cotenants.* Argue that there has been delivery.

☞ **Oral conditions:** Watch for a grantor who imposes an oral *condition* to the effectiveness of the deed. As long as the grantor intends the transfer to be immediately effective, the fact that the grantor has imposed some condition or delay to the effectiveness of the estate in land being transferred won't invalidate the transfer.

Example: G, a landowner, drafts a deed purporting to grant an undivided one-quarter interest in the parcel to C, grantor's chauffeur. G hands C the deed, and says, "Because you have been a good and faithful chauffeur, I'm giving you this deed. But you don't get your interest in the property until I die."

The transfer is likely to be construed as a present transfer of a future interest to become possessory on the grantor's death. In that event, the delivery is valid, despite the condition. Alternatively, however, a court might construe the condition as making the deed itself ineffective until G's death; in that event, the transfer would be completely invalid unless it satisfied the requirements for a will (e.g., notarized and witnessed).

☞ **Remains in the grantor's control:** Look for facts showing that the grantor still has *control over the deed* and is *free to change his mind.* This would mean that delivery did not occur.

☞ **Agent of grantor:** This can happen in fact patterns where the grantor enlists an *agent* to take transfer the deed — while the deed is still in the agent's possession, it probably hasn't been "delivered" yet, since the grantor still has power to terminate the agency and get the deed back.

Example: G gives a deed to her chauffeur, C, and says, "I want you to give this deed to my niece, N. I also want you to go to the bank and the grocery store. Be sure and call me before you come home." C goes to the bank and the grocery store, then checks in with G to find out whether there is anything else she wants him to do. He is told that G died shortly after he left the house. Since C was G's employee, G retained the right and power to change her mind. Consequently, there was no delivery of the deed. The property will instead pass according to G's will.

☞ **Ready to be mailed:** Similarly, a fact pattern may indicate that a deed is ready to be mailed (e.g., it has been placed on the dining room table and the grantor intends to mail it the next morning). If the grantor dies before it is mailed, there has been no delivery.

☞ **Escrow agent:** A grantor who deposits a deed with an *escrow agent* no longer has control over the deed. In this situation, the deed is to be delivered to the grantee upon the happening of a condition outside the grantor's control, and title will pass automatically upon the happening of the specified condition. Consequently, if the grantor dies (or tries to revoke) after the escrow deposit, the transfer will still be *effective.*

☞ **Acceptance:** "*Acceptance*" of the deed is also required. But remember that if a conveyance is beneficial, it is *presumed* to be accepted

☞ **Returned for safekeeping:** Watch for a fact pattern where the grantee *returns the* *deed* to the grantor. If the return is just for safekeeping, this will not equal a lack of acceptance.

Example: G gives Z a deed. Z examines the deed, thanks G, and hands the deed back to G, asking that G hold it for safekeeping. The deed has been accepted by Z, and is thus effective.

☛ **Interest conveyed:** A deed that is silent as to the *type of interest* conveyed, but is otherwise complete, is presumed to convey *whatever interest the grantor holds* at the time of conveyance.

   ☞ **Quitclaim:** Likewise, a *quitclaim deed* conveys only the interest which the grantor holds at the time of its execution. The most important thing about a quitclaim deed is that it includes *no implied warranties* of title.

   ☞ **Estoppel by deed:** Look for a fact pattern where a party attempts to convey an estate which he does not have but *subsequently acquires* title to. The *estoppel-by-deed* doctrine causes the after-acquired title to *pass directly to the grantee.*

      Example: O purports to sell realty to A, who immediately records the deed. O's grandmother is the true owner of the realty. Later, O's grandmother dies, devising the realty to O. Then O deeds the realty to C for full satisfaction of a debt owed to C by O.

      In a contest between A and C, A will win. Under the doctrine of estoppel by deed, title to the realty passed to A immediately upon O's grandmother's death, so there was nothing for O to deed to *C.*

Covenants of title

Covenants of title are not tested very often. A couple of things to look for:

☛ **Breach of covenants as to title, generally:** Most covenant problems relate to the *"present"* covenants (covenants of *seisin*, right to convey and against encumbrances). These are representations that the grantor has a right to convey the title which he purports to convey. The present covenants are breached *only at the time the deed is delivered*, and only the *grantee* can bring an action for damages.

      Example: G grants a fee simple absolute to O, under a warranty deed. O then grants a fee simple to A. It turns out that X, not G, had title to the property. A may not bring an action against O for breach of warranty, because only the grantee may sue for breach of the covenant of seisin. Same result if the breach was because X had an undisclosed easement over the property (breach of covenant against encumbrances).

☛ **Easement:** Sometimes you'll have to know whether the presence of an *easement* in favor of a third party constitutes a breach of the seller's covenant against *encumbrances*.

   ☞ **Buyer unaware:** If the buyer was *unaware* of the easement at the time she took the deed, clearly the easement's existence is a breach of the covenant.

   ☞ **Buyer aware:** If the buyer was aware of the easement at the time she took the deed, courts are split, but many recognize a breach of the covenant here, too.

CHAPTER 12

THE RECORDING SYSTEM AND TITLE ASSURANCE

Introductory note: In this chapter, we examine the various statutory schemes, called recording acts, which govern most priority disputes in real estate. Then we treat various ways in which the buyer of property may be assured that her title is valid; the most significant among these is the title insurance policy.

I. COMMON-LAW PRIORITIES

A. Conflicts in real estate: The vast majority of situations in which there are two or more conflicting claims to a particular piece of real estate are resolved by use of recording acts, discussed below. However, occasionally the recording act will not govern a particular situation, and it becomes important to understand the *common-law* system of priorities.

1. **First in time, first in right:** The only common-law rule of priorities that you need to know is *"first in time, first in right."* In other words, in a contest between successive grantees, the one who received her interest first *has priority over any later taker.* DKA&S, p. 560. This rule applies not only to conflicts between two grantees of estates in land, but also to a conflict between a grantee of an estate and the recipient of an encumbrance like a mortgage or an easement.

    Example: O borrows $100,000 from Bank, and gives Bank a mortgage on Blackacre, which O owns in fee simple. O then sells Blackacre to *B* for the fair market value it would have if unencumbered. *B* has no idea that a mortgage is outstanding. At common law, Bank's mortgage, since it's earlier in time, has priority over *B*'s interest. Therefore, under the common-law approach, if *B* doesn't pay the mortgage, Bank can foreclose.

II. RECORDING STATUTES

A. General function of recording acts: The weaknesses of the common-law scheme in dealing with conflicting claims are readily apparent. Since that scheme generally operates *in favor of the earlier interest,* a prospective buyer has no assurance that he is getting a valid title. He can, of course, make inquiries about whether there has been a prior transaction, but if the seller falsely denies that there has been such a transaction, the later purchaser is out of luck (though he may be able to sue the seller for fraud). The above example, where *B* is subordinated to a prior mortgage he knew nothing about, is a good illustration of the danger to subsequent buyers.

The principal function of *recording acts*, in force in every jurisdiction, is to give this second purchaser a way to *check* whether there has been an earlier transaction. If the earlier transaction is not recorded, the later purchaser will gain priority (though he will probably have to take without actual knowledge of the earlier transaction, and in some courts he will have to record before the earlier transaction is recorded).

> **Example:** Under virtually any modern recording act, if Bank in the prior example did not record, *B* would, as one who took without actual notice of Bank's mortgage and paid valuable consideration, not be subject to Bank's mortgage, assuming *B* recorded promptly after buying.

1. **Bona fide purchasers (BFPs):** Modern recording acts generally protect only *"bona fide purchasers"* (*"BFPs"*). In brief, a person is a BFP, and is thus eligible for protection against an unrecorded prior interest, only if the person took *"for value"* and *"without notice"* of the prior interest. We examine the "for value" requirement *infra*, p. 361, and the "without notice" requirement *infra*, p. 365. For now, just remember that only BFPs are protected.

2. **Relations between original parties:** The recording acts only govern the relationship between a grantee and a subsequent purchaser of the same property, *not the relation between the grantor and grantee under a particular conveyance.*

> **Example:** D conveys the timber located on a particular tract to P. Then, he sells the same timber to X, who promptly records his deed before P has recorded his. Because of the recording act, X's deed takes priority over P's. P sues D for his double-dealing.
>
> *Held*, for P. The recording act has no effect upon the relations between both parties to a particular deed, i.e., P and D. Therefore, P may recover in quasi-contract for the amount by which D was unjustly enriched from his double-dealing (since D should not be allowed to keep the purchase price from P and the purchase price from X for the same property). *Patterson v. Bryant*, 5 S.E.2d 849 (N.D. 1939).

B. **Different types of acts:** There are three basic types of recording acts, the so-called *"pure race"* statues, the *"pure notice"* statues, and the *"race-notice"* statutes. To these three may be added a fourth which is a variant of either the race-notice or pure notice types: the *"period of grace"* statute.

1. **Pure race statute:** A *race* statute places a premium on the *race to the recorder's office.* The subsequent purchaser must *record before the earlier purchaser*, but he is protected *whether or not he has actual notice* of the earlier conveyance.

    a. **Few remain:** Although most of the earliest recording acts were of this nature, very few pure race statutes remain on the books. So you can essentially *ignore* this category of statute.

2. **Pure notice statute:** A pure *notice* statute provides that an unrecorded instrument is invalid as against *any* subsequent purchaser without notice and for value, whether or not the subsequent purchaser records prior to the first purchaser.

    a. **Sample text:** Here is the phrasing of a typical pure notice statute: "No conveyance or mortgage of real property shall be *good against subsequent purchasers for value and without notice* unless the same be *recorded according to law.*"

3. **Race-notice statute:** A *race-notice* statute protects the subsequent purchaser only if he meets *two* requirements: (1) he records *before* the earlier purchaser records; and (2) he takes *without actual notice* of the earlier conveyance.

    a. **Sample text:** Here is the phrasing of a typical *race-notice* statute: "No conveyance or mortgage of real property shall be good against subsequent purchasers for value and without notice, *who shall first record.*"

        i. **Difference:** Notice that the text is exactly the same for this race-notice statute as for the pure notice statute above, except for the addition of the phrase *"who shall first record."* In other words, the race-notice statute simply *adds a second requirement* for the subsequent purchaser who wants to get the benefit of the recording act — not only must the second purchaser take "for value and without notice," but she must "first record" (i.e., *record before the prior interest holder* — against whom the recording act would operate — records).

Illustration: Here's an illustration of how each of the three types of statute would operate: Assume that in 2005, *O* conveys Blackacre to *A*. In 2006, *O* conveys to *B*. In 2007, *B* records. In 2008, *A* records. Here is how the rights of *A* and *B* to Blackacre would be resolved under the three statute types:

    Race: Under a pure race statute, *B* wins automatically, without regard to whether he had actual notice of the earlier conveyance to *A* — *B* recorded his deed before *A* did, so that is the end of the matter. (Had *A* recorded in 2007 and *B* in 2008, *A* would have won, even though at the time *B* took, he had no way to find out about the earlier conveyance to *A*.)

    Notice: Under a pure notice statute, *B* wins. In fact, *B* would have won even if he never recorded at all, or recorded after *A* — the mere fact that *B* took after *A*, and without notice of *A*'s interest, would be enough to give him the victory.

    Race-notice: Under a race-notice statute, *B* will win only if he took without actual notice of *A*'s interest. Furthermore, if *B* had recorded after *A* (instead of before *A*, as really happened), *B* would have lost due to his late recording even if he took without actual notice of *A*'s interest. So under the race-notice statute (probably the most common kind of statute), the subsequent purchaser (here, *B*) has two obstacles to overcome: (1) he must record first; and (2) he must take without actual notice of the earlier interest.

4. **Grace period statute:** There is a fourth type of statute: a *"period-of-grace"* statute protects the first grantee for a *set period* of time *whether or not he records*. If he still has not recorded at the end of the period, he loses this special protection. The period of grace is combined with one of the other types of statutes, usually notice or race-notice. Period of grace provisions were common in earlier days, when it might take days or weeks to get to the recorder's office. Most such statutes have now been repealed.

C. **Mechanics of recording:** It is worth understanding a little bit about the mechanics of recording.

    1. **Deposit with recorder:** The grantee (or the grantee's *title insurance company*) brings the deed to the recording office, which is generally located in the *county where the land lies*. The recorder stamps the date and time of deposit, and usually microfilms the deed;

then, the original deed is returned to the grantee. The copy is then placed in a chronological book containing all recorded deeds. (A separate book may be kept for each of the various types of land interests, e.g., a book for mortgages, a book for tax-sale deeds, a book for ordinary private deeds, etc.; or, all may be consolidated into one book.)

2. **Indexing:** Then, the deeds are *indexed*. A grantor index is almost always prepared, which enables a searcher to find all conveyances made by a given grantor. A grantee index is also almost always made, which permits the searcher to find all conveyances made *to* a particular grantee. In some localities, a *tract* index is prepared; this is extremely valuable, because it enables a searcher to find all transactions involving the particular tract of land in question. How a title searcher uses each of these indexes is discussed extensively *infra*, p. 365.

D. **What instruments must be recorded:** Recording acts generally apply to nearly every instrument by which an interest in land, *whether legal or equitable*, is created or modified. Thus not only fee simple conveyances, but also mortgages, restrictive covenants, tax liens, etc., are brought within the recording act. Furthermore, any instrument *modifying* any of these (e.g., a satisfaction of mortgage) is brought with the act. Thus all of these documents must be recorded, or their holder runs the risk of having his interest subordinated to that of a later purchaser.

1. **Unrecordable interests:** However, there are a few sorts of interests which do not have to be recorded. In any priority dispute involving such an interest, the recording acts become *irrelevant*, and the conflict is governed by common-law principles.

     a. **Adverse possession:** The most important category of interests which do not have to be recorded (and which in fact are not recordable) are *titles based upon adverse possession*. Adverse possession, of course, does not give rise to an instrument at all; therefore, the adverse possessor does not have to record.

         i. **Adverse possessor has priority:** In a priority dispute between an adverse possessor and the grantee of a conveyance executed after the adverse possessor's claim ripened, the *adverse possessor will prevail* based upon the common-law rule that the earlier in time of two interests takes priority. (See *supra*, p. 357.)

2. **Written but unrecordable interests:** In addition to the above non-documentary interests, there are a few types of interests which are represented by instruments, but which are nonetheless treated as *non-recordable* by the particular recording act.

     a. **Short leases:** For instance, in many states, a *short-term lease* (e.g., less than three years), may not be recorded. If so, that lease will be valid against a subsequent *bona fide* purchaser. 4 A.L.P. 551.

     b. **Executory contract:** Similarly, some states do not permit executory *contracts of sale* to be recorded. If so, the buyer suffers no statutory penalty by failing to record (but even under common-law principles, his equitable interest will be subordinate to that of a subsequent legal claimant who takes without notice).

         i. **Contract of sale:** On the other hand, most states *allow* a contract of sale to be recorded (assuming that the contract otherwise meets the jurisdiction's requirements for a recordable interest in land, such as being signed, witnessed and/or notarized) even though they don't *require* recordation. In such a state, if the contract is recorded the rights of the contract vendee to close under the contract will be *superior* to the rights of any subsequent grantee, mortgagee, judgment creditor, etc., of the vendor.

    (1) Typical scenario: A typical scenario is where the contract is properly recorded, and the vendor then grants a mortgage to, or suffers a judgment lien by, someone else. In such a scenario, the rights of the contract vendee prevail over the later-created interest.

    Example: On Feb. 1, Ven contracts to sell Blackacre to Pur, in a document that meets local requirements for recording (e.g., it's notarized). On Feb. 2, Pur records the contract. On Feb. 3, Ven borrows $100,000 from Bank, giving Bank a mortgage on the property which Bank immediately records. Pur has priority over Bank, so on the closing date Pur can tender a check for the purchase amount to Ven and receive clear title (whether or not Ven pays over the first $100,000 of proceeds to Bank).

    (2) Incentives: Notice that the *vendee* will usually have an *incentive to record*, and the *vendor* will usually have an incentive to *prevent recording* (e.g., by refusing to have the contract witnessed or notarized, a precondition to recording in most states).

E. Parties protected: If a grantee fails to record, what groups of persons may claim the benefit of the recording act? We put aside the possible requirement that the subsequent grantee record (a requirement imposed by race and race-notice jurisdictions). Also, we defer for later discussion (beginning *infra*, p. 364), the issue of what constitutes "notice" in a notice or race-notice jurisdiction. The issue we focus on here is the requirement that the subsequent grantee either be a *"purchaser for value"* or a creditor meeting certain standards.

    1. Purchaser for value: In the substantial majority of states, a grantee receives the benefit of the recording act (i.e., he may take priority over an earlier unrecorded conveyance) only if he *gives value* for his interest. As the idea is usually put in these statutes, the earlier unrecorded conveyance is "void as against any subsequent purchaser in good faith and *for a valuable consideration*."

    2. Donee: Under the typical statute requiring that the subsequent grantee have taken "for value" (i.e., paid consideration), a *donee* will *not be protected* by the act. Furthermore, many statutes which do not expressly require payment of consideration by the subsequent grantee have been *judicially interpreted* to include such a requirement.

        Example: *O* conveys to *A*. *O* then purports to give the property, for no consideration, to *B*. *B* records, *A* never does. Under most statutes, *B* still loses to *A*, because *B* — although he is a subsequent grantee who recorded first — did not give valuable consideration.

    3. Less than market value: Though the grantee is typically required to have given consideration for the conveyance, that consideration does *not* have to be an amount *equal to the market value of the property.* 4 A.L.P. 557.

a. Nominal consideration: On the other hand, most courts hold that it is **not** enough that the grantee paid merely **nominal** consideration, or that the deed **recites** substantial payment of value when in fact **no value was paid**.

4. Creditors: **Creditors** of a landowner may also come within the protection of the recording acts.

a. Mortgage creditors: **Lenders** or other creditors who obtain a lien against the property by means of a **mortgage** often will be deemed to have given value, so that they can receive the protection of the recording act. But it makes a difference whether the lender/creditor gave "new value" in exchange for the mortgage, or instead got the mortgage on account of an "antecedent debt" without giving any new value.

i. Mortgage given for simultaneous loan: If a person **makes a loan** on the property in return for a **simultaneously-issued** mortgage, and then records the mortgage, the making of the loan clearly counts as "giving value." The lender is therefore entitled to the protection of the recording act.

Example: *O* conveys Blackacre to *A*. *A* doesn't record. *O* borrows $100,000 from *B*, and gives *B* a mortgage. *B* records the mortgage. *A* then records. *B* will be deemed to have "given value" in return for the mortgage. Therefore, if *O* doesn't repay the loan, *B*'s right to foreclose will be superior to *A*'s later-filed deed.

ii. Mortgage given for antecedent debt: On the other hand, if an unsecured creditor receives a fresh **mortgage** from the debtor on behalf of an **antecedent debt**, the creditor must generally meet the consideration requirement anew.

(1) "New value" satisfied: This means that if the mortgagee is giving something of **new value** (e.g., cancelling part of the debt in return for the mortgage, or extending the debtor's time to pay), he will probably be deemed to have given consideration, and will thus be protected against a prior unrecorded conveyance.

(2) "New value" not satisfied: But if mortgagee merely **retains** the same non-mortgage-related rights he always had (to be paid the full amount of his debt, at the time promised), then he is *not* giving new value, and his newly-issued mortgage will **not be protected** against a prior unrecorded conveyance.

b. Unsecured creditors: An **unsecured**, general, creditor gains **no protection at all** from the recording acts.

Example: O, in return for receiving a loan from Bank, simultaneously gives Bank a mortgage on O's house. Bank does not promptly record. Finance Co. then makes an unsecured loan to O, not knowing of Bank's mortgage. Now, Bank finally records.

Even though Bank had not recorded prior to Finance Co's extending unsecured credit to O, Finance Co. doesn't get the benefit of the recording act, because Finance Co's unsecured loan has not been recorded (and, indeed is not eligible to be recorded, because it's not an interest in O's real property). Therefore, Bank's interest has priority under the common-law "first in time" principle (*supra*, p. 357).

c. **Judgment creditors:** A pre-existing creditor who obtains and files a *judgment* gets a *lien* against the debtor's property. This lien may or may not be protected under the recording act against a prior unrecorded purchase or mortgage, depending on how the statute is drafted.

    i. **Lien creditor loses:** Under most statutes, the judgment lien creditor will *lose*. Sometimes, this is because he won't be deemed to have given "value." Alternatively, in the most common case where the recording statute protects only "purchasers for value," the judgment lien creditor *won't be deemed to be a "purchaser"* at all (whether he gets credit for having given value or not), so he won't get the protection of the act.

    ii. **Where judgment lien creditor takes first and records promptly:** In any event, where the judgment lien creditor takes his interest *first*, and records first, *you don't have to worry about whether the judgment lien creditor has bona fide purchaser status.* That's because recording acts can only protect a *second* purchaser (not a first purchaser), and the BFP concept (see *supra*, p. 358) only affects those who try to get protection from recording acts.

        Example: Cred, an unsecured creditor of O, gets a judgment against O on July 1, and immediately records that judgment as a lien against O's house, as permitted by local lien law. The state's recording act protects only one who takes "for value and without notice." On Aug. 1, O sells the house to Buy, who takes for value and without actual notice of Cred's judgment lien.

        Cred's lien has priority over Buy's title. And that's true whether Cred would have qualified for the protection of the recording act (i.e., whether he would be deemed to have taken "for value") had he taken after Buy took. Since Cred "took" *first* and filed first, the recording act's requirement that those to be protected must take for value is *irrelevant* — since a recording act protects only the later-in-time interests, the act's "take for value" requirement *never applies to the earlier-in-time interest.*

      (1) **After-acquired property:** A common sub-variant of the "judgment lien creditor takes first" scenario is that the judgment lien creditor takes *before the debtor even owns the property in question,* and the debtor *later acquires* the property. Typically, a judgment creditor's lien is valid against *subsequently-acquired property* of the debtor for some period of time (e.g., 10 years). If so, the judgment creditor will always *win,* except if the subsequent claimant is a purchase-money mortgagee. [1]

---

1. Nearly all states give a special priority to *purchase-money mortgages.* If a judgment debtor or other person with liens against him *buys new property* with the help of a purchase-money mortgage (i.e., a mortgage securing a loan made to help the debtor acquire the property), the *purchase-money lender has priority over all prior lienholders.* Otherwise, a person with outstanding judgments and liens against him could never buy real estate without paying full price in cash, because no lender could safely lend to facilitate the acquisition. Such a result would violate the public policy of encouraging people to buy real estate, especially homes.

F. Recording first in a race or race-notice state: Always remember to check the possibility that the second purchaser has *failed to win any required race by recording before the prior interest was recorded.*

1. **Second buyer must win the race:** Recall, *supra*, p. 359, that many states have race-notice statutes, under which *the second purchaser,* in order to get the protection of the recording act, *must record before the first one does.* So if your problem involves a race-notice statute, make sure that the second purchaser indeed recorded first.

   Example: The recording statute says that "No conveyance or mortgage of real property shall be good against subsequent purchasers for value and without notice, who shall first record." On Feb. 1, *O* conveys to *A* as a gift. On Feb. 2, *O* conveys for value to *B*, who does not know of the conveyance to *A*. On Feb. 3, *A* hears about the conveyance to *B*, and rushes to the courthouse and records. On Feb. 4, *B* records.

   A wins — *B* is second-in-time, so she loses unless the recording act protects her. Under this race-notice statute *B* could win only if she (1) took without notice of the earlier conveyance to *A*; (2) took for value; and (3) recorded before *A* recorded. *B* didn't satisfy (3), so she loses.

G. Formal requirements for recording: In a race or race-notice jurisdiction, the subsequent purchaser will of course be protected only if he records his deed. Furthermore, the instrument must be one which is in fact *eligible to be recorded.* If it is not, the purchaser will not be protected even if the recording clerk makes a mistake and accepts the document.

Example: O conveys to P, who does not record. O then conveys to X, but the deed is improperly acknowledged (because O does not appear before the notary). Since the improper acknowledgment is not apparent from the face of the deed, the recorder accepts it for recording. X then conveys to D, who records. Only after that does P record his deed.

Held, D is not entitled to the benefit of the recording act as against P, because a deed in D's chain of title (the deed to D's grantor) was not capable of being recorded even though it was in fact recorded. *Messersmith v. Smith*, 60 N.W.2d 276 (N.D. 1953).

1. **Must record whole chain of title:** The *Messersmith* case also illustrates that in a race or race-notice jurisdiction, the subsequent grantee must see to it that his *entire chain of title* is recorded, not just his own conveyance. (This requirement is discussed further *infra*, p. 368.) Normally, this is not an unreasonable requirement to place on the subsequent grantee. But in a case like *Messersmith*, where there was no way D could have known that the earlier deed in his chain was not properly recordable even though it was recorded, the result seems harsh and unfair; certainly P, who had failed to record his deed, was not in any way prejudiced by the "unrecordability" of the deed to X.

2. **Forged deeds:** Recording acts do not protect purchasers (even BFPs) who receive *forged deeds.*

   Example: In 2005, *O* is the record owner of Blackacre. In 2006, *A* forges a deed reading "from *O* to *A*," and records it. In 2007, *A* purports to sell Blackacre to *B* (and receives from *B* the full market value of the property), via a deed reading "*A* to *B* in fee simple." *B* records. In an action between *O* and *B*, *B* loses, even though *B* is a BFP and has perfect record title.

a. **Satisfaction of mortgage:** The same principle operates in connection with a forgery of a *release or satisfaction of a mortgage.* In other words, if the owner of mortgage property forges a satisfaction-of-mortgage document from the lender and records it, any purchaser of the property from that owner *takes subject to the mortgage.*

b. **Title insurance:** Gaining protection against forged deeds and forged satisfactions-of-mortgage earlier in the chain of title is one of the main purposes of buying *title insurance*, discussed *infra*, p. 376.

H. Notice to subsequent claimants: In all jurisdictions except those having pure race statutes, the most important question is likely to be: was the subsequent purchaser put on *notice* of the earlier deed? (Even in a pure race jurisdiction, the existence of notice via filing will be relevant.) There are generally considered to be three types of notice: (1) *actual* notice; (2) *record* notice; and (3) *"inquiry"* notice. We discuss each of these in a separate section below.

I. Actual notice: If the subsequent purchaser is shown to have had *actual notice* of the existence of the prior unrecorded interest, he will not gain the protection of the recording act in a notice or a race-notice jurisdiction.

J. Record notice: One function of the recording acts is to assure the holder of an interest that if he records it, he will not be vulnerable as against any subsequent interest. Therefore, *adequate recording* will always constitute notice (called *"record notice"*) to subsequent claimants. However, the mere fact that a deed is recorded somewhere in the public records does not mean that the recording is adequate.

1. **Defective document:** A document which is *not entitled to be recorded* will not give record notice, even if the document is in fact mistakenly accepted for recording. For instance, a document that is *not acknowledged*, in a jurisdiction which requires acknowledgement, will not give record notice.

   a. **Curative acts:** However, most states have adopted *"curative"* acts. These provide that after the expiration of a certain period of time following recording, the failure to conform to certain formal requirements for recording ceases to be material. Typically, these acts apply to defective acknowledgement, lack of signature, irregularity in a probate proceeding, or infirmity in a tax sale or judicial sale of the property.

2. **Mechanics of title examination:** Proper recording places subsequent purchasers on notice even if they *never actually see* the document that has been filed. That is, the court imputes to the subsequent purchaser that knowledge which he *would have obtained* had he conducted a *diligent title search*. To know what documents a diligent title searcher would find, it is necessary to have a fairly detailed understanding of the mechanics of title examination.

   a. **Two indexes:** All recording offices maintain two vital sets of indexes. One of these is the *grantor* index, which lists in alphabetical order all persons who have become grantors, the date upon which they did so, the grantee, perhaps a brief description of the property, and a reference to the book in which the full instrument is recorded. The other major index is the *grantee* index, which is similar to the grantor index except that it is organized by alphabetical order of grantees. Thus if one were interested in a deed from John Smith to William Doe, one could locate it by looking in the grantor index under "Smith" or by looking in the grantee index under "Doe"; either of these indexes would point to the same bound volume and page number where the deed itself was recorded.

b. Tracing back to root: The first step in searching title is to establish a *"root"* from which the title can be traced back down to the present. One begins by deciding upon a *time limit* for the search. Typically, only the *most recent 50 or 60 years* of ownership of the property are searched, since it is unlikely that a defect in the chain of title from before that time will have present implications. C&L, pp. 878-80. Then, it is necessary to find out *who owned the property, say 50 years ago*. This person, once he can be found, is the "root."

    i. Use of grantee index: The way the "root" is located is by use of the grantee index. The title searcher of course knows the name of the present potential seller. Let us assume that his name is David Drew. At some point, obviously, David Drew should have become a grantee of the property, so his name will be listed in the grantee index. Searching the grantee index, we find that the property was conveyed to Drew by Charles Crow. Now checking Crow in the grantee index, we find that he took from Bernard Bird, and checking Bird, we find that he took from Abner Ax. If we find that Abner Ax had record title to the property 50 years ago, he will be our "root."

    ii. Breaks in chain: In this checking backward process, there are likely to be breaks in the chain. The grantee index included only those who took by *inter vivos* conveyance. Thus one who has obtained his title by *will* or *intestacy* will not be shown; instead, the local *probate records* will have to be checked. (This may be difficult, since we don't know the name of the decedent; all we can do is to hope that it is the same surname as that of the person we believe took by the will or intestacy.) Similarly, a *tax sale* might break the chain, so the registry of tax deeds would have to be checked on the chance that there was such a sale.

c. Tracing forward to present: Once the "root" has been located, the title searcher starts the really important part of his task. It is now necessary to trace the title *back down through the present*, making sure that *each grantee did not dispose of the property except via the chain of title that leads to present prospective seller.*

Example: Assume that by the tracing-backwards-through-the-grantee-index procedure, we have established that Abner Ax is our root, and that he took the property in 1952. Using the *grantor* index, we check to see if Ax made any conveyances of the property at any time after 1952. If we are in luck, we will find that he made no conveyances of the property before conveying to Bernard Bird (who, it will be recalled, was part of our backwards chain of title) in 1968. The deed from Ax to Bird will be scrutinized, to see whether it indicated any defect in title (e.g., that the property is subject to a restrictive covenant in favor of Ax).

Then, Bernard Bird's name will be searched in the grantor index for the period from 1968 until his first conveyance of the property (which, we hope, will be to Charles Crow). Suppose that the conveyance to Crow is indeed the first, and that it occurred in 1983. Then Crow will be searched in the grantor index from 1983 until the conveyance to David Drew (the prospective seller). If Drew took in 2000, his name will have to be searched in the grantor index from 2000 down to the present, to make sure that he has not already disposed of the property.

d. Mortgages: During the search, it may develop that the property was **mortgaged** at various times. There ought to be a **satisfaction of mortgage** recorded for each of these mortgages except for the one held by the present seller. But if there is a lack of a mortgage satisfaction, it may not be fatal if the mortgage itself dates back more than a certain period; the period is usually related to the statute of limitations, and is established by local title-searching custom.

e. Probate proceedings: If one of the links in the chain is a **probate proceeding**, the will will have to be examined to see who was entitled to the property.

f. Tract indexes: In a few jurisdictions, the recorder's office maintains a **tract index**, i.e., an index showing all transactions in connection with a particular tract of land (e.g, a city block). This renders the title searcher's job much easier, since: (1) there is less chance of confusion from similar grantor or grantee names, or from the fact that a grantor has had interests in several parcels in the same county; and (2) one can go further back, and trace the title of each grantee all the way down to the present without undue effort, so that many of the "chain of title" problems, discussed *infra*, are eliminated. Even where the recorder's office does not maintain a tract index, the title companies maintain a "plant," or abstract, for each parcel, which amounts to the same thing (see *infra*, p. 376).

3. **"Chain of title" problems:** As the above discussion of the mechanics of title searching makes clear, the searcher is heavily dependent upon the grantor and grantee indexes, and upon the need to search these indexes only for the time that a grantor appears on the record to have title. Since any search is conducted only within these limits, it is quite possible that the search will not find a deed which in fact affects the title, but which is "lost" within the vastness of the recorder's office. In general, the recording of an instrument gives record notice to a subsequent searcher only if that searcher **would have found the document** using the generally-accepted searching principles discussed above. A recorded instrument which would not be found by these principles is said to be **outside of the searcher's "chain of title."** Here are a few of the important scenarios raising issues about whether a recorded instrument is within or outside the chain of title.

a. Unrecorded links: Recall that once the searcher has established a "root" of title, he then traces title by using the grantor index, checking that index for each person known to have been a grantee. If there is an **unrecorded deed** from a known grantee to a third person, then even if the deed from that third person to someone else, and all subsequent deeds, are recorded, the searcher will have no way of finding them, and these deeds will not be of record notice to him.

Example: *A* owns Blackacre. *A* conveys to *B*, and *B* records. *B* conveys to *C*, and *C* does not record. *B* conveys a second time, to *D*, and *D* records. *C* conveys to *E*, and *E* records his own deed, but not the deed from *B* to *C*. *D* now wants to sell to *F*. *F* checks the records. He will find the deed from *B* to *C*, and the deed from *A* to *B*. But *F* will never have occasion to discover that there was an unrecorded deed from *B* to *C*. F will also therefore never look in the grantor index under *C*, so he'll fail to find the *C*-to-*E* deed even though that deed is recorded.

i. **"Wild" or "fugitive" deed:**   An instrument issued by a grantor whose own source of title is not recorded is commonly referred to as a *"wild"* or *"fugitive"* instrument. In the above example, the *C* to *E* deed is wild.

ii. **B.F.P. must record whole chain:** Sometimes, it is the holder of the *prior* instrument who runs afoul of the rule that the entire chain of title must be recorded. But the requirement that the whole chain be recorded must also be observed by a ***subsequent bona fide purchaser*** who wishes to gain the recording act's protection against prior unrecorded instruments. That is, the *bona fide* purchaser must see that his ***entire chain of title*** is recorded, if he is to prevail against a prior unrecorded document. (This can be thought of as an illustration of the general rule that the subsequent *bona fide* purchaser gains the protection of the recording act only if the deed was both recorded and properly recordable; see *supra*, p. 364.)

b. **Misindexing:** The theory behind the "chain of title" rules is that a searcher will rely heavily upon the grantor and grantee indexes. This being the case, one would think that if the recorder's office ***misindexed*** a deed, this would place the deed outside the chain of title. However, in the substantial majority of states, the grantor and grantee indexes are ***not always required by statute***. In these states, the courts have almost always held that a ***mistake in indexing*** does ***not*** remove the deed itself from the chain of title. 4 A.L.P. 603-05.

c. **Early-recorded documents:** The title searcher will always begin checking the grantor index under a particular owner ***only from the date on which that owner gained title***. Normally this will be adequate, but there is one situation (in some states) where a conveyance made by a grantor ***before*** he became owner of the property may have an effect upon the title.

i. **Estoppel by deed:** This situation is caused by application of the common-law doctrine of ***estoppel by deed***. That doctrine holds that where a person (call him O) makes a conveyance of property to another (call him *A*) before he has ever obtained title, and then subsequently the grantor (O) does obtain title, this title ***passes immediately*** to the grantee (*A*). The name "estoppel by deed" arises from the fact that the grantor is "estopped" from denying the validity of his earlier deed.

ii. **Effect on title searcher:** If the estoppel by deed doctrine is applied, and the estoppel is held to be binding upon a subsequent *bona fide* purchaser, then that purchaser's failure to check the records prior to the date the owner of record obtained title will be ***ruinous***.

Example: O is the son of X, the record owner of Blackacre, who has promised to leave the property to O in X's will. In 2004, while X is still alive, O purports to convey the property to *A*; *A* believes O is already the owner, and gives valuable consideration. *A* properly records the deed. In 2005, X dies and, as promised, leaves the property to O. In 2006, O conveys to *B*, who is a purchaser for value and is without notice of the prior O-to-*A* transfer. Right before taking, *B* checks the grantor index to make sure that O didn't convey the property at any time after he took in 2005 (but *B* feels no need to check the index for conveyances by O prior to the date in 2005 when X left the property to O). The jurisdiction applies the estoppel-by-deed doctrine, at least as between the grantor and the grantee.

The estoppel-by-deed doctrine means that as soon as O took in 2005, title was deemed immediately vested in *A*. Yet *B*, even though he has checked the grantor index for all times when O was the record owner, never had reason to discover the O-to-*A* deed. If the O-to-*A* deed is deemed to be within O's chain of title, then *B* loses (since recording acts protect only against conveyances that have not been properly recorded within the grantor's chain of title), even though he "did everything right" when he checked the records.

iii. Majority view: Because of the unfairness of the scenario shown in the above example, a *majority* of courts hold that even though the estoppel by deed doctrine may apply as between the original grantor and grantee (e.g., as between O and *A* in the above example), the doctrine is *not binding against a subsequent good-faith purchaser*. This seems to be a much better rule, since it means that a title searcher does not have to check the grantor index under a particular owner's name *until the date on which that person is shown to have become the owner* of record.

Example: So on the facts of the above example, under the majority approach the O-to-*A* deed is not within *B*'s chain of title, and *B* therefore gets the protection of the recording act as against *A*. (It was up to *A* to make sure that his grantor, O, really was the owner at the time O purported to convey to *A*.)

d. Easements and servitudes prior to subdivision: The owner of a parcel may sell part of it, and in so doing give the grantee rights against the grantor's remaining property (e.g., an *easement* or the benefit of an *equitable servitude*). When the grantor then sells his remaining land, the purchaser will not necessarily discover the existence of these interests.

i. Split: The courts are about *evenly split* as to whether the purchaser of the land retained by the grantor is on record notice of these interests.

e. Effect of actual or inquiry notice: Keep in mind that even though an instrument may be outside the title searcher's chain of title, either *actual* or *"inquiry"* notice may exist as to that instrument. For instance, suppose the deed to the buyer states that the title being conveyed is "subject to any land-use restrictions imposed by a previous deed to X." This will be enough to put the buyer on inquiry notice of any equitable restrictions in the deed to X, and the fact that the deed to X is not in P's chain of title will be irrelevant. Inquiry notice is discussed immediately below.

K. Inquiry notice: Even if the purchaser has neither record nor actual notice of a prior unrecorded conveyance, he may be found to have been on *"inquiry" notice* of it. Inquiry notice exists where the circumstances are such that a purchaser is in *possession of facts which would lead a reasonable person in his position* to make an *investigation*, which would in turn advise him of the existence of the prior unrecorded right. Just as a purchaser is on record notice even though he never sees the prior recorded instrument, so a purchaser is on inquiry notice *even if he does not in fact make the investigation*.

1. **Only what search would have disclosed:** However, even where there are facts which would lead the purchaser to make an investigation, he will be responsible for *only those facts which the investigation would have disclosed*. 4 A.L.P. 566-67.

2. **Notice based on possession of property:** The most important source of inquiry notice is *possession* of the parcel in question by a person who is *not the record owner*. Therefore, to be safe:

   [1] the purchaser must *view* the property, to see whether it is in the possession of someone other than the record owner; and

   [2] if there is such a possessor, the purchaser must *inquire as to the source* of the possessor's rights in the property.

   > **Example:** *O* conveys a house to *A* as a gift. *A* doesn't record, but takes possession and lives at the house. *O* then conveys the house to *B*. *B* pays fair value, and at the time of closing does not have actual knowledge of *A*'s unrecorded deed (or of the fact that *A* is in possession of the premises). After the closing, *B* discovers *A*'s deed and possession.
   >
   > In a contest between *A* and *B*, *A* will win if the court concludes (as it probably would) that *A*'s possession put *B* on inquiry notice of *A*'s interest. That is, the court would likely conclude that if *B* had inspected the premises before closing, he would have discovered *A*'s presence, and would have asked questions that would have led him to learn of *A*'s paramount title. In this scenario, *B* would not be a subsequent purchaser "without notice," and would therefore lose the protection of the recording act.

   a. **Easements:** Often the inquiry-notice issue comes up in connection with an *easement*. If the second grantee would have seen *visible evidence of the easement's existence* had she viewed the property (e.g., a *driveway* or well-worn *path*), then that second grantee will be deemed to be on inquiry notice of the easement even if she had no actual notice of it.

   b. **Possession consistent with record title:** Suppose the prospective purchaser views the property, and discovers that it's possessed by someone other than the record owner. In that situation, if the possession of property is *consistent with the record title*, the purchaser is generally entitled to assume that the possessor has *no additional, unrecorded, rights*.

   > **Example:** The record shows that title to Blackacre is held by *A* and *B* as tenants in common. *B* conveys his undivided one-half interest to *A*, but the deed is not recorded. *A* is in sole possession. *B* then purports to convey his one-half interest to C, who does not have actual knowledge of *B*'s unrecorded conveyance to *A*. Despite *A*'s sole possession of the property, C was not put on inquiry notice; he was entitled to ignore *A*'s possession, since that possession was consistent with the record title (because either tenant in common has the right to full possession and use of the property; see *supra*, p. 147). 4 A.L.P. 580.

      i. **Exception for tenant:** However, an exception to the "possession consistent with record title" rule is usually made where the possessor is shown by the record to be a *tenant*. The reason for this is that informal unrecorded modifications of lease rights (e.g., an extension to the term of the lease, or an option to purchase the leased premises) are so common that the usual assumption that the possessor has no rights not shown in the record is unwarranted. See generally 4 A.L.P. 577.

L. Purchaser from one without notice: Assume that a purchaser takes without notice of a prior unrecorded instrument. When he *resells* the property (or makes a gift of it), what is the effect of knowledge either by him, or by the new purchaser/donee, of the unrecorded document?

   1. Protection of seller's market: In order to protect the innocent purchaser's market for the property, the courts uniformly hold that the new purchaser or donee is to be treated as a *bona fide* purchaser who may claim the benefit of the recording act, *even if he buys or takes with actual notice*, 4 A.L.P. 567-58. That is, once an interest is purged by its acquisition by one without notice of the prior unrecorded document, the interest remains "clean."

> **Example:** In a jurisdiction with a race-notice statute, *O* conveys to *A*. *A* does not record. *O* conveys to *B* for value; *B* does not know of the conveyance to *A*. *B* records. *A* then finally records. *B* gifts the property to *C*, who at the time he takes knows of the late-recorded deed to *A*.
>
> In a contest between *A* and *C*, *C* wins because *B*'s act of taking without notice of the grant to *A*, and for value, plus her prompt recording, cut off all rights of *A*. Therefore, *B* can and does pass fee simple to *C*, regardless of whether *C* took for value and/ or took without notice of the late-recorded deed to *A*.

III. TITLE REGISTRATION (THE TORRENS SYSTEM)

   A. Nature of registration: In the recording systems which we have examined thus far, the record merely furnishes *evidence* of title. In parts of the U.S., by contrast, a quite different optional system is available, in which *the title itself* is registered. This system, called the *title registration* system or *Torrens* System, enables the owner of a parcel to obtain a *certificate of title*, similar to an automobile certificate of title. When the holder of the certificate wishes to sell the property, his prospective purchaser merely has to inspect the certificate itself (on which nearly all encumbrances must be noted), and a lengthy title examination is unnecessary.

      1. American use: The Torrens System has never really caught on in most of the U.S. Today, there are only five states that have a substantial amount of land registered under the Torrens System: Hawaii, Illinois (Cook County), Massachusetts, Minnesota (Hennepin and Ramsey Counties) and Ohio (Hamilton County). See DKA&S, p. 617.

         a. Never required: In no place is the owner of land *required* to register under the Torrens System (though once an owner does so, subsequent owners must continue under the System).

   B. How the System works: Because the Torrens System is entirely optional, the registration process begins with an *application* by a person claiming ownership of a parcel to have it registered.

      1. Notice to all record interests: The registration clerk, after receiving the registration application, inspects the ordinary land records to ascertain the names of all persons who

Figure 12-1
Determining Who Wins under a Recording Act

Use this chart to figure out who wins in a contest between two grantees. A is the first (in time) to receive a grant; B is the second to receive the grant. A and B do not necessarily have to have received their grant from the same grantor to be covered by this chart. (For the special problems if they've taken from different grantors, see box [17] and the footnote thereto.) ("C/L" = "common law.")

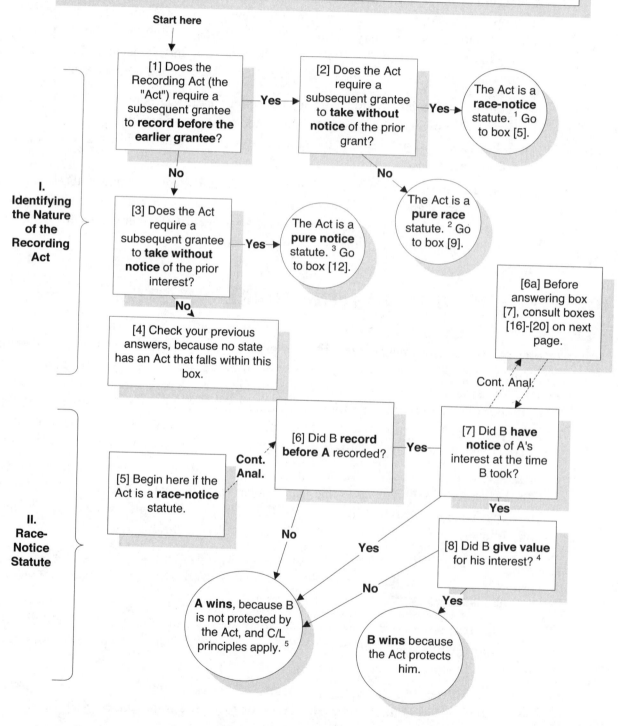

Start here

I. Identifying the Nature of the Recording Act

[1] Does the Recording Act (the "Act") require a subsequent grantee to **record before the earlier grantee**?

[2] Does the Act require a subsequent grantee to **take without notice** of the prior grant?

The Act is a **race-notice** statute.[1] Go to box [5].

[3] Does the Act require a subsequent grantee to **take without notice** of the prior interest?

The Act is a **pure notice** statute.[3] Go to box [12].

The Act is a **pure race** statute.[2] Go to box [9].

[4] Check your previous answers, because no state has an Act that falls within this box.

[6a] Before answering box [7], consult boxes [16]-[20] on next page.

II. Race-Notice Statute

[5] Begin here if the Act is a **race-notice** statute.

Cont. Anal.

[6] Did B **record before A** recorded?

[7] Did B **have notice** of A's interest at the time B took?

Cont. Anal.

[8] Did B **give value** for his interest?[4]

A wins, because B is not protected by the Act, and C/L principles apply.[5]

B wins because the Act protects him.

Notes start on page after next.

Figure 12-1 (cont.)
Determining Who Wins under a Recording Act

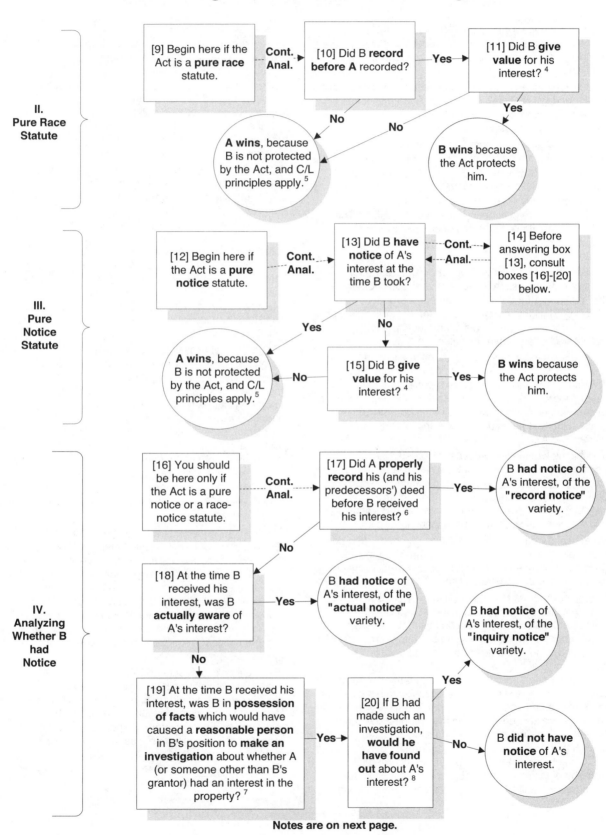

Notes are on next page.

Notes to
Figure 12-1 (Determining Who Wins under a Recording Act)

[1] Typical language for a race-notice statute: "No conveyance or mortgage of real property shall be good against subsequent purchasers for value and without notice, who shall first record."

[2] Typical language for a pure race statute: "No conveyance or mortgage of real property shall be good against a subsequent purchaser who shall first record." (There are very few pure race statutes left on the books.)

[3] Typical language for a pure notice statute: "No conveyance or mortgage of real property shall be good against subsequent purchasers for value and without notice unless the same be recorded according to law."

[4] In the substantial majority of states (though not in all), the recording act protects only "purchasers for value." The most significant thing to watch out for is that a donee -- one who receives the property as a gift -- is not a purchaser for value.

If the grantee has received the property in return for paying real, but less than market-value, consideration, the "purchaser for value" requirement is probably satisfied. Similarly, a mortgage lender who makes a loan to the "grantor" and receives a mortgage in return qualifies as a "purchaser for value."

[5] Recording acts by their nature are only designed to protect the later grantee (B), not the earlier one (A). Therefore, if B does not qualify for protection, the Act simply doesn't apply. Then, the case is decided according to common-law principles. At common law, the first-granted interest takes priority over the later-granted interest, so A wins.

[6] In deciding whether A "properly" recorded, the most important thing to worry about is whether A recorded his whole "chain of title." That is, A must have recorded any previously-unrecorded deeds leading to his deed, in a way that would have enabled a searcher in B's position to find A's deed using standard searching principles.

Be especially careful about whether A properly recorded his whole chain when A and B took from different grantors, because that's when the chain-of-title concept is likely to make the most difference.

Example: Al owns Blackacre. Al conveys to Bert, and Bert records. Bert conveys to Charlie, and Charlie does not record. Bert conveys a second time, to Dave, and Dave records. Charlie conveys to Ed, and Ed records his own deed, but not the deed from Bert to Charlie. Dave now wants to sell to Fred. Fred checks the records. He will find the deed from Bert to Dave, and the deed from Al to Bert. But Fred will never have occasion to discover that there was an unrecorded deed from Bert to Charlie. Fred will therefore also never look in the grantor index under Charlie, so he'll fail to find the Charlie-to-Ed deed even though that deed is recorded. Therefore, on these facts Ed will be found not to have "properly" recorded his deed, since he didn't record his whole chain. Thus Fred will not have "record notice" of Ed's interest, and Fred will win

under the recording act vis a vis Ed.

[7] There are two main ways in which B may know facts that would cause a reasonable person to make an investigation: (1) there are references, in the recorded deeds that are part of A's chain of title, to another interest, which is either completely unrecorded or recorded outside A's chain of title; or (2) the property is in the physical possession of someone who is not the record owner, and whose possession is inconsistent with the record title.

Example 1 (reference in recorded deed): O conveys mineral rights on O's property to X. The mineral-rights deed is never recorded. O then conveys the fee simple to A. This deed mentions that the conveyance is "subject to the mineral rights previously conveyed by O to X." The O-to-A deed is properly recorded. A now conveys to B, who promptly records. B then discovers that X is mining the minerals, and sues to stop X. B will be found to have been in possession, at the time he took from A, of facts that would have led a reasonable person in his position to make an investigation about the mineral rights.

Example 2 (possession): Same basic facts as Example 1. Now, however, assume that the O-to-A deed is silent about mineral rights, but further assume that X has built a large oil well on the property that, at the time B buys from A, is busy pumping away. Here, too, B will be found to have been in possession of facts that would have led a reasonable person in his position to make an investigation about the mineral rights -- courts presume that a reasonable buyer will conduct a physical inspection of the property.

[8] Generally, on exam questions, the answer to this question will be "yes."

Example 1: Same facts as Example 1 in note 7. Once B knew of the reference in the O-to-A deed to the O-to-X minerals conveyance, inquiry of either A, O or X (or even physical inspection of the now-mined property) would almost certainly have caused B to learn that the mineral rights had indeed been conveyed to X. In that event, B would be deemed to be on inquiry notice, and he wouldn't be a purchaser without notice. Consequently, in a notice or race-notice state, he'd lose in a contest with X.

Example 2: Same facts as Example 2 in note 7. Once B physically inspected the property, he would see the oil well, would be able to find out who was operating the well, and would learn that X, the operator, had a valid interest. Therefore, B would be deemed to be on inquiry notice, and he wouldn't be a purchaser without notice. As in Example 1, consequently, B would lose in a contest with X, in a notice or race-notice state.

appear to have an interest in the property. ***Notice*** is given to them, and is also usually published.

2. **Judicial proceeding:** Then, a court hears the claim of any person asserting an interest in the property. If the court is satisfied that the applicant indeed has good title, it orders a ***certificate of title*** to be issued to him. Also noted on the certificate are any encumbrances which the court has concluded to be valid. A ***duplicate copy*** of the certificate of title is ***kept in the registration clerk's office***.

3. **Subsequent conveyances:** When the holder of the first certificate of title (or the holder of a subsequent certificate) wishes to sell the property, he shows the certificate to the prospective purchaser, who can quickly see the state of the title by a simple examination. (Because of the possibility that there have been ***involuntary*** encumbrances against the property, the purchaser should probably also check with the registration clerk's office; see *infra*.)

   a. **Transfer of title:** Execution and delivery of a ***deed*** by the registration holder to the purchaser is ***not sufficient*** to transfer title. Rather, the transfer occurs when the parties go to the registration clerk, tender the original certificate, and receive a new one from the clerk. At the same time, of course, the clerk's copy of the old certificate is marked void, and a copy of the new certificate is entered in the clerk's records. Any encumbrances noted on the old certificate, if they are still in effect, are carried over onto the new certificate.

4. **Involuntary liens or transfers:** Tax liens, judgment liens, and mortgage foreclosure sales are examples of interests created ***without the consent*** of the owner of the property. If the owner's title is embodied by his certificate, how is the holder of the lien or the purchaser at the foreclosure sale to obtain this certificate and get the new interest noted on it? The answer is that an application must be submitted to the ***registration clerk*** to have the involuntary interest noted on the registrar's copy of the certificate. Once the notation is made, the fact that it is not necessarily embodied upon the owner's copy becomes irrelevant (which is why the purchaser must be sure to check the registrar's copy before parting with his money).

IV. METHODS OF TITLE ASSURANCE

A. **Various methods:** Apart from examination of the land records themselves, there are various means by which the purchaser of land can attempt to assure himself of a valid title.

B. **Covenants for title:** One method, of course, is by having the seller give ***covenants for title***. However, as we saw *supra*, p. 336, covenants for title, as a method of title assurance, have at least two very severe drawbacks: (1) they rely upon the personal solvency of the seller; and (2) the measure of damages applied by the courts is often woefully inadequate to compensate for the real loss caused by a breach.

C. **Examination by a lawyer:** A prospective purchaser of land could conceivably examine the land records himself. But apart from the large amount of time this would take, he would not know how to interpret the documents. Therefore, in many areas of the country, title examination is performed by the ***buyer's lawyer***. Occasionally, the lawyer himself does the examination of the title records. More commonly, however, the lawyer obtains an ***abstract*** of title from an abstract company. (Usually, the sale contract requires the seller to buy the abstract and supply it to the buyer's lawyer.)

1. **Nature of abstract:**   The abstract is a summary of the salient date on each conveyance in the chain of title, and each encumbrance of record. The abstract is compiled by the abstract company not via a *de novo* search of the records, but rather, from a ***private tract index*** kept by the abstract company. The lawyer then reviews the abstract, and gives the client a written ***opinion*** as to the state of the title.

2. **Lawyer's liability:**   The lawyer is not liable for any misstatement contained in the abstract itself. (This is the abstract company's responsibility, and it may be liable for negligence to the buyer.) The lawyer is, however, liable for his own negligence in rendering an opinion on the title as it is presented in the abstract. Thus if the abstract exposes a major defect (e.g., an unpaid tax lien), and the lawyer does not warn his client about it, he is likely to be held liable on a negligence theory for any loss sustained by the client.

D. **Title insurance:**   The leading means by which a buyer of property can assure himself of a good title is ***title insurance***. Whereas a lawyer's opinion based upon an abstract of title gives rise to only negligence liability, the title insurer's liability is absolute (apart from the exceptions noted in the policy).

1. **Practical importance:**   This means that the insured will be able to recover from a title insurer (but not from a lawyer or abstract company) if the title is bad for any of the following illustrative reasons: ***disability*** of a grantor in the chain of title; ***forgery*** of an instrument in the chain; fraudulent representation of ***marital status*** by a grantor (so that the spouse's inchoate right of dower perseveres); undisclosed heirs of an owner/decedent; and defects in the conveyances in the chain of title due to ***lack of delivery***. See Cribbet, p. 327. All of these are defects which could affect the validity of the buyer's title, but which would not be found even by the most careful title searcher.

    a. **Litigation costs:**   The policy will also cover the insured's ***litigation costs*** in defending his title, even if the defense is successful.

    b. **Liability for subsequent warranties:**   The policy typically also covers any loss which the insured may sustain if he gives ***covenants of title*** when he re-sells the property. Thus when the insured sells the property, his policy is transformed from an owner's policy to a ***warrantor's policy***. (But the new purchaser of the property is not covered by the policy, unless he pays the company a supplementary fee.)

2. **The "title plant":**   When the title company receives (usually from the buyer's lawyer) an application for a title policy, the company does not conduct a *de novo* search of the public land records. Instead, the company has built over the years a *"title plant."* The title plant is, in effect, a ***tract index***; every parcel has its own index entry, and all conveyances or encumbrances affecting that parcel are noted on the index. The company also keeps photocopies of the recorded documents themselves, so that these can be examined without the need to return to the public records. The system is maintained by a "take-off" person, who photocopies the newly-filed documents at the recording office each day.

3. **Scope of coverage:**   As noted, title insurance covers risks which would not be disclosed even by a competent examination of the public records, and also the risk of errors made by the company in its title examination. Nonetheless, most title policies do contain a number of *exceptions*. In fact, one of the buyer's lawyer's major functions is to evaluate the exceptions demanded by the title company and to be sure that these do not swallow up the bulk of the protection being sought.

   a. **Facts which survey would show:**   Nearly all policies exclude facts *which an accurate survey of the property would disclose*. Thus *encroachments* (either by the insured onto adjacent property or vice versa) and violations of *setback* rules are not generally covered.

      i. **What is "correct" survey:**   However, a survey is considered *"correct"* so long as it *corresponds to the description of the property as it appears in the deed* from the seller to the insured. The fact that the description recited in the seller's deed to the insured and relied on by the surveyor is itself wrong will not prevent the survey from being "correct".

         Example: O is the owner of Blackacre, a 10-acre parcel. O conveys two of the acres to X. O then conveys Blackacre to P, keeping the metes and bounds description as if the two-acre conveyance to X had never been made. At the time of the O-P conveyance, P gives D (P's title company) a survey that corresponds to the metes and bounds shown on the proposed O-P deed. P buys Blackacre. After X shows that X owns the two acres, and that P owns only eight, not 10, acres, P sues D under the title policy.

         If D defends on the grounds that a "correct" survey would have shown that the two acres belong to X rather than P, D will lose with this assertion — so long as the survey matches the description in P's deed (which it does), the survey will be deemed "correct," and the standard title policy exclusion for facts "which an accurate survey of the property would disclose" does not come into play.

   b. **Possession:**   Also, rights of *parties in possession* not shown by the public records are usually excluded. Thus the title policy *does not protect against a claim of adverse possession*, at least if the physical possession still exists at the time the policy is written. Accordingly, the buyer must still inspect the property.

   c. **Charges not shown as liens:**   The policy also usually excludes taxes or special assignments which, at the time the policy is issued, do *not yet appear as liens* on the public record.

4. **Effect on value:**   Title insurance generally protects the insured only from defects clouding *title*; it does not usually insure against defects that merely reduce the property's *value*. For instance, a title policy will usually be held not to protect the insured against the existence of a *restrictive covenant* (or against a violation of that restrictive covenant), even though the existence or violation of the restrictive covenant diminishes the value of the property. Similarly, a title policy will almost never be held to protect the insured against the presence of *hazardous waste* on the site.

   Example: P buys 30 acres of land from X. In connection with the purchase, P buys a title insurance policy from D (a title company). Before issuing the policy, D causes a survey and inspection to be made; the inspector notices various tanks, pumps, pipes and other improvements, but does not suspect a hazardous waste problem. After closing, P discovers hazardous waste on the property, and is forced to spend large sums to clean it up, both to protect the property's value and to avoid the state's right to put a lien on the property to guarantee payment of cleanup costs. P asserts that D should have to pay for the cleanup, under the title policy.

Held, for D. No clause in the policy obligates D to pay for cleanup costs. The clause guaranteeing that P's title would be "marketable" is not breached by the pollution, because P's *title* is perfectly marketable, even though the land itself is not marketable due to the waste on it. Similarly, the clause protecting against "encumbrances on title" is not violated, because although such a clause protects against existing liens, it does not protect against the possibility that the state might in the future get a lien to cover cleanup costs. *Lick Mill Creek Apartments v. Chicago Title Insurance Co.,* 283 Cal.Rptr. 231 (Cal.Ct.App. 1991).

5. **Zoning and building code violations:** Most title policies exclude coverage for violations of *zoning ordinances*, *building codes*, and the like. So it is up to the insured and his lawyer, not the title company, to guard against the possibility that, say, the property is an office building located in an area that is zoned residential.

   a. **Exception for litigation:** But some courts have held that where a zoning or building code violation has already led to *litigation* by the date the policy is issued, the exclusion for code violations does not apply.

6. **Duty to make reasonable search:** Apart from the insurance company's liability on the policy itself, it has potential liability for the *way in which it prepares the title report*. The title report, which is submitted to the buyer's lawyer before the policy itself is issued, is essentially a summary of the state of the title. As a practical matter, this title report is often as important to the buyer's lawyer as the eventual policy.

   a. **Some cases find duty of care:** A few cases have held that the insurer has an implied duty to make a *reasonable search* and to *disclose to the customer* the findings that would result from a reasonable search. Under these cases, if the insurer fails to make the reasonable search and disclosure, it may be liable for *negligence, even as to an item which has been excluded from coverage by the policy.* C,S&W, p. 875.

   b. **Majority does not find tort liability:** But *most* cases do *not* impose an implied duty of reasonable care as to the title search, and hold that only if the title company *expressly agrees* to perform a search and disclose its results to the insured will there be liability in tort. See, e.g., *Walker Rogge, Inc. v. Chelsea Title & Guaranty Co.,* 562 A.2d 208 (N.J. 1989) (in New Jersey, "a title company's liability is limited to the policy and . . . the company is not liable in tort for negligence in searching records").

7. **Damages:** If the insured does sustain loss as the result of a covered title defect, his claim is limited to the *face amount* stated in the policy, usually the *purchase price*. This means that if the defect does not come to light until after the property has greatly appreciated in value, the insured may not be made whole.

   a. **Difference in value:** But the courts do, however, generally give the insured the difference between the value the property would have had upon the date of the policy had it been free of defects, and its actual value, including the defects, on that date (up to the amount of the face value, of course).

Quiz Yourself on

THE RECORDING SYSTEM AND TITLE ASSURANCE

94. Oliver conveyed Whiteacre to Arkin in 2000; Arkin did not record at the time. Oliver then conveyed to Beacon in 2002. Beacon did not know about the deed to Arkin at the time he took. In 2003, Arkin recorded, without knowledge of the conveyance by Oliver to Beacon. In 2004, Beacon discovered the conveyance to Arkin by doing a title search, and immediately recorded. If the jurisdiction has a "race notice" statute, who has title as between Arkin and Beacon, and why? _____

95. Oliver conveyed Whiteacre to Arkin, for value, in 2005. Through negligence, Arkin did not record at the time. Oliver, who was aware of Arkin's failure to record, sold the property to Beacon in 2007. Just before the conveyance to Beacon, Oliver told Beacon, "I conveyed to Arkin in 2005, but Arkin has not recorded. As long as you record before Arkin can, you'll be safe." Beacon paid almost full value for the property, and immediately recorded (still in 2007). In 2008, Arkin suddenly realized, with panic in his heart, that he had failed to record, and that Beacon had recorded. Arkin immediately recorded. In a race-notice jurisdiction, who has priority, Arkin or Beacon, and why? _____

96. Oliver conveyed Whiteacre to Arkin in 2005. At the time, Arkin did not record. Oliver then conveyed Whiteacre to Beacon in 2007. Beacon did not record. Beacon, at the time he took, did not have actual knowledge of the conveyance to Arkin. In 2008, Arkin recorded. Beacon has never recorded. In a "pure notice" jurisdiction, who has priority, Arkin or Beacon, and why? _____

97. In 1980, Odell conveyed Blackacre to Arias. Arias did not record at the time. In 1990, Odell conveyed to Beck. At the time of the conveyance, Beck had actual notice of the earlier conveyance to Arias. Beck recorded immediately after receiving his deed. In 2000, Beck conveyed to Cabbott. Cabbott had neither actual nor constructive notice of the conveyance by Odell to Arias, and Cabbott paid Beck fair value. In 2005, Arias finally recorded. In 2007, Cabbott recorded. The jurisdiction has a race-notice statute. As between Arias and Cabbott, who has title? _____

98. In 1980, Osborn gave a gift of Whiteacre to Abrams. At the time, Abrams did not record the deed. In 1990, Osborn purported to give Whiteacre as a gift to Boone. At the time Boone received his deed, he had no knowledge of the earlier gift to Abrams. Boone immediately recorded. In 2010, Abrams recorded. The jurisdiction has a race-notice statute. As between Abrams and Boone, who has title?

---

99. In 1990, Orcini conveyed Blackacre to Arlen for value. Arlen never recorded his deed. In 2000, Arlen conveyed to Bishop. Bishop paid fair value, and promptly recorded. In 2010, Orcini conveyed Blackacre to Chavez. Chavez had no knowledge of the earlier Orcini-Arlen conveyance, or of the Arlen-Bishop conveyance. Chavez paid fair value, and immediately recorded. The jurisdiction has a race-notice statute. In a dispute between Bishop and Chavez, who has superior title to Blackacre? _____

100. In 1980, O'Neill conveyed Blackacre to Arens. At the time, this deed was not recorded. In 1990, Arens conveyed to Burrows. This deed was not recorded at the time. In 2000, O'Neill conveyed to Craft. This deed was never recorded. In 2005, Craft conveyed to Dempsey. Dempsey promptly recorded his deed from Craft. Neither Craft nor Dempsey, at the time each took his conveyance, had any actual knowledge of the O'Neill-to-Arens-to-Burrows line of conveyances. In 2009, the O'Neill-to-Arens and the Arens-to-

Burrows deeds were recorded by Burrows. The jurisdiction has a race-notice statute. In a contest between Burrows and Dempsey, who has priority? _____

101. In 1995, Oakley conveyed Blackacre to Andrews for value. Andrews never recorded the deed. In 2011, Oakley conveyed the same property to Burns for value. Burns promptly recorded. At the time Burns took, Andrews was in possession of the property (as, indeed, he had been since 1995), and the property (a farm) contained a mailbox with Andrews' name prominently displayed on it. Burns lived far away from the property, and never visited it before he took. If he had visited it, he would have seen signs of Andrews' possession. If he had spoken to Andrews, Andrews would have explained that he was the owner. The jurisdiction has a pure notice statute. In a contest between Andrews and Burns, who has superior title?

_____

102. In 1980, Olivia conveyed Blackacre to Albright. At the time, Albright did not record his deed. In 1990, Olivia conveyed Blackacre to Brown. Brown took without any notice (actual or record) of the earlier conveyance to Albright. Brown promptly recorded. In 1995, Albright belatedly recorded. In 2010, Brown conveyed to Crystal. Crystal bought for value. Brown, being an honest sort, disclosed to Crystal before the sale that there was an earlier conveyance by Olivia to Albright, and that that conveyance had been subsequently recorded. (Crystal paid a somewhat lower price to reflect the possible uncertainty about title.) Crystal promptly recorded her deed. The jurisdiction has a race-notice statute. In a contest between Albright and Crystal, who wins? _____

103. Barnes contracted to purchase Blackacre from Selish. As part of the contract, Selish provided Barnes with a metes-and-bounds survey of the property, which was in fact an accurate description of the property which Selish intended to sell and Barnes intended to buy. The survey did not disclose that the garage located principally on the property encroached three feet onto the neighboring property; in fact, the survey did not show the garage structure at all. However, if Barnes (or his lawyer) had measured the distance from the house to the garage, and compared this with the distance from the house to the rear property line, they would have seen by looking at the survey that the garage must encroach on the neighbor's property. In any event, Barnes bought the property without being aware of the encroachment. At the time of the closing, Barnes purchased from Title Co. a standard title insurance policy on the property. The policy excluded any "any facts which an accurate survey of the property would disclose." The title report that accompanied the policy did not refer in any way to the fact that the garage encroached or might encroach on the neighbor's property. Three years after the purchase, Barnes was sued by the neighbor, who obtained a court order compelling Barnes to remove the encroaching garage, at a cost of $40,000. If Barnes sues Title Co. for $40,000, will Barnes recover? _____

Answers

94. Arkin, because he recorded first. Under a race-notice statute, the second grantee (Beacon) will prevail over the earlier grantee (Arkin) only if the second satisfies two requirements: (1) he records before the earlier purchaser records; and (2) he took without notice of the earlier conveyance. Here, Beacon flunked the first of these requirements. (The fact that Beacon had notice at the time he recorded is irrelevant; what counts is whether Beacon had notice at the time he received his deed, which he did not on the facts here.)

95. Arkin. A race-notice statute requires that the subsequent purchaser record before the earlier purchaser, and take without notice of the earlier conveyance. (See answer to prior question.) Here, Beacon failed the second of these requirements, since he knew of the conveyance to Arkin at the time he, Beacon, took. Therefore, Beacon's having recorded first does not save him. (The fact that Oliver lied about the way the recording statute works should not insulate Beacon from his own failure to comply with the statute.)

96. Beacon. Under a "pure notice" statute, the sole issue is whether the subsequent grantee had actual or constructive notice of the prior grant at the time the subsequent grantee took. At the time Beacon took in 2007, he had neither actual nor constructive notice of the grant to Arkin (the facts tell you he did not have actual notice, and the lack of recordation means that he did not have constructive notice). Therefore, the fact that Arkin later recorded, and that Beacon never recorded, is irrelevant.

97. Cabbott, probably. Ordinarily, the second grantee under a race-notice statute must fulfill two requirements to take priority over a prior grantee: (1) he must record before the earlier grantee records; and (2) he must have taken without notice of the earlier grant. Here, Cabbott has not fulfilled the first of these requirements, since Arias recorded before he (Cabbott) did. However, most statutes requiring a race require it only where the contest is *between grantees from a common grantor*. Since Arias and Cabbott are claiming under different grantors, Cabbott's failure to record before Arias probably will not be fatal. Allowing Cabbott to win fulfills the goal of encouraging reliance on the public record: at the time Cabbott took from Beck, paying full value, Cabbott had no practical way to know of the earlier conveyance to Arias, so there is a strong interest in protecting him even though he was negligent by waiting to record. (Obviously, Cabbott could have protected himself fully by recording immediately, so that he would have won the race-to-record with Arias, even though he never knew of Arias' existence.) So the court will probably find for Cabbott.

98. Abrams. Boone appears to have fulfilled the two requirements for taking priority over a prior grantee under a race-notice statute: he took without notice of the prior grant, and he recorded before the prior grantee recorded. However, in the vast majority of states, a grantee receives the benefit of the recording act (i.e., he gets to take priority over an earlier unrecorded conveyance) only if he *gives value* for his interest. Here, Boone did not give value, but rather received a gift. Therefore, he gets no benefit from the recording act, and the usual principle of "first in time, first in right" applies. This is true even though Abrams similarly received a gift and thus did not give value.

99. Chavez. At first, Chavez appears to violate one of the two requirements for taking ahead of a prior grantee: Chavez failed to win the "race" to record before Bishop did. But in reality, Bishop will be deemed never to have recorded at all. A grantee records only when he *adequately* records. The mere fact that a deed is recorded somewhere in the public records does not mean that the recording is "adequate" — the document must be recorded *in such a way that a reasonable searcher would find it*. Here, only if a searcher would have found the document using the grantor and grantee indexes would Bishop's deed be adequately recorded.

A searcher in Chavez's position would have started with a "root" of Orcini (or one of Orcini's predecessors in recorded title); Chevez would then never have found the Orcini-to-Arlen deed because that deed was never recorded. Thus he would not have known to look in the grantor index to find that Arlen later conveyed to Bishop, and he consequently would never have found the deed to Bishop. In other words, Bishop would be deemed to have adequately recorded only if Bishop made sure that not only was his own deed recorded, but also *the deed by which his grantor took* (the Orcini-to-Arlen deed), and so forth back in the chain at least 50 or 60 years. Since Bishop is in a position equivalent to not having recorded at all, Chavez is the first to "adequately" record, and he is thus the first grantee; it is Bishop who is the second grantee, and he loses because he did not adequately record first.

100. Burrows. Dempsey's fatal mistake was that although he made sure that his own conveyance (Craft-to-Dempsey) was promptly recorded, he did not make sure that his whole chain of title was recorded. That is, he failed to make sure that the O'Neill-to-Craft deed was recorded. The entire line running from O'Neill through Arens through Burrows was then recorded (in 2009) at a time when Dempsey had still not "adequately" recorded. Therefore, Dempsey, as the second grantee, has not fulfilled one of the two requirements for a subsequent grantee to take under a race-notice statute: he did not win the race to record, because one wins that race only by "adequately" recording, which Dempsey has never done. So just as Question 99 illustrates that the earlier grantee may lose the protection of the recording acts by not seeing to it that his entire chain of title is recorded, so the subsequent grantee may lose the protection of the recording acts by failing to see to it that *his* entire chain of title is recorded.

101. Andrews. Under normal principles, Burns would get the benefit of the recording act because he took without actual or record notice of the prior grant (the unrecorded deed to Andrews). But Burns loses because of the doctrine of *"inquiry"* notice. Even if the subsequent purchaser has neither record nor actual notice of a prior unrecorded conveyance, he will be found to have been on inquiry notice of it if at the time he took he was in possession of facts which would have led a reasonable person in his position to make an investigation, which would in turn have advised him of the existence of the prior unrecorded right.

Most courts hold that the subsequent grantee has a duty to *view the property*, and if it is in possession of someone other than the record owner, he must inquire as to the source of the latter's rights in the property. Here, the facts tell us that if Burns had viewed the property, he would have discovered Andrews, and that if he had discovered Andrews, Andrews would have told him that he, Andrews, had an unrecorded deed. Therefore, Burns is charged with inquiry notice of Andrews' deed, and Burns is thus a grantee "with knowledge" of that deed (thereby removing him from the protection of the notice statute).

102. Crystal. Brown, at the time he took, met the two requirements for a subsequent grantee to take priority in a race-notice jurisdiction: he won the race to record ahead of Albright, and he took without notice of Albright's deed. That being the case, not only Brown's own "ownership," but his ability to *resell* his property, is protected by courts construing the recording acts. That is, once an interest is purged by its acquisition by one without notice of the prior unrecorded document, the interest remains "clean" when resold, *even if the new purchaser has actual or record notice*.

103. Yes, probably. Title Co. will probably argue that it is exculpated by the clause in the title policy excluding facts which an accurate survey of the property would disclose. But even if Title Co. persuades the court that this exclusion covers the garage, Title Co. will probably be liable for *negligence* for not having called Barnes' attention to the encroachment. See, e.g., *Shotwell v. Transamerica Title Ins. Co.*, 558 P.2d 1359 (Ct.App.Wash. 1976), holding that the title insurer could be liable for negligence in the search even as to an item (an easement) which was excluded from coverage by the policy.

Exam Tips on
THE RECORDING SYSTEM AND TITLE ASSURANCE

The most important things to remember in this area:

☛ **Types of statutes:** You must recognize and identify the applicable statute, and be able to analyze how it works.

   ☞   **Recognition:** Be aware of the standard verbal formulations for each of the three main types of statutes. Your exam question usually *won't* say, "The jurisdiction has a race-notice statute." Instead, the question will typically contain **actual statutory language**, and it's **up to you to recognize** the language as constituting, say, a race-notice statute.

☞ **Typical formulations:** For each of the three main types of statute, here's a typical chunk of statutory language that you'll have to identify:

❑ **Pure notice:** "No conveyance of real property is effective against a subsequent purchaser for value and without notice unless the same be recorded." (Notice that there's nothing requiring the first purchaser to record first in order to get protection; that's why it's not a race-*notice* statute.)

❑ **Pure race:** "In determining the priority of conflicting interests in land, the first such interest to have been recorded shall have priority." (Observe that there's no requirement that the second purchaser take without notice in order to get protection; that's why it's not a *race*-notice statute.)

❑ **Race-notice:** "No conveyance or mortgage of real property shall be good against subsequent purchasers for value and without notice, **who shall first record.**" (Notice that the second purchaser won't win unless she *both* takes without notice and records first.)

☞ **Discuss all possible outcomes:** Many times a fact pattern will not mention what type of recording statute is in effect, and the question asks you to analyze the rights of various parties to a parcel. If this happens, discuss the differing outcomes that would result based on the application of the three main types of statutes.

☛ **Purchaser for value:** Make sure to notice whether the statute requires that a purchaser give **value** for his interest (a/k/a **"consideration"**). If so, check the fact pattern to see whether there is any indication of value being given. Often, the pattern will not say "there was no consideration given in return," but will indicate a gift by circumstantial evidence (as in the above example, where the facts tell you that O "hands" the deed to her employee).

☞ **Release of debt:** Sometimes, property is transferred in return for the **cancellation of a preexisting debt** (a loan from grantee to grantor). In that instance, the grantee is generally deemed to have given consideration.

☛ **Notice:** The question of whether a subsequent purchaser has been put on **notice** of the earlier deed is one you'll commonly need to answer. If a party does not have **actual** notice then look for:

☞ **Record notice:** The recording of an instrument gives **"record notice"** to a subsequent purchaser, but only if that searcher **would have** found the document using generally-accepted searching principles. A conveyance **outside the chain of title** is treated as an unrecorded conveyance. Make sure every grantor appears as a grantee in the land records to reflect when he received the property, and then as a grantor when he conveys it away.

☞ **Wild deed:** Where a party gets a deed from a person whose own deed was never properly recorded (a **"wild deed"**), make sure the new grantee promptly records her **whole chain** of title. If that subsequent grantee does **not** record her whole chain, she'll probably forfeit the protection of the statute as against a prior unrecorded (or late-recorded) deed.

Example: The jurisdiction has a race-notice statute. *A* conveys a parcel to *B*. Later, *A* conveys the same parcel to *C*, who does not record the deed. *C* then conveys to *D*, who records immediately. (*D* does not know about the *A*-to-*B* deed). *B* then records. *D* discovers that *C*'s deed from *A* is unrecorded, so she obtains it from him and records it. Since *D* had a "wild deed," and did not record her whole chain of title before *B* recorded her deed, *B* will probably have priority to the realty. That is, in a race or race-notice jurisdiction, *D* will not be deemed to have "recorded" prior to *B* (even though D promptly recorded his own deed), and will lose the protection given to a subsequent good-faith purchaser who records first.

☞ **Inquiry notice:** Look for facts which would cause a reasonable person to conduct an *investigation* which, if taken, would had led her to discover the existence of the prior unrecorded deed. In this situation, the person is said to be on "inquiry notice."

   ☞ **Possession:** The key clue that typically triggers the prospective buyer's duty to make further inquiries is that the property is in the *possession* of someone other than the prospective seller, and the buyer has not been told that there's a tenant on the property.

   Example: O conveys a house to *A*. *A* doesn't record, but takes possession by moving in to the house. *O* then conveys to *B*, making no mention of any tenant on the property. *B* will be probably be deemed to be on "inquiry notice" of *A*'s deed — *B* had a duty to inspect the property, and at least to ask the possessor about the source of his possession; had *B* done this, *B* would almost certainly have learned from *A* about the *O*-to-*A* deed.

   ☞ **Quitclaim deed:** In some jurisdictions, the fact that the grantee is being given a *quitclaim deed* places her on inquiry notice.

   ☞ **What a reasonable inspection would show:** Before you conclude that a grantee is on inquiry notice, make sure that a *reasonable inspection* of the property and *questioning* of the grantor would have led to discovery of the prior interest. For instance, if the land is vacant and there is no other way of finding out about the prior deed, then there is no inquiry notice.

☛ **Common-law rule:** When a recording statute does not cover a situation, apply the common-law rule, i.e., *first in time, first in right.*

☞ **Tip:** This may occur when a grantee receives the property as a *gift*, and the recording statute protects only a subsequent purchaser "for value."

   Example: O borrows money from L and executes a note secured by a mortgage on his realty. O later deeds the realty to his son, S, as a birthday present. S records his deed; L then records his mortgage. The statute gives protection to a subsequent grantee against a prior unrecorded interest only if the grantee is a "purchaser for value."

   Since S was not a purchaser for value, S does not get the protection of the recording act. Therefore, the common-law rule — first in time, first in right — applies, making L's interest, received first, superior.

CHAPTER 13

RIGHTS INCIDENT TO LAND

Introductory note: In this chapter, we consider several rights which one holds by virtue of being a landowner: (1) the right not to have one's *use and enjoyment of the land* unreasonably interfered with (*nuisance*); (2) the right to have lateral and subjacent *support* for one's property; (3) the right to control "diffused surface water" (*drainage*); (4) the right to *water* flowing through or near one's property; and (5) the right to the *air space* above one's property.

I. NUISANCE

A. Nuisance generally: The subject of *nuisance* is usually covered more closely in the course on Torts. See Emanuel on *Torts*. Therefore, we examine it here only in a cursory fashion.

   1. Public vs. private nuisance: The term "nuisance" is used to cover two quite different types of harms, one called "public" nuisance and the other usually called "private" nuisance. Public nuisance is an interference with a right common to the general public. Our primary interest here is in *private* nuisance, i.e., an interference with a private landowner's *use and enjoyment of his land*.

   2. Distinguished from trespass: Whereas *trespass* is an interference with the plaintiff's right to *exclusive possession* of his property, nuisance is an interference with his right to *use and enjoy* it.

B. Interference with use: The interference with the plaintiff's use and enjoyment must be *substantial*.

   1. Inconvenience: If the plaintiff is personally injured, or his property is physically damaged, the interference will always be *"substantial."* But if the plaintiff's damage consists in his being *inconvenienced* or subjected to unpleasant smells, noises, etc., this will be substantial damage only if a person in the community of *normal sensitivity* would be seriously bothered.

C. Defendant's conduct: There is *no* general rule of *"strict liability"* in nuisance. In other words, the plaintiff must show that the defendant's conduct was *negligent*, *intentional*, or *abnormally dangerous*.

   1. Intentional: Most nuisance claims arise out of conduct by the defendant that can be called *"intentional"*. This does not mean that the defendant has *desired* to interfere with the plaintiff's use and enjoyment of his land, but simply that he *knows with substantial certainty* that such interference will occur. For instance, a factory owner whose plant spews pollutants and smoke into the air over plaintiff's property will be held to have intended this interference, at least if the plaintiff can show that he put the defendant on notice of what was happening by making a complaint.

2. Unreasonableness: Even if the defendant's conduct is intentional, the plaintiff may not maintain his nuisance suit unless he shows that the defendant's actions were also **unreasonable**.

   a. Significance: This means that even if the defendant intentionally interferes with the plaintiff's rights, he will have a kind of "privilege" to do so, as long as the interference is not unreasonable.

   b. Nature of neighborhood: In determining what is reasonable, the **nature of the neighborhood** is likely to be quite significant. A steel mill located in an otherwise completely residential area is obviously much more likely to be found to be an unreasonable interference with the rights of surrounding landowners than is a steel mill in the middle of an industrial park.

      i. Zoning: The **zoning** of the area will be important to the court's determination of the nature of the neighborhood. Indeed, some courts have given almost complete deference to the local municipality's decision to zone for certain uses.

D. Defenses: The defendant may raise a number of **affirmative defenses** to a private nuisance claim.

   1. Assumption of risk: The most significant of these, for our purposes, is the defense of **assumption of risk**. Most frequently, the defense applies in zoning cases where the plaintiff has purchased his property with **advance knowledge** that the nuisance exists. In such a case, he is said to have **"come to the nuisance"**.

      a. Not absolute defense: Older cases sometimes treated the fact that the plaintiff "came to the nuisance" as an **absolute** defense. The modern tendency, however, is to treat this as merely **one factor** in evaluating the reasonableness of the defendant's conduct. See Restatement (Second) of Torts, §840D.

      b. Locality: The court is much more likely to hold that "coming to the nuisance" is a defense if the defendant's activity is **suitable** for the area where it occurs, and the plaintiff's own use is out of step with that area.

      Example: D has operated a cattle feed lot (producing "over a million pounds of wet manure per day") for many years, in a completely rural area outside Phoenix. P, a developer, builds a development called "Sun City", one portion of which adjoins the feed lot. The flies and odor make this portion of the development unhealthy and almost unusable for residential purposes.

      Held, P has "come to the nuisance", and if its interests were the only ones at stake, it would not be entitled to an injunction. But since the rights of innocent third parties (the inhabitants of Sun City) are also involved, D will be enjoined from operating the feed lot, and forced to move. However, again because it has come to the nuisance, P will have to **indemnify** D for its costs in moving. *Spur Industries, Inc. v. Del E. Webb Development Co.*, 494 P.2d 700 (Ariz. 1972).

E. Remedies: The plaintiff may have one or more of three possible **remedies** for private nuisance.

1. **Damages:** If the harm has already occurred, he can recover **compensatory damages**. If it is not clear whether the harm will continue in the future, he can usually recover only for the damages sustained up till the time of suit, and he must bring successive actions for subsequent harm. But if it appears that the nuisance will probably be a permanent one (e.g., a polluting factory that is likely to stay in business), he can and must recover all damages, past and **prospective**, in one action.

2. **Injunction:** If the plaintiff can show that damages would not be a sufficient remedy, he may be entitled to an **injunction** against continuation of the nuisance. (Since courts typically regard every parcel of land as having a unique use, the plaintiff will frequently be able to make the showing that compensatory damages are not an adequate remedy.)

   a. **Balancing test:** To get an injunction, the plaintiff must show that the harm to him actually **outweighs** the utility of the defendant's conduct. (He probably does not have to make such a showing for damages, so long as the defendant's conduct is unreasonable.)

      Example: D operates a large cement plant, which employs over 300 people and which cost more than $45,000,000. The Ps, neighboring landowners, sue for nuisance, because of dirt, smoke and vibrations from the plant.

      Held, an absolute injunction against D should not issue, in view of the great disparity between the economic consequences to D and its employees (as well as the local economy) in closing down the plant, and the consequences to the plaintiffs in allowing it to continue. However, it is fair to require D to pay for the harm it causes, regardless of the utility of the plant. Therefore, a temporary injunction will be issued, to be suspended if D makes payment of permanent damages to the Ps.

      A dissent argued that the majority's holding "is the same as saying to the cement company, you may continue to do harm to your neighbors for so long as you pay a fee for it." Also, the dissent noted, once such permanent damages are paid, the incentive to alleviate the wrong would be eliminated, thereby continuing air pollution of the area. *Boomer v. Atlantic Cement Co., Inc.*, 257 N.E.2d 870 (N.Y. 1970).

3. **Self-help abatement:** In some situations, the plaintiff may have the right to use the **"self-help"** remedy of **"abatement"**. That is, he may have the right to enter the defendant's land to remove the nuisance. But he may use only reasonable force to do this, and must ordinarily first complain to the defendant and wait for the latter to refuse to remedy the condition himself.

II. LATERAL AND SUBJACENT SUPPORT

A. **Nature of interest:** Every landowner is entitled to have his land receive the necessary **physical support** from adjacent and underlying soil. The right to support from adjoining soil is called the right of "**lateral** support"; the right to support from underneath the surface (applicable only where there has been a severance of the surface and sub-surface rights) is known as the right to "**subjacent** support". Our focus here is principally upon lateral support, with a few words *infra*, p. 388, as to subjacent support.

Example: *A* and *B* are adjoining landowners. *A* constructs a large excavation extending almost to the edge of his property. This causes *B*'s soil to run into *A*'s excavation, impairing the surface of *B*'s property. *B*'s right to lateral support has been violated, and he may recover damages.

B. Ground for liability: The right to lateral support is **absolute**. That is, once support has been withdrawn and injury occurs, the responsible person is liable **even if he used utmost care** in his operation. 6-A A.L.P. 100.

1. **Building on land:** However, the absolute right to lateral support exists only with respect to land in its **natural state**. If the owner has constructed a **building**, and the soil under the building subsides in part due to the adjacent owner's acts, but also in part **because of the weight of the building itself**, the adjacent owner is **not liable** (in the absence of negligence).

   a. **Weight of building not factor:** Suppose, however, that the soil caves in and the building is damaged, but the owner is able to show that the cave-in would have occurred **even had the building not been present**. The adjacent landowner is obviously liable for damage to the soil, but is he liable for damage to the building? A substantial number of American courts (perhaps even a majority) hold that the excavator is **not** liable for damage to the building. *Id.*, at 117. But English courts, and the remaining American courts, hold that he **is** liable for the damage to the building, just as he is for the harm to the land.

2. **Withdrawal of water:** Suppose the adjacent landowner, pursuant to his excavation, causes **water** to flow from beneath P's land, thereby weakening the surface of P's property. The courts are in dispute about whether P's right to lateral support has been violated in this situation. A number of courts which follow English Rule allowing absolute privilege to withdraw groundwaters (see *infra*, p. 392) hold that the right to lateral support is not violated. But Rest. 2, Torts §818 provides that even though one may be privileged to withdraw water or other substances from underneath another's land, this does not give rise to a privilege to cause subsidence of the other's surface.

3. **Statutory modifications:** Statutes have been enacted in a number of states, and ordinances in many municipalities, contracting or expanding the common-law right of lateral support. A frequent type of provision grants the owner of a building limited protection from damage, even if the building's weight contributes to the subsidence of his land. For instance, a California statute provides that an excavator is strictly liable for damages to a neighbor's structure, but only if the foundation of the neighbor's structure exceeds the "standard depth" of nine feet. Cal. Civ. Code §832.

4. **Contractual arrangements:** Adjoining landowners are always free to make **private contractual arrangements** expanding or contracting the common-law right of lateral support. For instance, the owners of adjacent buildings often make a **party wall agreement**, whereby each agrees not to do anything to disturb a wall that is common to the two structures.

C. Subjacent support: The right to **subjacent** support arises only where sub-surface rights (i.e., mineral rights) are **severed** from the surface rights. When such a severance has taken place, the owner of the surface interest has the right not to have the surface subside or otherwise be damaged by the carrying out of the mining. 6-A A.L.P. 127. This right is similar to the right of lateral support; the principal difference is that the surface owner has a right to support not only of unimproved land, but of ***all structures existing on the date when the severance took place***. *Id.* at 128-29.

III. WATER RIGHTS (INCLUDING DRAINAGE)

A. **Drainage (diffused surface waters):** *"Diffused surface waters"* are waters that are spread over the surface of the ground without observable channels or banks, and which have no predictable flow. Thus they are distinguished from water in watercourses (e.g., streams and lakes), discussed *infra*, p. 389. Diffused surface waters may come from rainfall, melting snows, springs, etc. Although there are rules as to the landowner's right to make use of surface waters on his property, the principal body of law concerning these waters relates to the owner's right to ***drain*** them from his property.

   1. **Three theories:** Three distinct theories governing drainage rights have been recognized:

      a. **"Common enemy" rule:** The common-law view, recognized in almost half of the states, is that diffused surface waters are the *"common enemy"* of man. Therefore, an owner is privileged to ***dam*** against them, throw them back upon the land they came from, or deflect them onto adjoining lands. 6-A A.L.P. 189.

      b. **Civil-law doctrine:** By a doctrine adopted from the civil-law countries, and used in a substantial minority of states, exactly the opposite rule applies. That is, an owner may ***not*** channel the drainage, or otherwise change its ***natural flow*** in any way. *Id*, at 190-91.

      c. **"Reasonable use" doctrine:** Neither of the two above views is economically efficient, since the "common enemy" rule may result in a landowner having his land ruined by another owner's dumping excessive water on it, and the "natural flow" view prevents an owner from adjusting the drainage so as to render his own land usable. Therefore, many courts have implicitly or explicitly rejected both of the above rules, and hold that in ***all instances the test is whether the owner's handling of the surface waters is reasonable***. See, e.g., *Armstrong v. Francis Corp.*, 120 A.2d 4 (N.J. 1956) (the prior rule in New Jersey, that a landowner may increase the volume of the drainage as much as he wants so long as it flows to the same place it otherwise would have, is rejected; instead, the "reasonable use" rule will be followed).

B. **Water in watercourses (streams and lakes):** Whereas diffused surface water is seldom desired or appropriated by landowners, the opposite is true of water in ***watercourses*** (i.e., ***streams and lakes***). As to these, disputes between landowners will center on who has the right to ***use*** the water. There are two fundamentally distinct and incompatible approaches to this conflict: (1) the common-law *"riparian rights"* theory; and (2) the statutory *"prior appropriation"* theory.

   1. **Nomenclature:** First, as a matter of nomenclature, the word "riparian" is formally used only to refer to land abutting a ***stream***. The word *"littoral"* is used to describe land abutting a ***lake***. However, since the rights of riparian and littoral owners are virtually indistinguishable, the term "riparian" is used exclusively in the following discussion.

2. Common-law riparian rights: In all parts of the country except for about 17 western states, the common-law *"riparian rights"* theory is in force. The key to this theory is that *no advantage is gained by priority of use.* 6-A A.L.P. 159. The fact that a riparian owner has used stream- or lake-water for a certain purpose for many years (e.g., to run a mill) does not give him any greater rights than if he were making this use for the first time.

    a. "Natural flow" vs. "reasonable use": Within courts following the common-law approach, there is a split as to what use the owner may make, comparable to the split among courts on the drainage problem. Some courts purport to apply a *"natural flow"* approach, by which each waterfront owner is entitled to the flow of streams and level lakes in their *natural condition*, without material reduction in quantity or quality as the result of other riparian or non-riparian owners. *Id.* at 162.

    b. "Reasonable use": But most courts follow the *"reasonable use"* approach to riparian rights. A riparian owner, under this view, is entitled to only so much of the water as he can put to *beneficial use* upon his land, with due regard for the equal and correlative rights of other riparian owners. Thus whereas an owner under the "natural flow" theory may sue at least for nominal damages if the flow of water to him is materially interfered with (even if the owner would not have had a use for the water anyway), the owner in a "reasonable use" state may sue only if he has a beneficial use for the water with which the actions of another person (either another riparian owner or a non-riparian person) have interfered. *Id.* at 163-64. Since the "reasonable use" theory is more frequently applied, our remaining discussion of riparian rights assumes that this approach is in force.

    c. "Natural" vs. "artificial" uses: In determining what constitutes a reasonable use, the courts distinguish between so-called *"natural"* and *"artificial"* uses. Each riparian owner has an *absolute right* to all or any part of the water for *"natural"* uses, without regard to the effect which his use has upon other (usually downstream) owners. Thus as to natural uses, the upstream owner has *preferred status*.

        i. Artificial uses: But with respect to *"artificial"* uses, each owner must follow two rules: (1) he may not take *any* water for such uses, until the "natural" needs of *all* other riparian owners (upstream and down-stream) have been satisfied; and (2) if water is available after satisfaction of everyone's "natural" uses, each owner's rights to take for artificial uses is *equal*. *Id.* at 165.

    d. What is "natural" use: Water for drinking and bathing, and for the raising of farm animals, is always considered *"natural"*. Most courts hold that use of small quantities for *irrigation* of small areas of farmland is also "natural", but that large-scale irrigation is an artificial or "commercial" use. 6-A A.L.P. 165. (However, in relatively arid areas, even large-scale irrigation may be given a preference over other types of commercial uses. *Id.* at 166.)

        i. Pollution: An owner's use will generally not be considered reasonable (regardless of whether it is "natural" or "commercial") if it results in a material *pollution* of the water source. *Id.* at 168.

    e. Who is "riparian owner": *Only riparian owners* are entitled to make use of the water, under the riparian rights doctrine. A "riparian owner" is one whose land *abuts* the stream or lake, at least in part. Thus one whose land is not contiguous with the water at any point may not carry the water by pipe or ditch to his property. (Furthermore, courts have imposed a number of other limitations; for instance, if a person owns a large tract of land, part of which abuts the water and part of which is beyond the watershed, only the part within the watershed may benefit from the water use. *Id*. at 160.)

3. Prior appropriation doctrine: Seventeen *arid* states (all of them west of the Mississippi) have adopted a completely different theory, called the ***prior appropriation*** doctrine. In about half of these states, this doctrine is the only source for water rights; in the remainder, rights may derive either from the common-law riparian doctrine or from the prior appropriation theory.

    a. History: The prior appropriation theory dates from the mid-nineteenth century, when gold miners (who were trespassers on the land they worked anyway) adopted the custom of diverting streams without regard to the needs of those working downstream. Miners' groups, to preserve the peace, instituted a system of "first come first served"; that is, damming and diversion of streams was protected in order of priority of use. In 1866, Congress enacted a mineral law formalizing this system, and most of the western states enacted similar statutes of their own.

    b. How the system works: In some of the prior appropriation states, an application for a ***permit*** must be made; if the application is accepted by the governing agency, the user's priority dates from the time of application. See, e.g., Cal. Water Code, §1450-51. In other states, the right to appropriate is ***absolute*** (i.e., no permit is required) and the priority of the right dates from the time the appropriator begin construction of the necessary works to take the water. 6-A A.L.P. 174.

    c. Riparian ownership not required: A key feature of the prior appropriation system is that water may be appropriated by a ***non-riparian owner***. (However, he will have to procure an easement across the property of at least one riparian owner in order to transport the water to his own property.) See e.g., *Coffin v. Left Hand Ditch Co.*, 6 Colo. 443 (1882), holding that a non-riparian landowner may transport water from a stream to a point outside the stream's watershed, in order to irrigate his property; once he does so, his use gains priority over the subsequent use by one who abuts the stream.

    d. Rationale for prior appropriation theory: In the arid states where it applies, the prior appropriation theory works much better than the riparian-rights theory. In these states, water is an extremely valuable commodity; there are many worthwhile water-related projects which require large amounts of capital, and which will not be carried out unless the investors know that their right to the necessary water is assured.

    e. Coexistence of two theories: In California, Texas and seven other states, the doctrine of prior appropriation exists ***side by side*** with the riparian-rights doctrine. These states have evolved a complicated system for adjusting conflicts between those persons having rights by appropriation and those having rights by virtue of their status as riparian owners; in general, riparian rights are limited, because of the greater suitability of the prior appropriation system. 6-A A.L.P. 172-73.

C. Groundwater: Still another series of doctrines has been developed to deal with ***groundwater***, i.e., water below the surface. Underground streams or springs that are clearly attached to surface streams or lakes are treated the same way the surface water would be treated (i.e., either by the riparian rights doctrine or by prior appropriation, as the case may be). Where the subsurface water is not connected to any surface watercourse, there are three principal approaches:

1. **"English" rule:**   In England, and in some American states, a landowner is given an ***absolute interest*** in all the water which he can draw to the surface of his own land. Even though the water may come from a larger pool that is partially ***below the surface of other owners' property***, the owner is free to draw as much as he wishes, even the entire pool. This is true even if this injures the neighboring landowner, and even if the water is then transported to serve other, distant, lands held by the same owner. The sole limitation is that the owner may not extract the water "maliciously" (or, as the idea is sometimes put, he may not wantonly ***"waste"*** the water).

2. **American "reasonable use":**   In most American states, an owner may make only ***"reasonable use"*** of groundwater drawn from under his property. It is deemed "reasonable" for use to use as much of the water as he wishes for applications on the parcel which sits on top of the pool; but he may ***not divert*** the water to other property which he may own. 6-A A.L.P. 196.

3. **Appropriation rights:**   In about half of the states which follow the doctrine of ***prior appropriation*** for surface waters, the prior appropriation theory is followed as to groundwater as well. B.C&S, p. 212.

4. **Subsidence of neighboring lands:**   Suppose that *A*, by removing large quantities of water from his land, not only dries up the aquifer beneath *B*'s property (the most common kind of injury) but also causes the ***surface*** of *B*'s property to ***fall***. Most courts have held that this subsidence does not change the applicable rule. Thus, the courts following the "English" rule hold that as long as there is no malice, *A* can remove so much water that *B*'s land subsides, even if this leads to flooding or erosion; those following the American "reasonable use" rule generally hold that there is no liability so long as the amount of water taken is not unreasonably great (though the determination of "reasonableness" may be influenced by the fact that the land has subsided).

IV. AIR RIGHTS

A. Airplane flights: The old English common law purported to follow the dictum *"cujus est solum, ejus usque ad coelum,"* literally, "he who owns the soil owns upward into Heaven". With the age of aviation, it quickly became obvious that even if this saying applied to some uses of airspace, it could not apply to airplane flights. Landowners have seldom brought suit against the operators of individual airplanes; rather, most litigation on the consequence of airplane flights has been against the operators of ***airports***, which are usually government-owned facilities. These suits have generally been in "inverse condemnation" (*supra*, p. 298).

1. **Direct overflights:**   When the airport permits flights to occur ***directly over*** a landowner's property, and within the ***"immediate reaches"*** of his land, the landowner may sue in ***tres-***

pass. If sovereign immunity prevents a trespass action, the landowner may nonetheless claim that the direct overflights constitute a ***taking*** of his property, which under the federal Constitution cannot be done without compensation. In *U.S. v. Causby*, 328 U.S. 256 (1946), the Supreme Court agreed that direct overflights within the immediate reaches of an owner's property would constitute a compensable taking, provided that there was interference with the owner's actual (not just potential) use of the property.

2. **Flights in adjacent areas:** In the *Causby* case, the Supreme Court also indicated that airspace ***outside*** the "immediate reaches" of the surface has been transformed by federal statutes and regulations into a ***public highway***. The effect of this statement is that such flights (usually construed to be those which do not violate FAA ***minimum altitude*** regulations) do ***not*** constitute a trespass. However, the courts are not in agreement about whether the lack of a formal trespass prevents the overflights from being a taking for which compensation must be made.

   a. **Recovery allowed:** The Restatement of Torts takes the position that if flights outside the immediate reaches of an owner's property nonetheless result in an ***unreasonable interference*** with the owner's ***use and enjoyment*** of his land, this will constitute a ***nuisance*** (not trespass). Rest. 2d of Torts, §159, Comment m. A number of state courts have followed this theory further, and have held that the existence of a nuisance means that (in the case of a publicly-operated airport) a ***taking has also occurred***.

B. **Other air-rights issues:** The courts have recently faced several other issues concerning air rights.

   1. **Right to build tall building:** An owner generally has the right to build as ***high a building as he wishes*** (assuming, of course, that it satisfies all applicable zoning requirements and building restrictions.)

   2. **Cloud seeding:** Does a landowner have a right to the ***weather conditions*** which would naturally obtain over his property? The issue usually arises in connection with ***cloud seeding***. Where the cloud seeding flights do not directly cross over the owner's property, the courts that have faced the issue have almost always held that he has no cause of action (even though the seeding may result in less rain falling on his land.) But where the flight itself crosses the plaintiff's property, some courts have allowed recovery.

   3. **Solar cases:** In these days of burgeoning interest in solar energy, landowners are bound to assert a property interest in the ***sunlight*** which would naturally strike their property. Generally, American courts have been hostile to the assertion of rights to sunlight. For instance, they have seldom permitted a landowner to acquire an easement of "light and air" by implication or even by necessity.

      a. **Solar energy:** Where a landowner uses sunlight as a source of ***energy***, courts will probably be more willing to hold that he has a protectable property interest. It is too soon to know much about how disputes between *A*'s solar collector and *B*'s sunlight-blocking building will be resolved. But as the following example shows, at least one court has concluded that the law of ***private nuisance*** (*supra*, p. 385) may furnish a means by which the sunlight-collecting owner may gain relief.

Example: P has built a residence that makes extensive use of solar collectors for energy. D buys the vacant lot next door, and proposes to construct a building which would substantially block the sunlight from reaching P's collectors. D's proposed home satisfies all current zoning requirements.

Held, the private nuisance doctrine should be applied to this controversy. Therefore, if P can show that D's building would "unreasonably interfere" with P's use or enjoyment of his property, P will be entitled to enjoin the construction. In determining the "reasonableness" of D's proposed conduct, the lower court should consider such matters as the extent of the harm to P, the suitability of solar heat in this particular neighborhood, the availability of alternatives for P, and the cost to D of avoiding the harm (e.g., by building the house on a different part of his lot.) The fact that D's plans comply with zoning law does not automatically bar a nuisance claim (nor does the fact that P could have avoided the harm by building on a different part of his property). *Prah v. Maretti*, 321 N.W.2d 182 (Wisc. 1982).

A dissent in *Prah* made several arguments against treating D's use as a nuisance, including: (1) a nuisance is a non-trespassory "invasion" of another's use or enjoyment of land, and D's act of blocking the sunlight would not be an "invasion," especially since the building would satisfy all zoning ordinances; and (2) the solar heating system is an "unusually sensitive use," and such uses cannot be protected by the law of nuisance.

Quiz Yourself on
RIGHTS INCIDENT TO LAND

104. Plotnick and Duffy were adjacent property owners. Plotnick's land had a six-story building on it, built in conformity with applicable building codes (including ones governing the depth and strength of the foundation). Duffy's property was undeveloped. Duffy decided to build his own building. He was a very conservative sort. Therefore, he dug an unusually deep foundation (15 feet). Duffy dug only up to his property line. He proceeded without negligence, and in conformity with all codes dictating how to excavate and build a foundation. However, because of the geography of the land, and the unusual nature of Plotnick's foundation, Plotnick's foundation cracked and his building was severely damaged once there was no longer supporting soil on the Plotnick-Duffy border. Plotnick sued Duffy for the damage. Duffy proved at trial that if there had been no building on Plotnick's property, Plotnick's land would not have caved in. May Plotnick recover? _____

105. Phillips and Decker each own a parcel that abuts on the Bountiful River in the state of Ames. Decker is upstream from Phillips. Since 2006, Decker has operated a private hydro-electric plant. To maintain the necessary pressure, Decker has built a dam on the river, which has the effect of diverting the water through the hydro-electric plant's turbines, and then out onto a pond at the rear of Decker's property. Beginning in 1975, Phillips, a farmer, had been irrigating a five-acre parcel of his property. This worked well until Decker built his dam in 2006; since then so little water has been present in the Bountiful River by the time it reaches Phillips' property, that the pressure needed to perform useful irrigation is not present. Assuming that Ames follows the common-law approach to relevant matters, if Phillips sues Decker for improperly using the water, will Phillips prevail? _____

106. Same facts as prior question. Now, assume that as in the prior question, Decker's use (for hydro-electric) commenced in 2012, but that Phillips did not begin trying to use his property for irrigation until 2012.

Ames follows the common-law approach to relevant matters. May Phillips recover against Decker for improper use of water? _____

107. Same facts as prior question. Assume, however, that Ames is one of the 17 states that have abolished the common-law riparian rights doctrine, and that Ames has replaced that doctrine with the most common alternative. Would Phillips win in a suit against Decker for improper water use? _____

108. Pringle and Delaney are adjacent landowners. At the time Pringle bought his property in 1970, a six-story office building was already present on that lot. This building goes up nearly to the eastern property line (and does not violate any zoning rules). Delaney has owned his lot (which is to the east of Pringle's property) since 1990. The land has been vacant. Now, Delaney proposes to build a 12-story office building on the western side of his property. This building would conform with all applicable zoning laws. However, the effect of this building will be to deprive Pringle's tenants (at least those in the eastern side of the building) of nearly all of the sunlight and view which they have always had, since the two buildings will only be three feet apart. If Pringle sues Delaney to enjoin Delaney from placing the building so close to the property line that Pringle's tenants' light and view will be cut off, will the court grant Pringle's request? _____

_____

Answers

104. No, probably. Plotnick had an absolute right to *"lateral support."* However, this absolute right exists only with respect to land in its *natural state*. If the owner has constructed a building, and the soil under the building subsides in part due to the adjacent owner's acts, but also in part because of the weight of the building itself, the adjacent owner is not liable in the absence of negligence. Therefore, since Duffy's acts would not have caused Plotnick's land to cave in had the land been vacant, and Duffy behaved non-negligently, Duffy does not have to pay for damage accruing to Plotnick's structure.

105. Yes, probably. In a common-law jurisdiction, each riparian owner has an absolute right to all or any part of the water for "natural" uses (regardless of the effect on downstream owners), but an owner may take for *"artificial"* uses only after all natural uses have been satisfied, and then only in parity with other artificial users. Irrigation of small areas of farmland is generally considered "natural," whereas use for hydroelectric power is almost certainly artificial. Therefore, Phillips has priority over Decker; Phillips can recover damages, obtain an injunction, or both. (The fact that Phillips was using the water first does not matter to the result.)

106. Yes, probably. Courts following the common-law approach do not grant any advantage based on priority of use. So the fact that a riparian owner has used stream water for a certain purpose for many years does not give him any greater rights than if he were making this use for the first time. Thus the problem is solved the way it is in the prior answer (with Phillips winning because his use is "natural" and Decker's is "artificial").

107. No, probably. The 17 arid states that have abolished the common-law riparian rights doctrine have generally adopted the *"prior appropriation"* doctrine instead. In some of these states, a water user must apply for a permit in order to get priority; in these states, the issue would be decided based on who got a permit first (which the facts don't disclose). But in the remaining "prior appropriation" states, the right to appropriate is absolute (i.e., no permit is required) and the priority of the right dates from the time the appropriator began construction of the necessary works to take the water. In such a state, Decker, as the first user, would prevail.

108. No. Generally, courts hold that an owner may build as tall as he wants, and as close to his property line as he wants, so long as he does not violate zoning rules. In particular, courts almost never recognize an owner's right to sunlight or view. For instance, courts almost never recognize that a landowner has acquired an easement of "light and air" by implication or even by necessity. So Pringle is almost certainly out of luck. (His remedy was to build his own building far enough in from his property line that even a neighboring building later built right up to that property line would not block his own light completely.)

Exam Tips *on*
RIGHTS INCIDENT TO LAND

When this subject appears on an exam, it will generally be as a sub-issue, not a major issue. Things to keep in mind:

☛ **Water rights:** Most courts follow the *"reasonable use"* approach to riparian rights. Look for an indication that consumption by a riparian owner is more than what is reasonably necessary. Make sure that the reasonable use does not significantly interfere with a similar or more beneficial use of the water: domestic use is "higher" than agricultural use.

☛ **Nuisance:** Remember that for a nuisance to occur, there has to be a *substantial* interference with the plaintiff's use and enjoyment of his property.

   Examples of interferences great enough to be "substantial":

   ❑ D hooks up a sewer to a sewer line passing through P's property, causing the sewer line to be overloaded and to back up onto P's land;

   ❑ D, angry that P has refused to comply with deed restrictions regarding house style, puts up a 20-foot-high brick wall adjacent to and parallel to the entire boundary with P's lot, paints the side of the wall facing P's lot black and coats it with a foul-smelling preservative.

   ☞ **Coming to the nuisance:** The fact that the condition existed before the plaintiff came into possession of the property (*"coming to the nuisance"*) is a factor making nuisance more likely, but it is not dispositive of the issue. The issue is always whether the interference is "unreasonable" (as well as substantial), and a condition that existed before P moved in can still be unreasonable.

   ☞ **Nature of neighborhood:** Also, remember that the *nature of the neighborhood* counts in determining reasonableness.

      Example: An odorous pig farm is more likely to be "unreasonable" (and thus a nuisance) in a primarily-residential neighborhood than in a neighborhood dominated by farms or factories.

MULTISTATE-STYLE EXAM QUESTIONS

Here are 25 multiple-choice questions, in a Multistate Bar Exam style. These questions are taken from *Strategies & Tactics for the Finz Multistate Method*, written by the late Professor Steven Finz and published by Wolters Kluwer Law & Business. To learn more about this book and other study aids, go to **www.wolterskluwerlb.com** and click on "Education."

Questions 1-2 are based on the following fact situation.

Givers executed a deed to his realty known as Givacre, which contained the following clause:

"To Senior Center, for so long as the realty shall be used as a home for the elderly, but if racial discrimination is practiced in the admission of residents to said home, to Senior Life for so long as the realty shall be sued as a home for the elderly."

Senior Center and Senior Life were both charitable institutions devoted to the needs of indigent elderly persons.

1. On the day after the deed was executed, Givers' interest in Givacre is best described as

   (A) a valid reversion.

   (B) a valid possibility of reverter.

   (C) a valid right of re-entry.

   (D) void under the Rule Against Perpetuities.

2. On the day after the deed was executed, Senior Life's interest in Givacre is best described as a

   (A) valid contingent remainder.

   (B) valid executory interest.

   (C) void contingent remainder.

   (D) void executory interest.

Questions 3-4 are based on the following fact situation.

On March 1, Marcel conveyed a tract of realty to her daughters Andrea and Bessie as joint tenants. On April 1, Marcel purported to sell the same tract of realty to Parton by general warranty deed. Parton paid cash for the property, and was unaware of the prior conveyance to Marcel's daughters. Andrea and Bessie recorded their deed on April 3. Parton recorded his deed on April 5. Andrea died on April 7.

3. Assume for the purpose of this question only that the jurisdiction has ONE of the following statutes:

   I. "No conveyance of real property is effective against a subsequent purchaser for value and without notice unless the same be recorded."

   II. "Every conveyance of real estate is void as against any subsequent purchaser in good faith and for value whose conveyance is first duly recorded."

   Is Bessie's right superior to Parton's on April 8?

   (A) Yes, only if the jurisdiction has Statute I.

   (B) Yes, only if the jurisdiction has Statute II.

   (C) Yes, if the jurisdiction has Statute I or Statute II.

   (D) No.

4. Assume for the purpose of this question only that the jurisdiction has a statute which provides, "In determining the priority of conflicting interests in land, the first such interest to have been recorded shall have priority." Who has priority on April 8?

   (A) Bessie, because the conveyance to Andrea and Bessie was recorded before the conveyance to Parton was recorded.

   (B) Bessie, because the realty was conveyed to Andrea and Bessie before the conveyance to Parton was recorded.

   (C) Parton, because Bessie's interest was recorded.

   (D) Parton, because Marcel conveyed to him by general warranty deed.

5. After working twenty years for the People's Trust Company, Singer was promoted from assistant manager of the Twin Oaks branch located in another state. When he learned that Bryant was moving to Twin Oaks to replace him as assistant manager, he offered to sell Bryant his home in Twin Oaks for $60,000. After inspecting the premises, Bryant accepted the offer. They entered into a written contract of sale calling for closing of title six weeks after the signing of the contract. Because their employer was eager to have them both start at their new positions as soon as possible, the contract contained a clause permitting Bryant to move into the house immediately. Bryant did so a few days after signing the contract of sale. Singer kept the fire insurance policy on the house in effect, planning to cancel it upon conveying title to Bryant. In addition, Bryant purchased a policy of fire insurance on the house immediately after contracting for purchase of the house. Two weeks after Bryant moved in, a fire of unknown origin partially destroyed a portion of the roof, the entire kitchen, and parts of the exterior of the house. Bryant immediately notified Singer that he was unwilling to complete the transaction at the price originally agreed upon, but that he would be willing to renegotiate to determine a new price based on the diminished value of the real estate as the result of the fire.

If Singer sues for damages based upon Bryant's anticipatory repudiation of the contract of sale, the court should find for

   (A) Singer, since the risk of loss passed to Bryant when he took possession of the premises pursuant to the contract.

   (B) Singer, since Bryant purchased a policy of fire insurance covering the premises prior to the contract.

   (C) Bryant, since Singer had a policy of insurance insuring him against fire damage to the house.

   (D) Bryant, since the risk of loss never passed to Bryant.

Questions 6-8 are based on the following fact situation.

Several years ago, the Johnson Chemical Company developed a plan to use underground pipes for the purpose of transporting non-poisonous chemical wastes to a waste storage center located several miles away from its plant. At that time, it began negotiating for the right to lay an underground pipeline for that purpose across several tracts of realty. In return for a cash payment, the owner of Westacre executed a right-of-way deed for the installation and maintenance of the pipeline across his land. The right-of-way deed to Johnson Chemical Company was properly recorded. Westacre passed through several intermediate conveyances until it was conveyed to Sofield about fifteen years after the recording of the right-of-way deed. All of the intermediate deeds were recorded, but none mentioned the right-of-way.

Two years later, Sofield agreed to sell Westacre to Belden, by a written contract in which, among other things, Sofield agreed to furnish Belden with an abstract company, to prepare the abstract. Titleco prepared an abstract and delivered it to Sofield. The abstract omitted any mention of the right-of-way deed. Sofield delivered the abstract of title to Belden. After examining the abstract, Beldon paid the full purchase price to Sofield who conveyed Westacre to Belden by a deed which included covenants of general warranty and against encumbrances. At the time of closing,

Sofield, Belden, and Titleco were all unaware of the existence of the right-of-way deed. After possessing Westacre for nearly a year, Belden was notified by the Johnson Chemical Company that it planned to begin installation of an underground pipeline on its right-of-way across Westacre.

6. Assume for the purpose of this question only that Belden subsequently asserted a claim against Titleco for damages which Belden sustained as a result of the existence of the right-of-way. The court should find for

   (A) Titleco, because it was unaware of the existence of the right-of-way deed.

   (B) Titleco, because the right-of-way deed was outside the chain of title.

   (C) Belden, because Belden was a third party beneficiary of the contract between Sofield and Titleco.

   (D) Belden, because the deed executed by Sofield contained a covenant against encumbrances.

7. If Belden sues Sofield because of the presence of the right-of-way, the most likely result will be a decision for

   (A) Sofield, because Belden relied on the abstract of title prepared by Titleco in purchasing Westacre.

   (B) Sofield, because Sofield was without knowledge of any defects in the title to Westacre.

   (C) Belden, because the covenants in Sofield's deed to Belden were breached.

   (D) Belden, because Sofield negligently misrepresented the condition of title to Westacre.

8. Assume for the purpose of this question only that Belden sued for an injunction prohibiting the installation of the underground pipeline across Westacre. Which one of the following additional facts or inferences, if it was the only one true, which would be most likely to lead the court to issue the injunction?

   (A) The Johnson Chemical Company sold its entire business to another company which was planning to continue operating the business exactly as Johnson had operated it, and it was the new company which was attempting to install the underground pipeline.

   (B) The Johnson Chemical Company's operation had changed since the conveyance of the right-of-way, and it was now planning to use the pipeline for the transportation of poisonous wastes.

   (C) No use of the right-of-way has been made since the conveyance eighteen years ago, and the law of the jurisdiction sets a ten year period for acquiring title by adverse possession or acquiring an easement by prescription.

   (D) In purchasing Westacre Belden detrimentally relied on the absence of any visible encumbrances, and the installation of an underground pipeline will result in substantial reduction in the value of the realty.

9. Lance Industries completed construction of a new office building and rented the entire ground floor to Tollup, an attorney, under a three year lease which fixed rent at six hundred dollars per month. Lance was unable to obtain a tenant to rent any other space in the building. Six months later, Tollup vacated the premises. In a claim by Lance against Tollup for rent for the balance of the term, which one of the following additional facts if it were the only one true, would be most likely to result in a judgment for Tollup?

   (A) The day after Tollup vacated, Lance rented the ground floor to another attorney on a month-to-month basis at a rent of five hundred dollars per month.

   (B) The day after Tollup vacated, Lance began using the ground floor as a management office for the building.

   (C) The reason Tollup vacated was that the building was located in a part of town not easily accessible by public transportation, and as a result many of Tollup's client refused to travel to see him there.

(D) The reason Tollup vacated was that he had been disbarred and was disqualified from the practice of law.

10. Lardner rented a warehouse to Torrelson pursuant to a lease which fixed the rent at five hundred dollars payable at the beginning of each month. The lease contained a provision stating that in the event Torrelson failed to pay rent as agreed, Lardner had the right to terminate the tenancy and re-enter the premises. After Torrelson missed two rent payments, Lardner threatened to institute an eviction proceeding unless the unpaid rent was paid immediately. The following day, Torrelson moved out, sending Lardner a check for one thousand dollars in payment of rent already owing. Also enclosed was a letter which stated that it was Torrelson's intention to surrender the premises immediately, and an additional check for five hundred dollars in payment of the following month's rent. Lardner made no attempt to re-rent the warehouse, and it remained vacant for the balance of the term of Torrelson's lease. Upon its expiration, Lardner asserted a claim against Torrelson for unpaid rent from the date Torrelson vacated until the end of the lease term.

In deciding Lardner's claim against Torrelson, the court should find for

(A) Lardner, since Torrelson failed to pay the rent as agreed.

(B) Lardner, since the lease reserved a right of re-entry.

(C) Torrelson, since the lease reserved Lardner's right of re-entry.

(D) Torrelson, since, in effect, he gave Lardner a month's notice of his intention to vacate.

11. The City of Hampshire owned land known as Hampshire Heights which was located outside the city limits, east of the city itself. Because the Hampshire River ran along the western edge of Hampshire Heights, the City of Hampshire built a bridge across the river more than fifty years ago.

The eastern part of Hampshire Heights had once been used as a storage yard for city maintenance equipment, and was surrounded by an eight foot chain link fence. The part of Hampshire Heights between the fenced yard and the bridge had been used primarily as a dirt road connecting the bridge to the storage yard.

Due to periodic flooding of the Hampshire River, the City of Hampshire stopped using the Hampshire Heights storage yard and bridge thirty years ago. At that time, Adpo built a wooden shack on that portion of Hampshire Heights which had formerly been used as a dirt road between the storage yard and the bridge. Since then, Adpo has been living in the shack, and has been raising donkeys on the land formerly used as a dirt road. In addition, he planted a vegetable garden which produced food for himself and his donkeys.

Earlier this year, the City of Hampshire decided to begin using the Hampshire Heights storage yard again, and demanded that Adpo remove himself and his possessions. Adpo refused, asserting that by adverse possession he had become the owner of the land which he occupied. A statute in the jurisdiction conditions ownership by adverse possession on twenty years' continuous, hostile, open and notorious possession.

If the City of Hampshire institutes a proceeding to eject Adpo from Hampshire Heights, the outcome is most likely to turn on whether

(A) the City of Hampshire had knowledge that Adpo was in possession of part of Hampshire Heights.

(B) the jurisdiction permits the acquisition of city property by adverse possession.

(C) Adpo paid taxes on the land which he occupied.

(D) Adpo occupied Hampshire Heights under color of title.

12. Soon after Harold and Wilhemina married, they became interested in the purchase of a home with a price of $75,000. Because neither of them had been employed for very long, they were unable to

find a bank to lend them money for the purchase. The seller indicated that he would be willing to accept a note for part of the purchase price if Harold and Wilhemina could obtain an acceptable co-signor.

Wilhemina's mother Marion said that she would give them the money for the down payment and co-sign the note if Wilhemina and Harold promised to make all payments on the note as they came due, and if the three of them took title to the property as joint tenants. All agreed. On the day title closed, Marion paid $25,000 cash to the seller, and she, Harold, and Wilhemina all signed a note promising to pay the balance, secured by a mortgage on the realty which they all executed. The seller executed a deed conveying the realty to Harold, Wilhemina, and Marion as joint tenants.

Harold and Wilhemina moved into the house, but Marion never did. The following year Marion died, leaving a will purporting to devise her interest in the realty to her husband Allan. The year after that, Wilhemina and Harold were divorced. Wilhemina subsequently executed a deed purporting to convey her interest in the realty to Bernard. Harold subsequently executed a deed purporting to convey his interest in the realty to Charles.

Which of the following best describes the interests of Allan, Bernard, and Charles in the realty?

(A) Allan, Bernard, and Charles are tenants in common, each holding a one-third interest.

(B) Bernard and Charles are tenants in common, each holding a one-half interest.

(C) Bernard and Charles are joint tenants as to a two-thirds interest, and tenants in common as to a one-third interest.

(D) Allan, Bernard and Charles are joint tenants, each holding a one-third interest.

13. Larrick executed a document purporting to lease a parcel of real estate to Teeter for fifty years at an annual rent of $1,000. Twenty years before the scheduled expiration of the lease, the entire par-

cel was taken by the state for the construction of a reservoir. At a condemnation proceeding, the trier of the facts found that the balance of Teeter's leasehold was valued at $30,000. Of the total condemnation award, Teeter should receive

(A) $30,000, but Teeter will be required to pay Larrick a sum equivalent to the rent for the balance of the lease term.

(B) nothing, because Teeter's interest violates the Rule Against Perpetuities.

(C) $30,000, and Teeter will have no further obligation to Larrick.

(D) $30,000 minus a sum equivalent to the rent for the balance of the lease term, and Teeter will have no further obligation to Larrick.

Questions 14-15 are based on the following fact situation.

Upton is the owner of a hillside parcel of realty known as Slopeacre, on which he grows apples for sale to a company which makes juice from them. For several years, Upton has been irrigating his apple trees with water from a stream which flows across Slopeacre. After flowing across Slopeacre, the stream flows through Flatacre, a parcel of realty located in the valley below Slopeacre. Downey, who owns Flatacre, lives there with his family. Downey's family uses water from the stream for household purposes. This year, Upton informed Downey that he was planning to build a small dam across the stream so that he would be able to pump water out of it more easily for irrigating his apple trees. Downey immediately instituted a proceeding to prevent Upton from constructing the dam.

The jurisdiction determines water rights by applying the common law.

14. If it were the only one true, which of the following additional facts or inferences would be most likely to cause a court to grant the relief requested by Downey?

(A) Construction of a dam will increase Upton's

consumption of water from the stream.

(B) Construction of a dam will change the natural flow of the stream.

(C) Construction of a dam will cause Upton to consume more water from the stream than is reasonably necessary for the enjoyment of Slopeacre.

(D) Upton can continue to pump water from the stream without constructing a dam.

15. Assume for the purpose of this question only that because of a drought there is enough water in the stream to satisfy the needs of either Flatacre or Slopeacre, but not both, and that there are no other riparian owners. Who is entitled to use the water?

(A) Upton, because he is the upstream owner.

(B) Upton, because he needs the water for agricultural use.

(C) Downey, because he needs the water for household use.

(D) Downey, because he is the downstream owner.

16. When Fletcher died he left his farm to his son Sam for life with remainder to Unity Church. Because Fletcher had been a farmer, Sam tried farming the land for a while, but found the work unpleasant. Although gravel had never before been mined or removed from the land, Sam learned that he could derive a substantial income by doing so. He therefore dug a deep and extensive pit on the land from which he began removing gravel for sale to builders and other commercial purchasers.

If Unity Church asserts a claim against Sam because of his removal of gravel the court should

(A) grant Unity Church a proportionate share of any profits derived from the sale of gravel removed from the land.

(B) issue an injunction against further removal of gravel and order Sam to account to

Unity Church for profits already derived from the sale of gravel removed from the land.

(C) deny relief to Unity Church, because no right of action will accrue until Unity Church's interest becomes possessory at the termination of Sam's estate.

(D) deny relief to Unity Church, because a life tenant is entitled to remove minerals from an open pit.

17. Oscar, the owner of a summer beach cabin, conveyed it to his daughter Debra as a gift for her sixteenth birthday. Two years later, on her eighteenth birthday, Debra went to the cabin for the first time and found Adamo in possession of it. When she asked what he was doing there, Adamo said, "Anyone who lives around here can tell you that I've been coming here every summer." In fact, Adamo had occupied the beach cabin every summer for the past ten years, but had not occupied the cabin during other seasons. Debra instituted a proceeding to evict Adamo. In defense, Adamo claimed that he had acquired title to the cabin by adverse possession. Statutes in the jurisdiction fix the period for acquiring title to realty by adverse possession at 10 years and the age of majority at 18 years.

Has Adamo acquired title by adverse possession.

(A) No, because computation of the period of adverse possession begins anew each time there is a change in ownership of the realty.

(B) No, because for the past two years the owner of the cabin was under a legal disability.

(C) Yes, if occupancy only during the summer was consistent with the appropriate use of the cabin.

(D) Yes, if Adamo had Oscar's permission to occupy the cabin during the summers.

18. Lenox was the owner of a commercial building which he leased to Ashdown for use as a retail

shoe store for a period of five years. In the lease, Ashdown covenanted not to assign the premises without Lenox's written consent. A clause of the lease reserved Lenox's right to terminate the lease in the event of a breach of this covenant. Two years after Ashdown began occupancy, he sold the business to Boyer, his store manager. After obtaining Lenox's written consent, Ashdown assigned the balance of the lease to Boyer. Boyer operated the shoe store for several months and then sold it to Cole. As part of the sale, Boyer executed a document purporting to transfer to Cole all remaining rights under the lease. Boyer did not obtain Lenox's permission for this transfer. When Lenox learned of this transfer to Cole, he instituted a proceeding in which he sought Cole's eviction on the ground that the covenant not to assign had been violated.

Which of the following best states how the court will probably rule in Lenox's action?

(A) The covenant against assignment is void as a restraint against alienation.

(B) Lenox's only remedy is an action against Boyer for damages resulting from breach of the covenant.

(C) Lenox waived his rights under the covenant by consenting to the assignment by Ashdown to Boyer.

(D) The transfer by Boyer to Cole was not an assignment but a sublease.

Questions 19-20 are based on the following fact situation.

Owsley was the owner of a large tract of realty with its southernmost boundary fronting on a public road. Owsley divided the tract into two parcels, one to the north of the other. Owsley named the southernmost parcel, which fronted on the public road, Southacre. He named the northernmost parcel Northacre, and sold it to Archer. Northacre did not have road frontage, and was accessible only by a visible dirt road which crossed Southacre. The deed by which Owsley conveyed Northacre to Archer contained language granting a right-of-way easement over the

dirt road. Several years after purchasing Northacre, Archer purchased Southacre from Owsley. Archer never occupied Northacre and never used the dirt road which crossed Southacre.

19. Assume for the purposes of this question only that Archer subsequently sold Northacre to Barnhart by a deed which made no mention of a right-of-way easement across Southacre. If Barnhart claims that he received a right-of-way easement over Southacre, which of the following would be Barnhart's best argument in support of that claim?

(A) The visible dirt road across Southacre which provided access to Northacre was a quasi-easement.

(B) Since there was no other access to Northacre, Barnhart received an easement by implied reservation.

(C) Since there was no other access to Northacre, Barnhart received an easement by necessity.

(D) The grant of a right-of-way easement across Southacre contained in the deed by which Owsley conveyed Northacre to Archer benefits all subsequent purchasers of Northacre.

20. Assume for the purpose of this question only that Coates subsequently contracted to purchase Southacre from Archer, that Coates inspected Southacre and saw the dirt road which crossed it prior to contracting, and that the purchase contract made no mention of an easement or of the quality of title to be conveyed. Assume further that prior to closing of title, Coates refused to go through with the transaction on the ground that the existence of an easement across Southacre made Archer's title unmarketable. If Archer asserts a claim against Coates for breach of contract, which of the following would be Archer's most effective argument in support of his claim?

(A) A contract to purchase real property merges with the deed by which the title is conveyed.

(B) Coates had notice of the easement at the time he entered into the contract to purchase Southacre.

(C) The existence of an easement does not make title unmarketable.

(D) The purchase contract did not specify the quality of title to be conveyed.

Questions 21-23 are based on the following fact situation.

Zoning laws in Green City provided that all land on the north side of Main Street was restricted to residential use, and that commercial use was permitted on all land on the south side of Main Street. The zoning laws also provided that up two horses could be kept on any land zoned for residential use, but that no business could be operated on land zoned for residential use. Although all the other realty on the south side of Main Street was being put to commercial use, Homer owned and resided in a one story house located on the south side of Main Street.

Green Hills was a housing development located on the north side of Main Street. All deeds to realty in Green Hills contained language prohibiting the keeping of horses anywhere within the subdivision. The subdivision plan which had been filed when Green Hills was created provided that persons occupying realty in Green Hills were permitted to operate small businesses in their homes so long as such operation did not interfere with or annoy other residents in the subdivision.

21. Assume for the purposes of this question only that Typer operated a typing service from an office in her home in Green Hills, and that Foley entered into a contract to buy Typer's typing service and home. After entering into the contract of sale, however, Foley learned of the zoning law which prohibited the operation of any business in a residential zone. He immediately informed Typer that he would not go through with the purchase of Typer's home because of the zoning violation. If Typer asserts a claim against Foley for

breach of contract, the court should find for

(A) Foley, because the purchaser of realty cannot be forced to buy a potential litigation.

(B) Foley, but only if he could not have discovered the zoning violation by reasonable inquiry prior to entering into the contract of sale.

(C) Typer, because the zoning law which prohibited the operation of Typer's business existed before the contract of sale was formed.

(D) Typer, because her business was permitted by provisions of the Green Hills subdivision plan.

22. Assume for the purpose of this question only that Graves purchased the land owned by Homer, tore down the existing house, and began construction of a three story office building. Kaham, who operated a business known as a water slide on the adjacent realty, objected on the ground that the building which Graves was constructing would block off Kaham's air and light, thus diminishing the value of his realty. If Kaham commences an appropriate proceeding against Graves seeking an order which would prohibit construction of the building, the court should find for

(A) Graves if the construction of a three story office building is permitted by the zoning law.

(B) Graves because commercial use of the realty is the highest and best use.

(C) Kaham, because previous use by Homer created an implied easement for air, light, and view.

(D) Kaham, if residential use by Homer was a continuing non-conforming use.

23. Assume for the purpose of this question only that Equis, a resident of Green Hills, began keeping horses in his yard. If his neighbor, Ralph, commences a proceeding in which he seeks an order preventing Equis from keeping horses, the court should find for

(A) Equis because the zoning law permits the keeping of horses.

(B) Equis only if keeping horses is part of ordinary residential use.

(C) Ralph because of the language in Equis's deed which prohibits the keeping of horses.

(D) Ralph only if keeping horses is a nuisance.

Questions 24-25 are based on the following fact situation.

Olsen conveyed a parcel of realty "to Geller so long as liquor is not sold on the premises, but if liquor is sold on the premises, to the Foundation for Hereditary Diseases." Two years later, Geller began selling liquor on the premises.

24. Which of the following best describes Geller's interest in the realty on the day before he began selling liquor on the premises?

(A) void, since the interest of the Foundation for Hereditary Diseases could have vested more than 21 years after the death of all persons who were in being at the time of the conveyance.

(B) fee simple absolute.

(C) fee simple determinable, since Geller's interest will terminate if liquor is ever sold on the premises.

(D) fee simple subject to a condition subsequent, which will ripen into a fee simple absolute if liquor is not sold during a period measured by a life or lives in being plus twenty-one years.

25. Which of the following best describes the interest of the Foundation for Hereditary Diseases in the realty on the day after Geller began selling liquor on the premises?

(A) fee simple absolute if the Foundation for Hereditary Diseases is a charity.

(B) right of re-entry.

(C) no interest, since at the time of the conveyance it was possible that the interest which the deed purported to grant to the Foundation for Hereditary Diseases would not vest within a period measured by a life or lives in being plus twenty-one years.

(D) shifting executory interest which will not become possessory until the Foundation for Hereditary Diseases takes some step to exercise its right.

ANSWERS TO
MULTISTATE-STYLE EXAM QUESTIONS

1. **B**   A reversion is a future interest of the grantor which will automatically follow a prior estate which will inevitably terminate (e.g., a life estate; a leasehold). A possibility of reverter is a future interest of the grantor which will automatically follow a prior estate which will not inevitably terminate (e.g., fee simple determinable). A right of re-entry is a future interest of the grantor which does not revert automatically, but which requires some act by the grantor in order for him/her to re-acquire a possessory right, and which follows an estate which will not inevitably terminate. Since the property was conveyed only for so long as it is used as a home for the elderly, it will automatically revert to the grantor if that use is ever discontinued. It is, thus, either a reversion or a possibility of reverter. Since it is not certain that it ever will cease to be used as a home for the elderly, however, the prior estate is not one which will inevitably terminate. For this reason, the grantor's interest is a possibility of reverter. **B** is, therefore, correct, and **A** is, therefore, incorrect. **C** is incorrect because if the property ever ceases to be used as a home for the elderly, no act of the grantor is necessary to make his interest possessory. **D** is incorrect because the Rule against Perpetuities does not apply to a grantor's interest.

2. **B**   A remainder is a future interest in a grantee which will automatically become possessory following a prior estate which will terminate inevitably (e.g., a life estate). An executory interest is a future interest in a grantee which will not automatically become possessory and which follows a prior estate which will not terminate inevitably. Since the interest of Senior Life will only become possessory if racial discrimination is practiced by Senior Center, and since this may never happen, the interest of Senior Life is best classified as a executory interest. **A** and **C** are, therefore, incorrect. Under the Rule Against Perpetuities, no interest is good unless it must vest, if at all, during a period measured by a life or lives in being plus 21 years. Since Senior Center might begin practicing racial discrimination after the period proscribed by the Rule, the interest of Senior Life seems to violate the Rule. Because of an exception, however, the Rule Against Perpetuities does not apply to the interest of a charity which follows the interest of a charity. Since Senior Center and Senior Life are both charitable institutions, the Rule Against Perpetuities does not apply, and the interest of Senior Life is valid. **B** is, therefore, correct, and **D** is, therefore, incorrect.

3. **B**   Under Statute I (a pure notice type statute), Parton's interest would be superior to Bessie's because while Bessie's interest was unrecorded, he purchased for value and without notice of the prior conveyance. Under Statute II (a race-notice type statute) Bessie's interest would be superior even though Parton purchased for value and in good faith (i.e., without notice of the prior conveyance), because Parton's interest was not recorded before Bessie's.

4. **A**   Under this recording statute (a pure race type statute), the first interest recorded is superior. Bessie's interest derives from the deed which was recorded on April 3. Since Parton's deed was not recorded until April 5, Bessie's interest had priority.

   B is incorrect because under a race type statute, all that matters is the order in which the interests were recorded. **C** is incorrect because Bessie's interest derives from the deed which was recorded on April 3. The general warranty deed by which Marcel conveyed to Parton will determine Parton's rights against Marcel. But **D** is incorrect because the recording statute determines the rights of Marcel and Bessie as against each other.

5. **A**   Whether they apply the doctrine of equitable conversion, the Uniform Vendor and Purchaser Risk Act, or some other system for apportioning the risk of loss under a real estate sales contract, all jurisdictions agree that the risk of loss from causes other than the fault of the vendor passes to the vendee when he takes possession of the realty prior to closing.

B and **C** are incorrect because passage of the risk of loss does not depend on the purchase of fire insurance by either party. **D** is incorrect because the risk of loss passed to Bryant when he took possession of the realty.

6. **C**   Some jurisdictions hold that an abstractor of title impliedly warrants the abstract to be accurate; all jurisdictions agree that there is at least an implied warranty that the service will be performed in a reasonable manner. Since the right-of-way deed was properly recorded, Titleco's failure to include it in the abstract which it furnished was a breach of either the promise to perform reasonably or the implied warranty of accuracy. In either event, since Belden was an intended creditor beneficiary of the contract between Sofield and Titleco, Belden can enforce it.

If there was an implied warranty of accuracy **A** is incorrect because liability is imposed without fault for its breach. If there was no implied warranty of accuracy, **A** is incorrect because liability may be imposed if Titleco's lack of awareness of the right-of-way resulted from its failure to act reasonably. Since the right-of-way deed from the owner of Westacre to Johnson Chemical Company was properly recorded before any of the grants of Westacre took place, it was not outside the chain of title, and **B** is incorrect. **D** is incorrect because the liability of Titleco does not depend on covenants made by Sofield.

7. **C**   The covenant against encumbrances is a representation that there are no easements or liens burdening the realty. If the realty is, in fact, burdened by such an encumbrance, the covenant is breached and liability is imposed on the covenantor.

This is so even though the purchaser relied on assurances in addition to the covenant, and even though the grantor was unaware of the existence of the encumbrance at the time he executed the covenant. **A** and **B** are, therefore, incorrect. **D** is incorrect because there is no indication that Sofield failed to act reasonably (i.e., was "negligent").

8. **B**   The holder of an easement may not unreasonably burden the servient estate by using it in a way not contemplated when the easement was created. Since the dangers incident to the possible leakage of poisonous materials are much greater than those incident to the possible leakage of non-poisonous materials, the change in Johnson's intended use would unreasonably burden the estate of Belden.

Since most jurisdictions agree that commercial easements in gross may be freely alienated, **A** is incorrect. Non-use of an easement created by express grant is not sufficient to terminate it, so unless the holder of the easement extinguishes it by a deed that was properly recorded, the easement remains effective; **C** is therefore incorrect. Belden had constructive notice of the easement when he purchased, and would not have been justified in relying on the absence of visible encumbrances. **D** is, therefore, incorrect.

9. **B**   Ordinarily, a tenant who abandons the premises before the expiration of the lease is liable for rent for the balance of the term. If, however, the landlord accepts a *surrender* of the tenant's interest under the lease, the tenant will be free from liability for the balance of the term. A surrender generally takes place when the landlord occupies the premises for its own purposes.

Reletting the premises for the balance of the term might also result in a surrender, but this depends on the intent of the landlord. Here, there was much other vacant space in the building, and the landlord has relet the premises for rent lower than provided in the lease, and on a month-to-month basis. Therefore, it is not likely that Lance's intent was to surrender its rights, but rather, to relet for Tollup's account (as a mitigation of damages). **A** is, therefore, incorrect. The agreement between Lance and Tollup did not restrict use of the premises to any particular activity. For this reason, the fact that the premises are not well suited to the activity which Tollup had in mind, or that Tollup is no longer licensed in the practice for which he planned to use them, is irrelevant to his liability under the lease. **C** and **D** are, therefore, incorrect.

10. **A**   Ordinarily, a tenant who abandons the premises before the expiration of the lease is liable for rent for the balance of the term.

The lease may reserve to the landlord the right to terminate the tenancy and re-enter in the event of non-payment, but **B** is incorrect because this is alternative to the right to collect rent, not the source of it. A landlord who elects to terminate the tenancy, will not be entitled to collect rent for the balance of the term. **C** is incorrect, however, because a landlord may elect not to terminate, as did Lardner, and hold the tenant for rent. **D** is incorrect because neither party to a lease may avoid obligations under it merely by giving notice, unless the lease so provides.

11. **B**   Adpo has been in continuous possession for twenty years. His possession was hostile, because it was contrary to the rights of the City of Hampshire, the land's true owner. It was open and notorious because it was not hidden, and knowledge of his possession could have been obtained by anyone who looked. Having fulfilled all the statutory requirements, he would ordinarily be correct in his assertion that he has acquired title by adverse possession. Most jurisdictions, however, prohibit the acquisition of city or state property by adverse possession. This being the only legal obstacle to Adpo's assertion, the outcome will most likely depend on whether the jurisdiction permits the acquisition of city property by adverse possession.

A is incorrect because if the possession was open and notorious as described above, it does not matter whether the actual owner ever really knew of it. Some adverse-possession statutes establish a condition that the adverse possessor pay taxes on the realty during the period of his adverse possession. **C** is incorrect, however, because this statute did not contain such a requirement. An adverse possessor who occupies land under color of title may become the owner of all the land which he believed he owned, including that which he did not actually occupy. Since Adpo asserts ownership only of the land which he occupied, however, color of title is irrelevant, and **D** is incorrect.

12. **B**   Joint tenancy is a form of co-ownership in which the joint tenants have the right of survival. This means that upon the death of one joint tenant, the others receive equal shares in her interest. When Marion died, Harold and Wilhemina received equal shares of her

interest. The joint tenancy of Harold and Wilhemina continued, but each held a one-half interest in the whole instead of a one-third interest. Joint tenants may convey their interests inter vivos without each other's consent, but a joint tenant's grantee takes as a tenant in common with the remaining owners. Thus, upon Wilhemina's conveyance to Bernard, Bernard became a tenant in common with a one-half interest; and upon Harold's conveyance to Charles, Charles became a tenant in common with a one-half interest.

A is incorrect because as a joint tenant, Marion could not effectively pass her interest by will. Since a conveyance by a joint tenant makes the grantee a tenant in common, neither Bernard nor Charles received a joint tenancy in any part of the estate. **C** is, therefore, incorrect. **D** is incorrect for this reason, and because Allan received no interest at all under Marion's will.

13. **D** If leased realty is taken by eminent domain, the leasehold and the reversion merge in the taker, the leasehold is terminated, and the obligation to pay rent ceases. Since both the lessor and the lessee have had something of value taken for public use, each is entitled to receive just compensation for what s/he has lost. The lessor is entitled to receive the value of the leased premises (including the value of rent to be received) minus the value of the leasehold interest which he has already conveyed. The lessee is entitled to receive the value of the leasehold. If not for the condemnation, however, the lessee would have been required to pay rent in order to enjoy the benefits of her leasehold. Since the condemnation terminates that obligation, the rent which the lessee otherwise would have been required to pay should be deducted from the value of her leasehold.

A is incorrect because the taking terminates the leasehold, and with it, the obligation to pay rent. The Rule Against Perpetuities provides that no interest is good unless it must vest if at all within a period of time measured by a life or lives in being plus twenty-one years. Since a lessee's interest in leased premises vests at the moment the lease is executed, the Rule Against Perpetuities is inapplicable to it. **B** is, therefore, incorrect. Since the condemnation terminates Teeter's obligation to pay rent for the balance of the lease term, allowing her to keep the entire $30,000 would result in her receiving more than she has actually lost. For this reason, **C** is incorrect.

14. **C** Those who own land adjacent to a flowing body of water (i.e., riparian owners) have some rights to use that water. Under modern common law, each riparian owner has the right to make reasonable use of the water. If construction of a dam would result in the consumption of more water than is reasonably necessary, a court might hold that Upton has no right to build the dam.

A is incorrect because Upton's increased use of the water might still be reasonable. At one time it was said that no riparian owner was permitted a use which altered the natural flow of the stream. If "natural flow" is given a literal meaning, this would make it virtually impossible for anyone but the furthest downstream owner to use the water. For this reason, the natural flow rule has given way to a rule which bases riparian rights on reasonable use. Thus, even if the dam altered the natural flow, Upton would have a right to construct it so long as his use was reasonable. **B** is, therefore, incorrect. Under the reasonable use test, Upton may dam the stream so long as doing so would not make his water use unreasonable. **D** is incorrect because this would be so even if he could accomplish the same without damming the stream.

15. C   Under the existing reasonable use doctrine, when it is necessary to determine which riparian owner is entitled to water which is in limited supply, the courts consider many factors. Most important, however, is the use to which each owner puts the water. Although agricultural use is considered "higher" than most other uses, domestic or household use is universally acknowledged to be the "highest" use of all, entitling it to priority over all other uses. Since the choice to be made is between Upton's agricultural use and Downey's household use, Downey's rights will prevail.

        A is incorrect because upstream owners do not ordinarily have greater rights than downstream owners. **B** is incorrect because household use is a higher use than agricultural use. **D** is incorrect because with the retreat from the natural flow doctrine, downstream owners do not have greater rights than upstream owners.

16. B   Voluntary waste consists of some act by a possessory tenant which diminishes the value of the realty or otherwise "injures the inheritance." One of the ways in which it is committed is by removing minerals from the land. Ordinarily, when a life tenant commits voluntary waste, the holder of a vested remainder is entitled to bring an immediate action at law for damages. In the alternative, the remainderman may be entitled to the equitable remedies of injunction and an accounting for profits already derived from the sale of such minerals.

        Although it is understood that a possessory tenant may remove minerals from realty which is good for no other purpose, or may continue removing minerals from a mine which was open when his tenancy began, neither of these exceptions applies under the facts in this case. **B** is, therefore, correct. A possessory tenant who commits voluntary waste is not entitled to retain any of the profits from his activity. For this reason, Unity Church is entitled to all profits derived from the sale of gravel, rather than merely to a proportionate share. **A** is, therefore, incorrect. It is sometimes held that the holder of a contingent remainder or a remainder subject to defeasance has no right to sue for waste until its interest vests indefeasibly. Since the remainder interest held by Unity Church is already vested, however, **C** is incorrect. The rule which permits a possessory tenant to continue removing minerals from a mine which was open when he began his tenancy is sometimes known as the "open pit" doctrine. **D** is incorrect, however, because the facts indicate that gravel had never before been mined or removed from the land.

17. C   Title to property may be acquired by adverse possession if the person claiming such title occupies the realty openly, notoriously, hostilely, and continuously for the statutory period. Possession is "open and notorious" if the possessor has, in general, behaved as an owner. Since Adamo occupied the premises every summer, his possession was open and notorious. Possession is "hostile" if it is contrary to the rights of the owner. Since the facts do not indicate that Adamo had the owner's permission to occupy the cabin, his occupancy was hostile. Although possession must be "continuous," it is not necessary that it be without interruptions, so long as the interruptions are consistent with the appropriate use of the realty. Since this was a summer cabin, occupancy only during the summers might have been consistent with its appropriate use. If it was, Adamo has acquired title by adverse possession. **C** is, therefore, correct. Once the period of possession has begun, it continues to run in spite of conveyances or other changes in ownership. Thus, **A** is an inaccurate statement and is, therefore, incorrect. If the owner of realty is under a legal disability at the time adverse possession begins, computation of the period of possession does not start until the disability ends. If, however, the owner is

not under a legal disability at the time adverse possession begins, subsequent legal disability or legal disability of a subsequent owner does not interrupt the running of the period. **B** is, therefore, incorrect. Because of the requirement that adverse possession be hostile to the rights of the owner, one who occupies with permission of the owner cannot acquire title by adverse possession. **D** is, therefore, incorrect.

18. **C**   Under the "Rule in Dumpor's Case," many jurisdictions hold that if a landlord consents to an assignment by the tenant, the covenant against assignment is thereafter waived and the assignee may in turn assign to another without being bound by the covenant. Although it is not certain that the court in this jurisdiction would apply the rule, **C** is the only option listed which could possibly be effective in Cole's defense, and is, therefore, correct. Courts strictly construe restraints against the alienation of leasehold interests. This means that a covenant against assignments does not prevent subleases, and vice versa. **A** is incorrect, however, because although such covenants are strictly construed, they are not void. Ordinarily, an assignment made in violation of a covenant not to assign is valid, and the landlord has no remedy other than an action for damages resulting from the breach. Where, as here, however, the landlord reserves the right to terminate the lease in the event of a violation of the covenant, the assignment is voidable at the landlord's election. **B** is, therefore, incorrect. An assignment is a transfer of all remaining rights under a lease; a sublease is a transfer of less than all remaining rights. Since Boyer transferred all remaining rights to Cole, the transfer was an assignment, and **D** is incorrect.

19. **C**   An easement is a right to use the land of another. If the right benefits a parcel of realty, that parcel is known as the dominant estate. The parcel which is burdened by the easement is known as the servient estate. If the dominant estate and the servient estate were owned by the same person, and if a right-of-way easement across the servient estate is necessary to provide access to the dominant estate, the sale of either parcel results in an implied easement by necessity. Since Northacre and Southacre were both owned by Archer, and since the only access to Northacre was over the dirt road which crossed Southacre, Barnhart received an implied easement by necessity over Southacre when he purchased it. **C** is, therefore, correct. When the common owner of two parcels uses one of them for the benefit of the other, and when signs of that use are visible, a quasi-easement may exist which passes by implication to the buyer of the parcel which received the benefit of such use. **A** is incorrect, however, because Archer never actually used Northacre or the dirt road which crossed Southacre. A grantor of realty may reserve for himself an easement to use it, and under some circumstances (e.g., strict necessity), such a reservation may be implied. **B** is incorrect, however, because only a grantor can receive an easement by reservation. Ordinarily, an easement of record benefits subsequent owners of the dominant estate even if it is not mentioned in the deeds by which the dominant estate was conveyed to them. When the dominant estate and the servient estate merge (i.e., are owned by the same person), however, all existing easements terminate. **D** is, therefore, incorrect.

20. **B**   Although the existence of an easement may make title to realty unmarketable, most courts hold that this is not so where the buyer was aware of the easement at the time he contracted to purchase the realty. Since Coates saw the dirt road prior to contracting, it is likely that a court would hold that its existence does not prevent the title from being marketable. While it is not certain that a court would come to this conclusion, the argu-

ment in **B** is the only one listed which could possibly provide support for Archer's claim. **B** is, therefore, correct. If a buyer accepts a deed which does not conform to the requirements of the purchases contract, he has waived his rights under the contract because the contract is said to merge with the deed. **A** is incorrect, however, because Coates did not accept the deed and so is still protected by the terms of the contract. Marketable title means title that is reasonably secure against attack. Since the existence of an easement would provide the holder of a dominant estate with a ground to attack the rights of the holder of the servient estate, an undisclosed easement is usually sufficient to render title to the servient estate unmarketable. **C** is, therefore, incorrect. A covenant to deliver marketable title is implied in a contract for the sale of realty unless some other quality of title is specified. Since the contract between Archer and Coates did not specify the quality of title to be conveyed, Archer is required to convey marketable title. **D** is, therefore, incorrect.

21. **A**   Every contract for the sale of realty contains an implied covenant by the seller that he will deliver marketable title. Marketable title means title which is reasonably secure against attack. It is generally understood that title to property which is being used in violation of a zoning law is not marketable. If a seller is unable to deliver marketable title, the buyer is not required to complete the transaction because no person should be required to purchase potential litigation. Since Foley's agreement to purchase the house was connected with his purchase of the business, it is likely that a court would find that the zoning violation constitutes a defect which excuses Foley from going through with the purchase. Although it is not certain that a court would come to this conclusion, **A** is the only option which could possibly be correct. **B** and **C** are incorrect because the courts usually hold that an existing zoning violation makes title unmarketable. **D** is incorrect because a public law which prohibits a particular activity takes precedence over a private rule which permits it.

22. **A**   Ordinarily zoning laws determine the use to which land may be put. Thus, if the zoning law permits the construction of a three story office building, Graves may construct it. **A** is, therefore, correct. **B** is incorrect because there is no rule which requires a court to permit the highest and best use of realty. Although an easement for air, light, and view may be created by express grant, **C** is incorrect because courts do not recognize an implied easement for air, light, or view. If land was being used in a way which violates a zoning law passed after the use began, the non-conforming use is permitted to continue. **D** is incorrect, however, because the non-conforming use is never *required* to continue.

23. **C**   Developers are permitted to create conditions on the use of land in their subdivisions which are more restrictive than public laws. Thus, even where zoning law permits a particular activity, deed restrictions may validly prohibit it. Since restrictions contained in all the deeds to land in Green Hills prohibit the keeping of horses, a court will enforce these restrictions, and Ralph should receive the relief which he seeks. **C** is, therefore, correct, and **A** is, therefore, incorrect. Where a zoning law restricts land to residential use but does not define that use, the resolution of a dispute about whether that activity can be conducted there will depend on whether that activity is part of ordinary residential use. **B** is incorrect, however, because the deed restrictions in Green Hills clearly prohibit the keeping of horses. Although a court may enjoin a nuisance, **D** is incorrect because a court may enforce the deed restrictions without regard to whether keeping horses is a nuisance.

24. **C** A fee simple determinable is a fee interest which will terminate automatically upon the happening of a specified event. Courts almost always hold that a grant to a particular grantee "so long as" something does not happen creates this interest. **C** is, therefore, correct. Although an interest which might vest after a period measured by a life or lives in being plus twenty one years is void under the Rule Against Perpetuities, this does not affect the validity of any prior estate. For this reason, even if the interest of the Foundation for Hereditary Diseases violates the Rule, that has no effect on the validity of Geller's interest. **A** is, therefore, incorrect. A fee simple absolute is complete ownership which is not subject to defeasance. **B** is incorrect because of the special limitation created by the phrase "so long as." A fee simple subject to a condition subsequent is an interest which is subject to defeasance on the happening of a specified event, but which does not terminate until the holder of the future interest takes some step to make his/her interest possessory. **D** is incorrect because the phrase "so long as" results in an automatic termination upon the happening of the specified event and because the period described by the rule against perpetuities has no effect on an interest which is already possessory.

25. **C** Under the Rule Against Perpetuities, no interest is good unless it must vest, if at all, during a period measured by a life or lives in being plus twenty one years. Since liquor might be sold on the premises after the expiration of this period, it is possible that the interest of the Foundation for Hereditary diseases would vest beyond the period of perpetuities. For this reason, its interest is void. **C** is, therefore, correct. The future interest of a charity is not subject to the Rule Against Perpetuities if it follows the estate of another charity. Otherwise, the Rule applies as it would to any other grantee. **A** is incorrect because there is no indication that Geller is a charity. **B** is incorrect because only a grantor can hold a right of re-entry. An executory interest is a future interest which follows an estate which is not certain to terminate. If it follows the estate of a grantor, it is a springing executory interest. **D** is incorrect, however, because the interest of the Foundation for Hereditary Diseases is void as explained above.

ESSAY EXAM
QUESTIONS AND ANSWERS

The following Essay Questions are taken from the *Real Property* volume of *Siegel's Essay & Multiple-Choice Questions and Answers*, published by Wolters Kluwer Law & Business. The full volume contains 30 essays (with model answers), as well as 114 multiple choice questions (Most of the essay questions were originally asked on the California Bar Exam, and are copyright the California Board of Bar Examiners, reprinted by permission.) The book is available from your bookstore, or by clicking on "Education" at **www.wolterskluwerlb.com**.

QUESTION 1

Landlord rented a furnished apartment in his building to Tenant, a law student, for two years, beginning June 1. When Tenant arrived at the apartment on June 1, Ralph (the prior tenant) was still there. Tenant complained to Landlord and Landlord was able to evict Ralph on June 15. Tenant went into possession of the apartment on June 16. During early July, some children playing baseball broke a windowpane in Tenant's apartment. Tenant demanded that Landlord replace the windowpane, but Landlord refused. Rain, which subsequently came through the broken pane, caused damage to the living room floor, which began to warp.

The apartment above Tenant's was occupied by Charlie, a member of a famous rock group (The Charles River). The daily rehearsals (typically 2:00-6:00 p.m.) of this group interfered with Tenant's law studies so much that he complained repeatedly to Landlord. On July 15, three of Charlie's friends (the other members of Charlie's band) were arrested at Charlie's apartment and charged with possession of narcotics. The noise stopped immediately thereafter.

On August 30, Tenant discovered that the stove in his apartment was no longer functioning. On August 31, Tenant, disgusted with all these events, knocked on Landlord's door, tendered the key to Landlord, and said, "This place is a zoo; I wouldn't live here if you paid me!" Landlord took the key without saying a word. Landlord now comes to you wanting to sue Tenant for the accrued (Tenant has yet to pay any rent) and prospective rent. What would you advise Landlord? Discuss.

QUESTION 2

Alice has just shown you a deed which was recorded 40 years ago. This document reads as follows:

In consideration of love and affection, I hereby grant Sweetholm to my friend Josiah and the heirs of his body, this conveyance to take effect 10 years from the date hereof, provided that if Josiah dies without issue the estate is to go to my brother Ludwig and his heirs, and further provided that if animals, birds or children are ever kept on the property, the estate is to cease and determine.

[Signed] Vladimir

You ascertain from Alicia that her house, with its surrounding grounds of about 10 acres, is known as Sweetholm. Alicia tells you that she bought Sweetholm from Josiah's niece, Jennifer, 11 years ago. The deed transferred to Alicia "all my right, title and interest in Sweetholm." Alicia also tells you that when she bought the property the guest house near the southwest boundary of the estate was occupied by Danny, Jennifer's cousin. Danny had visited Jennifer 12 years ago and decided to stay to work on a novel. Jennifer had asked Alicia to let Danny stay there for awhile, "since he was finding himself." Alicia said it would probably be "all right, if Danny did not get in my way." Alicia thought it might be a good idea to have a male on the property to frighten away prospective thieves. Soon after Jennifer vacated Sweetholm, Danny built a separate mailbox outside the guest house and placed a doormat in front of the entrance, which read "Welcome to Danny's."

It seems that the estate bordering Sweetholm on the west, Laurel Hill, had been purchased 14 years ago by Wilson, a scientist doing research on the territorial habits of wild dogs, coyotes and wolves. Wilson had captured several wolves and brought them to Laurel Hill. When Alicia took over the property from Jennifer, Wilson talked to her about the wolves. Alicia promised him, in a valid writing, that she would allow the wolves to wander freely over Sweetholm. The wolves soon manifested their territorial behavior and took up residence on the southwest corner of Sweetholm.

Unfortunately, when Danny saw one of the animals wandering around near the guest house about 2 months ago, he suddenly took it into his head that it would make a nice pet. He enticed it into his enclosed patio and kept it there, even when it resisted his first efforts to make friends and bit his hand when he tried to feed it.

About a week ago Alicia received an unpleasant visit from Trivers, Wilson's co-experimenter, who had purchased Laurel Hill from Wilson last summer. Trivers threatened to sue Alicia because Danny had tampered with a subject involved in his experiment. Alicia became upset with the whole thing and evicted both Danny and the wolves from Sweetholm that very evening. Alicia hastily had a chicken wire fence constructed on the western boundary of Sweetholm so that the wolves could not get back in. Last night, (1) Danny called and claimed that he owned the guest house, and (2) Trivers called and threatened to obtain an injunction requiring Alicia to remove the chicken wire fence.

Alicia asks you whether Trivers and Danny really have any viable claims against her. She also wants to know whether there are any other people who might show up to claim an interest in Sweetholm.

In response to initial questioning from you, Alicia tells you that Vladimir is dead and Josef is his sole heir; that Ludwig is dead and Richard is his sole heir; and that Josiah is also dead, but Jennifer, his niece and only heir, is still alive. You have also learned that the Statute of Limitations for actions to recover real property is 10 years. Please evaluate the possible claims of Danny, Trivers, and any other person(s) you think might have a plausible claim to some interest in Sweetholm.

QUESTION 3

Art was the record owner of Greenacre, a vacant tract of land. Art and Bob discussed the sale of this land to Bob, and they orally agreed on a purchase price of $5,000 in cash. Art then typed up a statement setting forth all the terms that had been agreed upon, including the fact that Art would deliver to Carl, a real estate broker, a warranty deed conveying Greenacre to Bob and that Carl would hand deliver the deed to Bob if Bob gave Carl the purchase price within one month.

Art placed one copy of this statement, unsigned, unwitnessed and undated, in an envelope and mailed it to Bob. Upon receiving it, Bob telephoned Art and told him that the statement accurately reflected his understanding and that he would deliver $5,000 in cash to Carl within the month in accordance with their agreement.

Art then executed the warranty deed, complete in all respects, and gave it to Carl with a copy of his statement.

One week later, Art learned that a highway was to be built near Greenacre, greatly increasing its value. Art immediately wrote to Carl, telling Carl he had changed his mind and wanted the deed returned to him.

One day later and before Carl had received Art's last letter, Bob called Carl and said he had to show the deed to his bank to obtain a loan for the $5,000. Carl sent the deed to Bob, who promptly recorded it and immediately executed and delivered a warranty deed for Greenacre to Dale.

Bob has disappeared and has not paid the $5,000 to Art or Carl.

(1) In an action to quiet title between Art and Dale, who prevails? Discuss.

(2) What are the rights of Art and Dale against Carl? Discuss.

ANSWERS

ANSWER TO QUESTION 1

Assumptions: The lease was written and signed by Tenant (and so there is no Statute of Frauds problem even though the lease in question exceeded one year).

To advise Landlord ("LL") of his rights against Tenant ("T") it is initially necessary to determine if T can successfully assert any defenses against LL.

Duty to Deliver Possession: Under the English rule, a landlord has the obligation to assure his/her tenant that no other party will be in possession of the premises when the lease term commences. T might assert that LL breached his duty, since Ralph was in the apartment when T's lease term began. However, even assuming this jurisdiction adheres to this rule that the landlord must evict holdover tenants, T has probably waived (voluntarily relinquished a known right) this breach by going into possession of premises after Ralph moved out. At most, T can probably deduct the rent attributable to the period from June 1 through June 15. If the American view is followed, LL has the duty only to deliver *legal* possession, not actual possession, so the holdover (Ralph) would be T's problem.

Constructive Eviction ("CE"): A CE occurs where there is a substantial interference with a tenant's right of quiet enjoyment by reason of some cause for which the landlord is responsible, and the tenant vacates within a reasonable time thereafter. T might argue that a CE occurred by reason of (i) the noise caused by Charlie's friends, (ii) the broken window pane and warped floor, and (iii) the stove's malfunction.

In response, however, LL could assert the following arguments. With respect to the noises caused by Charlie's band, LL is not responsible for the activities of other tenants. In some states, where the lease contains a provision permitting the landlord to evict lessees who are disturbing other tenants, the landlord has been deemed responsible for the former. However, there is nothing in the given facts to indicate such a clause exists. Additionally, even assuming the band noise persisted from June 15th through July 15th (when 3 persons in the band were arrested), this probably did not constitute a substantial deprivation of T's right to the beneficial enjoyment of the premises since it occurred during daylight hours (rather than in the evening), when other tenants would be trying to sleep. Finally, LL could probably successfully argue that T waived the right to assert a CE by waiting 45 days after the noise had ceased to vacate the premises.

As to the broken window pane and consequent warped floor, LL could argue that, at common law, it is T's duty to make repairs, so T cannot complain about being deprived of the beneficial enjoyment of the premises when the condition which made them unsuitable was T's fault. As to the malfunctioning stove, LL could argue (1) again, this was T's responsibility, and (2) T apparently never even advised LL about this problem, and so he did not have the requisite opportunity to remedy this situation.

The Implied Warranty of Habitability: Many states recognize an implied warranty of habitability that leased premises will not become uninhabitable by reason of the landlord's failure to make repairs attributable to the natural deterioration of the premises. (A few jurisdictions limit this doctrine to situations involving housing code violations.) T might argue that defects vital to the use of the premises existed by reason of (i) the broken pane and consequent warping, and (ii) the malfunctioning stove.

The warping was the result of the failure to repair the window; so whoever had the responsibility for repairing would be liable for the warped floor. LL can argue that the widows should have been repaired by T since (1) the pane was broken by other persons (the children playing ball), as opposed to the natural deterioration of the premises, and (2) a broken window is not a defect which causes premises to become uninhabitable. As to the non-functioning stove, LL can argue that the stove would not cause premises to fall below the bar living requirements. Finally, LL was (apparently) never even informed of this event.

LL should prevail against T on this issue too.

Surrender: T will also probably argue that LL's acceptance of the keys to the apartment constituted a surrender, so that therefore T is not liable for any rent accruing after August 31. However, the fact that LL merely permitted T to hand the keys to him probably does not, without more, demonstrate a willingness to permit T to avoid his prospective obligations under the lease.

Advice/Extent of LL's Recovery: (We'll assume that rent was payable monthly, and that the lease did *not* have an accelerated rent or liquidated damage clause.)

LL should be able to recover T's unpaid rent, and for the additional rentals as they become due. However, LL should probably attempt to locate a new tenant for the premises since (1) many states require a landlord to mitigate a tenant's liability, and (2) it may be difficult for LL to recover any judgment against T (even if one were obtained). Finally, LL should be advised to notify T that any subletting is being done for T's account. This precaution would preclude T from contending that a surrender of the premises had occurred via the subletting.

ANSWER TO QUESTION 2

Adverse Possession ("AP"): One obtains title to real property by AP where he/she, under a claim of right, enters upon and exclusively occupies another's land in an open, notorious and hostile manner throughout the requisite statutory period. Danny ("D") could claim that by remaining at Sweetholm after the sale to Alicia ("A") without the latter's explicit permission, the "claim of ("A") without the latter's explicit permission, the "claim of right" and "hostile" elements are satisfied. Additionally, creating a separate mailbox and putting out a welcome sign which bore his name met the "open" and "notorious" requisites. Finally, D's occupation of the guest house continued for a period of time in excess of the applicable Statute of Limitations. Thus, D could assert ownership to the guest house (along with an easement hereto and therefrom) under AP.

In some jurisdictions, the claim of right requirement is not satisfied unless the adverse claimant went upon the land with the belief that he/she was entitled to possess it. If this were such a jurisdiction, D's claim of AP would fail. In most states, however, the claim of right element is satisfied merely by the adverse possessor being aware that his/her habitation of the land in question was without the owner's permission. If this jurisdiction adhered to the latter view, A could contend that Jennifer ("J") had presumably advised D of her statement that it would be "all right" for D to remain on Sweetholm. If it could be shown that J had so informed D, A should prevail on this issue.

A could alternatively claim that D's occupation of the guest house was ***not*** "hostile." While this element is usually satisfied by the claimant's use of the land in an "open and notorious" manner, an exception to this rule exists where the rightful owner would not necessarily recognize that the adverse possessor's occupation of the land is hostile to his/her ownership interest (even though aware of it). In such situations the adverse claimant must communicate (via clear words or actions) that the land is being held in derogation of the legal owner's rights thereto. Holdover tenancies often constitute such a situation, since a holdover tenant is usually deemed to be occupying the premises with the landlord's implicit permission.

A could contend that D should be viewed as either having been her guest (i.e., a continuation of the relationship which D enjoyed with J) or a tenant at sufferance. In either event, D would have been obliged to either (1) inform A that his occupation of the guest house was hostile to A's claim of ownership thereto, or (2) have done acts which clearly communicated this view (i.e., prevented A from entering the structure, built a fence around it, etc.). The mailbox would not suffice, since A could have presumed that while D had felt comfortable in permitting J (his cousin) to receive his mail, he would not have the same trust in a stranger. Finally, A would assert that the doormat was not adequate to inform her that D was claiming superior title to the guest house.

A would probably prevail upon the "hostile" issue, and therefore it is unlikely that D would prevail upon his claim of AP.

If, however, D's claim of AP were successful, he would have a right of action against A for evicting him. D would probably be entitled to recover the reasonable rental value of the land during his eviction, as well as any other costs and expenses attendant upon the interference with his right to possession.

Injunction sought by Trivers ("T"): T might initially contend that A had granted an express easement to Wilson ("W") to permit animals involved in the experiment to roam throughout Sweetholm, and easements will automatically run with the benefitted estate.

A would initially argue that the right given to W was a license. An easement is ordinarily described as the right of one person to make a particular use of another's land. A license, however, is usually defined as the right to do a particular thing on another's land. A could assert that no right was granted to W to ***use*** her land. Rather, A merely indicated that W's wolves could randomly traverse Sweetholm. Thus, A would contend that the grant made to W was a license, and such interests are (1) ordinarily ***not*** assignable, and (2) revocable at any time by the licensor (subject to the licensee's right to recover for monetary damages resulting from the revocation). However, T could argue in rebuttal that since he was engaged in an experiment whereby the wolves wandered onto A's land, W (and now T) was actually **using** the land for a particular purpose (i.e., to record the results of an experiment).

Even assuming the grant to W was an easement, A could contend that it was an easement in gross (rather than an appurtenant easement). Many courts view easements in gross as ordinarily being non-assignable. Easements in gross are those which **personally** benefit the holder thereof (as opposed to easements appurtenant, which primarily benefit the latter's **land**). The grant in question appears to have been made for the purpose of facilitating W's experiment (rather than enhancing the use or accessibility of Laurel Hill). While T could argue that the use of Laurel Hill is enhanced by having the right to permit animals involved in experimentation to cross into adjoining land, A's grant would probably be characterized as an easement in gross.

T might contend, however, even assuming the grant to W was deemed to be an easement in gross, it should be viewed as being "commercial" in nature. Such interests have been deemed to be assignable where, for example, a severe disruption to a utility (i.e., telephone and sewer lines) would otherwise occur. Although T could contend that maintenance of the fence by A would disrupt an experiment which has been carried on for a 14-year period, it is unlikely that T's easement in gross would be considered "commercial." Thus, A would probably prevail on this question.

Finally, T might argue that A's written statement to W, whereby A had agreed that she would take no action to prevent W's animals from coming upon Sweetholm, constituted a covenant which ran with the benefitted land. Since T is seeking an injunction, the covenant must be analyzed as an equitable servitude ("ES"). For the benefit of an ES to run against the covenantor: (1) the original parties must have intended it to run, and (2) it must touch and concern (affect the value or use) of the burdened land. Although there was no "successors, heirs and assigns" language, some courts take the view that where the promise touches and concerns the burdened parcel, the original parties probably intended for the covenantor's promise to run with the benefitted land. The value and use of Sweetholm is arguably diminished by the fact that wild animals could roam free on a portion of the land. However, A could probably successfully contend in rebuttal that there was no intent that the promise run with the land since it was given specifically to **W** for the purpose of permitting the latter to complete **his** experimentation.

Thus, T probably **cannot** obtain an injunction against A.

Ownership of Sweetholm: Richard (Ludwig's sole heir) could contend that the conveyance by Vladimir to Josiah was a fee tail (since the grant to Josiah is followed by the words "and the heirs of his body"). Therefore, when Josiah died without issue (J was merely his niece, rather than a lineal descendant), Sweetholm became the property of Ludwig (and his heirs).

A could argue in rebuttal that in many states the fee tail has been abolished entirely, and it is viewed as a fee simple absolute. In such case, Josiah would have been entitled to transfer the property to J. In other jurisdictions, however, the failure to have issue results in the estate terminating upon the death of the originally designated party. Under the latter view, Ludwig's heirs (Richard) would obtain title to Sweetholm upon Josiah's death. However, in such instance A could probably claim superior title to Sweetholm through AP. While it is not clear when Josiah died and J succeeded to possession of Sweetholm, the facts do indicate that A has apparently occupied the realty for 11 years and paid taxes on it. Having purchased the land from J, A presumably went into possession of Sweetholm under color of title. It therefore appears that A could defeat any claim of Richard to the property. Richard's remainder is vested, so it is not subject to the RAP.

Josef could, however, contend that J had a fee simple determinable or fee simple subject to a condition subsequent with respect to the provision pertaining to animals, and that the triggering event occurred when D retained one of the animals for a two-week period. However, A could contend in rebuttal that whichever future interest was held by Josef is unenforceable because implicit in the grant was that the **grantee** (rather than some other person who undertook such conduct without the owner's knowledge or consent) would not "keep" animals on Sweetholm. A should prevail on this argument, and therefore it is unlikely that Josef could presently claim paramount title to Sweetholm.

ANSWER TO QUESTION 3

(1) ***Dale v. Art (quiet title action):*** In an action by Dale ("D") to quiet title to Greenacre ("G/A") against Art ("A"), A can be expected to contend that Bob ("B") could not have conveyed G/A to D because no conveyance of G/A was made to B; and thus B had nothing to transfer to D. A transfer of land does not occur until there is delivery (completion of a valid deed by the grantor, with the intention that it be immediately operative) and

acceptance of the deed by the grantee. Where an escrow has been established, there is usually a presumption that the grantor intended that the deed *not* be immediately operative until the conditions of the escrow are satisfied. Since the condition precedent to the deed being operative (the payment of $5,000 by B) never occurred, B never acquired title to G/A to transfer to D.

D, however, could contend that A should be equitably estopped from denying that the transfer to D was invalid. Some states have adopted the rule that where a grantee wrongfully acquires a deed from an escrow holder chosen by the grantor and then conveys the land to a bona fide purchaser ("BFP"), the grantor is estopped from denying the validity of the transfer against the latter. Assuming D parted with present consideration to acquire G/A (the facts are silent on this point), D would seem to be a BFP (since the land was vacant, a visit to G/A would not have put D upon inquiry notice of A's ownership interest). Also, since A had given B a warranty deed (as opposed to a quitclaim deed), D would have no reason to investigate B's title beyond a search of the grantor-grantee index.

Assuming D were a BFP, D would additionally contend that there is a maxim in the law that where one of two innocent parties must suffer, the loss should fall upon the more blameworthy person; and that such person is A since (1) A chose Carl, who incorrectly parted with possession of the deed, and (2) by giving Carl a "clean" deed (one with no conditions upon the face of it), A should have realized that it would be possible for B, if he ever obtained the deed from Carl, to "sell" G/A. While A might contend in rebuttal that escrows are a common device for transferring ownership of land and that Carl, as a real estate broker, should have been well aware of the potential for harm if the deed left his possession, D should prevail in his quiet title action against A (even though no actual conveyance took place).

(2a.) *Art v. Carl ("C")*: A would probably sue C for breach of contract and negligence. With respect to the former, C could contend that he has no liability because (1) no contract ever arose between him and A, since C (apparently) received no consideration, and (2) in any event, the Statute of Frauds (which pertains to the sale of land) was never satisfied, since C never signed the statement prepared by A. However, it would probably be implied into the A-C arrangement that the latter would receive a reasonable compensation for this efforts on behalf of A and B. Additionally, equitable estoppel could probably be successfully asserted to overcome these contentions, since A detrimentally relied upon C to act as escrow agent.

While C might next assert that A's damages are limited to $5,000 (the amount he would have received if the escrow had closed), rather than the enhanced value of the land, A should be able to successfully argue in rebuttal that since the conditions for the close of the escrow were never satisfied, he would have been able to recover the deed back. Therefore, he should be able to recover the present fair market value of G/A from C.

A would also contend that C, by agreeing to act as escrow agent, assumed a duty to A that he would not leave A in a worsened position; and so when C did, he became liable to A in negligence. While C might contend that he could only foresee damages of $5,000, A could probably successfully argue in rebuttal that C should have foreseen that (1) misdelivery of the deed could result in greater damages to A since A would have obtained the deed back at the conclusion of the escrow period, and (2) G/A might appreciate in value. Thus A's damages would again be the reasonable value of G/A.

(2b.) *D v. C:* If D paid consideration for the deed received from B and lost his quiet title action against A, he would probably sue C in negligence for permitting B to obtain control of A's deed; and thereby defraud D of whatever consideration he paid to B. While C might argue that he had no duty to D (who did not rely upon C) and that B's fraudulent actions were the actual cause of D's loss, D should be able to recover from C the consideration which was given to B (C should have reasonably foreseen that B might misuse A's deed, especially since it was absolute on its face).

TABLE OF CASES

SUBJECT MATTER INDEX